Edition

5

Issues and Ethics
in the Helping Professions

Edition

5

Issues and Ethics in the Helping Professions

◆ **Gerald Corey**
California State University, Fullerton
Diplomate in Counseling Psychology,
American Board of Professional Psychology

◆ **Marianne Schneider Corey**
Private Practice

◆ **Patrick Callanan**
Private Practice

Brooks/Cole Publishing Company

I(T)P® *An International Thomson Publishing Company*

Pacific Grove • Albany • Belmont • Bonn • Boston • Cincinnati • Detroit • Johannesburg • London
Madrid • Melbourne • Mexico City • New York • Paris • Singapore • Tokyo • Toronto • Washington

Sponsoring Editor: *Eileen Murphy*
Marketing: *Jean Thompson/Margaret Parks*
Editorial Assistant: *Susan Carlson*
Production Coordinator: *Tessa McGlasson*
Production: *Cecile Joyner*
Manuscript Editor: *Kay Mikel*

Interior and Cover Design: *Sharon L. Kinghan*
Indexer: *Glennda Gilmour*
Typesetting: *Bookends Typesetting*
Printing and Binding: *R. R. Donnelley & Sons/ Crawfordsville, Indiana*

Copyright © 1998 by Brooks/Cole Publishing Company
A Division of International Thomson Publishing Inc.
I(T)P The ITP logo is a registered trademark under license.

For more information, contact:

BROOKS/COLE PUBLISHING COMPANY
511 Forest Lodge Road
Pacific Grove, CA 93950
USA

International Thomson Publishing Europe
Berkshire House 168-173
High Holborn
London WC1V 7AA
England

Thomas Nelson Australia
102 Dodds Street
South Melbourne, 3205
Victoria, Australia

Nelson Canada
1120 Birchmount Road
Scarborough, Ontario
Canada M1K 5G4

International Thomson Editores
Seneca 53
Col. Polanco
11560 México, D.F., México

International Thomson Publishing GmbH
Königswinterer Strasse 418
53227 Bonn
Germany

International Thomson Publishing Asia
221 Henderson Road
#05-10 Henderson Building
Singapore 0315

International Thomson Publishing Japan
Hirakawacho Kyowa Building, 3F
2-2-1 Hirakawacho
Chiyoda-ku, Tokyo 102
Japan

Printed in the United States of America

10   9   8   7   6   5   4   3   2

Library of Congress Cataloging-in-Publication Data

Corey, Gerald.
    Issues and ethics in the helping professions / Gerald Corey, Marianne Schneider Corey, Patrick Callanan.—5th ed.
        p.   cm.
    Includes bibliographical references and index.
    ISBN 0-534-34689-8
    1. Psychotherapists—Professional ethics.   2. Counselors—Professional ethics.   I. Corey, Marianne Schneider, [date].
II. Callanan, Patrick.   III. Title.
RC455.2.E8C66   1998
174'.2—dc21   97-9363
                                                          CIP

Dedicated to
the legion of friends, colleagues, clients, and
students who opened our eyes to the complexities
and subtleties of ethical thinking and practice

◆ **Gerald Corey** is a licensed psychologist and is Professor of Human Services and Counseling at California State University at Fullerton, where he was the Coordinator of the Human Services Department for nine years. He received his doctorate in counseling from the University of Southern California. He is a Diplomate in Counseling Psychology, American Board of Professional Psychology, a National Certified Counselor, a Fellow of the American Psychological Association (Counseling Psychology), and a Fellow of the Association for Specialists in Group Work.

Jerry received the Outstanding Professor of the Year Award from California State University at Fullerton in 1991. He teaches both undergraduate and graduate courses in ethics and professional issues and, in addition, teaches undergraduate human services courses in the theory and practice of counseling, group counseling, and courses in experiential groups. With his colleagues he has conducted workshops in the United States, Canada, Germany, Belgium, Scotland, Mexico, and China, with a special focus on training in group counseling. He often presents workshops for professional organizations and at various universities. Along with his colleagues, Jerry offers weeklong residential training and supervision workshops each summer. In his leisure time, Jerry likes to travel, hike and bicycle in the mountains, and drive his 1931 Model A Ford.

Recent publications by Jerry Corey—all with Brooks/Cole Publishing Company—include:

- *Becoming a Helper*, Third Edition (1998, with Marianne Schneider Corey)
- *Groups: Process and Practice*, Fifth Edition (1997, with Marianne Schneider Corey)
- *I Never Knew I Had a Choice*, Sixth Edition (1997, with Marianne Schneider Corey)
- *Theory and Practice of Counseling and Psychotherapy*, Fifth Edition (and *Manual*) (1996).
- *Case Approach to Counseling and Psychotherapy*, Fourth Edition (1996)
- *Theory and Practice of Group Counseling*, Fourth Edition (and *Manual*) (1995)
- *Group Techniques*, Second Edition (1992, with Marianne Schneider Corey, Patrick Callanan, and J. Michael Russell)

Along with his daughters, Cindy Corey and Heidi Jo Corey, he is the co-author of an orientation to college book entitled *Living and Learning* (1997), published by Wadsworth. He is also co-author (with Barbara Herlihy) of two books: *Boundary Issues in Counseling: Multiple Roles and Relationships* (1997) and *ACA Ethical Standards Casebook*, Fifth Edition (1996), both published by the American Counseling Association.

◆ ***Marianne Schneider Corey*** is a licensed marriage and family therapist in California and is a National Certified Counselor. She received her master's degree in marriage, family, and child counseling from Chapman College. She is a Fellow of the Association for Specialists in Group Work and a clinical member of the American Association for Marriage and Family Therapy. She holds memberships in the California Association of Marriage and Family Therapists, the American Counseling Association, the National Organization for Human Service Education, the Association for Spiritual, Ethical, and Religious Values in Counseling, and the Association for Specialists in Group Work.

Marianne is actively involved in providing training and supervision workshops in group process for human-services students and professionals, regularly facilitates a self-exploration group for graduate students in counseling, and co-facilitates weeklong residential workshops in personal growth. She is an adjunct faculty member of the Counseling Department at California State University at Fullerton. Along with Jerry, Marianne has conducted workshops, continuing education seminars, and personal-growth groups in Germany, Belgium, Mexico, and China as well as regularly doing these workshops in the United States. In her free time Marianne enjoys traveling, reading, visiting with friends, and hiking.

Marianne has co-authored the following books (published by Brooks/Cole Publishing Company):

- *Becoming a Helper,* Third Edition (1998, with Gerald Corey)
- *Groups: Process and Practice,* Fifth Edition (1997, with Gerald Corey)
- *I Never Knew I Had a Choice,* Sixth Edition (1997, with Gerald Corey)
- *Group Techniques,* Second Edition (1992, with Gerald Corey, Patrick Callanan, and J. Michael Russell)

Marianne and Jerry have been married since 1964. They have two adult daughters, Heidi and Cindy, and have made their home in the mountain community of Idyllwild, California. Marianne grew up in Germany and has kept in close contact with her family there.

◆ ***Patrick Callanan*** is a licensed marriage and family therapist in private practice in Santa Ana, California, and is a National Certified Counselor. In 1973 he graduated with a bachelor's degree in Human Services from California State University at Fullerton, and then received his master's degree in professional psychology from United States International University in 1976. In his private practice he works with individuals, couples, families, and groups. As part of his private practice, Patrick leads different time-limited groups.

Patrick is on the part-time faculty of the Human Services Program at California State University at Fullerton, where he regularly teaches an internship course. He also offers his time each year to the university to assist in training and supervising group leaders, co-leads weeklong residential growth groups, and co-teaches an undergraduate course in ethical and professional issues. Patrick is a consultant for mental-health practitioners, and he presents workshops and training groups at conventions and for professional organizations. He is a member of the California Association of Marriage and Family Therapists, the Association for Specialists in Group Work, and the American Counseling Association. Along with Marianne Schneider Corey and Gerald Corey, he received an Award for Contributions to the Field of Professional Ethics by the Association for Spiritual, Ethical, and Religious Values in Counseling in 1986.

Patrick co-authored *Group Techniques*, Second Edition (1992). In his free time, Partick enjoys reading, antique hunting, cycling, and playing racquetball, tennis, and golf.

Contents

Preface

Issues and Ethics in the Helping Professions is written for both graduate and undergraduate students in the helping professions. This book is suitable for courses in counseling, human services, marriage and family therapy, psychology, and social work. It can be used as a core textbook in courses such as practicum, fieldwork, internship, and ethical and professional issues or as a supplementary text in courses dealing with skills or theory. Because the issues we discuss are likely to be encountered throughout one's professional career, we have tried to use language and concepts that will be meaningful both to students doing their fieldwork and to professionals interested in improving their skills through continuing-education seminars or independent reading.

In this book, we involve readers in learning to deal with the professional and ethical issues that most affect the actual practice of counseling and related helping professions. We raise the following questions: How do therapists' values and life experiences affect the therapeutic process? What are the rights and responsibilities of both the client and the counselor? As professionals, how can we determine our level of competence? How can we provide quality services for culturally diverse populations? What major ethical issues face practitioners in marital and family therapy? in group work? in community agencies? in private practice?

Our goal is both to provide a body of information and to teach readers a process of thinking about and resolving the basic issues they will face throughout their careers. For most of the issues we raise, we present various viewpoints to stimulate discussion and reflection. We also present our views, when appropriate, to challenge readers to formulate their own positions.

The ethical codes of various professional organizations offer some guidance for practice. However, these guidelines leave many questions unanswered. We believe that students and professionals alike must ultimately struggle with the issues of responsible practice, deciding how accepted ethical principles apply in the specific cases they encounter.

We have tried to make this book a personal one that will involve our readers in an active and meaningful way. To this end we have provided many opportunities to respond to our discussions and to draw on personal experiences. Each chapter begins with a self-inventory designed to help readers focus on the key topics to be discussed in the chapter. Within the chapters we frequently ask readers to think about how the issues apply to them. Open-ended cases and situations are presented to stimulate thought and to assist readers in formulating their own positions. We also cite related literature when exploring ethical and professional issues.

This book combines the advantages of both the textbook and a student manual. Instructors will find an abundance of material and suggested activities, surely more than can be covered in a single course. An *Instructor's Resource Manual* is available that contains chapter outlines, suggestions for teaching an ethics course, test items, additional exercises and activities, and study guide questions. An electronic version of the *Instructor's Resource Manual* is available for all platforms. The publisher will also provide a set of transparency masters upon request.

This fifth edition of *Issues and Ethics in the Helping Professions* has been extensively revised and updated. It provides new topics and more comprehensive coverage than the previous editions. Here is a chapter-by-chapter look at some of the changes and new material you will find in this edition.

In Chapter 1, an introduction to ethics issues:

◆ updated coverage on new codes of ethics and the purpose they serve
◆ new material on the feminist model for ethical decision making and on including the client in the process of working through ethical concerns

In Chapter 2, evaluating the counselor as a person and as a professional:

◆ new discussion of the role of therapy for both trainees and professional counselors
◆ new material on counselor impairment

For Chapter 3, which deals with values in the helping relationship:

◆ a new and expanded section on the role of spiritual and religious values in counseling
◆ updated and expanded coverage on ethical and legal issues involved in end-of-life decisions
◆ discussion of ethical and value issues in counseling gay and lesbian clients

For Chapter 4, which concentrates on client rights and counselor responsibilities:

◆ new and expanded coverage of informed consent
◆ new section on documentation and record keeping practices
◆ new section on the counselor's responsibilities in a managed care system

- revised and expanded discussion of malpractice issues in counseling practice
- recent landmark case: lawsuit of a managed care company

For Chapter 5, the discussion of ethical and legal issues of confidentiality:

- updated and expanded coverage of confidentiality and privileged communication
- updated coverage of codes of ethics as applied to confidentiality and duty to warn and to protect
- recent landmark case expanding client-therapist privilege
- new material on the duty to warn and to protect
- new discussion of duty to protect versus confidentiality as it applies to AIDS-related psychotherapy

For Chapter 6, which examines theory, practice, and research:

- extensively revised section on assessment and diagnosis
- new discussion of implications of DSM-IV
- increased focus on cultural factors to consider in assessment, diagnosis, testing, intervention techniques, and research

For Chapter 7, on boundary issues and balancing multiple roles:

- more extensive coverage of multiple relationships, boundary issues, uses and abuses of power, and multiple roles and responsibilities
- new material on perspectives on managing multiple roles and relationships
- expanded discussion of nonsexual dual and multiple relationships
- more on considerations involving bartering, gift giving, and social relationships with current and former clients

In Chapter 8, which addresses professional competency and training:

- updated coverage of codes of ethics as applied to competence and training
- new section on specialties within the counseling profession
- new discussion of generalist versus specialist orientation

In Chapter 9, which focuses on supervision and consultation:

- new material on supervisor's roles and responsibilities
- new material on dual and multiple relationships in supervision
- new section on competence for supervisors
- new section on multicultural supervision

In Chapter 10, on acquiring a multicultural perspective:

- addition of new multicultural counseling competencies
- new material on perspectives on multicultural training
- discussion of new ethical codes pertaining to diversity issues

In Chapter 11, which highlights counselors at work in the community:

- expanded coverage of ways of working in the community
- new coverage of ethics codes pertaining to community and society
- new section on role of counselors and community intervention

In Chapter 12, addressing ethical concerns of marital and family therapy:

- new material on ethical issues facing marriage and family therapists
- new section on gender-sensitive marital and family therapy

In Chapter 13, on the ethical issues surrounding group work:

- revised material on ethics in group work
- new material on ethical issues in training group counselors

In the References and the Appendices you will find:

- an updated survey of the literature dealing with ethical and professional issues with emphasis on recent journal articles
- the revised codes of ethics of *five* professional organizations

A note on terminology: We frequently use the terms mental-health professional, practitioner, counselor, therapist, and helper. We generally use these interchangeably, but we have also tried to reflect the differing nomenclature of the various professions that we cover.

Acknowledgments

We would like to thank the following people who reviewed the manuscript and made valuable suggestions for this edition: Ken Johnson, Amber University; Terence Patterson, University of San Francisco; Barbara Herlihy, University of New Orleans; Lisa De Prato, University of Phoenix; John Norcross, University of Scranton; Shalynn Ford, Marycrest International University; Michelle Muratori, graduate student at Northwestern University; Harriet Glosoff, University of Southern Mississippi; Don McDonald, Seattle Pacific University; Joe Afanador, Seattle University; and Sheila Bell, graduate student at the University of Southern California.

We received extra help on selected chapters from several people. Yolanda Briscoe, graduate student at the University of San Francisco, evaluated the self-inventories at the beginning of each chapter. C. Emmanuel Ahia, Rider University, reviewed the discussion on confidentiality and the danger-to-self-or-to-others exception to confidentiality. Mark Homan, Pima Community College, and Sid Gardner, California State University at Fullerton, reviewed Chapter 11 on the counselor in the community. Judy Miranti, Our Lady of Holy Cross College, reviewed the discussion on spirituality in counseling.

The members of the Brooks/Cole team continue to offer support for all our projects. It is a delight to work with a dedicated staff of professionals who go out of their way to give their best. These people include: Eileen Murphy, the editor of counseling and psychology; Tessa McGlasson, production editor, who oversees the production of our books; Cecile Joyner, of the Cooper Company, who coordinated the production of this book; and Kay Mikel, the manuscript editor of this edition, whose fine editorial assistance kept this book reader friendly. We also want to recognize the work of the late Bill Waller, who edited three of the previous editions of *Issues and Ethics in the Helping Professions,* and whose influence has carried over into this edition. We appreciate Glennda Gilmour's work in compiling the index.

Gerald Corey
Marianne Schneider Corey
Patrick Callanan

Introduction to Professional Ethics

◆ *The Focus of This Book*

◆ *Ethical Decision Making*

◆ *Some Suggestions for Using This Book*

◆ *Self-Assessment: An Inventory of Your Attitudes and Beliefs about Professional and Ethical Issues*

◆ *Chapter Summary*

◆ *Suggested Activities*

The Focus of This Book

Working both independently and together, the three of us have, over the years, confronted a variety of professional and ethical issues that do not have clear-cut solutions. Exchanging ideas has helped us clarify our positions on these difficult issues, and conversations with students and colleagues have shown us that others wrestle with similar questions. We have become convinced that students in the helping professions should think seriously about these problems before they begin practicing.

We have discovered that many of the issues relevant to beginning professionals resurface later and take on different meanings at various stages of professional development. Therefore, this book will be useful both to experienced practitioners and to students about to embark on their professional careers. We have tried to avoid the trap of dispensing prescriptions or providing simple solutions to complex problems. Our main purpose is to give you the basis for formulating your own ethical guidelines within the broad limits of professional codes and divergent theoretical positions. We raise what we consider to be central issues, present a range of views on these issues, discuss our position, and provide you with many opportunities to refine your own thinking and actively develop your position.

As you read this book, you will realize that we have certain biases and viewpoints about ethical behavior. We hope you will see these stances as our points of view rather than the correct points of view. We try to keep our viewpoints open to revision. We state our position on issues not to sway you to adopt our view but to challenge you to devise your own position. In the end, you are responsible for your own ethical practice; however, don't think you are free to choose any set of ethical views merely because it "feels right."

The various mental-health professions have developed codes of ethics that are binding on their members. Every professional should know the ethical code of his or her specialty and should be aware of the consequences of practicing in ways that are not sanctioned by the organization. In addition, responsible practice requires that professionals use informed, sound, and responsible judgment. Professionals should consult with colleagues, keep themselves up to date through reading and continuing education, and continually examine their behavior.

Codes of ethics provide general standards, but these guidelines are not sufficiently explicit to deal with every situation. It is often difficult to interpret ethical codes, and opinions differ over how to apply them in specific cases. Consequently, practitioners retain a significant degree of freedom and will encounter many situations that demand the exercise of sound judgment to further the best interests of their clients.

In writing about responsible ethical decision making, Lanning (1997) reminds us that the decision one counselor makes when facing an ethical dilemma may be different from that of another practitioner:

> We can consult with our colleagues, call an ethics professor, read the ethics books, and more; but when we make the final decision, it is ours alone. We alone are

responsible and accountable for the consequences. Nevertheless, the ability to reason with the ethical principles and arrive at a decision for which we are willing to be accountable is what makes counseling practice ethical. That is a difficult but not impossible task and one that in many ways determines the level of our professionalism. (p. 113)

Be prepared to reexamine many of the issues discussed here throughout your professional life. Even if you resolve some of these issues at the initial stage of your development as a counselor, they may take on new dimensions as you gain experience, and minor questions may become major concerns as you progress in your profession. Many students burden themselves with the expectation that they should resolve all possible issues before they begin to practice. But we see the definition and refinement of such issues as an ongoing evolutionary process that requires an open and self-critical attitude. Our goal is to give you a flexible framework and a direction for working through ethical dilemmas. You must find your own answers to the questions we raise here.

Ethical Decision Making

Some Key Terms

The terms *ethics, values, morality, community standards, laws,* and *professionalism* are critical components in any discussion of professional ethics. Although *values* and *ethics* are frequently used interchangeably, the two terms are not identical. *Values* pertain to beliefs and attitudes that provide direction to everyday living, whereas *ethics* pertain to the beliefs we hold about what constitutes right conduct. Ethics are moral principles adopted by an individual or group to provide rules for right conduct. *Morality* is concerned with perspectives of right and proper conduct and involves an evaluation of actions on the basis of some broader cultural context or religious standard.

Bersoff (1996) describes *ethical conduct* as the result of a combination of knowledge and a clear conception of the philosophical principals that underlie an ethics code. Ethical conduct grows out of sound character that leads you to respond with maturity, judgment, discretion, wisdom, and prudence. *Community standards* (or *mores*) vary on an interdisciplinary, theoretical, and geographical basis. The standard for a counselor's social contact with clients may be different in a large urban area than in a rural area or between practitioners employing an analytic versus a behavioral approach. Community standards often become the ultimate *legal* criteria for determining whether practitioners are liable for damages.

Professionalism has some relationship to ethical behavior, yet it is possible to act unprofessionally and still not act unethically. For instance, showing up late for appointments with clients might be viewed as unprofessional, but it would probably not be considered unethical.

Some situations cut across these concepts. For instance, sexual intimacy between counselors and clients is considered unethical, unprofessional, immoral, and illegal. Keep the differences in the meanings of these various concepts in mind as you read.

Foundations of an Ethical Perspective

Ethical issues in counseling are often complex and multifaceted, and they defy simplistic solutions. There are many gray areas that require decision-making skills. This process entails not only learning information about ethical standards but also learning how to define and work through a variety of difficult situations.

Law and ethics.   Ethical issues in the mental-health professions are regulated by both laws and professional codes. Laws and ethical codes provide guidelines, yet neither offers clear-cut answers to situational problems. Law defines the minimum standards society will tolerate; these standards are enforced by government. Ethics represents aspirational goals, or the maximum or ideal standards set by the profession, and they are enforced by professional associations, national certification boards, and government boards that regulate professions (Remley, 1996). Although these minimum and maximum standards may differ, they are not necessarily in conflict.

Laws and ethical codes, by their very nature, tend to be reactive, emerging from what has occurred rather than anticipating what may occur. We hope that you will not limit your behavior to obeying statutes and following ethical standards but will develop a sensitivity to doing what is best for your clients by working toward the best standards of practice. It is very important that you acquire this ethical sense at the beginning of your professional program. Remember that the basic purpose of practicing ethically is to further the welfare of your clients.

At times there may be conflicts between the law and ethical principles, and in these cases the values of the counselor come into play. Conflict between professional codes and the law may arise in areas such as advertising, confidentiality, and clients' rights of access to their own files. One example of a potential conflict between legal and ethical standards pertains to breaking confidentiality of a client who is HIV-positive by informing a third party of his or her condition. A new standard has been added to the American Counseling Association's (ACA) *Code of Ethics* (1995) regarding contagious fatal diseases, which suggests that practitioners may be justified in reporting to an identifiable third party, under certain circumstances. However, there is no legal imperative or precedent to do so at this time. Practitioners may act in ways they deem to be ethical only to find that they have broken a legal standard (see the discussion in Chapter 5 of the duty to warn and to protect).

The American Psychological Association's ethics code (APA, 1995) indicates that in cases of conflicts between ethics and the law psychologists should seek to resolve the conflict in a way that complies with the law and at the same time most nearly conforms to the code. The American Counseling Association's *Code of Ethics and Standards of Practice* (ACA, 1995) defers to the law, which means that counselors must practice within the requirements of the law. In ethical dilemmas involving legal issues, seek legal advice from colleagues familiar with the law and from legal counsel (Remley, 1996). In those cases where neither the law nor an ethics code resolves an issue, therapists are advised to consider other professional and community standards and their own consciences as well.

In making ethical decisions, ask yourself these questions: "Which values should I rely on? What values do I hold? How do my values affect my work with clients? Why do I hold certain values?" We agree with Tennyson and Strom (1986) that acting responsibly is an inner quality, not something imposed by authority. The National Association of Social Workers *Code of Ethics* (NASW, 1996) specifies that a practitioner's decisions and actions should be consistent with the spirit as well as the letter of the code. This code cautions social workers to be aware of their clients' as well as their own personal values, cultural and religious beliefs, and practices when making ethical decisions. Acting responsibly implies recognizing any conflicts between personal and professional values and dealing with them effectively.

One way of conceptualizing professional ethics is to contrast lower level ethical functioning with higher level functioning. *Mandatory ethics* describes a level of ethical functioning wherein counselors merely act in compliance with minimal standards, acknowledging the basic "musts" and "must nots." *Aspirational ethics* describes the highest standards of conduct to which professional counselors can aspire and requires that counselors do more than simply meet the letter of the code. It entails an understanding of the spirit behind the code and the principles on which the code rests. Practitioners who comply at the first level, mandatory ethics, are generally safe from legal action or professional censure. At the higher level of ethical functioning, aspirational ethics, practitioners go further and reflect on the effects their interventions may have on the welfare of their clients. The ethics codes of both the ACA (1995) and the APA (1995) include a *mandatory* section (a set of enforceable standards intended to be specific enough to use as compelling rules and resulting in sanctions if they are broken) and an *aspirational* section (a higher set of standards reflecting ideal principles). For example, the 1995 ACA *Code of Ethics and Standards of Practice* together address both mandatory and aspirational ethics. Courts of law and state licensure boards now require the counseling profession to define minimal standards to which all counselors may be held accountable. The *Standards of Practice* does this; it is comparatively brief and specifies minimal behaviors required of professional counselors (mandatory ethics) that can be understood and evaluated by individuals outside the counseling profession. The *Code of Ethics* is lengthier, gives more detailed guidance regarding the standards of practice, and includes statements describing the best practice (aspirational ethics) that represents the ideals of the profession (Herlihy & Corey, 1996a).

When the word *unethical* is used, people too often think of gross violations of established codes. In reality, most violations of ethics probably happen quite inadvertently in counseling practice. If practitioners are not aware of the more subtle ways in which their behavior can adversely affect their clients, such behavior can go unnoticed, and the clients will suffer. For instance, a private practitioner whose practice is not flourishing may prolong the therapy of his clients and justify his actions on theoretical grounds. He is likely to ignore the fact that the prolongation of therapy is influenced by his financial situation. Or a counselor whose funding in an agency requires that she demonstrate that her work is effective may devote more attention to acquiring funding than to pursuing clients' goals. Practitioners can easily find themselves in an ethical quagmire based on competing role expectations. The best way to maintain a clear ethical position is to focus on your clients' best interests.

Many ethical violations are hard to detect. Clients' needs are best met when practitioners monitor their own ethics. Many ethical violations can go undetected because only the individual who committed the violation knows about it. Rather than just looking at others and proclaiming "That's unethical!" we encourage you to challenge your own thinking and apply guidelines to your behavior by asking yourself, "Is what I am doing in the best interests of my clients?"

The Role of Professional Codes

Various professional organizations have established codes of ethics that provide broad guidelines for mental-health practitioners. Some of the professional mental-health organizations that have formulated codes are: the American Counseling Association (ACA, 1995), the American Psychological Association (APA, 1995), the National Association of Social Workers (NASW, 1996), the National Organization for Human Service Education (NOHSE, 1995), and the American Association for Marriage and Family Therapy (AAMFT, 1991). The complete ethical codes of the organizations above are found in the Appendix. At this time we encourage you to review these standards and note their assets and limitations. Also, identify any areas of possible disagreement you might have with particular standards. This will help you to evaluate the issues we raise in the remaining chapters of this book.

Multiple codes of ethics exist for mental-health professionals. Each of the national professional organizations mentioned above has a different set of codes, emphasizing different themes. Also, national certification boards, other professional associations, specialty areas within the counseling profession, and state regulatory boards all have their own ethics documents. Herlihy and Remley (1995) have written about the problems associated with this proliferation of codes, indicating that multiple codes are counterproductive. They conclude: "When a single, unified code of ethics is universally accepted by the counseling profession, future revisions will be a much more manageable task, and the public and counselors themselves will be clearer regarding the ethical obligations of professional counselors" (p. 133).

Become familiar with the ethical codes of your specialization, but know that you will be challenged in the application of these codes in your practice.

The ethical codes offered by most professional organizations are broad and general rather than precise and specific. Your own ethical awareness and problem-solving skills will determine how you translate these general guidelines into your professional day-to-day behavior. Ethical codes are necessary, but not sufficient, for exercising ethical responsibility. It is essential that you be aware of the limitations of such codes (Bersoff, 1994; Herlihy & Corey, 1996a; Herlihy & Remley, 1995; Ibrahim & Arredondo, 1990; Lanning, 1997; Mabe & Rollin, 1986; Mappes, Robb, & Engels, 1985; Pope & Vasquez, 1991). Here are some of the problems you may encounter when you strive toward an ethically responsible practice:

limitations of ethical codes

- Some issues cannot be handled solely by relying on ethical codes.
- Some codes lack clarity and precision, which makes enforcement difficult.
- Simply learning the ethical codes and casebooks will not prepare counselors for ethical practice.
- Consumers of counseling services may not have the knowledge or experience to determine whether a therapist is practicing ethically.
- Codes are designed more to protect professionals than to protect the public.
- Conflicts sometimes emerge within ethical codes as well as among various organizations' codes.
- Practitioners who belong to multiple professional associations, are licensed by their state, and hold national certifications may be responsible to practice within the framework of numerous codes of ethics, yet these codes may not be uniform.
- Ethical codes tend to be reactive rather than proactive.
- A practitioner's personal values may conflict with a specific standard within an ethics code.
- Codes may conflict with institutional policies and practices.
- Ethical codes need to be understood within a cultural framework; therefore, they must be adapted to specific cultures.
- Because of the diverse viewpoints within any professional organization, not all members will agree with all proposed standards.

In the *Code of Ethics* of the National Association of Social Workers (NASW, 1996) the limits of the code are succinctly described:

> A code of ethics cannot guarantee ethical behavior. Moreover, a code of ethics cannot resolve all ethical issues or disputes, or capture the richness and complexity involved in striving to make responsible choices with a moral community. Rather a code of ethics sets forth values, ethical principals and ethical standards to which professionals aspire and by which their actions can be judged.

It is clear that codes are not intended to be a blueprint that removes all need for the use of judgment and ethical reasoning. Pope and Vasquez (1991) maintain that formal ethical principles can never be substituted for an active, deliberative, and creative approach to meeting ethical responsibilities. They remind us that ethical codes cannot be applied in a rote manner, mainly because each client's situation is unique and calls for a different solution. Final authority must rest with the helper. The most difficult part of being an ethical counselor is having to make decisions and then assuming personal responsibility for the consequences (Lanning, 1997).

Herlihy and Corey (1996a) suggest that codes of ethics fulfill three objectives. The basic purpose of ethics codes is to educate professionals about sound ethical conduct. Reading and reflecting on the standards can help practitioners expand their awareness, clarify their values, and find a direction in dealing with the challenges of their work. Second, ethical standards provide a mechanism for professional accountability. Practitioners are obliged not only to monitor their own behavior but also to encourage ethical conduct in their colleagues. One of the best ways for practitioners to protect themselves from malpractice suits is to practice within the spirit of the ethical codes. Third, codes of ethics serve as catalysts for improving practice. When practitioners must interpret and apply the codes in their own practices, the questions raised often help to clarify their positions on dilemmas that do not have simple or absolute answers.

Ethics codes are designed to safeguard the public and to guide professionals in their work so that they can provide the best service possible. The community standard (what professionals *actually* do) is generally less rigorous than the ethical standard (what professionals *should* do). Keep informed of what others in your local area and subspecialties are doing on a practical level. And if you decide to practice in violation of a specific code, be sure you have a reasonable rationale for your course of action. Realize also that there are consequences for violating the codes of your profession. Must you follow all the ethical codes of your profession to be considered an ethical practitioner? If you agree with and follow all the ethical codes of your profession, does this necessarily mean that you are an ethical professional? These are complex questions, and you may find that you answer them differently in different situations.

Development of Ethical Codes

Ethics codes for professional organizations are not static; they must be revised as new concerns arise. The first APA code of ethics was adopted in 1953. It was revised in 1959, 1963, 1965, 1972, 1977, 1981, 1989, 1992, and 1995. A casebook, *Ethics for Psychologists: A Commentary on the APA Ethics Code* (Canter, Bennett, Jones, & Nagey, 1994), provides examples of how the code applies to a range of situations.

The first ACA ethics code was adopted in 1961, and revisions were made in 1974, 1981, 1988, and 1995. The *ACA Ethical Standards Casebook* (Herlihy & Corey, 1996a) deals with how the 1995 code can be used to resolve a variety of ethical dilemmas.

The first version of the *Code of Ethics for Marriage Counselors* was developed in 1962. The eighth revision of the *Code of Ethics of the American Association for Marriage and Family Therapy* was adopted in 1991. There is also an *American Association for Marriage and Family Therapy Ethics Casebook* (Brock, 1994), which contains numerous vignettes for each standard and articles on applications of ethics to practice.

The codes of ethics of most of the other professional organizations have also undergone several revisions. The ACA, APA, and AAMFT codes cited here illustrate that such codes are established by a group of professionals for the purpose of protecting consumers and furthering the professional stance of the organizations. As such, these codes do not convey ultimate truth, nor do they provide ready-made answers for the ethical dilemmas practitioners must face. Casebooks can never replace the informed judgment and goodwill of the individual counselor. They are tools that must be used wisely in making difficult decisions in complex situations. We want to emphasize again the need for a level of ethical functioning higher than merely following the letter of the law or the code. For instance, you might avoid a lawsuit or professional censure by ignoring cultural diversity, but many of your ethnically diverse clients would most certainly suffer from your neglect.

Enforcement of Ethical Codes

Most professional organizations have ethics committees, elected or delegated bodies that oversee the conduct of members of the organization. Let us consider the ACA Ethics Committee as an example. The main purposes of the committee are to educate the association's membership about ethical codes and to protect the public from unethical practices. The committee meets regularly to process formal complaints against individual members of the association.

When a complaint is lodged against a member, the committee launches an investigation and deliberates on the case. Eventually, a disposition is reached. The complaint may be dismissed, specific charges within the complaint may be dismissed, or the committee may find that ethical standards have been violated and impose sanctions. Possible sanctions include a reprimand; probation or suspension for a specified period of time; a recommendation that the member be allowed to resign from the organization; a recommendation that the member be expelled; or a recommendation that a specific course of remedial action be taken, such as obtaining ongoing supervision or personal therapy. Expulsion or suspension of a member is a major sanction. Members have the right to appeal the committee's decision, and once the appeals process has been completed or the deadline for appeal has passed, the sanctions of suspension and expulsion are published in writing. Practitioners who are expelled from the association may also face the loss of their license or certificate to practice, but only if the state board conducts an independent investigation. National and state certification boards may revoke a counselor's certification, and state licensure boards have the power to prohibit practice or issue reprimands to professionals (Chauvin & Remley, 1996).

Models of Ethical Decision Making

Several writers have developed models for ethical decision making (Forester-Miller & Davis, 1995; Hill, Glaser, & Harden, 1995; Jordan & Meara, 1990; Keith-Spiegel & Koocher, 1985; Kitchener, 1984; Lanning, 1997; Loewenberg &

Dolgoff, 1992; Meara, Schmidt, & Day, 1996; Paradise & Siegelwaks, 1982; T. S. Smith, McGuire, Abbott, & Blau, 1991; Stadler, 1986a; Tymchuk, 1981). This section is an amalgamation of elements from these various models.

In a major article entitled "Principles and Virtues: A Foundation for Ethical Decisions, Policies, and Character," Meara, Schmidt, and Day (1996) differentiate between principle ethics and virtue ethics. Principle ethics is a set of obligations and a method that focuses on moral issues with the goals of (a) solving a particular dilemma or set of dilemmas and (b) establishing a framework to guide future ethical thinking and behavior. Principles typically focus on acts and choices, and they are used to facilitate the selection of socially and historically acceptable answers to the question, "What shall I do?"

A thorough grounding in principle ethics opens the way for another important perspective, virtue ethics. Virtue ethics focuses on the character traits of the counselor and nonobligatory ideals to which professionals aspire rather than on solving specific ethical dilemmas. Simply stated, principle ethics asks "Is this situation unethical?" whereas virtue ethics asks "Am I doing what is best for my client?" Even in the absence of an ethical dilemma, virtue ethics compels the professional to be conscious of ethical behavior. Meara and her colleagues (1996) maintain that it is not a question of subscribing to one or the other form of ethics. Rather, professional counselors should strive to integrate virtue ethics and principle ethics, which they believe results in better ethical decisions and policies.

Some counselors concern themselves primarily with avoiding malpractice suits rather than with thinking of what is best for their clients. Their practices are influenced by following the law and ethics codes so that they will stay out of trouble. Other counselors, although also concerned with avoiding litigation, are first and foremost interested in doing what is best for their clients. Such counselors would consider it unethical to use techniques that might not result in the greatest benefit to their clients or to use techniques in which they were not thoroughly trained, even though these techniques might not lead to a lawsuit. For example, a Gestalt therapist might refer a client to a cognitive-behavioral therapist because, in her opinion, the client is more suited to the latter approach. Although this therapist could legally and ethically justify seeing this client, it may be more "virtuous" to refer the client in this instance. As Jordan and Meara write, "The ideals of professional psychology must include conscientious decision making, but they also must include virtuous deciders, who emphasize not so much what is permitted as what is preferred" (1990, p. 112).

Meara et al. (1996) identify four core virtues (prudence, integrity, respectfulness, and benevolence) that are appropriate for professionals to adhere to in making ethical decisions. They also describe five characteristics of virtuous professionals, which they see as being at the heart of virtue ethics. Virtuous agents:

1. are motivated to do what is right for the right reasons. They are positively motivated to do what is right because they judge it to be right, not simply because they feel obligated or fear the consequences.

- possess vision and discernment, which involve sensitivity, judgment, and understanding and lead to decisive action. They know which principles to apply to a situation and how to apply them.
- possess compassion that involves a regard for the welfare of others and a sensitivity to the suffering of others. They are able to take actions to reduce their clients' pain.
- possess self-awareness. They have a capacity for self-observation; they know how their assumptions, convictions, and biases are likely to affect their interactions with others.
- are connected with and understand the mores of their community and the importance of community in moral decision making, policy setting, and character development. They understand the ideals and expectations of their community.

Virtue ethics focuses on ideals rather than obligations and on the character of the professional rather than on the action itself. To meet the goals, ideals, and needs of the community being served, both principles and virtues need to be considered, because both are important elements in thinking through ethical concerns.

◆ **A case illustrating virtue ethics.**   Your client, Kevin, is progressing well; then he informs you that he has lost his job and will not be able to continue seeing you because of his inability to pay your fees. Here is how four different therapists handled a similar situation:

Therapist A: I'm sorry but I can't continue seeing you without payment. I'm giving you the name of a local community clinic that provides low cost treatment.

Therapist B: It's not my policy to see people without payment, but I appreciate the difficulty you find yourself in through no fault of your own. I'll continue to see you, and you pay whatever portion of my fee you can afford. In addition I want you to seek out a community agency and do volunteer work in lieu of the full payment.

Therapist C: I suggest that you put therapy on hold until you can financially afford it.

Therapist D: I can't afford to see you without payment, but I am willing to suggest an alternative plan. Continue writing in your journal, and once a month I will see you for a half hour to discuss your journal. You pay what you can afford for these sessions. When your financial situation has been corrected, we can continue therapy as usual.

What are your reactions to the various therapists' responses? Which position appeals to you the most and why? Can you think of any other responses? Would you be willing to see a client without payment? Why or why not? Do you have any questions about the ethics of any of these therapists?

In considering what you might do if you were the therapist in this case, reflect on the provisions pertaining to *pro bono* services in the ethics codes of both NASW and ACA:

> Social workers elevate service to others above self-interest. Social workers draw on their knowledge, values, and skills to help people in need and to address social

problems. Social workers are encouraged to volunteer some portion of their professional skills with no expectation of significant financial return (pro bono service). (NASW, 1996)

Counselors contribute to society by devoting a portion of their professional activity to services for which there is little or no financial return (pro bono). (ACA, 1995).

If you did not want to abandon your client, you could refer Kevin to an agency that would see him without a fee, assuming such a facility exists in your area. You could also see him as part of your *pro bono* services (services you provide without your usual fee or for no fee). Ethically you are obliged to provide the best quality of care, however you may be part of a managed care system that limits the number of sessions and has a very limited focus of goals and treatment. Even though you want to do what is best for your client, you may be unable to provide *pro bono* care without creating other problems for yourself.

Basic moral principles in making ethical decisions.   Building upon the work of others, especially Kitchener (1984), Meara et al. (1996) describe six basic moral principles that form the foundation of functioning at the highest ethical level as a professional: autonomy, nonmaleficence, beneficence, justice, fidelity, and veracity. Applying these ethical principles and the related ethical standards is not as simple as it may seem, especially when dealing with culturally diverse populations. (See Chapters 10 and 11 for more on this issue.) Consider each of these six basic moral principles, which we have illustrated by citing a specific ethical guideline from the ACA *Code of Ethics* (1995) and by providing a brief discussion of the cultural implications of using each principle.

Autonomy refers to the promotion of self-determination, or the freedom of clients to choose their own direction. Respect for autonomy entails acknowledging the right of another to choose and act in accordance with his or her wishes, and the professional behaves in a way that enables this right of another person. The ACA guideline is: "Counselors encourage client growth and development in ways that foster the clients' interest and welfare; counselors avoid fostering dependent counseling relationships" (A.1.b.).

The helping services are based on traditional Western values of individualism, independence, self-determination, and making choices for oneself. However, many cultures stress a different set of values, such as interdependence and making decisions with the welfare of the family and community in mind. What are the implications of the principle of autonomy when it is applied to clients who do not place a high priority on the value of being autonomous? Does it constitute an imposition of values for counselors to steer clients toward autonomous behavior when such behavior could lead to problems with others in their family, community, or culture? What about promoting autonomy for those incapable of it (for example, dependent youths)?

Nonmaleficence means avoiding doing harm, which includes refraining from actions that risk hurting clients, either intentionally or unintentionally.

Professionals have a responsibility to avoid engaging in practices that cause harm or have the potential to result in harm. The ACA code states: "In the counseling relationship, counselors are aware of the intimacy and responsibilities inherent in the counseling relationship, maintain respect for clients, and avoid actions that seek to meet their personal needs at the expense of clients" (A.5.a.).

M.C.

What are the cultural implications of the principle of nonmaleficence? Traditional diagnostic practices can be inappropriate for certain cultural groups. For instance, a therapist may assign a diagnostic label to a client based on a pattern of behavior the therapist judges to be abnormal, such as inhibition of emotional expression, hesitation to confront, being cautious about self-disclosing, or not making direct eye contact while speaking. Yet these behaviors may be considered to be normal in certain cultures. If a culturally different client does not feel understood, or if a therapist gives an inappropriate diagnosis to the client, he or she may not return for any professional service. Practitioners need to develop cultural awareness and sensitivity in using assessment, diagnostic, and treatment procedures.

Beneficence refers to promoting good for others. Ideally, counseling contributes to the growth and development of the client, and whatever counselors do should be judged against this criterion. The following ACA guideline illustrates beneficence: "The primary responsibility of counselors is to respect the dignity and to promote the welfare of clients" (A.1.a.).

Consider the possible consequences if a counselor encourages a Japanese client to behave more assertively toward his father. The reality of this situation may be that the father would refuse to speak again to a son who confronted him. Even though counselors may be operating with good intentions and may think they are being beneficent, they may not always be doing what is in the best interest of the client. Is it possible for counselors to harm clients unintentionally by encouraging a course of action that has negative consequences? How can counselors know what is in the best interest of their clients? How can counselors determine whether their interventions will lead to growth and development in their clients?

Justice or fairness, means providing equal treatment to all people. Everyone, regardless of age, sex, race, ethnicity, disability, socioeconomic status, cultural background, religion, or sexual orientation, is entitled to equal access to mental-health services. To ensure that client populations have equal access to professional services, the ACA code encourages counselors to offer *pro bono* services: "Counselors contribute to society by devoting a portion of their professional activity to services for which there is little or no financial return (pro bono)" (A.10.d.).

Traditional mental-health services may not be just and fair to everyone in a culturally diverse society. If intervention strategies are not relevant to some segments of the population, justice is being violated. How can practitioners adapt the techniques they use to fit the needs of diverse populations? How can new helping strategies be developed that are consistent with the worldview of culturally different clients?

Fidelity means that professionals make honest promises and honor their commitments to those they serve. This entails fulfilling one's responsibilities of trust in a relationship. ACA's code encourages counselors to inform clients about counseling and be faithful in keeping commitments made to clients: "When counseling is initiated, and throughout the counseling process as necessary, counselors inform clients of the purposes, goals, techniques, procedures, limitations, potential risks, and benefits of services to be performed, and other pertinent information" (A.3.a.).

Fidelity involves creating a trusting and therapeutic relationship whereby people can search for their own solutions. However, what about clients whose culture teaches them that counselors are experts who have the function of providing answers for clients' specific problem situations? What if a client expects the counselor to provide a solution to a particular problem? If the counselor does not meet the client's expectations, is trust being established?

Veracity means truthfulness. Unless practitioners are truthful with their clients, the trust required to form a good working relationship will not develop. This principle of veracity is found in the following ACA guideline: "Counselors take steps to insure that clients understand the implications of diagnosis, the intended use of tests and reports, fees, and billing arrangements. Clients have the right to expect confidentiality and to be provided with an explanation of its limitations, including supervision and/or treatment team professionals; to obtain clear information about their case records; to participate in the ongoing counseling plans; and to refuse any recommended services and be advised of the consequences of such refusal" (A.3.a.).

Informed consent is a part of being truthful with clients. At times, underserved populations (including many ethnic and racial minorities and persons of low socioeconomic status) have not been as fully informed by professionals as those in more advantageous situations (Meara et al., 1996). What would you do to ensure that your clients understand the informed consent process? How can underserved populations be taught to be active consumers of social services? In what way is being truthful with clients especially important when working with underserved clients?

Therapists often need to function in the role of advocate, community organizer, consultant, or agent for change in the communities they serve. These roles are quite different from traditional psychotherapy, and practitioners should reexamine ethical issues in light of these unfamiliar roles. The six principles discussed here are a good place to start in determining the degree to which their practice is consistent with promoting the welfare of the clients they serve.

Finally, Meara et al. (1996) raise some cautions and caveats with regard to virtue ethics. First of all, "Who decides what is virtuous?" As ethical professionals, you must regularly reassess your concept of virtue. Avoid rationalizations and attempts to justify your actions under the guise of following the right path. Meara et al. suggest: "We need to reassess systematically our motives and perspectives and the virtues we encourage. We need, as well, to be open to exploring and even adopting virtues different from our own" (p. 47).

Steps in Making Ethical Decisions

Ethical decision making is not a purely cognitive and linear process that follows neatly step by step. Indeed, it is crucial to acknowledge that emotions play a part in how we make ethical decisions. As a practitioner, your feelings will likely influence how you interpret both your client's behavior and your own behavior. Furthermore, if you are uncomfortable with an ethical decision and do not adequately deal with this discomfort, it will certainly influence your future behavior with your client. An integral part of recognizing and working through an ethical concern is discussing your beliefs and values, motivations, feelings, and actions with a supervisor or a colleague.

In the process of making the best ethical decisions, it is also wise to involve your clients as fully as possible. Because you are making decisions about what is best for the welfare of your clients, you should discuss with them the nature of the ethical dilemma that pertains to them. The feminist model for ethical decision making (Hill et al., 1995) calls for maximum involvement of the client at every stage of the ethical decision-making process. The authors of the feminist model state that consultation with the client "as fully as is possible and appropriate" (p. 27) is an essential step in ethical decision making. Hill, Glaser, and Harden suggest that the client should be included throughout the process whenever possible, as can be seen in their seven-step model:

feminist process include client " doing with" not "doing to"

1. Recognizing a problem
2. Defining the problem (collaboration with client essential at this stage)
3. Developing solutions (with client)
4. Choosing a solution
5. Reviewing the process (with client) and rechoosing
6. Implementing and evaluating (with client)
7. Continuing reflection

In "The Counselor/Client Partnership in Ethical Practice," Walden (1997) suggests that important therapeutic benefits can result from inclusion of the client in the ethical decision-making process, and she offers some strategies for accomplishing this goal at both the organizational and individual levels. When we make decisions about a client *for* the client rather than *with* the client, Walden maintains that we rob the client of power in the relationship. When we create a collaborative therapeutic relationship, the client is empowered. By soliciting the client's perspective, we stand a good chance of achieving better counseling results and the best resolution for any ethical questions that arise. Not only are there potential therapeutic benefits to be gained by including clients in dealing with ethical concerns but such practices also imply functioning at the aspirational level. In fact, Walden questions whether it is truly possible to attain the aspirational level of ethical functioning *without* including the client's voice in ethical concerns. By adding the voice and the unique perspective of the consumers of professional services, we indicate to the public that we as a profession are genuinely interested in protecting the rights and welfare of those who make use of our services. Walden sees few risks in bringing the client into ethical matters, and there are many benefits to both the client and the professional.

Keeping in mind both the feminist model of ethical decision making and Walden's views on including the client's voice in ethical concerns, we present our approach to thinking through ethical dilemmas. Following these steps may help you think through ethical problems.

1. *Identify the problem or dilemma.* Gather as much information as possible that sheds light on the situation. Clarify whether the conflict is ethical, legal, professional, or moral—or a combination of any or all of these. The first step toward resolving an ethical dilemma is recognizing that a problem exists and identifying its specific nature. Because most ethical dilemmas are complex, it is useful to look at the problem from many perspectives and to avoid simplistic solutions. Ethical dilemmas do not have "right" or "wrong" answers, so you will be challenged to deal with ambiguity. Consultation with your client should begin at this initial stage and continue throughout the process of working through an ethical problem.

2. *Identify the potential issues involved.* After the information is collected, list and describe the critical issues and discard the irrelevant ones. Evaluate the rights, responsibilities, and welfare of all those who are affected by the situation. Part of the process of making ethical decisions involves identifying competing moral principles. Consider the basic moral principles of autonomy, nonmaleficence, beneficence, justice, fidelity, and veracity and apply them to the situation. It may help to prioritize these principles and think through ways in which they can support a resolution to the dilemma. Good reasons can be presented that support various sides of a given issue, and different ethical principles may sometimes imply contradictory courses of action.

3. *Review the relevant ethics codes.* Ask yourself whether the standards or principles of your professional organization offer a possible solution to the problem. Consider whether your own values and ethics are consistent with or in conflict with the relevant codes. If you are in disagreement with a particular standard, do you have a rationale to support your position? You can also call your professional organization and seek guidance on any specific concern relating to the interpretation of an ethical standard.

4. *Know the applicable laws and regulations.* It is essential for you to keep up to date on relevant state and federal laws that apply to ethical dilemmas. This is especially critical in matters of keeping or breaching confidentiality, reporting child or elder abuse, record keeping, testing and assessment, diagnosis, and grounds for malpractice. In addition, be sure you understand the current rules and regulations of the agency or organization where you work.

5. *Obtain consultation.* At this point, it is generally helpful to consult with a colleague or colleagues to obtain a different perspective on the problem. Consider consulting with more than one professional, and do not limit the individuals with whom you will consult to those who share your orientation. If there is a legal question, seek legal counsel. It is wise to document the nature of your consultation, including the suggestions provided by those with whom

you consulted. Because of your involvement in the situation, you may have trouble seeing the forest for the trees. Consultation can help you think about information or circumstances that you may have overlooked. In making ethical decisions, you must justify a course of action based on sound reasoning. Consultation with colleagues provides an opportunity to test your justification.

6. *Consider possible and probable courses of action.* Brainstorming is useful at this stage of ethical decision making. By listing a wide variety of courses of action, you may identify a possibility that is unorthodox but useful. Of course, one alternative is that no action is required. As you think about the many possibilities for action, discuss these options with your client as well as with other professionals.

7. *Enumerate the consequences of various decisions.* Ponder the implications of each course of action for the client, for others who are related to the client, and for you as the counselor. Again, a discussion with your client about consequences for him or her is most important. Consider using the six fundamental principles (autonomy, nonmaleficence, beneficence, justice, fidelity, and veracity) as a framework for evaluating the consequences of a given course of action.

8. *Decide on what appears to be the best course of action.* In making the best decision, carefully consider the information you have received from various sources. The more obvious the dilemma, the clearer is the course of action; the more subtle the dilemma, the more difficult the decision will be. After deciding, try not to second-guess your course of action. You may realize later that another action might have been more beneficial. But this hindsight does not invalidate the decision you made based on the information you had at the time. Once you have made what you consider to be the best decision, do what you can to evaluate your course of action. Follow up to determine the outcomes and see if any further action is needed. To obtain the most accurate picture, involve your client in this process.

The procedural steps we have listed here should not be thought of as a simplified and linear way to reach a resolution on ethical matters. However, we have found that these steps stimulate self-reflection and encourage discussion with your clients and colleagues. Using this process, we are confident that you will find your own best solution.

Some Suggestions for Using This Book

In this book we deal with the central professional and ethical issues you are likely to encounter in your work with clients. Our aim is to stimulate you to form your own opinions on these issues and to be able to justify them.

In writing this book we frequently imagined ourselves in conversations with our students. Whenever it seems appropriate, we state our own thinking and discuss how we arrived at the positions we hold. We think it's important to reveal our biases, convictions, and attitudes; then you can critically evaluate our stance. On many issues we present a range of viewpoints. Our hope is that you will give constant attention to ways of integrating your own thoughts and experiences with the positions we explore. In this way you will not only absorb information but also deepen your understanding.

The format of this book is different from that of most traditional textbooks. This is a personal manual that can be useful to you at various stages in your professional development. The many questions and exercises interspersed in the text are intended to stimulate you to become an active reader and learner. If you take the time to do the exercises and complete the surveys and inventories, you will have met the challenge to reflect personally on these issues, and you will have a record of your reactions to them.

We have intentionally provided an abundance of exercises in each chapter, more than can be integrated in one semester or in one course. We invite you to decide which questions and other exercises have the most meaning for you now. At a later reading of the book, you may want to consider questions or activities that you omitted on your initial reading.

We'd like to make several other specific suggestions for getting the most from this book and from your course. Many of these ideas come from students who have been in our classes. In general, you'll get from this book and course whatever you're willing to invest of yourself, so it's important to clarify your goals and to think about ways of becoming actively involved. Here are some suggestions that can help you become an active learner:

◆ *Be prepared.* You can best prepare yourself to become active in your class by spending time reading and thinking about the questions we pose. Completing the exercises and responding to the questions and open-ended cases will help you focus on where you stand on controversial issues.

◆ *Examine your expectations.* Students often have unrealistic expectations of themselves. You may think you should have all the right answers worked out before you begin to work with people. If you haven't had much experience in counseling clients, you can begin to become involved in the issues we discuss by thinking about situations in which friends have sought you out when they were in need of help. You can also reflect on the times when you were experiencing conflicts and needed someone to help you gain clarity. In this way you may be able to relate the material to events in your own life even if your counseling experience is limited.

◆ *Take the self-assessment survey.* The multiple-choice survey at the end of this chapter is designed to help you discover your attitudes concerning most of the issues we deal with in this book. We encourage you to take this inventory before you read the book to see where you stand on these issues at this time. We also suggest that you take the inventory again after you complete the book. You can then compare your responses to see what changes have occurred in your attitudes as a result of the course and your reading of the book.

◆ *Take the pre-chapter self-inventories.* Each chapter begins with an inventory designed to stimulate your thinking about the issues that will be explored in the chapter. You may want to bring your responses to class and compare your views with those of fellow students. You may also find it useful to retake the inventory after you finish reading the chapter to see whether your views have changed.

◆ *Think about the examples, cases, and questions.* Many examples in this book are drawn from actual counseling practice in various settings with different types of clients. We frequently ask you to consider how you might have worked with a given client or what you might have done in a particular counseling situation. We hope you'll take the time to think about these questions and briefly respond to them in the spaces provided.

◆ *Do the end-of-chapter exercises and activities.* Each chapter ends with exercises and activities intended to help you integrate and apply what you've learned. They include suggestions for things to do both in class and on your own. The purpose of these aids is to make the issues come alive and to help you apply your ideas to practical situations. We think the time you devote to these end-of-chapter activities can be most useful in helping you achieve a practical grasp of the material treated in the text.

◆ *Follow up with selected outside reading.* Near the end of the book, you'll find a reading list of additional sources you might want to consult. By developing the habit of doing some reading on issues that have meaning to you, you will gain insights that can be integrated into your own frame of reference.

As you read and think about the cases and end-of-chapter exercises and activities, formulate your own personal ethical perspective on the issues they raise. We encourage you to use this book in any way that involves you in the issues. Focus selectively on the questions and activities that have the most meaning for you at this time, and remain open to new issues as they assume importance for you. Our hope is that by reading this book and getting involved in your ethics course, you will discover other ways in which to work through the process of making ethical decisions.

Self-Assessment: An Inventory of Your Attitudes and Beliefs about Professional and Ethical Issues

This inventory surveys your thoughts on various professional and ethical issues in the helping professions. The inventory is designed to introduce you to issues and topics presented in this book and to stimulate your thoughts and interest. You may want to complete the inventory in more than one sitting, giving each question your full concentration.

This is not a traditional multiple-choice test in which you must select the "one right answer." Rather, it is a survey of your basic beliefs, attitudes, and values on specific topics related to the practice of therapy. For each question, write in the letter of the response that most clearly reflects your viewpoint at this time. In many cases the answers are not mutually exclusive, and you may choose more than one response if you wish. In addition, a blank line is included for each item so you can provide a response more suited to your thinking or qualify a chosen response.

Notice that there are two spaces before each item. Use the space on the left for your answer at the beginning of the course. At the end of the course, retake this inventory, placing your answer in the space on the right. Cover your initial answers so you won't be influenced by how you originally responded. Then you can see how your attitudes have changed as a result of your experience in this course.

You may want to bring the completed inventory to your beginning class session to compare your views with those of others in the class. Such a comparison might stimulate some debate and help get the class involved in the topics to be discussed. In choosing the issues you want to discuss in class, circle the numbers of those items that you felt most strongly about as you were responding. You may find it instructive to ask others how they responded to these items in particular.

b ___   1. The personal characteristics of counselors are
    a. not really that relevant to the counseling process.
    b. the most important variable in determining the quality of the counseling process.
    c. shaped and molded by those who teach counselors.
    d. not as important as the skills and knowledge the counselors possess.
    e. _____

b ___   2. Which of the following do you consider to be the most important personal characteristic of a good counselor?
    a. willingness to serve as a model for clients
    b. courage
    c. openness and honesty
    d. a sense of being "centered" as a person
    e. _____

c ___   3. Concerning counselors' self-disclosure to their clients, I believe that
    a. it is essential for establishing a relationship.
    b. it is inappropriate and merely burdens the client.
    c. it should be done rarely and only when the therapist feels that it would be of benefit to the client.
    d. it is useful for counselors to reveal how they feel toward their clients in the context of the therapy sessions.
    e. _____

d ___   4. If I were working with a client who could no longer continue because of his or her inability to pay my fees, I would most likely
    a. be willing to see this person at no fee until his or her financial position changed.
    b. give my client the name of a local community clinic that provides low-cost treatment.
    c. suggest some form of bartering of goods or services for therapy services.

d. lower my fee to whatever the client could afford.

e. _____

_C_ __ 5. Of the following factors, which is the most important in determining whether counseling will result in change?

a. the kind of person the counselor is

b. the skills and techniques the counselor uses

c. the motivation of the client to change

d. the theoretical orientation of the therapist

e. _____

_C_ __ 6. Of the following, which do you consider to be the most important attribute of an effective therapist?

a. knowledge of the theory of counseling and behavior

b. skill in using techniques appropriately

c. genuineness and openness

d. ability to specify a treatment plan and evaluate the results

e. _____

_a_ __ 7. For those who wish to become therapists, I believe that personal
psychotherapy

a. should be required for licensure.

b. is not an important factor in developing the capacity to work
with others.

c. should be encouraged but not required.

d. is needed only when the therapist has some form of psychological impairment.

e. _____

_d_ __ 8. To be an effective helper, I believe that a therapist

a. must like the client personally.

b. must be free of any personal conflicts in the area in which the
client is working.

c. needs to have experienced the same problem as the client.

d. needs to have experienced feelings similar to those being
experienced by the client. Universality of feelings

e. _____

_C_ __ 9. With regard to the client-therapist relationship, I think that

a. the therapist should remain objective and anonymous.

b. the therapist should be a friend to the client.

c. a personal relationship, but not friendship, is essential.

d. a personal and warm relationship is not essential.

e. _____

_d_ __ 10. I should be open and honest with my clients

a. when I like and value them.

b. when I have negative feelings toward them.

c. rarely, if ever, so that I will avoid negatively influencing the
client-therapist relationship.

d. only when it intuitively feels like the right thing to do.

e. _____

_c_ ___ 11. If I were faced with an ethical dilemma, the first step I would take would be to
   a. review the relevant ethical codes.
   b. consult with an attorney.
   c. identify the problem or dilemma.
   d. quickly decide on what appears to be the best course of action.
   e. _____

_b_ ___ 12. For me, being an ethical practitioner *mainly* entails
   a. acting in compliance with minimal ethical standards.
   b. reflecting on the effects that my interventions are likely to have on the welfare of my clients.
   c. avoiding obvious violations of my profession's ethical codes.
   d. thinking about the legal implications of everything I do.
   e. _____

_a_ ___ 13. If I were an intern and was convinced that my supervisor was encouraging trainees to participate in unethical behavior in an agency setting, I would
   a. first discuss the matter with the supervisor.
   b. report the supervisor to the director of the agency.
   c. ignore the situation for fear of negative consequences.
   d. report the situation to the ethics committee of the state professional association.
   e. _____

_b_ ___ 14. Practitioners who work with culturally diverse groups without having cross-cultural knowledge and skills
   a. are violating the civil rights of their clients.
   b. are probably guilty of unethical behavior.
   c. should realize the need for specialized training.
   d. can be said to be practicing ethically.
   e. _____

_c_ ___ 15. If I had strong feelings, positive or negative, toward a client, I think I would most likely
   a. discuss my feelings with my client.
   b. keep them to myself and hope they would eventually disappear.
   c. discuss them with a supervisor or colleague.
   d. accept them as natural unless they began to interfere with the counseling relationship.
   e. _____

_d_ ___ 16. I won't feel ready to counsel others until
   a. my own life is free of problems.
   b. I've experienced counseling as a client.
   c. I feel very confident and know that I'll be effective.
   d. I've become a self-aware person and developed the ability to continually reexamine my own life and relationships.
   e. _____

_a_ ___ 17. If a client evidenced strong feelings of attraction or dislike for me,
_or c_   I think I would
- a. help the client work through these feelings and understand them.
- b. enjoy these feelings if they were positive.
- c. refer my client to another counselor.
- d. direct the sessions into less emotional areas.
- e. _____

_b_ ___ 18. Practitioners who counsel clients whose sex, race, age, social class, or sexual orientation is different from their own
- a. will most likely not understand these clients fully.
- b. need to understand the differences between their clients and themselves.
- c. can practice unethically if they do not consider cross-cultural factors.
- d. are probably not going to be effective with such clients because of these differences.
- e. _____

_c_ ___ 19. When I consider being involved in the helping professions, I value most
- a. the money I expect to earn.
- b. the security I imagine I will have in the job.
- c. the knowledge that I will be intimately involved with people who are searching for a better life.
- d. the personal growth I expect to experience through my work.
- e. _____

_c_ ___ 20. If I were faced with a counseling situation where it appeared that there was a conflict between an ethical and legal course to follow, I would
- a. immediately consult with an attorney.
- b. always choose the legal path first and foremost.
- c. strive to do what I believed to be ethical, even if it meant challenging a law.
- d. refer my client to another therapist.
- e. _____

_d_ ___ 21. With respect to value judgments in counseling, therapists should
- a. feel free to make value judgments about their clients' behavior.
- b. actively teach their own values when they think clients need a different set of values.
- c. remain neutral and keep their values out of the therapeutic process.
- d. encourage clients to question their own values and decide on the quality of their own behavior.
- e. _____

_b_ ___ 22. Counselors should
      a. teach desirable behavior and values by modeling them for clients.
      b. encourage clients to look within themselves to discover values that are meaningful to them.
      c. reinforce the dominant values of society.
      d. very delicately, if at all, challenge clients' value systems.
      e. _____

_d_ ___ 23. In terms of appreciating and understanding the value systems of clients who are culturally different from me,
      a. I see it as my responsibility to learn about their values and not impose mine on them.
      b. I would encourage them to accept the values of the dominant culture for survival purposes.
      c. I would attempt to modify my counseling procedures to fit their cultural values.
      d. I think it is imperative that I learn about the specific cultural values my clients hold.
      e. _____

_c_ ___ 24. If a client came to me with a problem and I could see that I would not be objective because of my values, I would
      a. accept the client because of the challenge to become more tolerant of diversity.
      b. tell the client at the outset about my fears concerning our conflicting values.
      c. refer the client to someone else.
      d. attempt to influence the client to adopt my way of thinking.
      e. _____

_?_ ___ 25. With respect to a client's right to make his or her own end-of-life decisions, I would
      a. always use the principle of a client's self-determination as the key in any dilemma of this sort.
      b. tell my client what I thought was the right course to follow.
      c. suggest that my client see a clergy person or a physician.
      d. encourage my client to find meaning in life, regardless of his or her psychological and physical condition.
      e. _____

_c_ ___ 26. I would tend to refer a client to another therapist
      a. if I had a strong dislike for the client.
      b. if I didn't have much experience working with the kind of problem the client presented.
      c. If I saw my own needs and problems getting in the way of helping the client.
      d. if the client seemed to distrust me.
      e. _____

_a_ ___ 27. My ethical position regarding the role of values in therapy is that, as a therapist, I should

a. never impose my values on a client.
b. expose my values, without imposing them on the client.
c. teach my clients what I consider to be proper values.
d. keep my values out of the counseling relationship.
e. _____

_C_ __ 28. If I were to counsel lesbian and gay clients, a major concern of mine would be
a. maintaining objectivity.
b. not knowing and understanding enough about this lifestyle.
c. establishing a positive therapeutic relationship.
d. pushing my own values.
e. _____

_b_ __ 29. Of the following, I consider the most unethical form of therapist
∜ d   behavior to be
a. promoting dependence in the client.
b. becoming sexually involved with a client.
c. breaking confidentiality without a good reason to do so.
d. accepting a client who has a problem that goes beyond my competence.
e. _____

_C_ __ 30. Regarding the issue of counseling friends, I think that
a. it is seldom wise to accept a friend as a client.
b. it should be done rarely, and only if it is clear that the friendship will not interfere with the therapeutic relationship.
c. friendship and therapy should not be mixed.
d. it should be done only if it seems appropriate to both the client and the counselor.
e. _____

a+b __ 31. Regarding confidentiality, I believe that
a. it is ethical to break confidence when there is reason to believe that clients may do serious harm to themselves.
b. it is ethical to break confidence when there is reason to believe that a client will do harm to someone else.
c. it is ethical to break confidence when the parents of a client ask for certain information.
d. it is ethical to inform the authorities when a client is breaking the law.
e. _____

_C_ __ 32. A therapist should terminate therapy with a client when
a. the client decides to do so and not before.
b. the therapist judges that it is time to terminate.
c. it is clear that the client is not benefiting from the therapy.
d. the client reaches an impasse.
e. _____

_b_ __ 33. A sexual relationship between a *former* client and a therapist is
a. ethical if the client initiates it.
b. ethical only two years after termination of therapy.

c. ethical only when client and therapist discuss the issue and agree to the relationship.

d. never ethical, regardless of the time that has elapsed.

e. _____

_d_ ___ 34. Concerning the issue of physically touching a client, I think that touching

a. is unwise, because it could be misinterpreted by the client.

b. should be done only when the therapist genuinely thinks it would be appropriate.

c. is an important part of the therapeutic process.

d. is ethical when the client requests it.

e. _____

_a_ ___ 35. A clinical supervisor has initiated sexual relationships with former trainees (students). He maintains that because he no longer has any professional responsibility to them this practice is acceptable. In my view, this behavior is

a. clearly unethical, because he is using his position to initiate contacts with former students.

b. not unethical, because the professional relationship has ended.

c. not unethical but is unwise and inappropriate.

d. somewhat unethical, because the supervisory relationship is similar to the therapeutic relationship.

e. _____

_d_ ___ 36. Regarding the role of spiritual and religious values, as a counselor I would be inclined to

a. ignore such values for fear that I would impose my own beliefs on my clients.

b. actively strive to get my clients to think about how spirituality or religion could enhance their lives.

c. avoid bringing up the topic unless my client initiated such a discussion.

d. conduct an assessment of my client's spiritual and religious beliefs during the intake session.

e. _____

_a_ ___ 37. In the practice of marital and family therapy, I think

a. the therapist's primary responsibility is to the welfare of the family as a unit.

b. the therapist should focus primarily on the needs of individual members of the family.

c. the therapist should attend to the family's needs and try to hold the amount of sacrifice by any one member to a minimum.

d. the therapist has an ethical obligation to state his or her bias and approach at the outset.

e. _____

_b_ ___ 38. The practice of limiting the number of therapy sessions a client is entitled to under a managed care plan is
   a. unethical as it can work against a client's best interests.
   b. a reality that I expect I'll have to accept.
   c. an example of exploitation of a client's rights.
   d. wrong because it takes away the professional's judgment in many cases.
   e. _____

_c_ ___ 39. Regarding the issue of who should select the goals of counseling, I believe that
   a. it is primarily the therapist's responsibility to select goals.
   b. it is primarily the client's responsibility to select goals.
   c. the responsibility for selecting goals should be shared equally by the client and the therapist.
   d. the question of who selects the goals depends on what kind of client is being seen.
   e. _____

_a_ ___ 40. Concerning the role of diagnosis in counseling, I believe that
   a. diagnosis is essential for planning a treatment program.
   b. diagnosis is counterproductive for therapy, because it is based on an external view of the client.
   c. diagnosis is dangerous in that it tends to label people, who then are limited by the label.
   d. whether to use diagnosis depends on the theoretical orientation and the kind of counseling a therapist does.
   e. _____

_b_ ___ 41. Concerning the place of testing in counseling, I think that
   a. tests generally interfere with the counseling process.
   b. tests can be valuable tools if they are used as adjuncts to counseling.
   c. tests are essential for people who are seriously disturbed.
   d. tests can be either used or abused in counseling.
   e. _____

_a_ ___ 42. Regarding the issue of psychological risks associated with participation in group therapy, my position is that
   a. clients should be informed at the outset of possible risks.
   b. these risks should be minimized by careful screening.
   c. this issue is exaggerated because there are no real risks.
   d. careful supervision will offset some of these risks.
   e. _____

_d_ ___ 43. Concerning the counselor's responsibility to the community, I believe that
   a. the counselor should educate the community concerning the nature of psychological services.
   b. the counselor should attempt to change patterns that need changing.

c. community involvement falls outside the proper scope of counseling.

d. counselors should become involved in helping clients use the resources available in the community.

e. _____

_C_ ___ 44. If I were working as a counselor in the community, the major role I would expect to play would be that of

a. a change agent.

b. an adviser.

c. an educator or a consultant.

d. an advocate.

e. _____

_a_ ___ 45. As an intern, if I thought my supervisor was inadequate, I would

a. talk to my supervisor about it.

b. continue to work without complaining.

c. seek supervision elsewhere.

d. feel let down by the agency I worked for.

e. _____

_d_ ___ 46. My view of supervision is that it is

a. a place to get answers to difficult situations.

b. an opportunity to work on my personal problems.

c. valuable to have when I reach an impasse with a client.

d. a way for me to learn about myself and to get insights into how I work with clients.

e. _____

_a_ ___ 47. When it comes to working in institutions, I believe that

a. I must learn how to survive with dignity within a system.

b. I must learn how to subvert the system so that I can do what I deeply believe in.

c. the institution will stifle most of my enthusiasm and block any real change.

d. I can't blame the institution if I'm unable to succeed in my programs.

e. _____

_a_ ___ 48. If my philosophy were in conflict with that of the institution I worked for, I would

a. seriously consider whether I could ethically remain in that position.

b. attempt to change the policies of the institution.

c. agree to whatever was expected of me in that system.

d. quietly do what I wanted to do, even if I had to be devious about it.

e. _____

_a_ ___ 49. In working with clients from different ethnic groups, it is most important to

a. be aware of the sociopolitical forces that have affected these clients.

b. understand how language can act as a barrier to effective cross-cultural counseling.

c. refer these clients to some professional who shares their ethnic and cultural background.

d. help these clients modify their views so that they will be accepted and not have to suffer rejection.

e. _____

_a_ ___ 50. To be effective in counseling clients from a different culture, a counselor must

a. possess specific knowledge about the particular group he or she is counseling.

b. be able to accurately "read" nonverbal messages.

c. have had direct contact with this group.

d. treat these clients no differently from clients from his or her own cultural background.

e. _____

Chapter Summary

This introductory chapter has focused on the foundations of creating an ethical sense and has explored various perspectives on teaching the process of making ethical decisions. Professional codes of ethics are indeed essential for ethical practice, but merely knowing these codes is not enough. The challenge comes with learning how to think critically and knowing ways to apply general ethical principles to particular situations. We encourage you to become active in your education and training. We also suggest that you try to keep an open mind about the issues you encounter during this time and throughout your professional career. An important part of this openness is a willingness to focus on yourself as a person and as a professional as well as on the questions that are more obviously related to your clients.

Suggested Activities

1. As a practitioner, how will you determine what is ethical and what is unethical? How will you develop your guidelines for ethical practice? Make a list of behaviors that you judge to be unethical. After you've thought through this issue by yourself, you may want to explore your approach with fellow students.

2. Take the self-assessment survey of your attitudes and beliefs about ethics in this chapter. After you've taken the inventory, circle the five items that you had the strongest reactions to or that you had the hardest time answering. Bring these items to class for class discussion.

3. Look over the professional codes of ethics in the Appendix. What are your impressions of each of these codes? To what degree are they complete? To what degree do they provide you with the needed guidelines for ethical practice? What are the values of such codes? What limitations do you see in them? What do the various codes have in common?

4. In addition to becoming generally familiar with the ethics codes in the Appendix, consider getting at least one of the ethics casebooks for one of the professional organizations. These casebooks illustrate standards and apply them to specific situations. There are case vignettes, articles, and discussions of ways to interpret specific sections of the codes in practical ethical dilemmas. The casebooks you may want to consider are:

- ◆ **For the American Counseling Association**
  ACA Ethical Standards Casebook (Fifth Edition)
  Barbara Herlihy and Gerald Corey (1996)
  This casebook is designed to provide a foundation for analytic evaluation of the standards in applying these principles in work with diverse client populations. It contains illustrative vignettes that encourage discussion and distinguish ethical practice from questionable or unethical practice. Nineteen original case studies (written by various authors) clarify complex areas of ethical conduct.
  > Order from the American Counseling Association
  > 5999 Stevenson Avenue
  > Alexandria, VA 22304
  > 1-800-347-6647
  > ($17.95 for members; $21.95 for nonmembers)

- ◆ **For the American Psychological Association**
  Ethics for Psychologists: A Commentary on the APA Ethics Code
  Mathilda B. Canter, Bruce E. Bennett, Stanley E. Jones, and Thomas F. Nagy (1994)
  This casebook is a practical resource to help students and practitioners learn and apply the APA Ethics Code. It deals with the ethical decision-making process and provides commentaries to address questions that are likely to be raised by therapists with regard to a given standard. The last section puts the ethical principles in context by describing how psychology is regulated by professional organizations as well as by local, state, and federal laws.
  > Order from the American Psychological Association
  > Book Order Department
  > 750 First Street, NE
  > Washington, DC 20002-4242
  > 1-800-374-2721
  > ($19.95 for members/affiliates; list price is $24.95)

- ◆ **For the American Association for Marriage and Family Therapy**
  American Association for Marriage and Family Therapy Ethics Casebook
  Gregory W. Brock (Editor) (1994)

This casebook contains specific case examples and discussions illustrating ethical practices regarding relationships with clients, supervisees, employees, third-party payers, and colleagues. It includes essays on dual relationships, confidentiality, impaired therapists, the role of clergy therapists, defensive supervision, and a U.S. survey of ethical behavior and attitudes of marriage and family therapists.

Order from the American Association for Marriage
   and Family Therapy
1133 15th Street, NW, Suite 300
Washington, DC 20005-2710
(202) 452-0109
($24.95 for AAMFT members; $34.95 for nonmembers)

Note to the student.   We hope you won't feel the pressure or expectation to systematically think about and work on every suggested activity at the end of each chapter. We have deliberately provided a range of activities for instructors and students to choose from. Our purpose is to invite you to personalize the material and develop your own positions on the issues we raise. We suggest that you choose those activities that you find the most challenging and meaningful.

2

The Counselor as a Person and as a Professional

- Pre-Chapter Self-Inventory

- Introduction

- Self-Awareness and the Influence of the Therapist's Personality and Needs

- Personal Therapy for Counselors

- Transference and Countertransference

- Client Dependence

- Manipulation versus Collaboration

- Stress in the Counseling Profession

- Counselor Impairment

- Staying Alive Personally and Professionally

- Chapter Summary

- Suggested Activities

Pre-Chapter Self-Inventory

The pre-chapter self-inventories can help you identify and clarify your attitudes and beliefs about the issues to be explored in the chapter. Keep in mind that the "right" answer is the one that best expresses your thoughts at the time. We suggest that you complete the inventory before reading the chapter; then, after reading the chapter and discussing the material in class, retake the inventory to see whether your positions have changed in any way.

Directions: For each statement, indicate the response that most closely identifies your beliefs and attitudes. Use the following code:

5 = I *strongly agree* with this statement.
4 = I *agree* with this statement.
3 = I am *undecided* about this statement.
2 = I *disagree* with this statement.
1 = I *strongly disagree* with this statement.

_5_ 1. Unless therapists have a high degree of self-awareness, there is a real danger that they will use their clients to satisfy their own needs.

_2_ 2. Before therapists begin to practice, they should be free of personal problems and conflicts.

_4_ 3. Counselors or therapists should be required to undergo their own therapy before they are licensed to practice.

_4_ 4. Counselors who satisfy personal needs through their work are behaving unethically.

_4_ 5. Many professionals in the counseling field face a high risk of burnout because of the demands of their jobs.

_2_ 6. Counselors who know themselves can avoid experiencing overidentification with their clients.

_2_ 7. Strong feelings about a client are a sign that the counselor needs further therapy.

_2_ 8. Feelings of anxiety in a beginning counselor indicate unsuitability for the counseling profession.

_2_ 9. A competent counselor can work with any client.

_4_ 10. I fear that I'll have difficulty challenging my clients.

_5_ 11. A professional counselor will avoid getting involved socially with clients or counseling friends.

_2_ 12. A major fear of mine is that I'll make mistakes and seriously hurt a client.

_4_ 13. Real therapy does not occur unless a transference relationship is developed.

_4_ 14. I think it is important to adapt my therapeutic techniques and approaches to the cultural background of my clients.

_2_ 15. An experienced and competent counselor should not need either periodic or ongoing personal psychotherapy.

Introduction

A primary issue in the helping professions is the role of the counselor *as a person* in the therapeutic relationship. Because counselors are asking clients to look honestly at themselves and to choose how they want to change, counselors must open their own lives to the same scrutiny. They should repeatedly ask themselves these questions: "What makes me think I am capable of helping anyone? What do I personally have to offer others who are struggling to find their way? Am I doing in my own life what I urge others to do?"

Counselors and psychotherapists usually acquire an extensive theoretical and practical knowledge as a basis for their practice. But they also bring their human qualities and their life experiences to every therapeutic session. Professionals can be well versed in psychological theory and can learn diagnostic and interviewing skills and still be ineffective helpers. If counselors are to promote growth and change in their clients, they must be willing to promote growth in their own lives. This willingness to live in accordance with what they teach is what makes counselors "therapeutic persons." If counselors are stagnant themselves, it is doubtful that they can inspire clients to make life-affirming choices. Ethical problems can arise when therapists are unable to carry out this modeling role, which is critical in encouraging clients to change.

In this chapter we deal with some of the ways that client dependence and manipulation of clients can present ethical issues for the therapist. Clients have a right to expect that therapy will increase their chances of functioning independently. If they are manipulated by their therapists, clients hardly have a basis for acting autonomously.

It is difficult to talk about the counselor *as a professional* without considering personal qualities. A counselor's beliefs, personal attributes, and ways of living inevitably influence the way he or she functions as a professional. Some of the issues we address, however, are specifically related to the counselor's professional identity. Although these professional issues are dealt with throughout this book, in this chapter we take up problems that are closely linked to the counselor's personal life: self-awareness and the influence of the counselor's personality and needs, transference and countertransference, job stress, and the challenge of remaining vital both personally and professionally.

Self-Awareness and the Influence of the Therapist's Personality and Needs

Counselors have a personal responsibility to be committed to awareness of their own life issues. Moreover, without a high level of self-awareness, counselors will most likely obstruct the progress of their clients. The focus of the therapy will shift from meeting the client's needs to meeting the needs of the therapist. Consequently, practitioners should be aware of their own needs, areas of "unfinished business," personal conflicts, defenses, and vulnerabilities and how these may intrude on their work with clients. In this section we consider two specific areas that we think counselors need to examine: personal needs and unresolved conflicts.

Personal Needs of Counselors

One critical question counselors can ask themselves is, "What do I personally get from doing counseling?" There are many answers to this question. Many therapists experience excitement and a deep sense of satisfaction from being with people who are struggling to achieve self-understanding and who are willing to experience pain as they seek a better life. Some counselors enjoy the feeling of being instrumental in others' changes; others appreciate the depth and honesty of the therapeutic relationship. Still others value the opportunity to question their own lives as they work with their clients. In many ways therapeutic encounters serve as mirrors in which therapists can see their own lives reflected. As a result, therapy can become a catalyst for change in the therapist as well as in the client.

Therapeutic progress can be blocked, however, when therapists use their clients, perhaps unconsciously, to fulfill their own needs. Out of an exaggerated need to nurture others or to feel powerful, for example, people sometimes feel that they know how others should live. The tendency to give advice and to direct another's life can be especially harmful in a therapist because it leads to excessive dependence on the part of clients and perpetuates their tendency to look outside themselves for answers. Therapists who need to feel powerful or important may begin to think that they are indispensable to their clients or, worse still, try to *make* themselves so.

The goals of therapy can also suffer when therapists who have a strong need for approval focus on trying to win the acceptance, admiration, respect, and even awe of their clients. Some therapists may be primarily motivated by a need to receive confirmation from their clients of their value as persons and as professionals. It is within their power as therapists to control the sessions in such a way that these needs are continually reinforced. Because clients often feel a need to please their therapists, they can easily be drawn into taking care of their therapists' ego needs.

One of the goals of therapy, as we see it, is to teach the *process* of problem solving. When clients have learned the process, they have less and less need of their therapists. Therapists who tell clients what to do or use the sessions to buttress their own sense of self-worth diminish the autonomy of their clients and invite increased dependence in the future.

When therapists are not sufficiently aware of their own needs, they may abuse the power they have in the therapeutic situation. Some counselors gain a sense of power by assuming the role of directing others toward solutions instead of encouraging them to seek alternatives for themselves. A solution-oriented approach to counseling may also spring from the therapist's need to feel a sense of achievement and accomplishment. Some therapists feel ill at ease if their clients fail to make instant progress; consequently, they may push their clients to make decisions prematurely or even make decisions for them. This tendency can be encouraged even more by clients who express gratitude for this kind of "help."

Of course, therapists *do* have their own personal needs, but these needs don't have to assume priority or get in the way of client's growth. Most people who enter the helping professions do want to nurture others, and they do need to know that they are being instrumental in helping others to change. In this sense, they need to have a sense from clients that they are a significant force in their lives. But to keep these needs from interfering with the progress of their clients, therapists should be aware of the danger of working primarily to be appreciated by others instead of working toward the best interests of their clients. If therapists are open enough to recognize this potential danger, the chances are that they will not use their clients to meet their own needs.

As Kottler (1993) wrote, in the practice of psychotherapy our personal and professional roles can complement each other. Our knowledge and skills are equally useful with clients, friends, or family. Also, our life experiences, both joys and sorrows, provide the background for what we do in our therapeutic sessions with clients.

The rewards of practicing psychotherapy are many, but one of the most significant is the joy of seeing clients move from being victims to assuming control over their lives. Therapists can achieve this reward only if they avoid abusing their influence and maintain a keen awareness of their role as facilitators of others' growth. As you consider your own needs and their influence on your work as a therapist, you might ask yourself the following questions:

- How can I know when I'm working for the client's benefit and when I'm working for my own benefit?
- How much might I depend on clients to tell me how good I am as a person or as a therapist? Am I able to appreciate myself, or do I depend primarily on others to validate my worth and the value of my work?
- Do I always feel inadequate when clients don't make progress? If so, how could my attitude and feelings of inadequacy adversely affect my work with clients?

Unresolved Personal Conflicts

We have suggested that the personal needs of a therapist can interfere with the therapeutic process to the detriment of the client if the therapist is not self-aware. The same is true for personal problems and unresolved conflicts. This is not to say that therapists must resolve all their personal difficulties before they begin to counsel others; such a requirement would eliminate almost everybody from the field. In fact, it's possible that a counselor who rarely struggles or experiences anxiety may have real difficulty relating to a client who feels desperate or caught in a hopeless conflict. Moreover, if therapists flee from anxiety-provoking questions in their own lives, they probably won't be able to effectively encourage clients to face such questions. The important point is that counselors can and should be *aware* of their biases, their areas of denial, and the issues they find particularly hard to deal with in their own lives, especially as they influence the therapist's ability to effectively render services. APA (1995) has a guideline on the importance of recognizing personal problems and conflicts: "Psychologists recognize that their personal problems and conflicts may interfere with their effectiveness. Accordingly, they refrain from undertaking an activity when they know or should know that their personal problems are likely to lead to harm to a patient, client, colleague, student, research participant, or other person to whom they may owe a professional or scientific obligation" (1.13).

To illustrate, suppose that you're experiencing a rough time in your life. You feel unresolved anger and frustration. Your home life is tense, and you're wrestling with some pivotal decisions about what you want to do the rest of your life. Perhaps you're having problems with your clients or your spouse. You may be caught between fears of loneliness and a desire to be on your own, or between your fear of and need for close relationships. Can you counsel others effectively while you're struggling with your own uncertainty?

The critical point isn't *whether* you happen to be struggling with personal questions but *how* you're struggling with them. Do you see your part in creating your own problems? Are you aware of your alternatives for action? Do you recognize and try to deal with your problems, or do you invest a lot of energy in denying their existence? Do you find yourself generally blaming others for your problems? Are you willing to consult with a therapist, or do you tell yourself that you can handle it, even when it becomes obvious that you're not doing so? In short, are you willing to do in your own life what you challenge your clients to do?

If you are unaware of your own conflicts, you'll be in a poor position to pay attention to the ways in which your personal life influences your work with clients, especially if some of their problem areas are also problem areas for you. For example, suppose a client is trying to deal with feelings of hopelessness and despair. How can you intensively explore these feelings if, in your own life, you're busily engaged in cheering everybody up? If hopelessness is an issue you don't want to face personally, you'll probably steer the client away from exploring it. Or consider a client who wants to explore her feelings about homosexuality. Can you facilitate this exploration if you are homophobic? If you feel discomfort in talking about homosexual feelings and experiences and don't want to deal with your discomfort, can you stay with your client emotionally when she brings up this topic?

Because you'll have difficulty staying with a client in an area that you're reluctant or fearful to deal with, consider what present unfinished business in your own life might affect you as a counselor. What unresolved conflicts are you aware of, and how might these conflicts influence the way you counsel others?

◆ ***The case of Rollo.***   Rollo is an intern completing his clinical hours for licensure. He came from a family where both parents abused alcohol. The clinic specializes in the treatment of children from abusive homes. Rollo finds himself easily moved to tears as he works with the children. At times he becomes extremely angry at the parents of these children, and he often broods about the children's plight. He typically devotes extra time beyond the scheduled activities, and he often feels overextended. He finds difficulty in saying no to his clients, and his personal life is increasingly suffering as a result of this involvement. He looks tired, and it comes to the attention of his supervisor that he frequently seems stressed and short-tempered with other staff members. In their supervision hour, Rollo retorts that the agency is not doing enough for the children. He proceeds to tell his supervisor how much he is affected by them and how he is continually trying to come up with ways to help them. After listening to Rollo, his supervisor suggests that he consider personal therapy to further explore the way in which he is affected by these children.

- What, if anything, do you see as being unethical in Rollo's behavior? Is he necessarily depriving his clients of adequate help by the manner in which he involves himself with them? At what point do you see the dividing line between being helpful and unhelpful? How could Rollo determine when his own personal involvement was counterproductive?
- Do you agree with the supervisor's suggestion of personal therapy? Why or why not?   yes
- Do you think that Rollo's supervisor should advise him to discontinue working with these children until he has a better understanding of his own personal issues?   on-going / immediate help plus supervision
- What possible conflicts are you aware of in your life that might get in your way of helping certain clients through their difficulties? If you are moved to tears by your clients, does that imply that you have unresolved conflicts? Does anger directed toward abusive parents mean that you have unresolved conflicts with your parents?   yes

Personal Therapy for Counselors

Throughout this chapter we have stressed the importance of counselors' self-awareness. A closely related issue is whether those who wish to become counselors should themselves undergo psychotherapy and whether continuing or periodic personal therapy is valuable for practicing therapists. We are not speaking of therapy for remediation of deep conflicts but of therapeutic experiences aimed at increasing awareness of yourself in the world. There are many ways to accomplish this goal: individual therapy, group counseling, consultation with colleagues, continuing education (especially of an experiential nature), and reading. Other less formal avenues to personal growth are reflecting on and evaluating the meaning of your work and life, remaining open to the reactions of significant people in your life, enjoying music and the arts, traveling, experiencing different cultures, being outdoors, meditating, engaging in spiritual activities, enjoying physical exercise, and spending time with friends and family.

therapy plus
ther. experiences

Therapy during Training

There are several reasons potential counselors should be encouraged to experience their own therapy. First, those who expect to counsel others should know what the experience of being a client is really like. We don't assume that most potential therapists are "sick" and in need of being "cured," but then we don't make that assumption about most clients either. Therapy can help you take an honest look at your motivations in becoming a helper. It can help you explore how your needs influence your actions, how you use power in your life, what your values are, and whether you have a need to persuade others to be like you.

When students are engaged in practicum, fieldwork, and internship experiences and the accompanying individual and group supervision sessions, the following issues tend to surface:

◆ a need to tell people what to do
◆ a desire to take away all pain from clients
◆ a need to have all the answers and to be perfect
◆ a need to be recognized and appreciated
◆ a tendency to assume too much responsibility for the changes of clients
◆ a fear of doing harm, however inadvertently

As students begin to practice counseling, they sometimes become aware that they are taking on a professional role that resembles the role they played in their family. They may recognize a need to preserve peace by becoming the caretaker of others. During their childhood they may have assumed adult roles with their own parents by trying to take care of them. Now, as adults, they may continue to take on most of the responsibility for the changes their clients make. When students become aware of concerns such as these, individual therapy can provide a safe place to encounter the painful memories that are often associated with these personal issues. In the process, students experience firsthand what their clients experience in therapy. If counseling students do not experience this process of internal searching, it is unlikely that they will be able to facilitate an in-depth exploration by their clients. If they have not traveled the path, how can they serve as a guide for others?

Another reason for undergoing therapy is that most of us have blind spots and unfinished business that may interfere with our effectiveness as therapists. Most of us have areas in our lives that aren't developed and that keep us from being as effective as we can be, both as persons and as counselors. Although it is not necessary for counselors to have fully resolved all of their personal problems, they at least need to be aware of the nature of such problems and the ways in which those problems may affect their professional work. Personal therapy is one way of coming to grips with your dynamics as well as working through unresolved conflicts. The lack of personal therapy may become an ethical issue if it diminishes your effectiveness as a counselor.

Ideally, we'd like to see potential counselors undergo a combination of individual and group therapy, because the two therapy types complement each other. Individual therapy provides you with an opportunity to look at yourself in some depth. Many counselors will experience a reopening of old psychic wounds as they engage in intensive work with their clients. For example, their therapeutic work may bring to the surface guilt feelings that need to be resolved. If students are in private therapy while they are doing their internship, they can productively bring such problems to their sessions.

2.   (Group therapy,) in contrast, provides members with the opportunity to get feedback from others. It allows participants to become increasingly aware of their personal style and gives them a chance to experiment with new behaviors in the group setting. It also allows them to generalize their experiences and realize that they are not alone in what they think and feel. The reactions you receive from others can help you learn about personal attributes that could be either strengths or limitations in your work as a counselor.

Many training programs in counselor education recognize the value of having students involved in personal-awareness groups with their peers. A group can be set up specifically for the exploration of personal concerns, or such exploration can be made an integral part of training and supervision groups. Whatever the format, students will benefit most if they are willing to focus on themselves personally and not merely on their "cases." Unfortunately, some beginning counselors tend to focus primarily on client dynamics, and more unfortunately, so do many supervisors and educators. What they are learning by being in a group would be more meaningful if they were open to exploring questions such as: "How am I feeling about my own value as a counselor? Do I like my relationship with my client? What reactions are being evoked in me as I work with this client?" By becoming personally invested in the therapeutic process, students can use their training program as a real opportunity for expanding their own awareness.

It is important for teachers and supervisors to clarify the fine line between training and therapy in the same way that fieldwork agencies must maintain the distinction between training and service. Although these areas overlap, it is clear that the emphasis for students should be on training in both academic and clinical settings, and it is the educator's and supervisor's responsibility to maintain that emphasis.

Holzman, Searight, and Hughes (1996) conducted a survey to investigate the experience of personal therapy among clinical psychology graduate students. Nearly 75% of the respondents reported receiving personal therapy at some point in their lives, most during graduate school. Of those who had been in therapy prior to or during graduate school, 99% reported that they were still in therapy or would consider getting involved in therapy again. Among those receiving therapy, the average length of treatment was 1.5 years. Generally, they saw their experience in personal therapy as being positive, and they viewed this experience as important for practicing as a therapist. The students in this study entered personal therapy for a variety of reasons. Personal growth was endorsed by more than 70% of respondents as one reason for seeking therapy. Other reasons included desiring to improve as a therapist (65%), adjusting to a life transition or a developmental issue (56%), and dealing with depression (38%). The vast majority of the sample entered treatment voluntarily rather than meeting a requirement of their graduate program. These graduate students viewed therapy as something more than a way to deal with distress in their lives. They perceived their therapy as providing them with valuable experiential learning that complemented their education and supervision as clinical psychologists.

This study sheds a positive light on the degree to which many graduate students want therapy for personal enrichment and as a source of training. It challenges counselor education programs to work with therapy providers outside the program to offer psychological services to graduate students in their programs. Because of the ethical problems of counselor educators and supervisors providing therapy for their students and supervisees, faculty members have an obligation to become advocates for their students by identifying therapeutic resources students can afford. There are both practical and ethical reasons to prefer professionals external to a program (who are not part of a program and who do not have any evaluative role in the program) when providing psychological services for students. Practitioners from the community could be hired by a counselor-training program to conduct therapeutic groups, or students might take advantage of either individual or group counseling from a community agency, a college counseling center, or a private practitioner.

We think that counselor educators go too far in the direction of protecting the rights of counselor trainees in those instances where they refuse to require any form of self-exploratory experience as part of their program lest it invade the privacy of students. We are concerned about students' rights to privacy, but we are also very concerned about protecting the public. One way to ensure that the consumer will get the best help available is to prepare students both academically and personally for the challenges they will face when they become practitioners.

The ethical codes of some professional organizations caution against requiring personal therapy for trainees or converting supervision sessions into therapy sessions for supervisees. The codes emphasize the right of students and trainees to make informed decisions about disclosing personal matters. For example, both the ACA and the APA state that mixing personal counseling with education, training, and supervision constitutes what is known as a dual or multiple relationship. This can raise ethical issues if the counselor educator is required to evaluate the student. In the section dealing with teaching, training, and supervision, ACA's guideline states: "If students or supervisees request counseling, supervisors or counselor educators provide them with acceptable referrals. Supervisors or counselor educators do not serve as counselors to students or supervisees over whom they hold administrative, teaching, or evaluative roles unless this is a brief role associated with a training experience"(1995, F.3.c.).

Supervisors should not function as therapists for their supervisees, but good supervision is therapeutic in the sense that the supervisory process involves dealing with the supervisee's personal limitations, blind spots, and impairments so that clients are not harmed. For example, working with difficult clients or dealing with resistance tends to affect trainees in personal ways.

Certainly, it is a challenge for both trainees and experienced therapists to recognize and deal with transference in effective therapeutic ways. Counter-transference issues can work either in favor of or against the establishment of effective client-therapist relationships. A study by Sumerel and Borders (1996) indicates that a supervisor who is open to discussing personal issues with supervisees in an appropriate manner does not necessarily affect the supervisor-supervisee relationship negatively.

We agree with Vasquez's (1992) contention that an integral part of the supervision process is to promote the supervisee's self-awareness and ability to recognize personal issues that could negatively affect his or her work with clients. Supervisors are responsible for monitoring the progress of their super-visees, both for their training and to benefit and protect the public. But,

> the supervisee must not become the supervisor's therapy client; the supervisor must know how much to explore and when to refer the supervisee to therapy. This task is challenging because some aspects of supervision may share common aspects with some forms of therapy. (Vasquez, 1992, p. 199)

We believe that it is appropriate for supervisors to encourage their supervisees to consider personal therapy with another professional as a route to becoming more effective both personally and professionally.

Therapists need training that opens them up to themselves and teaches them about vulnerability, discipline, and freedom in their professional training (Aponte, 1994). In Aponte's person/practice model of training and supervising, trainees work to develop new perspectives on their personal lives and to understand how these changes are likely to affect their professional relationships. This kind of training helps trainees address their own struggles in ways that become useful reference points for working with clients. In Aponte's own words:

> Their personal work is meant to be therapeutic, not therapy, which is essentially an effort to resolve personal issues. Trainers commit to trainees' personal issues primarily to improve their performance as therapists. This point is lucidly illustrated in the help trainees receive to work with their *unresolved* issues. Even with personal issues that become resolved, the ultimate goal is not achieved until trainees learn to use the original struggle and the journey to resolution as resources for their work with clients. (1994, p. 5)

A more detailed exploration of the multiple roles and responsibilities of supervisors, along with ethical issues in combining therapy and supervision is included in Chapter 9. At this point, ask yourself:

◆ What kind of self-exploration have I engaged in prior to or during my training?
◆ How open am I to looking at personal characteristics that could be either strengths or limitations as a counselor?
◆ What am I willing to do to work through personal problems I have at this time?

◆ ***The case of a required personal growth group.*** Miranda is a psychologist in private practice who is hired by the director of a graduate program in counseling psychology. She assumes that the students have been informed that they will be required to attend her personal-growth class, and she is given the impression that the students are eagerly looking forward to it. When she encounters the students at the first class, however, she meets with resistance. They express resentment that they were not told that they would be expected to participate in a personal-growth group, and they say they have not really given their consent. They are attending out of fear that there will be negative consequences if they do not.

- If you were a student in this program, what might your reactions have been?
- Were there any ethical violations in the way in which this group experience was set up? *leader mislead; students mislead, anger, resistance.*
- Is it ever ethical to mandate self-exploration experiences?
- If you were the director of the program, how might you handle the situation?
- The students knew from their orientation and the university's literature that this graduate program included some form of self-exploration. Was this disclosure sufficient for ethical purposes? *no, interviews, advisors, etc.*
- If you were Miranda, what would you do in this situation? How would you deal with the students' objections? *vent, underst. their side. comply, give as much freedom of choice about what is shared as possible*

Ongoing Therapy for Practitioners

Experienced practitioners can profit from a program that will challenge them to reexamine their beliefs and behaviors, especially as these pertain to their effectiveness in working clients. Truly committed professionals engage in a lifelong self-examination as a means of remaining self-aware and genuine.

In a national survey of therapists as patients, Pope and Tabachnick (1994) found that of 84% who had been in personal therapy only two individuals described it as unhelpful. Respondents mentioned three outcomes as the most beneficial aspects of therapy: self-awareness or self-understanding, self-esteem or self-confidence, and improved skills as a therapist. The problem areas most often mentioned as being addressed in personal therapy were depression or general unhappiness, marriage or divorce, relationship concerns, self-esteem and self-confidence, anxiety, career, academics, and family of origin. Of those who had terminated, 63% reported that they were considering resuming therapy. Although only 13% of the respondents had been required by their graduate programs to participate in personal therapy, a substantial majority (70%) believed that graduate programs in psychology should "probably" or "absolutely" require therapy for therapists-in-training. A smaller majority (54%) believed that state licensing boards "probably" should make personal therapy a requirement for licensure.

Some licensing boards require therapy as a way for practitioners to recognize and monitor their countertransference. We think this provides a rationale for psychotherapy for both trainees and practitioners. J. D. Guy and Liaboe (1986a) suggest that a periodic course of psychotherapy may improve therapists' personal relationships and general well-being. The negative consequences that conducting therapy can have on therapists' interpersonal functioning include decreased emotional investment in their families, a reduction in their circle of friends, a tendency to socialize less with friends, and a tendency to become aloof and emotionally distant with friends and family. Guy and Liaboe maintain that both professional organizations and licensing and certification boards are ethically obligated to take an active role in monitoring professionals in the field. Such bodies should encourage, if not require, periodic supervision, consultation, or psychotherapy for practitioners. These measures can be instrumental in reducing or eliminating the potential negative consequences of practicing psychotherapy.

◆ **The case of Daniel.**   Daniel has a busy private practice, and he finds relief in sipping from a vodka bottle kept in his desk drawer. During a conversation with a colleague, he opens the desk drawer and has a sip. The colleague expresses her concern for him and the potential risks involved in his behavior. He reassures her that he never gets inebriated but that it helps him get through the day.

- ◆ What do you think of Daniel's habit of imbibing between sessions? Does it mean that he is abusing alcohol?   *yes*
- ◆ Does his assertion that "I never get inebriated" suffice to render the situation harmless?   *no*
- ◆ In his method of stress reduction acceptable and ethical? *no* Would you personally challenge him to seek personal therapy to deal with his stress and his use of alcohol?   *yes*
- ◆ As his colleague, what ethical obligation, if any, do you have to report the matter?   *to report problem to supervisor*
- ◆ Would it be appropriate for a licensing board to require therapy for Daniel as a condition for retaining his license?   *yes*

Therapists must be prepared to recognize and deal with their unresolved personal issues and their reactions to their clients. A high degree of self-awareness and a deep respect and concern for clients are safeguards. In the next section we will explore ways in which transference and countertransference can facilitate or interfere with therapy.

Transference and Countertransference

Although the terms transference and countertransference are derived from psychoanalytic theory, they are universally applicable to counseling and psychotherapy (Gelso & Carter, 1985). They are used to refer to the client's general reactions and orientation to the therapist and to the therapist's reactions in response. Conceptualizing transference and countertransference broadly,

Gelso and Carter assume that these processes are universal and that they occur, to varying degrees, in most relationships. The therapeutic relationship intensifies the natural reactions of both client and therapist, and how practitioners handle both their feelings and their clients' feelings will have a direct bearing on therapeutic outcomes. If these issues are not attended to, clients' progress will most likely be impeded. Therefore, this matter has implications from both an ethical and a clinical perspective.

Transference: The "Unreal" Relationship in Therapy

Transference is the process whereby clients project onto their therapists past feelings or attitudes they had toward significant people in their lives. Transference typically has its origins in early childhood and constitutes a repetition of past repressed material. Through this process, clients' unfinished business produces a distortion in the way they perceive and react to the therapist. The feelings clients experience in transference may include love, hate, anger, ambivalence, and dependency. The essential point is that these feelings are rooted in past relationships but are now directed toward the therapist. Gelso and Carter (1985) refer to transference as the "unreal" relationship because such projections are in error, even though the therapist's actions may serve to trigger them. Transference entails a misperception of the therapist, either positive or negative.

Watkins (1983) identified the following five transference patterns in counseling and psychotherapy:

1. *Counselor as ideal.* The client sees the counselor as the perfect person who does everything right, without flaws. Psychoanalytically, the counselor is given an idealized image, which may be the way the client viewed his or her parents at one time. The danger here is that counselors, their egos fed, can come to believe these projections! Yet not challenging clients to work through these feelings results in infantilizing them. When clients elevate the therapist, they put themselves down. They lose themselves by trying to be just like their ideal.

2. *Counselor as seer.* Clients view the counselor as an expert, all-knowing and all-powerful. They look to the counselor for direction, based on the conviction that the counselor has all the right answers and that they themselves cannot find their own answers. The counselor may feed on this projection and give clients advice based on his or her own need to be treated as an expert. The ethical issue here is that clients are then encouraged to remain dependent.

3. *Counselor as nurturer.* Some clients look to the counselor for nurturing and feeding, as a small child would. They play the helpless role, and they feel that they cannot act for themselves. They may seek touching and hugs from the therapist. The counselor may get lost in giving sympathy and feeling sorry for the client and become a nurturing parent, taking care of the client. In the process, the client never learns the meaning of personal responsibility.

4. Counselor as frustrator. The client is defensive, cautious, and guarded and is constantly testing the counselor. Such clients may want advice or simple solutions and may expect the counselor to deliver according to their desires. These clients become frustrated if they don't receive such prescriptions. Providing easy solutions will not help these clients in the long run, and counselors should be careful not to get caught in the trap of perceiving these clients as fragile. Also, it is essential that counselors avoid reacting defensively, a response that would further entrench clients' resistance.

5. Counselor as nonentity. In this form of transference the client regards the counselor as an inanimate figure without needs, desires, wishes, or problems. These clients use a barrage of words and keep their distance with these outbursts. The counselor is likely to feel overwhelmed and discounted. If counselors depend on feedback from their clients as the sole means of validating their worth as counselors, they may have difficulty managing cases in which this phenomenon exists.

The potential effects of transference, as shown in these examples, clearly demonstrate why counselors must be aware of their own needs, motivations, and personal reactions. If they are unaware of their own dynamics, they may avoid important therapeutic issues instead of challenging their clients to understand and resolve the feelings they are bringing into the present from their past.

Transference is not a catch-all intended to explain every feeling clients express toward their therapists. If a client expresses anger toward you, it may be justified. If you haven't been truly present for the client and have responded in a mechanical fashion, your client may be expressing legitimate disappointment. Similarly, if a client expresses affection toward you, these feelings may be genuine; dismissing them as infantile fantasies can be a way of putting distance between yourself and your client. Of course, most of us would be less likely to interpret positive feelings as distortions aimed at us in a symbolic fashion than we would negative feelings. But it is possible for therapists to err in either direction—being too quick to explain away negative feelings or too willing to accept whatever clients tell them, particularly when they are hearing how loving, wise, perceptive, or attractive they are. To understand the real import of clients' expressions of feelings, therapists must actively work at being open, vulnerable, and honest with themselves. Although therapists must be aware of the possibility of transference, they should also be aware of the danger of discounting the genuine reactions their clients have toward them.

We will now present a series of brief, open-ended cases in which we ask you to imagine yourself as the therapist. How do you think you would respond to each client? What are your own reactions?

◆ ***The case of Shirley.***   Your client, Shirley, seems extremely dependent on you for advice in making even minor decisions. It is clear that she does not trust herself and that she often tries to figure out what you might do in her place. She asks you personal questions about your marriage and your family life. Evidently, she has elevated you to the position of someone who always makes wise choices, and she is trying to emulate you in every way. At other times she tells you that her decisions typically turn out to be poor ones. Consequently, when faced with a decision, she vacillates and becomes filled with self-doubt. Although she says she realizes that you cannot give her the answers, she keeps asking you what you think about her decisions.

- How would you deal with Shirley's dependent behavior? *explore patterns of*
- What direction would you take in trying to understand her dependence and *dependency feelings?* lack of self-trust? *& feels?*
- How would you respond to her questions about your private life? *hold off/inappropriate*
- If many of your clients expressed the same thoughts as Shirley, is there anything in your counseling style that you may need to examine? *yes*

◆ **The case of Marisa.**   Marisa says she feels let down by you. She complains that you are not available and asks if you really care about her. She also says she feels that she is "just part of your caseload." She tells you that she would like to be more special to you.

- How would you deal with Marisa's expectations? *explore her feelings, present & past*
- How would you explain your position? *these feelings are! to explore.*
- How would you explore whatever might be behind her stated feelings instead of defending your position? *questions, reflection of feelings.*
- Would you be inclined to tell her how she affected you? *no*

◆ **The case of Carl.**   Carl treats you as an authority figure. He once said that you seem to judge him and that he is reluctant to say very much because you would consider much of what he said to be foolish. Although he has not confronted you directly since then, you sense many digs and other signs of hostility. On the surface, however, Carl seems to be trying very hard to please you by telling you what he thinks you want to hear. He seems convinced that you will react negatively and aggressively if he tells you what he really thinks.

- How would you respond to Carl? *confrontation*
- How might you deal with his indirect expressions of hostility? *openly + directly*
- How might you encourage him to express his feelings and work through them?

Countertransference: Ethical and Clinical Implications

So far we have focused on the transference feelings of clients toward their counselors, but counselors also have emotional reactions to their clients, some of which may involve their own projections. It is not possible to deal fully here with all the possible nuances of transference and countertransference. Instead, we will focus on improperly handling these reactions in the therapeutic relationship, a situation that directly pertains to ethical practice.

Countertransference can be considered, in the broad sense, as any projections by a therapist that can potentially get in the way of helping a client. For instance, counselor anxiety, the need to be perfect, or the need to solve a client's problems might all be manifestations of countertransference. Therapists must deal with these reactions in some form of supervision or consultation so that "their problem" does not become the client's problem. It may be helpful to consider the countertransference material being stirred up as a way of interpreting subtle messages from the client. The client might actually want a "cold therapist" because of a fear that more difficult material would surface if the therapist were warmer. If a therapist becomes frustrated with a client, it could be that this client, because of anxiety, wants progress to stop.

Countertransference can be either a constructive or a destructive element in the therapeutic relationship. A therapist's countertransference can illuminate some significant dynamics of a client. A client may actually be provoking reactions in a therapist by the ways in which he or she makes the therapist into a key figure from the past. The therapist who recognizes these patterns can eventually help the client change old dysfunctional themes. Destructive countertransference occurs when a counselor's own needs or unresolved personal conflicts become entangled in the therapeutic relationship, obstructing or destroying a sense of objectivity. In this way, countertransference becomes an ethical issue, as is illustrated in the case that follows.

◆ **The case of Lucy.**   Lucy is a Latina counselor who has been seeing Thelma, who is also a Latina. Thelma's presenting problem was her depression related to an unhappy marriage. Her husband, an alcoholic, refuses to come to counseling with Thelma. She works full time in addition to caring for their three children and her husband. Lucy is aware that she is becoming increasingly irritated and impatient with her client's "passivity" and lack of willingness to take a strong stand with her husband. During one of the sessions, Lucy says to Thelma: "You're obviously depressed, yet you're not willing to take action to change your situation. You've been talking about your miserable marriage for several months and blaming your husband for how you feel. You keep saying the same things, and nothing changes. Your husband refuses to seek treatment for himself or to cooperate with your therapy, yet you are not doing anything to change your life for the better." Lucy says this in an annoyed and critical way. Thelma seems to be listening but does not respond. When Lucy reflects on this session she becomes aware that she has a tendency to be more impatient and harsh with female clients from her own culture, especially over the issue of passivity. She realizes that she has not invited Thelma to explore ways that her cultural background and socialization have influenced her decisions. In talking about this case with a supervisor, Lucy explores why she seems to be triggered by women like Thelma. She recognizes that she has a good deal of unfinished business with her mother, whom she experienced as extremely passive. She also admits to her supervisor that she stayed in an oppressive marriage for many years out of fear of taking action.

◆ If you were Lucy's supervisor, what would you most want to say to her? *talk about passivity in her culture*
◆ Both the therapist and the client share a similar cultural background; to what extent should that have been examined?
◆ If you were Lucy's supervisor, would you suggest self-disclosure as a way *not necessarily* to help her client? What kind of therapist disclosure might be useful? Can *undergo pressures* you see any drawbacks to therapist self-disclosure in this situation? *yes*
◆ Because of Lucy's recognition of her countertransference with passive women, would you suggest that she refer Thelma to another professional? Why or why not? *not unless Lucy could not work through issues adequately.*
◆ What reactions do you have to the manner in which Lucy dealt with Thelma? Could any of Lucy's confrontation be viewed as therapeutic? *(yes)* What would make her confrontation nontherapeutic? *if Lucy remained lost or blurred by her own problems.*
◆ Are there any ways that Lucy's recognition of her own struggles with her mother and with her former husband could actually facilitate her work with women like Thelma? *possibly.*
◆ What are the main ethical dimensions in this case? If you found yourself in a situation where your unresolved personal problems and countertransference reactions were interfering with your ability to work effectively with a particular client, what actions do you think you'd take? *always refer if nec.*

Commentary. Regardless of how self-aware and insightful counselors are, the demands of practicing therapy are great. The emotionally intense relationships therapists develop with their clients can be expected to tap into their own unresolved conflicts. Because countertransference may be a form of identification with the client, the counselor can easily get lost in the client's world and be of little therapeutic value. In the case of Lucy, the ethical course of action would be for Lucy to involve herself in personal therapy to work through some of her unresolved issues. Supervision would enable her to monitor her reactions to certain behaviors of clients that remind her of aspects in herself that she despises. When counselors become overly concerned with meeting their own needs or pushing their own personal agendas, their behavior becomes unethical.

If countertransference is recognized by counselors, they can seek supervision to sort out their feelings. Ethical practice requires that counselors remain alert to their emotional reactions to their clients, that they attempt to understand such reactions, and that they do not meet their own needs at the expense of their clients' needs.

Countertransference can show itself in many ways. Each example in the following list presents an ethical issue because the therapist's effective work is obstructed by countertransference reactions:

1. *Being overprotective with a client* can reflect a therapist's deep fears. A counselor's unresolved conflicts can lead him or her to steer a client away from those areas that open up the therapist's painful material. Such counselors may treat some clients as fragile and infantile, softening their remarks and protect-

ing these clients from experiencing pain and anxiety. This may thwart clients in their struggle. If clients are not challenged to deal with their conflicts, they are likely to avoid them.

◆ Are you aware of reacting to certain types of people in overprotective ways? If so, what might this behavior reveal about you?
◆ Do you find that you are able to allow others to experience their pain, or do you have a tendency to want to take their pain away quickly?

2. *Treating clients in benign ways* may stem from a counselor's fear of their anger. To guard against this anger, the counselor creates a bland counseling atmosphere. This tactic results in exchanges that are superficial. Watkins (1985) mentions the danger of losing therapeutic distance, with the result that the client-counselor interchange degenerates into either a friendly conversation or a general "rap session."

◆ Do you ever find yourself saying things to guard against another's anger?
◆ What might you say or do if you became aware that your exchanges with a client were primarily superficial?

3. *Rejecting a client* may be based on the therapist's perception of the client as needy and dependent. Instead of moving toward the client to protect him or her, the counselor may move away from the client. The counselor remains cool and aloof, keeping distant and unknown, and does not let the client get too close (Watkins, 1985).

◆ Do you find yourself wanting to create distance from certain types of people?
◆ What can you learn about yourself by looking at those people whom you are likely to reject?

4. *Needing constant reinforcement and approval* can be a reflection of countertransference. Just as clients may develop an excessive need to please their therapists to feel liked and valued, therapists may have an inordinate need to be reassured of their effectiveness. Many beginning practitioners expect instant results with their clients. When they do not see immediate positive results, they become discouraged and anxious. If a client is not getting better, they fear that the client will not like them. They engage in self-doubt and wonder about their therapeutic effectiveness.

◆ Do you need to have the approval of your clients? How willing are you to confront them even at the risk of being disliked?
◆ What is your style of confronting a client? Do you tend to confront certain kinds of clients more than others? What does this behavior tell you about yourself as a therapist?

5. *Seeing yourself in your clients* is another form of countertransference. This is not to say that feeling close to a client and identifying with that person's struggle is necessarily countertransference. However, beginning therapists often identify with a client's problems to the point that they lose their objectivity. They become so lost in a client's world that they are unable to distin-

guish their own feelings. Or they may tend to see traits in their clients that they dislike in themselves. Sometimes the particularly "difficult" client can function as a mirror for the counselor. There are many "difficult" clients, a few of whom exhibit extreme resistance, silence, lack of motivation, and annoying mannerisms. The behaviors counselors react to most strongly in these clients are often the very traits that they dislike in themselves. Thus, an overly demanding client who never seems satisfied with what his or her therapist is doing can be a reminder of the therapist's own demanding nature.

◆ Have you ever found yourself so much in sympathy with others that you could no longer be of help to them? What would you do if you felt this way about a client?

◆ From an awareness of your own dynamics, list some personal traits of clients that would be most likely to elicit overidentification on your part.

abused
process Q

6. *Developing sexual or romantic feelings* toward a client exploits the vulnerable position of the client. Seductive behavior on the part of a client can easily lead to the adoption of a seductive style by the therapist, particularly if the therapist is unaware of his or her own dynamics and motivations. However, it's natural for therapists to be more attracted to some clients than to others, and these feelings do not necessarily mean that they cannot counsel these clients effectively. More important than the mere existence of such feelings is the manner in which therapists deal with them. Feelings of attraction can be recognized and even acknowledged without becoming the focus of the therapeutic relationship. The possibility that therapists' sexual feelings and needs might interfere with their work is one important reason therapists should experience their own therapy when starting to practice and should consult other professionals when they encounter difficulty due to their feelings toward certain clients. Besides being unethical and countertherapeutic, it is also illegal in many states to sexually act out with clients, a topic that we will discuss in detail in Chapter 7.

◆ What would you do if you experienced intense sexual feelings toward a client? *I would refer →*

◆ How would you know if your sexual attraction to a client was countertransference or not? *I'd know!*

7. *Giving advice compulsively* can easily be encouraged by clients who seek immediate answers to ease their suffering. The opportunity to give advice places therapists in a superior, all-knowing position, and they may delude themselves into thinking that they do have answers for their clients. Some therapists may find it difficult to be patient with their clients' struggles toward autonomous decision making. Such counselors may engage in excessive self-disclosure, especially by telling their clients how they have solved a particular problem for themselves. In doing so, the focus of therapy shifts from the client's struggle to the needs of the counselor. Even if a client has asked for advice, there is every reason to question whose needs are being served when a therapist falls into advice giving.

- Do you ever find yourself giving advice? What do you think you gain from it? In what ways might the advice you give to clients represent advice that you could give yourself?
- Are there any times when advice is warranted? If so, when?

8. *Desiring a social relationship with clients* may stem from countertransference, especially if it is acted on while therapy is taking place. Clients occasionally let their therapist know that they would like to develop a closer relationship than is possible in the limited environment of the office. They may, for instance, express a desire to get to know their therapist as "a regular person." Mixing personal and professional relationships often ends up souring the relationship and could lead to a lawsuit. This is a topic we will examine in Chapter 7. Ask yourself these questions:

- If I establish social relationships with certain clients, will I be as inclined to confront them in therapy as I would be otherwise? *no*
- Will my own needs for preserving these friendships interfere with my therapeutic activities and defeat the purpose of therapy? *yes*
- Am I sensitive to being called a "cold professional," even though I may strive to be real and straightforward in the therapeutic situation? *yes*
- Why am I inclined to form friendships with clients? Does this practice serve my own or my clients' best interests? *my own* .

Client Dependence

Clients have a right to expect that psychotherapy will enable them to move toward increased change and autonomy. Certainly, a therapist who fosters clients' dependence rather than autonomy is thwarting their progress. Clients frequently experience a period of dependence on therapy or on their therapist. This temporary dependence isn't necessarily a bad thing, nor does it take away from clients' autonomy. Some clients are people who have exaggerated the importance of being independent. They see the need to consult a professional as a sign of weakness. When these people do allow themselves to need others, their dependence doesn't necessarily mean that the therapist is unethical.

An ethical issue does arise, however, when counselors *encourage* dependence on the part of their clients. They may do so for any number of reasons. Counselor interns need clients, and sometimes they may keep clients coming to counseling longer than is necessary because they will look bad if they "lose" a client. Some therapists in private practice might fail to challenge clients who show up and pay regularly, even though they appear to be getting nowhere. Some therapists foster dependence in their clients in subtle ways out of a need to feel important. When clients play a helpless role and ask for answers, these counselors may readily tell them what to do. Dependent clients can begin to view their therapists as all-knowing and all-wise; therapists who have a need to be perceived in this way may act in ways that will keep their clients immature and dependent.

With the growth of managed care in this country as an alternative to traditional fee-for-service delivery systems, the client-counselor relationship is changing in many ways. In the relatively brief treatment and the restricted number of sessions allowed in most managed care plans, client dependence is often less of an issue than it might be with longer term therapy. However, even using short-term, problem-oriented therapy aimed at solutions, clients can still develop an unhealthy dependence on therapists, especially if therapists are willing to offer quick solutions to clients' problems.

Like many other ethical issues discussed here, encouraging dependence in clients is often not clear cut in practice. To stimulate you to think of possible ways that you might foster dependence or independence in your clients, let's consider an actual disciplinary action case that involved promoting client dependence. We will follow this with a couple of illustrative cases and ask you to respond to them.

Disciplinary Action Case

The following case was reported in *The California Therapist* (California Association of Marriage and Family Therapists, 1995, pp. 24–25). The therapist was a registered intern and an applicant for a marriage and family therapist license.

The therapist was charged with sexual misconduct, gross negligence, and incompetence in performing her professional duties. The therapist (whom we will call Sue) shared feelings about her sexual abuse and bisexual feelings with her client (whom we will call Bonnie) and gave Bonnie her home phone number and encouraged her to call her at home. Sue encouraged Bonnie to become dependent on her, and she agreed to become Bonnie's friend. Later, Bonnie revealed to Sue that she was in love with her.

Sue failed to set appropriate client-therapist boundaries, and she accepted a very expensive ring from her client. Bonnie entered a psychiatric hospital for one month, but Sue continued to encourage dependent behavior on her client's part. Sue told Bonnie that she would see her three times a week as a therapist and once a week as a friend. Then Sue began to hold Bonnie in her arms during therapy sessions. The therapist took Bonnie out to have a margarita even though Bonnie had a history of alcohol abuse.

Sue agreed to be Bonnie's friend and sister and invited her client to spend the weekends with her at her home. Although the therapist would sleep with Bonnie, she discouraged Bonnie's feelings for her. Eventually, Sue would not sleep with Bonnie and told her that she was not concerned with her. Bonnie attempted suicide and was returned to the hospital. After another hospitalization, Sue's husband contacted Bonnie and informed her that she would not get the ring back because she hadn't paid for her therapy. Thereafter, Bonnie began to see another therapist.

If you were Bonnie's new therapist and discovered that Bonnie was becoming increasingly more dependent on you, how would you handle it? What might you say to her? *what happened to Bonnie was illegal + unethical, + I would set strict personal boundaries + appropriate client/therapist boundaries.*

◆ **The case of Marcia.**   Marcia is single and almost ready to graduate from college. She tells you that she has ambivalent feelings about graduating because she feels that now she's expected to get a job and live on her own. This prospect frightens her, and she doesn't want to leave the security she has found as a college student. As she puts it, she doubts that she can "make it in the real world." Marcia doesn't trust her own decisions. When she does make choices, the results, in her eyes, are disastrous. Her style is to plead with you to advise her whether she should date, apply for a job, leave home, go on to graduate school, and so forth. Typically, Marcia gets angry with you because you aren't being directive enough. She feels that you have more knowledge than she does and should therefore give her more guidance. She says: "Why am I coming here if you won't tell me what to do? If I could make decent decisions on my own, I wouldn't need to come here in the first place!"

- How do you imagine you'd feel if Marcia were your client?
- How might you respond to her continual prodding for answers?
- How do you imagine you'd feel about her statement that you weren't doing your job and that you weren't being directive enough?
- What steps would you take to challenge her?
- In what ways do you think it would be possible for you to tie into her dependency needs and foster her dependence on you for direction instead of freeing her from you?
- If Marcia were covered under managed care, how might this affect how you would work with her?

◆ **The case of Ron.**   Ron, a young counselor, encourages his clients to call him at home any time they need to. He frequently lets sessions run overtime, lends money to clients when they're "down and out," devotes many more hours to his job than he is expected to, and is willing to take on a large caseload. He says that he lives for his work and that it gives him a sense of being a valuable person. The more he can do for people, the better he feels.

- How might his style of counseling either help or hinder a client?
- In what ways could Ron's style be keeping his clients dependent on him?
- What do you imagine his life would be like if there were no clients who needed him?
- If you were Ron's colleague and he came to you to talk about how "burnt out" he felt, what would you say to him?
- Can you identify with him in any ways? Do you see yourself as potentially needing your clients more than they need you?

Delaying Termination as a Form of Client Dependence

Most professional codes have guidelines that call for termination whenever further therapy will not bring significant gains, but some therapists have difficulty letting go of their clients. They run the risk of unethical practice because of either financial or emotional needs. On the financial issue, we contend that ethical practitioners should continually examine whether they are resistant to termination because it would mean a decline in income. Obviously, termination cannot be mandated by ethical codes alone; it rests on the honesty and the goodwill of the therapist. We agree with Kramer (1990) that more than at any other phase of therapy the ending demands that therapists examine and understand their own needs and feelings. Therapists are challenged to confront their own dependence and anxieties honestly. Kramer emphasizes the therapist's role in enabling clients to understand and accept the termination process: "A general philosophy that is respectful of patients and sees them as autonomous, proactive, and self-directive is essential if the therapist is to facilitate healthy, productive endings" (p. 3). In our view, the ultimate sign of an effective therapist is his or her ability to help clients reach a stage of autonomy, wherein they no longer need a therapist.

Most of the ethics codes of the various professions state that practitioners should terminate services to clients when such services are no longer required, when it becomes reasonably clear that clients are not benefiting from therapy, or when the agency or institution limits do not allow provision of further counseling services. Apply the general spirit of these codes to these questions:

- How can you determine when services are no longer required? *goal met, agreement*
- What criteria can you use to determine whether your client is benefiting from the therapeutic relationship? *goals*
- What should you do if your client feels he or she is benefiting from therapy but you don't see any signs of progress? *explore discrepancies*
- What should you do if you're convinced that your client is coming to you seeking friendship and not really for the purpose of changing? *confront/open + honestly*
- What are the ethical issues involved if your agency limits the number of sessions yet your client is clearly benefiting from counseling? What if termination is likely to result in harm to the client?

As a therapist, put yourself in each of the following two situations. Ask yourself what you would do, and why, if you were confronted with the problem described.

◆ **The case of George.**   After five sessions your client, George, asks: "Do you think I'm making any progress toward solving my problems? Do I seem any different to you now than I did five weeks ago?" Before you give him your impressions, you ask him to answer his own questions. He replies: "Well, I'm not sure whether coming here is doing that much good or not. I suppose I expected resolutions to my problems before now, but I still feel anxious and depressed much of the time. It feels good to come here, and I usually continue thinking about what we discussed after our sessions, but I'm not coming any closer to decisions. Sometimes I feel certain this is helping me, and at other times I wonder whether I'm just fooling myself."

- What criteria can you employ to help you and your client assess the value of counseling for him? *√ expectations + whether or not they're realistic*

- Does the fact that George continues to think about his session during the rest of the week show that he is probably getting something from counseling? Why or why not? *good sign*
- Does it sound as if George has unrealistic expectations about finding neat solutions and making important decisions too quickly? Is he merely impatient with the process? *Yes / yes*

◆ **The case of Joanne.**   Joanne has been coming regularly to counseling for some time. When you ask her what she thinks she is getting from the counseling, she answers: "This is really helping. I like to talk and have somebody listen to me. I often feel like you're the only friend I have and the only one who really cares about me. I suppose I really don't do that much outside, and I know I'm not changing that much, but I feel good when I'm here."

- If it became clear to you that Joanne wasn't willing to do much to change her life and wanted to continue counseling only because she liked having you listen to her, do you think you'd be willing to continue working with her? *no* Why or why not? Would you say that she is benefiting from the relationship with you? If so, how? *no*
- Is it ethical to continue the counseling if Joanne's main goal is the "purchase of friendship"? Why or why not? *no*
- Would it be ethical to terminate Joanne's therapy without exploring her need to see you? *no*
- If you thought Joanne was using her relationship with you to remain secure and dependent but that she believed that she was benefiting from the relationship, what might you do? How do you imagine you'd feel if you continued to see Joanne even though you were convinced that she wasn't changing? *not good*

Manipulation versus Collaboration

Psychotherapy is a process that teaches people how to be honest with themselves; therefore it is of the utmost importance for therapists to be honest with their clients. Unfortunately, there are many ways for therapists to deceive or manipulate clients, often under the guise of being helpful and concerned. Therapists who have plans for what they want their clients to do or be and who keep these plans hidden are manipulative. Other therapists may attempt to control their relationships with their clients by keeping therapy a mysterious process and maintaining a rigid "professional stance" that excludes the client as a partner.

To offset the danger of manipulating clients toward ends that they have not chosen, clients should be given an active role in deciding what happens to them in the therapeutic relationship. Some therapists use a contract containing specific goals and the criteria for evaluating when these goals have been met. Proponents say that a contract emphasizes the partnership of client and therapist.

Sidney Jourard (1968) contrasts manipulation with dialogue. He sees psychotherapy as "an invitation to authenticity" in which the therapist's role is to be an exemplar. Therapists can foster their clients' honesty and invite them to drop their pretenses only by dropping their own defenses and meeting their clients in an honest manner. According to Jourard, "the psychotherapist is the teacher in the therapeutic dance, and the patient follows the leader" (pp. 64–65). One of the best ways for therapists to demonstrate their goodwill is by avoiding manipulation and being open, trusting, and vulnerable to their clients. If counselors manipulate their clients, they can expect manipulation in return; if they are open, however, their clients may be open as well. As Jourard says:

> If I want [a client] to be maximally open, but I keep myself fully closed off, peeking at him through chinks in my own armor, trying to manipulate him from a distance, then in due time he will discover that I am not in that same mode; and he will then put his armor back on and peer at me through chinks in it, and he will try to manipulate me. (p. 641)

Manipulation can work in subtle ways. Consider the degree to which you think the behavior of the therapist in the following example is manipulative and unethical.

♦ **The case of Josephine.**   Among Clyde's patients is Josephine, a middle-aged widow. She has been seeing him for one year on a regular basis because of her loneliness and depression. Much of the dialogue of the sessions is now social in nature. Josephine continually tells Clyde how much she enjoys the sessions and how meaningful they are to her. She has connections with a professional sports franchise and has been able to obtain choice tickets for him. At times he lets it be known when he needs tickets for specific events.

- Is it unethical for Clyde to continue to see Josephine when the sessions are primarily social? *Yes*
- Is it ethical to continue to accept the tickets? *no*
- Could this arrangement be construed as a manipulation of the therapeutic relationship? *yes*
- Would mere enjoyment of the sessions warrant their continuation? *no*

Stress in the Counseling Profession
Warning: Bumpy Road

Burn-Out or Impairment

Counseling can be a hazardous profession, and its stresses stem both from the nature of the work and from the professional role expectations of counselors. Therapists are typically not given enough warning about the hazards of the profession they are about to enter. Many counselors-in-training look forward to a profession in which they can help others and, in return, feel a deep sense of self-satisfaction. They are not told that the commitment to self-exploration and to inspiring this search in clients is fraught with difficulties. Effective practitioners use their own life experiences and personal reactions to help them understand their clients and as a method of working with them. As you will recall, the process of working therapeutically with people opens up the therapist's own deepest issues. The counselor, as a partner in the therapeutic journey, can be deeply affected by seeing a client's pain. The activation of painful memories resonates with the therapist's own life experiences. Unfinished business is stirred up, and old wounds are opened. In short, working with clients who are in pain often opens up therapists to their own pain. If these countertransference issues are not recognized, they can have ethical implications. Counselors overburdened with stress cannot work effectively.

Many of the stressful client behaviors we will discuss in this section could easily be understood as countertransference issues of the therapist. When a therapist assumes full responsibility for a client's not making progress, for instance, the therapist is not giving the client enough responsibility for his or her own therapy. Instead of the therapist assuming he or she is to blame for the lack of progress, the therapist should first explore the situation with the client. As a result of this exploration, the therapist may discover that he or she is impeding the client's growth by too quickly assuming responsibility for such problems.

Practitioners who have a tendency to readily accept full responsibility for their clients often experience their clients' stress as their own. It is important to recognize the danger signs that indicate that stress is taking control. Be alert to the ways in which stress can lead to fatigue, distress, impairment and, eventually, burnout. Some signs to look for are irritability and emotional exhaustion, feelings of isolation, abuse of alcohol or drugs, reduced personal effectiveness, indecisiveness, compulsive work patterns, and drastic changes in behavior. Bennett, Bryant, VandenBos, and Greenwood (1990) raise the following questions that can help you assess the impact of stress on you both personally and professionally:

- Do you ignore your problems out of fear?
- Have you learned techniques for managing stress, such as time management and relaxation training?
- Are you able to take care of your personal needs?
- Are you aware of the signs and symptoms warning you that you are in trouble?
- Do you listen to your family, friends, and colleagues when they tell you that stress is getting the better of you?
- Do you consider seeking help when you notice you are exhibiting signs of stress?

Although it is not realistic to expect to eliminate the strains of daily life, you can develop practical strategies to recognize and cope with stress that is having adverse effects on you.

Sources of Stress

Deutsch (1984) and Farber (1983b) found surprisingly similar results in their surveys of therapists' perceptions of stressful client behavior. In both studies

Most Stressful Client Behaviors for Therapists

Deutsch's Findings
1. suicidal statements
2. anger toward the therapist
3. severely depressed clients
4. apathy or lack of motivation
5. client's premature termination

Farber's Findings
1. suicidal statements
2. aggression and hostility
3. premature termination of therapy
4. agitated anxiety
5. apathy and depression

therapists reported that clients' suicidal statements were the most stressful. The box above compares these two studies.

Other sources of stress that therapists reported in the Deutsch (1984) study included:

- being unable to help distressed clients feel better
- seeing more than the usual number of clients
- not liking clients
- having self-doubts about the value of therapy
- having professional conflicts with colleagues
- feeling isolated from other professionals
- overidentifying with clients and failing to balance empathy with appropriate professional distance
- being unable to leave client concerns behind when away from work
- feeling sexual attraction to a client
- not receiving expressions of gratitude from clients

A growing body of research suggests that many therapists experience negative effects with respect to their ability to relate meaningfully with family and friends (J. D. Guy & Liaboe, 1986a). More than half of the therapists in Farber's study (1983a, 1983b) reported that conducting therapy had decreased their emotional investment in their own families. In the area of friendships, some therapists reported that their work had hindered their ability to be genuine, spontaneous, and comfortable with friends (Farber, 1983b). Farber notes a trend for therapists to reduce their circle of friends and to socialize less during their career. One interpretation of these findings is that many therapists experience stress and negative consequences from their work.

Stress is related to irrational beliefs that many therapists hold. Practitioners with exceptionally high goals or perfectionistic strivings related to helping others often report a high level of stress. Deutsch (1984) gives the following examples of the three most stressful beliefs, all of which pertain to doing perfect work with clients:

- "I should always work at my peak level of enthusiasm and competence."
- "I should be able to cope with any client emergency that arises."
- "I should be able to help every client."

Some other irrational beliefs that lead to stress are:

- "When a client does not make progress, it is my fault."
- "I should not take off time from work when I know that a particular client needs me."
- "My job is my life."
- "I should be a model of mental health."
- "I should be 'on call' at all times."
- "A client's needs always come before my own."
- "I am the most important person in my client's life."
- "I am responsible for my client's behavior."
- "I have the power to control my client's life."

It is interesting to note that these beliefs are related to the basic reasons many people choose the helping professions. The needs of helpers are to be needed by others, to feel important, to have an impact on the lives of others, to have the power to control others, and to be significant. When helpers are able to do these things successfully, they are likely to feel that they are making a significant difference in the lives of their clients. When they feel that they are not making a difference and are not reaching clients, stress affects them more dramatically.

Deutsch (1984) makes the point that therapists' cognitions provide clues to the experience of stress. Beliefs that create stress are those that goad the counselor to constantly produce at maximum levels, a pace that eventually leads to burnout. When therapists do not live up to unrealistically high levels of performance, they often experience frustration. When they fall short of their own idealized expectations, they view the slow progress in their clients as evidence of their failure and lack of competence. The underlying assumption that creates stress is: "If I do not live up to my high expectations, I am personally incompetent and inadequate." From this vantage point, the crucial factor in therapists' experience of stress is not difficult client behaviors but the beliefs therapists hold about their role in helping others. If therapists assume that they are completely responsible for the success or failure of therapy, they are burdening themselves needlessly and creating their own stress. And, as we have said previously, they are also depriving their clients of their rightful share of responsibility for what they choose to do with their lives. The ethical and professional question is: To what degree does a therapist's behavior resulting from stress have negative implications for a client's progress?

Counselor Impairment

A number of factors can negatively influence a counselor's effectiveness, both personally and professionally, including substance abuse, physical illness, and burnout. According to Stadler (1990b), impaired counselors have lost the ability to resolve stressful events. They are not able to function professionally. Those therapists whose inner conflicts are consistently activated by client material may respond by trying to stabilize themselves rather than facilitating the growth of their clients.

Clearly, impaired practitioners contribute to the suffering of their clients rather than alleviating it. For example, the sexually exploitive behavior of counselors is often a manifestation of impairment (Emerson & Markos, 1996). Counselors who become sexually involved with clients show personality patterns similar to those of impaired counselors. Some of these shared characteristics are:

◆ fragile self-esteem
◆ difficulty establishing intimacy in one's personal life
◆ professional isolation
◆ a need to rescue clients
◆ a need for reassurance about one's attractiveness
◆ a substance abuse

Benningfield (1994) identifies other personal characteristics associated with impaired functioning. These signs include lack of empathy, loneliness, poor social skills, social isolation, discounting the possibility of harm to others, preoccupation with personal needs, justification of behavior, and denial of professional responsibility to clients and students. Herlihy (1996) points out that because a common characteristic of impairment is denial, professional colleagues may need to confront the irresponsible behavior of an impaired counselor. Herlihy suggests confronting the impaired counselor with sensitivity and respect. Benningfield maintains that the responsibility for addressing the assessment, remediation, and prevention of professional impairment lies not just with the impaired practitioner, ethics committees, or licensing boards but also with colleagues. Although most therapists know that supervision, consultation, and therapy are useful resources for dealing with personal problems, they may be hesitant to actually make use of these resources without the challenge from and encouragement of colleagues.

Colleagues can play a critical role in helping impaired practitioners recognize their condition and take remedial action. However, as Benningfield (1994) points out, all therapists have an ethical responsibility to themselves, their clients and students, and to their colleagues to monitor their own professional practice. She suggests that therapists should engage in an ongoing process of self-assessment to increase their awareness of problematic attitudinal and behavioral patterns that may lead to serious impairment. Some questions Benningfield offers for this self-assessment include:

◆ Is my personal life satisfying and rewarding? Are my relationships what I want them to be?
◆ To what degree am I taking care of myself, both physically and emotionally?
◆ Would I be willing for other therapists I respect to know about my professional conduct and decisions? Am I willing to express my vulnerabilities through consultation or peer supervision?
◆ Can I acknowledge and disclose my mistakes? Am I willing to acknowledge my limitations in my professional roles?

- Am I generally consistent in my practice?
- Do I think or fantasize about a relationship that goes beyond being a professional with some clients or students? Do I talk about subjects in therapy that are not related to clients' concerns?

In their investigation of psychologists' ethical beliefs about burnout and continued professional practice, Skorupa and Agresti (1993) found that psychologists perceive burnout to be a form of impairment. They also found that psychologists who believe that it is unethical to practice while impaired tend to see fewer clients per week and have greater knowledge about burnout prevention strategies than those who do not hold this belief as strongly. The investigators suggested several implications for practitioners. First, graduate training programs should include a course on burnout and prevention strategies. Second, practitioners need to monitor their professional practices, especially the number of client contact hours per week, as these may be related to burnout. Continuing education can be especially useful in learning self-monitoring. Third, therapists who work in mental-health agencies may be at greater risk for burnout than are private practitioners, and they may need to take special precautions to avoid burnout and impairment.

According to J. D. Guy (1987), although there is a need for better identification of impaired therapists and more effective remedial programs, there is an even greater need to prevent emotional distress and impairment *before* it results in professional incompetence:

> A proactive stance that attempts to address the causes of impairment would be far more effective and efficient than a reactive stance that focuses on the results of distress. Furthermore, such measures could prevent unnecessary patient harm and therapist suffering. Among the many possible preventive steps, those most often recommended include continued education, personal therapy, periodic supervision, and peer interaction. (p. 232)

We encourage you to reflect on the sources of stress in your life. What patterns do you see? How effectively are you managing stress? Do you see ways that this stress could lead to burnout or impairment? What steps can you take to recognize danger signals before you become an impaired practitioner? What preventive measures are you willing to take? Are you open to periodic supervision? Would you ask for help from peers or colleagues? Would you seek personal therapy if you recognized you were on a path leading to impairment? By developing a method of self-assessment for danger signs leading to impairment, you are taking important steps toward preventing problems for both yourself and your clients.

Staying Alive Personally and Professionally

Although burnout and the professional impairment associated with it have received much publicity from professional groups, many counselors have

Codes on Professional Impairment

Various codes of ethics address practitioner impairment and provide guidance for therapists whose unresolved personal problems intrude into their professional work. Here are three examples:

Social workers whose personal problems, psychosocial distress, legal problems, substance abuse, or mental health difficulties interfere with their professional judgment and performance should immediately seek consultation and take appropriate remedial action by seeking professional help, making adjustments in workload, terminating practice, or taking any other steps necessary to protect clients and others. (NASW, 1996, 4.05.b.)

When psychologists become aware of personal problems that may interfere with their performing work-related duties adequately, they take appropriate measures, such as obtaining professional consultation or assistance, and determine whether they should limit, suspend, or terminate their work-related duties. (APA, 1995, 1.13.c.)

Counselors refrain from offering or accepting professional services when their physical, mental, or emotional problems are likely to harm a client or others. They are alert to the signs of impairment, seek assistance for problems, and, if necessary, limit, suspend, or terminate their professional responsibilities. (ACA, 1995, C.2.g.)

avoided or denied their existence. In a discussion of counselor impairment, Stadler (1990b) reports that we know very little about the impact of burnout on clients, we have few data on counselor impairment, and there are few professionally sponsored avenues to help counselors suffering from burnout.

Graduate training programs in the helping professions should prepare students for the disappointments they will encounter in the course of their training and in the jobs they eventually secure. Students can be prepared for both the joys and the pains of the profession they are choosing. Students should learn about the rewards and frustrations of helping others, but they should also be informed about the hazards of this profession. If students are not adequately prepared, they may be especially vulnerable to early disenchantment and high rates of burnout due to unrealistic expectations. There is an ethical mandate for training programs to design strategies to prevent burnout and to teach students the importance of developing healthful attitudes.

What can you do not only to prevent yourself from becoming an impaired professional but also to become committed to promoting your own wellness from a holistic perspective? Perhaps the most basic way to retain your vitality as a person and as a professional is to realize that you are not a bottomless pit and cannot give and give without replenishing yourself. Counselors often ignore the signs that they are becoming depleted. They may view themselves as having unlimited capacities to give, and at the same time they may not pay attention to taking care of their own needs for nurturing, recognition, and support. However, simply recognizing that you cannot be a universal giver without getting something in return is not enough to keep you alive as a person and a professional. You need an action plan and the commitment to carry out this plan. Learning to cope with personal and professional sources of stress generally involves making some fundamental changes in your lifestyle. At this point, take some time to ask yourself what basic changes, if any, you are willing to make in your behavior to promote your own wellness.

Chapter Summary

One basic component in the practice of therapy and counseling is the counselor's own personality as an instrument in therapeutic practice. Counselors may possess knowledge and technical skills and still be ineffective in significantly reaching clients. The life experiences, attitudes, and caring that counselors bring to their sessions are crucial factors in establishing an effective therapeutic relationship. If counselors are unwilling to engage in self-exploration, it is likely that their fears, resistances, personal conflicts, and personal needs will interfere with their ability to be present for their clients. Therapists who are unaware of their personal dynamics will probably use their work primarily to satisfy their own unmet needs or will steer clients away from exploring conflicts that they themselves are unwilling to acknowledge. In our view, this lack of awareness on the part of therapists is a major ethical concern. Although the harm to clients that can result from unaware therapists is often of a subtle nature, it is indeed as real as some of the more flagrant ethical violations.

Personal therapy during training and throughout therapists' professional careers results in counselors who are better able to focus on the welfare of their clients. If our assumption is valid—that therapists are unable to take clients on any journey that they have not been on—ongoing self-exploration is critical. By focusing on their own personal development, counselor trainees and practitioners are better equipped to deal with the range of transference reactions their clients are bound to have toward them; they are also better able to detect countertransference on their part and have a basis for dealing with such reactions in a therapeutic manner. There is a potential for unethical behavior when therapists mismanage their countertransference. You may need to review your personal concerns periodically throughout your career. This honest self-appraisal is an essential quality of those who wish to be effective helpers.

Stress and the inevitable burnout that typically results from inadequately dealing with chronic sources of stress also raise ethical questions. How can therapists who are psychologically and physically exhausted adequately help their clients? Are counselors who have numbed themselves to their own pain able to deal with the pain of their clients? Are impaired practitioners doing more harm than good for those who seek their assistance? Although there is no simple answer to the question of how to stay alive personally and professionally, you are challenged to find your own path to maintaining your vitality and preventing burnout.

Suggested Activities

These activities and questions are designed to help you apply your learning. Many of them can profitably be done alone or with another person; others are designed for discussion either with the whole class or in small groups. We suggest that you select those that seem most significant to you and write on these issues in your journal.

1. In small groups in your class, explore your reasons for going into a helping profession. This is a basic issue, and it is one that many students have trouble putting into concrete words. What motivated you to seek this type of work? What do you think you can get for yourself? What do you see yourself as being able to do for others?

2. What personal needs of yours will be met by counseling others? To what degree might they get in the way of your work with clients? How can you recognize and meet your needs—which are a real part of you—without having them interfere with your work with others?

3. What major problems do you expect to face as a beginning counselor? What are some of your most pressing concerns?

4. In small groups share your own anxieties over becoming a counselor. What can you learn about yourself from a discussion of these anxieties?

5. This exercise deals with the fundamental question, "Who has a right to counsel anybody?" Form small groups of perhaps three persons, and take turns briefly stating the personal and professional qualities that you can offer people. Ask other group members for feedback. Afterward, explore any self-doubts you have concerning your ethical right to counsel others.

6. What results would you look for when working with clients? How would you determine the answers to questions such as: Is the counseling doing any good? Is my intervention helping my client make the changes he or she wants to make? How effective are my techniques?

7. Think of the type of client you might have the most difficulty working with. Then become this client in a role-playing fantasy with one other student. Have your partner attempt to counsel you. After you've had a chance to be the client, change roles and become the counselor. Your partner then becomes the type of client you just role-played.

8. In small groups explore the issue of how willing you are to disclose yourself to your clients. Discuss the guidelines you would use to determine the appropriateness of self-disclosure. What are some areas you would feel hesitant about sharing? How valuable do you think it is to share yourself in a personal way with your clients? What are some of your fears or resistances about making yourself known to your clients?

9. In small groups discuss some possible causes of professional burnout. Then examine specific ways you would deal with this problem. After you've explored this issue in small groups, reconvene as a class and make a list of the causes and solutions that your groups have come up with.

3

Values and the Helping Relationship

- Pre-Chapter Self-Inventory
- Introduction
- Clarifying Your Values and Their Role in Your Work
- The Ethics of Imposing Your Values on Clients
- Differences in Life Experiences and Philosophies
- Role of Spiritual and Religious Values in Counseling
- End-of-Life Decisions
- Values Pertaining to Sexuality
- Ethical and Value Issues in Counseling Gay and Lesbian Clients
- Chapter Summary
- Suggested Activities

Pre-Chapter Self Inventory

Directions: For each statement, indicate the response that most closely identifies your beliefs and attitudes. Use the following code:

5 = I *strongly agree* with this statement.
4 = I *agree* with this statement.
3 = I am *undecided* about this statement.
2 = I *disagree* with this statement.
1 = I *strongly disagree* with this statement.

__1__ 1. It is both possible and desirable for counselors to remain neutral and keep their values from influencing clients.

__1__ 2. Counselors should influence clients to adopt values that in their opinion seem to be in the clients' best interests.

__4__ 3. It is appropriate for counselors to express their values as long as they don't try to impose them on clients.

__1__ 4. Counselors should challenge clients to make value judgments regarding their own behavior.

__1__ 5. Before I can effectively counsel a person, I have to decide whether our life experiences and values are similar enough that I'll be able to understand that person.

__4__ 6. Clarifying values is a major part of the counseling process.

__4__ 7. I would never try to influence my clients to consider my values.

__4__ 8. I have a clear idea of what I value and where I acquired my values.

__2__ 9. I tend to have difficulty with people who think differently from the way I do.

__4__ 10. Ultimately, the choice of living or dying rests with my clients, and therefore I do not have the right to persuade them to make a different choice.

__4__ 11. I have an ethical obligation to ask myself when I would have to refer a client because of a conflict in our values.

__1__ 12. Sometimes it is ethical to impose my values on my clients, especially if I have their best interests at heart.

__2__ 13. To be helpful to a client, a counselor must accept and approve of the client's values.

__4__ 14. There are no fundamental conflicts between counseling and religion or spirituality; therefore it is possible to consider religious or spiritual concerns in a therapeutic relationship.

__2__ 15. If a client of mine subscribed to a dogmatic religion, I would be likely to challenge this person.

__3__ 16. If a client complained of having no meaning in life, I would be inclined to introduce a discussion of spirituality or religion as one way to find purpose.

__2__ 17. A Christian counselor should refer gay or lesbian clients to another professional.

__3__ 18. Gay and lesbian clients are best served by gay and lesbian counselors.

⟩19. I would have difficulty counseling either a lesbian or gay couple who
wanted support in adopting a child.
5 20. As a counselor, it is my ethical responsibility to learn about referral
resources for gay and lesbian clients and to make appropriate referrals
if I do not have the knowledge and skills to work effectively with
them.

Introduction

The question of values permeates the therapeutic process. In this chapter we
want to stimulate your thinking about your values and life experiences and the
influence they will have on your counseling. We ask you to consider the possible impact of your values on your clients, the effect your clients' values will
have on you, and the conflicts that may arise if you and your clients have different values.

The fundamental question is: Should therapists keep their values out of
their counseling sessions? In our view it is neither possible nor desirable for
counselors to be scrupulously neutral in this respect. Although it is not the
counselor's function to persuade clients to accept a certain value system, we do
think it's crucial for counselors to be clear about their own values and how
they influence their work and the directions taken by their clients. We also
think it's important for counselors to express their values openly when they are
relevant to the questions that come up in sessions with clients. As Bergin (1991)
writes, "It's vital to be open about values but not coercive, to be a competent
professional and not a missionary for a particular belief, and at the same time
to be honest enough to recognize how one's value commitments may not promote health" (p. 399).

Clarifying Your Values and Their Role in Your Work

When therapists disclose their values, they should clearly label them as their
own. Then values can be discussed in an open and noncoercive way, which can
assist clients in their exploration of their own values and the behavior that
stems from these values. Counselors may not agree with the values of their
clients, but it is essential that they respect the rights of their clients to hold a
different set of values. The way counselors deal with clients' values can raise
ethical issues. Bergin (1991) sees the core challenge as being able to use values
to enhance the therapeutic process without abusing the therapist's power and
exploiting the client's vulnerability:

> During treatment, therapists must make important decisions about how to enhance
> clients' functioning on the basis of professional values that are frequently implicit.
> At these decision points, therapist, client, and concerned others should collaborate
> in arriving at the goals toward which change is directed. (p. 396)

Not everyone who practices counseling or psychotherapy would agree with these views. At one extreme are counselors who have definite, absolute value systems. They believe that their job is to exert influence on their clients to adopt the *proper* values. These counselors tend to direct their clients toward the attitudes and behaviors that *they* judge to be in their clients' best interests. At the other extreme are counselors who are so anxious to avoid influencing their clients that they make themselves invisible. They keep themselves and their values hidden so they won't contaminate their clients' choices.

We don't view counseling as a form of indoctrination, nor do we believe that the therapist's function is to teach clients the right way to live. It's unfortunate that some well-intentioned counselors believe that their job is to help people conform to socially acceptable standards or to "straighten out" their clients. It seems arrogant to suppose that counselors know what's best for others. We question the implication that counselors have a greater wisdom than their clients and can prescribe ways of being happier. No doubt, teaching is a part of counseling, and clients do learn in both direct and indirect ways from the opinions and examples of their counselors. But counseling is not synonymous with preaching or instruction.

However, neither do we favor the opposite extreme of trying so hard to be "objective" that counselors keep their personal reactions and values hidden from clients. Counselors who adopt this style are unlikely to do more than mechanical therapy. In our opinion, clients demand a lot more involvement from therapists than mere reflection and clarification. Clients want and need to know where their therapists stand so they can test their own thinking. We believe that clients are helped by this kind of honest involvement.

Practitioners will inevitably incorporate certain value orientations into their therapeutic approaches and methods. Goals are usually based on values and beliefs, and clients may adopt goals that the therapist thinks are beneficial. If clients change the direction of their values without being aware of what they are doing, they are being deprived of self-determination (Brace, 1997).

However, it may be appropriate at times for the therapist to do more than merely watch clients make "bad decisions" without interference. Bergin (1991) asserts that it is irresponsible for a therapist to fail to inform clients about alternatives: "We need to be honest and open about our views, collaborate with the client in setting goals that fit his or her needs, then step aside and allow the person to exercise autonomy and face consequences" (p. 397).

Brace (1997) enumerates ten rules or ethical guidelines for counselors assisting clients in developing their own counseling goals: examine goals before they are adopted to be sure these goals are in the best interest of the client; ensure that goals are mutually consistent; justify the pursuit of end goals and the means to attain these goals; assess all causal and contributory factors that pertain to the goals; inform the client of their values, especially if such values are likely to influence the client's choice of goals; avoid or correct errors in clinical judgment; assess the risks that the client's goals might pose to the client or to others; consider how the client's goals may affect others; avoid deceiving clients; and honor any promises made to the client.

The following questions may help you to begin thinking about the role of your values in your work with clients:

- Some professionals consider it unethical to influence clients in specific value directions. What do you think? *I agree*
- Do you worry that openly discussing your values with certain clients might unduly influence their decision-making process? *yes*
- Is it possible for therapists to interact honestly with their clients without making value judgments? Is it desirable for therapists to avoid making such judgments? *yes, yes*
- If you were convinced that your client was making a "bad decision," would you express your concerns? *yes*
- Do you think the therapist is responsible for informing clients about a variety of value options? *yes*
- Do you need to see your clients adopt your beliefs and values? *no*
- Can you remain true to yourself and at the same time allow your clients the freedom to select their own values, even if they differ sharply from yours? *yes*
- How do you determine whether a conflict between your values and those of your client necessitates a referral to another professional? *if my ability to counsel is impaired*
- What specific values do you consider to be essential to the therapeutic process? *honesty, compassion, openness, directness*
- How does honestly exposing your clients to your viewpoint differ from subtly "guiding" them to accept your values? *keep boundaries clear*
- To what degree do you need to have had life experiences that are similar to those of your clients? Is it possible that too much similarity in values and life experiences might result in therapy that is not challenging for the client? *yes*

If your values will significantly affect your work with clients, it is incumbent on you to clarify them and the ways in which they enter the therapeutic process. For example, counselors who have "liberal" values may find themselves working with clients who have more traditional values. If these counselors privately scoff at conventional values, can they truly respect clients who don't think as they do? Or if counselors have a strong commitment to values that they rarely question, whether these values are conventional or unconventional, will they be inclined to promote these values at the expense of their clients' free exploration of attitudes and beliefs? If counselors rarely reexamine their own values, can they expect to provide a climate in which clients can reexamine their values?

From time to time your own values may present some difficulty for you in your work with clients. In the following sections we examine some sample cases and issues that can help you clarify what you value and how your values might influence the goals of counseling and the interventions you make with your clients. As you read these examples, keep the following questions in mind:

- What is my position on this issue?
- Where did I develop my views?

◆ Are my values open to modification?
◆ Am I open to being challenged by others?
◆ Do I insist that the world remain the same?
◆ Do I feel so deeply committed to any of my values that I'm likely to push my clients to accept them? Am I closed to clients with a different set of values?
◆ When would I feel the need to disclose my values to my clients? Why?
◆ How can I communicate my values without imposing those values on clients?
◆ Do my actions reveal that I respect the principle of client self-determination?
◆ How do my own values and beliefs affect what I say to clients regarding establishing their goals for counseling and for the manner in which I work with clients?
◆ Am I willing to make explicit to clients values of mine that could affect the development of goals in counseling? *don't understand*

The Ethics of Imposing Your Values on Clients

Counselors are cautioned to become aware of how their personal values influence their professional work. ACA's (1995) guideline reads, "Counselors are aware of their own values, attitudes, beliefs, and behaviors and how these apply in a diverse society, and avoid imposing their values on clients" (A.5.b.).

A national survey found a consensus among a representative group of mental-health practitioners that basic values such as self-determination are important for clients to become mentally healthy and to guide and evaluate the course of psychotherapy (Jensen & Bergin, 1988). Other basic values include: developing effective strategies for coping with stress; developing the ability to give and receive affection; increasing one's ability to be sensitive to the feelings of others; becoming able to practice self-control; having a sense of purpose for living; being open, honest, and genuine; finding satisfaction in one's work; having a sense of identity and self-worth; being skilled in interpersonal relationships; having deepened self-awareness and motivation for growth; and practicing good habits of physical health. These values were considered to be universal, and practitioners surveyed based their therapy on them.

healthy living

Even if you think it's inappropriate or unethical to impose your values on clients, you may still influence them in subtle ways to embrace your views. Indeed, some researchers have found that clients tend to change in ways that are consistent with the values of their therapists. It will be difficult to avoid communicating your values to your clients, even if you do not explicitly share them. What you pay attention to during counseling sessions will direct what your clients choose to talk about. The methods you use will provide them with clues to what you value.

Values are always at work

Your nonverbal behavior and body language also give clients indications of how you are being affected. If clients feel a need to have your approval, they may respond to these cues by acting in ways that they imagine will meet with your favor. Suppose, for example, that an unhappily married man knew or surmised that you really thought he was wasting good years of his life in the marriage. This client might be influenced to obtain a divorce simply because he thought you would approve. Although you may have decided not to coerce clients to believe and act in ways that agree with your own values, you still need to be sensitive to the subtle messages you may project that can be powerful influences on clients' behavior.

Value Conflicts: To Refer or Not to Refer

Know your limits in counseling

Tjeltveit (1986) suggests that referrals are appropriate when moral, religious, or political values are centrally involved in a client's presenting problems and when any of the following situations exist: the therapist's boundaries of competence have been reached, the therapist has extreme discomfort with a client's values, the therapist is unable to maintain objectivity, or the therapist has grave concerns about imposing his or her values on the client. In such cases it is appropriate to refer a client to a therapist who does not have such limitations or to one who shares the client's values. Merely having a conflict of values does not necessarily require a referral; it is possible to work through a conflict successfully.

referrals then are necessary

Some counselors believe that they can work with any client or with any problem. They may be convinced that being professional means being able to assist anyone. Other counselors are so unsure of their abilities that they are quick to refer anyone who makes them feel uncomfortable. Somewhere between these extremes are the cases in which your values and those of your client clash to such an extent that you question your ability to function in a helping way.

Counselors must honestly assess whether their values are likely to interfere with the objectivity they need to be useful to their clients. To make such an assessment, counselors must be clear about their feelings on value-laden issues. They must be honest about their own limitations, and they must be honest with clients or potential clients when they think value conflicts will interfere with the therapeutic relationship.

Consider the circumstances in which you would be inclined to refer a client to someone else because of a conflict of value systems. For each of the following, indicate the response that best fits you. Use the following code: A = I could work with this person; B = I would have difficulty working with this person; C = I could not work with this person.

A   1. a person with fundamentalist religious beliefs
A   2. a woman who claims to be seeking a way to put Christ at the center of her life, and if she could only turn her life to Christ, she would find peace
B   3. a person who shows little development of a conscience, who is strictly interested in his or her own advancement, and who uses others to achieve personal aims

A 4. a gay or lesbian couple hoping to work on conflicts in their relation-
      ship
A 5. a man who wants to leave his wife and children for the sake of sexual
      adventures with other women to bring excitement to his life
A 6. a woman who has decided to leave her husband and children to gain
      her independence but who wants to explore her fears of doing so
A 7. a woman who wants an abortion but wants help in confirming her
      decision
B 8. a teenager who is having unsafe sex and sees no problem with this
      behavior
B 9. a man who lives by extremely rigid "macho" expectations of what a
      man should be
D 10. a person who lives by logic and is convinced that feelings are confus-
      ing and should be avoided
B 11. a man who believes that the only way to discipline his children is
      through the use of corporal punishment
A 12. an interracial couple coming for premarital counseling
A 13. a husband and wife who seek counseling to discuss conflicts they are
      having with their adopted son, who is from a different culture
A 14. a lesbian couple wanting to adopt a child
A 15. a single parent wanting to adopt a child
B 16. a man who has found a way of beating the system and getting more
      than his legal share of public assistance
B 17. a woman who is unwilling to give up her affair but still wants to come
      in with her husband for couples counseling
A 18. an interracial couple wanting to adopt a child and being faced with
      their respective parents' opposition to the adoption
A 19. a client from another culture who has values very different from your
      own
C 20. a client who has values you strongly disapprove of or goals that you
      do not respect

Go back over the list, and pay particular attention to the items you marked
"C." Why do you think you'd have difficulty working with these people? What
other people or situations would pose problems for you because of a clash of
values?

Case Studies of Possible Value Conflicts

In this section we present some case studies of possible value conflicts. Try to
imagine yourself working with each of these clients. How do you think your
values would affect your work with them?

◆ **The case of Candy.**   Candy is a 14-year-old client you are seeing because
of family conflicts. Her parents have recently divorced, and Candy is having
problems coping with the breakup. Eventually, she tells you that she is having

sexual relations with her boyfriend. Moreover, she tells you that she's opposed to any birth-control devices because they seem so contrived. She assures you that she won't be one to get pregnant.

- What are your thoughts about Candy's having sex? *unprotected sex not*
  safe / at-risk
- If you sense that her behavior is an attempt to overcome her feelings of isolation, how might you deal with it? *help me see connection w/ time*
- Would you respond to her decision not to use birth-control measures? Why, or why not? *responsibility to unborn child*
- Is she a danger to herself or to others? *yes*

You've been working with Candy for a few months now, and she discovers that she is pregnant. Her boyfriend is 15 and declares that he is in no position to support her and a baby. She tells you that she has decided to have an abortion but feels anxious about following through on her decision. How would you respond? In the blanks put an "A" if you agree more than disagree with the statement, and put a "D" if you mainly disagree.

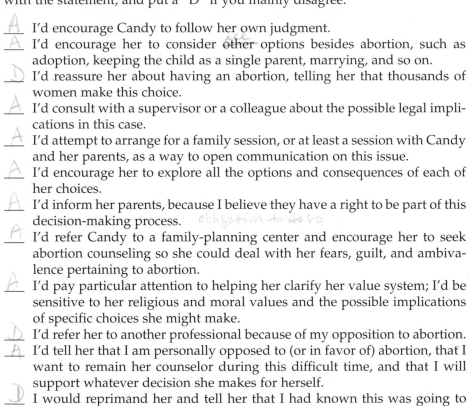

_A_ I'd encourage Candy to follow her own judgment.

_A_ I'd encourage her to consider *see* other options besides abortion, such as adoption, keeping the child as a single parent, marrying, and so on.

_D_ I'd reassure her about having an abortion, telling her that thousands of women make this choice.

_A_ I'd consult with a supervisor or a colleague about the possible legal implications in this case.

_A_ I'd attempt to arrange for a family session, or at least a session with Candy and her parents, as a way to open communication on this issue.

_A_ I'd encourage her to explore all the options and consequences of each of her choices.

_A_ I'd inform her parents, because I believe they have a right to be part of this decision-making process. *obligation to do so*

_A_ I'd refer Candy to a family-planning center and encourage her to seek abortion counseling so she could deal with her fears, guilt, and ambivalence pertaining to abortion.

_A_ I'd pay particular attention to helping her clarify her value system; I'd be sensitive to her religious and moral values and the possible implications of specific choices she might make.

_D_ I'd refer her to another professional because of my opposition to abortion.

_A_ I'd tell her that I am personally opposed to (or in favor of) abortion, that I want to remain her counselor during this difficult time, and that I will support whatever decision she makes for herself.

_D_ I would reprimand her and tell her that I had known this was going to happen.

Commentary.   Candy's case illustrates several thorny problems. What do you do if you feel that you cannot be objective because of your views on abortion? Do you refer Candy to someone else? If you do, might she feel that you think less of her because of her decision? If you're firmly opposed to abortion, could you support her in her decision to go ahead with it? Would you try to persuade her to have the baby because of your views on abortion? Ask yourself what your goals in working with her would be. What are your values in a case such as hers?

One possible course of action would be to tell Candy about your values and how you feel they would influence your work with her. If you felt that you couldn't work effectively with her, perhaps you should ask yourself why. Why is it crucial that her decision be compatible with your values? Do you necessarily have to approve of the decisions your clients make?

When the subject of abortion arises, some women may be reluctant to consider this option, either because of their value systems or because of feelings of guilt, shame, and fear. Other women may feel ambivalent and may want to explore all of their options. Ask yourself these questions:

◆ How would you react to not being allowed to explore abortion as one option for your client? *not good!*

◆ Do you think it is unethical to fail to discuss all of a client's options if this is her desire? *yes*

◆ What do you think about the behavior of a counselor who decides to ignore the federal prohibition and proceeds to provide abortion counseling for a client who has asked for this service? If this defiance were discovered and the agency lost its funding, what would be your reaction to the counselor's decision to explore all options?

◆ **The case of Paul.**   Paul comes to a counselor with many difficulties and anxieties, one of which is his antipathy toward interracial marriage. He expresses disappointment in his daughter and in himself as a father because of her engagement to a man of another race. Paul has gone as far as threatening to write her out of his will if she marries this man. What this client does not know is that the therapist herself is a partner in an interracial marriage. The therapist discloses this fact and lets him know of her difficulties with what she perceives as his prejudices.

◆ How do you react to her self-disclosure? (Was it ethical for her to do so? *yes* Would it have been ethical not to do so? Explain.) *yes.*

◆ What are your thoughts about the counselor's timing of her disclosure? *not good*

◆ Would a referral be in order? Why, or why not? *possibly – if they can't work thru the conflict*

◆ What are your values in this situation, and what might you do or say if you were the counselor?

Commentary.   Your views on racial issues can have an impact on your manner of counseling in certain situations. Take the following inventory, and think about what your responses tell you about how your values might operate in cases pertaining to racial concerns. In the space, put an "A" if you agree more than you disagree with the statement, and put a "D" if you disagree more than you agree.

_A_ I could effectively counsel a person of a different race.

_A_ I'd be inclined to refer a person of a different race to a counselor of that race because the client is bound to have more trust in a therapist of the same race.

_A_ My approach to counseling would entail modifying my practices and techniques in working with clients who are racially and culturally different.

_D_ Interracial marriages in this society are almost doomed to failure because of the extra pressures on them.

_A_ Interracial marriages pose no greater strain on a relationship than do interfaith marriages.

_D_ I have certain racial (cultural) prejudices that would affect my objectivity in working with clients of a different race (culture) from mine.

◆ ***The case of Lupe.***   Lupe is a social worker in a community mental-health agency. Her agency is sponsoring workshops aimed at preventing the spread of AIDS. The agency has attempted to involve the local churches in these workshops. One church withdrew its support because the workshops encouraged "safe" sexual practices, including the use of condoms, as a way of preventing AIDS. A church official contended that the use of condoms implied either homosexual behavior or promiscuous heterosexual activities, both of which are contrary to church teachings. Being a member of this church, Lupe finds herself struggling with value conflicts. She is in basic agreement with the teachings of the church, and she thinks that the official had a right to withdraw his support of these workshops. But she is also aware that many people in the community she serves are at high risk for contracting AIDS because of both drug usage and sexual practices. In her attempt to resolve her value conflicts she seeks out several of her colleagues, each of whom responds differently:

Colleague A: I would encourage you to tell your clients and others in the community that you agree with the position of the church. Then in your workshops actively attempt to change people's risky behavior. You could try to get them to give up their drug use, and you could steer them in the direction of monogamous sex practices.

Colleague B: I hope you will be up front with the people you come in contact with by telling them of your values and then providing them with adequate referrals so they can get information about prevention of this disease. But you do owe it to them not to steer them in the direction you think they should move.

Colleague C: I think it is best that you not disclose your values or let them know that you agree with the church's views. Instead, work toward changing their behavior and modifying their values directly. After all, in this case the end justifies the means.

Colleague D: More harm can come by your failure to provide necessary information. Even though your values are in sympathy with the church's position, ethically you owe it to the community to teach them methods of safe sex.

Commentary. If Lupe were to seek you out and ask for your advice, consider what you might say to her. In formulating your position, consider these questions:

◆ Which of her colleagues comes closest to your thinking, and why?
◆ With which colleague do you find yourself disagreeing the most, and why? Ⓐ
◆ Would Lupe be ethical if she did not disclose her values to her clients? Why or why not?   *yes*
◆ Given the gravity of this situation and the possibility of the spread of disease, is Lupe ethically bound to provide people who are at high risk with facts and information about prevention? *yes !*
◆ What advice would you be inclined to give Lupe, and what does this response tell you about your values?

Differences in Life Experiences and Philosophies

Many people contend that the life experiences and value systems of counselors must be similar to those of their clients. The idea is that counselors can understand and empathize with their clients' conflicts only if they have had the same kinds of subjective experiences. Thus, an elderly person may feel that a counselor who hasn't reached this stage of life cannot hope to understand what it means to cope with loss, physical decline, loneliness, and anxiety about the future. Many people who belong to racial or ethnic minorities think it is extremely important to seek counselors of their own ethnic group in the belief that counselors who haven't had to contend with discrimination and prejudice cannot really understand how they see the world. Similarly, many women are convinced that men's life experiences and biases prevent them from being able to understand women's needs. Lesbians and gay men may seek therapists with the same sexual orientation because they are convinced that heterosexual counselors lack the experience and understanding to work with them on their conflicts. Many drug addicts and alcoholics reveal failure after failure in their psychotherapy experiences with professionals who haven't experienced drug and alcohol problems.

The growth of self-help groups validates the idea that people who have encountered and resolved certain difficulties possess unique resources for helping others like themselves. Thus, overweight people share their problems in Overeaters Anonymous. Alcoholics who have chosen to live one day at a time without drinking provide support for fellow alcoholics who are trying to quit. Members of Recovery Incorporated find support in facing the world once they have left state mental hospitals.

To what degree do you share the view that you must have had life experiences similar to those of your clients? Can you help people whose experiences, values, and problems are different from yours by tuning in to their feelings and relating them to your own? Consider for a moment whether you can communicate effectively with:

- ◆ an elderly person
- ◆ a person of a different racial, ethnic, or cultural group
- ◆ a physically handicapped person
- ◆ a delinquent or a criminal
- ◆ a person who is abusing alcohol or drugs

Our position is that counselors need not have experienced each of the struggles of their clients to be effective in working with them. When the counselor and the client connect at a certain level, cultural and age differences can be transcended. It is possible for a relatively young counselor to work effectively with an elderly client. For example, the client may be experiencing feelings of loses, guilt, sadness, and hopelessness. The young counselor can empathize with these feelings even though the counselor's experiences that resulted in some of these same feelings were quite different. It is essential, however, that the counselor be sensitive to the differences in their backgrounds.

In *Counseling the Culturally Different: Theory and Practice,* D. W. Sue and Sue (1990) point out that many counselors are "culturally blind"; they perceive reality exclusively through the filters of their own life experiences. It is important, they contend, for counselors to become "culturally aware" so they can critically evaluate their conditioned values and assumptions and the conditioning of their clients. It is imperative that counselors have a broad perspective of diverse cultural value systems. D. W. Sue, Ivey, and Pedersen (1996) claim that the mental-health profession has been forced into serious soul-searching. They claim that mental-health services have often oppressed minority clients, and therapists have often failed to recognize the biased assumptions inherent in some theories of human behavior and counseling. Those counselors who remain victims of their own cultural conditioning risk further oppressing minority clients, a subject we examine in Chapter 10.

 To facilitate your reflection on whether you need to have life experiences or value systems that are similar to those of your clients, here are a number of situations you might face as a counselor. In each case, assess what factors in your life would either help or hinder you in establishing a good working relationship with the client.

◆ ***The case of Frances.***   Frances is a 60-year-old teacher who is thinking about going to law school because it's something she has wanted to do for a long time. She has taught government and history in community colleges for 30 years, and now she wants to retire early to take up a new profession. Frances wonders whether she has the stamina to endure long hours of study, and she is asking herself whether leaving teaching at this stage in life would be a wise move.

- ◆ What experiences have you had that could help you understand Frances's desires and conflict?   career move @ 42
- ◆ How do you respond to a person beginning law school at the age of 60?

great!

- Would you be inclined to encourage Francis to take a risk, or would you favor her staying with a secure job in her situation?
- How might your answers to the preceding questions affect the way you would counsel her, or how might they indicate your bias?

◆ ***The case of Alberto.***   Alberto, a Latino client, comes to a community mental-health clinic on the recommendation of one of his friends. His presenting problem is depression, chronic sleep disturbance, and the imminent threat of losing his job. During the initial session you are aware that he is extremely guarded. As a counselor, you may assume that self-disclosure and openness to feelings enhance life. Alberto discloses little about himself or how he is feeling. Although he will answer your questions briefly, you sense that he is withholding much information from you.

- How sensitive are you to your client's sense of privacy? Have you considered that keeping one's thoughts and feelings to oneself might be valued in certain cultures? How might this be a survival mechanism in some cultures?
- Assume that you succeed in getting Alberto to be more self-disclosing and expressive, not only with you but also within his environment. What potential hazards can you see in terms of his reentry into his environment?
- Is it ethical to convert Alberto to your point of view without first understanding the cultural context? Explain. *no.*
- One of your aims might be to teach Alberto to be more autonomous (to become less dependent on his parents and his extended family). How might this aim be an expression of your value system, and how might that affect your client as he attempts to deal with his family?
- How might your intervention reflect your lack of understanding of the importance of the extended family in certain cultures?
- Some might label Alberto's behavior as bordering on paranoia. How might his cautiousness be more adaptive than maladaptive?

◆ ***The case of Sylvia.***   At a community clinic Sylvia, who is 38, tells you that she is an alcoholic. During the intake interview she says: "I feel so much remorse because I've tried to stop my drinking and haven't succeeded. I'm fine for a while, and then I begin to think that I have to be a 'perfect' wife and mother. I see all the ways in which I don't measure up—how I let my kids down, the many mistakes I've made with them, the embarrassment I've caused my husband—and then I get so down I feel compelled to take that next drink to stop my shaking and to blur my depression. I see that what I'm doing is self-destructive, but I haven't been able to stop, in spite of going to Alcoholics Anonymous."

- What experiences have you had that would help you understand what it's like for Sylvia to feel compelled to drink?
- Do you see Sylvia as having a disease? as suffering from a lack of willpower? as an irresponsible, indulgent person?
- How does the fact that Sylvia is a woman affect your view of her problem?

- What is your reaction to Sylvia's being in Alcoholics Anonymous? Do you see it as a positive or negative adjunct to therapy?

◆ **The case of Jan.**   Jan is a physicist, born and educated in northern Europe. He has several degrees from prestigious universities. Jan's lifestyle and interests center on intellectual pursuits, and he tends to show very little affect in most situations. His wife is having an affair, and he seeks your counsel, not so much on his own initiative but because of the encouragement of colleagues who think he can use some guidance. He talks calmly about the potential breakup of his family and indicates that he has discussed the matter with his wife. In essence, he has asked her to decide the outcome. Jan is in your office to find a logical explanation for why the affair occurred. He does not display any strong emotional reactions to the situation. He gives no clues to how he is feeling about it.

- Would you consider Jan's cultural and educational background in dealing with his reaction to his situation? *yes*
- Would you immediately pursue the expression of feeling? Can you see yourself challenging him for intellectualizing? Why, or why not?

   Commentary.   This example is used to illustrate another type of cultural difference. Although we do not deny the value of expressing emotional reactions to a situation such as Jan's, we would be especially sensitive to his cultural background and his conditioning. In certain cultures openly admitting having been affected by a situation such as this is equivalent to a loss of face or pride. Jan might never show the degree of emotionality that we assume to be appropriate, but that does not mean that he cannot express an emotional reaction. To push for the norm of expressing feelings could be counterproductive and potentially unethical. Although this example could apply to many American men as well, it is even more representative of Jan's cultural conditioning not to share his feelings.

◆ **The case of Mike.**   You are the counselor for Mike, who has a history of being expelled from school. He has spent much of his life in and out of juvenile court. The rules of the gang he belongs to dictate how he lives. He is silent during most of your first session, but he does let you know that he doesn't really trust you, that he's only there because the court sent him, and that you can't possibly understand what his life is about.

- Have you had any life experiences that would qualify you to counsel Mike? *no*
- What are your immediate reactions to him? *tough life / hard*
- Would you want to change some of his values? For example, would you want to see him finish school? stop being involved in gang fights? take counseling seriously? *secretly, yes!*

potential probs for me.

- If you haven't had the kinds of experiences growing up that he has had, could you still communicate effectively with him and understand his view of the world? *I'm not sure, potentially yes*

◆ **The case of Luigi.**   Luigi is a middle-aged businessman who says that he is not seeking personal counseling but wants advice on how to manage his teenage daughter. According to Luigi, his daughter is immature and unruly. She isn't learning self-discipline, socializes too much, and works too little. She doesn't respect her parents, and in other ways she is a disappointment and a worry to him. In Luigi's eyes, the full responsibility for the conflict in his family rests with his daughter. You surmise that he doesn't see any need to examine his own behavior or his role in the problem.

- How do you imagine you might relate to Luigi? *I'm not sure*
- Would your own values get in the way of understanding his values? *yes*
- Do you think you might want to get him to look at his own part in the family disturbances? Would you want to challenge his values as they pertain to his daughter's behavior?
- Would you accept him as a client, even if he wanted to focus on how he could change his daughter? *yes*
- Would family therapy be indicated? *yes, I think*

    You can add your own examples of clients whom you might have difficulty counseling because of a divergence in values or life experiences. How would you deal with such clients? You could decide to refer most of them to other counselors, but you might also look at how to extend yourself so you could work with a wider range of personalities. If you have difficulty relating to people who think differently from the way you do, you can work on being more open to diverse viewpoints. This openness doesn't entail accepting other people's values as your own. Instead, it implies being secure enough in your own values that you aren't threatened by really listening to, and deeply understanding, people who think about life differently. It implies listening to your clients with the intent of understanding what their values are, how they arrived at them, and the meaning these values have for them and then communicating this acceptance. This kind of accepting attitude requires a willingness to let your clients be who they are without trying to convince them that they should see life the way you do. Achieving this acceptance of your clients can significantly broaden you as a person and as a professional. It does not require that you change your values.
    You have seen how differences in life experiences and values influence the interventions you make. As you counsel a variety of clients, you may find yourself struggling with how your beliefs affect the way you work with them. This is especially true with respect to the role of religious and spiritual values, end-of-life decisions, and value issues pertaining to sexual orientation. As you read the following sections, attempt to clarify your values in these areas and

think about how your views might either enhance or interfere with your ability to establish contact with certain clients.

Role of Spiritual and Religious Values in Counseling

The field of counseling and psychotherapy has been slow to recognize the need to address spiritual and religious concerns. This topic has been the subject of increasing debate in recent years however, and there is now widespread interest in the spiritual and religious beliefs of both counselors and clients and how such beliefs might be incorporated in therapeutic relationships (Younggren, 1993).

We are being challenged to incorporate spiritual and religious beliefs in both assessment and treatment practices. The American Psychological Association's Division 36 (Psychologists Interested in Religious Issues) has increased in membership, and the Association of Spiritual, Ethical, Religious Values in Counseling (ASERVIC) division of the ACA publishes the journal *Counseling and Values*, which features articles on ethics and values. Members of ASERVIC have done a great deal to promote awareness that the full range of a client's values is basic to the client-counselor relationship.

Bergin (1991) and many other researchers believe that discussing spiritual and religious values will result in a change in the focus of treatment away from symptom relief and toward more general changes in lifestyle. Spirituality is an important component of mental health, and its inclusion in psychotherapy renders the treatment process more effective. Spiritual and religious beliefs should be used to the client's benefit to enhance the therapeutic process (Mattson, 1994).

Spiritual and religious values play a major part in human life and in an individual's search for meaning. Exploring these values with clients may help them find solutions to their struggles. Spiritual and religious values can be integrated with other therapeutic tools to enhance the therapy process.

Some individuals claim to be deeply spiritual, yet they are not affiliated with any form of religion. Here are a few ideas put forth to distinguish between these two concepts:

◆ "*Spirituality* refers to a personal inclination or desire for a relationship with the transcendent or God; *religion* refers to the social or organized means by which persons express spirituality" (Grimm, 1994, p. 154).
◆ "Spirituality refers to a general sensitivity to moral, ethical, humanitarian, and existential issues without reference to any particular religious doctrine. Spiritually oriented individuals may or may not be affiliated with organized religion" (Genia, 1994, p. 395).
◆ "Spirituality from my perspective is larger than religion, although one's religious practices may be an expression of one's spirituality. For me, spirituality refers to a way of being in the world that acknowledges the existence of a transcendent dimension. It includes an awareness of the connectedness of

all that is, and accepts that all of life has meaning and purpose and is thus sacred" (Becvar, 1994, p. 13).

◆ "Spirituality may be defined as: the animating force in life, represented by such images as breath, wind, vigor, and courage. Spirituality is the infusion and drawing out of spirit in one's life. It is experienced as an active and passive process" (Summit on Spirituality, 1995, p. 30).

◆ "Spirituality is also described as a capacity and tendency that is innate and unique to all persons. This spiritual tendency moves the individual toward knowledge, love, meaning, hope, transcendence, connectedness, and compassion. Spirituality includes one's capacity for creativity, growth, and the development of a values system. Spirituality encompasses the religious, spiritual, and transpersonal" (Summit on Spirituality, 1995, p. 30).

Kelly (1995b) suggests that religion is the way people express their devotion to a deity or to an ultimate reality. In this sense, religion is expressed through Judaism, Christianity, Islam, Hinduism, Buddhism, Confucianism, and Taoism, as well as the many institutionalized variations within each of these world religions. Spirituality is generally seen to be less formal than this.

Some Commonalities and Differences

Religion and spirituality can be sources of healing and can provide strength in critical times by helping people find purpose in life. Both religion and counseling help people ponder questions of "Who am I?" and "What is the meaning of my life?" At their best, both counseling and religion are able to foster healing through an exploration of self: by learning to accept oneself; forgiving others and oneself; admitting one's shortcomings; accepting personal responsibility; letting go of hurts and resentments; dealing with guilt; and learning to let go of self-destructive patterns of thinking, feeling, and acting.

Religious beliefs and practices affect many dimensions of human experience, including how to handle guilt feelings, authority, and moral questions, to name a few. The key issues here are whether a counselor can understand the religious beliefs of the client and whether the counselor can work within the framework of the *client's* value system.

Although religion and counseling are comparable in many respects, some key differences exist. For example, counseling does not involve the imposition of counselors' values on clients, whereas religion often involves teaching doctrines and beliefs to which individuals are expected to conform. Some therapists, from Freud to Ellis, have been antagonistic toward religion. And some religious leaders have viewed therapy with suspicion. Religious leaders have reacted negatively to counseling as a secular force, and counselors have reacted negatively to religion, describing it as a defense mechanism or as a form of denial. The key is for counselors to be sensitive to the needs of their clients, to listen to them and let them lead the way, and to talk about areas they indicate they want or need to explore.

Personal Beliefs and Values of Counselors

Many counselors have a spiritual or religious orientation in their personal lives. In a national survey of counselor values, Kelly (1995a) reported that almost 64% of the respondents believed in a personal God, and another 25% believed in a transcendent or spiritual dimension to reality. Approximately 70% expressed some degree of affiliation with organized religion, with almost 45% indicating that they regularly participate in religious services.

It is clear that the value systems of therapists do influence their views of goals of treatment, the interventions used, and the topics explored during the sessions (Younggren, 1993). Indeed, no therapy is value free, but therapists must not attempt to indoctrinate clients with a particular set of spiritual or religious values (Grimm, 1994). Counselors who choose to practice from a spiritual and religious framework have an ethical responsibility to be aware of how their beliefs affect their work and to make sure they do not bring harm to clients (Younggren, 1993).

Your Personal Stance

What role does spirituality or religion play in your life? Does it provide you with a source of meaning? What connection, if any, do you see between spirituality and religion? What are your views concerning established and organized religion? Has religion been a positive, negative, or neutral force in your life?

Even if spiritual and religious issues are not the focus of a client's concern, these values may enter into the sessions indirectly as the client explores moral conflicts or grapples with questions of meaning in life. Can you keep your spiritual and religious values out of these sessions? How do you think they will influence the way you counsel? If you have little belief in spirituality or are hostile to organized religions, can you empathize with clients who view themselves as being deeply spiritual or who feel committed to the teachings of a particular church?

As you formulate your own position on the place of spiritual and religious values in the practice of counseling, reflect on these questions:

- Is it appropriate to deal with religious issues in an open and forthright manner as clients' needs arise in the counseling process?
- Do clients have the right to explore their religious concerns in their therapy?
- Are therapists forcing their values on their clients when they decide what topics can be discussed?

You may think that a client has accepted an unnecessarily strict and authoritarian moral code, but you need to understand what these beliefs mean to your client, whatever your own evaluation of them for yourself might be. Consider these examples as you think about your personal stance on the role of spiritual and religious values in counseling.

◆ **The case of Holly.** Holly is your client, and she is suffering from a major internal conflict. She is living with her boyfriend, whom she loves very much. But Holly knows her church would disapprove of the way she is living, and she is experiencing a great deal of guilt over what she sees as her transgressions.

- ◆ If you sharply disagreed with the values she accepted from her church or thought they were unrealistic, how might your views affect your counseling?
- ◆ Do you think you might try to persuade her that her guilt was controlling her and that she would be better off freeing herself from her religious beliefs? Why, or why not? *no*

◆ **The case of Susan.** Susan is a devout Catholic. After a marriage of 25 years, her husband left her. She has now fallen in love with another man, and very much wants a relationship with him. But because her church does not recognize divorce, Susan feels guilty about her involvement with another man. She sees her situation as hopeless, and she cannot find a satisfactory solution. Living alone for the rest of her life scares her. But if marries the man, she fears that her guilt feelings will eventually ruin the relationship.

- ◆ What are your values that pertain to this case, and how do you think they would influence your interventions?
- ◆ Would you recommend that Susan see a priest to help her resolve her guilt feelings? Explain. *Possibly, if I picked the priest!*
- ◆ If Susan asked you what she should do or what you think about her dilemma, what would you say to her? *This is extremely painful; your values are! to you. Let's think about the options carefully.*

◆ **The case of Jeremiah.** Jeremiah is in a group that you are leading. He calls himself a "born-again Christian," and he feels that he has found peace and strength in his own life. In a sincere and caring way, Jeremiah wants to pass on to other group members what has become very meaningful to him. Several members respond negatively, asserting that he is pushing his values on them and that he comes across in a superior way. *disruptive & controlling*

- ◆ As a group leader, how would you intervene? *block.*
- ◆ What reactions do you think you'd have toward Jeremiah, and how might your reactions either inhibit or enhance your ability to work with him?
- ◆ If your views were very similar to those of Jeremiah, what interventions might you make, and how might you react?

◆ **The case of Kieran.** Kieran is a counselor in private practice who has strong religious beliefs. He is open about this in his professional disclosure statement, explaining that his religious beliefs play a major part in his personal and professional life. Carmel comes to Kieran for counseling regarding what she considers to be a disintegrating marriage. Kieran has strong convictions that favor preserving the family unit. After going through an explanation of the informed consent document, Kieran asks Carmel if she is willing to join him in a prayer for the successful outcome of the therapy and for the preservation of the family. Kieran then takes a history and assures Carmel that everything can be worked out. He adds that he would like to include Carmel's husband in the sessions. Carmel leaves and does not return.

Kieran comes to you for consultation because he sees a pattern of clients who do not return after the first session.

♦ What would you want to say to Kieran? *he's influenced clients to his*
♦ Do you see any potential ethical violations on Kieran's part? *Pt of views.* *(yes!)*

Commentary. Although we applaud Kieran's frankness in presenting his values, we question his approach to Carmel. He does not assess the client's state of mind, her religious convictions, if any, the strength of her convictions, or her degree of comfort with his approach. Carmel may have felt pressured to agree with him in this first session, or she may not have had the strength to disagree openly. The ethical issue is captured in this question: Did Kieran take care of the client's needs or did he take care of his own needs at Carmel's expense?

Some Reasons to Include Spiritual and Religious Values in Counseling

Counseling can help clients gain insight into the ways their core beliefs and values are reflected in their behavior. Clients may discover that what they are doing is based on beliefs that are no longer functional, which implies that they will need to re-examine their values. Miranti and Burke (1995) suggest, "for counselors, the challenge is not whether the issue of spirituality should be addressed, but how it can best be addressed by well-prepared and sensitive professionals" (p. 3).

Miranti and Burke (1995) maintain that helpers must be prepared to deal with spiritual issues that lie at the very core of the client's being. The spiritual domain may offer clients in crisis solace and comfort. It is a major sustaining power that keeps people going when all else fails. The guilt, anger, and sadness that clients experience often results from a misinterpretation of the spiritual and religious realm, which can lead to depression and a sense of worthlessness. Counselors must remain open and nonjudgmental, for the spiritual beliefs clients hold can be a major source of strength as they make crucial life decisions.

Some cautions. Spirituality is an existential issue. Although it is important to be open to dealing with spiritual and religious issues in counseling, counselors should be cautious about introducing religious themes and be aware of the potential for countertransference. For example, a therapist who has a hostile attitude toward religion because of his or her own strict religious upbringing or a therapist with a strong religious faith could have intense reactions toward a client who portrays judgmental and critical attitudes of people who hold to a religion. Therapists must guard against making decisions for their clients or imposing their own values on clients. Some counselors may push their religious beliefs, and others may impose their nonreligious or anti-religious attitudes.

◆ **The case of Sheila.**   Sheila is a rational emotive behavior therapist who claims to be an agnostic. She has a strong bias against any kind of spiritual or religious influences, considering these beliefs to be irrational. Her client Brendan describes an unhappy marriage as one of the issues he struggles with. When she suggests to him that perhaps he should consider leaving his marriage, he replies that this is out of the question. He informs her that he has a deep spiritual conviction that this is his destiny. If he were to go against his destiny, he would suffer on some other level. Sheila replies: "Have you ever considered that your convictions may be unhealthy, not only for you but also for your children? Do you want to talk more about this?" Brendan seems taken aback. He tells the counselor, "I think that what you just said was insensitive to the way I believe. I'm not sure that you can help me." Brendan leaves abruptly.

- What do you think about Sheila's approach to Brendan?   *unethical "unhealthy beliefs" judged*
- Are any ethical issues raised in the way Sheila dealt with Brendan? If so, what are the issues?   *her values interfered w/ her ability to be competent*
- Would you be comfortable responding as Sheila did? Why, or why not?   *no (obj.) no.*
- Did Sheila take care of her needs or of Brendan's needs?   *hers*
- Would Sheila necessarily have to agree with Brendan's spiritual beliefs to work with him?   *no*
- How would you work with this client?   *explore ?s of unhappiness, "destiny"*

   Commentary.   We have concerns about Sheila's describing Brendan's spiritual beliefs as "unhealthy." Brendan's reasons for staying in his marriage (his spiritual values) should have been explored rather than being quickly judged. This kind of approach demonstrates the imposition of the therapist's values, not an exploration of the client's concerns.

◆ **The case of Rory.**   Rory, who has been in counseling for some time with Teresa, sees himself as unworthy and cannot move past his guilt. He keeps insisting that he cannot forgive himself for past sins. He is in great turmoil and berates himself for his aberrant ways. Teresa knows that Rory is a profoundly religious man and asks during one of the sessions: "How would you view and react to a person with a similar struggle as yours? What kind of God do you believe in? Is your God a punitive or loving God? What does your religion teach you about the forgiveness of sin?" Teresa is attempting to utilize Rory's convictions to reframe his thinking. Once he begins to look at his behavior through the eyes of his religious beliefs, his attitudes toward his own behavior change dramatically. Because Rory believes in a loving God, he finally learns to be more loving toward himself. Because his God is a forgiving God, he can be more forgiving of himself.

- How do you react to how Teresa worked with Rory? *good*
- Do you agree or disagree with using Rory's religious beliefs as an intervention? *yes*
- By doing this, was Teresa imposing her values? *no*

Commentary.   If Teresa had used her own religious beliefs to reframe Rory's thinking, we would have concerns. If she were his minister, rabbi, or priest, it would be acceptable for her to teach these values. But that is not the role of a counselor. However, Teresa noticed a discrepancy between Rory's religious beliefs and his assessment of his behaviors. By using the client's own belief system, she assisted him in reframing his self-assessment and in the process helped him to be true to his own belief system.

Spiritual and Religious Values in Assessment and Treatment

Traditionally, when a client comes to a therapist with a problem, the therapist explores all the factors that contributed to the development of the problem. Even though a client may no longer consider himself or herself to be religious or spiritual, a background of involvement in religion should be explored as part of the client's history. These beliefs may have been factors in the development of the problem, and thus could be part of the problem.

Faiver and O'Brien (1993) and Kelly (1995b) believe that it is essential to understand and respect the client's religious beliefs and to include such beliefs in their assessment and treatment practice. The first step is to include spiritual and religious dimensions as a regular part of the intake procedure and the early phase of the counseling process. Faiver and O'Brien devised a form to assess the religious beliefs of clients, which they use to glean relevant information on the client's belief system for diagnostic, treatment, and referral purposes. They suggest that the assessment process should include questions pertaining to spiritual and religious issues as they are relevant to a client's presenting problems, questions about the roles religion and spirituality have played or currently play in a client's life, and questions about how religious and spiritual beliefs might be related to the client's cognitive, affective, and behavioral processes. For example, is guilt an issue? What is the source of guilt, and does it serve any functional purpose?

In assessing a client Faiver and O'Brien think it is essential to consider the client's problems from a holistic perspective. Kelly (1995b) endorses the notion of including items pertaining to general information about the client's spirituality and religion that serve the purposes of (a) obtaining a preliminary indication about the relevance of spirituality and religion for each client, (b) gathering information that the helper might refer to at a later point in the helping process, and (c) indicating to the client that it is acceptable to talk about religious and spiritual concerns.

There are many paths toward fulfilling spiritual needs, and it is not the helper's task to prescribe any particular pathway. However, it is the helper's responsibility to be aware that spirituality is a significant force for many of their clients and it is especially important for practitioners to pursue spiritual concerns if clients initiate them. Practitioners should remain finely tuned to their clients' stories and to the reasons clients sought professional assistance.

◆ ***The case of Anami.***   Anami is a counselor in a university counseling center. A first-generation Asian American, Tai, is caught between the religion of his parents, who are Buddhist, and his emerging beliefs. Since entering the university environment, he has begun to question his Buddhist upbringing, yet he has not found anything to replace his parents' values. He feels lost and does not know what to believe.

Anami considers herself to be a holistic counselor, and she assesses clients from a holistic perspective, which includes asking questions about family history, personal history, religious and spiritual upbringing, life turning points, physical health, nutrition, and social relationships. In the process of the assessment, she discovers that many of the issues Tai is struggling with pertain to Buddhism. Anami tells Tai: "I think I can assist you in the things you struggle with, but I have limited knowledge of the Buddhist religion. With your permission I would like to consult with a colleague who is a Buddhist on some specific matters. I may also recommend a Buddhist teacher to you to help you clarify some specific beliefs you mentioned in the assessment. Is this acceptable to you?" Tai nods in agreement.

◆ What do you think of the way in which Anami handled this case? *great*
◆ Would you have done anything differently, and if so, what? *no*
◆ Do you think Anami should have referred Tai immediately because of her lack of familiarity with Buddhism? *not necessarily*

Commentary.   We find little to disagree with in the way Anami handled the case. We applaud her for recognizing and acknowledging her limitations, for being willing to educate herself on these matters, and also for being willing to consult with someone who has greater expertise than she does.

Training Programs for Counselors

Mental-health training programs have a long way to go in providing education and training dealing with religious and spiritual issues. In a national survey of counselor education programs, Kelly (1994) found that religious and spiritual issues are being dealt with as a course component in fewer than 25% of the programs. What may be more surprising is his finding that only about half the counselor educators who participated in the study believe that religious and spiritual issues are either "very important" or "important" in the education and training of counselors. A substantial number of state-affiliated programs in Kelly's study gave little or no attention to spiritual and religious issues. Clearly, if counselors are to meet the challenge of addressing the role of spirituality in the lives of their clients, they need training in both coursework and fieldwork as well as inspiration and leadership from their teachers.

At the Summit on Spirituality (1995) participants generated a list of competencies that all counselors should acquire as part of their training. Conceptual and practical strategies for inclusion of spiritual and religious concerns were also developed for infusion into the curriculum. Here are some of the counselor competencies in spirituality proposed for inclusion in the Standards of the Council for Accreditation of Counseling and Related Educational Programs (CACREP). Counselors should be able to:

- explain the relationship between religious, spiritual, and transpersonal phenomena
- describe religious, spiritual, and transpersonal beliefs and practices from the perspective of diversity
- describe their religious, spiritual, or transpersonal beliefs
- identify key events in their lives that contributed to the development of their belief system and explain how those events contributed
- engage in self-exploration of their religious, spiritual, and transpersonal beliefs that support or hinder respect and valuing of different belief systems
- demonstrate empathy for and understanding of a variety of religious, spiritual, and transpersonal phenomena
- acquire knowledge needed to better understand a client's religious and spiritual worldview by requesting information from the clients themselves or from outside resources
- assess the relevance of the religious, spiritual, and transpersonal domains in the client's therapeutic issues
- use a client's religious, spiritual, or transpersonal phenomena in pursuit of the client's therapeutic goals as befits the client's expressed preferences
- identify when their understanding or tolerance of religious, spiritual, or transpersonal worldview is insufficient to adequately serve the client
- seek consultation, seek further training or education, and demonstrate appropriate referral skills when their own limits of tolerance or competence are reached

How might these spirituality competencies best be attained? Spirituality and religious frameworks could be included in cultural diversity training for counselors. It is important for counselors-in-training to examine their biases, assumptions, and experiences with religious issues. Programs need to challenge students to look at what they believe and how their beliefs and values might influence their work.

End-of-Life Decisions

In March 1990 Bruno Bettelheim, a well-known psychoanalyst and author, stunned the psychological community when he took his own life. In an interview with Celeste Fremon (1991), Bettelheim shared some of his views on the right to take one's own life. He told Fremon that although he was not afraid of dying he did fear suffering. As people grow older, he contended, there is a greater likelihood that they will be kept alive without a purpose. At age 86, Bettelheim was no longer able to do most of the things that brought him enjoyment and meaning, such as hiking, reading, and writing. He made a decision to end his life. His situation highlights the issue of a person's right to choose the manner and time of death, especially in the event of terminal illness.

Your stance.   Might there come a time in your life when there was nothing for you to live for? Imagine yourself in a rest home, growing more and more senile. You are unable to read, to carry on meaningful conversation, or to go places, and you are partially paralyzed by a series of strokes. Would you want to be kept alive at all costs, or might you want to end your life? Would you feel justified in doing so? What might stop you?

Now apply this line of thought to other situations in life. If you accept the premise that your life is yours to do with as you choose, do you believe it is permissible to commit suicide at *any* period in your life? Suppose you felt like ending your life even after trying various ways of making your life meaningful, including getting intensive psychotherapy. Imagine that you felt as if nothing worked and that nothing changed. Would you continue to live until natural causes took over? Would you feel justified in ending your own life if your active search had failed to bring you peace? Put yourself in the following case as Andrew's counselor.

◆ **The case of Andrew.**   A young man in his 20s, Andrew is HIV positive but without any symptoms. He says that he wants to participate in a physician-assisted suicide before he gets to an intolerable state. Andrew has watched too many friends die agonizing deaths with full-blown AIDS. He vowed to himself that if he became HIV positive he would take active measures to make sure he would not die in the same way. Andrew wants to be remembered for the vital person that he is, not the person he fears he will eventually become. Because he is rational and knows what he wants, he believes that taking this action is reasonable and in accord with his basic human rights.

[handwritten margin note: This case brings me to my limits to my "rational" suicide]

- ◆ Because Andrew is rational and able to make decisions that affect his life, should he be allowed to take measures to end his life far before he becomes terminally ill? *[handwritten: no! not anymore than I would allow some to commit suicide w/o intervening.]*
- ◆ Because he is not yet seriously ill, should he be prevented from ending his life, even if it means taking away his freedom of choice? *[handwritten: yes consults, support. & eval,]*
- ◆ If Andrew were your client, would you respect his self-determination, or would you influence him to search for alternatives to suicide at this stage in his life? *[handwritten: yes]*
- ◆ As a counselor, if there were no legal mandates to report his intentions, would you feel justified in attempting to persuade Andrew to accept the priority you might place on life? *[handwritten: yes! talk w/ others who are HIV pos.]*

Suicide: A free and rational choice?   In their article on the need for ethical reasoning regarding physician-assisted suicide, Kiser and Korpi (1996) suggest that mental-health professionals may need to reconsider their views of suicide and how to treat suicidal clients. Instead of considering all individuals who are contemplating suicide as being "mentally ill" persons who should be prevented from ending their lives, certain individuals should be viewed as being capable of making autonomous and rational decisions. This alternative model would allow professionals to explore alternatives to suicide, while at the same time respecting the client's autonomy and freedom of choice.

As a counselor, you need to be willing to discuss end-of-life decisions when clients bring such concerns to you. If you are closed to any personal examination of this issue, you may interrupt these dialogues, cut off your clients' exploration of their feelings, or attempt to provide your clients with your own solutions based on your values and beliefs. Kiser (1996) has argued that counselors need to examine their own personal, moral, and ethical beliefs regarding rational suicide, and in particular, physician-assisted suicide. He contends that for those counselors whose belief systems do not condone rational suicide or physician-assisted suicide, the ethical course for them to follow is to disqualify themselves from such cases and refer the client to another competent professional qualified to assist the client.

Although there are no easy answers to right-to-die questions, Albright and Hazler (1995) remind us that counselors *do* face these situations *with* their clients. Counselors must clarify their own beliefs and values pertaining to end-of-life decisions so they can assist their clients in making decisions within the framework of their own belief and value systems. Once counselors understand their own perspectives on right-to-die issues, they can focus on the needs of their clients. Albright and Hazler point out some of the areas counselors need to explore from the worldview of their clients:

♦ Within what personal, religious and moral framework does the client exist?
♦ What are the client's religious and philosophical beliefs that are the source of meaning in life?
♦ What type of support system does the client have, and how do relatives view the client's decision?
♦ How hopeless is the client's illness?
♦ To what degree have alternatives and decisions been explored?
♦ What kind of decision-making skills does the client have, and can the counselor help improve those skills?
♦ What kind of referral resources are available if the counselor is unable or unwilling to handle the situation?

Albright and Hazler acknowledge that counselors will be faced with difficult decisions on what actions to take with clients who are doing their best to make decisions. Some of the following interventions aimed at providing direction for clients struggling with end-of-life situations, may be helpful:

helpful

- Learn as much as possible about the course of clients' illnesses, prognoses, and available treatments.
- Know the clients' family support systems and what their views are regarding end-of-life decisions.
- Realize that clients who are near death often need help coping with their psychological pain as well as their physical suffering. Explore clients' fears about dying, the impact of their religious beliefs on their decision or how religion provides them with meaning, and assist them in achieving closure on any unfinished business with others. *(Andrew is not "near" death)*
- Assume the role of a resource person for these clients.
- Help clients understand the importance of various personal and formal documents associated with the end of life.
- Regardless of the decisions clients make, offer compassion, acceptance, and understanding related to the difficulties in dealing with life and death issues.
- Realize the role of offering comfort to loved ones and friends after the death.

With these guidelines in mind, ask yourself where you stand with respect to key questions on end-of-life decisions and right-to-die issues. What is your position on an individual's right to decide about matters pertaining to living and dying? What religious, ethical, and moral beliefs do you hold that might enable you to support a client's decision about ending his or her life under certain circumstances? How might your beliefs get in the way of assisting your client in making his or her own decision? Are you aware of the laws of your state and the ethical guidelines of your professional organization concerning an individual's freedom to make end-of-life decisions?

Policy statement on end-of-life decisions.   The National Association of Social Workers developed a policy statement pertaining to client self-determination in end-of-life decisions (NASW, 1994). According to the NASW document, end-of-life decisions are the choices individuals make about terminal conditions regarding their continuing care or treatment options. These options include aggressive treatment of the medical condition, life-sustaining treatment, medical intervention intended to alleviate suffering (but not to cure), withholding or withdrawing life-sustaining treatment, voluntary active euthanasia, and physician-assisted suicide. A terminal condition is one where there is no reasonable chance of recovery and where the application of life-sustaining procedures would serve only to postpone the end of life. Here are some excerpts of the NASW's position concerning end-of-life decisions, which are based on the principle of client self-determination (the premise that choice should be intrinsic to all aspects of life and death):

from Andrew's case before

> Social workers have an important role in helping individuals identify the end-of-life options available to them. This role must be performed with full knowledge of and compliance with the law and in accordance with the *NASW Code of Ethics*. Social workers should be well informed about living wills, durable power of attorney for health care, and legislation related to advance health care directives.

A key value for social workers is client self-determination. Competent individuals should have the opportunity to make their own choices but only after being informed about all options and consequences. Choices should be made without coercion. Therefore, the appropriate role for social workers is to help patients express their thoughts and feelings, to facilitate exploration of alternatives, to provide information to make an informed choice, and to deal with grief and loss issues.

Social workers should be free to participate or not participate in assisted-suicide matters or other discussions concerning end-of-life decisions depending on their own beliefs, attitudes, and value systems. If a social worker is unable to help with decisions about assisted suicide or other end-of-life choices, he or she has a professional obligation to refer patients and their families to competent professionals who are available to address end-of-life issues.

It is inappropriate for social workers to deliver, supply, or personally participate in the commission of an act of assisted suicide when acting in their professional role. Doing so may subject the social worker to criminal charges. If legally permissible, it is not inappropriate for a social worker to be present during an assisted suicide if the client requests the socials worker's presence. The involvement of social workers in assisted suicide cases should not depend on race or ethnicity, religion, age, gender, economic factors, sexual orientation, or disability.

With this kind of policy statement by NASW, social workers have some general guidelines by which they can examine the ethical and legal issues pertaining to end-of-life decisions. The literature reveals an increase of professional interest in issues related to death and dying, yet despite this trend there do not seem to be any standard guidelines for counselors or psychologists when working with terminally ill individuals regarding the right to refuse treatment or to exercise choice in deciding to end their lives (Kiser, 1996; Farrugia, 1993). Kiser (1996) points out that the American Counseling Association has yet to establish guidelines for addressing a counselor's role and responsibility in relation to physician-assisted suicide for terminally ill individuals. In the Netherlands, physician-assisted suicide is a legal means of ending one's life (Kiser, 1996). Yet in the United States, physician-assisted suicide is a highly controversial issue. Ballot measures allowing terminally ill adults to obtain prescriptions from physicians for medications to end their lives were passed in Oregon, but they were later blocked from becoming law. Both Washington and California recently had measures legalizing assisted suicide on their ballots, but both initiatives failed.

The counseling profession faces the challenge of formulating ethical and procedural guidelines on right-to-die issues, especially in light of advances in medical technology, the aging of the population, and the AIDS epidemic. Counselors will increasingly be expected to assist clients in end-of-life decisions. It is essential for counselors to be both proactive and reactive to the needs of individual clients, families, and other professionals (Farrugia, 1993).

Potential conflicts between law and ethics.   Do you believe that client self-determination is a necessary and sufficient condition in making end-of-life decisions? Do you think that rational individuals who are suffering from terminal illnesses should be allowed to end their lives? Should competent individuals be allowed to participate in physician-assisted suicide after they have thoroughly examined all options and all aspects of their decisions? Does the state have a right to decide how individuals with terminal illnesses will die? What role do you think an individual's culture plays in shaping concepts of life and death? How might Western and Eastern cultures look differently at the belief that life is preferable to death? To what degree would you want to consider a client's religious and spiritual beliefs in any discussion of end-of-life decisions? What is your role when working with clients who are struggling with end-of-life decisions? with the families of such clients? Apply the ethical questions associated with end-of-life decisions that we have raised so far in the following cases.

◆ **The case of Festus.**   A counselor has been seeing a client named Festus who is now diagnosed with a fast-moving and painful cancer. After several sessions with chemotherapy and pain medications, Festus tells the counselor that nothing seems to work. He's in great pain and sees no reason to live in this pain. He tells the counselor that he's decided to end his life. They discuss this decision for several sessions, examining all aspects, and Festus becomes even clearer about his decision to end his life. Here are four counselors' responses to the decision Festus has made.

Counselor A: Both the law and my code of ethics require that I report this matter.

Festus: Do what you have to do. If you report me, I'll simply say that I was not seriously considering it, and I won't see you any more.

Counselor B: I have a great deal of difficulty accepting your decision. If you remain in counseling, I believe we can explore ways to find new meaning in your life in spite of your suffering. I'm asking you not to take any action for at least three weeks to give us time to talk about ways you might find meaning in this situation.

Counselor C: Although the law requires that I report you, it does not seem like the right or effective thing to do. Our relationship has come to mean a lot to both of us, especially at a time like this. You could always stop seeing me and kill yourself anyhow. I will continue to see you as long as you choose to come and I will help you in any way that I can.

Counselor D: Write a letter to me terminating therapy. Once I receive the letter, our relationship is over.

Consider each of these approaches, and then clarify what you would do in this situation.

◆ What are your thoughts about each counselor's response? Which one comes closest to your thinking?
◆ What other things might you want to say to Festus? *explore hospice*
◆ Is it ethical to impose your values on Festus in this exceptional case? Why, or why not? *no.*

Commentary.   Although the law is clear on this point—you must report—many therapists are likely to struggle with what they see as a conflict between choosing the ethical as opposed to the legal path. Following a strictly legal course, the therapist would be free from any lawsuit, and the counselor could exercise his or her duty to protect. If the counselor does report this situation, we think that his or her value to Festus would be limited. Festus might be put on a required 72-hour hold for psychiatric evaluation and then be released. He could then do whatever he intended to do.

We do not suggest that you ignore the law, but when you encounter this kind of case, the proper course is not always clear. If you don't report, you may be thinking of the client's autonomy, self-determination, and welfare. You could reason that your client is of sound mind and that he has a right to decide not to live in extreme pain. You could also think about providing him with the maximum degree of support as long as he wants this. However, if you don't report him and he does end his life, the family could sue you for breach of your professional duty. If you do report, and he terminates his therapy, you will not be in a position to offer support or to help him in other ways. If you follow the letter of the law, your therapeutic relationship with this client is likely to end.

(margin note: Even legal guidelines are not always blk + white decision-makers)

◆ **The case of Emily.**   Emily, who is in her early 40s, is suffering from advanced rheumatoid arthritis. She is in constant pain, and many of the pain medications have resulted in serious side effects. This is a debilitating disease, and she sees no hope of any improvement. She has lost her will to live and has expressed her desire to end her life, but her parents cling to hope. They deeply believe that it is always wrong to take your own life.

- If her parents were coming to you for counseling, what might you say to them?
- Do you feel that Emily has the right to end her life?
- What role should your beliefs play in your counseling?
- How might your values affect the things you say to the family?

Now assume that Emily herself comes to you, her therapist of long standing, and says: "I am in too much pain, and I don't want to suffer anymore. I don't want to involve you in it, but as my therapist, I would like you to know my last wishes." She tells you of her plan to take an overdose of pills, an action she sees as more humane than continuing to endure her suffering

- What legal implications are involved here?
- Do you see any conflict between ethics and the law in this case? *(margin note: suicide vs self-determination)*
- Do you have an ethical and legal responsibility to prevent Emily from carrying out her intended course of action?
- If you were in full agreement with her wishes, how might this feeling influence your intervention?
- What do you consider to be the ethical course of action?

◆   ***The case of Bettina.***   Bettina, who lives at boarding school, makes several suicidal overtures. Because these attempts seem to be primarily attention-getting gestures, her counselor feels manipulated and does not report them to her parents. During the last of these attempts, however, Bettina seriously hurts herself and ends up in the hospital.

- In this case, do you see any conflict between what is ethically right and what is legally right?
- Did the counselor take the "cry for help" too lightly?
- What are the ethical and legal implications for the counselor in deciding that Bettina's attempts were more manipulative than serious and therefore should be ignored?
- What can a counselor do in a situation in which he or she determines that the attempts are manipulative rather than serious?
- If the counselor told Bettina that she was going to inform the girl's parents about these suicidal attempts and Bettina had responded by saying that she would quit counseling if the counselor did so, what do you think the counselor should do?

Issues involved in end-of-life decisions.   Although the cases of Festus, Emily, and Bettina are different, they all raise similar issues of balancing what is ethically right with what is legally required.

- Do counselors have the responsibility and the right to forcefully protect people from the potential harm their own decisions may bring?
- Do helpers have an ethical right to block clients who have clearly chosen death over life? Do counselors have an ethical duty to respect clients' decisions?   *yes,*
- What are a counselor's legal obligations if a client decides to commit suicide?
- What should be done if what seems ethically right is not legal?
- If a course of action is legal but does not seem like the most ethical path to choose, what would you do?
- Once a therapist determines that a significant risk exists, must some action be taken?
- What are the consequences of failing to take steps to prevent clients from ending their lives? Do factors such as the age of the client, the client's level of competence, and the special circumstances of each case make a difference?

Values Pertaining to Sexuality

Examine your values with respect to sexual behavior. Do they tend to be restrictive or permissive? What is your attitude toward:

- the belief that sex should be reserved for marriage only
- sex as an expression of love and commitment

- casual sex
- group sex
- extramarital sex
- premarital sex
- homosexuality
- teenage sex

Can you counsel people who are experiencing conflict over their sexual choices if their values differ dramatically from your own? For example, if you have permissive views about sexual behavior, will you be able to respect the restrictive views of some of your clients? If you think their moral views are giving them difficulty, will you try to persuade your clients to adopt your views? How will you view the guilt clients may experience? Will you treat it as an undesirable emotion that they need to free themselves of? Conversely, if you have fairly strict sexual guidelines for your own life, will the more permissive attitudes of some of your clients be a problem? Can you be supportive of client choices that conflict with your own values?

◆ **The case of Virginia and Tom.**   Virginia and Tom find themselves in a marital crisis when Virginia discovers that Tom has had sexual affairs with several women during the course of their marriage. Tom agrees to see a marriage counselor. Tom says that he can't see how his affairs necessarily got in the way of his relationship with his wife, especially as they are not going on currently. He believes that what is done is done and that it is pointless to dwell on past transgressions. He is upset over his wife's reaction to learning about his affairs. He says that he loves his wife and that he does not want to end the marriage. His involvements with other women were sexual in nature rather than committed love relationships. Virginia says that she would like to forgive her husband but that she finds it too painful to continue living with him knowing of his activities, even though they are in the past.

Counselor A.   This counselor tells the couple at the initial session that from her experience extramarital affairs add many strains to a marriage, that many people tend to get hurt in such situations, and that affairs do pose some problems for couples seeking counseling. However, she adds that affairs sometimes actually have positive benefits for both the wife and the husband. She says that her policy is to let the couple find out for themselves what is acceptable to them. She accepts Virginia and Tom as clients and asks them to consider as many options as they can to resolve their difficulties.

- Is this counselor neutral or biased? Explain.
- Does it seem practical and realistic to expect the couple to make the decision by coming up with some alternatives?

Counselor B.   From the outset this counselor makes it clear that she sees affairs as disruptive in any marriage. She maintains that affairs are typically started because of a deep dissatisfaction within the marriage and are symptomatic of other real conflicts. With marital therapy, the counselor suggests that [↑ disagree] Tom and Virginia can get to the basics of their problem. She further says that she will not work with them unless Tom is willing to give up his affairs, be- [) agree] cause she is convinced that counseling will not work unless he is fully com- mitted to doing what is needed to work on his relationship with Virginia.

- Is this counselor imposing her values? *yes*
- Is it appropriate for the counselor to openly state her conditions and values from the outset?
- To what degree do you agree or disagree with this counselor's thinking and approach?
- After a year of working with them, if the counselor discovers that Tom has begun another affair, should she continue to work with them both? only with Virginia? or terminate the case altogether? *make an agreement while in therapy not to have another affair*

Counselor C. This counselor has a definite bias in favor of Tom. She points out that the couple seem to have a basically sound marriage and suggests that with some individual counseling Virginia can learn to accept and live with the past affairs.

- With her bias, is it ethical for this counselor to accept this couple for counseling? Should she suggest a referral to another professional? *yes*
- Is the counselor ignoring Virginia's needs and values? *yes*
- Is there an ethical issue for the counselor in siding with Tom? *failure to protect V.*
- Should the counselor have kept her values and attitudes to herself so that she would be less likely to influence this couple's decisions? *yes or refer if competence is jeopardized*

Ethical and Value Issues in Counseling Gay and Lesbian Clients

Working with lesbians and gay men often presents a challenge to counselors who hold traditional values. Even counselors who accept same-sex relationships intellectually may reject them emotionally. Counselors who have negative reactions to homosexuals are likely to impose their own values. Buhrke and Douce (1991) remind mental-health professionals that they have an ethical and moral obligation to address lesbian and gay issues in an affirmative manner. It is their professional responsibility to take the steps necessary to eliminate all forms of oppression. The ethical codes of the ACA, the APA, and the NASW clearly state that discrimination on the basis of minority status—be it race, ethnicity, gender, or sexual orientation—is unethical and unacceptable. If the profession is serious about meeting this guideline, it will need to train students to provide sensitive treatment of gays and lesbians (Buhrke & Douce, 1991). We highlight this topic because it illustrates not only the ethical problems involved in imposing values but also the problems of working with clients who have had different life experiences.

✱ Special training require

The American Psychiatric Association, in 1973, and the American Psychological Association, in 1975, stopped labeling homosexuality as a form of mental illness. Along with these changes came the assumption that therapeutic practices would be modified to reflect this viewpoint. After decades of discrimination, the mental-health system has begun to treat the problems of homosexuals rather than their sexual orientation (Fassinger, 1991b).

Although more clinicians are counseling gay and lesbian clients, Ritter and O'Neill (1989) write that a number of practitioners still view these clients as needing to be "cured." They propose that counselors develop therapeutic strategies that "can assist gay men and lesbian women in freeing their souls of the negativity and death-dealing emotions that may be preventing them from proceeding along their spiritual journeys" (p. 12).

what clinicians can do for gay lesbian clients

Before counselors can change their therapeutic strategies, they must change their attitudes toward lesbians and gays and acquire a body of knowledge about community resources for these clients. Unless counselors become conscious of their own faulty assumptions and homophobia, they may project their misconceptions and their fears onto their clients. Therapists must confront their personal prejudices, myths, fears, and stereotypes regarding sexual orientation. As part of the process of expanding their self-awareness, therapists need to acquire specialized knowledge about gay people in general and about the meaning of a gay identity to particular individuals (Sobocinski, 1990). They also need to find ways to continue to educate themselves about gay identity development and management and about affirmative counseling models (Shannon & Woods, 1991).

In an empirical study designed to examine common psychosocial assumptions pertaining to lesbian mothers, Falk (1989) found that discrimination had persisted in court decisions denying lesbian mothers' petitions for custody of their children. The courts often assume that lesbians are emotionally unstable or unable to perform in a maternal role. They also assume that children with lesbian mothers are more likely to be emotionally harmed, that they will be subject to molestation, that their role development will be negatively affected, or that they will themselves become homosexual. Falk concludes that "no research has identified significant differences between lesbian mothers and their heterosexual counterparts or the children raised by these groups. Researchers have been unable to establish empirically that detriment results to children from being raised by lesbian mothers" (p. 946).

The APA's Task Force on Bias in Psychotherapy with Lesbians and Gay Men conducted a survey of 2,544 licensed psychologists to identify their attitudes pertaining to homosexuals (Youngstrom, 1991a). Almost 95% of the psychologists reported that they had treated at least one lesbian or gay man. One of the purposes of the survey was to identify examples of both good and poor therapeutic practices with this population. The task force identified 25 themes that revealed biased, inadequate, or inappropriate practices and 20 themes indicating exemplary practices. Biased practices that may be unethical include:

Biases

- automatically attributing a client's problems to his or her sexual orientation
- discouraging lesbian or gay clients from having or adopting a child

Biases
con't

- expressing attitudes or beliefs that trivialize or demean gay and lesbian individuals or their experience
- showing insensitivity to the impact of prejudice and discrimination on gay and lesbian parents and their children
- providing or teaching inaccurate or biased information about lesbians and gay men

Exemplary practices include:

- not attempting to change the sexual orientation of a client without evidence that the client desires this change
- recognizing that gay and lesbian people can live happy and fulfilled lives
- recognizing the importance of educating professionals, students, super-visees, and others about gay and lesbian issues and attempting to counter bias and misinformation
- recognizing the ways in which social prejudices and discrimination create problems for clients and dealing with these concerns in therapy

Value Issues of Gay and Lesbian Clients

Like any other minority group, lesbians and gay men are subjected to discrimination, prejudice, and oppression, which manifests itself when gay people seek employment or a place of residence. But gay and lesbian clients also have special counseling needs. For instance, the U.S. Department of Defense does not permit openly homosexual individuals to serve in the military. Lesbians and gay men often bring to counseling the struggle between concealing their identity and "coming out." Dealing with family members is also of special importance to gay couples. They may want to be honest with their parents, yet they may fear hurting them or receiving negative reactions from them. With the reality of the AIDS crisis, gay men often face the loss of friends. Not only do gay men need to deal with death and loss but they may also want to explore their fears of becoming infected. Counselors who work with gay men need to be able to talk with their clients about safe-sex practices. In short, counselors need to listen carefully to their clients and be willing to explore whatever concerns they bring to the counseling relationship.

◆   ***The case of Myrna and Rose.***   Myrna and Rose are seeking relationship counseling, saying that they are having communication problems. They have a number of conflicts that they both want to work out. They clearly state that they are involved in a lesbian relationship and that their sexual orientation is not an issue they want to explore. They indicate that they are comfortable with their sexual orientation but need help in learning how to communicate more effectively.

Counselor A.   This counselor agrees to see the two women and work with them much as she would with a heterosexual couple. The counselor adds that if at any time the uniqueness of their relationship causes difficulties, it would be up to them to bring this up as an issue. She lets them know that if they are comfortable with their sexual orientation she has no need to explore it. What are your reactions to this counselor's approach? *good*

Counselor B. This counselor agrees to see the couple. During the initial session he realizes that he has strong negative reactions toward them. These reactions are so much in the foreground that they interfere with his ability to effectively work with the couple's presenting problem. He tells the two women about his difficulties and suggests a referral. He lets them know that he had hoped he could be objective enough to work with them but that this is not the case.

- Was this counselor's behavior ethical? *yes* Is he violating any of the ethical codes in refusing to work with this couple because of their sexual orientation? *yes* he needs some sensitivity train
- Given his negative reactions, should he have continued seeing the couple, or would this in itself have been unethical? *no*
- Would it be more damaging to the clients to refer them or to continue to see them? *con't to see them*
- Is it ethical for the counselor to charge the couple for this session? Explain your point of view. *no, because it is clearly a failure on the therapist's part.*

Counselor C. This counselor agrees to see Myrna and Rose, and during the first session he suggests that they ought to examine their homosexuality. He has concerns about excluding any issues from exploration in determining what the problem really is between them.

- Do you agree or disagree with this stance? *disagree*
- Because they made it clear over the telephone that they did not want to explore the issue of their sexual orientation, was the counselor's intervention appropriate? Explain. *no*

Commentary. In reviewing the approaches of these three counselors, which approach would be closest to yours? To clarify your thinking on the issue of counseling gay and lesbian clients, reflect on these questions:

- Therapists often find that the presenting problem clients bring to a session is not their major problem. Does it show the therapist's values to assume that a couple's homosexuality might be the real problem? Is the counselor justified in bringing up homosexuality as a therapeutic issue? *possibly in time*
- What are the ethical implications of a heterosexually oriented therapist working with homosexual couples?
- Is it an appropriate function for counselors to attempt to sway clients toward a sexual orientation that is deemed "acceptable" by the counselor? *no*
- Should the counselor make life decisions for clients, or should the counselor challenge clients to make their own decisions?
- What attitudes are necessary for therapists to be instrumental in helping gay men and lesbians accept their sexual orientations? *acceptance /respect & trust*

- Can a counselor who is not comfortable with his or her own sexuality possibly be effective in assisting homosexual clients to accept their identities? *no*

◆ **The case of Tanya and Liz.**   Maxine, a lesbian therapist, is seeing a lesbian couple, Liz and Tanya. It is customary for Maxine to see the partners individually on occasion. During Tanya's first individual session, she confesses to having affairs with several men. Tanya tells Maxine that she sees herself as bisexual, a fact that she has not disclosed to her partner. One of the issues that Liz and Tanya brought to therapy was problems with intimacy. During the individual session, Maxine suggests that this is one more way that Tanya avoids intimacy and begins to talk about this with her. At the end of the session, Tanya agrees with the therapist's interpretation and agrees to come back for further couples work with Liz.

- If you were the therapist, how would you have handled Tanya's disclosure?
- Do you see anything inappropriate or unethical in Maxine's approach? Why, or why not? *no*
- Is this an example of imposition of therapist values? Is Maxine's interpretation revealing a bias against bisexuality? *no*
- How will Maxine deal with the couple now that she shares a secret with Tanya? *ask Tanya to share secret w/ Liz*
- Was Maxine remiss in not exploring questions such as: Is Tanya gay with an intimacy issue? Is Tanya bisexual? Is Tanya ambivalent about her sexual orientation? *yes*

Religion and Homosexuality

A client's religious values can be a source of conflict to a person who is struggling with sexual identity issues. Of course, the religious and moral values of many counselors can also pose problems in maintaining objectivity when working with clients who want to explore their sexual feelings, attitudes, and behavior. Consider the case of Ronald as an example.

◆ **The case of Ronald.**   Ronald, in his early 20s, is a junior in college. He tells you that he wants to get into counseling with you to sort out conflicts he is experiencing between his sexual feelings and his religion. Ronald sees himself as a good Christian and a believer in the Bible. He has had very little experience dating and hasn't had any sexual relationships. He is troubled because he experiences far more intense feelings toward men than he does toward women. This is what he tells you:

> I haven't yet acted on my sexual feelings for other men because I feel that this would be morally wrong. My religious beliefs tell me that it's very wrong for me even to have sexual desires for other men, let alone to act on these desires! If I did have homosexual experiences, I'd feel extremely guilty. But I just don't have much interest in women. At the same time I'm intensely interested in having a close emotional and physical relationship with a man. I'm torn by what I feel I want to experience and what my religion tells me I *ought* to do. So, I was wondering whether

you think you can help me, and I'd also like to know what your views are about religion and about homosexuality.

From what you know about Ronald, would you want to accept him as a client? Do you think you could help him clarify his feelings and achieve some resolution of his conflict? What kind of answer would you give him concerning your view of homosexuality? What would you tell him about your religious values? How would your views either help or hinder him in resolving his struggle?

Let's examine the responses that three different counselors might make to Ronald. As you read these responses, think about the degree to which they represent what you might say if you were counseling him.

Counselor A.   "Well, Ronald, the answer to whether I can help you really depends on several factors. First of all, you need to know that I'm a Christian counselor, and I share many of your beliefs about religion, morality, and the Bible. I think that I could be very supportive in helping you work through some of your religious doubts. You should know that I believe my clients will find real serenity when they make Christ the center of their lives and when they live by the example He gave us. Next, you need to know that I cannot condone homosexuality because I do believe that it is immoral. I'm not implying that you're sinful for merely having homosexual wishes, but it would be morally wrong for you to act on these impulses."

◆ Do you share this counselor's views?   *no*
◆ Is this counselor imposing or merely exposing his beliefs?   *both*
◆ Do you think this counselor can work effectively with Ronald? Why, or why not?   *no*

Counselor B.   "Ronald, your sexual preference really doesn't affect me one way or the other. I'd want you to decide to do what you think is right for you. If you decide on a same-sex orientation, I'd be supportive, and I'd want to help you work through any problems that might arise as a result of your choice. Your religious views also don't affect me one way or the other. I realize that your religion is a part of you, and we could work on how your teachings might cause you difficulty in living the way you want to. I really don't see why it's important that I tell you my personal values. They won't be entering into our relationship that much, and I wouldn't want them to influence you. I want you to choose whatever way is right for you, and I'll support whatever that is."

◆ Is this counselor being neutral and passive or accepting and nonjudgmental?   *open + accepting*
◆ Do you think the counselor can keep his values out of the therapeutic relationship?
◆ What do you agree or disagree with in this counselor's approach?

Counselor C.   "I'm not sure whether I'm the counselor for you or not. You'll need to decide whether you want to work with me. Before you decide, you should know that I think that religion is a negative influence on most people. In your case, for example, you were taught to feel guilty about your sexual impulses. Guilt is a way of controlling people. If I worked with you, although I would respect your religious convictions, I'd probably challenge some of your religious values and the source of your guilt feelings. I'd have you look carefully at where you obtained your notions of right and wrong. As far as your homosexual feelings are concerned, I'd want to explore the relationship you had with your father and mother, and I'd challenge you to look at your motivations in not making more contact with women. Is it because you're afraid of them? Do you have enough experience with either sex to know whether you want to be homosexual or heterosexual?

- Do you agree or disagree with this counselor's thinking? *no*
- Do you think this counselor will impose her views on Ronald? *yes*
- Do you think this counselor's values will challenge Ronald to decide what he values?

After thinking about these three different approaches, how would you respond to Ronald? Would you have any reservations about accepting him as a client? Would you be able to accept his choice of homosexuality if that was what he wanted? Would you prefer that he not make this choice? Would you be more concerned about his religious struggles than about his sexual orientation?

Counseling Gay Parents and Their Children

You might become involved in counseling a gay parent, a child of a gay parent, or a heterosexual former spouse of a gay parent who is fighting for custody of their children. What values do you hold that might make it difficult for you to counsel any of these clients? What values do you possess that might facilitate building a relationship with your clients in each of these situations?

◆ ***The case of Ruby.***   Ruby is counseling Henry, who expresses extremely hostile feelings toward homosexuals and toward people who have contracted AIDS. Henry is not coming to counseling to work on his feelings about gay people; his primary goal is to work out his feelings of resentment over his wife, who left him. In one session he makes derogatory comments about gay people. He thinks they are all deviant and that it serves them right if they do get AIDS. Ruby's son is gay, and Henry's prejudice affects her emotionally. She is taken aback by her client's comments, and she finds that his views are getting in the way as she attempts to work with him. Her self-dialogue has taken the following turns:

- "Maybe I should tell Henry how he is affecting me and let him know I have a son who's gay. If I don't, I'm not sure I can continue to work with him."

- "I think I'll express my hurt and anger to a colleague, but I surely won't tell Henry how he's affecting me. Nor will I let him know I'm having a hard time working with him."
- "Henry's disclosures get in the way of my caring for him. Perhaps I should tell him I'm bothered deeply by his prejudice but not let him know that I have a gay son."
- "Because of my own countertransference, it may be best that I refer him without telling him the reason I'm having trouble with him."
- "Maybe I should just put my own feelings on a shelf and try to work with him on reducing his prejudice and negative reactions toward gays."

If Ruby came to you as a colleague and wanted to talk about her reactions and the course she should take with Henry, what might you say to her? In reflecting on what you might tell her, consider these issues:

- Is it ethical for Ruby to work on a goal that her client has not brought up? *Yes, in time*
- To what degree would you encourage Ruby to be self-disclosing with Henry? What do you think she should reveal of herself to him? And what do you think she should not disclose? Why? *I might not be as objct. I'd like because my son is gay –*
- Is it ethical for Ruby to continue to see Henry without telling him how she is affected by him? *I don't know – no*

Specialized Training in Counseling Gay and Lesbian Clients

Is it ethical to counsel gay and lesbian clients without having received specialized training with this population? Buhrke and Douce (1991) suggest ways gay and lesbian concerns might be integrated in both academic courses and internship experiences in a counseling program. Slater (1988) makes the point that myths surrounding homosexuality continue to abound. She sees it as the therapist's job to discourage such myths and to substitute reality. These myths and misconceptions tend to perpetuate the illness model and lead to discrimination, rejection, and even attacks on homosexuals. Slater concludes that it is essential that therapists who work with gays have a knowledge of developmental theories, be relatively free of homophobia, and be knowledgeable about what it means to be gay. Fassinger (1991b) contends that "we should deliberately create a gay affirmative approach that validates a gay sexual orientation, recognizes the oppression faced by gay people, and actively helps them overcome its external and internal effects" (p. 170). It is clear that practitioners need to critically examine any misconceptions they hold about gay men and lesbians and to obtain specialized training in working with gay clients.

One way for counselors to increase their awareness of ethical and therapeutic considerations in working with gay and lesbian clients is to take advantage of continuing education workshops sponsored by national, regional, state, and local professional organizations. Participants learn about referral resources as well as about specific interventions and strategies that are appropriate for gay and lesbian clients. You may not know the sexual orientation of a client until the therapeutic relationship develops, so even if you don't plan to work with a gay or lesbian population, you need to have a clear idea of your own values relative to this issue.

Chapter Summary

In this chapter we've looked at a variety of value-laden counseling situations and issues. Of course, you'll encounter many other value questions in your work. Our intent has been to focus your attention on the ways your values and those of your clients can affect your counseling relationships.

Counselors cannot be neutral in the area of values and should frankly acknowledge their values when they are related to issues their clients are struggling with. It takes honesty and courage to recognize how your values affect the way you counsel, and it takes wisdom to determine when you cannot work with a client due to a clash of values. Ongoing introspection and discussions with supervisors or colleagues are necessary to determine how to make optimal use of your values in the therapeutic relationship.

Suggested Activities

1. Have a panel discussion on the topic "Is it possible for counselors to remain neutral with respect to their clients' values?" The panel can also discuss different ways in which counselors' values may affect the counseling process.
2. Invite several practicing counselors to talk to your class about the role of values in counseling. Invite counselors who have different theoretical orientations. For example, you might ask a behavior therapist and a humanistic therapist to talk to your class at the same time on the role of values.
3. For a week or so keep a record of your principal activities. On the basis of what you do and how you use your time, list your values as they are reflected in your record in order of their priority. How do you think these values might influence the way you counsel others?
4. In class, do this exercise in pairs. First, discuss counseling situations that might be difficult for each of you because of a conflict of values. For example, one student might anticipate difficulty working with clients who have fundamentalist religious beliefs. Then choose one of these situations to role-play, with one student playing the part of the client and the other playing the part of the counselor. The client brings up some problem that involves the troublesome value area. It is important for you and your partner to really get into the frame of reference being role-played and to feel the part as much as possible.
5. As a variation on the preceding exercise, assume the role of a client whose values you have difficulty identifying with. For instance, if you think you'd have trouble counseling a woman who wanted an abortion, become this

client and bring her problem to another student, who plays the part of the counselor.

6. For this exercise, work in small groups. Discuss the life experiences you've had that you think will enable you to effectively counsel others. You might also talk about limitations in your life experiences that might hinder your understanding of certain clients.

7. Interview some practicing counselors about their experiences with values in the counseling process. You could ask questions such as: "What kinds of clients have you had difficulty working with because of your value system? How do you think your values influence the way you counsel? How are your clients affected by your values? What are the main value issues clients bring to the counseling process?"

8. Do this exercise in pairs. One student plays a counselor; the other plays a client. The counselor actively tries to convert the client to some value or point of view that the counselor holds. The job of the counselor is to try to persuade the client to do what the counselor thinks would be best for the client. This exercise can give you a feeling for what it's like to persuade a person to adopt your point of view and what it's like to be subjected to persuasion. Then switch roles.

4

Client Rights and Counselor Responsibilities

Pre-Chapter Self-Inventory

Directions: For each statement, indicate the response that most closely identifies your beliefs and attitudes. Use the following code:

5 = I *strongly agree* with this statement.
4 = I *agree* with this statement.
3 = I am *undecided* about this statement.
2 = I *disagree* with this statement.
1 = I *strongly disagree* with this statement.

___2___ 1. If there is a conflict between a legal and an ethical standard, a therapist must follow the law.

___2___ 2. Practitioners who do not use written consent forms are being unprofessional and unethical.

___5___ 3. To practice ethically, therapists must become familiar with the laws related to their profession.

___4___ 4. Clients in therapy should have the right of access to their files.

___5___ 5. Clients should be made aware of their rights at the outset of a diagnostic or therapeutic relationship.

___2___ 6. It is unethical for a counselor to alter the fee structure once it has been established.

___5___ 7. Ethical practice demands that therapists develop procedures to ensure that clients are in a position to make informed choices.

___4___ 8. Therapists have the responsibility to become knowledgeable about community resources and alternatives to therapy and to present these alternatives to their clients.

___4___ 9. Before entering therapy, clients should be made aware of the purposes, goals, techniques, policies, and procedures involved.

___5___ 10. Clients should be informed at the initial counseling session of the limits of confidentiality.

___3___ 11. Therapists have an ethical responsibility to discuss possible termination issues with clients during the initial sessions and to review these matters with them periodically.

___2___ 12. It is primarily the therapist's responsibility to determine the appropriate time for termination of therapy for most clients.

___4___ 13. A therapeutic relationship should be maintained only as long as it is clear that the client is benefiting.

___4___ 14. I would want to be sure that my clients were aware of both the possible benefits and the risks associated with counseling before we began a professional relationship.

___1___ 15. I would keep detailed clinical notes on my clients and share these notes with my clients because this can be therapeutic.

___4___ 16. We can easily make clients worse by attaching labels to them as part of therapy.

___3___ 17. It is appropriate for therapists who work with children and adolescents to serve as their advocates in certain legal situations.

___ 18. When a child is in psychotherapy, the therapist has an ethical and legal obligation to provide the parents with information they request.

___ 19. Minors should be allowed to seek psychological assistance regarding pregnancy and abortion counseling *without* parental consent or knowledge.

___ 20. A therapist should be aware of any client dependency, as this is counterproductive in therapy.

___ 21. Mystification of the client-therapist relationship tends to increase client dependence and decrease the client's ability to assert her or his rights in therapy.

___ 22. Involuntary commitment is a violation of human rights, even in those cases where individuals are unable to be responsible for themselves or their actions.

___ 23. Depending on the severity of their illness, mental patients in institutions should be consulted about the treatment they might receive.

___ 24. I should think about specific ways to protect myself from malpractice suits.

___ 25. If I follow the ethical codes of my profession, I should have few conflicts or difficulties carrying out my professional responsibilities to my clients and to those who are related to my clients.

Introduction

If we hope to practice in an ethical and legal manner, the rights of clients cannot be taken for granted. In this chapter we deal with ways of educating clients about their rights and responsibilities as partners in the therapeutic process. Special attention is given to the role of informed consent as well as ethical and legal issues that arise when therapists fail to provide for consent.

In this chapter we consider the impact that managed mental-health care is having on counseling practice, and we especially look at the balance between cost containment measures and providing quality care to consumers. We examine the ethical and legal implications of managed care as they apply to informed consent, appropriate levels of care, and outcome expectations for short-term interventions on a range of client problems. We also discuss some of the ethical and legal issues involved in counseling children and adolescents.

Part of ethical practice is talking with clients about their rights. Depending on the setting and the situation, this discussion can involve the circumstances that may affect the client's decision to enter the therapeutic relationship, the responsibilities of the therapist toward the client, the possibility of involuntary hospitalization, the possibility of being forced to submit to certain types of medical and psychological treatment, matters of privacy and confidentiality, the possible ramifications of a DSM-IV label, and the possible outcomes and limitations of therapy.

Frequently, clients don't realize that they have rights. Because they are vulnerable and sometimes desperate for help, they may unquestioningly accept

whatever their therapist says or does. There may be an aura about the therapeutic process, and clients may have exaggerated confidence in their therapists. It is much like the trust that many patients have in their physicians. For
most clients the therapeutic situation is a new one, and many people are
unclear about what is expected of them and what they should expect from the
therapist. For these reasons we think the therapist is responsible for protecting
clients' rights and teaching clients about these rights. The ethical codes of most
professional organizations require that clients be given adequate information
to make informed choices about entering and continuing the client-therapist
relationship. (See the box on page 113.) By alerting clients to their rights and
responsibilities, the practitioner is encouraging them to develop a healthy
sense of autonomy and personal power.

In addition to the ethical aspects of safeguarding clients' rights, legal
parameters also govern professional practice. At a conference we attended
dealing with ethical and legal issues in counseling, most of the counselors
expressed fears of lawsuits and were very concerned about what "exercising
sound professional judgment" really means. Indeed, some counselors seemed
more focused on protecting themselves than on helping their clients. We agree
with Bednar, Bednar, Lambert, and Waite (1991) that the exaggerated fears and
misconceptions surrounding legal liability are rarely the catalysts that bring
out the best qualities in practitioners.

You will surely want to protect yourself legally, but we hope you won't
allow this necessity to immobilize you and inhibit your professional effectiveness. Calfee (1997) informs us that lawsuits brought against mental-health professionals are few, but such cases are on the rise. Counseling is a risky venture,
and you must become familiar with the laws that govern professional practice.
However, we urge you to avoid becoming so involved in legalism that you
cease being sensitive to the ethical and clinical implications of what you do in
your practice.

The Client's Right to Give Informed Consent

One of the best ways to protect the rights of clients is to develop procedures to
help them make informed choices. Informed consent involves the right of
clients to be informed about their therapy and to make autonomous decisions
pertaining to it. Mental-health professionals are required by their ethics codes
to disclose to clients the risks, benefits, and alternatives to proposed treatment.
The intent of an informed consent document is to define and clarify the nature
of the therapeutic relationship. The process of informed consent begins with
the intake interview and continues throughout counseling. Informed consent
entails a balance between telling clients too much and telling them too little.
Although most professionals agree on the ethical principle that it is crucial to
provide clients with information about the therapeutic relationship, the manner in which this is done in practice varies considerably among therapists. It is
a mistake to overwhelm clients with too much detailed information at once,

The Rights of Clients and Informed Consent: Some Ethical Codes

American Psychological Association (1995):

> Psychologists obtain appropriate informed consent to therapy or related procedures, using language that is reasonably understandable to participants. The content of informed consent will vary depending on many circumstances; however, informed consent generally implies that the person (1) has the capacity to consent, (2) has been informed of significant information concerning the procedure, (3) has freely and without undue influence expressed consent, and (4) consent has been appropriately documented.

National Association of Social Workers (1996):

> Social workers should provide services to clients only in the context of a professional relationship based, when appropriate, on valid informed consent. Social workers should use clear and understandable language to inform clients of the purpose of the service, risks related to the service, limits to service because of the requirements of a third-party payor, relevant costs, reasonable alternatives, clients' right to refuse or withdraw consent, and the time frame covered by the consent. Social workers should provide clients with an opportunity to ask questions.

American Counseling Association (1995): ACA

> When counseling is initiated, and throughout the counseling process as necessary, counselors inform clients of the purposes, goals, techniques, procedures, limitations, potential risks, and benefits of services to be performed, and other pertinent information. Counselors take steps to ensure that clients understand the implications of diagnosis, the intended use of tests and reports, fees, and billing arrangements. Clients have a right to expect confidentiality and to be provided with an explanation of its limitations, including supervision and/or treatment team professionals; to obtain clear information about their case records; to participate in the ongoing counseling plans; and to refuse any recommended services and be advised of the consequences of such refusal.

but it is also a mistake to withhold important information that clients need if they are to make wise choices about their therapy program.

Professionals have a responsibility to their clients to make reasonable disclosure of all significant facts, the nature of the procedure, and some of the more probable consequences and difficulties. All clients have the right to have treatment explained to them. The process of therapy is not so mysterious that it cannot be explained in a way that clients can comprehend how it works. It is essential that clients give their consent *with* understanding. It is the responsibility of professionals to assess the client's level of understanding and to protect the client's free choice. Professionals need to avoid subtly coercing clients to cooperate with a therapy program to which they are not freely consenting. Generally, informed consent requires that the client be competent, have knowledge of what will occur, especially the risks, and be in treatment voluntarily (Anderson, 1996; Bennett et al., 1990; Crawford, 1994).

Legal Aspects of Informed Consent

Three elements are basic to the legal definition of informed consent: capacity, comprehension of information, and voluntariness (Anderson, 1996; Crawford,

1994; Stromberg & Dellinger, 1993). *Capacity* means that the client has the ability to make rational decisions. When this capacity is lacking, a parent or guardian is typically responsible for giving consent. *Comprehension of information* means that therapists must give clients information in a clear way and check to see that they understand it. To give valid consent, it is necessary for clients to have adequate information about both the procedure and the possible consequences. The information must include the benefits and risks of procedures, possible adverse effects from treatment, the risk of foregoing treatment, and available alternative procedures. *Voluntariness* means that the person giving consent is acting freely in the decision-making process and is legally and psychologically able (competent) to give consent. It implies that the professional and the client have discussed the nature of the problem and possible treatments for it. The therapist should explain to competent clients, who have not been ordered by the court to undergo evaluation or treatment, that they are free to withdraw their consent at any time for any reason.

Educating Clients about Informed Consent

It is a good practice for therapists to employ an educative approach by encouraging clients' questions about evaluation or treatment and by offering useful feedback as the treatment process progresses. Some questions therapists should answer at the outset of the counseling relationship are:

♦ What are the goals of the therapeutic program?
♦ What services will the counselor provide?
♦ What behavior is expected of the client?
♦ What are the risks and benefits of therapeutic procedures?
♦ What are the qualifications of the provider of the services?
♦ What are the financial considerations?
♦ How long is the therapy expected to last?
♦ What are the limitations of confidentiality?
♦ In what cases does the counselor have mandatory reporting requirements?

It is essential to give clients an opportunity to raise questions and to explore their expectations of counseling. We view clients as partners with their therapists in the sense that they are involved as fully as possible in each aspect of their therapy. Thus, education about the therapeutic process begins at the intake session and continues to the termination phase. The more clients know about how therapy works, including the roles of both the client and the therapist in the process, the more they will benefit from the therapeutic experience.

Besides the educative function, informed consent is also a means of sharing power with the client, which has clinical as well as ethical significance. Especially in the case of clients who have been victimized, issues of power and control can be central in the therapy process. The process of informing clients about therapy increases the chances that the client-therapist relationship will become a collaborative partnership and that both parties will have a clear idea of what is expected.

Practitioners are ethically bound to offer the best quality of service available, and clients have a right to know that managed care programs, with their focus on cost containment, may have adverse affects on the quality of care available. Prospective clients must be given clear information about the benefits to which they are entitled and clear information about the limits of treatment as the clinician envisions them (Haas & Cummings, 1991). I. J. Miller (1996) asserts that quality of care is likely to decline under restrictive managed care programs. Consumers in need of therapy may be denied service, clients who are treated may be systematically undertreated, and those with moderate to severe problems requiring longer term treatment may not receive it. Therapists have an obligation to educate consumers, and managed care programs that promote financial interests to the detriment of quality treatment should be held legally responsible for any adverse impact on clients (Newman & Bricklin, 1991).

Informed Consent in Practice

How do practitioners assist clients in becoming informed partners? Somberg, Stone, and Claiborn (1993) conducted a survey to assess therapists' practices pertaining to informed consent and found that informed consent procedures need to be considered within the context of the therapist's values, orientation, and work setting. Some practitioners use informed consent forms. Others talk with clients and report these discussion in their files. In either case, it is important to note that both the client and the therapist have the option to revise the therapeutic contract at any time. Due to considerations of documentation, ease of administering, and standardization, Somberg, Stone, and Claiborn (1993) recommend using a written approach to informed consent. is recommended

Bennett and his colleagues (1990) recommend that practitioners record the nature of the consent and suggest that a written consent form include the following information: date of discussion regarding consent; name of the practitioner and the client; a statement affirming that the client understood what was explained to him or her; a statement of the client's right to withdraw from treatment; likely benefits and inherent risks associated with therapy; a description of the kind of treatment that will be provided; issues of confidentiality, privilege, and their limits; and the signature of the client. Other aspects that might be included in a written informed consent document are: a statement describing the counselor's theoretical orientation and how this will affect treatment, a discussion about the purpose of counseling records and how they will be maintained, clarification pertaining to fees and charges, procedures for filing for insurance reimbursement, the therapist's policies and procedures, and a discussion of how a managed care system will affect the treatment process, if applicable. Consent forms are best viewed as merely one aspect of the ongoing dialogue between the therapist and client about the therapeutic process and its consequences (Bednar et al., 1991). Through the effective use of informed consent procedures, client misunderstanding is reduced, which also tends to reduce the chances of filing a liability claim. Both the therapist and the client benefit from this practice.

Two Cases for Discussion

We have emphasized the importance of the therapist's role in teaching clients about informed consent and encouraging clients' questions about the therapeutic process. With this general concept in mind, put yourself in the counselor's place in each of the following cases. Identify the main ethical issues in each case, and think about your stance if you were faced with these concerns.

◆ **The case of Dottie.**   At the initial interview the therapist, Dottie, does not provide an informed consent form and touches only briefly on the process of therapy. In discussing confidentiality, she implies that whatever is said in the office will stay in the office. Three months into the therapy, the client exhibits some suicidal ideation. Dottie has recently attended a conference at which malpractice was one of the topics of discussion and worries that she may have been remiss in not providing her client with adequate information about her services, including confidentiality and its limitations. She hastily reproduces an informed consent document that she received at the conference and asks her client to sign the form at the next session. This procedure seems to evoke confusion in the client, and he makes no further mention of suicide. After five more sessions, he calls in to cancel an appointment and does not schedule another appointment. Dottie does not pursue the case further.

- What are the ethical and legal implications of the therapist's practice? Do you think the therapist was remiss in not providing a written informed consent document at the first session? Why, or why not?   *yes*
- Did Dottie exacerbate the problem by introducing the document after therapy had already been under way for three months?   *yes*
- If you had been in Dottie's shoes, what might you have done instead of introducing a written document at that juncture?
- Would you have contacted this client after he canceled? Was it unethical for Dottie to ignore the situation by not following up on his case?   *yes*

◆ **The case of Hector.**   During the initial interview, Simone asks the counselor, Hector, how long she might need to be in therapy. Hector tells Simone that the process will take a minimum of two years of weekly sessions. She expresses dismay at such a lengthy process. Hector says that this is the way he works and explains that in his experience significant change is a slow process that demands a great deal of work. He tells Simone that if she cannot commit to this time period it would be best if she finds herself another therapist.

- Did Hector take care of the need for informed consent?   *no*
- Did Hector have an ethical and a professional obligation to explain his rationale for the two years of therapy?   *yes*
- Should Hector have been willing to explore alternatives to his approach to therapy, such as the possible values of short-term counseling?   *yes*
- Given Hector's statement of minimum length of therapy, would it have been ethical for him to offer short-term counseling to Simone?   *maybe not*

if he that she would benefit.

♦ Would it be ethical for this practitioner to accept clients under a managed care system or with an insurance provider that paid for only a very limited number of sessions?

Checklist for Informed Consent for Treatment

This checklist is from Wheeler and Bertram's (1994) American Counseling Association workshop entitled "Legal Aspects of Counseling: Avoiding Lawsuits and Legal Problems." The following topics are recommended for consideration when developing a written informed consent for treatment document:

1. *Voluntary Participation.* Clients voluntarily agree to treatment and can terminate at any time without penalty.
2. *Client Involvement.* What level of involvement and what type of involvement will be expected from clients?
3. *Counselor Involvement.* What will the counselor provide? How will this be provided? How can the counselor be reached in the event of an emergency?
4. *No Guarantees.* Counselors cannot guarantee results (namely, become happier, less tense or depressed, save the marriage, stop drug use, obtain a good job, and so forth).
5. *Risks Associated with Counseling.* Define what, if any, risks are associated with the counselor's particular approach to counseling.
6. *Confidentiality and Privilege.* Specify how confidentiality will be handled in couple counseling, family counseling, child/adolescent counseling, and group counseling situations. How may confidential and privileged information be released?
7. *Exceptions of Confidentiality and Privilege.* Define specific statutory circumstances where confidentiality and privilege cannot be maintained (namely, abuse reporting).
8. *Counseling Approach or Theory.* What is the counselor's counseling orientation or theoretical belief system? How will that affect treatment?
9. *Counseling and Financial Records.* What will they include? How long will they be maintained? How will they be destroyed?
10. *Ethical Guidelines.* What standards define the counselor's practice? How might a client obtain a copy of these guidelines?
11. *Licensing Regulations.* What license does the counselor hold? How may a client check on the status of the licensee?
12. *Credentials.* What education, training, and experience credential will the counselor need to provide counseling treatment, including any specialty credentials?
13. *Fees and Charges.* What are the specific fees and charges? How will fees be collected? How are financial records maintained?
14. *Insurance Reimbursement.* What responsibility will the counselor take for filing insurance forms? What fees, if any, are associated with insurance filing? How will co-payments be handled?

15. *Responsibility for Payment.* Who is responsible for payment of counseling charges? How will delinquent accounts be handled? What charges will be assessed for delinquent accounts?

16. *Disputes and Complaints.* How will fee or other disputes be resolved? Provide the address and phone number of the state licensing board for complaints if required by state licensing statute.

17. *Cancellation Policy.* How much notice for cancellation of a scheduled appointment is required? What fees will be charged for late cancellation?

18. *Affiliation Relationship.* Describe independent contractor or partnership relationship with other practitioners in office suite.

19. *Supervisory Relationship.* Describe any required supervisory relationship along with reason for the supervision. Provide supervisor's name and credentials.

20. *Colleague Consultation.* Indicate that, in keeping with generally accepted standards of practice, you frequently consult with other mental-health professionals regarding the management of cases. The purpose of consultation is to ensure quality care. Every effort is made to protect the identity of clients.

The Content of Informed Consent

The types and amounts of information, the specific content of informed consent, the style of presenting information, and the timing of introducing this information must be considered within the context of legal requirements, work setting, agency policies, and the nature of the client population. However, there is no assurance that practitioners can avoid legal action, even if they do obtain written informed consent. Rather than focusing on legalistic documents, we suggest that you develop informed consent procedures that increase client understanding and foster client-counselor dialogue about the counseling process. We now look in more detail at some of the topics about which clients should be informed.

The therapeutic process.   Although it may be difficult to give clients a detailed description of what occurs in therapy, some general ideas can be explored. We support the practice of letting clients know that counseling might open up levels of awareness that could cause pain and anxiety. Clients who want long-term counseling need to know that they may experience changes that could produce disruptions and turmoil in their lives. Some clients may choose to settle for a limited knowledge of themselves rather than risking this kind of disruption. We believe it is appropriate to use the initial sessions for a frank discussion of the chances for change and the personal and financial costs to the client of such change. Clients should have a knowledge of the procedures and goals of therapy, especially if any unusual or experimental approaches or techniques are to be employed. It is their right to refuse to participate in certain therapeutic techniques.

Because practitioners differ with respect to an orientation of long-term versus short-term therapy, it is important to inform clients of the basic assumptions underlying their orientation. In a managed care setting, Richardson and Austad (1991) believe that the therapeutic process will be determined largely by the health provider. Under this system, practitioners must have expertise in rapid assessment, identifying the core psychological issues quickly and matching each client with the most appropriate intervention. They will have to be competent in short-term strategies and be willing to have their work assessed by review committees. Part of informing clients about the therapeutic process entails giving them relevant facts about short-term interventions that may not always be in their best interests. Sometimes short-term interventions are appropriate, but in other situations long-term, intensive therapy is what a client needs.

Health maintenance organizations exert considerable influence over basic decisions that affect the therapy process, including length of treatment, number of sessions, and even the content of therapy (D. Smith & Fitzpatrick, 1995). Clients have a right to know how their health care program is likely to influence the course of their therapy as well as the limitations imposed by the program.

Background of the therapist. Therapists might provide clients with a description of their training and education, their credentials, licenses, any specialized skills, their theoretical orientation, and the types of clients and types of problems in which they have competence. If the counseling will be done by an intern or a paraprofessional, the clients should know this. Likewise, if the provider will be working with a supervisor, this fact should be made known to the client. This clear description of the practitioner's qualifications, coupled with a willingness to answer any questions clients have about the process, reduces the unrealistic expectations clients may have about therapy. It also reduces the chances of malpractice actions.

Costs involved in therapy. It is essential to provide information about all costs involved in psychological services at the beginning of these services, including methods of payment. Clients need to be informed about insurance reimbursement and any limitations of their health plan with respect to fees. For practitioners who are working with a managed care entity, clients have a right to know that a financial incentive exists to limit the amount or type of service provided (Newman & Bricklin, 1991). Managed care providers have assumed a more active role in the treatment planning process, and these providers impose many limitations on treatment, including the number of sessions allowed and the amount of money that will be reimbursed (Haas & Cummings, 1991).

Most ethics codes have a standard pertaining to establishing fees, as can be seen in these guidelines:

> In establishing fees for professional counseling services, counselors consider the financial status of clients and locality. In the event that the established fee structure

is inappropriate for a client, assistance is provided in attempting to find comparable services of acceptable cost. (ACA, 1995)

Marriage and family therapists make financial arrangements with clients, third
party payors, and supervisees that are reasonably understandable and conform to
accepted professional practices. (AAMFT, 1991)

When setting fees, social workers should ensure that the fees are fair, reasonable,
and commensurate with the service performed. Consideration should be given to
the client's ability to pay. (NASW, 1996)

As early as is feasible in a professional or scientific relationship, the psychologist
and the patient, client, or other appropriate recipient of psychological services
reach an agreement specifying the compensation and the billing arrangements.
(APA, 1995)

Matters of finance are delicate and, if handled poorly, can easily result in
a strained relationship between client and therapist. Thus, the manner in
which fees are handled has much to do with the tone of the therapeutic
partnership.

Some professional codes of ethics recommend a sliding fee standard
because the financial resources of clients are variable. Lien (1993) indicates that
there has been very little research on how using a sliding fee scale affects practice. She suggests that individual practitioners decide on the ethics of adopting
this practice, and that those who believe a sliding fee scale negatively affects
the therapeutic work should not feel bound to this practice.

In addition to adjusting fees to what clients can afford, many professionals
provide services to some clients for little or no financial compensation, making
their services available to some who could not otherwise afford help. ACA's
standard A.10.d. reads: "Counselors contribute to society by devoting a portion of their professional activity to services for which there is little or no financial return (pro bono)."

The length of therapy and termination.

Many agencies have a pol-
icy of limiting the number of sessions that a client can have. These clients
should be informed at the outset that they cannot receive long-term therapy
and should be informed no later than the next-to-last session that they will not
be allowed to return. Also, clients have the right to expect a referral so that they
can continue exploring whatever concerns initially brought them to therapy.
Under a managed care system, clients are often limited to 6 sessions, or a specified amount for a given year, such as 20 sessions. What becomes of the client
after this limit has been reached if he or she still needs treatment? If referrals
are not possible, what other alternatives exist?

Some therapists make it a practice to discuss with their clients an approx-
imate length for the therapeutic process. Other therapists maintain on theoretical grounds that because the problems that brought the client into therapy
are typically complex and long-standing, predicting the length of treatment
is often difficult. Psychodynamic therapists, for example, may be unwilling
to talk during the initial phase about the length of treatment because of their

conviction that individual differences among clients make such predictions impossible.

Regardless of the therapist's theoretical orientation, clients have a right to expect that their therapy will end when they have realized the maximum benefits from it or have obtained what they were seeking when they entered it. The issue of termination needs to be openly explored by the therapist and the client, and the decision to terminate ultimately should rest with the client.

Kramer (1990) reminds us that termination may do more than signal the end of therapy; it can be a new beginning for clients. Kramer contends that when termination issues are ignored or mishandled the whole of therapy is jeopardized. Termination is a crucial phase of therapy, yet it is also the least understood and most complex of all aspects of therapy. Kramer observes that there is a lack of consensus with regard to every aspect of termination, including the criteria for ending. Furthermore, there are few theoretical and practical guidelines for practitioners to follow as they assist their clients in working through issues pertaining to the termination of their therapy. Responsible practitioners discuss this phase of therapy with clients at critical junctures in the therapy process.

Consultation with colleagues.   Student counselors generally meet regularly with their supervisors and fellow students to discuss their progress and any problems they encounter in their work. Trainees need to do this at the outset with their clients both verbally and in writing. It is good policy for all counselors to inform their clients that they may be receiving supervision on their cases. Experienced clinicians often have scheduled consultation meetings with their peers to focus on how they are serving clients. Even though it is ethical for counselors to discuss their cases with other counselors, it's wise to routinely let clients know about this possibility. Clients will then have less reason to feel that the trust they are putting in their counselors is being violated. Counselors can explain that these discussions may well focus on what they are doing and feeling as counselors rather than on their clients as "cases."

Interruptions in therapy.   Most ethical codes specify that therapists should consider the welfare of their clients when it is necessary to interrupt or terminate the therapy process. NASW (1996) has two guidelines:

◆ "Social workers who anticipate the termination or interruption of service to clients should notify clients promptly and seek the transfer, referral, or continuation of services in relation to the clients' needs and preferences."
◆ "Social workers should make reasonable efforts to ensure continuity of services in the event that services are interrupted by factors such as unavailability, relocation, illness, disability, or death."

It is a good practice to explain at the first contact with clients the possibilities for both expected and unexpected interruptions in therapy and how they might best be handled. A therapist's absence might appear as abandonment to some clients, especially if the absence is poorly handled. As much as possible, therapists should make plans for any interruptions in therapy, such as vacations or long-term absences. Clients need information about the therapist's method of handling emergencies as part of their orientation to treatment. When practitioners know they will be on vacation, ethical practice entails providing the name and telephone number of another therapist in case of need. Of course, therapists should obtain clients' written consent to provide information to their substitutes (Bennett et al., 1990).

Clients' right of access to their files.   It is a good idea to inform clients that counseling records are kept for their benefit. Remley (1990) maintains that clients have a legal right to inspect and obtain copies of records kept on their behalf by professionals. To those therapists who believe that it may be harmful to the client to share the clinical records, Remley advises them to attempt to convince the client that he or she should not demand the records. Rather than automatically providing clients access to what is written in their files, some therapists give an explanation of the client's diagnosis and the general trend of what kind of information they are recording. Also, it is a good idea to write about a client in descriptive and nonjudgmental ways, keeping in mind that he or she could read these notes at some time.

Professionals have various views about sharing counseling records with a client. Some therapists are reluctant to share their notes, including the diagnosis, with their clients. They may operate on the assumption that their clients are not sophisticated enough to understand their diagnosis and the clinical notes, or they may think that more harm than benefit could result from disclosing such information to their clients. Others are more willing to grant their clients access to information in the counseling records they keep, especially if clients request specific information. ACA's (1995) guideline on this matter is: "Counselors recognize that counseling records are kept for the benefit of clients, and therefore provide access to records and copies of records when requested by competent clients, unless records contain information that may be misleading and detrimental to the client"(B.4.d.).

Giving clients access to their files seems to be consistent with the consumer-rights movement, which is having an impact on the fields of mental health, counseling, rehabilitation, and education. One way to reduce the growing trend toward malpractice suits and other legal problems is to allow patients to see their medical records, even while hospitalized. Later in this chapter we discuss procedures for keeping records.

Rights pertaining to diagnostic labeling.   One of the major obstacles to the open sharing of files with clients is the need to give clients a diagnostic classification as a requirement for receiving third-party reimbursement for psychological services. Some clients are not informed that they will be so labeled, what those labels are, or that the labels and other confidential material will be given to insurance companies. Clients also do not have control over who can receive this information, nor are they informed of their right not to be labeled (Mappes, Robb, & Engels, 1985). In a managed care system office workers will have access to specific information about a client, such as a diagnosis. Ethical practice involves informing clients that a diagnosis can become a permanent part of their file. Indeed, a diagnosis can have ramifications in terms of costs of insurance, long-term insurability, and employment. With this information, clients are at least in the position to decline treatment with these restrictions. Some clients have the means to pay for the kind of therapy they want and may choose not to use a third-party payor.

Greenhut (1991) contends that therapists often make clients worse by attaching labels to them. She believes that therapy sometimes becomes the exploitation of the exploited. For example, in treating incest survivors, rape victims, and those who have been physically abused, therapists can further oppress these victims by assigning them labels such as co-dependent, narcissistic, eating disordered, and chronically depressed. Greenhut urges therapists to encourage their clients to act on the basis of what they believe is best for themselves and, thus, to move beyond their labels. However, it is important for therapists to have assessment skills and to know that clients' behaviors can fit patterns or categories that may assist in the development of a treatment plan. The danger is in viewing a client entirely in terms of a diagnostic label, or in viewing a disorder as being static, with the end result that the client is left with the notion of being labeled forever.

The nature and purpose of confidentiality.   Clients should be educated regarding matters pertaining to confidentiality, privileged communication, and privacy (which we discuss in the following chapter). The effectiveness of the client-counselor relationship is built on a foundation of trust. If clients do not trust their therapists, it is not likely that they will engage in significant self-disclosure and self-exploration.

Part of establishing trust involves making clients aware of how certain information will be used and whether it will be given to third-party payors. Clients in a managed care program should be made aware that the confidentiality of their communications will be compromised to some extent. When a practitioner contracts with a third-party payor, a client's records come under the scrutiny and review of the system doing the reimbursing. Some clients may want to safeguard their privacy and confidentiality by seeking treatment that does not involve third-party reimbursement.

All the professional codes have a clause stating that clients have a right to know about any limitations of confidentiality from the outset. For example, NASW (1996) has this guideline: "Social workers should discuss with clients and other interested parties the nature of confidentiality and limitations of clients' right to confidentiality. Social workers should review with clients circumstances where confidential information may be requested and where disclosure of confidential information may be legally required. This discussion should occur as soon as possible in the social worker-client relationship and as needed throughout the course of the relationship." As you will see in the next chapter, confidentiality is not an absolute. Certain circumstances demand that a therapist disclose what was said by a client in a private therapy session or disclose counseling records.

Tape-recording or videotaping of sessions.   Many agencies require that interviews be recorded for training or supervision purposes. Clients have a right to be informed about this procedure at the initial session, and it is important that they understand why the recordings are made, how they will be used, who will have access to them, and how they will be stored. Therapists sometimes make recordings because they can benefit from listening to them or by having colleagues listen to their interactions with clients and give them feedback. It is essential for trainees or counselors to secure the permission of clients before making any kind of electronic recording. Most ethics codes have a provision for these matters, as does AAMFT (1991): "Marriage and family therapists obtain written informed consent from clients before videotaping, audio recording, or permitting third party observation." Clients are usually very willing to give their consent if they are approached in an honest way. Clients, too, may want to listen to a taped session during the week to help them remember what went on or to evaluate what is happening in their sessions.

Benefits and risks of treatment.   Clients should have some information about both the possible benefits and the risks associated with a treatment program. Due to the fact that clients are largely responsible for the outcomes of therapy, it is a good policy to emphasize the role of the client's responsibility. Clients need to know that no promises can be made about specific outcomes, which means that ethical practitioners avoid giving guarantees of cures to clients. Bednar and his colleagues (1991) comment that until more is known about risks, it is wise for practitioners to make every attempt to note negative reactions and begin to devise strategies for assisting clients in making more informed choices about their treatment.

no guarantees

Alternatives to traditional therapy.   According to the ethics codes of some professional organizations, clients need to know about alternative helping systems. Therefore, it is a good practice for therapists to learn about community resources so they can present these alternatives to a client. Alternatives to psychotherapy include: self-help programs, stress management, programs for personal-effectiveness training, peer self-help groups, bibliotherapy, twelve-step programs, support groups, and crisis-intervention centers.

This information about therapy and its alternatives can be presented in writing, through an audiotape or videotape, or during an intake session. An open discussion of therapy and its alternatives may, of course, lead some clients to choose sources of help other than therapy. Given the state of psychotherapy research, however, it is difficult to discuss the advantages of alternative treatments and make recommendations (Bednar et al., 1991). For practitioners who make a living providing therapy services, asking their clients to consider alternative treatments can produce financial anxiety. However, openly discussing therapy and its alternatives is likely to reinforce many clients' decisions to continue therapy. Clients have a right to know about alternative therapeutic modalities (such as different theoretical orientations and medication) that are known to be effective with particular clients and conditions.

The Counselor's Responsibilities in Record Keeping

Maintaining thorough clinical notes has a dual purpose: (a) to provide the best service possible for clients, and (b) to provide a basis for safeguarding practitioners in the event of a lawsuit. Many practitioners believe that accurate and detailed clinical records can provide an excellent defense against malpractice claims, and entire books and monographs are devoted to the subject. Professional ethics codes also outline the requirements of good record keeping (see the box on page 126).

Schaffer (1997) suggests that practitioners who fail to maintain adequate clinical records are putting themselves in great ethical and legal peril. Keeping records is not only required in all settings but is perhaps the least expensive and most effective form of liability insurance as well. Clinicians may not keep notes because they can remember what clients tell them, because they are concerned about breaching confidentiality, because they do not want to assume a legalistic stance in their counseling practice, or because they do not have time to keep notes on their clients. Regardless of the reason for not keeping records, Schaffer claims that it is a serious mistake. Failing to keep records deprives practitioners of evidence they will need to defend themselves should they become involved in a malpractice or disciplinary action. Even more important, it deprives clients of data needed for treatment. For example, clients may need to transfer to another therapist, or the therapist may die or retire. If notes were not kept, both the client and the therapist can be hurt. Because most agencies require clinicians to keep records, and because this is a requirement of managed care programs, practitioners must learn how to write and maintain notes about their client's progress. Ideally, good record-keeping practices will help practitioners provide quality service to their clients.

The Committee on Professional Practice and Standards of APA adopted a set of guidelines for record keeping in February 1993 (see Appendix B of Canter et al., 1994). Much of the material that follows is a summary and adaptation of the material approved by this committee.

In general, records should document the nature, delivery, and progress of psychological services. It is mandatory for managed care practitioners to keep accurate charts and notes, and by law they must provide this information to authorized chart reviewers. At a minimum, records should contain: client-identifying information; the name of the client's primary care physician, or an explanation for the absence of such a name; intake sheet; documentation of a mental status exam or assessment; signed informed consent for treatment form; the existence of treatment plans, containing specific target problems and goals; statements regarding the client's presenting problem; previous and present data from psychological tests; documentation of referrals to other pro-

> ### Codes on Record Keeping
>
> *American Psychological Association (1995):*
>
> Psychologists create, maintain, disseminate, store, retain, and dispose of records and data relating to their research, practice, and other work in accordance with law and in a manner that permits compliance with the requirements of this Ethics Code.
>
> *National Association of Social Workers (1996):*
>
> (a) Social workers should take reasonable steps to ensure that documentation in records is accurate and reflective of the services provided. (3.04.a.)
>
> (b) Social workers should include sufficient and timely documentation in records to facilitate the delivery of services and to ensure continuity of services provided to clients in the future. (3.04.b.)
>
> (c) Social workers' documentation should protect clients' privacy to the extent that it is possible and appropriate, and should include only that information that is directly relevant to the delivery of services. (3.04.c.)
>
> (d) Social workers should store records following the termination of service to ensure reasonable future access. Records should be maintained for the number of years required by state statutes or relevant contracts. (3.04.d.)
>
> *American Counseling Association (1995):*
>
> Counselors maintain records necessary for rendering professional services to their clients and as required by laws, regulations, or agency or institution procedures.

viders, when appropriate; signed and dated progress notes; types of services provided; precise times and dates of appointments made and kept; the use and completion of a discharge summary; and release of information obtained.

Case notes should *never* be altered or tampered with after they have been entered into the client's record. Tampering with a clinical record after the fact can cast a shadow on the therapist's integrity in court. Enter notes into a client's record as soon as possible after a therapy session, and sign and date the entry.

The content and style of a client's records are often determined by agency or institutional policy, state counselor licensing laws, or other regulatory bodies. The particular setting and the therapist's preference often determines how detailed the records will be. Remember that the information in the client's record belongs to the client, and a copy may be requested at any time. Thus, it is a prudent policy to write notes in a manner that is honest yet never demeaning of a client. In writing progress notes, use clear behavioral language. Focus on describing specific and concrete behavior and avoid jargon. It may help to assume that the contents of a record might someday be read in a courtroom with the client present.

Although professional documentation should be thorough, it is best to keep notes as concise as possible. Be mindful of the dictum, "If you didn't document it, then it didn't happen." Record client and therapist behavior that is clinically relevant. Include in clinical records interventions used, client responses to treatment strategies, the evolving treatment plan, and any follow-up measures taken.

Counselors are ethically and legally required to keep records in a secure manner and to protect client confidentiality. Counselors are responsible for taking reasonable steps to establish and maintain the confidentiality of information based on their own delivery of services, or the services provided by others working under their supervision. Clients' records must be maintained for the period of time required by relevant federal, state, and local laws. Organization policy often prescribes guidelines for maintaining records, including a time frame. In the absence of such laws, the general recommendation is that complete records should be kept for seven years. Whether records are active or inactive, counselors are expected to maintain and store them safely and in a way in which timely retrieval is possible. Extra care should be taken if information is stored on computer disks. Failure to maintain adequate client records could be the basis of a malpractice claim because it breaches the standard of care expected of a mental-health professional (B. S. Anderson, 1996).

◆ **_The case of Noah._**   Noah is a therapist in private practice who primarily sees relatively well-functioning clients. He considers keeping records to be basically irrelevant to the therapeutic process for his clients. As he puts it: "In all that a client says to me in one hour, what do I write down? And for what purpose? If I were seeing high-risk clients, then I certainly would keep notes. Or if I were a psychoanalyst, where everything a client said matters, then I'd keep notes." One of his clients, Sue, who had watched a television talk show in which clients rights were discussed, asked to see her file. Noah had to explain his lack of record keeping to Sue.

◆ What do you think of Noah's philosophy on record keeping? Do you consider it unethical? Why or why not?
◆ Taking into consideration the kind of clientele Noah sees, is his behavior justified? If you disagree, what criteria would you use in determining what material should be recorded?
◆ What if a legal issue arises during or after Sue's treatment? How would documenting each session help or not help both the client and the counselor?
◆ Assuming that some of Noah's clients will move to other locales and see new therapists, does the absence of notes to be transferred to the new therapists have ethical implications? Is it a burden and expense on the clients to have to cover old ground?
◆ How do you react to Noah's opinion that keeping notes is irrelevant in his practice? Would you consider that an indicator of incompetence on his part? How would you persuade him to do otherwise?

Counseling in a Managed Care Environment

Until the 1980s mental-health services were generally purchased through a traditional fee-for-service delivery system, wherein practitioners controlled both the supply and the demand dimensions of service delivery (Cummings, 1995). Practitioners decided what clients needed, how and when to treat them, and how long therapy would last. Individual practitioners billed insurance carriers on a fee-for-service basis, and there was little incentive for practitioners to reduce costs by increasing their efficiency and effectiveness. With large numbers of health care professionals entering the marketplace, the general expectation was that fees would fall. However, the opposite has been the case, and fees have risen.

Rapidly escalating costs, especially in inpatient care, and associated concerns for client treatment outcomes have led third-party payors to demand more effective cost and quality controls (see Broskowski, 1991; Cummings, 1995; Haas & Cummings, 1991; Hersch, 1995; Karon, 1995; I. J. Miller, 1996; Newman & Bricklin, 1991). Managed care has grown out of a demand by those who pay the bills (employers) for relief from the escalating costs of care (Hersch, 1995). Case reviews are expected to eliminate unnecessary and costly interventions, and a focus on prevention by health maintenance (HMOs) and preferred provider (PPOs) organizations should further reduce the costs of treatment (Karon, 1995). In large measure, the failure of mental-health professionals to control rising costs has led to the increase in external control by the managed care industry.

Psychological fees are often exorbitant, which means that only a small number of people can afford these services. On a personal note, consider the case of a student we know who wanted to enter couples therapy. She inquired about the fee schedule and was given this overview by the therapist:

> For a 90-minute session with a couple my fee is $290. I like to see the couple together for the first session to get a sense of how you interact as a couple. Then I see each partner individually for the second and third sessions. In the fourth session, I meet with you as a couple to establish your goals for therapy.

At this point the process has cost the couple $1,160, and if they are lucky, they have identified the goals for their work. This is a good example of an approach to treatment that has contributed to the rise of cost-containment systems for mental-health services. As intrusive and arbitrary as managed care can be, it may well be that therapists have otherwise priced themselves out of business.

Fee-for-Service Care versus Managed Care

Under fee-for-service care, some therapists operated from the assumption, "the longer, the better." The managed care dictum appears to be "the shorter, the better." In both systems, clients are vulnerable to the judgment of others (in the first instance the solo practitioner and in the second the HMO provider) regarding length of treatment, nature of treatment, techniques to be used, and content of treatment sessions.

In the fee-for-service approach, individual practitioners determined the costs and the length of treatment without any outside review. To think that this system was not abused would be naive. However, it is equally obvious that managed care does not focus on the best interests of the client, and judging from the reactions of practitioners, it is not in their best interests either.

As the managed care model stresses time-limited interventions, cost-effective methods, and a focus on preventive rather than curative strategies, this shift in values has, as Cummings (1995) points out, brought forth a fundamental redefinition of the role of the therapist. I. J. Miller (1996) reports that one major problem with managed care is that clients receiving therapy are undertreated, which leads to underdiagnosing important conditions, dangerously restricting hospital admissions, failing to make referrals, and providing insufficient follow-up.

Although managed health care was once a reasoned response to real problems, Karon (1995) asserts that current managed care practice is characterized more by an interest in reducing costs than by quality of service. He contends that owners and managers of the managed care system are primarily interested in cost containment as a route to profitability and are concerned only secondarily with consumer needs and preferences.

Shore (1996) states that managed care makes people powerless, depriving them of basic rights of choice, privacy, and decision making: "Managed care is simply a search on behalf of employers for the cheapest health plan—a search, by the insurer, for the least possible treatment performed by the cheapest, least-trained clinician" (p. 324). It is clear that financial considerations are driving decisions. While it is true that the costs of medical care have soared, does managed care cure the problem or simply create a new problem? What about what is best for the client? Again, Shore is critical of managed care, stating: "Managed care favors clinicians who generate a profit and cause no trouble. Skill, training, and ethics matter less than compliance with managed care procedures" (p. 324).

Of interest in this debate are the professional organizations. Although these organizations all have clauses in their codes of ethics pertaining to client welfare and competence of services, they are silent on the ethics of the operation of managed care. The question we consider to be at the core of this conflict is: Who is taking care of the client's interests?

One marriage and family therapist, in solo private practice for more than 31 years, wrote about the major changes he has experienced (Rubel, 1996): Under the fee-for-service system, therapists tended to think in terms of growth, actualization, and personal discovery. Under managed cost systems, therapists are required to attend to the goals of adjustment, with a focus on short-term treatment and an emphasis on how quickly clients can be stabilized. Prime consideration is given to cost containment. Rubel sees both advantages and drawbacks to the movement from the old system to the new system. The major drawbacks of managed care have to do with issues of ethics, confidentiality, and selling out to adjustment and conformity standards. But he admits to having been challenged to sharpen his skills and move faster in every aspect of working with clients. He has been able to see more people with a wider range of problems, even though he has had to see them for less time. Foos, Ottens, and Hill (1991) contend that with the limitations of managed care plans, counselors are forced to become more proficient in time-limited counseling.

Treatment plans must be formulated rapidly, goals must be limited in scope, and the emphasis is on attaining results.

In her discussion of the ethical issues in managed care, Austad (1996) points out that those who oppose managed care contend that it is inherently unethical because it gives providers a financial incentive to withhold treatment. Furthermore, the financial incentives inherent in managed care tempt both the practitioner and the payor to:

◆ deny and limit access to long-term therapy
◆ narrow the clients' choice of a therapist
◆ disrupt the continuity of care
◆ rely on less-qualified providers to provide services
◆ use less-qualified providers to review care
◆ breach client confidentiality by giving reviewers too much personal information about clients
◆ base practices on a business ethic instead of a professional ethic

Austad (1996) is not opposed to managed care. She makes a convincing case about the myth of long-term psychotherapy as the standard for ideal therapy. In fact, Austad contends that long-term therapy poses real problems for the fair distribution of psychological services to those who need care. Austad takes the position that what is good for the individual must be tempered by the common good; that is, it is better to give some therapy to those who need it rather than giving abundant therapy to a select few. Austad argues that short-term therapy can be highly effective, that it is not inferior to long-term treatment, and that brief therapy allows more people to be served. What the profession needs to develop, according to Austad, are therapy models that provide care to the largest number who need treatment. She concludes with:

> A change from an individual ethic to a societal ethic will lead to a change from long-term dominance to temporal eclecticism. And this change will command greater accessibility and universality for behavioral health care. Let us develop a societal ethic of psychotherapy whereby both patients and therapists know that they should take what they need and leave the rest for others. (p. 275)

Critical Ethical Issues Associated with Managed Care

As Newman and Bricklin (1991) have noted, ethical and professional guidelines for psychologists have been developed with little attention to the unique issues raised by managed care. Haas and Cummings (1991) identify the limitations imposed by managed care on a client's treatment as ethical concerns. In many HMOs, clients are limited to 20 sessions annually, with lifetime cost caps, and may be denied the care they need if it extends beyond their benefits. Although this makes financial sense, it can become ethically problematic. Haas and Cummings note that this policy shifts the risk to the therapist. Therapists are ethically obligated to offer a standard of care to clients, and they are not to abandon them. This puts the therapist who works with managed care in the position of referring a client if continued therapy is needed. As an alternative, therapists could offer *pro bono* service, which might put an unrealistic strain on their ability to survive financially. If referral resources are not readily available, and if therapists are not willing to abandon clients, how can therapists protect their financial interests and still serve the best interests of their clients?

Haas and Cummings (1991) consider other ethical issues for therapists involved in managed care programs. First is the issue of competence, which is crucial. Therapists must be capable of providing time-limited, effective services. Furthermore, therapists will have to assume a pragmatic and theoretically eclectic orientation, as they will need to demonstrate flexibility in the use of effective techniques in dealing with a variety of problems. Therapists who are not competent in short-term interventions should probably avoid involvement in a managed care program. Second, informed consent assumes particular importance under this system. It is critical that research be done to determine what treatments are effective. Only then can consumers make informed choices about the therapy they receive (Newman & Bricklin, 1991). Third, therapists clearly have divided loyalties between doing what is best for the client and the obligation to contain costs and restrict intervention to short-term, highly focused goals. It is important that the welfare of the client does not get put on the back burner in the interests of preserving the financial integrity of the system. Karon (1995) reminds us that competent and ethical therapists are primarily concerned with the well-being of their clients, which is an entirely different criterion from cost-effectiveness.

Karon (1995) considers psychotherapy under managed health care as "a growing crisis and a national nightmare." Although Karon admits that there are legitimate ways to save money without impairing the quality of care, he emphasizes that doing so requires careful thought and research; managed care companies are largely ignoring such reasonable and reasoned approaches. Stating that the aim of managed care is to provide as little psychological care as possible, while seemingly providing adequate mental-health care, Karon contends that ethical therapists are bound to encounter dilemmas. In a system where the median number of sessions is five or six, no matter what problem is presented, medication is often relied on to obviate the need for long-term therapy.

The Future of Mental-Health Care Delivery

Most who write about managed care seem to agree that the system is here to stay and that therapists will need to become trained or retrained in a body of knowledge and skills applicable to time-efficient and cost-effective therapies. All disciplines of mental-health services are facing and will continue to face major changes in the manner in which those services are delivered. Clearly certain demands must be met if professionals expect to survive in the era of managed care. Hersch (1995) notes the initial negative and defensive reactions on the part of practitioners and calls upon psychologists to use their existing organizational structures to form working alliances with other professional groups, consumer groups, and employers to influence the direction of health care reform. He concludes:

> If psychologists mobilize their resources constructively, they can occupy important leadership roles in reshaping the health care system in ways that enhance psychology's opportunities to serve the public's welfare." (p. 25)

Various writers have forecast the future of mental health services under managed care. Here is a sampling of their thoughts:

> In summary, the future doctoral practitioner will be an innovative clinician, a creative researcher, an inspired supervisor, a knowledgeable health psychologist, a caring skilled manager, and an astute business person. (Cummings, 1995, p. 15)

> Carefully selecting one's training, carefully selecting the plans one associates with, and carefully selecting the interventions one attempts with clients are likely to be the keys to satisfactory professional life in the "new era." (Hass & Cummings, 1991, p. 50)

> Managed care is now invading the fee-for-service plans and managed care is becoming nearly universal. There will be the same panic among professionals as there was 10 years ago, but patients will return no matter how irrational the system. Patients learned before, as they will again now, that six sessions for everything is not psychotherapy; that therapists who are willing to pretend that six sessions for everything is reasonable do not even do those six sessions well; and if they want help, they must escape managed care. (Karon, 1995, p. 9)

> The data necessary to evaluate the impact of managed care on the quality of services are not available. Legislation is required to ensure that the essential information about the functioning of managed care is open to public review; in the meanwhile, audits of managed care can identify and remedy some quality problems. (Miller, 1996, p. 360)

We certainly are not wise enough to predict the future of the therapy enterprise under a managed care paradigm. However, we wonder whether managed care might be improved, from an ethical dimension, if clients were included in the review process of their assessment and appropriateness for treatment. After six sessions, clients could be included in the discussion pertaining to their care.

Under both the old and the new systems, clients have had relatively little voice in decisions that are made about them. Under the old system a solo practitioner might tell them, "Your problem will require at least two years of therapy, or longer." With the new system the client is likely to hear, "Your treatment will be limited to six sessions." Regardless of the structure underlying the delivery of services, ethical practice demands that clients be given the maximum voice possible in agreeing to basic aspects of their treatment and in participating in the process of making decisions about the course of their therapy. Consider your responses to the following questions:

- What are the major ethical problems you might face under a managed care program?
- Is your role being determined or restricted by managed care? To what degree are you willing to accept the requirements imposed by a managed care approach?

◆ How might your ability to establish a working relationship with your clients be affected under managed care?
◆ How would you educate your clients about the benefits and limitations inherent in a managed care plan? Can you think of ways to increase the chances that your clients will have a voice in the process of their therapy?
◆ What steps can you take to become competent in rendering cost-effective treatments that do not compromise the welfare of your clients?

Counseling Children and Adolescents

Consistent with the increasing concern over children's rights in general, more attention is being paid to issues such as the minor's right of informed consent. Some of the legal and ethical questions faced by therapists who work with children and adolescents are:

◆ Can minors consent to treatment without parental consent?
◆ Can minors consent to treatment without parental knowledge?
◆ To what degree should minors be allowed to participate in setting the goals of therapy and in providing consent to undergo it?
◆ What are the limits of confidentiality in counseling with minors?
◆ What does informed consent consist of in working with minors?

We will consider some of these questions in this section and focus on the rights of children when they are clients.

The Right to Treatment

The parent's right to information about his or her child is different from a right to have access to a child's records. The general rule is that a parent is entitled to general information from the counselor about the child's progress in counseling (Stromberg and his colleagues, 1993). In most states parental consent is legally required for minors to enter into a relationship with health care professionals, but there are exceptions to this general rule. Some state statutes grant adolescents the right to seek counseling about birth control, abortion, substance abuse, and other crisis concerns.

A Virginia law of 1979 is the broadest statute in the country on the rights of children and adolescents to consent to therapy. This law implies that "mature minors" should be able to consent to psychotherapy independently on grounds of personal privacy and liberty (Melton, 1981b). More specifically, in Virginia a minor is deemed to be an adult for the purposes of consenting to:

◆ health services needed to determine the presence of or to treat venereal disease or any infections or contagious disease that the State Board of Health requires to be reported
◆ health services required for birth control, pregnancy, or family planning
◆ health services needed for outpatient care, treatment, or rehabilitation for substance abuse

◆ health services needed for outpatient care, treatment, or rehabilitation for mental or emotional illness

Counselors in Virginia have the duty to keep information in these areas confidential, even from parents. This duty challenges the commonly accepted premise that before counselors accept a minor as a client they are required to inform the parents and obtain their consent (Swanson, 1983).

The justification for allowing children and adolescents access to treatment without parental consent is that some might not otherwise seek needed treatment. There is some evidence that adolescents who seek help when given independent access might not have done so without the guarantee of privacy (Melton, 1981a). This is especially true in cases where the presenting problems involve family conflict, psychological or physical abuse, drug or alcohol abuse, and pregnancy or abortion counseling.

Counselors who are faced with the issue of when to accept minors as clients without parental consent must consider various factors. What is the competence level of the minor? What are the potential risks and consequences if treatment is denied? What are the chances that the minor will not seek help or will not be able to secure parental permission for needed help? How serious is the problem? What are the laws pertaining to providing therapy for minors without parental consent? If practitioners need to make decisions about accepting minors without parental consent, it is a good idea for them to know the relevant statutes in their state. They would also be wise to consult with other professionals in assessing the ethical issues involved in each case.

Informed Consent of Minors

Minors are not always able to give informed consent. On this matter the guideline provided by the APA (1995) is as follows: "When persons are legally incapable of giving informed consent, psychologists obtain informed permission from a legally authorized person, if such substitute consent is permitted by law."

The ACA (1995) Code of Ethics guideline suggests including family members in a minor's counseling, if appropriate: "When counseling clients who are minors or individuals who are unable to give voluntary, informed consent, parents or guardians may be included in the counseling process as appropriate. Counselors act in the best interests of clients and take measures to safeguard confidentiality."

Therapists who work with children and adolescents have ethical responsibilities to provide information that will help minors become active participants in their treatment. It is a good policy to provide children with treatment alternatives and to enlist their participation in defining goals for their therapy. There are both ethical and therapeutic reasons for involving minors in their treatment. By giving them the maximum degree of autonomy within the therapeutic relationship, the therapist demonstrates respect for them. Also, it is likely that therapeutic change is promoted by informing children about the process and enlisting their involvement in it.

If children lack the background to weigh risks and benefits and if they cannot give complete informed consent, therapists should still attempt to provide some understanding of the therapy process. If formal consent cannot be obtained, then even partial understanding is better than proceeding with therapy without any attempt to explain the goals and procedures of the process (Margolin, 1982).

At this point we suggest that you think about some of the legal and ethical considerations in providing therapy for minors.

- Many parents argue that they have a right to know about matters that pertain to their adolescent daughters and sons. They assert, for example, that parents have a right to be involved in decisions about abortion. What is your position?
- Some people argue for the right of minors to seek therapy without parental knowledge or consent because needed treatment might not be given to them otherwise. When, if at all, would you counsel a minor without parental knowledge and consent?
- What kinds of information should be provided to children and adolescents before they enter a therapeutic relationship?
- If therapists do not provide minors with the information necessary to make informed choices, are they acting unethically? Why, or why not?   yes

Counseling Reluctant Children and Adolescents

Some young people simply resent not having a choice about entering a therapeutic relationship. Adolescents often resist therapy because they become the "identified patient" and the focus is on changing them. These adolescents are frequently aware that they are only *part* of the problem in the family unit. Although many minors indicate a desire to participate in treatment decisions, few are given the opportunity to become involved in a systematic way. The message here is that resistance to therapy can at least be minimized if therapists are willing to openly and nondefensively explore the reasons behind this resistance.

◆ ***The case of Frank.***   Frank was expelled from high school for getting explosively angry at a teacher who, according to Frank, had humiliated him in front of his class. Frank was told that he would not be readmitted to school unless he sought professional help. His mother called a therapist and explained the situation to her, and the therapist agreed to see him. Although Frank was uncomfortable and embarrassed over having to see a therapist, he was nevertheless willing to talk. He told the therapist that he knew he had done wrong by lashing out angrily at the teacher but that the teacher had provoked him. He said that although he was usually good about keeping his feelings inside, this time he had "just lost it."

After a few sessions, the therapist determined that there were many problems in Frank's family. He lived with an extreme amount of stress, and to work effectively with Frank it would be essential to see the entire family. Indeed, he did have a problem, but he was not the problem. He was covering up many family secrets, including a verbally abusive stepfather and an alcoholic mother. Hesitantly, he agreed that it would be a good idea to have the entire family come in for therapy. When the therapist contacted the family, the other members totally rejected the idea of family therapy. The mother asserted that the problem was with Frank and that the therapist should concentrate her efforts on him. A few days before his next scheduled appointment his mother called to cancel, saying that they had put him on homebound study and that he therefore no longer required counseling.

- What are the ethical responsibilities of the therapist in this situation?
- Should Frank be seen as a condition of returning to school?
- What other strategies could the therapist have used?
- What would you have done differently, and why?
- Should the therapist have seen Frank and the teacher?
- Did the family interfere with Frank's right to treatment by being uncooperative?
- Should the therapist have encouraged Frank to continue his therapy even if his family refused to undergo treatment?

Commentary.   One ethical problem in this case was the treatment of the individual as opposed to the treatment of the family. There was an alcoholism problem within the family. Frank's expulsion from school could have been more a symptom of the family dysfunction than of his own disturbance. Indeed, he did need to learn anger management, as both the school and the mother contended, yet more was going on within this family that needed pressing attention. In this case it might have been best for the therapist to stick to her initial convictions of family therapy as the treatment of choice. If the parents would not agree to this, she could have made a referral to another therapist who would be willing to see Frank in individual counseling.

Specialized Training for Counseling Children and Adolescents

The ethical codes of the major professional organizations specify that it is unethical to practice in areas for which one has not been trained. Many human-service professionals have been trained and supervised in "verbal therapies," but there are distinct limitations in applying these therapeutic interventions to children. Practitioners who want to counsel children may have to acquire supervised clinical experience in play therapy, art and music therapy, and recreational therapy. These practitioners also must have a knowledge of developmental issues pertaining to the population with which they intend to work. They need to become familiar with laws relating to minors, to be aware of the limits of their competence, and to know when and how to make appropriate referrals. It is essential to know about community referral resources, such as the Child Protective Services.

Counselors working with children and adolescents must also have special training to deal with issues such as confidentiality. Therapists cannot guarantee minors blanket confidentiality. If the parents or guardians of minors request information about the progress of the counseling, the therapist is expected to provide some feedback. Information that will or will not be disclosed to parents or guardians must be discussed at the outset of therapy with both the child or adolescent and the parent or guardian. If the matter of confidentiality is not clearly explored with all parties involved, it is almost certain that problems will emerge in the course of therapy. In addressing confidentiality as it applies to children and adolescents, Hendrix (1991) writes that there are times when alternatives to absolute confidentiality must be applied. He maintains that counselors would do well to seek voluntary, informed consent, even when working with children under the age of 14. In the case of adolescents, the consensus of writers and judges appears to be that they have the same confidentiality rights as adults.

Involuntary Commitment and Human Rights

The practice of involuntary commitment of people to mental institutions raises difficult professional, ethical, and legal issues. Practitioners must know their own state laws and must be familiar with community resources before taking measures leading to involuntary hospitalization. Good practice involves consulting with professional colleagues to determine the appropriate length and type of treatment (Austin, Moline, & Williams, 1990). The focus of our discussion here is not on specific legal provisions but on the ethical aspects of involuntary commitment.

Under the social policy of "deinstitutionalization," which has gained popularity over the past 25 years, involuntary commitment is sought only after less restrictive alternatives have failed. The main purpose of involuntary hospitalization is to secure treatment for clients rather than to punish them. As it applies to mental-health practices, the legal doctrine of using the "least restrictive alternative" requires that treatment be no more harsh, hazardous, or intrusive than necessary to achieve therapeutic aims and to protect clients and others from physical harm (Bednar et al., 1991). Professionals are sometimes confronted with the responsibility of assessing the need to commit clients who pose a serious danger either to themselves or to others. The growing trend is for courts to recognize the therapist's duty to commit such clients. Under most state laws, involuntary civil commitment is based on the following criteria: mental illness, dangerousness to self or others, grave disability, refusal to consent, treatability, incapacity to decide on treatment, and compliance with the "least restrictive" criterion (Bednar et al., 1991).

Bennett and his colleagues (1990) offer specific recommendations pertaining to the commitment process, some of which are:

- Be familiar with your state laws and regulations pertaining to both voluntary and involuntary commitment.
- If you notice that a client's condition is deteriorating, consider consulting with colleagues.
- Carefully consider what you hope to obtain in recommending commitment. Assess the degree to which your client is a danger to self or others.
- Before deciding on a course leading to commitment, consider other options. Also, consider the advisability of referring your client to another professional for evaluation or treatment.
- Ask yourself how commitment might affect the client's attitude toward you as a therapist and toward therapy in general.
- If hospitalization is involuntary, know the procedural steps that must be followed under your state laws.
- Make certain that you can offer reasons for commitment.

Making a decision to commit a client is a serious matter that has implications for you, your client, and members of the client's family. It is essential that you obtain consultation if there is any doubt about the proper course to follow. You need to raise many questions about the appropriateness of choosing commitment over other alternatives. Some writers emphasize practices such as conducting ongoing psychiatric and psychosocial assessments and documenting all examinations and consultations in the client's record. Practitioners are advised to protect themselves from liability associated with involuntary hospitalization by documenting all the steps they take in making this decision (Austin et al., 1990; Bednar et al., 1991).

Imagine yourself as a counselor at a state mental hospital. The ward on which you work is overcrowded, and there aren't enough professionals on the staff to provide for much more than custodial services. You observe patients who seem to be psychologically deteriorating, and the unattractive surroundings reinforce the attitude of hopelessness that is so prevalent among the patients. You become aware that the rights of patients are often ignored, and you see many of the hospital's practices as destructive. When patients are given medication, for instance, there is rarely a consistent evaluation of the effects of the drug treatment and of whether it should be continued. Moreover, you recognize that some of the people who have been hospitalized against their will really don't belong there, yet institutional procedures and policies make it difficult for them to be released or placed in a more appropriate agency. Finally, although some members of the staff are both competent and dedicated, others who hold positions of power are incompetent.

What do you think you might do if you were involved in this situation? What is your responsibility, and what actions might you take? Check as many of the following statements as you think appropriate:

___ Because I couldn't change the people in power, I'd merely do what I could to treat the patients with care and dignity.

___ I'd bring the matter to public attention by writing to newspapers and talking with television reporters.

✓ I'd attempt to rectify the situation by talking to the top administrators and telling them what I had observed.   *supervisors or trusted admin.*

✓ I'd form a support group of my peers for collective action.

___ I'd keep my views to myself, because the problem is too vast and complex for me to do anything about it.

___ I'd encourage the patients to revolt and demand their rights.

___ I'd directly confront the people who I thought were incompetent or who were violating the rights of patients and attempt to change them.

___ I'd spruce up the environment.

Malpractice Liability in the Helping Professions

How vulnerable are mental-health professionals to malpractice actions? What are some practical safeguards against being involved in a lawsuit? In this section we examine these questions and encourage you to develop a prudent approach to risk management in your practice. It is easy to become swept up in a tide of anxiety over the possibility of being sued, but this is certainly not likely to bring out the best in us as practitioners. We hope that our discussion of malpractice will lead you to an increased awareness of the range of professional responsibilities and suggest ways meet those responsibilities as an ethical practitioner.

What Is Malpractice?

Malpractice is the failure to render professional services or to exercise the degree of skill that is ordinarily expected of other professionals in a similar situation. Malpractice is a legal concept involving negligence that results in injury or loss to the client. Professional negligence can result from unjustified departure from usual practice or not exercising due care in fulfilling one's responsibilities.

Practitioners are expected to abide by legal standards and adhere to the ethical codes of their profession in providing care to their clients. Unless they take due care and act in good faith, they are liable to a civil suit for failing to do their duties as provided by law. The primary problem in a negligence suit is determining which standards of care apply to determine whether a counselor has breached a duty to a client. Counselors are judged according to the standards that are commonly accepted by the profession. Although practitioners need not be infallible, they are expected to possess and exercise the knowledge, skill, and judgment common to other members of their profession.

Practitioners should try to maintain a reasonable view of the realities involved in dealing with high-risk clients:

> As professionals, we are expected to be clairvoyant only on rare and unreasonable occasions. We are usually held accountable only for failure to exercise the ordinary skill and expertise that can be expected from similarly trained professionals. Any of our beliefs that imply that more can be expected of us, or that it is against the law to make mistakes or have unfavorable client outcomes, only enhance the fear that deters quality clinical care. (Bednar et al., 1991, p. 18)

Malpractice is generally limited to six kinds of situations: (1) the procedure used by the practitioner was not within the realm of accepted professional practice; (2) the practitioner employed a technique that he or she was not trained to use; (3) the professional did not use a procedure that would have been more helpful; (4) the therapist failed to warn others about and protect them from a violent client; (5) informed consent to treatment was not obtained or not documented; or (6) the professional did not explain the possible consequences of the treatment (B. S. Anderson, 1996).

To succeed in a malpractice claim, these four elements of malpractice must be present: (1) a professional relationship between the therapist and the client must have existed; (2) the therapist must have acted in a negligent or improper manner, or have deviated from the "standard of care" by not providing services that are considered "standard practice in the community"; (3) the client must have suffered harm or injury, which must be demonstrated; and (4) there must be a legally demonstrated causal relationship between the practitioner's negligence or breach of duty and the damage or injury claimed by the client. The burden of proof that harm actually took place is the client's, and the plaintiff must demonstrate that all four elements applied in his or her situation. Let's take a closer look at each of these elements. This discussion is based on an adaptation of the work of several writers (B. S. Anderson, 1996; Austin et al., 1990; Bednar et al., 1991; Bennett et al., 1990; Calfee, 1997; R. L. Crawford, 1994).

1. *Duty.* There are two aspects of establishing a legal duty: one is the existence of a special relationship, and the other is the nature of that special relationship. A duty exists when a therapist implicitly or explicitly agrees to provide mental-health services.
2. *Breach of duty.* After the plaintiff proves that a professional relationship did exist, he or she must show that the duty was breached. Practitioners have specific responsibilities that involve using ordinary and reasonable care and diligence, applying knowledge and skill to a case, and exercising good judgment. If the practitioner failed to provide the appropriate standard of care, the duty was breached. This breach of duty may involve either actions taken by the therapist or a failure to take certain precautions.
3. *Injury.* Plaintiffs must prove that they were harmed in some way — physically, relationally, psychologically—and that actual injuries were sustained. Examples of such injuries include wrongful death (suicide), loss (divorce), and pain and suffering. Plaintiffs must show proof of actual injury.

4. *Causation.* Plaintiffs must demonstrate that the professional's breach of duty was the proximate cause of the injury they suffered. The test in this case lies in proving that the harm would not have occurred if it were not for the practitioner's actions or omissions.

In the case of suicide, for example, two factors determine a practitioner's liability: foreseeability and reasonable care. Most important is *foreseeability,* which involves assessing the level of risk. Failing to conduct a comprehensive risk assessment and to document this assessment would be a major error on the therapist's part. Practitioners need to demonstrate that their judgments were based on data observed and that these judgments were reasonable. The second factor in liability is whether *reasonable care* was provided. Once an assessment of risk is made, it is important to document that appropriate precautions were taken to prevent a client's suicide.

Reasons for Malpractice Suits

Violations of confidentiality and sexual misconduct have received the greatest attention in the literature as grounds for malpractice suits. To be liable in the first case, psychotherapists must have violated client confidentiality under circumstances outside the legitimate exceptions mandated by ethical guidelines or by state laws. This is a topic that we turn to in the next chapter. The topic of sexual relationships with clients is taken up briefly in the section below and in some detail in Chapter 7. Swenson (1997) identifies three general problem areas that pose the highest risks of malpractice lawsuits:

- violations of clients' personal rights (typically related to sex, privacy, or wrongful commitment)
- failure to protect others from clients (alleged in failure to warn, failure to commit, and wrongful release cases)
- incompetent treatment of clients (often alleged in suicide cases)

Many areas of a therapist's practice could lead to a legal claim, but eleven types of professional negligence commonly put therapists at legal risk. The discussion of these risk categories is an adaptation of malpractice liability and lawsuit prevention strategies suggested by various writers: (B. S. Anderson, 1996; Calfee, 1997; R. L. Crawford, 1994; Stromberg & Dellinger, 1993; Swenson, 1997).

Failure to obtain or document informed consent. Therapists need to recognize that they can be liable for failure to obtain appropriate informed consent even if their subsequent treatment of the client is excellent from a clinical perspective. Although written informed consent may not be needed legally, it is wise to have clients sign a form to acknowledge their agreement with the terms of the proposed therapy. Without a written document, it may be very difficult to ascertain whether counselors communicated clearly and effectively to clients about the therapeutic process and whether clients understood the information. As you recall, earlier in this chapter we discussed the content of informed consent and the importance of making this part of the client's record.

Client abandonment. Courts have determined that the following acts may constitute abandonment: failure to follow up on the outcomes with a client who has been hospitalized; not being able to be reached between appointments; failure to respond to a request for emergency treatment; or failure to provide for a substitute therapist during vacation times. Clients have a case for abandonment when the facts indicate that a therapist unilaterally terminated a professional relationship and that this termination resulted in some form of harm. Under managed care plans, therapists may be accused of abandonment if they terminate when doing so could result in harm to the client.

Marked departures from established therapeutic practices. If counselors employ unusual therapy procedures, they put themselves at risk. They bear the burden of demonstrating a rationale for their techniques. If it can be shown that their procedures are beyond the usual methods employed by most professionals, they are vulnerable to a malpractice action. If it is unlikely that an expert can be found to testify to the acceptability of a certain treatment approach, it would be prudent not to employ this approach (Calfee, 1997).

Practicing beyond the scope of competency. In some recent cases counselors have been held liable for damages for providing treatment below a standard of care. If the client relies on the advice given by a professional and suffer damages as a result, the client can initiate a civil action. Professional health care providers should be sure they work only with those clients and deliver only those services that are within the realm of their competence. Accepting a case beyond the scope of a counselor's education and training is not only a breach of ethics but also can result in a malpractice suit. If counselors have any doubts about their level of competency to work with certain cases, they should receive peer input or consultation. If a counselor is accused of unethical practice, the counselor must prove that he or she was properly prepared in that area of practice (Chauvin & Remley, 1996). Counselors who want to augment their skills can participate in continuing education, take additional graduate course work, and work under the direct supervision of a colleague who has clinical experience with such cases (Calfee, 1997).

Misdiagnosis. Giving a diagnosis that the therapist is not qualified or licensed to render could leave the practitioner vulnerable to subsequent liability for malpractice (B. S. Anderson, 1996). It is generally not the court's role to question the therapist's diagnosis. However, in cases where it can be shown through the therapist's records that a diagnosis was clearly unfounded and below the standard of care, a case of malpractice might be successful. In court an expert witness is often questioned to determine whether the therapist used appropriate assessment procedures and arrived at an appropriate diagnosis. It is wise for mental-health practitioners to require a prospective client to undergo a complete physical examination, as the results of this examination might have a bearing on the client's diagnosis and affect his or her treatment (Calfee, 1997).

Crisis intervention.   Crisis intervention strategies are used in emergency situations. People who need crisis counseling are often close to death or are seriously injured. From a legal perspective, the crisis worker is responsible for harm only if the failure to exercise reasonable care increased the risk of harm to another *and* if that failure increased the risk of harm or left the person in a worse condition than before the intervention (B. S. Anderson, 1996).

Repressed or false memory.   Articles in the professional literature on the ethical and legal issues surrounding past memories of child sexual abuse are increasing. B. S. Anderson (1996) cites the example of a jury in Ramsey County, Minnesota, that awarded more than $2.6 million to a woman who claimed she was injured by false memories of abuse induced after her psychiatrist suggested that she suffered from a multiple personality disorder, which most likely was the result of repeated sexual abuse by relatives. Certainly, the style in which a therapist questions a client can influence memories, particularly for young children. Repeated questioning can lead a person to believe in a "memory" that did not occur. A trusted therapist who suggests past abuse as a possible cause of problems or symptoms can greatly influence the client.

What is the best course for you to follow when you suspect that past sexual abuse is related to a client's present problem? How can you best protect the client, the alleged abuser, and other family members, without becoming needlessly vulnerable to a malpractice suit? Anderson (1996, pp. 54-55) recommends following these basic clinical and ethical principles:

- Be attentive to the kinds of questions you ask clients.
- Remain nonjudgmental and demonstrate empathy as you talk to a client about possible memories of abuse.
- Avoid prejudging the truth of the client's reports.
- If a client reports a memory, talk frankly about the clinical uncertainty of such memories at this time.
- Make use of standard assessment and treatment techniques.
- Avoid pressuring the client to believe events that may not have actually occurred.
- Do not suggest to clients that they terminate the relationship precipitously.
- If you are not specifically trained in child abuse assessment and treatment, consult with a supervisor or a professional with expertise in this area, or refer the client.

Unhealthy transference relationships.   The importance of understanding how transference and countertransference play out in the therapy relationship was considered in Chapter 2. The mere existence of countertransference is not an ethical and legal issue. However, if a therapist's personal reactions to a client cannot be managed effectively, the abuse of power is likely, and this can have both ethical and legal ramifications. In cases involving mishandling of a client's transference or counselor's countertransference, allegations have included inappropriate socialization with clients, burdening clients with a counselor's personal problems, and putting clients in awkward business situations. When a counselor gets involved in multiple relationships with a client, it is always the client who is more vulnerable to the abuse of power. When a client cannot be served in a professional manner due to a counselor's personal feelings about him or her, it is the therapist's responsibility to seek consultation, to undergo personal therapy, and perhaps to refer the client to another counselor (Calfee, 1997).

Sexual abuse of a client. Related to the topic of unhealthy transference relationships is the area of sexual misconduct, one of the most common grounds for malpractice suits. It is *never* appropriate for therapists to engage in sexual contact with clients or to become sexually and intimately involved with clients. This topic is explored in detail in Chapter 7. A finding of liability against therapists who have engaged in sexual contact with clients is highly likely. Court cases suggest that no act is more likely to create legal problems for therapists than engaging in a sexual relationship with a client. Furthermore, initial consent of the client will not be a defense against malpractice actions. Even in the case of sex between a therapist and a former client, courts do not easily accept the view that therapy has ended. More often than not, the court considers that a therapist has taken advantage of the client by changing a professional relationship into a romantic one (Stromberg & Dellinger, 1993).

Failure to control a dangerous client. Therapists have a duty to intervene in cases where clients pose a grave danger to themselves or to others. However, it is difficult to determine when a given client actually poses a danger to self or others. As Perlin (1997) reminds us, negligence lies in the therapist's failure to warn a third party who is threatened by imminent danger, not in the failure to predict violence.

Most states require mental-health professionals to warn intended victims of potential harm. Even in states where such a warning is not legally mandated, ethical practice demands a proper course of action on the therapist's part. A therapist can be liable in a wrongful death claim if the therapist failed to diagnose a client's suicidal condition and if the therapist failed to act in a way to prevent the suicide. However, the courts recognize that suicide and assaultive acts are difficult to predict, which means that liability for failing to anticipate such acts is relatively uncommon. Liability may be imposed, however, if the professional's decision can be shown to have departed from accepted professional practice or standards, or when the therapist did not base his or her assessment and treatment on sound clinical principles (Stromberg & Dellinger, 1993).

Managed care and malpractice. Mental-health managed care increases the potential for misdiagnosis, negligent treatment, and abandonment of the client. According to Stromberg and Dellinger (1993), two core issues of malpractice apply to managed care: standard of care and therapist liability. Is the standard of care by which a therapist's service is measured different, or lower, in a managed care plan? Some may argue that clients who participate in a less expensive health plan—one that offers only limited coverage for psychological services—should not be in a position to sue therapists who terminate treatment after a predetermined number of sessions. To date, there is no evidence that courts recognize a lower standard of competence for managed care versus fee-for-service care. This means that therapists who work under managed care must still do the best they can to provide the kind of service the client requires. Moreover, practitioners have a responsibility to anticipate the limited nature of services, and they should discuss the implications of this with their clients.

Are health care professionals liable for decisions to limit care that are specified by managed care plans? Some court rulings have established an ambiguous but important obligation for therapists: Although therapists need not disregard the utilization review standards of the managed care plan, they are likely to be legally required (1) to provide emergency psychological services regardless of payment, and (2) to energetically seek approval for additional services that the client genuinely needs.

Jones and Higuchi (1996) describe a landmark New Jersey lawsuit against one of the largest managed behavioral health care providers in the United States. Believed to be the first of its kind involving a managed behavioral health care company (MCC), the lawsuit alleged that MCC terminated therapists, purportedly without cause, when therapists requested more sessions for their clients than the managed care company was willing to provide. In their lawsuit, the plaintiffs claimed that in limiting the number of sessions provided, MCC was substituting its judgment for the therapist's professional judgment, contrary to client welfare and public policy, and that these policies unlawfully prevented psychologists from exercising appropriate standards of care and clinical judgment.

It is clear that managed care does have both ethical and legal implications for professional practice. Ethically, therapists must not abandon their clients, and they have a responsibility to render competent services. Legally, it appears that practitioners employed by a managed care unit are not exempt from malpractice suits if clients claim that they did not receive the standard of care they required. Therapists cannot use the limitations of the managed care plan as a shield for failing to render crisis intervention, to make appropriate referrals, or to request additional services from the plan.

Ways to Protect Yourself from Malpractice Suits

One of the best ways to protect yourself from a malpractice action is to restrict your practice to clients for whom you are prepared by virtue of your education, training, and experience. Pope and Vasquez (1991) point out that even when practitioners function within their legitimate specialty, they may attempt to work with specific populations or to use specific techniques that exceed the boundaries of their competence. Another precaution against malpractice is personal and professional honesty and openness with clients. Although you may not always make the "right choice" in every situation, it is crucial that you know your limitations and remain open to seeking consultation in difficult cases.

Calfee (1997) stresses the importance of understanding risk management techniques that can reduce the practice of unethical behavior and minimize the chance of litigation. She describes risk management as a four-step process whereby practitioners: (1) identify potential risks areas, (2) evaluate whether the risk area is serious enough to merit further attention, (3) employ preventive and risk control strategies in their work, and (4) review treatments periodically to ascertain their effectiveness.

Here are some additional safeguards against malpractice accusations:

- Define your particular areas of expertise and practice (Stromberg & Dellinger, 1993).
- Make use of informed consent procedures. Realize that there is a wide variation in age of consent, depending on what the client is consenting to. Present information to your clients in clear language.
- Provide clients with a professional disclosure statement that addresses basic policies and boundary issues in the counseling relationship. Recognize that the disclosure statement forms a contract between you and your client (Chauvin & Remley, 1996).
- In describing a treatment approach, explain its risks and benefits, as well as possible alternatives, in sufficient detail to ensure that the client understands the procedures (Bennett et al., 1990).
- Clearly define issues pertaining to fees at the outset of therapy. If it is your practice to increase your fees periodically, tell clients that fees are subject to change with notice. Some practitioners avoid raising fees for current clients.
- Collect fees for your professional services on a regular basis, preferably after each session. Avoid bringing a suit against a client for unpaid fees. A frequent basis of complaints lodged against counselors pertains to fee disputes (Chauvin & Remley, 1996).
- Terminate treatment carefully and for proper reasons (Stromberg & Dellinger, 1993). Clients should be informed that they have the right to terminate treatment any time they choose.
- Practice only in specific areas where you are competent. Refer clients whose conditions are obviously not within the scope of your competence. If you are in doubt, seek peer input to determine whether you are practicing outside the scope of your competency (Austin et al., 1990; Calfee, 1997; Pope & Vasquez, 1991).
- Take steps to maintain your competency, even if this is not required by state law.

- Carefully document a client's treatment plan. Records might include notes on symptoms, diagnosis, and treatment; documents verifying informed consent and relevant consultations; and a copy of the therapeutic contract (Austin et al., 1990; Remley, 1990).
- Maintain adequate business records. In case of a suit, if you admit that you don't keep records, you will probably be perceived as unprofessional. How detailed you make your clinical notes is a matter of preference (Austin et al., 1990; Remley, 1990).
- Recognize your professional and legal responsibility to preserve the confidentiality of client records. Know the circumstances under which you might be required to disclose counseling records: (1) when clients are a danger to themselves or others, (2) when clients request that records be released, and (3) when a court orders disclosure of records (Remley, 1990).
- Keep clients' complete records for seven years. Such records include homicide or suicide attempts or threats, written treatment plans, and clients' failure to follow major suggestions (Austin et al., 1990).
- Report any case of suspected child abuse as required by law.
- Before engaging in any dual relationship, talk with your client about the possible repercussions of such a relationship and the dangers to both of you of unfulfilled expectations and lack of objectivity (Herlihy & Corey, 1997). Be aware of your position of power, and avoid even the appearance of conflict of interest.
- Exercise caution in any situations where you might engage in bartering with clients. Realize that such exchanges often lead to resentment on both your part and your clients'.
- It is risky to accept gifts from clients. Although you can be friendly and personal with clients, your relationships should be primarily professional.
- Avoid sexual relationships with either current or former clients and with current supervisees and students.
- Absences on your part may appear to a client to be abandonment. Although you cannot always prevent this perception, you can ameliorate it (Bennett et al., 1990; Pope & Vasquez, 1991).
- Be sure to provide coverage for emergencies when you are going away. Consider an answering service so that you can be reached in times of crisis. The best way to avoid malpractice actions regarding allegations of abandonment is through proper documentation (Calfee, 1997).
- Consult with colleagues when you are in doubt. Because the legal standard is based on the practices of fellow professionals, the more consensus you have, the better chance you have of prevailing in a suit. Record these case consultations in the client's file.
- Before consulting with others about a specific client, obtain consent from the client for the release of information. However, some state laws allow emergency consultation without the client's consent (Austin et al., 1990; Bennett et al., 1990).

- In cases where you have limited experience or encounter cultural barriers, consult with a colleague experienced in treating this population and, if necessary, refer the client (Bennett et al., 1990).
- In accepting or making referrals, carry out your responsibility to obtain or transfer information pertaining to a client (Austin et al., 1990).
- Learn how to assess and intervene in cases in which clients pose a danger to themselves or others. Knowing the danger signs of potentially suicidal and violent clients is the first step toward prevention.
- If you make a professional determination that a client is dangerous, take the necessary steps to protect the client or others from harm (Austin et al., 1990; Bednar et al., 1991; Perlin, 1997).
- In counseling minors, be aware of sources to whom you can send them when they seek specific information about birth-control methods or abortion.
- Become aware of local and state laws that limit your practice, as well as the policies of an agency you may work for. Keep up to date with legal and ethical changes by becoming actively involved in professional organizations.
- Recognize that a counselor is a potential target for a client's anger or transference feelings. Keep the lines of communication open with clients, allowing them to express whatever they feel to you. Strive to avoid becoming defensive or personalizing issues that may belong to the client (Chauvin & Remley, 1996).
- Treat your clients with respect by attending carefully to your language and your behavior.
- Avoid undue influence over clients (such as imposing your values or making decisions for clients). Recognize that it is possible for you to unintentionally influence a client in an inappropriate way (Bennett et al., 1990).
- Have a clear theoretical orientation and a rationale for employing techniques as a guide in your practice.
- Create reasonable expectations about what psychotherapy can and cannot do. When initiating a new form of therapy or different method of treatment, make sure that you can support the choice with current professional journal articles attesting to its usefulness (Calfee, 1997).
- Realize that prevention is a less expensive option than a successful defense against a malpractice suit (Swenson, 1997).
- Have adequate professional-liability insurance.

In their very helpful book, *Professional Liability and Risk Management,* Bennett and his colleagues (1990) emphasize the importance of anticipating and recognizing potential problem areas and guarding against behaviors that might harm the client. They remind practitioners of their ethical and legal obligations and suggest risk management procedures. They urge clinicians to assess their own practices and to keep up to date on legal, ethical, and community standards affecting their profession and their client population.

Malpractice claims are not reserved exclusively for the irresponsible practitioner but may also be filed against any practitioner. Clients may make allegations of unethical conduct or file a legal claim due to negligence, even though the counselor may have acted ethically and appropriately. According to Chauvin and Remley (1996), relatively few counselors will be accused during their careers of unethical conduct, yet all professionals are susceptible to such charges. They write:

> Counseling is not conducted according to a formula, nor are there any step-by-step manuals that guide counselors in every situation. In exercising professional judgment, counselors may have every intention of doing the right thing professionally; however, a panel of other counselors, reviewing retroactively the actions of a colleague, may determine that the ethical standards of the profession were violated.

The best way to reduce the chance of being sued is to know the rules and to follow them. If the therapist develops too many forms of self-protection, however, the therapeutic relationship may be negatively affected. A client may infer that the counselor is not to be trusted. In turn, the client may be reluctant to engage in the self-disclosure that is so important for successful therapy.

Course of Action in a Malpractice Suit

Even though you practice prudently and follow most of the guidelines we have given, you may still be sued. In the event that you are sued, consider these recommendations given by Bennett and his associates (1990):

- Treat the lawsuit seriously, even if it represents a client's attempt to punish or control you.
- Do not attempt to resolve the matter with the client directly, because anything you do might be used against you in the litigation.
- Become familiar with your liability policy, including the limits of coverage and the procedures the company will use.
- If a client threatens to sue you or if you receive a subpoena notifying you of a lawsuit, contact your insurance company immediately.
- Never destroy or alter files or reports pertinent to the client's case.
- Promptly retain an attorney. In consultation with your attorney, prepare summaries of any pertinent events about the case that you can use.
- Do not discuss the case with anyone other than your attorney. Avoid making self-incriminating statements to the client or to his or her attorney.
- Determine the nature of support available to you from professional associations to which you belong.
- Do not continue a professional relationship with a client who is bringing a suit against you.

If you face going to court, you must have some basic knowledge and take steps to prepare yourself for your appearance. Helpful resources for understanding legal matters pertaining to mental-health practices, for avoiding counselor malpractice, and for preparing for court are Remley (1991) and R. L. Crawford (1994).

Legal Liability in an Ethical Perspective

Legal liability and ethical practice are not identical, but they do overlap. Legal issues give substance and direction to the evolution of ethical issues. Chauvin and Remley (1996) state that because ethics complaints may lead to civil or criminal lawsuits, the legal aspects of an ethical complaint dictate how counselors must conduct themselves. Thus, counselors need to know the relationship between ethics complaints and lawsuits, how boards process complaints, and the importance of seeking legal consultation.

The public's use of the legal system to resolve grievances against mental-health professionals is increasing. Private practitioners are becoming more vulnerable and are likely to find themselves involved in litigation more often than in the past. Consult an attorney about any questionable matters, and purchase professional-liability insurance. This increased scrutiny can have a positive effect, stimulating professionals to offer higher quality and more ethical service. However, increased use of the legal system can also lead to excessive caution on the part of therapists because of their concern about being sued. No professional is expected to be perfect, but it is beneficial to evaluate what you are doing and why you are practicing as you are.

Chapter Summary

The ethical codes of all mental-health organizations specify the centrality of informed consent. Clients' rights can best be protected if therapists develop procedures that aid their clients in making informed choices. Legally, informed consent entails the client's ability to act freely in making rational decisions. The process of informed consent includes providing information about the nature of therapy as well as the rights and responsibilities of both the therapist and the client. A basic challenge therapists face is to provide accurate and sufficient information to clients yet at the same time not to overwhelm them with too much information too soon. Informed consent can best be viewed as an ongoing process aimed at increasing the range of choices and the responsibility of the client as an active therapeutic partner.

In addition to a discussion of the rights of clients, this chapter has considered the scope of professional responsibility. Therapists have responsibilities to their clients, their agency, their profession, the community, the members of their clients' families, and themselves. Ethical dilemmas arise when there are conflicts among these responsibilities, for instance, when the agency's expectations conflict with the concerns or wishes of clients. Members of the helping professions need to know and to observe the ethical codes of their professional organizations, and they must make sound judgments within the parameters of acceptable practice. We have encouraged you to think about specific ethical issues and to develop a sense of professional ethics and knowledge of state laws so that your judgment will be based on more than what "feels right."

 Associated with professional responsibilities are professional liabilities. If practitioners ignore legal and ethical standards or if their conduct is below the expected standard of care, they may be sued. Practitioners who fail to keep adequate records of their procedures are opening themselves to liability. It is realistic to be concerned about malpractice actions, and professional practices that can reduce such risks have been described. But practitioners should not become so preoccupied with making mistakes that they render themselves ineffective as clinicians.

Suggested Activities

1. Form small groups in class and create an informed consent document. What does your group think clients must be told either before therapy begins or during the first few sessions? How might you implement your informed consent procedures?

2. Working in small groups in class, explore the topic of the rights clients have in counseling. One person in each group can serve as a recorder. When the groups reconvene for a general class meeting, the recorders for the various groups share their lists of clients' rights on a 3-point scale: extremely important, important, and somewhat important. What rights can your class agree on as the most important?

3. Select some of the open-ended cases presented in this chapter to role-play with a fellow student. One of you chooses a client you feel you can identify with, and the other becomes the counselor. Conduct a counseling interview. Afterward, talk about how each of you felt during the interview and discuss alternative courses of action that could have been taken.

4. Providing clients with access to their files and records seems to be in line with the consumer-rights movement, which is having an impact on the human-services professions. What are your own thoughts on providing your clients with this information? What information would you want to share with your clients? In what ways might you go about providing them with this information? What might you do if there were a conflict between your views and the policies of the agency that employed you?

5. Consider inviting an attorney who is familiar with the legal aspects of counseling practice to address your class. Possible questions for consideration are: What are the legal rights of clients in therapy? Legally, what are the main responsibilities of therapists? What are some of the best ways to become familiar with laws pertaining to counselors? What are the grounds for lawsuits, and how can counselors best protect themselves from being sued? What are some future projections concerning the link between the law and ethical counseling practices?

6. Interview practicing counselors about some of their most pressing ethical concerns in carrying out their responsibilities. How have they dealt with

these ethical issues? What are some of their legal considerations? What are their concerns, if any, about malpractice suits?

7. Read some of the recent literature on malpractice and on how to reduce the chances of being sued. Students can research different aspects of malpractice and bring the findings to class for a general discussion.

8. In small groups discuss your own concerns about professional liability. How worried are you about being sued someday? What can you do to lessen the chances of being accused of not having practiced according to acceptable standards?

Chapter

5

Confidentiality: Ethical and Legal Issues

- ◆ *Pre-Chapter Self-Inventory*

- ◆ *Introduction*

- ◆ *Confidentiality, Privileged Communication, and Privacy*

- ◆ *The Duty to Warn and to Protect*

- ◆ *Protecting Children from Harm*

- ◆ *Confidentiality and HIV/AIDS-Related Issues*

- ◆ *Chapter Summary*

- ◆ *Suggested Activities*

Pre-Chapter Self-Inventory

Directions: For each statement, indicate the response that most closely identifies your beliefs and attitudes. Use the following code:

5 = I *strongly agree* with this statement.
4 = I *agree* with this statement.
3 = I am *undecided* in my opinion about this statement.
2 = I *disagree* with this statement.
1 = I *strongly disagree* with this statement.

__2__   1. I worry a lot about what to tell my clients about confidentiality.
__1__   2. There are no situations in which I would disclose what a client had
          told me without the client's permission.
__1__   3. Absolute confidentiality is necessary if effective psychotherapy is to
          occur.
__4__   4. If I were working with a client whom I had assessed as potentially
          dangerous to another person, it would be my duty to warn the pos-
          sible victim.
__4__   5. Once I make an assessment that a client is suicidal or at a high risk of
          carrying out self-destructive acts, it is my ethical obligation to take
          action.
__2__   6. Counselors should make it more difficult for suicidal persons to reject
          responsibility for deliberately taking their own lives.
__2__   7. If a suicidal client does not want my help or actively rejects it, I would
          be inclined to leave the person alone.
__5__   8. As a helping professional, it is my responsibility to report suspected
          child abuse, regardless of when it occurred.
__4__   9. The reporting laws pertaining to child abuse sometimes in effect pre-
          vent therapy from taking place with the abuser.
__1__ 10. I think reporting child abuse should be left to the judgment of the
          therapist.
__4__ 11. To protect children from abuse, strict laws are necessary, and profes-
          sionals should be penalized for failing to report abuses.
__2__ 12. In the effort to protect children from child abuse, sometimes what is
          legal may not be ethical.
__4__ 13. If my client is HIV-positive, I have a duty to warn all of the person's
          identifiable sexual partners if my client refuses to disclose his or her
          HIV status.
__4__ 14. In counseling HIV-positive clients, I would be inclined to maintain
          confidentiality because failing to do so could erode the trust of my
          clients.
__5__ 15. If an HIV-positive client refused to disclose his or her HIV status
          to a partner, I would explore with my client the reasons for not doing
          so.

Introduction

Perhaps the central right of a client is the guarantee that disclosures in therapy sessions will be protected. As you will see, however, you cannot make a blanket promise to your clients that *everything* they talk about will *always* remain confidential. Consider the ethical and legal ramifications of confidentiality, and inform your clients from the outset of therapy of those circumstances that limit confidentiality.

Landmark court cases have shed new light on the therapist's duty to warn and to protect both clients and others who may be directly affected by a client's behavior. You have both ethical and legal responsibilities to protect innocent people who might be injured by a dangerous client. You also have responsibilities to assess and intervene effectively with clients who are likely to try to take their own lives. To help you think about your position when dealing with potentially dangerous or suicidal clients, we offer some guidelines and case illustrations.

The more you consider the legal ramifications of confidentiality, the clearer it becomes that most matters are not neatly defined. Even if therapists have become familiar with local and state laws that govern their profession, this legal knowledge alone is not enough to enable them to make sound decisions. Each case is unique, for there are many subtle points in the law and various and sometimes conflicting ways to interpret the law. Professional judgment always plays a significant role in resolving cases.

Confidentiality, Privileged Communication, and Privacy

An important obligation of practitioners in the various mental-health professions is to maintain the confidentiality of their relationships with their clients (see the box on page 156 for some specific guidelines). This obligation is not absolute, however, and practitioners must develop a sense of professional ethics for determining when the confidentiality of the relationship should be broken. Become familiar with the legal protection afforded the privileged communications of your clients as well as the limits of this protection.

Definition of Terms

Confidentiality, privileged communication, and privacy are related concepts, but there are important distinctions among them.

Confidentiality. Mental-health professionals have an ethical responsibility and a professional duty to safeguard clients from unauthorized disclosures of information given in the therapeutic relationship. Professionals must not disclose this information except when authorized by law or by the client to do so. However, there are limitations to the promise of confidentiality. Court deci-

Confidentiality in Counseling Practice

American Psychological Association (1995):

Psychologists have a primary obligation and take reasonable precautions to respect the confidentiality rights of those with whom they work or consult, recognizing that confidentiality may be established by law, institutional rules, or professional or scientific relationships.

National Association of Social Workers (1996):

Social workers should protect the confidentiality of all information obtained in the course of professional service, except for compelling professional reasons. The general expectation that social workers will keep information confidential does not apply when disclosure is necessary to prevent serious, foreseeable, and imminent harm to a client or other identifiable person or when laws or regulations require disclosure without a client's consent. In all instances, social workers should disclose the least amount of confidential information necessary to achieve the desired purpose; only information that is directly relevant to the purpose for which the disclosure is made should be revealed.

American Counseling Association (1995):

When counseling is initiated and throughout the counseling process as necessary, counselors inform clients of the limitations of confidentiality and identify foreseeable situations in which confidentiality must be breached.

American Association for Marriage and Family Therapy (1991):

Marriage and family therapists have unique confidentiality concerns because the client in a therapeutic relationship may be more than one person. Therapists respect and guard confidences of each individual client.

sions, for example, have underscored the therapist's duty to warn and to protect the client or others, even if it means breaking confidentiality. Also, because confidentiality is a client's right, psychotherapists may ethically reveal a client's confidences in those cases where a client waives this right. However, the waiver must be knowing and voluntary (Ahia & Martin, 1993).

The APA ethics code provides the following guidelines for disclosure of confidential information:

Psychologists disclose confidential information without the consent of the individual only as mandated by law, or where permitted by law for a valid purpose, such as (1) to provide needed professional services to the patient or the individual or organizational client, (2) to obtain appropriate professional consultations, (3) to protect the patient or client or others from harm, or (4) to obtain payment for services, in which instance disclosure is limited to the minimum that is necessary to achieve the purpose. (APA, 1995)

Privileged communication. Privileged communication is a legal concept that protects against forced disclosure in legal proceedings that would break a promise of privacy. All states have enacted into law some form of psychotherapist-client privilege, but the specifics of this privilege vary from state to state. These laws ensure that clients' disclosures of personal and sensitive information will be protected from exposure by therapists in legal proceedings. In other words, therapists can refuse to answer questions in court or refuse to produce a client's records in court. This privilege belongs to the client and is designed for the client's protection rather than for the protection of the professional. If a client knowingly and rationally waives this privilege, the professional has no legal grounds for withholding the information. Professionals are obligated to disclose information when the client requests it, but only the information that is specifically requested and only to the individuals or agencies that are specified by the client.

Because psychotherapist-client privilege is a legal concept, there are certain circumstances under which information must be provided by the therapist. Exceptions to confidentiality and the therapist-client privilege listed by Stromberg and his colleagues (1993) include:

- when the client consents to disclosure
- when the law requires reporting of certain information, such as child or elder abuse
- when there is a duty to warn or protect third parties
- when reimbursement or other legal rules require disclosure
- when the client is deemed to have waived confidentiality by bringing a lawsuit
- when an emergency exists

Recently, the basic principles of privileged communication have been reaffirmed by case law. On June 13, 1996, the United States Supreme Court ruled that communications between licensed psychotherapists and their clients in the course of diagnosis or treatment are privileged and therefore protected from forced disclosure in cases arising under federal law. The Supreme Court ruling in *Jaffee* v. *Redmond,* written by Justice John Paul Stevens, stated that "effective psychotherapy depends upon an atmosphere of confidence and trust in which the patient is willing to make frank and complete disclosure of facts, emotions, memories, and fears" (Morrissey, 1996; Seppa, 1996). According to Newman (1996), the high court's ruling recognizes the societal value of psychotherapy and the importance of confidentiality to successful treatment. This decision may signal the broadening of a trend toward stronger privileged communication statutes.

Generally speaking, the legal concept of privileged communication does not apply to group counseling. Members of a counseling group can assume that they could be asked to testify in court concerning certain information revealed in the course of a group session, unless there is a statutory exception. Similarly, couples therapy and family therapy are not subject to privileged communication statutes in many states. No clear judicial trend has emerged for communications that are made in the presence of third persons. It is best for therapists to assume that such communications are not privileged. Therapists should inform their clients of the ethical need for confidentiality and the lack of legal privilege concerning disclosures made in the presence of third persons (B. S. Anderson, 1996). It is important to note that from an ethical perspective confidentiality is still applicable when three or more clients are involved. It is privilege, from a legal perspective, that is not protected.

Privacy.   Privacy, as a matter of law, refers to the constitutional right of an individual to decide the time, place, manner, and extent of sharing oneself with others (Stromberg and his colleagues, 1993). In discussing some basic issues pertaining to privacy, Everstine and his colleagues (1980) raise the following questions:

◆ To what extent should beliefs and attitudes be protected from manipulation or scrutiny by others?
◆ How can it be decided who may intrude on privacy and in what circumstances privacy must be maintained?
◆ Assuming that privacy has been violated, what can be done to ameliorate the situation?
◆ Do people have a right to waive their privacy, even when their best interests might be threatened?

Practitioners should exercise caution with regard to the privacy of their clients. It is easy to invade a client's privacy unintentionally. Examples of some of the most pressing situations in which privacy is an issue include an employer's access to an applicant's or an employee's psychological tests, parents' access to their child's school and health records, and a third-party payor's access to information about a client's diagnosis and prognosis.

Most professional codes of ethics contain guidelines to safeguard a client's right to privacy. An example of such a standard is the APA (1995) ethics code: "In order to minimize intrusions on privacy, psychologists include in written and oral reports, consultations, and the like, only information germane to the purpose for which the communication is made."

One other area where privacy is an issue involves practitioners who also teach courses, offer workshops, write books and journal articles, and give lectures. If these practitioners use examples from their clinical practice, it is of the utmost importance that they take measures to adequately disguise their clients' identities. We think it is good practice to inform clients if you are likely to use your clinical experience in writing or in lectures. One relevant guideline on this issue of privacy is given by the NASW (1996): "Social workers should respect clients' right to privacy. Social workers should not solicit private information from clients unless it is essential to providing service or conducting social work evaluation or research. Once private information is shared, standards of confidentiality apply."

Privacy in a Small-Town Private Practice*

I practiced for many years as a marriage and family therapist in a small community. This situation presented a set of ethical considerations involving safe-

*This case is presented from the perspective of Marianne Corey.

guarding the privacy of clients. First, it was important that I choose an office that afforded privacy to clients as they entered and left. I considered leasing space in a small professional building in the center of town, but I quickly discovered that people would be uncomfortable making themselves that visible when seeking psychological help. A home office, which was remote from the center of the village, worked out well. However, I had to carefully schedule clients, allowing ample time between sessions so clients who might know each other would not meet in the office. When an office is located within a home, it is essential that a professional atmosphere be provided. Clients have a right to expect privacy and should not have to deal with intrusions by the therapist's family members.

I discussed with my clients the unique variables pertaining to confidentiality in a small community. I informed them that I would not discuss professional concerns with them should we meet at the grocery store or the post office, and I respected their preferences regarding interactions away from the office. Knowing that they were aware that I saw many people from the town, I reassured them that I would not talk with anyone about who my clients were, even when I might be directly asked. Another example of protecting my clients' privacy pertained to the manner of depositing checks at the local bank. Because the bank employees knew my profession, it would have been easy for them to identify my clients. Again, I talked with my clients about their preferences. If they had any discomfort about my depositing their checks in the local bank, I arranged to have them deposited elsewhere.

Now consider the following questions:

◆ What other ethical issues do you think apply to practicing in a small community?
◆ Can you apply any of the principles illustrated in this example to having a private practice in a large city or working in a community mental-health center?
◆ Is there room for flexibility in setting guidelines regarding social relationships and outside business contacts with clients in a small community?

Confidentiality and Privacy in a School Setting

Donna discussed with us some of the difficulties she encountered when she shifted her career from private practice to counseling in an elementary school. She was particularly surprised by the differences between private practice and school counseling with respect to confidentiality issues. She remarked that she was constantly fielding questions from teachers such as: "Whom do you have in that counseling group?" "How is Johnny doing?" "It's no wonder this girl has problems. Have you met her parents?"

Although Donna talked to the teachers about the importance of maintaining a safe, confidential environment for students in counseling situations, she would still receive questions from them about students, some of whom were not in their classes. In addition to the questions from teachers, Donna found that she had to deal with inquiries from school secretaries and other staff members, some of whom seemed to know everything that was going on in the school. They would ask her probing questions about students, which she, of course, was not willing to answer. For example, although she would not tell a secretary whom she was counseling, a teacher might have told the secretary that she was seeing one of his students. One secretary asked her: "Why are you working with Jimmy Smith? He doesn't have as many problems as some of the other students!"

Donna observed that principals and parents also asked for specific information about the students she was seeing. She learned the importance of talking to everyone about the need to respect privacy. If she had not exercised care, it would have been easy for her to say more than would have been wise to teachers, staff members, and parents. She also learned how critical it was to talk about matters of confidentiality and privacy in simple language with the schoolchildren she counseled.

Laws regarding confidentiality in school counseling differ. In some states, therapists in private practice are required to demonstrate that attempts have been made to contact the parents of children who are younger than 16, whereas school counselors are not required to do so. Schools that receive federal funding are generally bound by the provisions of the Family Educational Rights and Privacy Act of 1994 (FERPA). It is essential that school counselors exercise discretion in the kind and extent of information they reveal to parents or guardians about their children. Counselors working in schools are not required by FERPA to make their personal records available or disclose the substance of confidential counseling sessions to parents (B. S. Anderson, 1996).

If you were an elementary school counselor, how might you address these questions:

- If you were asked some of the questions that were posed to Donna, how would you respond?
- How might you protect the privacy of the students and at the same time avoid alienating the teachers and staff members?
- How might you explain the meaning of confidentiality and privacy to teachers? staff members? parents? administrators? the children?

Ethical and Legal Ramifications of Confidentiality and Privilege

The ethics of confidentiality rest on the premise that clients in counseling are involved in a deeply personal relationship and have a right to expect that what they discuss will be kept private. The compelling justification for confidentiality is that it is necessary to encourage clients to develop the trust needed for full disclosure and for the other work involved in therapy. Surely no genuine therapy can occur unless clients trust that what they say is confidential.

When it does become necessary to break confidentiality, it is a good practice to inform the client of the intention to take this action and also to invite the client to participate in the process. This step may preserve the therapeutic relationship and create the opportunity to resolve the issue between the individuals concerned (Mappes et al., 1985). For example, most states now have statutes that require professionals who suspect any form of child abuse or elder abuse to report it to the appropriate agencies, even when the knowledge was gained through confidential communication with clients. The failure to report often includes substantial fines, and even imprisonment (Ahia & Martin, 1993). Professionals who report suspected child abuse are immune from prosecution for breaching confidentiality.

The limits of confidentiality. The circumstances under which confidentiality cannot be maintained are not clearly defined by accepted ethical standards, and therapists must exercise their own professional judgment. When assuring their clients that what they reveal will ordinarily be kept confidential, therapists should point out that they have obligations to others besides their clients. All of the major professional organizations have taken the position that practitioners must reveal certain information when there is clear and imminent danger to an individual or to society; therapists are bound to act in such a way as to protect others from harm. The ACA's ethical guidelines state: "The general requirement that counselors keep information confidential does not apply when disclosure is required to prevent clear and imminent danger to the client or others or when legal requirements demand that confidential information be revealed. Counselors consult with other professionals when in doubt as to the validity of an exception" (1995).

It is the responsibility of therapists to clarify the ethical and legal restrictions on confidentiality. Exceptional circumstances in which it is permissible to share information with others in the interest of providing competent services to clients include:

- when clerical assistants handle confidential information, as in managed care
- when the counselor consults with experts or peers
- when the counselor is working under supervision
- when other mental-health professionals request information and the client has given consent to share

Other times when it is permissible (or required) to breach confidentiality include these circumstances (Ahia & Martin, 1993; Herlihy & Corey, 1996b):

- when a client poses a danger to self or others
- when a client discloses an intention to commit a crime
- when the counselor suspects abuse or neglect of a child, an elderly person, a resident of an institution, or a disabled adult
- when a court orders a counselor to make records available

The limitations of confidentiality may be greater in some settings and agencies than in others. If clients are informed about the conditions under which confidentiality may be compromised, they are in a better position to decide whether to enter counseling. If clients are involved in involuntary counseling, they can decide what they will disclose in their sessions. It is generally accepted that clients have a right to understand in advance the circumstances under which therapists are required or allowed to communicate information about the client to third parties. Unless clients understand the exceptions to confidentiality, their consent to treatment is not genuinely informed.

If you breach confidentiality in an unprofessional manner (in the absence of a recognized exception), you open yourself to both ethical and legal sanctions, including expulsion from a professional association, loss of certification, license revocation, and a malpractice suit. To protect yourself against such liability, Ahia and Martin (1993) recommend taking the following actions:

◆ As part of the written informed consent process, let your clients know about all counseling procedures and policies, including confidentiality and its exceptions.
◆ Become familiar with all applicable ethical and legal guidelines pertaining to confidentiality, including state privilege laws and their exceptions, child, elder, and disabled abuse reporting requirements, and the parameters of the duty-to-warn exceptions in your state.

◆ **The case of Larry.**   When he is 14 years old, Larry is sent to a family guidance clinic by his parents. He is seen by a counselor who has nine years of counseling experience. At the first session the counselor sees Larry and his parents together. She tells the parents in his presence that what she and Larry discuss will be confidential and that she will not feel free to disclose information acquired through the sessions without his permission. The parents seem to understand that confidentiality is necessary for trust to develop between their son and his counselor.

At first Larry is reluctant to come in for counseling, but eventually he begins to open up. As the sessions go on, he tells the counselor that he is "heavily into drugs." Larry's parents know that he was using drugs at one time, but he has told them that he is no longer using them. The counselor listens to anecdote after anecdote about Larry's use of dangerous drugs, about how "I get loaded at school every day," and about a few brushes with death when he was under the influence of drugs. Finally, she tells Larry that she does not want the responsibility of knowing he is experimenting with dangerous drugs and that she will not agree to continue the counseling relationship unless he stops using them. At this stage she agrees not to inform his parents, on the condition that he quit using drugs, but she does tell him that she will be talking with one of her colleagues about the situation.

Larry apparently stops using drugs for several weeks. However, one night when he is under the influence of PCP he has a serious automobile accident. As a result of the accident, Larry is paralyzed for life. Larry's parents angrily assert that they had a legal right to be informed that he was unstable to the

[handwritten margin note: even telling parents about drug using parented may not have prevented the accident]

point of committing such an act, and they file suit against both the counselor and the agency.

- What is your general impression of the way Larry's counselor handled the case? *[handwritten: handled well.]*
- Do you think the counselor acted in a responsible way toward herself? the client? the parents? the agency?
- If you were convinced that Larry was likely to hurt himself or others because of his drug use and his emotionally unstable condition, would you have informed his parents, even though doing so would probably have ended your counseling relationship with him? Why, or why not?
- Which of the following courses of action might you have taken if you had been Larry's counselor? Check as many as you think are appropriate:

  ✓ state the legal limits on you as a therapist during the initial session
  ✓ consult with the director of the agency
  ✓ refer Larry for psychological testing to determine the degree of his emotional disturbance
  ___ refer Larry to a psychiatrist for treatment
  ___ continue to see Larry without any stipulations
  ___ insist on a session with Larry's parents as a condition of continuing counseling
  ___ inform the police or other authorities
  ✓ request supervision and consultation from the agency
  ✓ document your decision-making process with a survey of pertinent research

- What other specific courses of action might you have pursued?

◆ ***Three short cases.***   The following cases deal with ethical and legal aspects of confidentiality. What do you think you would do in each of these situations?

1. You're a student counselor. For your internship you're working with college students on campus. Your intern group meets with a supervisor each week to discuss your cases. One day, while you're having lunch in the campus cafeteria with three other interns, they begin to discuss their cases in detail, even mentioning names of clients. They joke about some of the clients they're seeing, while nearby are other students who may be able to overhear this conversation. What would you do in this situation?

  ✓ I would tell the other interns to stop talking about their clients where other students could overhear them, and I would say that I thought they were behaving unprofessionally.
  ✓ I would bring the matter up in our next practicum meeting with the supervisor.
  ___ I wouldn't do anything because the students who could overhear the conversation would most likely not be that interested in what was being said.
  ___ I wouldn't do anything because it's natural to discuss cases and make jokes to relieve tension.

_____ I would encourage them to stop talking and to continue their discussion in a private place.

2. You're leading a counseling group on a high school campus. The members have voluntarily joined the group. In one of the sessions several of the students discuss the drug traffic on their campus, and two of them reveal that they sell marijuana and various pills to their friends. You discuss this matter with them, and they claim that there is nothing wrong with using these drugs. They argue that most of the students on campus use drugs, that no one has been harmed, and that there isn't any difference between using drugs (which they know is illegal) and relying on alcohol. What would you do in this situation?

_____ Because their actions are illegal, I'd report them to the police.

_____ I'd do nothing because their drug use doesn't seem to be a problem for them, and I wouldn't want to jeopardize their trust in me.

✓ I would report the situation to the school authorities but keep the identities of the students confidential. (because of harm to others)

_____ I would let the students know that I planned to inform the school authorities of their actions and their names.

_____ I wouldn't take the matter seriously because the laws relating to drugs are unfair.

✓ I would explore with the students their reasons for making this disclosure.

3. You're counseling children in an elementary school. Barbara is referred to you by her teacher because she is becoming increasingly withdrawn. After several sessions Barbara tells you that she is afraid that her father might kill her and that he frequently beats her as a punishment. Until now she has lied about obvious bruises on her body, claiming that she fell off her bicycle and hurt herself. She shows you welts on her arms and back but tells you not to say anything to anyone because her father has threatened a worse beating if she tells anyone. What would you do in this situation?

_____ I would respect Barbara's wishes and not tell anyone what I knew.

✓ I would report the situation to the principal and the school nurse.

_____ I would immediately go home with Barbara and talk to her parents.

_____ I would take Barbara home with me for a time.

_____ I would report the matter to the police.

_____ I would ask Barbara why she was telling me about the beatings if she didn't want me to reveal them to anyone else.

✓ I would tell her that I had a legal obligation to make this situation known to the authorities but that I would work with her and not leave her alone in her fears.

The Duty to Warn and to Protect

Mental-health professionals, spurred by the courts, have come to realize that they have a double professional responsibility: to protect other people from potentially dangerous clients and to protect clients from themselves. In this section we look first at therapists' responsibilities to warn and to protect potential victims and then at the problems posed by suicidal clients.

The Duty to Protect Potential Victims

Practitioners need to integrate legal and professional issues into their clinical practices in such a manner that care of clients is not compromised. Bednar and his colleagues (1991) maintain that counselors must exercise the ordinary skill and care of a reasonable professional in (1) identifying those clients who are likely to do physical harm to third parties, (2) protecting third parties from those clients judged potentially dangerous, and (3) treating those clients who are dangerous. They recommend that practitioners "take reasonable precautions in *record keeping* and collegial *consultations* that will most dramatically reduce the chances of successful malpractice suits" (p. 59). It is, in fact, this standard—what a *reasonable* professional in the community would do under similar circumstances—that often determines professional liability in a malpractice suit.

One of the main tasks therapists must grapple with is deciding whether a particular client is dangerous. Although practitioners are not generally legally liable for their failure to render perfect predictions of violent behavior of a client, a professionally inadequate assessment of client dangerousness can result in liability for the therapist, harm to third parties, and inappropriate breaches of client confidentiality. Therapists faced with potentially dangerous clients should take specific steps designed to protect the public and to minimize their own liability. They should take careful histories, advise clients of the limits of confidentiality, keep accurate notes of threats and other client statements, seek consultation, and record steps they've taken to protect others. Indeed, it is extremely difficult to decide when breaching confidentiality to protect potential victims is justified. Most states permit (if not require) therapists to breach confidentiality to warn or protect victims. In addition, many states grant therapists protection from being sued for breaching confidentiality if the therapist can demonstrate that he or she acted in good faith to protect third parties (Stromberg, Schneider, & Joondeph, 1993). Ahia and Martin (1993) state that there is clearly no exact way to determine who is a reasonably identifiable victim who must be warned of the dangerous behavior of a client. Counselors are advised to consult with a supervisor or an attorney because they may be subject to liability for either failing to warn those entitled to warnings or warning those who are not entitled.

The responsibility to protect the public from dangerous acts of violent clients entails liability for civil damages when practitioners neglect this duty by (1) failing to diagnose or predict dangerousness, (2) failing to warn potential victims of violent behavior, (3) failing to commit dangerous individuals, and (4) prematurely discharging dangerous clients from a hospital (APA, 1985). The first two of these legally prescribed duties are illustrated in the case of *Tarasoff* v. *Board of Regents of the University of California*, which has been the subject of extensive analysis in the psychological literature. The other two duties are set forth in additional landmark court cases.

The Tarasoff case.   In August 1969 Prosenjit Poddar, who was a voluntary outpatient at the student health service on the Berkeley campus of the university, was in counseling with a psychologist named Moore. Poddar had confided to Moore his intention to kill an unnamed woman (who was readily identifiable as Tatiana Tarasoff) when she returned from an extended trip in Brazil. In consultation with other university counselors, Moore made the assessment that Poddar was dangerous and should be committed to a mental hospital for observation. Moore later called the campus police and told them of the death threat and of his conclusion that Poddar was dangerous. The campus officers did take Poddar into custody for questioning, but they later released him when he gave evidence of being "rational" and promised to stay away from Tarasoff. He was never confined to a treatment facility. Moore followed up his call with a formal letter requesting the assistance of the chief of the campus police. Later, Moore's supervisor asked that the letter be returned, ordered that the letter and Moore's case notes be destroyed, and asked that no further action be taken in the case. Tarasoff and her family were never made aware of this potential threat.

Shortly after Tarasoff's return from Brazil, Poddar killed her. Her parents filed suit against the Board of Regents and employees of the university for having failed to notify the intended victim of the threat. A lower court dismissed the suit in 1974, the parents appealed, and the California Supreme Court ruled in favor of the parents in 1976, holding that a failure to warn an intended victim was professionally irresponsible. The court's ruling requires that therapists breach confidentiality in cases where the general welfare and safety of others is involved. This was a California case, and courts in other states are not bound to decide a similar case in the same way.

Under the *Tarasoff* decision, the therapist must first accurately diagnose the client's tendency to behave in dangerous ways toward others. This first duty is judged by the standards of professional negligence. In this case the therapist did not fail in this duty. He even took the additional step of requesting that the dangerous person be detained by the campus police. But the court held that simply notifying the police was insufficient to protect the identifiable victim (Laughran & Bakken, 1984).

In the first ruling, in 1974, the lower court cited a "duty to warn," but this duty was expanded by the California Supreme Court into a "duty to protect" third parties from dangerous clients. Therapists can protect others through traditional clinical interventions such as reassessment, medication changes, referral, or hospitalization. Other steps therapists may take include warning potential victims, calling the police, or informing the state child protection agency. Negligence lies in the practitioner's failure to warn a third party of imminent danger, not in failing to predict any violence that may be committed. Stromberg, Schneider, and Joondeph (1993) indicate that courts and legislatures tend to be sympathetic in predicting violence, identifying potential victims, and requiring therapists to protect third parties. In fact, few reported decisions have found mental-health professionals actually liable for failing to protect a threatened third party. Because psychology is not an exact science, predicting the likelihood of future dangerousness cannot be done in a highly reliable manner.

The *Tarasoff* decision made it clear that client confidentiality can be readily compromised; indeed, "the protective privilege ends where the public peril begins" (cited in Perlin, 1997). Issues of the welfare of the individual client are balanced against concerns for the welfare of society. As Bednar and his colleagues (1991) indicate, the mental-health professional is a double agent. Therapists have ethical and legal responsibilities to their clients, and they also have legal obligations to society. These dual responsibilities sometimes conflict, and they can create ambiguity in the therapeutic relationship. A number of state courts have not ruled on applications of *Tarasoff*, and practitioners remain uncertain about the nature of their duty to protect or to warn.

In their assessment of *Tarasoff*, Knapp and VandeCreek (1982) make the point that variations in state laws make the procedures involved in the "duty to warn" a difficult matter. In the *Tarasoff* case the identity of the victim was known. However, therapists are often concerned about legal responsibility when the identity of the intended victim is unknown. What are the therapist's obligations in cases of generalized statements of hostility? What is the responsibility of the therapist to predict future violence? Knapp and VandeCreek (1982) recommend that "psychotherapists need only follow reasonable standards in predicting violence. Psychotherapists are not liable for the failure to warn when the propensity toward violence is unknown or would be unknown by other psychotherapists using ordinary skill" (pp. 514–515). Their point is that therapists should not become intimidated by every idle fantasy, for every impulsive threat is not evidence of imminent danger. In their opinion recent behavioral acts can best predict future violence. In addition to warning potential victims, Knapp and VandeCreek suggest that practitioners consider other alternatives to diffuse the danger and, at the same time, satisfy their legal duty. They recommend seeking consultation with other professionals who have expertise in dealing with potentially violent people, and also documenting the steps taken.

In his assessment of *Tarasoff*, Fulero (1988) suggests that the issues raised by the decision are likely to continue generating litigation, legislation, and controversy for some time to come. To clarify the soundness of their professional practices, it is suggested that clinicians seek consultation. As mentioned earlier, therapists are not liable for a negative outcome unless their actions fall below the expected standard of care. Therapists can be deemed negligent for failing to protect potential victims in cases where a court finds that other therapists of average skill, exercising reasonable care, would have predicted the client's violent actions (Stromberg, Schneider, & Joondeph, 1993).

The Bradley case.   A second case illustrates the duty not to negligently release a dangerous client. In *Bradley Center* v. *Wessner* the patient, Wessner, had been voluntarily admitted to a facility for psychiatric care. Wessner was upset over his wife's extramarital affair. He had repeatedly threatened to kill her and her lover and had even admitted to a therapist that he was carrying a weapon in his car for that purpose. He was given an unrestricted weekend pass to visit his children, who were living with his wife. He met his wife and her lover in the home and shot and killed them. The children filed a wrongful death suit, alleging that the psychiatric center had breached a duty to exercise control over Wessner. The Georgia Supreme Court ruled that a physician has a duty to take reasonable care to prevent a potentially dangerous patient from inflicting harm (Laughran & Bakken, 1984).

The Jablonski case. A third legal ruling underscores the duty to commit a dangerous individual. The intended victim's knowledge of a threat does not relieve therapists of the duty to protect, as can be seen by the decision in *Jablonski* v. *United States.* Meghan Jablonski filed suit for the wrongful death of her mother, Melinda Kimball, who was murdered by Philip Jablonski, the man with whom she had been living. Earlier, Philip Jablonski had agreed to a psychiatric examination at a hospital. The physicians determined that there was no emergency and thus no basis for involuntary commitment. Kimball later again accompanied Jablonski to the hospital and expressed fears for her own safety. She was told by a doctor that "you should consider staying away from him." Again, the doctors concluded that there was no basis for involuntary hospitalization and released him. Shortly thereafter Jablonski killed Kimball. The Ninth U.S. Circuit Court of Appeals found that failure to obtain Jablonski's prior medical history constituted malpractice. The essence of *Jablonski* is a negligent failure to commit (Laughran & Bakken, 1984).

The Hedlund case. The decision in *Hedlund* v. *Superior Court* extends the duty to warn to anyone who might be near the intended victim and who might also be in danger. LaNita Wilson and Stephen Wilson had received psychotherapy from a psychological assistant, Bonnie Hedlund. During treatment Stephen Wilson told the therapist that he intended to harm LaNita Wilson. He later did assault her, in the presence of her child. The allegation was that the child had sustained "serious emotional injury and psychological trauma."

In keeping with the *Tarasoff* decision, the California Supreme Court held (1) that a therapist has a duty first to exercise a "reasonable degree of skill, knowledge, and care ordinarily possessed and exercised by members [of that professional specialty] under similar circumstances" in making a prediction about the chances of a client's acting dangerously to others and (2) that therapists must "exercise reasonable care to protect the foreseeable victim of that danger." One way to protect the victim is by giving a warning of peril. The court held that breach of such a duty with respect to third persons constitutes "professional negligence" (Laughran & Bakken, 1984).

In the Hedlund case the duty to warn of potentially dangerous conduct applied to the mother, not to her child, against whom no threats had been made. However, the duty to exercise reasonable care could have been fulfilled by warning the mother that she and her child might be in danger.

The Jaffee case.   In *Jaffee* v. *Redmond* the U.S. Supreme Court ruled on June 13, 1996, that communications between licensed psychotherapists and their clients are privileged and therefore protected from forced disclosure in cases arising under federal law. The 7–2 decision in this case represented a victory for mental-health organizations because it extended the confidentiality privilege.

An on-duty police officer, Mary Lu Redmond, shot and killed a suspect while attempting an arrest. The victim's family sued in federal court, alleging that the victim's constitutional rights had been violated. The court ordered Karen Beyer, a licensed clinical social worker, to turn over notes she made during counseling sessions with Redmond after the shooting. The social worker refused, asserting that the contents of her conversations with the police officer were protected against involuntary disclosure by psychotherapist-client privilege. The court rejected her claim of psychotherapist-client privilege, and the jury awarded the family $545,000.

The Court of Appeals for the Seventh Circuit then reversed this decision and concluded that the trial court had erred by refusing to afford protection to the confidential communications between Redmond and Beyer. Jaffee, an administrator of the victim's estate, appealed this decision to the Supreme Court.

The Supreme Court upheld the appellate court's decision, clarifying for all federal court cases, both civil and criminal, the existence of the privilege. The Court recognized a broadly defined psychotherapist-client privilege and further clarified that this privilege is not subject to the decision of a judge on a case-by-case basis. The Court's decision to extend federal privilege (which already applied to psychologists and psychiatrists) to licensed social workers leaves the door open for inclusion of other licensed psychotherapists, such as licensed professional counselors, mental-health counselors, and licensed marriage and family therapists. The issues in this case are critical for psychotherapists, and it is expected that this decision will have far-reaching consequences for licensed psychotherapists and their clients (Hinnefeld & Towers, 1996; Morrissey, 1996; Newman, 1996; Seppa, 1996).

Guidelines for Dealing with Dangerous Clients

Most counseling centers and community mental-health agencies now have guidelines regarding the duty to warn and protect when the welfare of others is at stake. These guidelines generally specify how to deal with emotionally disturbed individuals, violent behavior, threats, suicidal possibilities, and other circumstances in which counselors may be legally and ethically required to breach confidentiality.

The question raised by these documents is, "What are the responsibilities of counselors to their clients or to others when, in the professional judgment of the counselor, there is a high degree of probability that a client will seriously harm another person or destroy property?" Many counselors find it difficult to predict when clients pose a serious threat to others. Clients are encouraged to

engage in open dialogue in therapeutic relationships, and many clients express feelings or thoughts about doing physical harm to others. But few of these threats are actually carried out, and counselors should not be expected to routinely reveal all threats. Breaking confidentiality can seriously harm the client-therapist relationship as well as the relationship between the client and the person "threatened."

Such disclosures should be carefully evaluated; counselors should exercise reasonable professional judgment and apply practices that are commonly accepted by professionals in the specialty.

If a counselor determines that a client poses a serious danger of violence to others, the counselor is obliged to exercise reasonable care to protect the would-be victims. Costa and Altekruse (1994) offer the following guidelines for implementing duty to warn requirements:

- Get informed consent.
- Plan ahead through consultation.
- Develop contingency plans.
- Obtain professional liability insurance.
- Involve the client.
- Obtain a detailed history.
- Document in writing.
- Implement procedures to warn.

Costa and Altekruse conclude that the duty to warn and to protect presents a major challenge to counselors. Generally, the duty to warn and to protect is indicated when these three conditions are present: (a) a special relationship exists between client and therapist, (b) a reasonable prediction of harmful conduct (based on a history of violent behavior) is made, and (c) a potential victim can be identified.

Some additional guidelines for risk containment in duty to warn and protect cases are described by Monahan (1993):

- Develop risk assessment strategies. Become educated in risk assessment, stay current with developments in the field, and be conversant with the relevant laws.
- Develop risk management procedures. For cases that raise particular concerns about violence, consider intensification of treatment or hospitalization. Seek consultation from experienced colleagues.
- Document salient points of the treatment. Record the source, content, and date of significant information on risk and the rationale and dates of all actions taken to prevent violence.
- Develop policy statements and feasible guidelines for handling risk, and subject these guidelines to clinical and legal review.

Truscott, Evans, and Mansell (1995) present a model for clinical decision making to determine the best interventions for dealing with dangerous outpatient clients. Their model takes into account the degree of risk of violence and the strength of the therapeutic alliance. They suggest a periodic informal assessment of the therapeutic alliance and maintenance of detailed case notes pertaining to the alliance. Some specific aspects of the therapeutic relationship to be assessed include: the level of trust between the client and the counselor, the client's perception of feeling understood and accepted, indication of working toward shared goals, notes on the helpfulness of therapy and the value of the therapeutic process.

From the vantage point of limiting therapist exposure to duty to protect liability, Monahan (1993) emphasizes the role of documentation as a risk management strategy. Documentation should include a brief statement of the rationale for the actions taken. If a therapist becomes involved in a malpractice suit, what is not in the written record is considered not to exist. Unrecorded warnings to a client's family member that he or she has been threatened with harm are of no value when that person is dead as a result of the threatened violence. Under no circumstances should clinicians alter the record. If asked under oath whether any part of the records have been altered and such entries later come to light, the clinician is guilty of perjury, a criminal offense. Monahan writes: "It is, in short, much better to admit that you didn't keep good records and hope that the jury believes you when you tell them what happened than to manufacture good records after the fact at the cost of your own integrity and credibility" (p. 248).

Now let's turn to some case examples. As you think about these cases, ask yourself how you would assess the degree to which Marvin and Kevin are potentially dangerous. What would you do if you were the therapist in each case?

◆ **The case of Marvin.**   Marvin has been seeing Robin, his counselor, for several months. One day he comes to the therapy session somewhat drunk and very angry. He has just found out that a close friend is having an affair with his wife. He is deeply wounded over this incident. He is also highly agitated and even talks about killing the friend who betrayed him. As he puts it, "I'm so damn mad I feel like getting my gun and shooting him." Marvin experiences intense emotions in this session. Robin does everything she can to defuse his rage and to stabilize him before the session ends. The session continues for about two hours (instead of the usual hour), and she asks him to call her a couple of times each day to check in. Before he leaves, she contracts with him that he will not go over to this man's house and that he will not act out his urges. Because she knows him well and thinks that basically he is not a violent person, she decides to let him leave the session without discussing legal imperatives in this type of case. He follows through and calls her every day. When he comes to the session the following week, he admits to still being in a great deal of pain over his discovery, but he no longer feels violent. As he puts it, "I'm not going to land in jail because of this jerk!" He tells Robin how helpful the last session was in allowing him to get a lot off his chest.

◆ Do you think Robin followed the proper ethical and legal course of action in this case? no, she must discuss the legal + ethical imperatives

- Did she fulfill her responsibilities by making sure that Marvin called her twice a day? *partially*
- Some would say that she should have broken confidentiality and warned the intended victim. What might have been the consequences for Marvin's therapy had she followed this course? *devestating*
- What criteria could a therapist use to determine whether the situation is dangerous enough to warn a potential victim? What is the fine line between overreacting and failing to respond appropriately in this kind of case?
- Knowing what you do about the case, what actions might you have taken? Why? *set limits of confidentiality / realistically*
- If Robin had sought you out for consultation in this case immediately after the session at which Marvin talked about wanting to kill his friend, what would you have told her? *the above*

◆ ***The case of Kevin.***   You're working with Kevin, a young man who you think is potentially violent. During his sessions with you, Kevin talks about his impulses to hurt others and himself, and he describes times when he has seriously beaten his girlfriend. He tells you that she is afraid to leave him because she thinks he'll beat her even more savagely. He later tells you that sometimes he gets so angry that he comes very close to killing her. You believe that he is very likely to seriously harm and possibly even kill the young woman. Which of the following would you do?

____ I would notify Kevin's girlfriend that she might be in grave danger.
____ I would notify the police or other authorities. *if prior steps are not taken / last effort*
____ I would keep Kevin's threats to myself, because I couldn't be sure that he would act on them.
____ I would seek a second opinion from a colleague.
____ I would inform my director or supervisor.
____ I would refer Kevin to another therapist. *or psychiatrist for evaluation*
____ I would arrange to have Kevin hospitalized.

What else might you do?

The Duty to Protect Suicidal Clients

In the preceding discussion we emphasized the therapist's obligation to protect others from dangerous individuals. The guidelines and principles outlined in that discussion apply equally to the client who poses a danger to self. Many therapists inform their clients that they have an ethical and legal obligation to break confidentiality when they have good reason to suspect suicidal behavior. Even if clients argue that they can do what they want with their own lives, including taking them, therapists have a legal duty to protect suicidal clients. The crux of the issue is knowing when to take a client's hints seriously enough to report the condition. Certainly not every mention of suicidal thoughts or feelings justifies extraordinary measures.

The evaluation and management of suicidal risk is a source of great stress for most therapists. It brings to the surface many troublesome issues that clinical practitioners must face, such as their degree of influence, competence, level of involvement with a client, responsibility, legal obligations, and ability to make life-or-death decisions. Szasz (1986) has noted that failure to prevent suicide is now one of the leading reasons for successful malpractice suits against mental-health professionals and institutions.

Guidelines for Assessing Suicidal Behavior

Although it is not possible to prevent every suicide, it is possible to recognize the existence of common crises that may precipitate a suicide attempt and reach out to people who are experiencing these crisis. Counselors must take the "cry for help" seriously and have the necessary knowledge and skills to intervene once they make an assessment that a client is suicidal (Fujimura, Weis, & Cochran, 1985). Several researchers have suggested factors to consider when making an assessment (Fujimura et al., 1985; Pope, 1985b; Sommers-Flanagan & Sommers-Flanagan, 1995; Wubbolding, 1996). In an assessment interview, especially focus on evaluating depression, suicide ideation, suicide intention, and suicide plans. In crisis counseling, assess your clients for suicidal risk during the early phase of therapy, and keep alert to this issue during the course of therapy. Danger signs, such as those listed here, should be evaluated:

◆ Take direct verbal warnings seriously, as they are one of the most useful single predictors of a suicide.

◆ Pay attention to previous suicide attempts, as these are the best single predictor of lethality.

◆ Identify clients suffering from depression, a characteristic common to all suicide victims. Sleep disruption, which can intensify depression, is a key sign. For people with clinical depression the suicide rate is about 20 times greater than that of the general population.

◆ Be alert for feelings of hopelessness and helplessness, which seem to be closely associated with suicidal intentions. Individuals may feel desperate, guilt-ridden, and worthless.

◆ Monitor severe anxiety and panic attacks.

◆ Determine whether the individual has a plan. The more definite the plan, the more serious is the situation. Suicidal individuals should be asked to talk about their plans and encouraged to explore their suicidal fantasies.

◆ Identify clients who have a history of severe alcohol or drug abuse, as they are at greater risk than the general population. Alcohol is a contributing factor in one-fourth to one-third of all suicides.

◆ Be alert to client behaviors such as giving away prized possessions, finalizing business affairs, or revising wills.

◆ Determine whether clients have a history of previous psychiatric treatment or hospitalization. Clients who have been hospitalized for emotional disorders are more likely to be inclined to suicide.

♦ Question clients about their use of resource and support systems. Refusal to use these systems signifies a cutting off of communication and makes the intent more serious.

In addition to these factors, be aware of the categories of people who have an increased risk of suicide. Men are three times more likely than women to commit suicide (the rate rises rapidly until age 35 and is also high for men over 65). Single people are twice as likely as married people to commit suicide. And finally, factors such as unemployment increase the risk of suicide.

Wubbolding (1996) states that even veiled threats of suicide should be taken seriously and discussed in a clear and explicit manner. He suggests raising the following six generic questions as an approach to assessment of lethality and to open a frank discussion of whether further intervention is necessary:

♦ Are you thinking about killing yourself?
♦ Have you attempted suicide in the past?
♦ Do you have a plan?
♦ Do you have the means available to you?
♦ Will you make a no-suicide agreement to stay alive?
♦ Is there anyone close to you who could prevent you from killing yourself and to whom you could speak if you feel suicidal?

After these questions have been asked and answered, the final decision about the degree of suicidal risk is a subjective one that demands professional judgment.

The case for suicide prevention.   Suicidal individuals often hope that somebody will listen to their cry. Many are struggling with short-term crises, and if they can be given help in learning to cope with the immediate problem, their potential for suicide can be greatly reduced.

Therapists have the responsibility to prevent suicide if they can reasonably anticipate it. Once it is determined that a client is at risk, the professional is legally required to break confidentiality and take appropriate action. Liability generally arises when a counselor fails to act in such a way as to prevent the suicide or when a counselor does something that might contribute to it.

Successful lawsuits have been brought against therapists who did not follow standard procedures to protect a client's life (Austin et al., 1990). The following are recommendations for managing suicidal behavior (see Austin et al., 1990; Bednar et al., 1991; Bennett et al. 1990; Bonger, 1991; Fujimura et al., 1985, Pope, 1985b; Pope & Vasquez, 1991; Sommers-Flanagan & Sommers-Flanagan, 1995; Wubbolding, 1996):

♦ Know your personal limits; recognize the stresses involved in working with suicidal clients and the toll that they take on you personally.
♦ Work with the suicidal client to create a supportive environment.
♦ Attempt to secure a promise from the client that he or she will not try to commit suicide, either intentionally or unintentionally.

- Periodically collaborate with colleagues and ask for their views regarding the client's condition; realize that even for experienced practitioners two perspectives are better than one.
- Specify your availability to your clients; let them know how they can contact you during your absences.
- Obtain training for suicide prevention and for crisis-intervention methods. Keep up to date with current research, theory, and practice.
- Recognize the limits of your competence and know when and how to refer.
- Consider hospitalization, weighing the benefits, the drawbacks, and the possible effects. If the client does enter a hospital, pay particular attention to the increased risk of suicide immediately after discharge.
- Be clear and firm with the client, and do not allow yourself to be manipulated by threats. Give clear messages to the client.
- For services that take place within a clinic or agency setting, ensure that clear and appropriate lines of responsibility are explicit and are fully understood by everyone.
- Work with clients so that dangerous instruments are not within easy access. If the client possesses any weapons, make sure that they are in the hands of a third party.
- Consider increasing the frequency of the counseling sessions.
- Work with clients' strengths and desires to remain alive.
- Attempt to communicate realistic hopes.
- Be willing to communicate your caring. Suicidal people sometimes interpret the unwillingness of others to listen as a sign that they do not care. People may be driven to suicide by an avoidance of the topic on the part of the listener. Remember that caring entails some specific actions and setting of limits on your part.
- Do not make yourself the only person responsible for the decisions and actions of your clients. Your clients must share in the responsibility for their ultimate decisions.
- Attempt to develop a supportive network of family and friends to help clients face their struggles. Discuss this with clients and enlist their help in building this resource of caring people.

It is a good idea to document in writing the steps you take in crisis cases, for documentation may be necessary to demonstrate that you actually used sound professional judgment and acted within acceptable legal and ethical parameters. Remember that clients are ultimately responsible for their own actions and that there is only so much that you can reasonably do to prevent self-destructive actions. Even though you take specific steps to lessen the chances of a client committing suicide, the client may still take this ultimate step.

According to Sommers-Flanagan and Sommers-Flanagan (1995), two processes offer safeguards against malpractice liability in suicidal cases: consultation and documentation. Consultation gives professionals working with suicidal clients the support they need in dealing with the most stressful of all clinical activities. Consultation also provides feedback about the degree to which standards of practice are being met. Because documentation is especially important when working with suicidal individuals, Sommers-Flanagan and Sommers-Flanagan recommend that practitioners who conduct suicide assessments document that they have conducted a thorough assessment, obtained a relevant history, obtained previous treatment records, directly evaluated suicidal thoughts, consulted with one or more professionals, discussed the limits of confidentiality with the client, implemented appropriate suicide interventions, provided resources to the client, and contacted authorities and family members if a client is at high risk of suicide.

The case against suicide prevention.   Now that we have looked at the case for suicide prevention, we explore another point of view. Szasz (1986) challenges the perspective that mental-health professionals have an absolute professional duty to try to prevent suicide. He presents the thesis that suicide is an act of a moral agent who is ultimately responsible, and he opposes coercive methods of preventing suicide, such as forced hospitalization. Szasz argues that by attempting to prevent suicide, mental-health practitioners often ally themselves with the police power of the state and resort to coercion, therein identifying themselves as foes of individual liberty and responsibility. When professionals assume the burden of responsibility of keeping clients alive, they deprive their clients of their rightful share of accountability for their own actions. It is the client's responsibility to choose to live or to die. According to Szasz, if clients seek professional help for their suicidal tendencies, the helper has an ethical obligation—and in some cases a legal obligation—to provide the help being sought. However, if clients do not seek such help and actively reject it, the professional's duty is either to persuade them to accept help or to leave them alone. Here is the core of Szasz's argument in his own words:

> Because I value individual liberty highly and am convinced that liberty and responsibility are indivisible, I want to enlarge the scope of liberty and responsibility. In the present instance, this means opposing policies of suicide prevention that minimize the responsibility of individuals for killing themselves and supporting polices that maximize their responsibility for doing so. In other words, we should make it more difficult for suicidal persons to reject responsibility for deliberately taking their own lives and for mental health professionals to assume responsibility for keeping such persons alive. (p. 810)

It should be noted that Szasz is not claiming that suicide is always good or that it is a morally legitimate option; rather, his key point is that the power of the state should not be used to prohibit an individual from taking his or her own life. The right to suicide implies that we must abstain from empowering agents of the state to coercively prevent it.

Your stance on suicide prevention.   You will recall that in Chapter 3 we explored the issue of the right-to-die and end-of-life decisions. Your own value system will have a lot to do with the actions you would be likely to take.

Considering the arguments for and against suicide prevention, what is your stance on this complex issue? Where do you stand with respect to your ethical obligations to recognize, evaluate, and intervene with potentially suicidal clients? To what degree do you agree with the guidelines listed earlier? Which guidelines make the most sense to you? Do you take a contrary position on at least some cases of suicide? How do you justify your position? To what extent do you agree or disagree with the contention of Szasz that current policies of suicide prevention displace responsibility from the client to the therapist and that this needlessly undermines the ethic of self-responsibility? After clarifying your own values underlying the professional's role in assessing and preventing suicide, reflect on the following cases of clients who are contemplating suicide. If they were your clients, what actions would you take?

◆ ***The case of Rupe.***   Rupe, a 16-year-old high school student, is being seen by a therapist at the request of his parents. His school work has dropped off, he has become withdrawn socially, and he has expressed to his parents that he has thought of suicide, even though he has not made a specific plan. After the therapist has seen Rupe for several weeks of individual counseling, his concerned parents call and ask how he is doing. They wonder whether they should be alert to possible suicide attempts. Rupe's parents tell the therapist that they want to respect confidentiality and are not interested in detailed disclosures but that they want to find out if they have cause for worry. Without going into details, the counselor reassures them that they don't need to worry.

  ◆ Is the therapist's behavior ethical? Would it make a difference if Rupe were 25 years old?
  ◆ Does the therapist have an ethical obligation to inform Rupe of the conversation with his parents?   *yes*
  ◆ If the parents were to insist on having more information, does the therapist have an obligation to say more?   *no*
  ◆ If the therapist provides details to the parents, does the therapist have an obligation to inform Rupe before talking with his parents?   *yes*
  ◆ Other than doing what the therapist did, do you see other courses of action?   *no plan for suicide*
  ◆ If Rupe were indeed suicidal, what ethical and legal obligations would the therapist have toward the parents?   *determine risk take action document + consult   meds for depression*

◆ ***The case of Emmanuel.***   Emmanuel is a middle-aged widower who complains of emptiness in life, loneliness, depression, and a loss of the will to live any longer. He has been in individual therapy for seven months with a clinical psychologist in private practice. Using psychodiagnostic procedures (both objective tests and projective techniques), she has determined that he has serious depressive tendencies and is potentially self-destructive. Emmanuel came to her for therapy as a final attempt to find some meaning that would show him that his life had significance. In their sessions he explores the history of his failures, the isolation he feels, the meaninglessness of his life, and his bouts with feelings of worthlessness and depression. With her encouragement he experiments with new ways of behaving in the hope that he will find reasons to go on living. Finally, after seven months of searching, he decides that he wants to take his own life. He tells his therapist that he is convinced he has been deluding himself in thinking that anything in his life will change for the better and that he feels good about deciding to end his life. He informs her that he will not be seeing her again.

The therapist expresses her concern that Emmanuel is very capable of taking his life at this time because so far he has not been able to see any light at the end of the tunnel. She acknowledges that the decision to commit suicide is not a sudden one, for they have discussed this wish for several sessions, but she lets him know that she wants him to give therapy more of a chance. He replies that he is truly grateful to her for helping him to find his answer within himself and that at least he can end his life with dignity in his own eyes. He says firmly that he doesn't want her to attempt to obstruct his plans in any way. She asks that he postpone his decision for a least a week and return to discuss the matter more fully. He tells her he isn't certain whether he will keep this appointment, but he agrees to consider it.

The therapist does nothing further. During the following week she hears from a friend that Emmanuel has committed suicide by taking an overdose of sleeping pills.

- What do you think of the way the therapist dealt with her client? *not good*
- What is your view of suicide? *wrongly taking of life*
- What might you have done differently if you had been Emmanuel's therapist? *calls if needed/*
- How do you think your viewpoint regarding suicide would influence your approach with Emmanuel?
- Which of these actions might you have pursued if you had been Emmanuel's counselor?

    _____ committed him to a state hospital for observation, even against his will, for 72 hours

    ✓ consulted with another professional as soon as he began to discuss suicide as an option

    _____ respected his choice of suicide, even if you didn't agree with it

    ✓ informed the police and reported the seriousness of his threat

    ✓ informed members of his family of his intentions, even though he didn't want you to

    _____ bargained with him in every way possible in an effort to persuade him to keep on trying to find some meaning in life

either/or

Discuss in class any other steps you might have taken in this case.

Concluding thoughts.   In his discussion of malpractice liability for the suicidal client, Swenson (1997) writes that suicidal clients, like dangerous clients, pose a high risk for therapists. Although prediction of both danger to others and to self is difficult, courts impose liability on therapists who predict incorrectly. Swenson adds, "Even an hour of therapy can create a special relationship with a therapist and consequent duties to competently attempt to predict who will commit suicide and to take preventive steps. Although there is no *Tarasoff* duty to warn the next of kin of suicidal patients, therapists must warn if it is the best way to prevent the suicide" (p. 188). Given this caution, are you inclined to modify your stance on the issue of suicide prevention? If so, how?

Protecting Children from Harm

Whether you work with children or adults in your practice, you are expected to know how to assess potential abuse and then to report it in a timely fashion. Privileged communication does not apply in cases of child abuse and neglect. If children disclose that they are being abused or neglected, the professional is required to report the situation. If adults reveal in a therapy session that they are abusing or have abused their children, the matter must generally be reported.

In 1974 Congress enacted the National Child Abuse Prevention and Treatment Act (PL 93–247), which defines child abuse and neglect as follows:

> Physical or mental injury, sexual abuse or exploitation, negligent treatment, or maltreatment of a child under the age of eighteen or the age specified by the child protection law of the state in question, by a person who is responsible for the child's welfare, under circumstances which indicate that the child's health or welfare is harmed or threatened thereby.

If you have reason to suspect abuse or neglect, the law requires you to report the situation under penalty of fines and imprisonment.

Increasingly, states are enacting laws that impose liability on professionals who fail to report abuse or neglect. States also provide immunity by law from a civil suit that may arise from reporting suspected child abuse and neglect. Some states require that professionals complete continuing education workshops on assessment of abuse and proper reporting as a condition of license renewal.

Mandatory reporting laws differ from state to state (Youngstrom, 1991b). In Pennsylvania, for example, therapists are required to file a report if the client is a child who appears to be the victim of abuse. If the client is the abuser, however, the mandatory reporting law does not apply. In New York, therapists must report abuse whether they learn about the situation from the child in therapy, the abuser who is in therapy, or a relative. In 1989 Maryland changed its law, and it now requires therapists to report both present and past cases of child abuse that have been revealed by adult clients in therapy.

How effective are state laws in inducing professionals to report suspected child abuse? Many professionals do not adhere to mandatory reporting laws. In a study to assess psychologists' decisions to report suspected child abuse, Kalichman and Craig (1991) found that the age of the child, the child's behavior during a clinical interview, and the type of abuse influenced their decisions.

These investigators cite studies suggesting that clinicians may decide not to report because of concerns about the potential negative effect that reporting may have on therapy. Their review indicates that clinicians are hesitant to report unless they are fairly certain that abuse is occurring.

A study on confidentiality and its relation to child abuse reporting indicated that respondents were inconsistent in their procedures for informing clients of the limits of confidentiality (Nicolai & Scott, 1994). The findings of this study suggest the need to reassert the importance of providing clients with detailed information about the limits of confidentiality from the onset of therapy. Nicolai and Scott maintain that continuing education and peer-review processes should emphasize the ethical and legal obligations pertaining to child abuse reporting. The focus on training and supervision needs to be on both the associated risks as well as benefits involved in child abuse reporting.

Although therapists are likely to accept their professional responsibility to protect innocent children from physical and emotional mistreatment, they may have difficulty determining how far to go in making a report. It is often difficult to reconcile ethical responsibilities with legal obligations. Therapists may feel that they have been placed in the predicament of either behaving unethically (by reporting and thus damaging the therapy relationship) or illegally (by ignoring the mandate to report all cases of suspected child abuse). Sometimes therapists are uncertain about when they need to report an incident. Is it necessary to report adult clients who admit having abused a child years ago or who were abused as minors themselves? The laws of some states now require therapists to report disclosures by adult clients about child sexual abuse that occurred years before treatment.

A graduate student in counseling informed us that in her internship she learned that child abuse should be viewed in a cultural context. What constitutes "abuse" in American culture may not be viewed as abuse in another culture. Also, the language used to describe abuse differs from culture to culture. This student told us that she conducted an intake session and called the Child Protective Services because an African-American woman was talking about "whooping her kids" repeatedly. The Child Protective Services worker told the student that this was a cultural term and was not necessarily indicative of abuse. This illustration reminds us of the importance of taking into account the client's culture in making an assessment of child abuse.

Clinicians must develop a clear position regarding child abuse assessment and reporting. To clarify your ethical stance in dealing with the duty to protect children (and vulnerable adults) from abuse, consider these questions:

- What cultural factors might you consider in determining whether a situation indicates actual abuse? How would you account for cultural differences in assessing abuse?
- Can you think of a rationale for excluding therapists from mandatory reporting laws if their clients (abusers) voluntarily seek treatment?
- Some state laws require reporting all child abuse, regardless of when it occurred. What are your thoughts about such laws? Do they always serve to protect children from abuse? not in the past!

- Can you think of ways in which you could file a report on an adult abuser and continue working with the client therapeutically? *yes*
- What struggles, if any, have you encountered with respect to following the laws regarding reporting child abuse?
- If you follow the law in all cases are you also following an ethical course? What potential conflicts are there between doing what is legal and what is ethical?
- In what situations might encouraging the client to participate in reporting abuse actually enhance the therapeutic relationship? *owning responsibility*
- If an adult admits having abused a child, what are your thoughts about a therapist who argues that keeping the client in therapy is the best way to help him or her work through this problem, even if it means failing to report the abuse to authorities? *I don't agree; the protection of the child is paramount.*
- Do you think therapists should have some flexibility in deciding when it would be best to make a report? What policies might be in the best interests of the abused child?

One alternative to mandatory reporting is for therapists to document a clinical plan that adequately addresses the well-being of the children who are being abused as well as the treatment of the perpetrator (reported in Youngstrom, 1991b). What are your thoughts about this alternative? What other alternatives can you think of to mandatory reporting of all cases of child abuse?

To help you clarify your position with respect to situations involving child abuse, consider the following two case examples. In the first case, ask yourself how far you should go in reporting suspected abuse. Does the fact that you have reported a matter to the officials end your ethical and legal responsibilities? In the second case, look for ways to differentiate between what is ethical and what is legal practice. Ask yourself what you would be inclined to do if you saw a conflict between ethics and the law.

◆ **The case of Martina.**   Martina, a high school counselor, has reason to believe that one of her students is being physically abused. As part of the abuse, critical medication is being withheld from the student. Martina reports the incident to Child Protective Services and gives all the information she has to the caseworker. She follows up the phone conversation with the caseworker with a written report. A week later, the student tells her that nothing has been done.

- Has Martina adequately fulfilled her responsibility by making the report? Does she have a responsibility to report the agency for not having taken action?
- If the agency does not take appropriate action, does Martina have a responsibility to take other measures?
- Would it be ethical for Martina to take matters into her own hands and to call for a family session or make a house call, especially if the student requests it?

♦ Does Martina have an obligation to inform the administration? Does the school have a responsibility to see that action is taken?

♦ ***The case of Sally.***   One night, in a moment of rare intoxication, a father stumbles into his 12-year-old daughter's bedroom and briefly fondles her. Sally's cries bring her mother into the room, and the incident does not go further. Later, the father does not recall the incident. There has been no previous history of molestation. During therapy the family is able to talk openly about the incident and is working through the pain that resulted. Because of this incident, the father has enrolled in a substance abuse program. The family is adamant that this situation should not be reported to social services. The therapist knows that the statute in her state clearly specifies that she is required to report this incident, even if it had happened in the past and no further incidents had occurred. Listen to the inner dialogue of the therapist as she attempts to decide whether to report the incident, and think about your reactions to each course of action she considers:

> There are many hazards involved if I don't report this incident. If this family ever broke up, the mother or daughter could sue me for having failed to report what happened. I would be obeying the law and protecting myself by reporting it, and I could justify my actions by citing the requirement of the law.
>
> But this is a one-time incident. The father was intoxicated, and the situation did not progress beyond the fondling stage. The daughter was traumatized by the incident, but she seems to be able to talk about it in the family now. If I obey the law, my actions may be more detrimental to the family than beneficial.
>
> But the law is there for a reason. It appears that a child has been abused—that is no minor incident—and there was trauma for some time afterward.
>
> What is the most ethical thing to do? I would be following the law by reporting it, but is that the most ethical course in this case? Is it the best thing for this family now, especially as none of the members want it reported? My ethical sense tells me that my interventions should always be in the best interests of all three members of this family.
>
> I'm required to report only if I suspect or believe that abuse has occurred. Some could argue that no abuse has taken place, which is what the parents seem to indicate by their behavior.
>
> The family is now in therapy with me. If I do make a report, the family might terminate therapy. Is reporting this situation worth risking that chance?
>
> Child protective agencies are often overburdened, and only the most serious cases may be given attention. Because no abuse is presently going on, I wonder if this case will be followed up. Will it be worth risking the progress that has been made with this family?
>
> As an alternative to reporting this matter to the authorities, I could document a clinical plan of action that addresses therapeutic interventions with the father and also the well-being of the others. This course of action might be the best way to meet my legal and ethical obligations in this particular case.
>
> Before I act, perhaps I should consult an attorney for advice on how to proceed.
>
> I need to call Child Protective Services to find out what I must do.

I could call the Board of Ethics of my professional organization and get some advice on how to proceed.

I don't know what action to take. Maybe I should consult with a colleague.

Commentary.   This case illustrates some of the difficulties counselors can find themselves in when their inner ethical sense conflicts with the law or an ethical code. This counselor must struggle with herself to determine whether she will follow her clinical intuitions by doing what she thinks is in the best interests of this family or whether she will do what is required by the law. If she simply reported this case, she would be acting on the lower level of ethical functioning. Her actions would be characterized by compliance with the law and adherence to the ethical code of her profession.

If the therapist called the ethics committee of her professional organization or a colleague, she would be acting on a slightly higher level of ethical functioning because of her willingness to consult. Consulting colleagues is always recommended in cases such as this one. The consultation process would help from a legal perspective as well. If other professionals agreed with her course of action, she would have a good chance of demonstrating that she had acted in good faith and that she had met the professional standards of her peers. In addition, consulting colleagues would provide her with one or more different perspectives on a difficult case.

The therapist is acting on the highest level of ethical functioning in examining all the factors and special circumstances of this family before acting. She is struggling to act appropriately, not just to protect herself, and is truly concerned with the best interests of everyone in the family. The welfare of the family members does not require her to violate the law, but it does require her to think beyond merely obeying the law. It would be good for her to keep in mind that although she has the obligation to report the situation it is not her task to conclude whether abuse has actually taken place. Also, it is not her role to get involved in the actual investigation.

It may still be possible for her to continue her therapeutic relationship with the family even if she decides to make a report. If this therapist approached you for consultation, what suggestions would you give her? What are your views about this case?

Confidentiality and HIV/AIDS-Related Issues

AIDS affects a large population with diverse demographics and will continue to gain prominence as a public health and social issue. All mental-health practitioners will inevitably come in contact with people who have AIDS, with people who have tested positive as carriers of the virus, or with people who are close to these victims.

People who have tested HIV-positive (and those who have contracted AIDS) are usually in need of short-term help. They need to find a system to support them through the troubled times they will endure. Those who are

HIV-positive live with the anxiety of wondering whether they will come down with this incurable disease. Most also struggle with the stigma attached to AIDS. They live in fear not only of developing a life-threatening disease but also of being discovered and rejected by society and by friends and loved ones. In addition to feeling different and stigmatized, they typically have a great deal of anger, which is likely to be directed toward others, especially those who have given them the virus. Those at risk are often angry at health professionals as well. Because such clients are particularly vulnerable to being ostracized and suffering discrimination, it is critical that professionals obtain their informed consent and educate them about their rights and responsibilities.

Therapists need to be very clear in their own minds about the limits of confidentiality, matters of reporting, and their duty to warn and to protect third parties, and they need to communicate their professional responsibilities to their clients from the outset. If therapists decide that they cannot provide competent services to HIV-infected people, it is ethically appropriate that they refer these clients to professionals who can provide assistance. We recommend that you review the earlier discussion in this chapter regarding the therapist's duty to warn and to protect as it applies to people who have AIDS or are HIV-positive.

As a counselor you may indeed work with clients who are HIV-positive. You might accept a client and establish a therapeutic relationship, only to find out months later that this person had recently tested positive. If this were the case, would it be ethical to terminate the professional relationship and make a referral? Would the ethical course be to become informed so that you could provide competent help? What would be in the best interests of your client? If you are counseling HIV-positive individuals, do you have a duty both to your clients and to their sexual partners? Do you have a responsibility to warn and protect third parties in cases of those who are infected? As you think about these questions, we hope you will consider your ethical responsibilities to respond to this population before you encounter possible difficult situations. The three cases described here are designed to help you clarify your position on the ethical dimensions of counseling clients who have AIDS or are HIV-positive.

◆ ***The case of Al and Wilma.*** Al and Wilma are seeing Sarina for marital counseling. After a number of sessions Wilma requests an individual session, in which she discloses that she has tested HIV-positive as a result of several extramarital alliances. Sarina finds herself in a real dilemma: She has concerns for the welfare of the couple, but she is also concerned about Wilma's painful predicament, especially because Wilma has a sincere desire to make her marriage work. Part of Sarina's quandary is that she did not tell the couple her policy about handling confidentiality for private sessions.

◆ Does Sarina have a duty to warn Al? Why, or why not?
◆ Would such a duty supersede any implied confidentiality of the private session?
◆ What are some of the potential ethical violations in the manner in which Sarina handled this case?

◆ Would it be more therapeutic for Sarina to persuade Wilma to disclose her condition to Al rather than taking the responsibility for this disclosure herself? *Yes*

◆ If Wilma refused to inform her husband, should Sarina discontinue therapy with the couple? If she were to discontinue working with them, how might she ethically explain her decision? *duty to warn/protect*

◆ If she felt obligated to continue therapy with the couple, how would she handle the secret, and what would be the ethical implications of her practices? *compromised*

◆ Are there factors in this situation that would compel Sarina to treat Wilma's secret differently from other major secrets in couples therapy?

The case of Paddy. Paddy has been seeing a counselor for several months to deal with his depression. He comes to one session in a state of extreme anxiety. He has been in a gay relationship with Christopher for 15 years. On a recent business trip Paddy had a sexual encounter with another man. Paddy is now worried that he may have contracted the HIV virus, but he refuses to be tested. He is terrified of confirming his fear that he is HIV-positive. The counselor encourages Paddy to challenge his fears and be tested. He also encourages him to discuss this matter with Christopher. Paddy steadfastly refuses to consider either of the counselor's suggestions. When the counselor asks Paddy what he wants from him, he replies that he wants to be reassured that he is merely overreacting. He also would like to get over feeling depressed most of the time.

◆ What are the ethical dilemmas in this case?

◆ Are there any legal ramifications?

◆ How would you work with Paddy? Would you try to convince him to be tested, and would this be ethical? Would you try to persuade him to tell Christopher, and would your persuasion be ethical? *yes*

◆ What kind of referral might you make? What if Paddy refused a referral you suggested but insisted on continuing to see you? *I cannot unless...*

◆ How would you help him achieve his stated goal for seeing you? Do you have enough information to accomplish that goal? *not yet.*

◆ What values of yours might come into play in dealing with this situation?

◆ If Paddy consented to being tested and was found to be HIV-positive but still refused to disclose this fact to his partner, what ethical and legal concerns would now come into play? How would you proceed with this new information?

◆ If Paddy did not have a life-threatening disease but instead contracted a sexually transmitted disease (genital herpes), would your course of action be any different? If so, how might you proceed differently?

The case of Hershel. Hershel is a vice-president in a large company. He is married and has young children. Hershel's job necessitates transcontinental travel several times a year. During these trips he spends time with a lover. On his last trip she confided that one of the men that she had recently been sexually involved with had received an HIV-positive diagnosis. Hershel is panic stricken and seeks the help of a counselor, Blanche, who immediately recommends that he be tested. He follows her recommendation, and his test results are negative. He is elated and now sees no reason to continue therapy. Blanche makes no attempt to persuade him to explore other issues. She has no expertise in the treatment of AIDS clients and lacks essential knowledge pertaining to the latest AIDS research.

- Blanche appeared to take the ethical course in suggesting that Hershel be tested for AIDS, but was one test sufficient? What else needed to be done? *flips*
- Given this therapist's level of knowledge about AIDS, should she have referred Hershel? *yes*
- Although he was symptom-free and may not have transmitted the virus to his wife, there is a chance that he could be carrying the virus and that symptoms might not develop until much later. Given these facts, do you think that he presented a clear and imminent danger to his wife or to other sexual partners? *yes, yes*
- Did the therapist have a duty to warn his wife of the potential life-threatening situation to which she was exposed? *yes, but it is not the 1st step,*
- Did the therapist have a duty to notify the authorities, and if so, which authorities? *(circled) %*

- If Hershel had disclosed to Blanche that he and his wife were planning on having more children, how might that have affected the complexity of this case? *greatly*
- Did Blanche have an obligation to persuade him to discontinue his potentially life-threatening behavior?
- Did Blanche have an obligation to get him to discuss the matter with his wife because of the risk to her health? *yes*
- If Hershel had come to see you, what course of action would you have taken?

Ethical and Legal Considerations in AIDS-Related Cases

In the past few years much has been written about the conditions under which confidentiality might be breached in AIDS-related therapy situations. Up to now, courts have not applied the duty to warn to cases involving HIV infection, and therapists' legal responsibility in protecting sexual partners of HIV-positive clients remains unclear. Practitioners have few legal guidelines to help them determine when or how to inform a potential victim of the threat of HIV transmission (Erickson, 1993). Despite the lack of legal guidance on this issue, Erickson contends that there is some basis to consider this an exception to confidentiality issue. Calculated risks can be taken to ensure that unsuspecting individuals are protected from the definite possibility of infection by a contagious, fatal disease.

    In the last revision of its ethics code, ACA (1995) added a guideline pertaining to the ethical responsibility of practitioners who might deal with HIV-positive clients who are unwilling to inform their sexual or needle-sharing partners of their HIV status. ACA's standard pertaining to contagious, fatal diseases reads: "A counselor who receives information confirming that a client has a disease commonly known to be both communicable and fatal is justified in disclosing information to an identifiable third party, who by his or her relationship with the client is at a high risk of contracting the disease. Prior to making a disclosure the counselor should ascertain that the client has not already informed the third party about his or her disease and that the client is not intending to inform the third party in the immediate future" (B.1.d.).

Duty to protect versus confidentiality.   Earlier in this chapter we discussed the principles involved in situations where therapists may have a duty to warn and to protect innocent victims. The literature reveals some attempts at applying the *Tarasoff* decision to AIDS-related cases (Ahia & Martin, 1993; Cohen, 1997; Erickson, 1993; Gray & Harding, 1988; Hoffman, 1991a; Knapp & VandeCreek, 1990; Lamb, Clark, Drumheller, Frizzell, & Surrey, 1989; McGuire, Nieri, Abbott, Sheridan, & Fisher, 1995; Melton, 1988, 1991; Morrison, 1989; Totten, Lamb, & Reeder, 1990). The duty to warn and to protect may arise when a counselor has reason to believe that an HIV-positive client intends to continue to have unprotected sex, or to share needles, with unsuspecting but reasonably identifiable third parties (Ahia & Martin, 1993).

The HIV-positive duty to warn decision is one of the more controversial and emotion-laden issues practitioners might encounter. The complexity of this issue and a corresponding lack of case law may account for the large number of calls for help to the APA office on AIDS (Werth & Carney, 1994). For practitioners who work with HIV-positive clients, the choice is often between protecting the client-therapist relationship and breaching confidentiality to protect at-risk populations. This situation can put practitioners in a moral, ethical, legal, and professional dilemma. The duty to warn and to protect third parties is especially difficult because counselors face not only ethical and legal issues surrounding confidentiality of client communications but also specific statutory prohibitions against disclosure of HIV information (Ahia & Martin, 1993; VandeCreek & Knapp, 1994).

State laws differ regarding HIV and the limits of confidentiality. Oftentimes these state laws are different for medical professionals than for licensed psychotherapists. According to Pennsylvania law, therapists may not break confidentiality to warn that a client poses a threat to others through HIV/AIDS. Instead, therapists are expected to persuade clients to change their behaviors voluntarily (VandeCreek & Knapp, 1994). Some state laws forbid any disclosure of HIV status to third parties, and others allow some disclosure to at-risk third parties by physicians and psychiatrists but not by other mental-health professionals. Under many state laws, therapists who disclose a person's HIV-status to an unauthorized third party are subject to criminal charges and to malpractice action as well. Other states have yet to address this issue by statute.

Melton (1988) believes that the core ethical and legal issue is the duty to protect third parties from HIV infection with minimal violation of the client's privacy. Cohen (1997) contends that the HIV dilemma can be resolved by referring to legal precedent, state statutes, and professional codes of ethics. Counselors who disclose information about their client's HIV status to endangered third parties will break client-counselor confidentiality. However, counselors who keep this confidentiality may fail to prevent serious and preventable harm to the third party. Cohen proposes these ethical guidelines for deciding when to disclose confidential information about a client's HIV status:

- when there are sufficient factual grounds for considering risk of harm to the third party to be high
- when the third party is at risk of death or substantial bodily harm
- when the harm to the third party is not likely to be prevented unless the counselor makes the disclosure
- when the third party cannot reasonably be expected to foresee or comprehend the high risk of harm to self

Because preserving client confidentiality is a serious moral, ethical, and legal obligation, Cohen states that the case for breaching confidentiality must be strong before disclosure is justifiable.

Do Tarasoff principles apply in AIDS-related psychotherapy?

McGuire and colleagues (1995) assert that *Tarasoff* guidelines may be helpful in identifying critical factors in the ethical dilemma of having a client who is HIV-positive and who refuses to disclose his or her HIV status or otherwise warn sexual partners. They suggest that therapists should be extremely cautious regarding breaching confidentiality and should first consider less intrusive means of dealing with HIV-positive clients who indicate that they are not using safe sex practices and are not warning their partners of their HIV status. Several researchers have addressed breaching confidentiality related to the danger to others posed by HIV-positive clients (Ahia & Martin, 1993; Erickson, 1993; McGuire et al., 1995; Lamb et al., 1989). They provide these recommendations for therapists:

- All limits to confidentiality should be discussed with the client at the onset of treatment. When this is done early in the therapeutic relationship, it is less likely that therapists will lose clients because of breaching confidentiality. The implications of disclosing confidentiality, as well as other alternatives, can be explored with HIV-infected clients within the counseling context at this time.
- Therapists must be aware of the state laws regarding their professional interactions with HIV-positive clients and know the HIV confidentiality law of their state. Therapists should be aware that some state laws prohibit warning identifiable third parties of partners who are HIV-positive.
- Therapists need to keep current with regard to relevant medical information related to the transmission of HIV, know which sexual practices are safe and

which are not, and encourage their clients to practice safe sex. Because sharing a contaminated needle is another major means of HIV transmission, therapists should be up to date on approaches to drug education.

- Practitioners can seek training for intervening in the crises facing HIV-positive clients and those with AIDS.
- Therapists need to be aware of their own attitudes, biases, and prejudices as they relate to individuals who are at a higher risk of becoming infected.
- Therapists should speak directly and openly with their clients about their concerns regarding the danger of certain behaviors and the risk to third parties. They can use the therapeutic process to educate their clients as to the effects their behavior can have on others, teach safe sex practices, obtain commitments from the client to notify partners, and offer help in communicating information to partners.
- If the client continues to resist using safe sex practices or refuses to inform partners, then the therapist needs to determine what course of action to follow.
- Practitioners should consult with knowledgeable peers or attorneys, or both, to determine that their intended course of action is ethically and legally sound.
- If all other options have been exhausted and the therapist has decided to breach confidentiality by warning an identified partner, the client should generally be informed of this intention and the therapist should attempt to obtain the client's permission.
- In disclosing HIV information, therapists need to follow the statutory guidelines and safeguard the client's privacy as much as possible.

Several writers have applied *Tarasoff* as a framework for examining decisions about breaking confidentiality and protecting third parties (Lamb et al., 1989; McGuire et al., 1995; Totten et al., 1990). Therapists have a duty to protect when the following three conditions are met:

- There must be a *special client-therapist relationship* that entails the practitioner's responsibility for the safety of the client and also of other parties whom the therapist knows to be threatened by the client.

- *Clear and imminent danger* must exist. It is important to be certain that the client is HIV-positive. The degree of dangerousness of a client who has tested HIV-positive depends on several factors: the client's medical diagnosis, the extent to which the person engages in high-risk behaviors, and the use of safe sex techniques aimed at reducing the chances of transmission of the virus. Assessing dangerousness calls for an in-depth discussion of the client's drug use and sexual practices.

- There must be an *identifiable victim.* The duty to protect would probably extend to partners of an exclusive relationship but would not include anonymous partners unknown to the therapist. HIV-positive clients may have been sexually involved with many people in the past and may now have multiple sexual partners. This matter is complicated by the fact that the virus can remain dormant for years. Who are the potential victims? How should the therapist decide whom to inform?

Totten and her colleagues (1990) found that some clinicians used the criteria of degree of dangerousness and identifiability of a third party in determining when to break confidentiality. These researchers found that dangerousness appeared to be a more relevant factor than identifiability of a victim. Those clinicians who had had professional contact with people with HIV or AIDS were less likely to favor breaking confidentiality than those practitioners who had not had such contact.

If an HIV-infected individual is engaging in high-risk behavior with an identifiable, unsuspecting partner, then it appears that the three criteria under the *Tarasoff* decision may be met. However, many states have not adopted *Tarasoff*, which places the professional responsibility on each practitioner to examine his or her personal and professional values in weighing the ethical, legal, and moral implications of any proposed course of action.

Special Training on HIV-Related Issues

Hoffman (1991b), who describes approaches to training mental-health counselors to respond to the AIDS crisis, begins with the premise that all counselors will eventually work in some capacity with people who are affected by it. We think that mental-health professionals have an ethical obligation to be knowledgeable about the disease so they can ask the right questions. You can start by reading about AIDs-related issues and by attending a workshop on the subject. You can also contact one of the clinics being started all over the country, which are useful resources for treatment and referrals. In many communities, groups of volunteers have been organized to work with AIDS clients.

Werth and Carney (1994) emphasize the importance of incorporating HIV-related issues into graduate student training. They cite several surveys that show that most students are not receiving HIV-related training in their graduate programs and are unprepared to handle ethical, legal, and professional issues pertaining to HIV situations. Specifically, on the topic of the duty to protect versus confidentiality, they find the reaction of their students is to breach confidentiality too soon, without giving adequate consideration to other alternatives or to the potential consequences. In training students in this area, Werth and Carney introduce several discussion activities. They review case scenarios, discuss the implications of the *Tarasoff* case, and review ethical and legal cases. They pose the following questions for discussion:

- ◆ What is the therapist's role (watchdog, change agent, client advocate)?
- ◆ To whom does the therapist have a primary responsibility?
- ◆ How is this situation similar or different from the *Tarasoff* case?
- ◆ What options and courses of action are available?
- ◆ Where can the therapist go for consultation?

In addition to exploring these issues, Werth and Carney provide other examples of content areas they believe should be infused into graduate training: assessment and diagnosis, counseling diverse populations, and research design.

Erickson (1993) puts the challenge to the profession well when she writes: "Society must come to view AIDS as a deadly disease, rather than a stigma, and must grapple with the legal and ethical issues involved. But, until society responds, and clear legal and ethical guidelines are established, each mental-health counselor must carefully consider all pertinent professional issues and then make an individual decision for appropriate action" (pp. 129–130).

In summary, dealing responsibly with the dilemmas posed in this section demands an awareness of the ethical, legal, and clinical issues involved in working with clients with AIDS and AIDS-related disorders. There are no simple solutions to the many complex issues practitioners may face, and this topic is surely one of the more challenging ones. Consulting with colleagues is an excellent practice that can help you make appropriate decisions.

Chapter Summary

Along with their duties to clients, therapists also have responsibilities to their agency, to their profession, to the community, to the members of their clients' families, and to themselves. Ethical dilemmas arise when there are conflicts between responsibilities. Members of the helping professions should know and observe the ethical codes of their professional organizations and make sound judgments that are within the parameters of acceptable practice. We have encouraged you to think about specific ethical issues and to develop a sense of professional ethics and knowledge of state laws so that your judgment will be based on more than what "feels right."

Court decisions have provided an expanded perspective on the therapist's duty to protect the public. As a result of the *Tarasoff* case, therapists are now becoming aware of their responsibility to the potential victims of a client's violent behavior. This duty spans interventions from warnings to threatened individuals to involuntary commitment of clients. Therapists are vulnerable to malpractice action when they demonstrate negligent failure to diagnose dangerousness, negligent failure to warn a known victim once such a diagnosis has been made, negligent failure to commit a dangerous person, or negligent failure to keep a dangerous client committed.

Therapists also have a duty to protect clients who are likely to injure or kill themselves. Practitioners must develop skills in making accurate assessments of potentially suicidal persons. Once a client is diagnosed as a danger to himself or herself, the therapist is responsible for preventing suicide by acting in professionally acceptable ways. A dissenting opinion on this issue is that of Szasz (1986), who challenges the assumption that therapists should be held accountable for a client's decision to die. He believes that suicide is an ultimate right and responsibility of the client and that it is unethical for therapists to employ coercive measures aimed at preventing it.

All states have laws that require professionals to report child abuse whenever they suspect or discover it in the course of their professional activities. Clients have a right to know that therapists are legally and ethically bound to breach confidentiality in situations involving child abuse.

The duty to protect has also been applied to HIV/AIDS cases. Because state laws vary on breaching confidentiality to warn victims of a client's HIV status, practitioners are advised to know their state laws and to consult professional colleagues, and perhaps an attorney, before they take the action of informing an identified partner of an HIV-infected client. This should be the last option, implemented only after less obtrusive measures have failed.

Suggested Activities

1. In small groups discuss the cases and guidelines presented in this chapter on the duty to protect victims from violent clients. If you found yourself faced with a potentially dangerous client, what specific steps might you take to carry out this duty?
2. Structure a class debate around the arguments for and against suicide prevention. Failure to prevent suicide is one of the main grounds for successful malpractice suits against mental-health professionals and institutions (Szasz, 1986). Consider debating a specific case of a client who is terminally ill with AIDS and decides that he wants to end his life because of his suffering and because there is no hope of getting better. Divide the class into teams for an exchange on the therapist's responsibility to prevent this suicide.
3. Ask several students to investigate the laws of your state pertaining to confidentiality and privileged communication and present their findings to the class. What kinds of mental-health providers in your state can offer their clients privileged communication? What are the exceptions to this privilege? Under what circumstances are you legally required to breach confidentiality? Regarding confidentiality in counseling minors, what state laws should you know?
4. In small groups discuss specific circumstances in which you would break confidentiality, and see whether you can agree on some general guidelines.
5. Discuss some ways in which you can prepare clients for issues pertaining to confidentiality. How can you teach clients about the purposes of confidentiality and the legal restrictions on it? Examine how you would do this in various situations, such as school, group work, marital and family counseling, and counseling with minors.
6. In a class debate, have one side take the position that absolute confidentiality is necessary to promote full client disclosure. The other side can argue for a limited confidentiality that still promotes effective therapy.

Chapter

6

Issues in Theory, Practice, and Research

◆ *Pre-Chapter Self-Inventory*

◆ *Introduction*

◆ *Developing a Counseling Stance*

◆ *The Division of Responsibility in Therapy*

◆ *Deciding on the Goals of Counseling*

◆ *Diagnosis as a Professional Issue*

◆ *Using Tests in Counseling*

◆ *The Use of Techniques in Counseling and Therapy*

◆ *Ethical Issues in Psychotherapeutic Research*

◆ *Chapter Summary*

◆ *Suggested Activities*

Pre-Chapter Self-Inventory

Directions: For each statement, indicate the response that most closely identifies your beliefs and attitudes. Use the following code:

5 = I *strongly agree* with this statement.
4 = I *agree* with this statement.
3 = I am *undecided* about this statement.
2 = I *disagree* with this statement.
1 = I *strongly disagree* with this statement.

__4__ 1. I should adhere to a definite theory of counseling.

__3__ 2. I would rather combine insights and techniques derived from various
theoretical approaches to counseling than base my practice on a single
model.

__4__ 3. People are basically capable of and responsible for changing their
behaviors.

__3__ 4. What happens in counseling sessions is more my responsibility than it
is my client's.

__4__ 5. I would find it difficult to work for an agency if I were expected to perform functions that I didn't think were appropriate to counseling.

__4__ 6. I should have the power to define my own role and professional identity as a counselor.

__4__ 7. Clients should always select the goals of counseling.

__4__ 8. I'd be willing to work with clients who didn't seem to have any clear
goals or reasons for seeking counseling.

__4__ 9. Competent diagnosis is necessary for planning appropriate treatment.

__2__ 10. The drawbacks associated with diagnosis in counseling outweigh the
values.

__4__ 11. Testing can be a very useful adjunct to counseling.

__2__ 12. The medical model of mental health can be applied effectively in counseling and psychotherapy.

__4__ 13. The theory I hold and the techniques I employ must be compatible
with the demands of a managed care system.

__4__ 14. Skill in using a variety of techniques is one of the most important qualities of a therapist.

__2__ 15. Theories of counseling can limit counselors by encouraging them to
pay attention only to behavior that fits their particular theory.

__4__ 16. Counselors should develop and modify their own theory of counseling as they practice.

__2__ 17. There are major shortcomings in applying most of the contemporary
counseling theories to diverse ethnic and cultural groups, such as
Asian Americans, Latinos, Native Americans, and African Americans.

__4__ 18. Although people are not responsible for creating their problems, I
believe they are responsible for finding ways to deal effectively with
these problems.

4 19. It can be unethical for practitioners to fail to do some type of assessment and diagnosis, especially with high-risk (suicidal or dangerous) patients.

4 20. It is critical to take cultural factors into consideration in assessment and diagnosis if the therapist hopes to gather accurate data and come up with a valid perspective on a client.

Introduction

Professional counselors need to be able to conceptualize what they are doing in their counseling sessions and why they are doing it. Too often practitioners are unable to explain why they use certain counseling procedures. When you meet a new client, for example, what guidelines would you use in structuring your first interview? What do you want to accomplish at this initial session? Rank in order of importance the following factors that you would be interested in knowing about your client:

✓ the presenting problem (the reason the client is seeking counseling)
___ the client's style of coping with demands, stresses, and conflicts
___ early experiences as a child, particularly in relation to parents and siblings
___ ego strength
___ functional strengths and weaknesses
___ history of successes and failures
✓ developmental history
___ the client's struggle with current choices
✓ the client's cultural background
___ goals and agenda for counseling
___ current support system
___ motivation to change
___ level of reality testing

In this chapter we focus on how therapists' theoretical positions and conceptual biases influence their actual practice. Ideally, theory should help you make sense of what you do in your counseling sessions. Another way of thinking about this issue is to imagine a client asking you to explain your view of counseling in clear and simple terms. Could you tell your client what you most hoped to accomplish and how you would go about it? Ethical practice is grounded in a solid theoretical and research base. Practitioners who operate in a theoretical vacuum, with little or no interest in the practical applications of psychotherapeutic research, may be engaging in ethically questionable behavior.

You might consider how open you are to challenging your theoretical stance and how this openness or lack of it might influence the therapeutic outcome for your clients. Think about how your theoretical viewpoint influences your stand on questions such as these: What are some goals for counseling? What is the proper place of diagnosis and testing in the counseling process?

Explain your view of counseling briefly

What techniques are most appropriate in reaching certain goals of counseling? In your assessment and treatment of clients, how do you make provisions for cultural diversity? What is the place of research in counseling practice? In what ways are issues pertaining to theory, practice, and research interrelated?

Developing a Counseling Stance

Developing a counseling stance is more complicated than merely accepting the tenets of a given theory. We believe that the theoretical approach you use to guide your practice is an expression of your uniqueness as a person and an outgrowth of your life experience. Further, because a theory of counseling is often an expression of the personality of the theorist, we believe that a theoretical approach becomes more useful and meaningful after you've taken a critical look at the theorist who developed it as well as its key concepts. Blindly following any single theory can lead you to ignore some of the insights that your life opens up to you. This is our bias, of course, and many would contend that providing effective therapy depends on following a given theory. Ultimately your counseling stance must be appropriate for the type of counseling you do and the unique needs of your clients.

Theories of counseling are based on worldviews, each with its own values, biases, and assumptions of how best to bring about change in the therapeutic process (Ivey, Ivey, & Simek-Morgan, 1997). Contemporary theories of therapeutic practice are grounded in assumptions that are part of Western culture, and they emphasize choice, the uniqueness of the individual, self-assertion, and ego strength. Many of these assumptions are inappropriate for evaluating clients from non-Western cultures. By contrast, some non-Western cultures focus on interdependence, downplay individuality, and emphasize losing oneself in the totality of the cosmos. From an Asian perspective, for example, basic life values are associated with a focus on inner experience and an acceptance of one's environment.

Whereas the Western therapeutic approaches are oriented toward individual change, non-Western approaches focus more on the social framework than on development of the individual. The Western model of therapy has limitations when it is applied to many ethnic and cultural groups, such as Asian Americans, Latinos, Native Americans, and African Americans. It is not customary for many client populations to seek professional help, and they will typically turn first to informal systems (family, friends, community).

D. W. Sue, Ivey, and Pedersen (1996) write that because there are shortcomings in contemporary theories of counseling and psychotherapy there is a need to develop a theory of multicultural counseling and therapy that addresses all aspects of human behavior. In addition to dealing with the feeling, thinking, and behaving dimensions familiar to Western theorists, a multicultural approach emphasizes the social and cultural facets of human existence. This approach takes into account that we are all biological, spiritual, and political beings as well.

So it is! for us to look critically at a counseling theory in order to make it authentically my own.

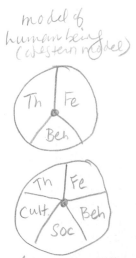

model of human being (western model)

(multicult. model)

When developing or evaluating a theory, a major consideration is the degree to which that perspective helps you understand what you're doing with clients. Does your framework provide a broad base for working with diverse clients in different ways, or does it restrict your vision and cause you to ignore variables that don't fit the theory? Are you able to make the culture of the client a central variable in your counseling approach? If you hold steadfastly to one theory, you might expect your clients to conform to your expectations. It's important, therefore, to evaluate what you are emphasizing in your counseling work. The following questions may help you make this evaluation:

◆ Where did you acquire your theory? Did you incorporate many of the views of your instructors or training supervisors? Has one theory intrigued you to the point that it is the sole basis for your orientation?

◆ Does your theory evolve and change as you gain clinical experience with a variety of clients?

◆ Do you embrace a particular theory because it is a justification of your own experiences and values? For instance, do you adopt a theory that stresses an active, didactic role for the therapist because you see your role as prescriptive? What does your approach stress, and why does it appeal to you?

◆ To what degree does your theory challenge your own previous frame of reference? Does it cause you to test your hypotheses, beliefs, and assumptions? Does it encourage you to think of alternatives? To what degree does your theory reinforce your present worldview? Does it force you to extend your thinking, or does it merely support your biases?

◆ Does your theory make room for cultural factors? Can you apply your theory to a wide range of clients, many of whom will have different expectations in seeking help? Does the range of interventions available to you based on your theoretical orientation accommodate cultural diversity?

◆ How do your own life experiences influence your counseling style? In what ways have your life experiences caused you to modify your theoretical viewpoint?

◆ What are the ethical implications for a counselor practicing without a theoretical orientation? Does ethical practice demand having a rationale for the interventions you make?

Your assumptions about the nature of counseling and the nature of people have a direct impact on your manner of practice. The goals that you think are important in therapy, the techniques and methods you employ to reach these goals, the way in which you see the division of responsibility in the client-therapist relationship, your view of your role and functions as a counselor, and your view of the place of diagnosis and testing in the therapeutic process are all largely determined by your theoretical orientation.

Practicing counseling without an explicit theoretical rationale is somewhat like flying a plane without a map and without instruments. A theoretical orientation (or a counseling stance) is not a rigid structure that prescribes specific steps of what to do in a counseling situation; rather, it is a set of general guidelines that counselors can use to make sense of what they are doing.

The Division of Responsibility in Therapy

Many beginning counselors deprive their clients of their rightful responsibility for their therapy by anxiously taking too much of this responsibility on themselves. If clients don't progress fast enough, these counselors may blame themselves for not knowing enough, not having the necessary skill and experience, or not being sensitive or caring enough. They may worry constantly about their adequacy as counselors and transmit this anxiety to their clients. If only they were better therapists, their clients would be changing in more positive directions. This may be true, of course, but overly anxious counselors frequently fail to see the role their clients play in the outcome of their own therapy, whether for better or for worse.

Counselors do well to bring up the question of responsibility during the initial sessions, allowing clients to begin thinking about their part in their own therapy. One way to clarify the sharing of responsibility in a therapeutic relationship is by a contract. A contract is based on a negotiation between the client and the therapist to define the therapeutic relationship. A contract, which can be an extension of the informed consent process discussed in Chapter 4, tends to encourage the client and the therapist to specify the goals of the therapy and the methods likely to be employed in obtaining these goals. Other aspects of a contract include the length and frequency of sessions, the duration of therapy, the cost and method of payment, provisions for renegotiating the contract, any factors limiting confidentiality, the extent of responsibility for each partner, and ways of determining the effectiveness of the therapeutic relationship. If you work within a managed care system, the HMO or PPO provider determines many of these issues, including what kinds of problems are acceptable for treatment, how long treatment will last, the number of sessions, and the focus of the work. Under this system, practitioners must be accountable to the managed care company by demonstrating that specific objectives have been met. At the very least, therapists need to discuss with clients how being involved with managed care will influence the division of responsibility among the HMO, the client, and the therapist.

From our own perspective, therapy is a joint venture of the client and the therapist. Both have serious responsibilities for the direction of therapy, and this needs to be clarified during the initial stages of counseling. Counselors who typically decide what to discuss and are overdirective run the risk of perpetuating their clients' dependence. Clients should be encouraged from the start to assume as much responsibility as they can. Directive therapies, such as the cognitive-behavioral approaches, emphasize client-initiated contracts and homework assignments as ways in which clients can fulfill their commitment to change. These devices help to keep the focus of responsibility on the clients by challenging them to decide what they want from therapy and what they are willing to do to get what they want.

As you consider the range of viewpoints on the division of responsibility in therapy, think about your own position on this issue. What is your responsibility, both to your client and to yourself? What do you expect from your client? Do you burden yourself with the total responsibility for what happens in therapy?

◆ ***The case of Ivan.***   Ivan is a member of a weekly group. At the sixteenth meeting he unexpectedly tells the group that he has often thought of suicide, although he has never developed a detailed plan. But suicide is weighing heavily on his mind, and it frightens him. Consider three possible responses that a group leader could make to Ivan:

Counselor A: This is a surprise. I'd like you to tell me more about what's going on in your life now. Perhaps you can address the members in the group and give each person a reason why life isn't worth living. This will give you an opportunity to explore at a deeper level the meaning of your suicidal thinking. [At the end of the session, the therapist adds] Ivan, you are ultimately responsible for your life, but I'd like to make myself available to you to explore and understand what you are experiencing. I think you could also use this group as a tool to help you in this struggle.

Counselor B: Ivan, this is news to me! I'm very willing to work with you on your suicidal ideation, but I hold you responsible for your life. If you choose to kill yourself, that is your responsibility. If you choose to challenge yourself and live, that, too, is your responsibility. I refuse to burden myself with the responsibility of your life.

Counselor C: Ivan, this really surprises me! If I'd known this, I wouldn't have put you in the group. I'd like to switch you from group treatment to individual treatment twice a week. Furthermore, I'll check in with you by telephone every day, and I'd like you to call me at any time if you become frightened by your impulses. Perhaps later on, when you have worked through this problem, you may be able to be in a group again.

In reviewing these three approaches, consider your own stand:

◆ Are any legal issues involved in this case? If so, what are they?
◆ Which approach are you most likely to take, and why?
◆ Imagine yourself as Ivan. Which of these approaches would you find most helpful? least helpful? Why?
◆ How can this case help you formulate your own ideas about the division of responsibility in counseling?

Deciding on the Goals of Counseling

Aimless therapy is unlikely to be effective, yet too often practitioners fail to devote enough time to thinking about the goals they have for their clients and the goals clients have for themselves. In this section we discuss possible aims of therapy, how goals are determined, and who should determine them. Counselors' answers to these questions are directly related to their theoretical orientations.

When considering therapeutic goals, it is important to keep in mind the cultural determinants of therapy. The aims of therapy are specific to a particular culture's definition of psychological health. In describing their theory of multicultural counseling and therapy, D. W. Sue, Ivey, and Pedersen (1996) develop a number of propositions that are considered to be basic assumptions underlying their metatheory. Two of these assumptions have particular relevance for the topic of therapeutic goals. Sue and his colleagues claim that multicultural counseling is more effective when counselors use modalities and define goals that are consistent with the life experiences and cultural values of the client. They stress that no single approach is equally effective in working with all client populations. The ultimate goal of training practitioners to be mulitculturally competent, regardless of their theoretical orientation, is to expand the range of therapeutic strategies they can apply to culturally diverse client groups. A second proposition of their multicultural theory pertains to its basic goal, which is the liberation of consciousness. This approach goes beyond the limitations of the traditional goals of Western psychotherapy and emphasizes the family, group, and cultural aspects of counseling. Ultimately, this theory considers the person-in-relation and the cultural context as essential aspects in developing appropriate goals for the helping process.

In most counseling approaches, effective counseling does not result when the therapist imposes goals; rather, goals should be set by the client and the therapist working together. However, some therapists believe that they know what is best for their clients and try to persuade their clients to accept certain goals. Others are convinced that the specific aims of counseling ought to be determined entirely by their clients. Who sets the goals of counseling must be seen in the light of the theory you operate from, the type of counseling you offer, the setting in which you work, and the nature of your clientele. Your theoretical orientation influences generic goals, such as insight versus behavior change, and if you are not clear about your general goals, your techniques will be random and arbitrary.

Other factors can also affect the determination of goals. For example, if you work with clients in a managed care system, the goals will need to be highly specific, limited to reduction of problematic symptoms, and often aimed at teaching coping skills. If you work in crisis intervention, your goals are likely to be short term and practical, and you may be very directive. If you're working with children in a school, you may combine educational and therapeutic goals. As a counselor with elderly people in an institution, you may stress coping skills and ways of relating to others in this environment. What your goals are and how actively involved your client will be in determining them depend to a great extent on the type of counseling you provide and the type of client you see.

Diagnosis as a Professional Issue

Cognitive-behavioral therapies place heavy emphasis on the role of assessment as a prelude to the treatment process. The rationale is that specific therapy goals cannot be designed until a thorough picture of the client's past and present functioning is formed. Other theories, such as the relationship-oriented approaches, tend to view the process of assessment and diagnosis as external to the immediacy of the client-counselor relationship, a process that can remove the therapist from understanding the subjective world of the client. Both clinical and ethical issues are associated with the use of assessment procedures and diagnosis as part of a treatment plan.

Assessment consists of evaluating the relevant factors in a client's life to identify themes for further exploration in the counseling process. Diagnosis, which is sometimes part of the assessment process, consists of identifying a specific category of psychological or behavioral problem based on a pattern of symptoms. The main purpose of the diagnostic approach is to allow the therapist to plan treatments tailored to the special needs of the client. There are different kinds of diagnosis. *Medical diagnosis* is the process of examining physical symptoms, inferring causes of physical disorders or diseases, providing a category that fits the pattern of a disease, and prescribing an appropriate treatment. *Psychodiagnosis* (or *psychological diagnosis*) is a general term covering the process of identifying an emotional or behavioral problem and making a statement about the current status of a client. This process also includes identification of possible causes of the person's emotional, psychological, and behavioral difficulties, suggestions for appropriate therapy techniques to deal effectively with the identified problem, and estimates of the chances for a successful resolution. *Differential diagnosis* is the process of distinguishing one form of disease or psychological disorder from another by determining which of two (or more) diseases or disorders with similar symptoms the person is suffering from. The fourth edition of the American Psychiatric Association's (1994) *Diagnostic and Statistical Manual of Mental Disorders* (DSM-IV) is the standard reference for pathology. DSM-IV is the most exhaustive and widely used system for identifying, classifying, and describing mental and emotional disorders in the world (Wylie, 1995).

Whether diagnosis should be part of psychotherapy is a controversial issue. Some mental-health professionals see diagnosis as an essential step in any treatment plan, but others view it as an inappropriate application of the medical model of mental health to counseling and therapy:

> Psychologists' track record on assessment is the source of an ongoing debate. Many argue that in the last few decades the profession has developed new tools that have greatly heightened the precision of clinical assessment. Others assert that clinicians cloud their diagnoses with inflated confidence, personal biases and overreliance on their intuition. (Sleek, 1996, p. 30)

Some contend that clients in managed care systems can no longer trust their therapists' motives, so they are faced with making significant life decisions without professional guidance (Shore, 1996). The constant refrain of those who oppose a diagnostic model is that DSM labels and stigmatizes people; yet those who designed DSM assert that it classifies illnesses, not people (Wylie, 1995).

Although you may not yet have had to face the practical question of whether to diagnose a client, you will probably need to come to terms with this issue at some point in your work. Let's briefly review some of the arguments for and against the use of diagnosis in therapy. Then you can consider how valuable diagnosis is from your point of view.

Arguments for Psychodiagnosis

Practitioners who favor the use of diagnostic procedures in therapy generally argue that such procedures enable the therapist to acquire sufficient knowledge about the client's past and present behavior to develop an appropriate plan of treatment. Diagnosing a client can be likened to putting together a jigsaw puzzle—it involves piecing together small bits of information to build an overall picture of the individual (Sleek, 1996). This approach stems from the medical model of mental health, according to which different underlying causal factors produce different types of disorders.

Psychoanalytically oriented therapists favor psychodiagnosis, because this form of therapy was patterned after the medical model of mental health and stresses understanding the past situations that have contributed to a dysfunction. Some psychological assessment devices used in psychodiagnosis involve projective techniques that rest on psychoanalytic concepts.

For different reasons, practitioners with a behavioristic orientation also favor a diagnostic stance. Although they may not follow the medical model, these practitioners value observation and other objective means of appraising both a client's specific symptoms and the factors that have led up to the client's malfunctioning. Such an appraisal, they argue, enables them to use the techniques that are appropriate for a particular disorder and to evaluate the effectiveness of the treatment program.

Those who argue for the usefulness and necessity of diagnosis often make some of the following points:

- There is no third-party reimbursement without an acceptable diagnosis. For example, under a managed care system, formulating a diagnosis is a basic first step to qualify for further therapy sessions.
- As a prerequisite to being able to treat clients effectively, it is essential that an accurate diagnosis be established. It is difficult to formulate a meaningful treatment plan without clearly defining the specific problems that need to be addressed.
- To function effectively in most mental-health agencies, practitioners need to be skilled in understanding and utilizing diagnostic procedures.
- In working with a professional team, diagnosis is essential so that all team members have a common language and a common frame of reference.

- Diagnosis points the way to appropriate treatment strategies for specific disorders and is helpful in predicting the course of the disorder.
- Diagnosis allows therapists to rule out possible medical conditions as causes for psychological problems.
- Therapists have a legal, professional, and ethical obligation to assess whether clients may pose a danger to themselves or to others. They also need to screen for organic disorders, bipolar disorders, and psychotic states.
- Diagnosis provides a framework for research into various treatment approaches. Responsible delivery of psychological services depends on data-based clinical outcome studies; accurate diagnosis is necessary to these outcome studies.

In his article on ethical concerns about diagnosis, Hamann (1994) makes a case for the usefulness of diagnosis:

> When I take my car to the mechanic, I expect him or her not to fix my brakes if my transmission is faulty. If I go to my family doctor with a complaint of chest pain, I do not want him or her to treat me for a broken leg. In the same manner, I do not believe professionals providing clinical care can simply treat without first determining what is the problem. Clearly, treatment varies depending on the disorder. As clinicians we must be able to diagnose accurately before we can treat effectively. (p. 259)

In his experience with both public and private mental-health agencies, Hamann (1994) has found that all clinicians have the responsibility for diagnosing. Practitioners who work in an agency setting have the initial contact with most clients. They are expected to take a history as part of the intake session and must arrive at a diagnosis. Such clinicians often have a caseload of at least 100 clients, and they are expected to define the client's problem and develop a treatment plan to alleviate the problem—typically in one session. From Hamann's perspective, graduate programs involved in training therapists need to teach diagnosis. Because mental-health agencies assume that those they employ will be proficient in diagnosis, training programs have a responsibility to see that students acquire competence in understanding a diagnostic framework.

Brammer, Shostrom, and Abrego (1989) see diagnosis as being broader than simply labeling clients with some diagnostic category. They argue in favor of diagnosis as a general descriptive statement identifying a client's style of functioning. Such information can motivate clients to change their behavior. They contend that practitioners must make some decisions, do some therapeutic planning, and be alert for signs of pathology to avoid serious mistakes in therapy. They propose that a therapist "simultaneously understand diagnostically and understand therapeutically." In favoring this broad type of diagnostic process, which involves developing hunches, Brammer and his colleagues caution against accepting a narrow and rigid diagnostic approach.

Even though you may not find diagnosis necessary or useful in your practice, it may behoove you to know enough about diagnosis to refer a client.

For example, once you've made a diagnosis of a client who is chronically depressed with possible suicidal tendencies, you are in a position to make an appropriate referral if you do not have the competence to deal with this problem area.

Those who support traditional forms of diagnosis agree that present classification systems have limitations and that some of the problems mentioned by the critics of diagnosis do exist. Rather than abandoning diagnostic classifications altogether, however, they favor updating diagnostic manuals to reflect improvements in diagnosis and treatment procedures.

Arguments against Psychodiagnosis

Many professionals see diagnosis as an essential component of psychotherapy, but others view it as unnecessary or harmful. Rogers (1961) consistently maintained that diagnosis was detrimental to counseling because it tended to pull clients away from an internal and subjective way of experiencing themselves and to foster an objective and external conception about them. The result was an increased tendency toward dependence, with clients acting as if the responsibility for changing their behavior rested with the expert and not with themselves.

Client-centered therapy is grounded in the belief that clients are in the best position to understand and resolve their personal difficulties. Existential or relationship-oriented therapists generally fall into this group of clinicians who see diagnosis as being restrictive or who oppose diagnosis. Arguments against diagnosis include the following:

- Diagnosis is typically done by an expert observing a person's behavior and experience from an external viewpoint, without reference to what they mean to the client.
- Diagnostic categories can minimize the uniqueness of the client.
- Reducing people to the sum of their symptoms ignores natural capacities for self-healing.
- Because the emphasis of DSM is on pathology, deficits, limitations, problems, and symptoms, individuals are not encouraged to find and utilize their strengths, competencies, and abilities.
- Diagnosis can lead people to accept self-fulfilling prophecies or to despair over their condition.
- Diagnosis can narrow therapists' vision by encouraging them to look for behavior that fits a certain disease category.
- DSM is based on the assumption that distress in a family or social context is the result of individual pathology, whereas a systemic approach views the source of the distress as being within the entire system.
- Although DSM-IV makes some reference to ethnic, cultural, environmental, and class factors in understanding and interpreting dysfunctional behavior, it deals largely with culture-bound syndromes and does not adequately

take into account culture, age, gender, and other ways of viewing health and sickness.

◆ The best vantage point for understanding another person is through his or her subjective world, not through a general system of classification.

◆ Many therapists do not possess the competence to use DSM diagnosis appropriately.

Our Position on Assessment and Psychodiagnosis

We believe that both assessment and diagnosis, broadly construed, are legitimate parts of the therapeutic process. The kind of diagnosis we have in mind is the result of a joint effort by the client and the therapist. Both should be involved in discovering the nature of the client's difficulty, a process that commences with the initial sessions and continues until therapy is terminated. Even practitioners who oppose conventional diagnostic procedures and terminology unavoidably make an assessment of clients based on questions such as these:

◆ What is going on in this client's life at this time?

◆ What are the client's resources for change?

◆ What are the client's strengths and vulnerabilities?

◆ What does the client want from therapy, and how can it best be achieved?

◆ What should be the focus of the sessions?

◆ What factors are contributing to the client's problems, and what can be done to alleviate them?

◆ In what ways can an understanding of the client's cultural background shed light on developing a plan to deal with the problems?

◆ What specific family dynamics might be relevant to the client's present struggles and interpersonal relationships?

◆ What are the prospects for meaningful change?

From our perspective, diagnosis should be associated with treatment, and it should help the practitioner conceptualize a case. The counselor and the client can discuss key questions as part of the therapeutic process. Counselors will develop hypotheses about their clients, and they can talk about these conjectures with them. Diagnosis does not have to be a matter of categorizing clients; rather, counselors can describe behavior and think about its meaning. In this way, diagnosis becomes a process of thinking *about* the client *with* the client.

It is not so much a simple question of whether to diagnose or not. Using DSM-IV nomenclature is a reality that most practitioners must accept, especially if they work within a managed care system. For therapists who must work with a diagnostic framework, the challenge is to use diagnosis as a means to the end of providing quality service to clients rather than as an end in itself that leads to a justification for treatment. As one clinician put this struggle: "It's hard *not* to think in terms of DSM when I have to use it every day for managed care. The language seeps into my brain, into the way I look at clients, even when I know better" (Wylie, 1995, p. 68).

Clarifying your stance.   What is your position on diagnosis? The following questions may help you clarify your thinking on this issue:

◆ After reviewing the arguments for and against psychodiagnosis, what position do you tend to support? Why? *in favor / it can open up understanding*
◆ Some contend that clients have a right to know their diagnoses on the ground of informed consent, whereas others maintain that clients should not be told their diagnoses because of dangers of their living up to a self-fulfilling prophecy. What is your thinking on this matter?
◆ If you were working for an agency that relied on managed care programs, how would you deal with the requirement of quickly formulating a diagnosis and a treatment plan? How would you work with the limitations of being able to see clients for no more than six visits?
◆ Some writers have taken the position that practitioners should take a stand against classification and coding for the purpose of third-party payments unless clients know of their diagnoses and agree to provide this information to insurance companies. Do you see an ethical issue in this practice? *duty / upheld / views of / right to / privacy*
◆ Do you agree or disagree that therapists who do not accept the medical model, yet who provide diagnoses for reasons of third-party payments, are compromising their integrity? Are there any ethical issues here?
◆ What ethical and professional issues can you raise pertaining to diagnosis? In your view what is the most critical issue? *whether or not the client has a right to know*

Ethical and Legal Issues in Diagnosis

Ethical dilemmas are often created when diagnosis is done strictly for insurance purposes, which often entails arbitrarily assigning a client to a diagnostic classification, sometimes merely to qualify for third-party payment. Many insurance carriers will not pay for treatment that is not defined as an "illness" for which treatment is medically necessary. Wylie (1995) gives the example of the V-codes, a grab bag of diagnostic leftovers at the back of DSM-IV that rarely qualify for reimbursement. If a therapist treats a couple for marital difficulties and submits a claim with a V-code diagnosis, chances are that the claim will be rejected. Some therapists may agree to see a couple or a family but submit a claim for an individual as the "identified patient," using an acceptable DSM diagnosis. According to Wylie, not only is this practice technically unethical and inaccurate but it may be illegal. Wylie suggests an alternative approach:

> A more honest and possibly promising, but time-consuming, practice is to attempt to educate the managed care company about the value of systems therapy by providing, along with an individual DSM diagnosis, a comprehensive report detailing the impact of family, work and school factors on the individual presumably under treatment. (p. 33)

unethical ben

Hamann (1994) stresses that under no circumstances should clinicians compromise themselves regarding the accuracy of a diagnosis to make it "fit" criteria accepted by an insurance company. This behavior is not only unethical but is also fraudulent. Some practitioners who are opposed to a diagnostic framework take the path of least resistance and give every client the same diagnosis. A related matter is the fact that many insurance companies pay only for psychological services that have been approved under an acceptable diagnosis. Presumably, clients who consult therapists regarding problems that don't fit a standard category will not be reimbursed for their psychotherapy.

With some managed care mental-health companies, a therapist may call the company with a diagnosis. A technician then looks up "appropriate" treatment strategies to deal with the identified problem (if, indeed, the diagnosis even meets the criteria for reimbursement). This raises significant ethical issues. In such cases important treatment decisions may be made by a nonprofessional who has never seen the client.

this is the tight rope walk of the dx's + honest dx

Practitioners who submit claims to managed care companies must often wrestle with practical versus ethical decision making. If a therapist submits an honest diagnosis, but one not classified as an illness in DSM, there will be no reimbursement. However, if the diagnosis is selected mainly on the basis that it is one the company will accept, the therapist runs the risk of deceptive practice. "Therapists are forever trying to fit their diagnosis to the procrustean bed of official DSM terminology and managed care's interpretation of it" (Wylie, 1995, p. 32).

Competence is another central ethical issue in making assessments. If therapists do not understand how to work within a diagnostic framework, it is likely that they will develop inappropriate treatment plans. Unless practitioners have full diagnostic pictures of their clients, they cannot be certain that they are ethically providing the most appropriate treatment. For example, unless a practitioner knows that a client has had a manic episode, he or she may proceed incorrectly by treating depression alone. We also think it is an ethical (and sometimes legal) obligation of therapists to screen clients for life-threatening problems such as organic disorders, schizophrenia, manic-depression, and suicidal types of depression. Students need to learn the clinical skills necessary to do this type of screening, which is a form of diagnostic thinking.

Practitioners may bring harm to clients if they begin to treat their clients in restrictive ways because they have diagnosed them on the basis of a pattern of symptoms. Therapists can actually behave toward clients in ways that make it very difficult for the clients to change. Furthermore, it is essential that practitioners who use the DSM-IV be trained in its use. This training implies learning more than diagnostic categories; it involves knowing personality theory and seeing how it relates to therapeutic practice. Now let's look at two specific cases where diagnosis and treatment options had to be evaluated.

◆ ***The case of Irma.***   Irma has just accepted her first position as a counselor in a community agency that is part of a managed care system. An agency policy requires her to conduct an intake interview with each client, determine a diagnosis, and establish a treatment plan—all in the first session. Once a diagnosis is established, clinicians have a maximum of five more sessions with a given client. After three weeks, she lets a colleague know that she is troubled by this timetable. Her colleague reassures her that what she is doing is acceptable and that the agency's aim is to satisfy the requirements of the HMO. Irma does not feel reassured and cannot justify making an assessment in so short a time.

- Do you share Irma's concern? Are there ethical difficulties with this agency's policies?
- Is it ever justified to provide a person with a diagnosis mainly for the purpose of obtaining third-party payment? How can you ethically satisfy the demands of insurance companies that a psychiatric disorder be identified and treated?
- If Irma retains her convictions, is she ethically obliged to discontinue her employment at this agency? What other alternatives, if any, do you see for her situation?
- In the course of a client's treatment, if the original diagnosis becomes obsolete, would you continue to use that diagnosis simply because your client wishes to see you?

◆ **The case of Bob.**   Bob displays symptoms of anxiety and lethargy. After 12 weeks of treatment, Felicita realizes that her client has all the symptoms of a major depression and that he is showing no improvement. She is inclined to double the number of weekly sessions to accelerate her client's progress. *wrong*

- What do you think of Felicita's plan? Is it justified?
- Should she have done a more thorough assessment earlier in the treatment? Might the results have indicated alternative treatments?   *possibly*
- Is Felicita obligated to refer Bob for a psychiatric evaluation to determine whether or not antidepressant medication is indicated? Is she obliged to refer him if he so desires?   *yes.*
- What are her ethical obligations if he refuses to see a psychiatrist? *terminate*
- Do you see any other ethical issues in this case?

Cultural Issues in Diagnosis

In its *Code of Ethics and Standards of Practice*, ACA (1995) recognizes that cultural sensitivity is essential in making a proper diagnosis:

> Counselors take special care to provide proper diagnosis of mental disorders. Assessment techniques (including personal interview) used to determine client care (e.g., locus of treatment, type of treatment, or recommended follow-up) are carefully selected and appropriately used. (E.5.a.)

> Counselors recognize that culture affects the manner in which clients' problems are defined. Clients' socioeconomic and cultural experience is considered when diagnosing mental disorders. (E.5.b.)

The APA's (1995) *Ethical Principles* also provides general guidance in applying the assessment process with special populations:

> Psychologists attempt to identify situations in which particular interventions or assessment techniques or norms may not be applicable or may require adjustments in administration or interpretation because of factors such as individuals' gender, age, race, ethnicity, national origin, religion, sexual orientation, disability, language, or socioeconomic status. (2.04.c.)

If counselors fail to consider ethnic and cultural factors in certain patterns of behavior, a client may be subjected to an erroneous diagnosis. Due to the methods used to identify meaning in diagnosis, the cultural and gender aspects of the presenting problem frequently are not considered (Sinacore-Guinn, 1995), and certain behaviors and personality styles may be labeled neurotic or deviant simply because they are not characteristic of the dominant culture.

Itai and McRae (1994) recommend caution in diagnosis as it applies to cross-cultural situations, especially when English is not the client's primary language. Some cultural differences are easily misunderstood and misdiagnosed. Itai and McRae give the example of Japanese Americans to whom appearing foolish or crying in front of people would mean a loss of face. A therapist could inappropriately assign a DSM diagnosis of "Avoidant Personality Disorder" if the cultural imperative of not displaying emotion in public were not considered. Japanese American people tend to let their parents make important decisions for them. Such clients could be misdiagnosed as "Dependent Personality Disorder" if the therapist did not understand the value placed on interdependence, respect, and conformity in Japanese culture.

The APA's (1993) guidelines for serving culturally diverse populations address the importance of modifying assessment and treatment approaches to meet the needs of ethnic minorities, recommending that providers of psychological services "need knowledge and skills for multicultural assessment and intervention" (p. 45), "recognize ethnicity and culture as significant parameters in understanding psychological processes" (p. 46), and "consider not only differential diagnostic issues but also the cultural beliefs and values of the client and his/her community in providing intervention" (p. 46).

DSM-IV also incorporates cautions so that misdiagnoses are less likely with culturally diverse populations:

> Diagnostic assessment can be especially challenging when a clinician from one ethnic or cultural group uses the DSM-IV classification to evaluate an individual from a different ethnic or cultural group. A clinician who is unfamiliar with the nuances of an individual's cultural frame of reference may incorrectly judge as psychopathology those normal variations in behavior, belief, or experience that are particular to the individual's culture. (American Psychiatric Association, 1994, p. xxiv)

Whenever clinicians assess clients with different ethnic or cultural backgrounds, it is important to be aware of unintentional bias and to keep an open mind to the possibility of distinctive ethnic and cultural patterns.

Using Tests in Counseling

As is true of diagnosis, the proper use of testing in counseling and therapy is the subject of some debate. Generally, those who use therapeutic approaches that emphasize an objective view of counseling are inclined to use testing procedures as tools to acquire information about clients or as resources that clients themselves can use to help them in their decision making. Therapists who employ client-centered and existential approaches tend to view testing in much the same way that they view diagnosis—as an external frame of reference that is of little use in counseling situations.

We think the core issue is not whether you will use tests but rather under what circumstances and for what purposes. Tests are available that measure aptitude, ability, achievement, intelligence, values and attitudes, vocational interests, or personality characteristics. Unfortunately, these tests are often misused. They may be given routinely to unwilling clients, given without providing feedback to clients, used for the wrong purposes, or given by unqualified testers. The following questions will help you think about the circumstances under which you might want to use tests for counseling purposes.

◆ What do you know about the tests you may use? It is important for counselors to be familiar with any tests they use and to have taken these tests themselves. They should know the purpose of each test and how it measures what it purports to measure. Sometimes mental-health workers find that they are expected to give and interpret tests as a basic function of their jobs. If they have not had adequate training in this area, they are in an ethical bind. In-service training and continuing education programs are ways of gaining competence in using psychological assessment devices.

◆ Do you follow the codes of ethics with respect to competence in working with tests? The ACA (1995) indicates the importance of a counselor recognizing the limits of competence to use and interpret tests: "Counselors recognize the limits of their competence and perform only those testing and assessment services for which they have been trained." The APA's *Ethical Principles* (1995) stresses the importance of competence in assessment: "Psychologists who develop, administer, score, interpret, or use psychological assessment techniques, interviews, tests, or instruments do so in a manner and for purposes that are appropriate in light of the research on or evidence of the usefulness and proper application of the techniques" (2.02.a.).

◆ How much involvement should clients have in the selection of tests? Should counselors assume the responsibility, or should clients decide whether they want to take certain tests?

◆ Do you know why you want to use a particular test? Does your agency require that you administer certain tests? Are you giving tests because they will help you understand a client better? Do you administer tests mainly when clients request them? Whatever your reasons, you should be able to state them clearly.

◆ When clients request testing, do you explore their reasons? Some clients may think that a test will provide them with answers in making important decisions. Clients need to be aware that tests are merely tools that can provide useful information about themselves, which they can then explore in their counseling sessions. They also need to know clearly what the tests are designed for. These points are particularly relevant in testing culturally diverse populations.

◆ How do you integrate test results into the counseling sessions? In general, it's best to give test *results*, not simply test *scores*. In other words, you should explore with your clients the meaning the results have for them. Evaluate your clients' readiness to receive and accept certain information and be sensitive to the ways in which clients respond to the test results. The interpretation and discussion of test data should be understandable and relevant to the needs of ethnically and culturally diverse client populations (APA, 1993).

◆ Are you concerned about maintaining the confidentiality of test results? Results may be handled in different ways, depending on the purpose and type of each test. Nevertheless, your clients need to feel that they can trust you and that test results will neither be used against them nor revealed to people who have no right to this information.

◆ Are you critical in evaluating tests? Too often mistakes are made because counselors have blind faith in tests. Know the limitations of the tests you use, and keep in mind that a test can be useful and valid in one situation but inappropriate in another. On this point, the APA (1993) guidelines for working with diverse populations caution psychologists to consider the validity of a given test and to interpret test data in the context of the cultural and linguistic characteristics of the individual being tested. Be aware of the reference population of the test, and recognize the possible limitations of such an instrument with other populations.

The ACA (1995) has developed a number of specific standards governing the ethical use of tests in counseling. Clients being tested should know what the test is intended to discover, how it relates to their situation, and how the results will be used. Test results should be placed in proper perspective and read in the context of other relevant factors. Furthermore, in interpreting tests it is essential for counselors to recognize the effects of socioeconomic, ethnic, linguistic, and cultural factors that might affect scores. The ACA warns counselors to proceed with caution when testing culturally diverse client populations and to avoid inappropriate testing that may be outside the client's socialized behavioral or cognitive patterns. Clients from culturally diverse backgrounds may react to testing with suspicion if tests have been used to discriminate against them in schools and employment. To minimize such negative reactions, it is a good practice to explore a client's views and feelings about testing and to work with him or her in resolving attitudes that are likely to affect the outcome of a test. ACA's guideline on diversity in testing reads:

> Counselors are cautious in using assessment techniques, making evaluations, and interpreting the performance of special populations not represented in the norm

group on which an instrument was standardized. They recognize the effects of age, color, culture, disability, ethnic group, gender, race, religion, sexual orientation, and socioeconomic status on test administration and interpretation and place test results in proper perspective with other relevant factors. (E. 8.)

Many clients seek tests in the hope of finding "answers." It is important to explore why a person wants to take a battery of tests and to teach the person the values and limitations of testing. If that is done, there is less chance the tests will be undertaken in a mechanical fashion or that unwarranted importance will be attributed to the results. Perhaps the most basic ethical guideline for using tests is to keep in mind the primary purpose for which they were designed: to provide objective and descriptive measures that can be used by clients in making better decisions. And it is wise to remember that tests are tools that should be used in the service of clients, not against clients.

The Use of Techniques in Counseling and Therapy

Your view of the use of techniques in counseling and therapy is closely related to your theoretical model. What techniques, procedures, or intervention methods would you use, and when and why would you use them? Some counselors are very eager to learn new techniques, treating them almost as if they were a bag of tricks. Others, out of anxiety over not knowing what to do in a given counseling situation, may try technique after technique in helter-skelter fashion. Counselors should have a rationale for using particular methods of intervention, and we question the benefit to the client of an overreliance on technique.

Lambert and Cattani-Thompson (1996) reviewed studies on counseling effectiveness and found little evidence of specific efficacy for particular techniques or counseling theories. However, a number of significant implications for counseling practice did come to light. For example, some specific techniques appear to be more effective with particular symptoms and disorders, especially for certain behavioral disorders. However, Lambert and Cattani-Thompson assert that successful client outcome is largely determined by client characteristics, such as motivation, severity of symptoms, and acceptance of personal responsibility for change. Other predictors of successful outcomes of counseling involve client-therapist relationship factors. Practitioners would do well to pay attention to the way they interact with clients and the manner in which they participate in the therapy, providing high levels of empathy, respect, and collaboration. It appears that the techniques counselors employ, although important, are less crucial to therapy outcomes than are the interpersonal factors operating in the client-counselor relationship.

We believe that the purpose of techniques is to facilitate movement in a counseling session and that your counseling techniques really cannot be separated from your personality and your relationship with your client. When counselors fall into a pattern of mechanically employing techniques, they are not responding to the particular individuals they're counseling. To avoid this

Be careful

pitfall, pay attention to the ways you tend to use techniques. You may try a technique that you've observed someone else using very skillfully only to find that it fails for you. In essence, your techniques should fit your counseling style, and they should be tailored to the specific needs of your client. When working with culturally diverse client populations, it is clinically and ethically imperative that you use interventions that are consistent with the values of your client. It is best if you adapt your techniques to the needs of your clients rather than expecting your clients to fit into your techniques.

Ethical Issues in Psychotherapeutic Research

Most of the questions we have raised in this chapter have a direct relationship to a therapist's therapeutic approach. Specialized techniques, the balance of responsibility in the client-therapist relationship, the functions of the therapist, and the goals of treatment are all tied to a therapist's theoretical orientation. But at some point we must ask: Does a given psychotherapeutic approach or technique work? To answer these kinds of questions we must rely on the findings of psychotherapeutic research.

Although the ethical implications of conducting research in counseling and psychotherapy are vast, we want to address a few selected issues and encourage you to think about your responsibilities in this area. For example,

?!

no

- ◆ In conducting research in a counseling setting, must the participants always give informed consent? Can you think of situations in which it might be justified not to obtain informed consent for the sake of a better research design?
- ◆ Is it ever ethical to use deception in psychological research? Is deception justified if the subjects are given accurate details after the research study is completed?
- ◆ Can practitioners be considered ethical if they practice without conducting any research on the techniques they use or without having them empirically validated?

Ethics and Research: Some Situations

Ethical issues in research project

Considering the vast number of studies on psychotherapeutic research, there is little discussion in the literature of the ethical problems encountered in designing and conducting studies. Yet there are critical ethical issues in this field that deserve the careful attention of investigators (Imber et al., 1986). In this section we consider some of these issues, including informed consent, using deception in psychological research, withholding treatment, using placebos, research with training and personal-growth groups, and cultural diversity in research.

(1)

Situations involving informed consent. We defined informed consent as the participant's assent to being involved in a research study after having received full information about the procedures and their associated risks and benefits. NASW (1996) provides this guideline on informed consent with research participants:

> Social workers engaged in evaluation or research should obtain voluntary and written informed consent from participants, when appropriate, without any implied or actual deprivation or penalty for refusal to participate, without undue inducement to participate, and with due regard for participants' well-being, privacy and dignity. Informed consent should include information about the nature, extent, and duration of the participation requested and disclosure of the risks and benefits of participation in the research. (5.02.e.)

Informed consent is important for a variety of reasons: it protects people's autonomy by allowing them to make decisions about matters that directly concern them; it guarantees that the participants will be exposed to certain risks only if they agree to them; it decreases the possibility of an adverse public reaction to experimenting with human subjects; and it helps researchers scrutinize their designs for inherent risks (Lindsey, 1984). The researcher might be guided by asking: "What would clients who are interested in their own welfare need to know before making a decision? With these points in mind consider the following situation to determine the ethics of the researcher's behavior.

◆ ***The case of Hannah.***   Hannah is committed to designing research procedures to evaluate the process and outcome of her treatment programs. She is convinced that to obtain valid data she must keep the research participants ignorant in many respects. Thus, she thinks that it is important that the clients she sees be unaware that they are being studied and be unaware of the hypotheses under investigation. Although she agrees that some ethical issues may be raised by her failure to inform her clients, she believes that good research designs call for such procedures. She does not want to influence her clients and thus bias the results of her study, so she chooses to keep information from them. She contends that her practices are justified because there are no negative consequences or risks involved with her research. She further contends that if she is able to refine her therapeutic techniques through her research efforts with her clients, both they and future clients will be the beneficiaries.

- What are your thoughts about Hannah's ethics and the rationale she gives for not obtaining informed consent? *not good*
- Assume that she was interested in studying the effects of therapists' reinforcement of statements by clients during sessions. If the clients knew she was using certain procedures and studying certain behaviors, would it bias the results? *?*
- If the value of the research seems to be greater than the risks involved to participants, do you think researchers are justified in not obtaining the informed consent of participants? *No.*

Commentary.   Although some of Hannah's contentions have merit, we don't think the ends are justified by the means she employs. Further, although she might be justified in withholding some of the details of her research studies (or the hypotheses under investigation), it seems unethical for her to fail even to mention to her clients that she is actually doing research with them as part of her therapeutic approach. Because Hannah's clients are investing themselves both emotionally and financially in their therapy, they have the right to be informed about procedures that are likely to affect them. Furthermore, they have the right to agree or refuse to be a part of her study. Her approach does not allow them to make that choice.

(2) ***Situations involving deception.*** Individuals who participate in a research project have a right to know what they will be voluntarily agreeing to. One of APA's (1995) guidelines on deception in research is: "Psychologists never deceive research participants about significant aspects that would affect their willingness to participate, such as physical risks, discomfort, or unpleasant emotional experiences" (6.15.b.). ACA's (1995) standard on deception reads: "Counselors do not conduct research involving deception unless alternative procedures are not feasible and the prospective value of the research justifies the deception. When the methodological requirements of a study necessitate concealment or deception, the investigator is required to explain clearly the reasons for this action as soon as possible" (G.2.b.).

The case against deception in psychological research has been strongly made, and ethics codes prohibit deception that undermines an individual's rights. Deception violates the individual's right to voluntarily choose to participate, abuses the trusting relationship between experimenter and subject, contributes to deception as a societal value, is contrary to the professional roles of educator or scientist, and will eventually erode trust in the profession of psychology (Adair, Dushenko, & Lindsay, 1985). With these points in mind, consider the following situation and determine whether deception is justified.

◆ ***The case of Vincent.*** Vincent, a family therapist, routinely videotapes his initial session with families without their knowledge. He does so on the ground that he wants to have a basis for comparing the family's behavior at the outset with their behavior at the final session. He assumes that if the family members knew they were being videotaped at the initial session they would behave in self-conscious and fearful ways. At the beginning of therapy he does not think that they could handle the fact of being taped. Yet he likes to have families look at themselves on videotape at their final session, at which time he tells them that he taped their initial session and explains why he did not inform them of this procedure.

- ◆ Because Vincent eventually does tell families that they were taped at the initial session, do you think he is guilty of deception? Explain. *yes*
- ◆ To what degree do you think that the practice of taping clients without their knowledge affects the trust level in the therapeutic relationship? Are the possible benefits of this practice worth the potential risks to the practitioner's reputation? *destroy it / no*

Commentary. Vincent's policy of videotaping clients without their knowledge and consent is ethically questionable. Most of the professional codes of the national organizations explicitly state that such a practice is to be avoided. Because the therapeutic relationship is built on goodwill and trust, we oppose any practices that are likely to jeopardize that trust.

(3)   **Situations involving withholding treatment.**   Is it ethical to withhold treatment from a particular group so that it can be used as a control group? Consider this situation.

◆ **The case of Hope.**   Hope works with people diagnosed as depressive psychotics in a state mental hospital. In the interest of refining therapeutic interventions that will help depressed clients, she combines therapy and research procedures. Specifically, she employs cognitive-behavioral approaches in a given ward. Her research design specifies treatment techniques for a particular group of patients, and she carefully monitors their rate of improvement as part of the treatment program. Hope says that she believes in the value of cognitive-behavioral approaches for depressive patients, yet she feels a professional and ethical obligation to empirically validate her treatment strategies. For her to know whether the treatment procedures alone are responsible for changes in the patients' behaviors, she deems it essential to have a comparable group of patients who do not receive the treatment. When she is challenged on the ethics of withholding treatment from a particular group of patients on the ward, she justifies her practice on the ground that she is working within the dictates of sound research procedures.

♦ Some researchers contend that they are necessarily caught in ethical dilemmas if they want to use a control group. Do you see an apparent contradiction between the demands of sound research methodology and sound ethical practice?   *yes*

♦ Do you think Hope was acting ethically in withholding treatment so that she could test her therapeutic procedures? Would it be better for her to simply forget any attempts at empirical validation of her procedures and devote her efforts to treating as many patients as she can?   *no / yes*

♦ Would it be ethical for her to use procedures that are untested?   *yes*

◆ **A modification of the case.**   In a second case Hope uses placebo controls. That is, rather than merely denying treatment to a group or keeping members on a waiting list, she meets with a control group whose members think they are receiving therapy but actually are not receiving standard treatment. In short, the group is led to believe that it is benefiting from therapy.

♦ What are the ethics of using placebos in counseling and clinical research?

♦ Does the placebo approach by its very nature constitute deception of patients?   *yes unless they agree it*

♦ Can you think of any situations that justify the use of this approach?   *w/ informed consent*

does group know they may not be treated at all except w/ placebos?

(4) **Situations involving research with training and personal growth.** In many graduate programs it is common for trainees in counseling internships to participate in personal-growth groups. Sometimes these groups are integrated with training or supervision groups in which the interns are encouraged to explore their own personal issues that arise in conjunction with their placements in the field.

◆ **The case of Wesley.** A professor, Wesley, makes it a practice to conduct research on the process and outcomes of the personal-growth groups he leads for counselor trainees. To begin with, all the students in his graduate counseling program are required to attend the sessions of a personal-growth group for a full acacemic year. In addition to leading these growth groups for trainees, he also teaches theory courses and supervises students writing master's theses and doctoral dissertations. His primary theoretical orientation is Gestalt therapy, with an emphasis on other experiential and role-playing techniques. He expects the students to come to the sessions and be willing to work on personal concerns. These personal concerns often pertain to issues that arise as a result of problems they encounter with difficult client situations in their internship. At the beginning of the group Wesley asks students to take psychological tests that assess traits such as openness, dogmatism, degree of self-acceptance, level of self-esteem, and other dimensions of personality that he deems to be related to one's ability to counsel others. He again administers these same devices at the end of the year so that he has a comparison. During the year he asks a group of experts to observe his trainees in the group sessions at various points. This is done so that outsiders can assess the level of growth of individuals at different points as well as get a sense of the progress of the group as a whole. N

As part of informed consent, Wesley tells the trainees what he is attempting to evaluate during the year, and he discusses fully with them the rationale for using outsiders to observe the group. He also promises the students that he will meet with them individually at any time during the semester if they want to discuss any personal issues. He also meets with them individually at the end of the group to discuss changes in scores on the psychological tests. As a way to correct for his bias in the investigation, he submits his research design to a university committee. The function of this committee is to review his design for any ethical considerations and to give him suggestions for improving his study.

◆ Do you think it is ethical for a program to require student attendance at personal-growth groups? And is it ethical for the leader of such a group to also have these same students in academic classes and to evaluate and supervise them?
◆ What research practices, if any, would you say are ethically questionable?
◆ Do you think it is ethically sound to have observers as a part of the design? The students know about these outsiders, but the observers will be part of the process even if some students do not like the idea. Do you see pressure being exerted? If so, is it justified in this case?

♦ What recommendations can you make for improving Wesley's research design as well as improving the quality of the learning experience for the students?

Cultural Diversity Aspects of Research

Although research is considered basic to the development of theory, cultural factors are often neglected in both research and theory. It is critical that research designs be based on culturally sensitive principles. ACA's (1995) guideline on the use of human subjects is as follows: "Counselors plan, design, conduct, and report research in a manner consistent with pertinent ethical principles, federal and state laws, host institution regulations, and scientific standards governing research with human subjects. Counselors design and conduct research that reflects cultural sensitivity appropriateness" (G.1.a.). Another guideline is given on diversity: "Counselors are sensitive to diversity and research issues with special populations. They seek consultation when appropriate" (G.1.f.).

The APA's *Guidelines for Providers of Psychological Services to Ethnic, Linguistic, and Culturally Diverse Populations* (1993) calls for a conceptual framework that will enable service providers to organize and accurately assess the value and utility of current and future research involving diverse ethnic and cultural populations. These guidelines include an exploration of several research issues:

♦ the impact of ethnic and racial similarity in the counseling process
♦ minority groups' use of mental-health services
♦ the relative effectiveness of directive and nondirective styles of therapy
♦ the role of cultural values in treatment
♦ appropriate counseling models
♦ competence in skills for working with specific ethnic populations

In a discussion of new approaches to cultural diversity, C. C. Lee (1997b) contends that research evidence must guide counseling. Based on reviews of what has been accomplished in research on cross-cultural counseling, he proposes the following three areas for future research:

♦ New process and outcome research in the area of multicultural counseling. Evaluation of culturally responsive methods must be made an integral part of practice in various settings.
♦ Normal human development research from a cross-cultural perspective. New studies might focus on coping skills among diverse groups of people.
♦ Research on intragroup differences due to factors such as level of ethnic identity, level of acculturation, and socioeconomic status.

Inventory of Your Position on Research

As a way of concluding this discussion, we suggest that you clarify your own thinking on the matter of balancing scientific rigor with ethical rigor. If you agree more than you disagree with the following statements, place an "A" in the space provided; if you disagree more than you agree, place a "D" in the space. After you've finished the inventory, discuss some of your answers with fellow students.

A 1. To use therapeutic techniques or interventions that lack a sufficient research base is irresponsible and unethical.

D 2. Deception is sometimes a necessary evil in psychological research.

A 3. Failure to obtain the informed consent of participants in research is always unethical.

D 4. If a research study contains any risks to the participants, its design should be changed, for by its very nature it is unethical.

A 5. The use of placebo groups can be justified. If these controls are not used, practitioners will have difficulty evaluating the efficacy of the intervention they use.   c) informed consent

A 6. Researchers will ultimately get the best results if they are open and honest about the research design with the participants in the study.

D 7. If individuals are "debriefed" afterward, deception during the study can be justified.

D 8. Practitioners should use no techniques that have not been empirically shown to be of value.

D 9. To produce sound research studies of therapy, we must be willing to tolerate some ethical violations.

D 10. It is ethical to justify research in educational settings solely on the basis of the potential benefits of the research itself.

Chapter Summary

Issues in theory, practice, and research are necessarily interrelated. From an ethical perspective, therapists need to anchor their practices to both theory and research. Without a theoretical foundation, practitioners are left with little rationale to formulate therapeutic goals and develop techniques to accomplish these goals. Practitioners are sometimes impatient when it comes to articulating a theory that guides practice. Some are riveted to concrete techniques to deal with every conceivable problem clients may present. However, a good theory is highly practical, for theoretical concepts help clinicians understand what they are doing. Just as clinicians sometimes have little use for theory, some do not see the practical applications of research. Without understanding how to translate current research findings into their practices, therapists have little basis for deciding what techniques to use with different clients. Thus, an appreciation of how theory and research can enhance how therapists function may result in ethical and effective practice.

We do not advocate that you subscribe to one established theory, because therapeutic techniques from many theoretical approaches may be useful in your practice. However, we hope you will develop clear views pertaining to these questions: How does change come about? What is your view of human

handwritten margin notes: "practices shld be anchored in both theory & research"; "has can theory & research enhance practice"; "Be clear"

nature? How does the therapeutic relationship lead to change? What is the role of diagnosis and assessment as a prelude to designing a treatment plan? When might tests be useful in the counseling process? How can research help practitioners determine the degree to which a therapy program is working? Ideally, your theoretical orientation will serve as a basis for reflecting on matters such as goals in counseling, the division of responsibility between the client and the counselor in meeting these goals, and techniques that are most appropriate with specific clients in resolving a variety of problems.

Suggested Activities

1. Do this exercise in dyads. Describe your theoretical stance, and tell your partner how you view human nature. How will this view determine the way you counsel?

2. How do you determine for yourself the proper division of responsibility in counseling? How might you avoid assuming responsibility that you think belongs to your client? How might you ensure that you will accept your own share of responsibility?

3. If you were applying for a job as a counselor and were asked, "What are the most important goals you have for your clients?" how would you respond?

4. In class, debate the role of diagnosis in therapy. Have one person make a case for diagnosis as a valuable part of the therapeutic process, and have the other person argue against the use of diagnosis. Or have a class discussion on trends in diagnosis, its uses and abuses, and its purpose and value.

5. Suppose that a client came to you and asked you to administer a battery of interest, ability, and vocational tests. How would you respond? What questions would you ask the client before agreeing to arrange for the testing?

6. What is your position on the use of techniques in counseling? When do you think they are appropriate? How can you determine for yourself whether you're using techniques as gimmicks to allay your anxiety or as extensions of your personal style as a counselor?

7. Interview at least one practicing therapist and discuss how his or her theoretical orientation affects that therapist's practice. Ask the practitioner the kinds of questions that were raised in this chapter. Bring the results of your interview to class.

8. Suppose you were applying for a job in a community mental-heath center. How would you respond to these questions during the interview:

   ♦ Many of our clients represent a range of diverse cultural and ethnic backgrounds. To what degree do you think you will be able to form positive therapeutic relationships with clients who are culturally different from you?

   ♦ How do you think your own acculturation will influence the way you counsel ethnically and culturally diverse clients?

♦ Can you think of any factors that might get in the way of forming trusting relationships with clients who are culturally different from you?

9. In dyads, have one person argue that a thorough assessment (diagnosis) is not necessary with a majority of clients in outpatient counseling. The other person can argue that without a thorough assessment of each client it is not ethically possible to proceed with an appropriate treatment plan.

10. What interventions might you make during your initial session in getting to know your client? How would you structure future sessions? Explore the following questions:

♦ Would you begin with a detailed case history? Why, or why not?

♦ Do you consider a comprehensive assessment and a diagnosis necessary prerequisites to counseling? Why, or why not?

♦ Are tests important as a prerequisite to counseling? Would you decide whether to test, or would you allow your client to make this decision?

♦ How much would you structure the session to obtain current information about your client's life? How much would you want to know about the client's past?

♦ Would you do most of the talking? Why, or why not?

♦ How would you incorporate a cultural perspective into your work? How would your client's cultural and ethnic background influence the development of your relationship?

♦ Who would set the goals of therapy? Who would be primarily responsible for what was discussed? Why?

♦ Who would take the greater responsibility for directing the initial session? Would you ask many questions? Would you encourage your client to structure the session?

♦ Would you develop a contract with your client specifying what the client could expect from you, what the client wanted from counseling, and what the client was willing to do to meet these goals? Why, or why not?

♦ Would you be inclined to use directive, action-oriented techniques, such as homework assignments? Why, or why not?

♦ What aspects of the client's life would you stress?

11. Videotape or tape-record sessions with several clients. Instead of focusing your attention on what your client said or did, examine your own responses and how you relate to clients.

♦ Do you ask many questions? If so, are the questions mainly to get information or are they open-ended ones designed to challenge your client?

♦ Do you tend to give advice and work quickly toward solutions? Or do you allow your client to explore feelings in depth rather than focusing on solutions to problems?

♦ Do you consider cultural factors in your use of techniques?

♦ How much support and reassurance do you give? Do you allow your clients to fully express what they're feeling before you offer support?

- Do you challenge your clients when you think they need it? Do your interventions get them to think about what they're saying on a deeper level?
- Who does most of the talking? Do you hear yourself as pushing or persuading? Are you responsive to what your client is saying?
- Are you asking questions just to keep the sessions moving?
- How often do you clarify what you hear? Do you check to be sure you're hearing what your client means to express?
- Do you reflect back to your clients what you hear them saying? If so, is your reflection done mechanically, or does it encourage a deeper self-exploration?
- Do you interpret much, telling your clients what you think certain behaviors mean? Or do you leave it to clients to discover what their behaviors mean from their own perspectives?
- Do you use techniques primarily to get clients moving, or do you use interventions aimed at enabling clients to explore thoughts or feelings that they bring up?
- Do you use techniques that you're comfortable using? Have you experienced these techniques yourself as a client?
- Are the procedures you use drawn from one counseling approach? Or do you borrow techniques from various approaches and use them when they seem appropriate?
- When you use a particular technique, does it seem mechanical to you? Or do you feel that your techniques are appropriate and unforced?
- Do you see your favorite techniques as being applicable to all clients?
- How do your clients generally respond to the techniques you use? Do they react negatively to any of your counseling methods?

Monitoring your own work in light of these questions can help you discover your counseling style, understand the interventions you make, and evaluate the impact these counseling procedures have on your clients. This willingness to reflect on the effects your interventions have on clients is of the utmost importance.

Chapter

7

Managing Boundaries and Multiple Relationships

◆ *Pre-Chapter Self-Inventory*

◆ *Introduction*

◆ *Dual and Multiple Relationships in Perspective*

◆ *Controversies on Boundary Issues*

◆ *Bartering for Professional Services*

◆ *Social Relationships with Clients*

◆ *Sexual Attractions in the Client-Therapist Relationship*

◆ *Sexual Relationships: Ethical and Legal Issues*

◆ *A Special Case: Nonerotic Physical Contact with Clients*

◆ *Dealing with Unethical Behavior in Dual Relationships*

◆ *Chapter Summary*

◆ *Suggested Activities*

Pre-Chapter Self-Inventory

Directions: For each statement, indicate the response that most closely identifies your beliefs and attitudes. Use the following code:

5 = I *strongly agree* with this statement.
4 = I *agree* with this statement.
3 = I am *undecided* about this statement.
2 = I *disagree* with this statement.
1 = I *strongly disagree* with this statement.

_5_ 1. A good therapist gets involved in the client's case without getting involved with the client emotionally.

_4_ 2. Touching, whether erotic or not, is best avoided in counseling, because it can easily be misunderstood by the client.

_4_ 3. Therapists who touch clients of only one sex are guilty of sexist practice.

_1_ 4. Although it may be unwise to form social relationships with clients while they are in counseling, there should be no ethical or professional prohibition against social relationships after counseling ends.

_1_ 5. If I were a truly ethical professional, I would never be sexually attracted to a client.

_4_ 6. If I were counseling a client who was sexually attracted to me, I might refer this client to another counselor.

_2_ 7. I might be inclined to barter my therapeutic services for goods if a client could not afford my fees.

_2_ 8. If a client initiated the possibility of exchanging services in lieu of payment, I would consider bartering as an option.

_4_ 9. Sexual involvement with a client is never ethical, even after therapy has ended.

_4_ 10. Topics such as nonerotic touching, dealing with sexual attractions, and sexual dilemmas should be addressed throughout the counselor's training program.

_4_ 11. Unethical behavior is anything that results in harm to the client.

_2_ 12. If another professional was doing something I considered to be unethical, I would report him or her to the state licensing agency.

_5_ 13. It is essential that I monitor my own behavior and think of ways to lessen the chances of unethical behavior on my part.

_2_ 14. I would never accept a gift from a client, for doing so constitutes crossing appropriate boundaries.

_4_ 15. It is essential to consider the cultural context in deciding on the appropriateness of bartering, accepting gifts, and the counselor assuming multiple roles with a client.

_2_ 16. Dual or multiple relationships are almost always problematic and therefore should be considered unethical.

_4_ 17. Because dual relationships are so widespread, they should not be considered as either inappropriate or unethical in all circumstances but should be decided on a case-by-case basis.

_2_ 18. I would have no trouble accepting a close friend as a client if we had a clear understanding of how our personal relationship could be separated from our professional one.

_1_ 19. As long as my client felt comfortable about developing a social relationship with me once therapy was over, I would have little difficulty forming such a relationship.

_4_ 20. I think that it will be relatively easy for me to establish clear and firm boundaries with my clients.

Introduction

Ethical problems are often raised when counselors blend their professional relationship with a client with another kind of relationship. The ethics codes of most professional organizations have increasingly paid attention to the potential for crossing boundaries and exploiting clients when dual or multiple relationships occur. Because of the complex nature of combining various roles and relationships, the term *multiple relationships* is often more accurate than *dual relationships* in capturing the many forms that can occur.

Dual or multiple relationships occur when professionals assume two or more roles at the same time or sequentially with a client. This may involve assuming more than one professional role (such as instructor and therapist), or blending a professional and nonprofessional relationship (such as counselor and friend or counselor and business partner). Other examples of dual relationships include bartering therapy for goods or services, providing therapy to a relative or a friend's relative, socializing with clients, attending a social event of a client, accepting gifts from clients, becoming emotionally or sexually involved with a client or former client, or combining the roles of supervisor and therapist. Mental-health professionals must learn how to effectively and ethically manage multiple relationships, including dealing with the power differential that is a basic part of most professional relationships, managing boundary issues, and striving to avoid the misuse of power (Herlihy & Corey, 1997).

The underlying theme of this chapter is the need for therapists to be honest and self-searching in determining the impact of their behavior on clients. Some of the issues and cases we present may seem clear-cut to you, but others are not. In ambiguous cases it becomes a personal challenge to make an honest appraisal of your behavior and its effect on clients. Resolving the ethical dilemmas we pose requires personal and professional maturity and a willingness to continue to question your own motivations. A key question is: Whose needs are being met, the therapist's or the client's? To us, behavior is unethical when it reflects a lack of awareness or concern about the impact of the behavior on clients. Some counselors may place their personal needs above the needs of their clients, engaging in more than one role with clients to meet their own financial, social, or emotional needs.

This chapter deals with the subject of boundary issues in counseling practice, dual and multiple relationships, role blendings, a variety of nonsexual dual relationships, and sexual issues in therapy. We examine the more subtle aspects of sexuality in therapy, including sexual attractions and the misuse of power. Multiple relationship issues cannot be resolved with rules alone, and we advocate for the value of learning how to think through the ethical and clinical dimensions involved in a wide range of boundary concerns.

Dual and Multiple Relationships in Perspective

During the 1980s sexual relationships received considerable attention in the professional literature. Sexual relationships with clients are clearly unethical, and all of the major professional ethics codes have specific prohibitions against them. However, *nonsexual* relationships have also been arousing increased interest (see Herlihy & Corey, 1997). The codes of ethics of most professional organizations warn of the potential hazards of dual and multiple relationships (see the box on page 227). These codes typically take a dim view of becoming involved in dual relationships, and the standards caution professionals against any involvement with clients that might impair their judgment or result in exploitation.

Differing perspectives.   There is a wide range of viewpoints on dual relationships. If you are intent on clarifying your position on this issue, you will encounter conflicting advice. Some writers focus on the problems inherent in dual relationships. St. Germine (1993) maintains that although dual relationships are not always harmful to clients it is essential for professionals to recognize the potential for harm associated with any kind of blending of roles. She mentions that errors in judgment may occur when a professional's self-interest becomes involved. Pope (1985a) and Pope and Vasquez (1991) contend that dual relationships tend to impair the therapist's judgment, increasing the potential for conflicts of interest, exploitation of the client, and blurred boundaries that distort the professional nature of the therapeutic relationship. Pope and Vasquez note that therapists often try to justify, trivialize, or discount their practices of engaging in more than one role with clients. Therapists may block out awareness of the potential for serious harm; may focus on the beneficial aspects of such relationships; may assert that these practices are widely prevalent, inevitable and unavoidable, and reflect tradition; and may emphasize the right of clients to enter into relationships of their choice. Such skillful rationalizations allow the professional to evade responsibility for designing acceptable alternative approaches.

Those who take a more moderate view see the entire discussion of dual relationships as subtle and complex, defying simplistic solutions or absolute answers. In many situations, it is not possible to remain within the context of a

Ethical Standards for Dual and Multiple Relationships

The AAMFT (1991) ethical code standard dealing with dual relationships states:

> Marriage and family therapists are aware of their influential position with respect to clients, and they avoid exploiting the trust and dependency of such persons. Therapists, therefore, make every effort to avoid dual relationships with clients that could impair professional judgment or increase the risk of exploitation. When a dual relationship cannot be avoided, therapists take appropriate professional precautions to ensure judgment is not impaired and no exploitation occurs.

In the ACA's *Code of Ethics and Standards of Practice* (1995), counselors are encouraged to avoid dual relationships when possible:

> Counselors are aware of their influential positions with respect to clients, and they avoid exploiting the trust and dependency of clients. Counselors make every effort to avoid dual relationships with clients that could impair professional judgment or increase the risk of harm to clients. (Examples of such relationships include, but are not limited to, familial, social, financial, business, or close personal relationships with clients.) When a dual relationship cannot be avoided, counselors take appropriate professional precautions such as informed consent, consultation, supervision, and documentation to ensure that judgment is not impaired and no exploitation occurs. (A.6.a.)

NASW's *Code of Ethics* (1996) focuses on factors of risk of exploitation or potential harm to clients:

> Social workers should not engage in dual or multiple relationships with clients or former clients in which there is a risk of exploitation or potential harm to the client. In instances when dual or multiple relationships are unavoidable, social workers should take steps to protect clients and are responsible for setting clear, appropriate, and culturally sensitive boundaries. (1.06.c.)

Although the *Ethical Standards of the National Organization for Human Services Education* (NOHSE, 1995) point to the unequal power and status in the helping relationship, dual or multiple relationships are not prohibited:

> Human service professionals are aware that in their relationships with clients, power and status are unequal. Therefore, they recognize that dual or multiple relationships may increase the risk of harm to, or exploitation of, clients, and may impair their professional judgment. However, in some communities and situations it may not be feasible to avoid social or other nonprofessional contact with clients. Human services professionals support the trust implicit in the helping relationship by avoiding dual relationships that may impair professional judgment, increase the risk of harm to clients, or lead to exploitation.

APA's (1995) standard on multiple relationships points to the potential for impairing a professional's objectivity:

> In many communities and situations, it may not be feasible or reasonable for psychologists to avoid social or other nonprofessional contacts with persons such as patients, clients, students, supervisees, or research participants. Psychologists must always be sensitive to the potential harmful effects of other contacts on their work and those persons with whom they deal. A psychologist refrains from entering into or promising another personal, scientific, professional, financial, or other relationship with such persons if it appears likely that such a relationship reasonably might impair the psychologist's objectivity or otherwise interfere with the psychologist's effectively performing his or her functions as a psychologist, or might harm or exploit the other party. (1.17.a.)

single role. Tomm (1993) believes that standards in the ethics codes that address dual relationships tend to be narrow and deceptive. In his view, the AAMFT's (1991) code gives the impression that practitioners should maintain professional distance and that all dual relationships lead to exploitation and are wrong. He makes an excellent observation when he points out that simply avoiding dual relationships does not prevent exploitation. Counselors can misuse their power and influence in a variety of ways that can harm clients. Tomm contends that maintaining interpersonal distance focuses on the power differential, promotes an objectification of the therapeutic relationship, and tends to promote a vertical hierarchy in the relationship.

From a psychoanalytic perspective, Hedges (1993) maintains that transference, countertransference, resistance, and interpretation necessarily involve some form of dual relationship. He points out the beneficial aspects of therapy that can be a consequence of a dual relationship.

Herlihy and Corey (1997) suggest that dual relationships are inherent in the work of all helping professionals, regardless of work setting or client population. Despite certain clinical, ethical, and legal risks, some blending of roles is unavoidable, and it is not necessarily unethical or unprofessional. Although the ethical codes of most professions caution against engaging in dual relationships, not all such relationships can be avoided, nor are they necessarily harmful. For example, "mentoring" involves blending roles, yet both mentors and learners can certainly benefit from this relationship.

Designing safeguards to protect clients.   Herlihy and Corey (1997) conclude that there is no clear consensus regarding nonsexual relationships in counseling. It is the responsibility of practitioners to monitor themselves and to examine their motivations for engaging in such relationships. In rural areas, for instance, mental-health practitioners may find it more difficult to maintain clear boundaries than do those who work in large cities. They may have to blend several professional roles and functions, and they may attend the same church or community activities as the clients they serve. In an isolated area a priest or a minister may seek counseling for a personal crisis from the only counselor in the town—someone who also happens to be a parishioner.

Schank and Skovholt (1997) conducted interviews with psychologists who lived and practiced in rural areas and small communities. They found that all of the psychologists in their study acknowledged concerns involving professional boundaries. Some of the major themes were the reality of overlapping social or business relationships, the effects of overlapping social relationships on members of the psychologist's own family, and the dilemma of working with more than one family member as clients or with clients who have friendships with other clients. Although the psychologists knew the content of the ethics codes, they admitted that they often struggled in choosing how to apply those codes to the ethical dilemmas they faced in rural practice.

Sleek (1994) also describes ethical dilemmas that plague rural practice. For example, if a therapist shops for a new tractor, he risks violating the letter of the ethics code if the only person in town who sells tractors happens to be a client. However, if the therapist were to buy a tractor elsewhere, this could strain relationships with the client because of the value rural communities place on loyalty to local merchants. Or consider clients who wish to barter goods or services for counseling services. Some communities operate substantially on swaps rather than on a cash economy. This does not necessarily have to become problematic, yet the potential for conflict exists in the therapeutic relationship if the bartering agreements do not work well.

In the same vein, Kitchener and Harding (1990) contend that dual relationships range from those that are potentially seriously harmful to those that have little potential for harm. They maintain that even in cases where there is a low risk of damage, practitioners have an obligation to evaluate the risk and *always* act responsibly:

> Only after concluding that the risks of harm are small should they engage in relationships that have dual expectations. They should never enter into such relationships when the potential for harm is high unless there are strong offsetting, ethical benefits for the consumer and the risks are clearly discussed. (p. 153)

Certain behaviors of professionals have the potential for creating a dual relationship, but they are not inherently considered to be dual relationships. Examples of these behaviors include accepting a client's invitation to a special event such as a graduation, bartering goods or services for professional services, accepting a small gift from a client, attending the same church activities as a client, or giving a supportive hug after a difficult session. Some writers (Gabbard, 1994, 1995; Gutheil & Gabbard, 1993; D. Smith & Fitzpatrick, 1995) caution that engaging in boundary crossings paves the way to boundary *violations* and to becoming entangled in complex multiple relationships. Gutheil and Gabbard (1993) distinguish between boundary *crossings* (changes in role) and boundary *violations* (exploitation of the client at some level). A boundary crossing is a departure from commonly accepted practices that could potentially benefit clients, while a boundary violation is a serious breach that results in harm to clients. They note that not all boundary crossings should be considered boundary violations. Interpersonal boundaries are fluid; they may change over time and may be redefined as therapists and clients continue to work together. Yet behaviors that stretch boundaries can become problematic if boundary crossings lead to a pattern of blurring the professional boundaries. There is real potential for harm in these multiple relationship entanglements (Herlihy & Corey, 1997).

Consistent, yet flexible, boundaries are often therapeutic and can help clients develop trust in the therapy relationship. Borys (1994) suggests that many clients require the structure provided by clear and consistent boundaries. Such a structure is like "a buoy in stormy, chaotic seas; that is, the only stable object to cling to for miles" (p. 270).

Strasburger, Jorgenson, and Sutherland (1992) contend that therapists who push nonsexual boundaries are more likely to become sexually involved with clients. They recommend avoiding this slippery slope to prevent sexual misconduct. Inherent in the concept of the "slippery slope" is the warning that clinicians need to exercise caution before entering into all types of multiple relationships, even if they are not harmful in themselves.

A concept related to that of maintaining appropriate boundaries is role blending. Certainly, blending some roles is indefensible, such as blending the roles of therapist and lover or therapist and business partner. But other roles that professionals play involve an inherent duality. For example, counselor educators serve as instructors, but they also act as therapeutic agents for their students' personal development. At different times, counselor educators may function in the roles of teacher, therapeutic agent, mentor, evaluator, and supervisor. The roles supervisors play are another example. Although supervision and psychotherapy are two different processes, they share some common aspects. The supervisor may need to assist supervisees in identifying ways that their personal dynamics are blocking their ability to work effectively with clients. Herlihy and Corey (1997) assert that role blending is inevitable in the process of educating and supervising counselor trainees and that this role blending can present ethical dilemmas that involve a loss of objectivity or conflicts of interest. They state that role blending is not necessarily unethical, but it does call for vigilance on the part of the professional to ensure that exploitation does not occur.

Functioning in more than one role involves thinking through potential problems before they occur and building safeguards into practice. Whenever a potential for negative outcomes exists, professionals have a responsibility to design safeguards to reduce the potential for harm. Herlihy and Corey (1997) and St. Germaine (1993) identify the following measures aimed at minimizing the risks inherent in dual or multiple relationships:

Safeguards

- set healthy boundaries from the outset
- secure the informed consent of clients and discuss with them both the potential risks and benefits of dual relationships
- remain willing to talk with clients about any unforeseen problems and conflicts that may arise
- consult with other professionals to resolve any dilemmas
- seek supervision when dual relationships become particularly problematic or when the risk for harm is high
- document any dual relationships in clinical case notes
- examine your own motivations for being involved in dual relationships
- when necessary, refer clients to another professional

In *Boundary Issues in Counseling: Multiple Roles and Responsibilities* Herlihy and Corey (1997) identify ten key themes surrounding multiple roles in counseling. We present these themes here as a summary of critical issues in thinking about dual and multiple relationships.

1. Multiple relationship issues affect virtually all mental-health practitioners, regardless of their work setting or clientele.
2. All professional codes of ethics caution against dual relationships, but newer codes acknowledge the complex nature of these relationships.

3. Not all multiple relationships can be avoided, nor are they necessarily always harmful.

4. Multiple role relationships challenge us to monitor ourselves and to examine our motivations for our practices.

5. Whenever you consider becoming involved in a dual or multiple relationship, seek consultation from trusted colleagues or a supervisor.

6. There are few absolute answers that can neatly resolve dual or multiple relationship dilemmas.

7. The cautions for entering into dual or multiple relationships should be for the benefit of our clients or others served, rather than to protect ourselves from censure.

8. In determining whether to proceed with a dual or multiple relationship, consider whether the potential benefit outweighs the potential for harm.

9. It is the responsibility of counselor preparation programs to introduce boundary issues and explore multiple relationship questions. It is important to teach students ways of thinking about alternative courses of action.

10. Counselor education programs have a responsibility to develop their own guidelines, policies, and procedures for dealing with multiple roles and role conflicts within the program.

We find it useful to frame the discussion of dual or multiple relationships within the context of boundaries. Professionals often get into trouble when their boundaries are ill defined and when they attempt to blend roles that do not mix well, such as therapy and friendships or therapy and business. A gradual erosion of boundaries can lead to very problematic multiple relationships that bring harm to clients. Gabbard (1994) cites the well-known "slippery slope" phenomenon as one of the strongest arguments for carefully monitoring boundaries in psychotherapy.

Consider where you stand on issues involving blending roles, boundary crossing, and multiple relationships. How might certain dual or multiple relationships be unavoidable at times, and what can you do in these situations? What kinds of relationships might place you in professional jeopardy? Rather than unequivocally condemning bartering or refusing to attend a social event of a client, consider how these situations could complicate the therapeutic relationship—then think about circumstances in which you may decide to stretch the boundaries. In your struggle to determine what constitutes appropriate boundaries, you are likely to find that certain role blendings are inevitable. Therefore, it is crucial to learn how to manage boundaries, how to prevent boundary crossings from turning into boundary violations, and how to develop safeguards that will prevent exploitation of clients.

Controversies on Boundary Issues

Lazarus (1994a) has developed the position that certain boundaries and ethics actually diminish therapeutic effectiveness. He contends that some well-intentioned ethical standards can be transformed into artificial boundaries that result in destructive prohibitions and undermine clinical effectiveness. In this section, we present some of his key arguments along with some responses to Lazarus's ideas.

When taken too far, Lazarus argues that some well-intentioned guidelines can backfire. He admits that he has socialized with some clients, played tennis with others, taken walks with some, graciously accepted small gifts, and given gifts (usually books) to some of his clients. Lazarus emphasizes that he is clearly opposed to any form of disparagement, exploitation, abuse, harassment, or sexual contact with clients. He is not advocating elimination of all boundaries and espousing a thoughtless laissez-faire approach. Indeed, certain boundaries are essential. Rather than being driven by rules, however, Lazarus calls for a process of negotiation in many areas of nonsexual multiple relationships that some would contend are in the forbidden zone.

Lazarus argues that the current frenzy over avoiding malpractice litigation tends to make therapists leery, almost to the extent of viewing every client as a potential adversary or litigant. Professionals who hide behind rigid boundaries often fail to be of genuine help to their clients. He concludes with these words:

> If I am to summarize my position in one sentence, I would say that one of the worst professional or ethical violations is that of permitting current risk-management principles to take precedence over humane interventions. By all means drive defensively, but try to practice psychotherapy responsibly—with compassion, benevolence, sensitivity, and caring. (p. 260)

Lazarus's (1994a) keynote article caused a good deal of controversy, as can be seen by the number of authors who were invited to respond to his article. These authors included Bennett, Bricklin, and VandeCreek (1994); Borys (1994); L. S. Brown (1994); Gabbard (1994); Gottlieb (1994); and Gutheil (1994).

Bennett, Bricklin, and VandeCreek (1994) remind us of the unfortunate reality that too many practitioners have difficulty distinguishing where appropriate boundary lines should be drawn. They point out that beyond a few clear prohibitions most ethics codes offer little real guidance. Bennett and his colleagues agree with Lazarus that competent therapists will use clinical judgment rather than a cookbook approach when working with clients. However, they fear that less experienced therapists than Lazarus will misinterpret his position as granting them license to minimize the importance of respecting boundary issues in therapy.

In her response, Borys (1994) takes Lazarus to task for associating ethics and boundaries with traits such as rigidity, dehumanization, artificiality, and the absence of flexibility. She sees it as a mistaken notion to equate confusing clear boundaries with coldness. Instead, Borys draws a parallel between good parents and good therapists—both need to set limits in a firm but nonauthoritarian fashion and still be empathic and warm:

> A therapist who is comfortable with these boundaries, and experiences and understands them as promoting effective, safe treatment, will find them to be allies in the process and to be safeguards that actually allow greater levels of spontaneity and

warmth by helping to keep nontherapeutic needs and impulses of the clinician within their proper parameters. (p. 273)

In her response to Lazarus's article, L. S. Brown (1994) maintains that the goal of ethical decision making is to take a position where potential for abuse and exploitation are minimized. She recognizes how easy it is for therapists to misuse the power they have and suggests that therapists consider the impact of their behavior on clients. Brown questions the clinical purpose of Lazarus's extraoffice encounters with his clients, such as playing tennis, eating meals, and going for walks, and wonders if he has taken into account the entire therapeutic relationship before deciding to engage in any of these extraoffice contacts. Brown takes the position that violations of boundaries tend to profoundly imbalance the power of an already power-imbalanced relationship by placing the needs of the more powerful person, the therapist, in a paramount position.

Gabbard (1994) expresses concern over Lazarus's "cavalier attitude" about disregarding boundaries. The crux of Gabbard's response is that Lazarus is "teetering on the precipice." Failing to establish clear boundaries can be very dangerous to both the client and the therapist. Gabbard sees boundaries as providing safety for clients: "Professional boundaries provide an envelop within which a warm, empathic holding environment can be created" (p. 285). He further states that the mental-health professions' established guidelines (or boundaries) are aimed at minimizing the opportunity for therapists to use their clients for their own gratification.

Gottlieb (1994) asserts that Lazarus "argues his point to the extreme and in the process trivializes serious ethical and clinical issues" (p. 287). Gottlieb criticizes Lazarus for:

◆ ignoring literature of ethical decision making that provides clear guidelines to help therapists protect clients
◆ discounting the historical context in which risk management has developed
◆ failing to apply basic ethical principles to clinical practice
◆ disregarding the subtle ways ethical decisions affect clinical outcome

From Gottlieb's perspective, clients appreciate a clear structure that is explained from the outset of therapy. He adds that using informed consent procedures when ethical issues arise in the midst of treatment can serve as grist for the therapeutic mill.

Gutheil (1994) criticizes Lazarus for not considering the impact of his interventions on the client. He also stresses his belief that sound risk management is not antithetical to spontaneity, warmth, humanitarian concerns, or flexibility of approach, as Lazarus contends. One of Gutheil's main points is that sound and valid risk management principles need to rest on a solid clinical foundation.

In Lazarus's rejoinder (1994b), he comments on the risk-benefit ratio of transcending therapeutic boundaries. From his perspective, the major difference between his views and those of the respondents is that they dwell mostly on the potential costs and risks, whereas he focuses mainly on the potential advantages that may occur when certain boundaries are transcended.

Before you read about the various forms of multiple relationships therapists may encounter, clarify your thinking on these issues:

◆ What do you think of Lazarus's contention that certain boundaries can diminish therapeutic effectiveness?
◆ Do you think the ethical codes of the various professional organizations as they pertain to boundary issues and multiple relationships are too rigid and may compromise therapeutic effectiveness?
◆ What kinds of boundaries would you want to establish with your clients?
◆ How can you assess the impact your interventions and behavior have on your clients?
◆ Are you concerned with the potential for becoming involved in a malpractice suit if you relax certain boundaries?
◆ What topics pertaining to managing boundaries, multiple roles, and multiple relationships would you want to address with your clients from the initial session?

As you read the rest of this chapter, imagine yourself in these situations. What challenges might you encounter in managing multiple relationships?

Bartering for Professional Services

When a client is unable to afford therapy, he or she may offer a bartering arrangement. For example, a mechanic might exchange work on a therapist's car for counseling sessions. However, if the client was expected to provide several hours of work on the therapist' car in exchange for one therapy session, this client might become resentful over the perceived imbalance of the exchange. If the therapist's car was not repaired properly, the therapist might harbor resentment against the client. This could damage the therapeutic relationship. In addition, problems of another sort can occur with dual relationships, especially when clients clean house, perform secretarial services, or do other personal work for the therapist. Clients can easily be put in a bind when they are in a position to learn personal material about their therapists. Certainly, many problems can arise from these kinds of exchanges for both therapists and clients.

Ethical Standards on Bartering

In the last edition of this book we stated that most professional codes did not have a specific standard on bartering. Just five years later this has changed, and now most ethics codes address the complexities of bartering (see the box on page 235). We agree with the general tone of these standards, although we would add that bartering should be evaluated within a cultural context. In some cultures and in certain communities, bartering is an accepted practice. Before bartering is entered into, both parties should talk about the arrangement, gain a clear understanding of the exchange, and come to an agreement.

Ethical Codes and Standards for Bartering

The APA ethics code (1995) includes a standard that discourages bartering as a general rule but also delineates circumstances when psychologists might become involved in such an arrangement:

> Psychologists ordinarily refrain from accepting goods, services, or other nonmonetary remuneration from patients or clients in return for psychological services because such arrangements create inherent potential for conflicts, exploitation, and distortion of the relationship. A psychologist may participate in bartering *only* if (1) it is not clinically contraindicated, and (2) the relationship is not exploitative. (1.18.)

ACA's (1995) code also discourages bartering:

> Counselors ordinarily refrain from accepting goods or services from clients in return for counseling services because such arrangements create inherent potential for conflicts, exploitation, and distortion of the professional relationship. Counselors may participate in bartering only if the relationship is not exploitive, if the client requests it, if a clear written contract is established, and if such arrangements are an accepted practice among professionals in the community. (A.10.c.)

NASW (1996) has the following guideline on bartering:

> Social workers should avoid accepting goods or services from clients as payment for professional services. Bartering arrangements, particularly involving services, create the potential for conflicts of interest, exploitation, and inappropriate boundaries in social workers' relationships with clients. Social workers should explore and may participate in bartering only in very limited circumstances where it can be demonstrated that such arrangements are an accepted practice among professionals in the local community, considered to be essential for the provision of service, negotiated without coercion and entered into at the client's initiative and with the client's informed consent. Social workers who accept goods or services from clients as payment for professional services assume the full burden of demonstrating that this arrangement will not be detrimental to the client or the professional relationship. (1.13.b.)

It is also important that potential problems that might develop be discussed and that alternatives be examined. Using a sliding scale to determine fees or making a referral are two possible alternatives that might have merit. Bartering is an example of a dual relationship that we think allows some room for practitioners to use their professional judgment and to consider the cultural context in which they practice.

Forester-Miller (1997) writes about the difficulties involved in avoiding dual relationships in rural communities. She reminds counselors that values and beliefs may vary significantly between urban dwellers and their rural counterparts and suggests that counselors need to work to ensure that they are not imposing values that come from a cultural perspective different from that of their clients. She uses bartering as an example of one way of providing counseling services in some regions to individuals who could not otherwise afford counseling. Forester-Miller gives an example of adapting her practices in the Appalachian culture, where individuals pride themselves on being able to provide for themselves and their loved ones. Forester-Miller once counseled an adolescent girl whose single-parent mother could not afford her usual fee, nor could she afford to pay a reduced fee, as even a small amount would be a drain on this family's resources. When Forester-Miller informed the mother that she would be willing to see her daughter for free, the mother stated that this would not be acceptable to her. However, she asked the counselor if she would accept a quilt she had made as payment for counseling the daughter. The mother and the counselor discussed the monetary value of the quilt and decided to use this as payment for a specified number of counseling sessions. Forester-Miller reports that this was a good solution because it allowed the adolescent girl to receive needed counseling services and gave the mother an opportunity to maintain her sense of pride that she could pay her own way.

If you had a client who could not afford to pay even a reduced fee, might you be inclined to engage in bartering goods for your services? What kind of understanding would you need to work out with your client before you agreed to a bartering arrangement? Would your decision be dependent on whether you were practicing in a large urban area or a rural area? How might you take the cultural context into consideration when making your decision?

Some professionals strongly disapprove of bartering, and others consider the practice unethical, regardless of the context in which it occurs. The California licensing board is one group that disapproves of bartering. In 1990, it distributed a pamphlet to all licensed therapists that stated that bartering goods or services to pay for therapy is an "inappropriate behavior and misuse of power." Bartering was considered just as inappropriate as hiring a client to do work for the therapist (Hall, 1996).

Therapists who are considering entering into a bartering arrangement would do well to consider Hall's (1996) recommendations prior to establishing such an arrangement:

- Evaluate whether the bartering arrangement will put you at risk of impaired professional judgment or have a negative impact on your performance as a therapist.
- Determine the value of the goods or services in a collaborative fashion with the client at the outset of the bartering arrangement.
- Determine the appropriate length of time for the barter arrangement.
- Document the bartering arrangement, including the value of the goods or services and a date on which the arrangement will end or be renegotiated.

To this list of suggestions, we add the importance of consulting with experienced colleagues or a supervisor if you are considering some form of bartering in lieu of payment for therapy services. The opinions of others might prove helpful in pinpointing potential problems associated with certain kinds of proposed bartering arrangements. Also, colleagues may offer alternatives that you and your client have not considered.

Consider these cases and apply the ethical standards we have summarized to your analysis. What ethical issues are involved in each case? What potential problems do you see emerging from these cases? What alternatives to bartering can you think of?

◆ ***The case of Barbara.*** Barbara is 20 years old and has been in therapy with Sidney for over a year. She has developed respect and fondness for her therapist, whom she sees as a father figure. She tells him that she is thinking of discontinuing therapy because she has lost her job and simply has no way of paying for the sessions. She is obviously upset over the prospect of ending the relationship, but she sees no alternative. Sidney informs her that he is willing to continue her therapy even if she is unable to pay. He suggests that as an exchange of services she can become the baby-sitter for his three children. She gratefully accepts this offer.

After a few months, however, Barbara finds that the situation is becoming difficult for her. Eventually, she writes a note to Sidney telling him that she cannot handle her reactions to his wife and their children. It makes her think of all the things she missed in her own family. She writes that she has found this subject difficult to bring up in her sessions, so she is planning to quit both her services and her therapy.

1st lowering fee
2nd referral to another community organization

◆ What mistakes, if any, do you think Sidney made? *not considering the impact of the services upon her.*
◆ How might you have dealt with this situation?
◆ Was it unethical for the therapist to suggest that Barbara do baby-sitting for him? In doing so, to what degree did Sidney take into consideration the nature of the transference relationship? *Yes, it was self-serving* *he did not.*

◆ ***The case of Olive.*** Olive is a massage therapist in her community. Her services are sought by many professionals, including Gerard, a local psychologist. In the course of a massage session, she confides in him that she is experiencing difficulties in her marriage. She would like to discuss with him the possibility of exchanging professional services. She proposes that in return for marital therapy she will give both him and his wife massage treatments. An equitable arrangement based on their fee structures can be worked out, she says, and they will save some money on taxes as well. Gerard might make any one of the following responses:

Response A: That's fine with me, Olive. It sounds like a good proposal. Neither one of us will suffer financially because of it, and we can each benefit from our expertise.

Response B: Well, Olive, I feel OK about the exchange, except I have concerns about the dual relationship.

Response C: Even though our relationship is nonsexual, Olive, I do feel squeamish about seeing you as a client in marital therapy. I certainly could refer you to a competent marital therapist.

◆ What do you think about each of these responses?
◆ What are your thoughts about Olive's proposal? What are the ethical implications, or possible violations, in this case? *not accepted practice in the community!*
◆ If you were in this situation, how would you deal with Olive? *# 1 in 2 steps*

#C

236

Commentary.   Pope and Vasquez (1991) point out a particular problem with exchanging services: "The therapist who is treating a patient in exchange for some services may find himself or herself manipulating or otherwise influencing the patient to provide better services or might became so critical of the patient's seemingly poor services that the therapeutic process becomes destructive for the patient" (p. 116). To what degree do you think this statement fits these two cases? What implications do you see?

Social Relationships with Clients

Do social relationships with clients necessarily interfere with therapeutic relationships? Some would say no, contending that counselors and clients are able to handle such relationships as long as the priorities are clear. They see social contacts as particularly appropriate with clients who are not deeply disturbed and who are seeking personal growth. Some peer counselors, for example, maintain that friendships before or during counseling are actually positive factors in establishing trust.

Other counselors take the position the counseling and friendship should not be mixed. They argue that attempting to manage a social and professional relationship simultaneously can have a negative effect on the therapeutic process, the friendship, or both. Here are some reasons for discouraging the practice of accepting friends as clients or of becoming socially involved with clients: (1) counselors may not be as confrontive with clients they know socially; (2) counselors' own needs to be liked and accepted may lead them to be less challenging, lest the friendship or social relationship be jeopardized; (3) counselors' own needs may be enmeshed with those of their clients to the point that objectivity is lost; and (4) counselors are at greater risk of exploiting clients because of the power differential in the therapeutic relationship.

The cultural context can play a role in evaluating the appropriateness of dual relationships. In his article dealing with multicultural perspectives on multiple relationships, D. W. Sue (1997) makes it clear that some cultural groups may value multiple relationships with helping professionals. Some of Sue's points are worth considering in determining when multiple relationships might be acceptable:

◆ In Asian culture it is believed that personal matters are best discussed with a relative or a friend. Self-disclosing to a stranger (the counselor) is considered taboo and a violation of familial and cultural values. Thus, some Asian clients may prefer to have the traditional counseling role evolve into a more personal one.

◆ Gift giving is a common practice in many Asian communities to show gratitude and respect and to seal a relationship. Although such actions are culturally appropriate, Western-trained professionals may believe that accepting a gift would distort boundaries, change the relationship, and create a conflict of interest. If the therapist were to refuse the gift, it is likely that this client would feel insulted.

♦ Clients from many cultural groups prefer to receive advice and suggestions from an expert. They perceive the counselor to be an expert, having higher status and possessing superior knowledge. To work effectively with these clients, the counselor may have to play a number of different roles. Yet counselors may view playing more than one of these roles as engaging in dual or multiple relationships. (See Chapter 10 for a more extensive discussion of alternatives to traditional roles for professionals who work in the community.)

Sue (1997) admits that the guidelines that discourage multiple relationships are well-intentioned and basically sound, yet he emphasizes that they must not be rigidly applied to all situations. For him, it is essential to take into consideration community characteristics, multicultural redefinitions of counseling roles, and cultural perceptions of helping practices.

In a survey of dual relationships between therapist and client (Borys & Pope, 1989), psychologists, psychiatrists, and social workers rated the following practices as being "never ethical":

♦ accepting a client's invitation to a special occasion (6.3%)
♦ becoming friends with a client after termination (14.8%)
♦ inviting clients to an office or clinic open house (26.6%)
♦ going out to eat with a client after a session (43.2%)
♦ inviting a client to a personal party or social event (63.5%)

In a study on the beliefs and behaviors of therapists (Pope, Tabachnick, & Keith-Spiegel, 1987), 42.1% of respondents said that they never became friends with a former client, and 6.4% considered the behavior unethical. Regarding inviting clients to a party or social event, 82.9% said they had never engaged in the behavior, and 50% viewed this behavior as unethical.

Although some therapists take the position that socializing with *current* clients is ethically and clinically problematic, they may be more accepting of forming social relationships with certain *former* clients. What are the ethics involved in nonromantic posttherapy relationships between therapists and former clients? In their study on this topic, Anderson and Kitchener (1996) found little consensus among professionals regarding how ethical these contacts are. Some therapists believe the client-therapist relationship continues in perpetuity, however the majority of study participants suggested that posttherapy relationships were ethical if a certain time period had elapsed. Others proposed that such relationships were ethical if the former client decided not to return to therapy with that therapist and if the posttherapy relationship did not seem to hinder later therapy with other therapists.

In Salisbury and Kinnier's (1996) research on counselors' behaviors and attitudes regarding friendships with former clients, they found that many counselors have engaged in posttermination friendships and believe that under certain circumstances such relationships are acceptable. Fully 70% of the study participants believed that posttermination friendships were ethical approximately two years after termination of the professional relationship.

Our position on socializing with clients.   It is our view that blending social and personal relationships is an open issue. We question the assertion that some social involvements with a client other than in the office implies an unwillingness to challenge the client and automatically makes the therapist less objective. Although the possibility exists that a therapist may be less confrontive because of the fear of losing the relationship, we do not think that all forms of out-of-office contact necessarily preclude honest and effective confrontation. However, even though making friends with former clients may not be unethical, the practice may be unwise. In the long run, former clients may need you more as a therapist at some future time than as a friend. If you develop a friendship with a former client, then he or she is no longer eligible to use your professional services. Counselors should be aware of their own motivations, as well as the motivations of their clients, and they must objectively assess the impact a social relationship might have on the client-therapist relationship. Consider this case example.

◆ **The case of a counselor intern.**   Imagine that you are an intern in a college counseling center, and one of your clients says to you: "I really like working with you, but I hate coming over here to this cold and impersonal office. I always feel weird waiting in the lobby as if I were a 'case' or something. Why can't we meet outside on the lawn? Better yet, we could get away from campus and meet in the park nearby. I'd feel more natural and uninhibited in a more informal setting."

- Would you agree to meet your client outside the office? *no*
- Would your decision depend on how much you liked or were attracted to your client? *no*
- Would your client's age and sex have much to do with your decision? *no*

Later, your client invites you to a party and lets you know that it would mean a lot if you were to come. Your client says: "I'd really like to get to know you on a personal basis because I'm being so deeply personal in here. I really like you, and I'd like more time with you than the hour we have each week."

- What are your immediate reactions? *no*
- Assuming that you like your client and would like to go to the party, do you think it would be wise to attend? *no*
- What would you say to your client? How would you support your decision?
- What effect do you think meeting your client on a social basis would have on the therapeutic process? *no good, boundaries crossed*

It would damage our prof. relationship

Commentary.   Certainly, there are problems when professional and social relationships are blended. Such arrangements demand a great deal of honesty and self-awareness on the part of the therapist. No matter how clear the therapist is on boundaries, if the client cannot understand or cannot handle the social relationship, such a relationship should not be formed—with either current or former clients. When clear boundaries are not maintained, both the professional and the social relationship can sour. Clients may well become inhibited during therapy out of fear of alienating their therapist. They may fear losing the respect of a therapist with whom they have a friendship. They may censor their disclosures so that they do not threaten this social relationship.

Your position on socializing with clients.   There are many types of socializing, ranging from dating a client to having a cup of tea or coffee with a client. There are differences between a social involvement initiated by a client and one instigated by a therapist. Another factor to consider is whether the social contact is ongoing or occasional. The degree of intimacy is also a factor. For instance, there is a difference between meeting a client for coffee or for a candlelight dinner. In thinking through your own position on establishing a dual relationship with a current client, consider the nature of the social function, the nature of your client's problem, the client population, the setting where you work, the kind of therapy being employed, and your theoretical approach. If you are psychoanalytically oriented, you are likely to adopt stricter boundaries and will be concerned about polluting the transference relationship should you blend any form of socializing with the therapy. If you are a behavior therapist helping a client to stop smoking, it may be possible to have social contact at some point. Weigh the various factors and consider this matter from both the client's and the therapist's perspective.

Ethics codes do not address the issue of friendships with former clients. What are your thoughts on this topic? Should ethics codes address nonromantic and nonsexual posttherapy relationships specifically? Under what circumstances might such relationships be unethical? When do you think these relationships might be considered ethical?

Sexual Attractions in the Client-Therapist Relationship

In a pioneering study, "Sexual Attraction to Clients: The Human Therapist and the (Sometimes) Inhuman Training System," Pope, Keith-Spiegel, and Tabachnick (1986) developed the theme that there has been a lack of systematic research into the sexual attraction of therapists to their clients. This silence gives the impression that therapists are incapable of being sexually attracted to those they serve or that the phenomenon is a regrettable aberration limited to the few who sexually act out with clients. Many therapists feel that if they do experience sexual attractions toward clients, they are guilty of therapeutic errors. Pope and his colleagues provide clear evidence that attraction to clients is a prevalent experience among both male and female therapists and investigated the following questions:

◆ What is the frequency of sexual attraction to clients by therapists?
◆ Do therapists feel guilty or uncomfortable when they have such attractions?
◆ Do they tend to tell their clients about their attractions?

- Do they consult with colleagues?
- Do therapists believe that their graduate training provided adequate education on attraction to clients?

Pope and his colleagues studied 585 respondents and only 77 reported never having been attracted to any client. The vast majority (82%) reported that they had never seriously considered actual sexual involvement with a client. An even larger majority (93.5%) reported never having had sexual relations with their clients. Therapists gave a number of reasons for having refrained from acting out their attractions to clients, including a need to uphold professional values, a concern about the welfare of the client, and a desire to follow personal values. Fears of negative consequences were mentioned, but they were less frequently cited than values pertaining to client welfare. Most respondents (69%) believed that sexual attractions to clients were useful or beneficial, at least in some instances, to the therapy. With respect to the client's being aware of the therapist's attraction, 71% believed that the client was probably not aware. Most therapists (81%) believed that the attraction had been mutual. Over half (55%) indicated that they had received no education on the subject of sexual attraction to clients in their graduate training and internships; 24% had received "very little"; 12 % had received "some"; and 9% thought that they had received adequate preparation in dealing with sexual attraction to clients. Those who had some graduate training in this area were more likely to have sought consultation (66%) than were those with no such training.

Another study on the beliefs and behaviors of psychologists as therapists sheds light on the topic of sexual attractions in therapy (Pope et al., 1986). In this study only 9.2% of the respondents said they had never been "sexually attracted to a client," and 11.2% considered this behavior unethical. With respect to "engaging in sexual fantasy about a client, 27% said they had never engaged in this behavior and 18.9% considered this behavior to be unethical. With respect to telling a client "I'm sexually attracted to you," 78.5% said they had never done so and 51.5% considered this behavior to be unethical.

According to Pope, Sonne, and Holroyd (1993), the tendency to treat sexual feelings as if they are taboo has made it difficult for therapists to acknowledge and accept attractions to clients. They found that the most common reactions of therapists to sexual feelings in therapy were:

- surprise, startle, and shock
- guilt
- anxiety about unresolved personal problems
- fear of losing control
- fear of being criticized
- frustration at not being able to speak openly—or at not being able to make sexual contact
- confusion about tasks
- confusion about boundaries and roles
- confusion about actions

- anger at the client's sexuality
- fear or discomfort at frustrating the client's demands

It is not surprising that many therapists want to hide rather than to acknowledge and deal with sexual feelings by consulting a colleague or by bringing this to their own therapy.

There is a distinction between finding a client sexually attractive and being preoccupied with this attraction. If you find yourself sexually attracted to your clients, it is important that you examine these feelings. If you are intensely aroused and attracted often, you may need to deal with this issue in your own therapy and supervision. Consider these questions: What's going on in my own life that may be creating this intense need for sexual attractions? What might I be missing in my personal life?

Although transient sexual feelings are normal, intense preoccupation with clients is problematic. Pope, Keith-Spiegel, and Tabachnik (1986) found that 57% of the psychologists in their study sought consultation or supervision when attracted to a client. Seeking help from a colleague or supervision or personal therapy can give therapists access to guidance, education, and support in handling their feelings. Pope, Sonne, and Holroyd (1993) believe that exploration of sexual feelings about clients is best done with the help, support, and encouragement of others. They maintain that practice, internships, and peer supervision groups are ideal places to talk about this topic, which is often treated as though it were nonexistent.

Bennett, Bryant, VandenBos, and Greenwood (1990) and Gill-Wigal and Heaton (1996) offer these suggestions on how therapists can deal with powerful attractions to clients:

- Acknowledge the feelings of attraction.
- Explore the reasons you are attracted to a client. Ask if there is something about this person that meets one of your needs.
- Never act out feelings of attraction. Be careful of actions that might foster the attraction, such as sitting close to the client, hugging the client, or prolonging the sessions.
- Seek out an experienced colleague, supervisor, or personal therapist who might be able to help you decide on a course of action.
- Seek personal counseling, if necessary, to help you resolve your feelings about this client and to uncover the issues in your life that you may not be dealing with.
- Monitor boundaries by setting clear limits on physical contact, self-disclosure, and client requests for personal information.
- If you are unable to resolve your feelings appropriately, terminate the professional relationship and refer the client to another therapist.

Consider this situation: You are sexually attracted to one of your clients. You're aware that your client has sexual feelings toward you and would be willing to become involved with you. You often have difficulty paying attention during sessions because of your fantasies. How would you interpret this situation?

- This is a sure sign of the beginning of countertransference.
- My feelings are acceptable and can easily be hidden from the client.
- I must discuss this immediately with my client, with a strong recommendation for referral.
- My own needs have become more important than my client's needs.
- I need to consult with a colleague.
- I have serious problems.

What do you think your response would be?

- I can ignore my feelings for the client and my client's feelings toward me and focus on other aspects of the relationship.
- I will tell my client of my feelings of attraction, discontinue the professional relationship, and then begin a personal relationship.
- I will openly express my feelings toward my client by saying: "I'm glad you find me an attractive person, and I'm strongly attracted to you as well. But this relationship is not about our attraction for each other, and I'm sure that's not why you came here."
- If there were no change in the intensity of my feelings toward my client, I would arrange for a referral to another therapist.
- I would consult with a colleague or seek professional supervision.

Which of the above courses of action would you take, and why? Can you think of another direction in which you might proceed? Why would you choose this direction?

◆ **The case of Diana.** Diana's husband, a police officer, was killed in the line of duty, leaving her with three young children. She seeks professional help from Clint and works through her grief, in the process uncovering some deep-rooted abandonment issues pertaining to other areas in her life. After three years of therapy, she and Clint discuss termination. During this final stage of therapy she confesses to him that she is finding it increasingly difficult to think of not seeing him anymore. She has grown fond of him. She finds herself constantly thinking about him, and she wonders if they could continue to see each other socially, maybe even romantically.

At first Clint is taken aback. But he also realizes that throughout the course of therapy he has come to admire and respect Diana, and he discloses his fondness for her. He explains to her that because of their professional relationship, he is bound by ethical guidelines not to become involved with his clients socially or romantically. He proposes to her that they not see each other for a year. If their feelings persist, he will then consider initiating a personal relationship. Diana expresses her disappointment at the year's delay but agrees to the stipulation rather than having no hope at all. They embrace, and Diana leaves the office.

- What are your thoughts about Clint's way of handling the situation? Do you see any possible ethical violations in how the case evolved?
- Are there any therapeutic issues that Clint did not explore? *transference after*
- If Clint was attracted to Diana but had withheld this information for thera- *death*
  peutic reasons, would you consider that to be ethical behavior? Why, or why not? *w/ supervision/consult.*
- What if Clint has no feelings of attraction or desire to continue any sort of relationship but said what he did to avoid a difficult ending? How ethical would that be? If you were in a similar situation and did not want to pursue the relationship, how might you deal with your client's disclosure? *the lawyer/insured*
  code of ethics
  binds
- What are your reactions to their embrace at the end?

misleading → handshake
warmly given

Sexual Relationships: Ethical and Legal Issues

The issue of erotic contact in therapy is not simply a matter of whether or not to have sexual intercourse with a client. Even if you decide intellectually that you wouldn't engage is such intimacies, it's important to realize that the relationship between therapist and client can involve varying degrees of sexuality. Therapists may have sexual fantasies, they may behave seductively with their clients, they may influence clients to focus on romantic or sexual feelings toward them, or they may engage in physical contact that is primarily intended to arouse or satisfy their sexual desires. Their behavior is clearly sexual in nature and can have much the same effect as direct sexual involvement would have. Sexual overtones can easily distort the therapeutic relationship and become the real focus of the sessions. It is crucial that practitioners learn to accept their sexual feelings and consciously decide how to deal with them in therapy. Olarte (1997) makes the point that as therapists none of us are immune from the possibility of engaging in an inappropriate relationship with a client. We need to be aware of the effects of our sex-related socialization patterns and how they may influence possible countertransference reactions.

During the past decade a number of studies have documented the harm that sexual relationships with clients can cause. As you will see in Chapter 9, there has also been considerable writing on the damage done to students and supervisees when educators and supervisors enter into sexual relationships with them. Later in this section we discuss the negative effects on clients that typically occur when the client-therapist relationship becomes sexualized.

The Scope of the Problem

Sexual contact with current clients is explicitly prohibited in the codes of ethics of the various professional organizations. Yet even with this clear proscription, sexual boundary violations have been documented in various groups of health professionals (Olarte, 1997). Sexual misconduct is considered to be one of the most serious of all ethical violations for a therapist, and it is the most common allegation in malpractice suits. Therapist-client sexual contact is arguably the most disruptive and potentially damaging boundary violation (D. Smith & Fitzpatrick, 1995).

In her review of research on the sexually abusive therapist, Olarte (1997) notes that a majority of sexual boundary violations (approximately 88%) occur between male therapists and female clients. Sixty-five percent of offending therapists reported being "in love" with their clients, 33% were repeat offenders, 40% regretted instances of sexual contact with clients, and 41% consulted colleagues. Therapists who engage in sexual misconduct are typically described as being in a "lovesick" state, which tends to cloud their judgment. The typical composite of a therapist who becomes involved in sexual boundary violations is a middle-aged man who is experiencing personal distress, is isolated professionally, and overvalues his healing abilities. His methods are unorthodox, and he inappropriately discloses personal information that is irrelevant to therapy.

Many professional journals review disciplinary actions regarding therapists who violate ethical and legal standards. *The California Therapist*, for example, carries a section on disciplinary actions in each issue. A cursory review of this section reveals that most therapists who are subject to disciplinary actions by both the Board of Behavioral Science Examiners and the Board of Psychology have been charged with sexual misconduct. The four charges described here provide a picture of how therapists can manipulate clients to meet their own sexual or emotional needs.

◆ A licensed clinical social worker was charged with gross negligence in the performance of clinical social work; engaging in sexual relationships with a client; and dual relationships. The therapist commenced a professional relationship with a client that evolved into a social and friendship relationship. The therapist admitted to her client that she loved her, in response to a similar statement by the client. At the therapist's invitation, the client attended a birthday party for the therapist, at which time the therapist introduced her client to other clients. She also offered to loan her client money so that she could attend graduate school. Later the therapist attended a housewarming party given by her client. The therapist subsequently engaged in sexual relations with another client. The client abruptly terminated counseling. About two weeks after counseling ended, the therapist and client became lovers and remained lovers for about a year and a half, when the client ended this relationship. (California Association of Marriage and Family Therapists, 1996a, p. 18)

◆ A licensed counselor treated a female client for about ten years. The counselor asked his client how she felt about taking her clothes off during therapy sessions. She indicated that she would feel very embarrassed. About three months later, he urged her to remove her clothing, proposing to use "Reichian" therapy. The client removed her clothes, except her underwear, but told her counselor about her discomfort in doing this. He assured her that this technique would help her in dealing with her sexual problems. Later, she agreed to take off all her clothes and was nude during her sessions. This occurred between 6 and 12 times and constituted gross negligence on the counselor's part. (California Association of Marriage and Family Therapists, 1996b, p. 25)

◆ A licensed marriage, family, and child counselor permitted and encouraged a client's therapy relationship to develop into a personal and sexual relationship, including hugging, kissing, and sexual intercourse. The therapist also provided the client with marijuana and alcohol in the course of his personal relationship with her, despite his knowledge that some of the problems for which she was in therapy were related to drugs and alcohol. The therapist also loaned the client about $1000. (California Association of Marriage and Family Therapists, 1996b, p. 26)

◆ A licensed counselor told a female client that she needed to have and to express her oedipal sexual feelings toward her father as a child in a safe place, that he would be that safe place, that she should have sexual feelings for someone other than her father, and that she needed to be sexually attracted to him. During a session in the early phase of her therapy, the counselor instructed the client to sit on his lap and tell him what she wanted to do with him sexually. Later the counselor kissed the client on the mouth. Although she did not experience this kiss as sexual, she did not feel it was right. The therapist later tried to convince her that the kiss was on the cheek and not on the lips. She eventually terminated therapy because she felt that the situation surrounding the kiss operated against any therapeutic gain in continuing therapy with this counselor. (California Association of Marriage and Family Therapists, 1996c, p. 34)

Clients who are the victims of sexual misconduct suffer dire consequences. Studies continue to demonstrate that therapists strongly disapprove of erotic contact in therapy and contend that it should never occur in a professional relationship. Practitioners typically take the position that erotic contact is totally inappropriate and is an exploitation of the relationship by the therapist. Sexual contact with clients is viewed by most practitioners as being unprofessional, unethical, and clinically harmful. Not only does sexualizing a therapy relationship result in harm to clients but therapists who engage in sexual intimacies with clients (or former clients) risk negative consequences for themselves, both personally and professionally. Among these consequences are: being the target of a lawsuit, being convicted of a felony, having their licenses revoked, being expelled from professional organizations, losing their insurance coverage, and losing their jobs. They may also be placed on probation, be required to undergo their own psychotherapy, be closely monitored if they are allowed to resume their practice, and be required to obtain supervised practice.

A Continuum of Sexual Contact with Clients

Coleman and Schaefer (1986) write that sexual abuse of clients by counselors can best be considered along a continuum ranging from psychological abuse to covert and overt abuse. In *psychological abuse* the client is put in the position of becoming the emotional caretaker of the counselor's needs. A therapist may meet his or her own needs for intimacy through the client, reverse roles with

Sexual Contact and the Therapeutic Relationship

◆ "Sexual intimacy with clients is prohibited" (AAMFT, 1991).
◆ "Counselors do not have any type of sexual intimacies with clients and do not counsel persons with whom they have had a sexual relationship" (ACA, 1995).
◆ "Psychologists do not engage in sexual intimacies with current patients or clients" (APA, 1995).
◆ "Psychologists do not accept as therapy patients or clients persons with whom they have engaged in sexual intimacies" (APA, 1995).
◆ "Social workers should under no circumstances engage in sexual activities or sexual contact with current clients, whether such contact is consensual or forced" (NASW, 1996).
◆ "Social workers should not provide clinical services to individuals with whom they have had a prior sexual relationship. Providing clinical services to a former sexual partner has the potential to be harmful to the individual and is likely to make if difficult for the social worker and individual to maintain appropriate professional boundaries" (NASW, 1996).

the client, or self-disclose without aiding the client. In *covert abuse* the counselor's boundary confusion with the client becomes more pronounced as he or she displays behaviors with intended sexual connotations. The result is a further intrusion into the client's intimacy boundaries. Common forms of this level of abuse include sexual hugs, professional voyeurism, sexual gazes, over-attention to the client's dress and appearance, and seductiveness through dress and gestures. At the far end of the continuum are *overt forms of sexual misconduct.* This category includes the most clearly recognized forms of counselor abuse: sexual remarks, passionate kissing, fondling, sexual intercourse, oral or anal sex, and sexual penetration with objects. Coleman and Schaefer state that such contact is totally inappropriate and is an exploitation of the relationship by the therapist. Erotic contact with clients is unprofessional, unethical, and antitherapeutic.

Ethical Standards on Sexual Contact with Clients

Virtually all of the professional organizations now have a specific statement prohibiting sexual intimacies in the therapeutic relationship (see the box above). Many of the ethical codes also specify that if therapists have had a prior sexual relationship with a person, they should not accept this person as a client. It is clear from the statements of the major mental-health organizations that these principles go beyond merely condemning sexual relationships with clients. The existing codes are explicit with respect to sexual harassment and sexual relationships with clients, students, and supervisees. However, they do not, and maybe they cannot, define some of the more subtle ways that sexuality may be a part of professional relationships.

Harmful Effects of Sexual Contact with Clients

Bouhoutsos, Holroyd, Lerman, Forer, and Greenberg (1993) suggest that when sexual intercourse begins, therapy as a helping process ends. When sex is involved in a therapeutic relationship, the therapist loses control of the course of therapy. Sexual contact is especially disruptive if it begins early in the relationship and if it is initiated by the therapist. Of the 559 clients in their study who became sexually involved with their therapists, 90% were adversely affected. This harm ranged from mistrust of opposite sex relationships to hospitalization and, in some cases, suicide. Other effects of sexual intimacies on clients' emotional, social, and sexual adjustment included negative feelings about the experience, a negative impact on their personality, and a deterioration of their sexual relationship with their primary partner. Bouhoutsos and her colleagues conclude that the harmfulness of sexual contact in therapy validates the ethical codes barring such conduct and provides a rationale for enacting legislation prohibiting it.

Coleman and Schaefer (1986) describe other negative outcomes of inappropriate sexual contact in therapy, including depression and other emotional disturbances, impaired social adjustment, and substance abuse. Many clients found that their primary relationships deteriorated. Even though these clients felt that their emotional problems had increased, they also found it more difficult to seek out further therapy because of their previous negative experience. According to Coleman and Schaefer, the psychological and covert forms of abuse may be more damaging than overt abuse. In cases involving overt actions there is no question about the ethical violation, and clients often feel justified in considering themselves abused. With either psychological or covert abuse, however, clients are likely to feel confusion, guilt, and shame. Olarte (1997) identifies these harmful effects of sexual boundary violations: distrust of the opposite sex, distrust for therapists and the therapeutic process, guilt, depression, anger, feeling of rejection, suicidal ideation, and low self-esteem. It is generally agreed that sexual boundary violations remain harmful to clients no matter how much time elapses after termination of therapy.

Pope (1988) describes a syndrome that is associated with sexual contact between therapist and client, which bears a striking relationship to the rape syndrome, the battered-spouse syndrome, and responses to child abuse. Some aspects of the therapist-client syndrome are ambivalence, guilt, emptiness and isolation, sexual confusion, an impaired ability to trust, identity and role confusion, suppressed rage, increased suicidal risk, and cognitive dysfunction. After an extensive survey of the research on the harmful consequences of sexual intimacies with clients, Pope (1988) concludes that awareness of this problem can help professionals avoid the temptation to act out sexual attractions to clients. This awareness can challenge mental-health professionals to create effective measures to ensure that clients are protected from exploitive therapists, and it can help other professionals recognize and respond therapeutically to victims who have experienced distress over this abuse.

The APA's Committee on Women in Psychology (1989) asserts that sexual relationships between therapists and clients are never the fault of the client, that such relationships are never appropriate or helpful in therapy, and that therapists can never be excused for sexual misconduct. This committee contends that sexual contact destroys the objectivity that is necessary for effective therapeutic relationships and that it damages not only clients' trust in the therapist but also their trust in other people, including other therapists. Although the negative impact may be apparent almost immediately, often it does not become evident until later. Clients typically feel taken advantage of and may discount the value of any part of their therapy. They may become embittered and angry, and they may terminate therapy with psychological scars. The problem is compounded if they are deterred from initiating therapy with anyone else because of their traumatic experience.

Legal Sanctions against Sexual Violators

Clients have sued therapists who engaged in sex with them. Therapists found guilty of sexual malpractice have been given sanctions, have been expelled from their professional organizations, have had their licenses revoked or suspended by the state, and have been ordered to undergo therapy to resolve their problems. Austin, Moline, and Williams (1990) reviewed relevant court cases and came to the conclusion that therapists who had engaged in sex with their clients had few arguments they could use in court. Courts have rejected claims of consent by clients, mainly because of the vulnerability of clients and the power of the transference relationship.

Some states have legal sanctions in cases of sexual misconduct in the therapeutic relationship. Sexual intimacy with client is a felony in the states of Colorado, Wisconsin, Minnesota, Missouri, Texas, Washington, and Florida, to mention a few. In Minnesota it is a felony to have sexual contact with a client during the therapy session, and in certain cases the counselor may be found guilty of sexual misconduct even if the contact occurred outside the session. Client consent cannot be used as a defense.

Some states have passed legislation making it easier to remove licenses in situations involving sexual misconduct. In those states it is no longer necessary to prove that damage has resulted from sexual intimacy with a therapist; the only question is whether the sexual misconduct occurred (Holroyd & Bouhoutsos, 1985). These laws place the ultimate ethical and legal burden of responsibility to avoid sexual relationships squarely on the licensed professional. Consistent with such laws is the position of Coleman and Schaefer (1986) that the counselor must take responsibility for setting appropriate sexual boundaries for the client, communicate these boundaries, and keep the relationship professional rather than personal. Professionals cannot argue that their clients seduced them. Even if clients behave in seductive ways, it is clearly the professional's responsibility to maintain appropriate boundaries. Regardless of the client's pathology, the responsibility to hold to ethical standards in a therapy relationship rests solely with the therapist (Olarte, 1997).

Ethical Sanctions

The procedures for filing and processing ethical complaints against psychologists are codified and are dealt with by the state professional associations and by the APA's Committee on Scientific and Professional Ethics and Conduct. Sanders and Keith-Spiegel (1980) summarize the investigation of one psychologist who was accused of becoming sexually involved with his female client after two years of therapy. The psychologist promptly terminated the therapeutic relationship, according to the client, yet no attempt was made to resolve the therapeutic issues remaining. The sexual relationship continued for about a year, on a weekly basis, until it was finally cut off by the client because of her guilt and disgust over the situation. The psychologist made two attempts to resume the affair, but the client refused to become involved.

Although the psychologist at first flatly denied the client's charges, he eventually admitted that they were true. He also said that he loved his client, that he was struggling with a midlife crisis, and that he was having severe marital problems. He added that he was willing to seek personal therapy to work on his problems.

The state psychological association voted to monitor this psychologist's personal therapy and have his practice reviewed for one year. In his hearing before the APA's ethics committee, the therapist gave a progress report on his personal therapy and attempted to convince the committee members that the insights he had gained would preclude any recurrence of this sort of ethical violation. The committee offered a stipulated resignation from the APA for five years, after which he might reapply if no further ethical violations had been brought to the association. Consider these questions:

- Should this psychologist have been allowed to continue his professional practice? Why, or why not? *a year + tell ... periodic reviews thereafter.*
- If you had been a member of the ethics committee that reviewed this case, what action would you have recommended? *very serious — once done prob.*
- If the psychologist was aware that he had fallen in love with his client and *do again & again.* wanted to become sexually involved with her (yet had not done so), what *but & possibly* ethical course of action could he have taken? Is termination of the professional relationship enough? *no personal rela may be taken up.*

Assisting Victims in the Complaint Process

The number of complaints of sexual misconduct against therapists has risen dramatically, but women are still reluctant to file complaints for disciplinary action against their therapists, educators, or supervisors (Gottlieb, 1990; Hotelling, 1991; Howard, 1991; Riger, 1991). Many clients do not know that sexual contact between counselors and clients in unethical and illegal. They are often unaware that they can file a complaint, and they frequently do not know the avenues available to them to address sexual misconduct. Hotelling (1988) describes ethical, legal, and administrative options for individuals who have been victims of professional misconduct. Clients can file an ethical complaint with a professional association or with the therapist's licensing board. Another option is to lodge a complaint with the counselor's employer. There are also legal alternatives: civil suits or criminal actions. A malpractice suit on civil grounds seeks compensatory damages for the client for the cost of treatment and for the suffering involved. Each option has both advantages and disadvantages, and it is ultimately up to clients to decide what is best for them.

Mental-health professionals have an obligation to help increase public awareness about the nature and extent of sexual misconduct and to educate the public about possible courses of action. Gottlieb (1990) describes some institutional barriers within the profession that lead women to feel intimidated and deterred. He suggests the need to establish an organizational structure to help them. Howard (1991) focuses on the need for written policies and consistent, accessible grievance procedures for addressing sexual violations. Asserting that the profession has an obligation to do more than merely process ethical complaints, Gottlieb (1990) encourages creation of a Committee for Complaint Assistance within each state or provincial professional association. The main goal of the committee would be to reach out to clients, students, and trainees who have been abused by professionals. Another function would be to educate the public and the profession.

Sexual Relationships with Former Clients

What are the ethics of beginning a sexual relationship once therapy has ended? Gutheil (1989) asserts that many professionals wrongly operate on the assumption that sexual relationships are permissible if a client's therapy has ended or if there is a termination with a referral. To avoid a possible legal or ethical conflict, Gutheil emphasizes that practitioners should not establish a social or sexual relationship with either a present or a past client. But what do the ethics codes have to say with respect to sexual relationships with former clients? (See the box on page 253 for specific statements on this topic.)

The American Counseling Association, the American Psychological Association, and the American Association for Marriage and Family Therapy all agree that sexual contact before two years after termination is unethical. The National Association of Social Workers does not specify a time period. All four of these organizations state that in the exceptional circumstance of sexual relationships with former clients—even after a two-year interval—the burden of demonstrating that there has been no exploitation clearly rests with the therapist. The factors that need to be considered include: the amount of time that has passed since termination of therapy; the nature and duration of therapy; the circumstances surrounding termination of the professional-client relationship; the client's personal history; the client's competence and mental status; the foreseeable likelihood of harm to the client or others; and any statements or actions of the therapist suggesting a romantic relationship after terminating the professional relationship.

With regard to posttermination sexual relationships, the question that is always unclear is when the professional relationship actually terminated (Foster, 1996). Foster summarizes some points made by Gary Schoener, who raises some very useful questions to help practitioners evaluate posttermination relationships:

Sexual Relationships with Former Clients

♦ "Counselors do not engage in sexual intimacies with former clients within a minimum of two years after terminating the counseling relationship. Counselors who engage in such relationships after two years following termination have the responsibility to examine and document thoroughly that such relations did not have an exploitative nature, based on factors such as duration of counseling, amount of time since counseling, circumstances of termination, client's personal history and mental status, adverse impact on the client, and actions by the counselor suggesting a plan to initiate a sexual relationship with the client after termination" (ACA, 1995).

♦ "Psychologists do not engage in sexual intimacies with a former therapy patient or client for at least two years after cessation or termination or professional service" (APA, 1995).

♦ "Social workers should not engage in sexual activities or sexual contact with former clients because of the potential for harm to the client. If social workers engage in conduct contrary to this prohibition or claim that an exception to this prohibition is warranted due to extraordinary circumstances, social workers—not their clients—assume the full burden of demonstrating that the former client has not been exploited, coerced, or manipulated, intentionally or unintentionally" (NASW, 1996).

♦ "Sexual intimacies with former clients for two years following the termination of therapy is prohibited" (AAMFT, 1991).

♦ What was the length and level of therapeutic involvement?
♦ How much transference, dependency, or power inequity remains after termination?
♦ Was there any deception or coercion, intentional or unintentional by the therapist indicating that sex is generally acceptable after termination of therapy?
♦ Was there an actual termination? Was the decision to terminate a mutual one? Did the therapist end the professional relationship to make it possible to enter into a romantic or sexual relationship with a client?
♦ Who initiated posttermination contact?
♦ What was the extent of the discussion of the pros and cons of engaging in a romantic or sexual relationship?
♦ What kind of consultation, if any, took place?

Some counselors maintain: "Once a client, always a client." Although a blanket prohibition on sexual intimacies, regardless of the time that has elapsed since termination, might clarify the issue, some would contend that this is too extreme of a measure. Others point out that there is a major difference between an intense, long-term therapy relationship and a less intimate, brief-term one. A blanket prohibition ignores these distinctions.

Although the question of whether sexual relationships with former clients are ever acceptable has not been resolved, there appears to be a trend toward strongly discouraging, if not prohibiting, this behavior. In exceptional circumstances when a therapist is considering becoming involved in a personal relationship with a former client, it is essential that the therapist be willing to seek consultation or personal therapy to explore his or her motivations and the possible ramifications of transforming a professional relationship into a personal one. Bennett and his colleagues (1990) offer several suggestions to those considering initiating a relationship with a former client:

- Be aware that developing a personal relationship with a former client is illegal in some jurisdictions and that therapists have been sued for malpractice for engaging in this practice.
- Reflect on the reasons for termination. If you, the client, or both of you experienced an attraction before ending therapy, was the professional relationship terminated for an appropriate reason or so that a sexual relationship could develop?
- Ask yourself about the potential benefits and risks of developing a personal relationship with a former client.
- Before initiating such a relationship, consider discussing the matter with a colleague.

At this point, reflect on your own stand on the controversial issue of forming sexual relationships once therapy has ended. Consider these questions in clarifying your position:

- Should counselors be free to formulate their own practices about developing sexual relationships with former clients?
- Does the length and quality of the therapeutic relationship have a bearing on the ethics involved in such a personal relationship? If a client was in therapy for several years and struggled with an intense transference relationship with her therapist, for example, would it be ethical for them to establish a personal relationship two years after her therapy had ended? If a client saw her counselor for only six sessions to learn how to cope with stress, would it be ethical for them to get involved personally two years after her final session?
- Are sexual relationships with former clients unethical regardless of the elapsed time or the type of therapy? Do you see any exceptions that might justify developing intimate relationships with former clients?
- What guidelines can you come up with to determine the ethics of personal relationships with former clients?
- Although it might not be illegal in your state, is it wise to engage in sex with former clients?
- React to the statement, "Once a client, always a client."

Educating Counselor Trainees to Deal with Sexual Dilemmas

As you can see from the previous discussion, sexual contact in the therapeutic relationship has harmful effects on both client and therapist (Bates & Brodsky, 1989; Bouhoutsos et al., 1983; Brodsky, 1986; Pope, 1988, 1990b; Pope & Bouhoutsos, 1986). Although counselor-client sexual contact is one of the most common ethical violations, most training programs spend little or no time addressing the prohibition. Nor do these programs devote much time to dealing with sexual attraction to clients (Pope, 1987; Pope et al., 1986; Pope, Sonne, & Holroyd, 1993; Rodolfa, Kitzrow, Vohra, & Wilson, 1990; Vasquez, 1988). Moreover, little attention has been given to the ethical aspects of nonerotic physical contact (Holub & Lee, 1990) (see the next section).

Counselors need to ask themselves how they support their choices clinically, and they especially need to ask how they are able to set boundaries when sexual attraction occurs. Heiden (1993) writes that counselors must ask themselves about how they treat clients in different ways, especially with reference to time spent, intimacy, and touch. It is well for counselors to think about how their own needs for intimacy are being met by clients and about ways to set boundaries when sexual attraction to a client occurs.

To reduce sexual misconduct, Stake and Oliver (1991) recommend a multifaceted approach, including changes in legal codes, consumer education, and training for therapists. They suggest that the best approach is for training programs to include the topic of sexual misconduct as a basic component of ethics education and to provide continuing education for therapists.

We think that training programs have a responsibility to help students identify and openly discuss their concerns pertaining to sexual dilemmas in counseling practice. Prevention of sexual misconduct is a better path than remediation. Gutheil (1989), for example, suggests that students should receive explicit instruction on the ethical, legal, and clinical issues pertaining to sexual abuses. Holub and Lee (1990) recommend that these issues be addressed in clinical supervision, in ethics seminars, in continuing education programs, in in-service training, and formally by ethics committees. They also recommend that trainees experience personal therapy as a way to better clarify their own needs and motivations.

Rodolfa and his colleagues (1990) describe training seminars on sexual dilemmas wherein small groups typically explore cases such as these:

- a therapist feels sexually attracted to a client
- a supervisor and a supervisee are mutually attracted to each other
- a therapist feels attracted to a former client
- during an intake session, a client reports a sexual involvement with a previous therapist

Topics that are generally covered during these seminars include:

- an overview of sexual dilemmas and the distinction between having sexual feelings and acting on them
- how to deal with an attraction between client and therapist and respond in ethical and therapeutic ways
- how to intervene with a client who has been sexually involved with another therapist
- how to intervene with a therapist who is sexually attracted to a client or sexually involved with a client

◆ attraction between supervisees and supervisors
◆ feelings during sex therapy and sexual assessments

These seminars encourage interns to work through some of the complex issues involved. The aim is to assist them to think flexibly and to develop options that satisfy professional responsibilities and adhere to ethical standards. Most therapists will encounter sexual dilemmas during their careers, and some formal training in this area is vital.

Vasquez (1988) suggests specific strategies for preventing counselor-client sexual contact: provide students with knowledge, conduct experiential activities that promote self-awareness, and encourage a climate that enhances the development of ethical values and behavior. Students need to learn about the legal and professional consequences of sexual misconduct. They especially need to know about the deleterious consequences for clients. Experiential activities are particularly useful in dealing with issues such as touching in counseling, maintaining proper boundaries, and managing sexual feelings. Role-playing situations can heighten a trainee's sensitivity to the complexity of relationship issues. Vasquez also underscores the place of modeling of ethical behavior by faculty members and clinical supervisors. Educational programs should provide a safe environment where students can acknowledge and explore matters such as sexual attraction and learn how to respond ethically.

It is the responsibility of training programs to help students identify and openly discuss their concerns about sexual temptations. Ignoring this subject in training sends a message to students that the subject should not be talked about, which will inhibit their willingness to seek consultation when they encounter sexual dilemmas in their practice.

A Special Case: Nonerotic Physical Contact with Clients

Although we contend that acting on sexual feelings and engaging in erotic contact with clients is unethical, we do think that nonerotic contact is often appropriate and can have significant therapeutic value. It is important to stress this point, because some counselors perceive a taboo against touching clients. Therapists may hold back when they feel like touching their clients affectionately or compassionately. They may feel that touching can be misinterpreted as sexual or exploitive; they may be afraid of their impulses or feelings toward clients; they may be afraid of intimacy; or they may believe that to express closeness physically is unprofessional. With the current attention being given to sexual harassment and lawsuits over sexual misconduct in professional relationships, some counselors are likely to decide that it is not worth the risk of touching clients at all, lest their intentions be misinterpreted. Although touching does not necessarily constitute a dual relationship, we include this discussion here because certain kinds of touching can lead to dual relationships. A therapist's touch can be a genuine expression of caring, or it can be done primarily to gratify the therapist's own needs.

There are two sides to the issue of touching: some practitioners support it, and others do not. After reviewing both research and clinical data, Willison and Masson (1986) found some indication that touching could be therapeutic when used appropriately. They also found little evidence of any negative effects from appropriate touching. (By appropriate touching they mean non-sexual contact aimed at fostering therapeutic progress and serving the client's needs.) Some clinicians, however, oppose any form of physical contact between counselors and clients on the grounds that it can promote dependency, can interfere with the transference relationship, can be misread by clients, and can become sexualized.

Although research into the use of touching in therapy has produced mixed findings, there do appear to be some therapeutic benefits to nonerotic physical contact. In writing about a men's therapy group, Rabinowitz (1991) cites research findings indicating that appropriate touching can foster self-exploration, increase verbal interaction, increase the client's perception of the expertness of the counselor, and produce more positive attitudes toward the counseling process.

There is also evidence that most psychologists do not consider it unethical to hug a client or a student. In one study only 13.4% of the therapists reported that they had never hugged a client, and only 4.6% viewed hugging a client as unethical (Pope et al., 1987). In another study, 28.4% of educators said that they had never hugged a student, and only 5.6% of them viewed such behavior as unethical (Tabachnick, Keith-Spiegel, & Pope, 1991). Of course, hugging clients or students can be sexual or nonsexual, and the two participants may interpret the hug differently.

Holub and Lee (1990) maintain that good therapists who are concerned with the best interests of distressed clients may choose to reach out with the healing power of touch. But they add this caution: "It should not be done unthinkingly or without considering the therapist's motives and the client's possible reaction" (p. 117). Stake and Oliver (1991) remind us that therapists may not accurately and objectively judge the erotic side of their behavior.

In their discussion, Holub and Lee (1990) assert that the decision to touch or not to touch clients involves more than considering its effectiveness in helping clients or engaging them in therapy. They maintain that this decision should also include deliberating over the correctness, motivations, and interpretations of the touching. The power differential between therapist and client should be considered, and touching often elicits different feelings in men than it does in women. The practice of male therapists' touching only female clients might be interpreted as sexist or at least as poor judgment.

Holroyd and Brodsky (1980) explored the question, "Does touching patients lead to sexual intercourse?" Their results indicate that respondents who admitted having had sexual intercourse with their clients more often advocated and participated in nonerotic contact with opposite-sex clients but not with clients of the same sex. Also, male therapists who had had intercourse with clients were likely to have used and to advocate affectionate touching with women but not with men, even though the men might have initiated contact. Based on data from questionnaires received from 347 male therapists and 310 female therapists, Holroyd and Brodsky came to the following conclusions:

- Touching that does not lead to intercourse is associated with older and more experienced therapists.
- It is the practice of restricting touching to opposite-sex clients, not touching itself, that is related to intercourse.

Holroyd and Brodsky (1980) observe that it is difficult to determine where "nonerotic hugging, kissing, and affectionate touching" leave off and "erotic contact" begins. They conclude: "The use of nonerotic touching as a mode of psychotherapeutic treatment requires further research. Moreover, the sexist implications of differential touching of male and female patients appear to be an important professional and ethical issue" (p. 810).

Rabinowitz (1991) describes some therapeutic values of embracing in a men's group. He points out that it may be safer for a hug to occur in group therapy rather than in individual counseling because there are witnesses to the context of the touching, leaving less room for misinterpretation. However, counselors are still responsible for being sensitive to each member of the group and for avoiding meeting their own needs at the expense of the members. Rabinowitz adds: "Despite the cultural taboo for men to engage in physical touching, the act of embracing another man, in the context of the therapy group, does seem to encourage the expression of deeper feelings and lessen the isolation men often feel in our competitive society" (p. 576).

Bennett and his colleagues (1990) suggest that if touching is consistently and actively used in therapy, it is wise to explain this practice to clients and their families, if appropriate, before therapy begins. They recommend that practitioners consider how clients are likely to react to touching and that they ask themselves questions such as:

- How well do I know the client?
- What makes me think that touch is indicated?
- Could the touch be misinterpreted by the client (or the client's family) as a sexual overture?
- Is touching appropriate in this circumstance?

In our view, touching should be a spontaneous and honest expression of the therapist's feelings. We think it is unwise for therapists to touch clients if this behavior is not congruent with what they feel. A nongenuine touch will be detected by clients and could erode their trust in the relationship. Counselors need to be sensitive to when touching could be counterproductive. There are times when touching clients can distract them from what they are feeling. There are also times when a touch that is given at the right moment can convey far more empathy than words can. Therapists need to be aware of their own motives and to be honest with themselves about the meaning of physical contact. They also need to be sensitive to factors such as the client's readiness for physical closeness, the client's cultural understanding of touching, the client's reaction, the impact such contact is likely to have on the client, and the level of trust that they have built with the client.

Think about your position on the ethical implications of the practice of touching as part of the client-therapist relationship by answering these questions:

- What criteria could you use to determine whether touching your clients was therapeutic or countertherapeutic?
- Do you think that some clients may never be ready to engage in touching in therapy? *yes, part. abused clients*
- How could you honestly answer the question, "Are my own needs being met at the expense of my client's needs?" What might you do if you hugged a client whom you felt needed this kind of physical support and the client suggested that you were meeting your own needs? *I usually let client initiate hug.* *Would think I had*
- To what degree do you think your professional training has prepared you to determine when touching is appropriate and therapeutic? *≈*
- What factors should you consider in determining the appropriateness of touching clients? (Examples are age, gender, the type of client, the nature of the client's problem, and the setting in which the therapy occurs.)
- Do you agree or disagree with the conclusions of Holroyd and Brodsky concerning the sexist implications of differential touching of male and female clients? *?*
- Imagine your first session with a same-sex client who is crying and in a state of crisis. Might you be inclined to touch this person? Would it make a difference if the client asked you to hold him or her? Would it make a difference if this client were of the opposite sex? *I can't be a friend + counselor.*
- If you are favorably inclined toward the practice of touching clients, are you likely to restrict this practice to opposite-sex clients? to same-sex clients? to attractive clients of either sex? Explain.

◆ ***The case of Ida.***   Tu Chee is a warm and kindly counselor who routinely embraces his clients, both male and female. One of his clients, Ida, has had a lonely life, has had no success in maintaining relationships with men, is now approaching her fortieth birthday, and has come to him because she is afraid that she will be alone forever. She misreads his friendly manner of greeting and assumes that he is giving her a personal message. At the end of one session when he gives his usual embrace, she clings to him and does not let go right away. Looking at him, she says: "This is special, and I look forward to this time all week long. I so much need to be touched." He is surprised and embarrassed. He explains to her that she has misunderstood his gesture, that this is the way he is with all of his clients, and that he is truly sorry if he has misled her. She is crestfallen and abruptly leaves the office. She cancels her next appointment.

- What are your thoughts on this counselor's manner of touching his clients?
- Was Tu Chee guilty of insensitivity in not picking up Ida's reactions to him at an earlier point? *Yes – more caution is necessary (circumspection)*
- If Tu Chee explained at the outset of therapy that his touching was part of his style, would that be acceptable? *better but still not great*

- Was the manner in which he dealt with Ida's clinging to him ethically sound? *he was honest + said she was nuisance — but the fact she cancelled her next appt suggests it had gone*
- What obligations, if any, do you think Tu Chee had when Ida canceled her appointment? *redress the situation, ask to talk* *too far already* *about it.*

Dealing with Unethical Behavior in Dual Relationships

In our classes and workshops many students have raised the question, "What should I do when I know of other therapists who are engaging in unethical behavior?" To sharpen your thinking on this question, reflect for a few moments on the possibility of your being involved in the following situations:

- You are aware that a clinical supervisor has made it a practice to have sexual relationships with several of her supervisees. Some of these students are friends of yours, and they tell you that they felt pressure to comply because they were in a vulnerable position. What would you do?
- You know a student intern who initiates social relationships with his clients. He says that his clients are consenting adults, and he argues that by dating them he actually gets to know them better, which helps him in his role as a therapist. What would you do?
- Several of your friends tell you that a counseling professor makes it a practice to date former students. When colleagues confronted him in the past, he maintained that all of these students were adults, that none of them were his students when he dated them, and that what he did in his private life was strictly his own business. What is your view of his behavior? If his behavior were not known to his colleagues, would you report him? Why, or why not?
- You have heard unsettling reports from several clients about another therapist in an agency where you work. They say that he touches them frequently and that he behaves seductively. When you confront this therapist, he becomes defensive, telling you that he is not hung up on touching and that he likes to express his feelings spontaneously. What would you say to him? If you felt you were not getting through to him, what might you do next?
- Imagine yourself as a student in a training program. One of your professors makes several inappropriate and unwelcome advances to you. How might you react? What would you do?

You may wonder whether it is your place to judge the practices of other practitioners. Even if you are convinced that the situation involves clear ethical violations, you may be in doubt about the best way to deal with it. Should you first discuss the matter with the person? Assuming that you do and that the person becomes defensive, should you take any other action or simply drop the matter? When would a violation be serious enough that you would feel obligated to bring it to the attention of an appropriate local, state, or national committee on professional ethics? Most professional organizations have specific ethical standards that clearly place the responsibility for confronting recognized violations squarely on members of their profession. Ig-

Unethical Behavior by Colleagues

◆ "Counselors expect professional associates to adhere to the Code of Ethics. When counselors possess reasonable cause that raises doubts as to whether a counselor is acting in an ethical manner, they take appropriate action" (ACA, 1995, H.2.a.).

◆ "When counselors have reasonable cause to believe that another counselor is violating an ethical standard, they attempt to first resolve the issue informally with the other counselor if feasible, providing that such action does not violate confidentiality rights that may be involved" (ACA, 1995, H.2.d.).

◆ "When an informal resolution is not appropriate or feasible, counselors, upon reasonable cause, take action such as reporting the suspected ethical violation to state or national ethics committees, unless this action conflicts with confidentiality rights that cannot be resolved" (ACA, 1995, H.2.e.).

◆ "Social workers should take adequate measures to discourage, prevent, expose, and correct the unethical conduct of colleagues" (NASW, 1996, 2.11.).

◆ "Human service professionals respond appropriately to unethical behavior of colleagues. Usually this means initially talking directly with the colleague and, if no resolution is forthcoming, reporting the colleague's behavior to supervisory or administrative staff and/or to the professional organization(s) to which the colleague belongs" (NOHSE, 1995, Statement 24).

◆ "When psychologists believe that there may have been an ethical violation by another psychologist, they attempt to resolve the issue by bringing it to the attention of that individual if an informal resolution appears appropriate and the intervention does not violate any confidentiality rights that may be involved" (APA, 1995, 8.04.).

noring an ethical violation is considered to be a violation in itself (see the box above).

The APA's (1995) ethics code makes it clear that professionals have an ethical obligation to be familiar with the ethics code. Furthermore, not being aware of the code or misunderstanding an ethical standard is not an adequate defense to a charge of unethical conduct. Professionals also have an obligation to deal with colleagues when they suspect unethical conduct—first by informally dealing with the person, and if that does not work, then using more formal methods of addressing the situation. Generally, the best way to proceed when you have concerns about the behavior of colleagues is to tell them directly. Then, depending on the nature of the complaint and the outcome of the discussion, reporting a colleague to a professional board would be one of several options open to you.

In a survey of APA-approved clinical training programs, graduate students were asked what they *should* do in a hypothetical situation in which a friend and colleague had violated APA ethical principles; they were then asked what they *would* do (Bernard & Jara, 1986). Approximately half of these students said they would not live up to their own interpretation of what the ethical codes required of them as professionals. Bernard and Jara contend that the problem in training professionals is not how to communicate ethical codes to students but rather how to motivate them to apply their knowledge of ethical standards. "Psychologists need to carefully examine this question and to arrive at ways to reorder priorities so that their responsibility to monitor their own practices is taken more seriously" (p. 315).

It is sometimes easier to see the faults in others and to judge their behavior than to examine your own behavior. Make a commitment to continually reflect on what you are doing personally and professionally. Being your own judge is more realistic and more valuable than being someone else's judge.

Chapter Summary

Sexual relationships with clients are an obvious detriment to their welfare. However, it is important that you not overlook some of the more subtle and perhaps insidious behaviors of the therapist that may in the long run cause as much damage to clients.

It is unwise, unprofessional, unethical, and in many states illegal to become sexually involved with clients. This is not to say that as a counselor you aren't also human or that you will never have strong feelings of attraction toward certain clients. You are probably imposing an unnecessary burden on yourself if you believe that you shouldn't have such feelings for clients or if you try to convince yourself that you shouldn't have more feeling toward one client than toward another. What is important is how you decide to deal with these feelings as they affect the therapeutic relationship. Referral to another therapist isn't necessarily the best solution, unless it becomes clear that you can no longer be effective with a certain client. Instead, you may recognize a need for consultation or, at the very least, for an honest dialogue with your colleagues. It may also be appropriate to have a frank discussion with the client, explaining that the decision not to act on your sexual feelings is based on a commitment to the primacy of the therapeutic relationship.

Becoming a therapist doesn't make you perfect or superhuman. You'll make some mistakes. But we want to stress the importance of reflecting on what you're doing and on whose needs are primary. A willingness to be honest in your self-examination is your greatest asset in becoming an ethical practitioner.

Suggested Activities

1. Investigate the ethical and legal aspects of dual relationships as they apply to the area of your special professional interests. Look for any trends, special problems, or alternatives in your area of specialization. Once you have gathered some materials and ideas, consider presenting your findings in class.
2. Some say that dual relationships are inevitable, pervasive, and unavoidable and have the potential to be either beneficial or harmful. Form two teams and debate the core issues. Have one team focus on the potential benefits of dual relationships and argue that they cannot be dealt with by

simple legislative or ethical mandates. Have the other team argue the case that dual relationships are unethical because they have the potential for bringing harm to clients and that there are other and better alternatives.

3. Write a brief journal article on your position on dual relationships in counseling. Take some small aspect of the problem, develop a definite position on the issue, and present your own views. Consider submitting this article to one of the professional journals. If your article is accepted, you are already on the road to professional writing. If your article is rejected, you have had the experience of writing a position paper and actually going through the process of submission and review. Consider doing this project jointly with one of your professors. (That way, if the article is rejected, you can always blame the professor.)

4. What are your views about forming social relationships with clients during the time they're in counseling with you? after they complete counseling?

5. What guidelines would you employ to determine whether nonerotic touching was therapeutic or countertherapeutic? Would the population you work with make a difference? Would the work setting make a difference? How comfortable are you in both receiving and giving touching? What are your ethical concerns about touching?

6. Take some time to review the ethical codes in the Appendices as they apply to two areas: (a) dual relationships in general and (b) sexual intimacies with present or former clients. Have several students team up to analyze different ethical codes, make a brief presentation to the class, and then lead a discussion on the code's value.

7. Review the discussion on sexual relationships with former clients. Form two teams, and debate the issue of whether sexual and romantic relationships with former clients should be allowed after a specific length of time.

8. What unethical behaviors by your colleagues do you think you would report, if any? How might you proceed if you knew of the unethical practice of a colleague?

9. Form small groups to explore the core issues involved in some of the cases in this chapter. Role-play the cases, and then discuss the implications. Acting out the part of the therapist and the client is bound to enliven the discussion and give you a different perspective on the case. Feel free to embellish on the details given in the cases.

10. Divide the class into a number of small groups, and brainstorm one case other than the ones we have presented in this chapter. The case should illustrate some ethical dilemma in the general area of dual relationships. Come up with a title for your case, creative names for the therapist and the client, and interesting points that will make the case a good discussion tool. Each group can act out its case in class and lead a general discussion.

Professional Competence and Training

Pre-Chapter Self-Inventory

Directions: For each statement, indicate the response that most closely identifies your beliefs and attitudes. Use the following code:

5 = I *strongly agree* with this statement.
4 = I *agree* with this statement.
3 = I am *undecided* about this statement.
2 = I *disagree* with this statement.
1 = I *strongly disagree* with this statement.

__5__ 1. Counselors are ethically bound to refer clients to other therapists when working with them is beyond their professional training.

__2__ 2. Ultimately, practitioners must create their own ethical standards.

__4__ 3. Possession of a license or certificate from a state board of examiners shows that a person has therapeutic skills and is competent to practice psychotherapy.

__4__ 4. Professional licensing protects the public by setting minimum standards of preparation for those who are licensed.

__3__ 5. The present processes of licensing and certification encourage the self-serving interests of the groups in control instead of protecting the public from incompetent practice.

__4__ 6. Continuing education should be a requirement for renewal of a license to practice psychotherapy.

__4__ 7. Health care professionals should be required to demonstrate continuing competency in their field as a prerequisite for license renewal.

__4__ 8. Institutions that train counselors should select trainees on the basis of both their academic record and the degree to which they possess the personal characteristics of effective therapists (as determined by current research findings).

__3__ 9. I think that the arguments for licensing counselors and therapists outweigh the arguments against licensing.

__4__ 10. Peer review, or the analysis and judging of a professional's practice by other practitioners, provides a high degree of assurance to consumers that they will receive competent services.

__3__ 11. A major problem of the peer-review process is the difficulty in determining the qualifications of the reviewer.

__4__ 12. I think that candidates applying for a training program have a right to know the criteria for selecting trainees.

__4__ 13. Once students are admitted, a graduate training program is ethically obliged to continue to assess them to determine their suitability to complete the requirements.

__3__ 14. Trainees who display rigid and dogmatic views about human behavior should not be allowed to continue in a training program.

__4__ 15. It is unethical for a program to train practitioners in only one therapeutic orientation without providing an unbiased overview of other theoretical systems.

_3_ 16. The process of licensing and certification tends to pit professional specializations against one another.

_3_ 17. Rather than having all the counseling specialties, it is best to have only counseling generalists.

_4_ 18. Competent practice implies that counselors are both generalists and have at least one specialty.

_4_ 19. It is unethical for counselors to practice without continuing their education.

_1_ 20. For myself, I might not seek out workshops, seminars, courses, and other postgraduate learning activities if continuing education were not required as a stipulation for maintaining my practice.

Introduction

In this chapter we focus on the ethical and legal aspects of professional competence and the education and training available for mental-health professionals. We discuss issues related to professional licensing and certification as well as approaches to continuing education. We also look at the controversy over a generalist versus a specialty approach to professional counseling.

Ability is not an easy matter for practitioners to assess. To maintain their competence, practitioners must keep up to date on new developments in their specialties. They also need to sharpen their skills and find ways to meet the needs of new populations. Areas such as eating disorders, sexual abuse, substance abuse, gerontological counseling, and AIDS all present challenges that demand that practitioners do more than boast of what they learned in their training programs. Continuing education is particularly important in emerging areas of practice.

Training is given special attention because of the unique ethical issues involved in counselor training. Indeed, ethical issues must be considered from the very beginning, starting with admission and screening procedures for graduate programs. One key issue is the role of training programs in safeguarding the public when it becomes clear that a trainee has problems that are likely to interfere with professional functioning.

Therapist Competence: Ethical and Legal Aspects

In this section we examine what therapist competence is, how we can assess it, and what some of its ethical and legal dimensions are. We pose questions such as: What ethical standards do the various mental-health professions have regarding competence? What ethical issues are involved in training therapists? To what degree is professional licensing an accurate and valid measure of competence? What are the ethical responsibilities of therapists to continue to upgrade their knowledge and skills?

Professional Codes of Ethics on Competence

American Association for Marriage and Family Therapy (1991):

Marriage and family therapists do not diagnose, treat, or advise on problems outside the recognized boundaries of their competence.

American Psychological Association (1995):

Psychologists provide services, teach, and conduct research only within the boundaries of their competence, based on their education, training, supervised experience, or appropriate professional experience.

National Association of Social Workers (1996):

Social workers should accept responsibility or employment only on the basis of existing competence or the intention to acquire the necessary competence. (4.01.a.)

Social workers should strive to become and remain proficient in professional practice and the performance of professional functions. Social workers should critically examine, and keep current with, emerging knowledge relevant to social work. Social workers should routinely review professional literature and participate in continuing education relevant to social work practice and social work ethics. (4.01.b.)

American Counseling Association (1995):

Counselors practice only within the boundaries of their competence, based on their education, training, supervised experience, state and national professional credentials, and appropriate professional experience. Counselors will demonstrate a commitment to gain knowledge, personal awareness, sensitivity, and skills pertinent to working with a diverse client population.

Perspectives on Competence

We begin this discussion of competence with an overview of specific guidelines from various professional associations. They are summarized in the box above.

The guidelines leave several questions unanswered. What are the boundaries of one's competence, and how do professionals know when they have exceeded them? How can practitioners determine whether they should accept a client if they lack the experience or training they would like to have? What should be the minimal degree required for entry level for professional counseling? To be competent to practice with a variety of client populations, does a counselor have to be both a generalist and a specialist?

These questions become more complex when we consider the criteria used in evaluating competence. Many people who complete a doctoral program lack the skills or knowledge needed to carry out certain therapeutic tasks. Obviously, a degree alone does not guarantee competence for any and all psychological services. Practitioners must also assess how far they can safely go with clients and when to refer them to other specialists. Similarly, it's important to learn when to consult another professional if the counselor hasn't had extensive experience working with a particular problem.

However, if you were to refer all the clients with whom you encountered difficulties, you'd probably have few clients. Keep in mind that many beginning counselors have doubts about their general level of competence; in fact, it's not at all unusual for highly experienced therapists to wonder seriously at times whether they have the personal and professional abilities needed to work with some of their clients. Thus, difficulty working with some clients doesn't by itself imply incompetence.

One way to develop or upgrade your skills is to work with colleagues or professionals who have more experience than you do. You can also learn new skills by going to conferences and conventions, by taking additional courses in areas you don't know well, and by participating in workshops that combine didactic work with supervised practice. The feedback you receive can give you an additional resource for evaluating your readiness to undertake certain therapeutic tasks. In addition to having a basic preparation as a generalist, you might also want to acquire advanced training in a specialty area, a topic we deal with later in this chapter.

Making Referrals

It is crucial for professionals to know the boundaries of their own competence and to refer clients to other professionals when working with them is beyond their professional training or when personal factors would interfere with a productive working relationship. After counseling with a client for a few sessions, for example, you may determine that he or she needs more intensive therapy than you're qualified to offer. Even if you have the skills to undertake long-term psychotherapy, the agency you work for may, as a matter of policy, permit only short-term counseling. Or you and a client may decide that because of value conflicts or for some other reason your relationship isn't productive. The client may want to continue working with another person rather than discontinue counseling. For these and other reasons you will need to develop a framework for evaluating when to refer a client, and you'll need to learn how to make this referral in such a manner that your client will be open to accepting your suggestion. Most codes of ethics have a standard pertaining to conditions for making a referral, for example:

> Social workers should refer clients to other professionals when other professionals' specialized knowledge or expertise is needed to serve clients fully, or when social workers believe they are not being effective or making reasonable progress with clients and additional service is required. (NASW, 1996, 2.06.a.)

To make the art of referral more concrete, consider the following exchange between a client and her counselor. Helen is 45 years old and has seen a counselor at a community mental-health center for six sessions. She suffers from periods of deep depression and frequently talks about how hard it is to wake up to a new day. In other respects it is very difficult for Helen to express what she feels. Most of the time she sits silently during the session.

The counselor decides that Helen's problems warrant long-term therapy that he doesn't feel competent to provide. In addition, the center has a policy of referring clients who need long-term treatment to therapists in private practice. The counselor therefore approaches Helen with the suggestion of a referral:

Counselor: Helen, during your intake session I let you know that we're generally expected to limit the number of our sessions to six visits. Since today is our sixth session, I'd like to discuss the matter of referring you to another therapist.

Helen: Well, you said the agency generally limits the number of visits to six, but what about exceptions? I mean, after all, I feel as if I've just started with you, and I really don't want to begin all over again with someone I don't know or trust.

Counselor: I can understand that, but you may not have to begin all over again. I could meet with the therapist you'd be continuing with to talk about what we've done these past weeks.

Helen: I still don't like the idea at all. I don't know whether I'll see another person if you won't continue with me. Why won't you let me stay with you?

Counselor: Well, there are a couple of reasons. I really think you need more intensive therapy than I'm trained to offer you, and, as I've explained, I'm expected to do only short-term counseling.

Helen: Intensive therapy! Do you think I'm that sick?

Counselor: It's not a question of being sick. But I am concerned about your prolonged depressions, and we've talked about my concerns over your suicidal fantasies. I'd just feel much better if you were to see someone who's trained to work with depression.

Helen: You'll feel better, but I sure wouldn't! The more you talk, the more I feel crazy as though you don't want to have anything to do with me.

Counselor: I wish I could make you understand that it isn't a matter of thinking you're crazy; it's a matter of being concerned about many of the things you've talked about with me. I want you to be able to work with someone who has more training and experience than I do, so that you can get the help you need.

Helen: I think you've worked with me just fine, and I don't want to be passed around from one counselor to another. If you won't let me come back, then I'll just forget counseling.

This exchange reflects a common problem. What do you think of the way Helen's counselor approached his client? Would you have done anything differently? If you were Helen's counselor, would you agree to continue seeing her if she refused to be referred to someone else? Why, or why not?

If you didn't want Helen to discontinue counseling, a number of alternatives would be open to you. You could agree to see her for another six sessions, provided that your director or supervisor approved. You could let her know that you would feel a need for consultation and close supervision if you were to continue seeing her. Also, you could say that although this might not be the appropriate time for a referral, you would want to work toward a referral eventually. Perhaps you could obtain Helen's consent to have another therapist sit in on one of your sessions so that you could consult with him or her. There may be a chance that Helen would eventually agree to begin therapy with this person. What other possibilities can you envision? What would be the consequences if you refused to see Helen or could not obtain approval to see her?

Ethical Issues in Training Therapists

Training is a basic component of practitioner competence. Our discussion of the central ethical and professional issues in training is organized around questions pertaining to selection of trainees, diversity, content of training program, best approaches to training, evaluating students, and accreditation.

Selection of Trainees

A core ethical and professional issue involves formulating policies and procedures for selecting appropriate candidates for a training program. Here are some issues to consider:

- What criteria should be used for admission to training programs?
- Should the selection of trainees be based solely on traditional academic standards, or should it take into account the latest findings on the personal characteristics of effective therapists?
- To what degree is a candidate for training open to learning and to considering new perspectives?
- Does the candidate have problems that are likely to interfere with training and with the practice of psychotherapy?
- What are some ways to increase applications to programs by underrepresented groups?
- How open are we to diversity? How open are we to including people who will challenge us as trainers?
- Which populations do you desire to work with, and which do you not want as clients? Why?
- What is the importance of a thorough orientation to a program?

Training programs have an ethical responsibility to establish clear selection criteria, and candidates have a right to know the nature of these criteria when they apply. Although grade-point averages, scores on the Graduate Record Examination, and letters of recommendation are often considered in the selection process, relying on these measures alone does not provide a comprehensive picture of a candidate. Many programs ask candidates to write a detailed essay that includes their reasons for wanting to be in the program, their professional goals, an assessment of their personal assets and liabilities, and life experiences that might be useful in their work as counselors. We recommend conducting group interviews with candidates. A number of programs have both faculty members and graduate students on the reviewing committee. If many sources are considered and if more than one person makes the decision about whom to select for training, there is less likelihood that people will be screened out on the basis of some personal whim.

As part of the screening process, ethical practice implies that candidates are given information about what will be expected of them if they enroll in the program. Just as potential therapy clients have a right to informed consent, students applying for a program have a right to know the material they will be expected to learn and the manner in which education and training will take place. With this kind of knowledge, students are better equipped to decide if they want to make a commitment to a program.

Screening is a two-way process. As faculty screen candidates and make decisions on whom to admit, candidates may also be screening the program to decide if this is right for them. ACA's (1995) guideline on orientation is:

> Prior to admission, counselors orient prospective students to the counselor education or training program's expectations, including but not limited to the following: (1) the type and level of skill acquisition required for successful completion of the training, (2) subject matter to be covered, (3) basis for evaluation, (4) training components that encourage self-growth or self-disclosure as part of the training process, (5) the type of supervision settings and requirements of the sites for required clinical field experiences, (6) student and supervisee evaluation and dismissal policies and procedures, and (7) up-to-date employment prospects for graduates. (F.2.a.)

African Americans and Hispanics are severely underrepresented in graduate programs in the mental-health professions. Data on the ethnic distribution of counseling doctorates show that most students in the programs are Caucasians. Thus, it appears that efforts to redress racial and ethnic imbalances in training programs have not been effective (Zimpfer & DeTrude, 1990). Diversity in programs is endorsed by ACA's *Code of Ethics* (1995): "Counselors are responsive to their institution's and program's recruitment and retention needs for training program administrators, faculty, and students with diverse backgrounds" (F.2.i.). If the faculty is made up of diverse individuals, the chances are increased that the program will emphasize the desirability of attracting a diverse student population—and a wider range of potential students will likely feel encouraged to enroll in the program.

◆ ***The case of Leo.***   Julius is on a review committee in a graduate counseling program. Leo has taken several introductory courses in the program, and he has just completed an ethics course with Julius. It is clear to this professor that Leo displays a rigid and dogmatic approach to human problems, particularly in areas such as interracial marriage, same-sex relationships, and abortion. Over the course of the semester, Leo appeared to be either unwilling or unable to modify his thinking. When challenged by other students in the class about his views, Leo argued that certain behaviors were simply "never proper" and that it was the task of the counselor to point this out to clients. In meeting with the committee charged with determining whether candidates should be advanced in the program, Julius expresses his strong concern about retaining

Leo in the program. His colleagues share this concern, and Leo is denied advancement.

- What concerns, if any, do you have about the manner in which this case was handled? Were any of Leo's rights violated? *Leo was not included on*
- Was it clear to Leo that when he expressed his ideas in his classes they could be held against him? Is there an ethical issue in that situation? *yes*
- Could the committee determine so early in the program that Leo would not change his ideas in the course of his education? *no*
- Were any other avenues open in dealing with him short of disqualifying him from the program? *expectations/requirements/values/not imposing*
- If his values reflected his minority cultural background, would that make a difference? Would the committee be culturally insensitive for rejecting him from the program?
- What if Leo said that when he eventually obtained his license he intended to work exclusively with people from his cultural and religious background? Should he be denied the opportunity to pursue a degree in counseling if his career goal was to work with a specific population that shared his views and values?
- Using the criteria seemingly espoused by this selection committee, would a minister from a fundamentalist background who was attempting to get a master's degree in counseling be rejected?
- If you were on the committee, how would you handle candidates who exhibited racism, homophobia, and absolutist thinking?

Content of a Program

What is the content of a training program and how is it decided? Is the curriculum determined by the preferences of the faculty, or is it based on the needs of the people being served, or both? Lazarus (1990) writes that "most graduate programs socialize their students into delimited schools of thought" (p. 351). In his lectures to professional audiences, he often warns of the limitations of rigidly following a particular theory and then stretching clients to fit its preconceptions rather than adapting the techniques that flow from a theory to fit the unique needs of each client. He argues that a multimodal, systematic, technically eclectic model can point the way to a genuinely scientific approach to the training of therapists. Thus, training programs would do well to offer students a variety of therapeutic techniques and strategies that can be applied to a wide range of problems with a diverse clientele.

Some programs are structured around a specific theoretical orientation. Other programs have a broader content base and are aimed at training generalists who will be able to step into future positions that present evolving challenges. Some think that all specialty training should be abolished. They are concerned about training practitioners in only one therapeutic orientation (without also providing unbiased introductions to other models). There is merit in an analytically trained therapist's learning about alternative approaches such as behavior therapy or a systemic model. By the same token, a behavior therapist and a systemic therapist should be able to recognize the role of transference and countertransference in the therapeutic process. Therapists should learn when a particular approach is contraindicated, especially if it is their own specialty. From an ethical perspective, counselor educators and trainers are expected to present varied theoretical positions:

> Counselors present varied theoretical positions so that students and supervisees may make comparisons and have opportunities to develop their own positions. Counselors provide information concerning the scientific bases of professional practice. (ACA, 1995, F.2.f.)

We recommend that students be exposed to the major contemporary counseling theories and that they be taught to formulate a rationale for the therapeutic techniques they employ. It is a good idea to teach students the strengths and limitations of these contemporary counseling theories. Some writers point out the limitations of basing training mainly on these standard counseling models and call for training in alternative theoretical positions that apply to diverse client populations (D. W. Sue, Ivey, & Pedersen, 1996). For an overview of the contemporary counseling theories see G. Corey, 1996b; Corsini and Wedding, 1995; Ivey, Ivey, and Simek-Morgan, 1997; and Sharf, 1996.

In deciding what to teach, certain questions are worth considering:

- Is the curriculum based on a monocultural or a multicultural set of assumptions?
- Is there a universal definition of mental health, or is mental health culturally defined?
- Should therapy help clients adjust to their culture? Or might it encourage them to find ways of constructively changing within their culture?
- Does the curriculum give central attention to the ethics of professional practice?
- Is it ethical to leave out training in ethics? Is it enough to hope that ethical issues will be addressed through the supervision process alone?
- What is the proper balance between academic course work and supervised clinical experience?
- What core knowledge should be taught in counselor education programs?
- What is the appropriate balance between basic preparation and advanced specialization?

In training programs for various mental-health professions, general content areas are part of the core curriculum. For example, in counseling programs the following areas are typically required for all students: professional orientation, human growth and development, social and cultural foundations, counseling theory and practice, group counseling, lifestyle and career development, appraisal of individuals, and research and evaluation.

It is our opinion that training programs need to be designed so that students can learn a good deal more about themselves as well as acquire theoretical knowledge. Ideally, students will be introduced to various content areas, will acquire a range of skills they can utilize in working with diverse clients, will learn how to apply theory to practice through supervised fieldwork experiences, and will learn a great deal about themselves personally. A good program does more than impart knowledge and skills essential to the helping process. In a supportive and challenging environment, the program encourages students to build on their life experiences and personal strengths and provides opportunities for expanding their awareness of self and others.

Ethics deserves prominent attention in any program geared to educating and training mental-health practitioners. We are aware of an APA-accredited doctoral program in clinical psychology in which a separate ethics course is not required! Although the content of ethics is supposedly incorporated in a number of required courses, seminars, and practicum and internship experiences, we believe that the lack of systematic coverage of ethical issues will hinder these students, both as trainees and later as professionals. ACA's (1995) standard on teaching ethics is: "Counselors make students and supervisees aware of the ethical responsibilities and standards of the profession and the students' and supervisees' ethical responsibilities to the profession" (F.2.d.). We think the topics we address in this book deserve a separate course as well as infusion throughout all courses and supervised fieldwork experiences.

How Can We Best Train?

Programs geared to educating and training counselors should be built on the foundation of the natural talents and abilities of the students. Ideally, as we have said, programs teach people the knowledge and skills they need to work effectively with diverse populations. In addition, students need a core set of attitudes and values that are congruent with carrying out their role as helping professionals. In his provocative article "Can Psychotherapists Transcend the Shackles of Their Training and Superstitions?" Lazarus (1990) contends that formal education and training in psychological diagnosis and treatment often undermine the natural talents and skills of trainees. In illustrating his point, he describes a friend who was "an absolute natural when it came to understanding people and showing genuine warmth, wisdom, and empathy" (p. 352). When Lazarus brought his own problems to his friend, he found the experience to be "amazingly therapeutic." After his friend obtained a Ph.D. in psychology, however, Lazarus was able to receive only "a string of platitudes and labels." He maintains that as his friend took courses in assessment, diagnosis, and treatment, his natural talents were destroyed. Of course, Lazarus does not believe that training necessarily erodes natural talent, but he does warn that "one of the main shackles under which many therapists labor comes from the almost endless list of proscriptions that they are handed" (p. 353).

In our view, one of the best ways to teach students how to effectively relate to a wide range of clients, many of whom will differ from themselves, is for faculty to model healthy interpersonal behavior. Teachers and supervisors should display cohesive relationships among themselves and treat students in a collegial manner with respect. This is not always the case, however. In some programs the faculty functions somewhat like a dysfunctional family with behavioral characteristics of power plays, unaddressed interpersonal conflict, and even hostile behavior. Conflict among faculty members may be obvious, and students are sometimes drawn into these rivalries, being expected to side with a particular faculty member. In an effective program, differences are discussed openly and there is an atmosphere of genuine respect and acceptance of diversity of perspectives. If faculty practice the principles they teach, they are demonstrating powerful lessons about interpersonal relating that students can apply to their personal and professional lives.

- What problems would you encounter if you found yourself in a program characterized by dysfunctional behavior? How would you deal with the problems you might face?
- How would you react to a student who said, "I don't care what they do; I just want to get my degree and get out of here"?
- If you were concerned about the ethics of this program as a student, what actions would be open to you besides quitting?

Effective programs combine academic and personal learning, weave together didactic and experiential approaches, and integrate study and practice. A program structured exclusively around teaching academics does not provide important feedback to students on how they function with clients. In experiential learning and in fieldwork, problem behaviors of trainees will eventually surface and can be ameliorated. Evaluation is an important component of this process. The policies and procedures pertaining to how students will be evaluated and how decisions will be made about their advancement or dismissal from a program should be known by all students. Evaluation criteria is the topic we turn to next.

Evaluation Criteria

Every training institution has an ethical responsibility to screen candidates so that the public will be protected from incompetent practitioners. Programs clearly have a dual responsibility: to honor their commitment to the students they admit and also to protect future consumers who will be served by those who graduate. Just as the criteria for selecting applicants to a program should be clear, the criteria for successful completion and the nature of the evaluation process need to be spelled out as objectively as possible.

The ACA (1995) addresses the evaluation process in counselor education and training programs in this way:

> Counselors clearly state to students and supervisees, in advance of training, the levels of competency expected, appraisal methods, and timing of evaluations for both didactic and experiential components. Counselors provide students and supervisees with periodic performance appraisal and evaluation feedback throughout the training program. (F.2.c.)

! for Leo ↓ p271

We strongly support the ACA's position. In addition to evaluating candidates when they apply to a program, we favor periodic student reviews to determine whether trainees should be retained.

Students need feedback on their progress so they can build on their strengths or remediate problem areas. Ideally, trainees will also engage in self-evaluation to determine whether they are "right" for the program and the program is suitable for them. We are uncomfortable with a judgment such as "You'll never be a counselor." If shortcomings are sensitively pointed out to trainees, they can often correct them.

Sometimes students have personal characteristics or problems that interfere with their ability to function effectively, yet when this is pointed out to them, they may deny the feedback they receive. A program has an ethical responsibility to take action and not simply pass on a student with serious academic or personal problems. ACA's *Code of Ethics* (1995) addresses this issue:

> Counselors, through ongoing evaluation and appraisal, are aware of the academic and personal limitations of students and supervisees that might impede performance. Counselors assist students and supervisees in securing remedial assistance when needed, and dismiss from the training program supervisees who are unable to provide competent service due to academic or personal limitations. Counselors seek professional consultation and document their decisions to dismiss or refer students or supervisees for assistance. Counselors assure that students and supervisees have recourse to address decisions made, to require them to seek assistance, or to dismiss them. (F.3.a.)

It has become clear to us that many counselor educators are hesitant to dismiss students. This is especially true if the concerns are about personal characteristics or problematic behavior, even in cases where the faculty are in agreement regarding the lack of suitability of a given student. Some counselor educators have expressed fears of becoming embroiled in a lawsuit, either personally or as a program, if a student is not allowed to continue. Faculty who are in the business of training counselors should be credited with the ability to have accurate perceptions and observations pertaining to personality characteristics that are counterproductive for becoming effective counselors. If a student has good grades but has serious unresolved personal conflicts or demonstrates dysfunctional interpersonal behavior, action needs to be taken. Dismissal from a program is a measure of last resort. We would hope this option would not be employed unless all other attempts at remediation had failed.

Counseling programs can be held legally liable for turning out incompetent counselors (Custer, 1994). If the counselors who graduate from a program are proven to be incompetent, the program can be sued. If it can be demonstrated that a program failed to adequately train an individual, the university is responsible for the harm the graduate inflicts on clients. Custer describes a lawsuit involving a master's level counselor who graduated from Louisiana Tech's College of Education. A female therapy client named Louisiana Tech in a suit, claiming that the program allowed an incompetent practitioner to graduate from the program. The client claimed that her life had been destroyed by incompetent therapy. The claim was that the program itself was inadequate in that it simply did not adequately prepare her counselor. The counselor was named in the malpractice action along with her supervisor and the university. The initial lawsuit was settled in 1994 for $1.7 million. A case such as this makes it clear that specific competency standards for retaining and graduating counseling students are not only useful but necessary.

Donigian (1991) takes the provocative position that the consumer's trust in the profession is violated if counselors are not psychologically prepared for the challenges they will confront as they undertake their work. He suggests that preparation programs should take responsibility for evaluating students' emotional and psychological readiness to become practitioners.

If faculty groups assume the role of examining and evaluating both the academic and personal fitness of students to graduate, the question ought to be raised: Who evaluates and examines the examiners? Assume that several advanced students approach the dean of their graduate school to express their concern about the seeming discrepancies between what they are experiencing in their internships and supervised sessions and what they are being taught in their counseling classes. They complain that their professors live in an ivory tower, and they point out that not one of their professors is a counseling practitioner. The dean replies that all of the faculty members are properly credentialed. Although they are not seeing clients, they have had practical experience in the past.

- Is it important for counselor educators to have current hands-on experience with clients?
- Every program evaluates students and their suitability for the counseling profession. Is it equally important to evaluate the evaluators and their suitability to make such assessments?

Professional Licensing and Credentialing

Most states have established specific requirements of supervised practice beyond the receipt of a master's or doctor's degree for licensing and certification in areas such as clinical social work, clinical or counseling psychology, rehabilitation counseling, mental-health counseling, and marriage and family therapy. In this section we focus on some of the issues pertaining to competence both as a generalist and in an advanced specialization; basic assumptions of the practice of licensing; arguments for and against licensing and certification for mental-health professionals; professional jealousy and turf battles; and the value of professional collaboration.

Purposes of Legislative Regulation of Practice

Sweeney (1995) describes credentialing as an approach to identifying individuals by occupational group, involving at least three methods: registry, certification, and licensure. In its simplest form, *registry* is generally a voluntary listing of individuals who use a title or provide a service. Registration represents the least degree of regulation of practice. Both certification and licensure involve increased measures designed to regulate professional practices.

Although licensing and certification differ in their purposes, they have some features in common. Both require applicants to meet specific requirements in terms of education and training and acceptance from practicing professionals. Both also generally rely on tests to determine which applicants have met the standards and deserve to be granted a credential.

Certification is a voluntary attempt by a group, such as the National Board for Certified Counselors (NBCC), to promote a professional identity. Broadly conceived, certification is a process of verifying the truth of one's assertion of qualifications as a professional counselor. It implies that the practitioner has met a set of minimum standards established by the certification agency. Although certification gives practitioners the right to use a specific title, it does not assure quality practice, nor does it govern practice (Hosie, 1995).

Unlike certification, *licensure* statutes determine and govern professional practice. Licensure acts, sometimes called practice acts, specify what the holder of the license can do and what others cannot do (Remley, 1995). Licensure is generally viewed as the most desirable form of legislative regulation of professional practice because it tends to highlight the uniqueness of an occupation and restricts both the use of the title and the practice of an occupation (Sweeney, 1995).

Licensure and certification assure the public that the practitioners have completed minimum educational programs, have had a certain number of hours of supervised training, and have gone through some type of evaluation and screening. Licenses and certifications do not, and probably cannot, ensure that practitioners will competently do what their credentials permit them to do. The main advantages of licensure and certification are the protection of the public from grossly unqualified and untrained practitioners and the formal representation to the public that practitioners are part of an established profession.

Most licenses and credentials are generic; that is, they usually don't specify the clients or problems practitioners are competent to work with, nor do they specify the techniques that they are competent to use. A licensed psychologist may possess the expertise needed to work with adults yet lack the training necessary to work with children. The same person may be qualified to do individual psychotherapy yet have neither the experience nor the skills required for family counseling or group therapy. Most licensing regulations do specify that licensees are to engage only in those therapeutic tasks for which they have adequate training, but it is up to the licensee to put this rule into practice. Such a broad definition of practice also applies to many other professions.

Arguments for and against Professional Licensing and Credentialing

Four main arguments have been put forth in favor of legislation to regulate the delivery of mental-health services. The first is that the public is protected by setting minimum standards of service and holding professionals accountable if they do not measure up. This argument contends that the consumer would be harmed by the absence of such standards because incompetent practitioners can cause long-term negative consequences. Second, the regulation of practitioners is designed to protect the public from its ignorance about mental-health services. This argument rests on the assumption that the consumer who needs psychological services typically does not know how to choose an appropriate practitioner or how to judge the quality of services received. Most people do not know the basic differences between a licensed psychologist, a psychiatrist, a licensed clinical social worker, a licensed marital and family therapist, and a licensed professional counselor. Third, because insurance companies frequently reimburse clients for the services of licensed practitioners, licensing means that more people can afford mental-health care. Finally, there is the view that licensing allows the profession to define for itself what it will and will not do. In fact, licensure itself is perceived to enhance the profession and is a sign of maturity.

The arguments for licensure revolve around the contention that the consumer's welfare is better safeguarded with legal regulation than without it. Those who challenge this assumption often maintain that licensing is designed to create and preserve a "union shop" and that it works more as a self-serving measure that creates monopolistic helping professions than as a protection for the public from misrepresentation and incompetence (Davis, 1981). Others are skeptical when it comes to setting up criteria for regulating mental-health practitioners. Carl Rogers (1980) maintained that as soon as criteria are set up for certification the profession inevitably becomes frozen in a past image. He noted that there are as many certified charlatans as there are uncertified competent practitioners. Another drawback to licensing, from his viewpoint, is that professionalism builds up a rigid bureaucracy.

In our view, the process of licensing often contributes to professional specializations' pitting themselves against one another. Instead of fostering a collaborative spirit between licensed clinical social workers and licensed marriage and family counselors or between licensed psychologists and licensed professional counselors, the licensing process of each group too often promotes working in isolation.

Specialties within the Counseling Profession

Some training programs offer specialty training and encourage students to enroll in a specific track at all levels of education, from associate of arts to doctoral programs. For example, students can be trained and certified as substance abuse counselors in associate of arts programs. At the master's level counseling program, students can specialize in a given area such as school counseling, rehabilitation counseling, or marriage and family counseling. Doctoral programs offer specializations in community and multicultural counseling, organizational development, and human development, to mention a few. At the doctoral level specializations also exist within each of the major mental-health professions of social work, psychology, marriage and family therapy, and counseling.

Within the counseling profession, a specialty is officially recognized when it achieves either a specialty accreditation through a group such as the Council for Accreditation of Counseling and Related Educational Programs (CACREP) or certification through an organization such as the National Board for Certified Counselors (NBCC) or the Commission on Rehabilitation Certification (CRCC) (Myers, 1995b). At this time eight counseling specialties have been recognized by ACA. They are:

- career counseling (Engels, Minor, Sampson, & Splete, 1995)
- college counseling (Dean & Meadows, 1995)
- gerontological counseling (Myers, 1995a)
- school counseling (Paisley & Borders, 1995)
- marriage and family counseling (R. L. Smith, Carlson, Stevens-Smith, & Dennison, 1995)
- mental-health counseling (H. B. Smith & Robinson, 1995)
- rehabilitation counseling (Leahy & Szymanski, 1995)
- addictions counseling (Page & Bailey, 1995)

In addition to these eight specialties, there is a proposal to create a new specialty area in sports counseling (Miller & Wooten, 1995). The reference given with each specialty is a good place to start if you want to know more about a special area.

Within the counseling profession, some argue in favor of specialty licensing and some argue against it. Should states adopt legislation to regulate the practice of counseling specializations? Although Remley (1995) sees a need to recognize counselors who possess specialized knowledge and training, he opposes state regulation of the practice of counseling specializations as being not in the best interests of either the public or the profession. Remley contends that only the general practice of counseling should be regulated by the state; specialty practice should be addressed through credentialing. He adds: "I propose that state counseling boards vigorously enforce the requirements that professional counselors restrict their practices to the areas in which they are qualified and move toward official recognition of legitimate private counseling specialization credentials" (p. 129).

At the present time the proliferation of specialties has led to confusion and a lack of unity in determining specialization (Bradley, 1995; Hosie, 1995; Remley, 1995; Sweeney, 1995). Hosie (1995) challenges the assumption that specialties are necessary to provide competent practice to specific client types. He makes a case for basic preparation required to be a competent generalist rather than viewing advanced specialization as necessary for employment as a counselor and for competent practice with clients. In her discussion of certification and licensure issues, Bradley (1995) indicates the need to unify credentialing standards. She writes: "If certification and licensure problems are ignored, I believe the counseling profession will become fragmented and vulnerable" (p. 186). Pate (1995) makes the point that if there is no counseling generalist then specialties become separate professions and not specializations. He indicates that counseling is a single profession with individual practitioners who have skills and expertise that make them competent in assisting clients with concerns in a number of identifiable areas of practice and specializations.

Practitioners who argue for the need for specializations within the counseling field point to the current realities and complexities of counseling practice in diverse settings, with various client problems, and with a range of client populations. Practitioners who have expressed concern over certification of specialties are asking for a basis to bring unity to the counseling field. According to Pate (1995), a number of issues surround specialty certification: counseling is a profession with specific practice settings; counselors desire specializations and argue that they should benefit consumers; specialization should be part of an understandable credentialing system; and advanced training and qualifications deserve to be recognized by a separate credential.

We hope that consumers do not get forgotten in the heated debates surrounding certification and licensure issues and professional specialties. Also, we hope these issues will not separate professionals, a topic we address in the next section.

Turf Battles or Interprofessional Collaboration?

The process of registration, certification, and licensure can promote a sense of professional identity. It can also be the basis for professional jealousy over turf and can lead to restrictive regulation that is motivated by competition for access to the marketplace. How has interprofessional bickering manifested itself? According to Cummings (1990), professional psychology has struggled with the psychiatric profession to retain its turf in the areas of hospital privileges, licensure to prescribe drugs, and inclusion in Medicare. Cummings asserts that a major contribution of psychology to the other mental-health professions was designing and implementing the freedom-of-choice amendments to state insurance codes. Psychology has also recently made great strides in expanding mental-health services to the elderly and to residents of rural areas through revisions in Medicare regulations.

Just as psychology has struggled with psychiatry for turf, clinical psychologists often contend that their scientific discipline makes them preeminent over other disciplines (Cummings, 1990). They have opposed the licensing efforts of social workers, mental-health counselors, and marriage and family therapists. Some writers warn about the dangers of competition to the welfare of the client; they contend that such fighting among professions can lead to an erosion in the quality of services and that those who stand to suffer most are the consumers (Garcia, 1990; Ivey & Rigazio-DiGilio, 1991). Brooks and Gerstein (1990) also decry the competition within and among the various professional fields, and they urge professionals to join forces and collaborate. They add that interprofessional bickering must cease if mental-health professionals, their associations, and the respective licensing boards are to achieve their goal of delivering the best services possible. The more that money is a factor, the more vigorous the "ideological" turf battles are bound to become.

Continuing Education and Demonstration of Competence

Most professional organizations support efforts to make continuing education a mandatory condition of relicensing. Professionals are encouraged to engage in ongoing education and training in their specializations. ACA's *Code of Ethics* (1995) states the following on continuing education:

> Counselors recognize the need for continuing education to maintain a reasonable level of awareness of current scientific and professional information in their fields of activity. They take steps to maintain competence in the skills they use, are open to new procedures, and keep current with the diverse and/or special populations with whom they work. (C.2.f.)

Many professional organizations have voluntary programs. All clinical members of the AAMFT, for example, are encouraged to complete 150 hours of continuing education every three years. The association regards the program, known as Continuing Education in Family Therapy, as part of an ongoing process of professional development with the goal of maintaining high-quality services to consumers. Most other professionals are required to demonstrate, as a basis for relicensure, that they have completed a minimal number of continuing education activities.

To assume that our skills never deteriorate or that we know everything we need to know upon graduation is naive. If we rarely or never seek continuing education, how are we to justify this lack of initiative? Learning never ceases; new clients present new challenges. New areas of knowledge and practice demand ongoing education. Even recent graduates may have significant gaps in their education that will require them to take workshops or courses in the future. You may also need to seek supervision in working with various client populations or to acquire skills in certain therapeutic modalities. For example, your job may require you to conduct groups, yet your program may not have included even one group course in the curriculum. When continuing education is tailored to your personal and professional needs, it can keep you on the cutting edge of your profession.

Individual practitioners have an ethical responsibility to seek out ways to keep current with new developments in their field, and administrators of mental-health agencies also have responsibilities to provide continuing education activities for the staff. Some of these activities can take the form of in-service workshops and training at the agency site; other activities will require therapists to go outside the agency. NASW'S *Code of Ethics* (1996) has this guideline on continuing education and staff development:

> Social work administrators and supervisors should take reasonable steps to provide or arrange for continuing education and staff development for all staff for whom they are responsible. Continuing education and staff development should

address current knowledge and emerging developments related to social work practice and ethics. (3.08.)

Apply the principles of supervision and the development of competence as an ongoing process to the following case of a therapist who believes that competence can be attained once and for all.

◆ ***The case of Conrad.***   Dr. Conrad Hadenuf has been a licensed psychologist for 20 years and has always maintained a busy practice. He sees a wide variety of clients. As a condition of license renewal, he is required to attend a 15-hour retraining program on substance abuse. He is indignant. "I have a Ph.D., I have 3000 hours of supervised experience, and I have years of experience with all sorts of problems," he says. "This is just a money-making gimmick for those who want to generate workshops!" Knowing that he has no choice if he wants to retain his license, Conrad grudgingly attends the workshop, sits in the back of the room, takes no notes, takes longer breaks than scheduled, and leaves as soon as the certificates of attendance are available.

◆ What are your reactions to Conrad's statements? Is his rationale for not wanting to participate in the workshops justified? *pick ones he's interested in*

◆ Even though Conrad says he has no desire to deal with substance abuse, can he realistically say that he will never be confronted with clients with drug abuse problems?

◆ How do you view mandated continuing education as a condition for license renewal? *good*

◆ Are practitioners being ethically responsible to their clients if they never upgrade their knowledge and skills?

Clarifying your stance.   We hope that you have thought about ways to maintain and enhance your competence. Use the following questions to clarify your thinking on the issues we have raised. What is your own strategy for remaining professionally competent?

continued requirement for relicensure

◆ What effects on individual practitioners do you think the trend toward increased accountability is likely to have? How might this trend affect you?

◆ Do you think it is ethical to continue practicing if you do not continue your education? Why, or why not? *no, always learn something new*

◆ What are some advantages and disadvantages to using continuing education programs solely as the basis for renewing license? is continuing education enough? Explain. *if courses, work shops, new techniques, new advances. Keeps you on cutting edge.*

◆ What are your reactions to competence examinations (oral and written) for entry-level applicants and as a basis for license renewal? What kinds of exams might be useful?

◆ Should evidence of continuing education be required (or simply strongly recommended) as a basis for recertification or relicensure? If you support mandatory continuing education, who do you think should determine the nature of this education? What standards should be used in making this judgment? *if you take prof code seriously, you would enjoy.*

◆ What kinds of continuing education would you want for yourself? Through what means do you think you can best acquire new skills and keep abreast of advances in your field?

The Role of Peer Review and Peer Support

Peer review is an organized system by which practitioners within a profession assess one another's services. This approach is gaining in popularity and provides some assurance to consumers that they will receive competent services. In addition to providing peer review, colleagues can challenge practitioners to adopt a fresh perspective on problems they encounter in their practice. In one survey it was found that psychologists rated informal exchanges among colleagues as the most effective resource for promoting effective and ethical practice (Pope, Tabachnick, & Keith-Spiegel, 1987). Such networks were perceived as being more valuable in fostering ethical practice than laws, committees, research, continuing education, or professional codes of ethics.

Regarded as a means rather than an end in itself, the ultimate goals of peer review are to determine whether a practitioner's professional activity is adequate and to ensure that future services will be acceptable. Peer review continues a tradition of self-regulation.

Peer-consultation groups.   Borders (1991) described the value of structured peer groups that foster the development of skills, conceptual growth, participation, instructive feedback, and self-monitoring. Borders maintains that peer-supervision groups are useful for counselors at all levels of experience. For trainees, peer groups offer a supportive atmosphere and help them learn that they are not alone with their concerns. For counselors in practice, peer-consultation groups provide an opportunity for continued professional growth.

Peer-consultation groups can also function as an informal and voluntary form of review in which individual cases and ethical and professional issues are examined (G. J. Lewis, Greenburg, & Hatch, 1988). These groups provide additional safeguards to consumers and a greater measure of accountability, which government agencies often require. Furthermore, being part of a peer-consultation group offers reassurance to private practitioners who are concerned about malpractice litigation.

Consider your own stance as you answer these questions about peer review:

◆ Can you think of both advantages and disadvantages to basing license renewal strictly on peer-review procedures?
◆ What are some potential difficulties with the peer-review model? For instance, who would decide on the criteria for assessment?
◆ Assume that the peers who reviewed you had been chosen because they had a similar orientation to counseling (behavioral). Would they be assessing your competence or your fidelity to the tenets of a particular school? If the

peers who reviewed your work had a different theoretical orientation from yours (psychoanalytic), how competent would they be to assess you within the framework of your practice?

◆ What are your thoughts about a peer-consultation group for yourself? If you would like to be involved in such a group, how might you take the initiative to form one?

Concluding commentary.   Before closing this discussion of competence, we want to mention the danger of rarely allowing yourself to experience any self-doubt and being convinced that you can handle any therapeutic situation. Some therapists feel this way. They tell themselves they have it made and attend conventions to show off how much they know and impress their colleagues with their competence. Sidney Jourard (1968) warns about this delusion that one has nothing new to learn. He maintains that exciting workshops or contact with challenging colleagues can keep therapists growing. He urges professionals to find colleagues whom they can trust so that they can avoid becoming "smug, pompous, fatbottomed and convinced that they have the word. [Such colleagues can] prod one out of such smug pomposity, and invite one back to the task" (p. 69).

We support the view that supervision is a useful tool throughout one's career. Along with Jourard, we also see the development of competence as an ongoing process, not a goal that counselors ever finally attain. This process involves a willingness to continually question whether you're doing your work as well as you might and to search for ways of becoming a more effective person and therapist.

Chapter Summary

Clients' welfare is directly affected by ethical issues in the training of therapists, the debate over whether professional licensure and credentialing are adequate signs of competence, the role of peer review and peer-consultation groups in ensuring professional competence, and the importance of continuing one's education.

Counselors must acquire new knowledge and skills throughout their professional career. This is particularly true for practitioners wishing to develop a specialty area dealing with certain client populations or problems. In addition to continuing education activities, peer-consultation groups are useful routes to maintaining professional competence.

A core ethical and professional issue in training involves the question of how to develop policies and procedures for selecting the candidates who are best suited for the various mental-health professions. The challenge is to adopt criteria for choosing people who have the life experiences that will enable them to understand the diverse range of clients with whom they will work. The personal characteristics of trainees, such as attitudes and beliefs, are critical in deciding whom to admit to training programs.

Another important issue is the effectiveness of professional licensing and credentialing as a sign of an individual's competence. Although most practitioners will need to acquire competence as generalists, the counseling profession has been characterized by the emergence of specialty areas of practice. These areas of specialization need to be clarified without destroying the unity within the profession.

The issues are complex, yet the goal is to focus licensure and certification more on protecting consumers than on protecting professional specializations. Increased collaboration among the various mental-health professions can enhance this process. Isolation too often creates turf battles and professional jealousies that benefit no one.

Suggested Activities

1. Invite several practicing counselors to talk to your class about the ethical and legal issues they encounter in their work. You might have a panel of practitioners who work in several different settings and with different kinds of clients.

2. In small groups explore the topic of when and how you might make a referral. Role-play a referral, with one student playing the client and another the counselor. After a few minutes the "client" and the other students can give the "counselor" feedback on how he or she handled the situation.

3. In small groups explore what you think the criteria should be for determining whether a therapist is competent. Let a student role-play an "incompetent" therapist and defend himself or herself. Make up a list of specific criteria, and share it with the rest of the class. Are you able as a class to come up with some common criteria?

4. Several students can look up the requirements for licensure or certification of the major mental-health specializations in your state. What are some of the common elements? Present your findings to the class.

5. Work out a proposal for a continuing education program. In small groups, develop a realistic model to ensure competency for professionals once they have been granted a license. What kind of design most appeals to you? a peer-review model? competency examinations? taking courses? other ideas?

6. Assume that you are applying for a job or writing a resume to use in private practice. Write up your own professional disclosure statement in a page or two. Bring your disclosure statements to class and have fellow students review what you've written. They can then interview you, and you can get some practice in talking with "prospective clients." This exercise can help you clarify your own position and give you valuable practice for job interviews.

7. As a class project several students can form a committee to investigate some of the major local and state laws that apply to the practice of psychotherapy. You might want to ask mental-health professionals what major conflicts they have experienced between the law and their professional practice.

8. Form a panel to discuss procedures for selecting appropriate applicants for your training program. Your task as a group is to identify specific criteria for candidates. Consider these questions: In addition to grade-point averages, scores on the Graduate Record Examination, and letters of recommendation, what other criteria might you establish? What life experiences would your group look for? What personal qualities are essential? What attitudes, values, and beliefs would be congruent with becoming a counseling professional? What personal characteristics, if any, would you use as a basis for rejecting an applicant? What process should the program use in making selections? Would you recommend individual interviews? interviews conducted in small groups?

9. Assume that you are a graduate student who is part of the interviewing team for applicants for your training program. Identify six questions to pose to all applicants. What are you hoping to learn about the applicants from your questions?

10. Interview professors or practitioners in schools, agencies, or work settings that interest you. Ask them what they most remember about their training programs. What features were most useful for them? What training do they wish they had had more of, and what would they like to have had less of? How adequately do they think their graduate program prepared them for the work they are now doing? What continuing education experiences do they most value?

11. Form a small group for role-playing a licensing board that will interview candidates for a professional license. Meet out of class for the time it takes to draw up a list of questions to pose to the "practitioners" who will be examined by your group. Several students in the class can volunteer to sit for the interview.

12. Consider the advantages of forming a peer-support group within one of your own classes. Several of you could make a commitment to meet to explore ways to get the most from your training and education. The group could also study together and exchange ideas for future opportunities.

9

Issues in Supervision and Consultation

Pre-Chapter Self-Inventory

Directions: For each statement, indicate the response that most closely identifies your beliefs and attitudes. Use the following code:

5 = I *strongly agree* with this statement.
4 = I *agree* with this statement.
3 = I am *undecided* about this statement.
2 = I *disagree* with this statement.
1 = I *strongly disagree* with this statement.

_5_ 1. To protect the client, the supervisor, and the supervisee, ethical guidelines are needed to govern the conduct of counselor supervisors.

_5_ 2. Supervisors should be held legally accountable for the actions of the
trainees they supervise.

_5_ 3. Supervisors have the responsibility to monitor and assess a trainee's
performance in a consistent and careful manner.

_5_ 4. Working under supervision is one of the most important components
for my development as a competent practitioner.

_5_ 5. Supervisors must be sure that trainees fully inform clients about the
limits of confidentiality.

_5_ 6. The focus of supervision should be on my progress as a practitioner
rather than on the client's problems.

_5_ 7. Ideally, supervisory sessions should not be aimed at providing therapy
for the trainee.

_5_ 8. It is clearly unethical for counselor educators to date their students or
other students who are involved in the training program.

_4_ 9. It is acceptable for a supervisor or educator to date former students,
once they have completed the program.

_5_ 10. Supervisees and trainees should have a right to know what is expected
of them and how they will be evaluated. They also have a right to periodic feedback and evaluation from supervisors so that they have a
basis for improving their clinical skills.

_4_ 11. It is unethical for counseling supervisors to operate in multiple roles
such as mentor, adviser, teacher, and evaluator.

_5_ 12. Ethically, supervisors need to clarify their roles and to be aware of
potential problems that can develop when boundaries become
blurred.

_5_ 13. It is unethical for supervisors or counselor educators to provide therapy to a current student or supervisee.

_5_ 14. It is essential that consultants subscribe to ethical standards to ensure
that their services are competent and that the consumer receives professional service.

_5_ 15. Consultants are obligated to determine with certainty who the consultee is.

_5_ 16. Before initiating a contract, consultants may ethically investigate the
goals of the agency to determine whether they can support them.

_4_ 17. When consultants become aware of value clashes that cannot be resolved, ethical practice dictates that they decline to negotiate a contract.

_5_ 18. Consultants need to make an ethical determination whether they are sufficiently trained to offer the services they contract to perform.

_3_ 19. In consulting it is almost impossible to avoid dual relationships, because the work involves blending teaching skills and counseling skills as needed in the situation.

_5_ 20. Ethical practice requires that consultants inform their consultees about the goals and process of consultation, the limits to confidentiality, the voluntary nature of consultation, the potential benefits, and any potential risks.

Introduction

Supervision is an integral part of training helping professionals and is one of the ways in which trainees can acquire the competence needed to fulfill their professional responsibilities. As we mentioned in the last chapter, professional competence is not attained once and for all. Remaining competent demands not only continuing education but also a willingness to obtain periodic supervision when faced with an ethical dilemma. By consulting experts, practitioners show responsibility in obtaining the assistance necessary to provide the highest quality of care for clients. As practitioners, we can never know all that we might like to know, nor can we attain all the skills required to effectively intervene with all client populations or all types of problems. This is where the processes of supervision and consultation come into play.

Counselors are often expected to function in the roles of both supervisor and consultant. To carry out these roles ethically and effectively, they must have proper training in both areas. The skills used in counseling are not necessarily the same as those needed to adequately supervise trainees or to advise other helping professionals. This chapter explores dilemmas frequently encountered in supervision and consultation and provides some guidelines for ethical and legal practice in these areas.

Ethical and Legal Issues in Clinical Supervision

The relationship between the clinical supervisor and the trainee (or student of psychotherapy) is of critical importance in the development of competent and responsible therapists. If we take into consideration the dependent position of the trainee and the similarities between the supervisory relationship and the therapeutic relationship, the need for guidelines describing the rights of trainees and the responsibilities of supervisors becomes obvious. Although specific guidelines for ethical behavior between a supervisor and trainee have not been delineated in the ethical codes of all professional associations, the

Association for Counselor Education and Supervision (ACES) has developed "Ethical Guidelines for Counseling Supervisors" (ACES, 1993), which address issues such as client welfare and rights, supervisory role, and program administration role.

Harrar, VandeCreek, and Knapp (1990) distinguish between the ethical and legal aspects of clinical supervision. The *ethical* issues are supervisors' qualifications, their duties and responsibilities, dual relationships, the consent of trainees' clients, and third-party payments. The *legal* issues involve direct and vicarious liability, confidentiality and the supervisor's duty to protect, and standards of care. Sherry (1991) also discusses ethical issues in supervision and includes responsibility, the welfare of clients and supervisees, confidentiality, competence, moral and legal standards, and professional relationships.

One of the main ethical issues in supervision is managing the rights of supervisees and the responsibilities of supervisors. Tyler and Tyler (1997) maintain that many of the ethical standards pertaining to the client-therapist relationship also apply to the supervisor-supervisee relationship. They believe that it is beneficial to discuss the rights of supervisees in much the same way as the rights of clients are addressed early in the therapy process. If this is done, Tyler and Tyler maintain, the supervisee is empowered to express expectations, make decisions, and become an active participant in the supervisory process. Tyler and Tyler propose a "bill of rights" for supervisees that defines the parameters of the supervision process, creates an equitable and mutual relationship, and ensures quality supervision. Specific rights of supervisees include the right to:

♦ a supervisory session free from interruptions and distractions
♦ be fully informed of supervisors' approaches to supervision
♦ confidentiality with regard to supervisee's disclosure as well as that of clients, except as mandated by law
♦ continual access to any records maintained during the supervisory relationship
♦ provide feedback to supervisors concerning the helpfulness of supervision
♦ seek consultation from other professionals as necessary

Informed consent regarding supervision is as essential as informed consent in counseling (which was discussed in Chapter 4). Supervisees have a right to begin their supervisory experience knowing the conditions that dictate their status and progress. Supervisees need to clearly understand what their responsibilities are and what the supervisors' are (Bernard & Goodyear, 1992).

The Supervisor's Roles and Responsibilities

Supervisors have a responsibility to provide training and supervised experiences that will enable supervisees to deliver ethical and effective services. Supervisors must be well trained, knowledgeable, and skilled in the practice of clinical supervision (Vasquez, 1992). If they do not have training in clinical supervision, it will be difficult for supervisors to ensure that those they supervise are functioning effectively and ethically.

Supervisors are ultimately responsible, both ethically and legally, for the actions of their trainees. Therefore, they are cautioned not to supervise more trainees than they can responsibly manage at one time. They must check on trainees' progress and be familiar with their caseloads. Just as practitioners keep case records on the progress of their clients, supervisors should maintain records pertaining to their work with supervisees. The trainee has the right to know about training objectives, assessment procedures, and evaluation criteria. Supervisees have a right to know what is expected of them and how they will be evaluated. It is the responsibility of supervisors to inform trainees about these matters at the beginning of supervision (ACA, 1995; ACES, 1993; Bernard & Goodyear, 1992; Pope & Vasquez, 1991; Tyler & Tyler, 1997).

Trainees have an ethical and legal right to periodic feedback and evaluation so that they have a basis for improving their clinical skills (ACA, 1995; ACES, 1993). Supervision is perhaps the most important component in the development of a competent practitioner. It is within the context of supervision that trainees begin to develop a sense of professional identity and to examine their own beliefs and attitudes regarding clients and therapy.

Counseling or clinical supervisors have a position of influence with their supervisees; they operate in multiple roles as teacher, evaluator, counselor, model, mentor, and adviser. It is essential that supervisors monitor their own behavior so as not to misuse the inherent power in the supervisor-supervisee relationship. According to Sherry (1991), there are three main reasons why supervisors are ethically vulnerable: (1) the power differential between the participants, (2) the "therapylike" quality of the supervisory relationship, and (3) the conflicting roles of the supervisor and supervisees. He points to the multiple roles that supervisors are expected to play. Although the requirements of these roles overlap in some cases, they may also conflict. Supervisors are faced with the responsibility of protecting the welfare of the clients, the supervisees, the public, and the profession. Sherry maintains that the clients' welfare comes first, followed by that of the supervisees. He also reminds us that because supervision is like therapy in some ways, there is a risk of harm to both the client and the supervisee from a supervisor's blurred objectivity, impaired judgment, or exploitation. Supervisors are responsible for ensuring compliance with relevant legal, ethical, and professional standards for clinical practice (ACES, 1993). They can demonstrate these standards through the behavior they model in the supervisory relationship.

Responsibilities to supervisees and clients.   Here are some responsibilities of supervisors to supervisees and some specific ways in which supervisors can promote counselor development:

- being qualified to supervise and providing adequate supervision
- stating the purposes and nature of supervision
- negotiating mutual decisions about the needs of the trainee

- performing the role of teacher, counselor, or consultant as they are appropriate
- clarifying the supervisory role
- promoting competency for supervisees
- integrating knowledge of supervision with one's interpersonal style
- meeting with supervisees on a regular basis to give ongoing evaluation and feedback
- promoting the supervisee's ethical knowledge and behavior
- interacting with counselor trainees in a manner that facilitates their self-exploration, problem-solving ability, and confidence
- promoting the knowledge and skills required to effectively work with clients from ethnically and culturally diverse populations
- assisting supervisees in recognizing their personal limitations to protect the welfare of the clients seen by supervisees
- being aware of the clients being treated by supervisees and maintaining records on them
- teaching and modeling ethical and professional behavior
- being familiar with the goals and techniques being employed by the trainees
- being aware of subtle cues that a client may be at risk
- maintaining confidentiality of clients

Because supervisors are the gatekeepers of the profession, it is essential that they be involved with ethical standards for practice. They need to put ethics in the foreground of their supervisory practices. The primary responsibility of supervisors is to model what they hope to teach (Bernard & Goodyear, 1992).

Methods, techniques, and styles of supervision. The standards of both ACA (1995) and ACES (1993) require that supervisors demonstrate a conceptual knowledge of supervisory methods and techniques and that they be skilled in using this knowledge to promote the development of trainees. However, we believe that the most important element in the supervisory process is the kind of person the supervisor is. The methods and techniques supervisors use are less important than their ability to establish an effective and collaborative working relationship with supervisees. In much the same way that effective therapists create a climate in which clients can explore their conflicts, supervisors need to establish a collaborative relationship that encourages trainees to reflect on what they are doing. Fogel (1990), who considers herself a "rebellious supervisor," makes an urgent plea to teach trainees the value of doubting and of creative innovation:

> My whole purpose in supervision has been to create such a safe environment that the trainee can function in his/her own style and feel cherished enough to ask for help when the going gets rough. We can then reflect, explore options, and discover together the process which feels suited to the trainee's present psychic state and skills. (p. 61)

Supervisees at different stages in their professional development require different types of supervision. Overholser (1991) points out that an important element in the supervisory process is balancing a directive style and a permissive one. A supervisor's task is to strive for an optimal level of challenge, promoting autonomy without overwhelming the supervisee. Although supervisees may need more direction when they begin their training, it is a good idea to foster a reflective and questioning approach that leads to self-initiated discovery. Overholser applies the Socratic method to supervision, assuming that trainees achieve more insight when they discover a relationship on their own than when it is explained to them. The Socratic supervisor functions more as a catalyst for exploration than as a lecturer and helps trainees realize that the answers lie within themselves.

Focus on the supervisory process.   When we supervise, we focus on the dynamics between ourselves and our trainees. Our style of supervision can be grasped by the questions we explore: What is going on with you? How are you reacting to your clients? How is your behavior affecting them? Which clients bring out your own resistances? How are your values manifested by the way you interact with your clients? How might our relationship, in these supervisory sessions, mirror your relationships with your clients? Are you feeling free enough to bring into these supervisory sessions any difficulties you are having with your clients?

Supervisors must look beyond the cases that trainees bring to the supervisory sessions and focus on the interpersonal and intrapersonal variables. Although we see supervision as a separate process from psychotherapy and do not attempt to make training sessions into therapy sessions, we think that the supervisory process can be therapeutic and growth-producing. Vasquez (1992) writes that one of the most important goals for clinical supervisors is to promote the supervisee's self-awareness and ability to recognize personal characteristics that could negatively impact the therapeutic relationship.

Legal Aspects of Supervision

Three legal considerations in the supervisory relationship are informed consent, confidentiality and its limits, and liability. First, supervisors must see that trainees provide the information to clients that they need to make informed choices. Clients must be fully aware that the counselor they are seeing is a trainee, that he or she is meeting on a regular basis for supervisory sessions, that the client's case may be discussed in group supervision meetings with other trainees, and that sessions may be taped or observed. As Bernard and Goodyear (1992) indicate, by virtue of supervision, supervisors have a relationship with the trainee's clients. Therefore, it is necessary that the client be informed of that relationship in detail. McCarthy, Sugden, Koker, Lamendola, Maurer, and Renninger (1995) discuss a practical guide to informed consent in clinical supervision. They recommend addressing the following areas in a written informed consent document: purpose of supervision, professional disclosure statement, practical issues, supervision process, administrative issues, ethical and legal issues, and statement of agreement. McCarthy and her colleagues view informed consent as a crucial aspect of clinical supervision. They suggest that this process is best implemented through written documents and discussion between supervisees and supervisors. By attending to informed consent in the supervision process, supervisees professional development will be enhanced and the quality of client care will be fostered.

Second, supervisors have a legal and ethical obligation to respect the confidentiality of client communications. There may be certain exceptions, however, such as cases when the supervisor determines that the client is potentially dangerous to himself or herself or to others. Supervisors must make sure that clients are fully informed about the limits of confidentiality, including those situations in which supervisors have a duty to warn or a duty to protect.

Third, supervisors ultimately bear legal responsibility for the welfare of those clients who are counseled by their trainees. Cormier and Bernard (1982) assert that supervisors must be familiar with each case of every supervisee to avoid being negligent. This requirement may not be practical in the sense that supervisors cannot be cognizant of all details of every case, but they should at least know the direction in which the cases are being taken. Also, university training programs have a responsibility to clients to make some kind of formal assessment of each trainee before allowing the person to counsel clients. Harrar and his colleagues (1990) indicate that supervisors bear both direct liability and vicarious liability. *Direct liability* can be incurred if supervisors are derelict in the supervision of their trainees, if they give trainees inappropriate advice about treatment, or if they give tasks to trainees that exceed their competence. *Vicarious liability* pertains to the responsibilities that supervisors have because of the actions of their supervisees. From both a legal and ethical standpoint, trainees should not assume final responsibility for clients; rather, their supervisors must carry the decision-making responsibility and liability.

Competence of Supervisors

From both an ethical and legal standpoint, it is essential that supervisors have the education and training to adequately carry out their roles. This implies taking course work in theories of supervision, working with difficult supervisees, working with culturally diverse supervisees, and methods of supervision. Besides course work, counselors need to be provided with training in supervision. Unfortunately, many who function as supervisors have not had the academic and training background that will allow them to deal with the challenges they will face as supervisors. If supervision courses were not part of their program, it is essential that they acquire the specific knowledge and skills that will enable them to function effectively as clinical supervisors.

Supervisors not only need specialized training in methods of supervision but also need to have an in-depth knowledge of the specialty area in which they will provide supervision. Storm (1994) contends that marriage and family therapy supervisors assume a central position in educating their supervisees about marital and family issues. However, she cites studies indicating that most supervisors who work with trainees in marriage and family therapy have themselves not had an academic background in marriage and family therapy. In her view, the unique context of marriage and family therapy creates special considerations for supervisors as they attempt to carry out their roles in an ethical and effective manner. Storm identifies several areas in which marriage and family therapy supervisors have ethical responsibilities. These include: providing timely and adequate supervision, assessing the supervisee's readiness for supervision, managing multiple relationships, maintaining confidentiality, emphasizing professional development in supervision, and monitoring and evaluating the supervisee's competence.

Multicultural Issues in Supervision

Ethical supervision must include the ways in which individual differences can influence the process. The ACA's standards dealing with supervision and training (1995) call for counselor educators and supervisors to demonstrate knowledge of individual differences with respect to gender, race, ethnicity, culture, sexual orientation, disability, and age and to understand the importance of these characteristics in supervisory relationships and training. The term *multicultural supervision* implies a broad perspective of culture that includes race, ethnicity, socioeconomic status, sexual orientation, religion, gender, and age (Fukuyama, 1994). Supervisors who are functioning ethically and competently are cognizant of and address the salient issues that apply to multicultural supervision (Bernard, 1994). The topic of competence in supervision is incomplete without taking into consideration the role of cultural factors in the supervisory relationship and the competence of supervisors in this area. Bernard and Goodyear (1992) identified the following dimensions of a good model of multicultural supervision: (a) a pluralistic philosophy, (b) cultural knowledge, (c) consciousness raising, (d) experiential training, (e) contact with racial and ethnic minorities, and (f) practicum or internship with minorities. Certainly, supervisors have an ethical responsibility to become aware of the complexities of a multicultural society (see Chapter 10).

Racial issues in supervision. There is a price to be paid for ignoring racial and ethnic factors in supervision. If supervisors do not assist supervisees in addressing racial issues, their clients may be denied the opportunity to explore these issues in their therapy. D. A. Cook (1994) calls for routinely including discussions of racial identity attitudes as part of both therapy and supervisory relationships. The supervisor's recognition of racial issues can serve as a model for supervisees in their counseling relationships. Reflecting on racial interactions in supervision offers a cognitive framework for supervisees to generalize to their counseling practices. Cook suggests that supervisors might raise questions such as: "When did you notice the client's race?" "How did this affect you?" "What did you do in response to the client's race?" According to Cook, unspoken assumptions regarding race and cultural influences of those involved in the supervision process can affect all aspects of supervision including: establishment of the relationship and expectations for supervision, assignment of clients, conceptualization of clients and treatment planning, recommendations for client referrals, and the evaluation of supervisees.

Priest (1994) focuses on the supervisor's role in enhancing the supervisee's respect for diversity. He points out that too often supervisors emphasize client similarities and minimize racial and cultural differences. If trainees do not understand the cultural context in which their clients live, Priest believes that the chances are increased that trainees' behavior will result in clients' prematurely terminating counseling.

Toward multiculturally effective supervision.   In her pilot study to define the issues in multicultural supervision with visible ethnic minority trainees, Fukuyama (1994) explored critical incidents in multicultural supervision. Respondents were asked how to make supervision more multiculturally sensitive and effective. Their suggestions included:

- Have supervisors initiate discussion of multicultural issues as a basic part of supervision.
- Provide increased training for supervisors in working with multicultural issues, including opportunities to tape supervision sessions for self-reflection.
- Provide more multicultural supervisors.
- Make use of all personnel within an agency for multicultural training.
- Train supervisors to develop a genuine respect for and acceptance of cultural diversity. Caution them about the problems involved in trying to be "politically correct" and overemphasizing diversity issues.
- Provide a training model for "prejudice reduction" that could be used with trainees' clients to help them deal with racism and prejudice.
- Discuss multicultural issues in an intern seminar under the training director's guidance.

Fukuyama (1994) found two emerging themes in multicultural supervision: culture and cultural differences, and racism and racial identity issues. It is essential that supervisors receive training in multicultural issues, including having course work and practical experiences in supervision and multicultural counseling (Fukuyama, 1994; Priest, 1994).

Implications for training and supervision.   Bernard (1994) suggests the following parameters of training and supervision to achieve multicultural competence:

- Supervisees must be at least as multiculturally sensitive as their clients, and supervisors must be at least as multiculturally competent as their supervisees.
- Training programs need to determine a trainee's readiness for clinical experience and for entry-level practice.

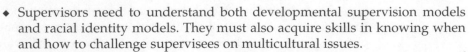

- Supervisors need to understand both developmental supervision models and racial identity models. They must also acquire skills in knowing when and how to challenge supervisees on multicultural issues.
- Supervisors themselves need supervision if they hope to enhance their own multicultural development.

Bernard underscores the importance of competent multicultural supervision when she writes: "I do not consider it an overstatement to assert that the development of the profession and the relevance of counselor education programs will be severely compromised if we do not advance the knowledge and practice of multicultural supervision" (p. 170).

On a more personal note, one of our former students, who is now in a doctoral program in counseling, shared her views with us about the importance of including multicultural considerations in supervision. She reported an experience in a group supervision session with a fellow student (an Asian American whom we will call Hoa). The supervisor, who was generally a sensitive person, perceived Hoa's quiet nature in a negative light and questioned her level of empathy. Hoa attributed her style of relating to colleagues and clients to her cultural background. This is but one example of how supervisors may hold assumptions that are out of their awareness that can be detrimental to both supervisees and to their clients. This also illustrates the need for supervisors to participate in their own supervision as a way to detect their blind spots.

To develop the knowledge and skills to work effectively in multicultural counseling situations, trainees need to understand their own level of racial and cultural identity. Furthermore, they need to recognize how their attitudes and behaviors affect their clients. Good supervision will allow trainees to explore the impact diversity issues may have on their counseling style.

Multiple Roles and Relationships in the Supervisory Process

The ACES standards (1993) imply that counseling supervisors possess the personal and professional maturity to play multiple roles. Ethically, supervisors need to clarify their roles and to be aware of potential problems that can develop when boundaries become blurred. As Herlihy and Corey (1997) point out, unless the nature of the supervisory relationship is clearly defined, both the supervisor and the supervisee may find themselves in a difficult situation at some point in their relationship. If supervisor's objectivity becomes impaired, the supervisee will not be able to make maximum use of the process. If the relationship evolves into a romantic one, the entire supervisory process becomes confounded, with the supervisee likely to feel exploited sooner or later.

The crux of the issue of multiple role relationships in the training and supervisory process is the potential for abuse of power. Like therapy clients, students and supervisees are in a vulnerable position and can be harmed by an educator or supervisor who exploits them, misuses power, or crosses appropriate boundaries. The ACA (1995) standard is relevant to this discussion:

> Counselors clearly define and maintain ethical, professional, and social relationship boundaries with their students and supervisees. They are aware of the differential in power that exists and the student's or supervisee's possible incomprehension of that power differential. Counselors explain to students and supervisees the potential for the relationship to become exploitative. (F.1.b.)

In their study of faculty-student relationships, Bowman, Hatley, and Bowman (1995) assessed both faculty and student perceptions regarding dual or multiple relationships in mentoring, friendships, monetary interactions, informal social interactions, and romantic-sexual relationships. They admit that certain multiple relationships are unavoidable in most training programs. Bowman and her colleagues propose that rather than viewing multiple relationships as inherently unethical it is best to examine the behavior of the persons who are involved in these relationships. Apart from sexual dual relationships with students and supervisees, which are clearly unethical, a wide range of dual and multiple relationships exist that are part and parcel of supervision and training of therapists. Rather than lumping these nonsexual dual or multiple relationships with unethical sexual relationships, professional training ought to deal with learning how to manage situations involving multiple roles and relationships.

Supervisors play a critical role in helping counselor trainees understand the dynamics of balancing multiple roles and managing dual relations. Although students may learn about dual relationships during their academic work, it is generally during the time they are engaged in fieldwork experiences and internships that they are required to grapple with boundary issues (Herlihy & Corey, 1997).

Supervisors must not exploit students and trainees or take unfair advantage of the power differential that exists in the context of training. Managing multiple roles ethically is the responsibility of the supervisor. Next we look at sexual dual relationships in training and supervision.

Sexual Intimacies during Professional Training

As in the case of sexual relations between therapists and clients (which was explored in Chapter 7), sex in the supervisory relationship can result in an abuse of power because of the difference in status between supervisees and supervisors. Further, there is the matter of poor modeling for trainees for their future relationships with clients.

In a study of the beliefs and behaviors of psychologists as educators, only 23.9% of the educators surveyed said they had never been "sexually attracted to a student"; 15.4% of them considered this behavior unethical. With respect to "engaging in sexual fantasies about students" 39.8% said they had never engaged in this behavior; 20% considered this behavior unethical. With respect to telling a student, "I'm sexually attracted to you," 92.7% said they had never done so; 68.9% considered this behavior unethical (Tabachnick, Keith-Spiegel, & Pope, 1991).

In their national survey on sexual intimacy in counselor education and supervision, G. M. Miller and Larrabee (1995) found that counseling professionals who were sexually involved with a supervisor or an educator during their training later viewed these experiences as being more coercive and more harmful to a working relationship than they did at the time. Perceptual changes took place over time with respect to how students were affected by becoming sexually involved with people who were training them, which raises questions about their willingness to freely consent to such relationships and how prepared they were to deal with the ethics of such intimacies. Moreover, it seems clear that educators and supervisors have professional power and authority long after direct training ends.

Hammel, Olkin, and Taube (1996), who studied student-educator sex in doctoral training programs in psychology, also found that respondents were, in retrospect, more likely to view sexual relationships as coercive, ethically problematic, and a hindrance to the working relationship compared to how they viewed them at the time they occurred. Clear power differentials exist between educators and students. The typical relationship is between an older male professor and a younger female graduate student. Both G. M. Miller and Larrabee (1995) and Hammel and his colleagues (1996) take the position that engaging in sexual behavior with students and supervisees is highly inappropriate and contrary to the spirit of the ethical codes of most professional organizations.

Additionally, Hammel et al. make a strong recommendation for the APA to take a clearer and more encompassing stand against sexual relationships during training and to forbid them outright (see the box on page 301). Miller and Larrabee suggest that educators and supervisors be aware of their position of power and function as professional role models. They add that because of the detrimental impact of sexual involvements during training, educators and supervisors ought to refrain from any sexual involvements with students and supervisees.

Supervisory relationships have qualities in common with instructor-student and therapist-client relationships. In all of these professional relationships, it is the professional who occupies the position of greater power. Thus, it is the professional's responsibility to establish and maintain appropriate boundaries and to explore with the trainee (student, supervisee, or client) ways to prevent potential problems associated with boundary issues. If problems do arise, the professional has the responsibility to take steps to resolve them in an ethical manner.

Bartell and Rubin (1990) emphasize the supervisor's responsibility to create an ethical climate for self-exploration. It is essential that supervisees believe that they can explore difficult topics, such as sexual feelings for clients, without having to fear that the discussion will be perceived by the supervisor as an invitation to some kind of sexual involvement (Pope et al., 1986).

The core ethical issue is the difference in power and status between educator and student or supervisor and supervisee and the exploitation of that

Standards for Practice in Counselor Education and Supervision

♦ "Supervisors should not participate in any form of sexual contact with supervisees. Supervisors should not engage in any form of social contact or interaction which would compromise the supervisor-supervisee relationship. Dual relationships with supervisees that might impair the supervisor's objectivity and professional judgment should be avoided and/or the supervisory relationship terminated" (ACES, 1993).

♦ "Counselors do not engage in sexual relationships with students or supervisees and do not subject them to sexual harassment" (ACA, 1995, F.1.c.).

♦ "Social workers should not engage in any dual or multiple relationships with supervisees in which there is a risk of exploitation of or potential harm to the supervisee" (NASW, 1996, 3.01. c.).

♦ "Marriage and family therapists do not engage in sexual or other harassment or exploitation of clients, students, trainees, supervisees, employees, colleagues, research subjects, or actual or potential witnesses or complainants in investigations and ethical proceedings" (AAMFT, 1991, 3.5.).

♦ "Psychologists do not engage in sexual relationships with students or supervisees in training over whom the psychologist has evaluative or direct authority, because such relationships are so likely to impair judgment or be exploitative" (APA, 1995, 1.19. b.).

power. Because of the vulnerable position of supervisees, many would argue that the supervisee is not in a position to give free consent. The developmental level of supervisees may also be related to their vulnerability to sexual contact with a supervisor (Bartell & Rubin, 1990). When supervisees first begin counseling, they are typically naive and uninformed with respect to the complexities of therapy. They frequently regard their supervisors as experts, and thus, they have a dependence on their supervisors that may make it difficult to resist sexual advances. Supervisees may disclose personal concerns and intense emotions during supervision, much as they might in a therapeutic situation. The openness of supervisees and the trust they place in their supervisors can be exploited by supervisors who choose to satisfy their own psychological needs at the expense of their supervisees.

Assume that you are a trainee and that your clinical supervisor consistently harasses you sexually, both verbally and behaviorally. During your individual supervision sessions the supervisor frequently acts around you in flirtatious ways. You get the distinct impression that your evaluations will be more favorable if you "play the game." What course of action might you take in such a situation? Is there a difference between sexual harassment and consensual sexual relationships, or are all sexual advances in unequal power relationships really a form of sexual harassment? Do you agree or disagree with the assumption that sexual relationships between students or supervisees and their professors or supervisors cannot be equated with sexual relationships between a client and a therapist?

♦ ***The case of Augustus.*** Augustus meets weekly with his professor, Amy, for individual supervision. With only three weeks remaining in the semester,

Augustus hesitantly confesses to having a strong attraction to Amy and says he finds it difficult to maintain professional distance with her. Amy discloses that she, too, feels an attraction. But she is sensitive to the professional boundaries governing their relationship, and she tells him it would be inappropriate for them to have any other relationship until the semester ends. She lets him know that she would be open to further discussion about a dating relationship at that point. She says that even though he will still be in the program, she will no longer have a supervisory role with him, nor will she be evaluating his status in the program.

- What ethical implications do you see in this situation? List them and say why you see them as ethical concerns.
- Do you think that Amy handled her attraction to Augustus in the best way possible? Would it have been better for her to wait until the semester was over before she acknowledged her feelings of attraction? Would that have been ethical?
- If you were a colleague of Amy's and heard about this situation from another student, what would you do, if anything?
- Is the fact that Amy will no longer be supervising Augustus sufficient to eliminate the imbalance of power in the relationship? Do you think that it would be appropriate for them to date each other while he is still a student in the program? after he graduates?

Ethical Issues in Combining Supervision and Counseling

Supervisors play multiple roles in the supervision process, and the boundaries between therapy and supervision are not always clear. In a national survey on dual relationships, 75% of the respondents said that providing therapy to a current student or supervisee was either "never ethical" or "ethical under rare conditions" (Borys & Pope, 1989). In the literature on supervision, there seems to be basic agreement that the supervision process should concentrate on the supervisee's professional development rather than on personal concerns and that supervision and counseling have different purposes. However, there is a lack of consensus and clarity about the degree to which supervisors can ethically deal with the personal issues of supervisees.

Wise, Lowery, and Silverglade (1989) contend that supervision cannot provide supervisees with the kinds of personal-growth experiences that are afforded through personal counseling. They assert: "Ethical concerns, as well as differences between supervision and counseling, lead to the conclusion that personal counseling as a component of counselor training should be offered by professionals other than the supervisor or counselor education faculty member" (p. 328).

Supervisory relationships are a complex blend of professional, educational, and therapeutic relationships. It is the supervisor's responsibility to help trainees identify how their personal dynamics are likely to influence their work with clients, yet it is not the proper role of supervisors to serve as personal counselors for supervisees. Combining the roles of supervising and counseling often presents conflicts (Corey & Herlihy, 1996c; Pope & Vasquez, 1991; Whiston & Emerson, 1989).

As personal problems or limitations of supervisees and students become evident, training professionals are ethically obliged to encourage and challenge trainees to face and deal with these barriers that could inhibit their potential as helpers (Herlihy & Corey, 1997).

However, this discussion should emanate from the work of the trainee with the client. The purpose of discussing a trainee's personal issues, which may appear like therapy, is to facilitate the trainee's ability to work successfully with clients. When personal concerns are discussed in supervision, the goal is not to solve the trainee's problem. This generally requires personal therapy. The goal is to facilitate the therapeutic relationship between trainee and client. If the trainee needs or wants personal therapy, the best course for supervisors to follow is to make a referral to another professional. Now let's consider two specific cases.

◆ **The case of Hartley.**   During a supervision hour, Hartley confides to his supervisor that his five-year relationship has just ended and that he is in a great deal of pain. As he describes in some detail what happened, he begins to sob. Hartley expresses his concern about his ability to be present and work with clients, especially those who are struggling with relationships. Here are how three supervisors might have dealt with Hartley's concerns:

Supervisor A: I'm sorry you're hurting, but I am ethically bound to use this time to help you work with your clients. Hartley, hard as it may sound, they really have priority.

Supervisor B: [After listening to Hartley for some time and acknowledging his pain] I know it is difficult for you to work with your clients. I know you are in therapy, and I suggest that you increase the frequency of your sessions to give you an opportunity to deal with your own pain.

Supervisor C: That must be very painful. Do you want to talk about it? Since what is going on with you interferes with your ability to be present with clients, I think it is essential that we work with your pain. [The more the supervisor works with Hartley's pain, the more they tap into earlier issues of abandonment. Three weeks later the supervision time still involves Hartley's hurt and crisis.]

- Which of the three responses comes closest to your own, and why?
- Can you think of another way a supervisor could have responded to Hartley?
- Is there an ethical issue involved when supervision turns into personal therapy, even during times of personal crisis? *does it take away from primary objective to welfare of client?*

◆ **The case of Greta.**   Ken is a practicing therapist as well as a part-time supervisor in a counseling program. One of his supervisees, Greta, finds herself in a personal crisis after she learns that her mother has been diagnosed with inoperable cancer. Much of her internship placement involves working with hospice patients. In tears, she approaches Ken and lets him know that she feels unable to continue doing this work. He is impressed with her therapeutic skills and thinks that it would be most unfortunate for her to interrupt her education at this point. He also assumes that he can more expeditiously deal with her personal crisis because of their trusting relationship. For the next four supervision sessions, Ken focuses exclusively on Greta's personal problems. As a result of his help, Greta recovers her stability and is able to continue working with the hospice patients, with no apparent adverse affects for either them or her.

- Given Greta's crisis, was Ken justified in blending the roles of supervisor and counselor? If it was clear that her personal crisis was affecting her ability to function therapeutically with her clients, was it acceptable for Ken to assume the role of counselor for four sessions? Does the fact that Ken's interventions worked in just four sessions ethically justify the action he took?
- What ethical issues, if any, would you see if Ken had recommended that Greta temporarily discontinue her field placement and enter therapy with him in his private practice?
- If Ken recommended that Greta see another therapist for her personal therapy but she refused on the ground that he knew her best and that she would like him as her therapist, would that make his acceptance ethical?
- What alternatives do you see for dealing with this situation both ethically and effectively?
- Is it ever appropriate for supervisors to blend the roles of supervisor and therapist? Why, or why not?

Commentary.   It is our position that the emphasis of supervision needs to be on the enhancement of supervisees' work with their clients. Because we believe in the notion of countertransference, we think that trainees' own issues can be stimulated by their clients. Therefore, the task of supervision sometimes involves attending to the personal dynamics of supervisees. We see this as a necessary part of supervision. However, we disagree with the in-depth exploration of any personal issues that may be triggered. For instance, with Greta, we would attend to the pain that is triggered by her work, yet we would not explore unfinished business she might have with her mother. With Hartley, we would be sensitive to his pain, yet we would not pursue the historical issues of abandonment. Supervision requires a focus on the here and now. Past concerns are more appropriately explored in personal therapy.

Educators Who Counsel Students

There is no clear answer to the ethical question raised by counselor educators who provide counseling for their students. As we mentioned in Chapter 2, many professional programs strongly recommend, if not require, a personal therapeutic experience. Some programs expect students to undergo individual therapy for a time, and other programs provide a growth-group experience. At the very least, students have a right to know of these requirements before they make a commitment to begin a program. Further, we think that students should generally be allowed to decide what type of therapeutic experience is most appropriate for them.

The practice of faculty members' providing counseling for students for a fee is highly questionable, and Stadler (1986b) contends that the dual relationship standard of ethical conduct can and should be used to establish limits on the methods used to train counselors. On the issue of educators' serving as counselors for their students, Stadler concludes that there are many negative repercussions that can sour student-faculty relationships.

Some situations are not so clear-cut, however. Once students complete a program, for example, what are the ethics of a psychology professor taking them on as clients? Can it still be argued that the prior role as educator might negatively affect the current role as therapist? If the former student and the professor/therapist agree that there are no problems, is a therapeutic relationship ethically justified? To clarify your position on this issue, reflect on this case.

I think so.

◆ **The case of Brent.**   A psychology professor, Hilda, teaches counseling classes, supervises interns, and also provides individual therapy at the university counseling center. One of her graduate students, Brent, approaches her with a request for personal counseling. Even though she tells him of her concern over combining roles, he is persuasive and adds that he trusts her and sees no problem in being both her student and her counselee. He also informs her that he will be in her internship class next semester.

◆ Would Hilda be acting unethically if she accepted Brent as a client, given his feelings about the matter? *yes!*
◆ Would you see any difference if he approached her for counseling after he had completed the course with her? *yes!*
◆ Would the situation take on a different ethical dimension if the professor had a private practice? Is the matter partly one of the professor's charging a fee for her service? *no   dual rela/ dif of power (evaluator + counselor)*
◆ Assume that Hilda was leading a therapy group during the semester and that Brent wanted to join the group. Do you think that being a client in a group is different from being an individual client? Would it be unethical for her to accept Brent into the group? Would it be unethical for Hilda to reject him on the ground that he was a student, especially if she believed that the group would benefit him? *I feel dif about a grp*
◆ What is the potential for exploitation in this case?
◆ Do you think that the lack of availability of other resources in the area should make a difference in whether Hilda accepts Brent as a client? *yes*

Clarifying your stance.   What is your position on the ethical and legal issues raised in this section? Specifically, take a stand on the following situations:

◆ Your supervisor does not provide what you consider to be adequate supervision. You are left mainly on your own with a difficult caseload. The staff members where you work are all overloaded, and when you do get time with a supervisor, the person feels burdened with many responsibilities. Thus, you do not get enough time to discuss your cases. What would you be inclined to do? *talk about it w/ supervisor*

- ◆ You have a conflict with your supervisor over the most ethical way to deal with a client. What would you do? *I wonder.... I would feel more comfortable —*
- ◆ You do not get adequate feedback on your performance as a trainee. At the end of the semester your supervisor gives you a negative evaluation. What ethical and legal issues are involved? What might you do or say?

be clear about self — no feedback no chance for change — unfair

- ◆ Do you think it is unethical for a supervisor to initiate social or sexual relationships with trainees after they have graduated (and when the supervisor has no professional obligations to the trainee)? Explain your position.
- ◆ If during the course of your supervision you became aware that personal problems were interfering with your ability to work effectively with clients, what would you be inclined to do? If you trusted your supervisor, would you feel that it might be appropriate to discuss your personal concerns? *yes*
- ◆ What are the main problems with multiple relationships in supervision? Can you think of ways to avoid problems that might arise from certain dual relationships? Do you think that all such relationships in supervision should be avoided entirely? *I don't think they can be entirely —*
- ◆ What possible benefits, if any, do you see when supervisors combine a multiplicity of roles such as teacher, mentor, counselor, consultant, evaluator, and supervisor? Can you think of ways to maximize potential benefits and also to decrease the potential for harm from such multiple relationships?

Ethical and Professional Issues in Consultation

Consultation is becoming a specialized professional process, and it is being carried out by many different groups in diverse work settings. For the most part, professionals who function in the role of consultants are involved in collaborative forms of consultation that aim at improving the mental health of individuals and the functioning of organizations (Brown, 1993). Consultants often work with individuals and small groups in schools, agencies, and businesses. Consultation often involves sharing expertise with others in the helping professions so that they can better serve their own clients. This process is aimed at helping people work more effectively on the individual, group, organizational, or community level. Consultants assist consultees with immediate problems and also try to improve their ability to solve future problems. Dougherty (1995, pp. 9–10) found general agreement on these common characteristics of consultation:

- ◆ Consultants help practitioners better serve their own clients.
- ◆ Participation in the consultation process should be voluntary by all the parties involved.
- ◆ Consultees have the freedom to decide what they will do with the suggestions and recommendations of the consultant.

- The relationship between the consultee and the consultant, at its best, is a collaboration of peers who are equal in power.
- Consultation is a temporary process aimed at helping consultees move toward autonomy and independence.
- Consultation is primarily aimed at problems with work or caretaking as opposed to personal concerns (such as the consultee's marital discord or depression). For example, consultants might provide training workshops for counselors and social workers in an agency. The focus of consultation could be on learning to recognize and deal effectively with job-related stress that can easily interfere with one's professional functions.
- Consultants can take on a variety of roles in consultation.
- Consultation typically occurs in an organizational context.

Ethical Standards for Consultants

At the present time, formal ethical guidelines specific to the practice of consultation are not available, and the existing ethical codes of most mental-health professions offer only limited guidance to consultants. Consultants carry a heavy responsibility for their actions and the decisions they make. It would be a step forward if consultants had a set of ethical standards to ensure that consumers received professional service.

Because ethical codes are lacking, qualified professionals often do not know how to deal with ethical dilemmas they may face. Such dilemmas are particularly serious because of the potentially large number of people who are indirectly affected by a consultant's ethical principles and decisions. With these problems in mind, Gallessich (1982) asserts that a code of ethics for consultants is urgently needed to protect the public. Other writers agree with the need for guidelines for consultants, yet they argue that the responsibility for ethical and professional behavior ultimately rests with the consultant (Brown, 1993; Dougherty, 1995; Newman, 1993; Robinson & Gross, 1985; Tokunaga, 1984; Wubbolding, 1991).

Wubbolding (1991) mentions several pitfalls facing consultants and offers some useful guidelines for responsible practice:

- Consultants need to identify their real client, for the expectations of the manager and of the participants are frequently quite different.
- The cultural context in which consultation occurs is important. In Asian cultures, for example, consultants may be expected to assume a more directive role in their dealings with consultees.
- Creating a job for oneself is a pitfall that a consultant needs to monitor. The goal is to help people acquire skills that will lead to independence rather than to create a niche for the consultant.
- Even though the optimal consultant-consultee relationship is an equal one, the potential for dual relationships exists; these can be problematic from both a business and a professional perspective.

Dougherty (1995) describes six ethical and professional issues that pertain to consultation in the human-services professions: values, competence, training, the consultation relationship, the rights of consultees, and consultation in groups. Let's look more closely at each of these ethical issues in consultation. Our discussion is based on material from a variety of sources (Brown, 1993; Dougherty, 1992, 1995; Jackson & Hayes, 1993; Newman, 1993; Remley, 1993).

Values issues in consulting.   A major professional issue for consultants is the degree to which their personal values will have an impact on their actions and decisions in the consultation process. It is essential that consultants be aware that their values play a fundamental role in guiding their behavior. Newman (1993) puts this matter well:

> To ignore or deny the central role of values in the practice of consultation is naive at best, and from an ethical perspective, dangerous. It is imperative that consultants identify their personal and professional values and use them in conjunction with established ethical standards to guide their practice. (p. 151)

Before initiating a contract, consultants should investigate the goals of the organization to determine whether they can support them. When consultants become aware of differences in values that cannot be resolved, ethical practice dictates refusing to negotiate a contract. This approach prevents arriving at an insoluble value conflict in the middle of the consulting contract. Because of a difference between the values of the consultant and the consultee, referral is sometimes in order.

Value conflicts can arise at any stage of the consultation process. Consulting involves multiple parties with diverse and often competing interests and priorities, and it can be expected that value conflicts will occur among various sectors within an organization. It is critical that difficult choices be made *with* consultees rather than *for* them by the consultant acting alone.

Competence in consultation.   Consultants must have adequate education and training to perform the services for which they intend to contract. Furthermore, they are ethically bound to assume responsibility for keeping abreast of theoretical and technical developments in their field. The codes of ethics of the ACA (1995) and the APA (1995) make reference to consultants' delivering only those services that they are competent to perform. Consultants should present their professional qualifications to avoid misrepresenting themselves. It is also essential for consultants to recognize their own limitations, which entails knowing and appreciating the boundaries of their competence. Furthermore, consultants must be reasonably certain that the organization employing them has the resources to give the kinds of help that its clients need and that referral resources are available.

Consultant training.   Closely related to the issue of competence is determining whether consultants have an adequate level of training to perform contracted services. Dougherty (1995) lists five topics in which all consultants should receive training: (1) theoretical foundations of various models of consultation, (2) the range of possible consultant roles and functions, (3) a generic model of consultation, (4) organizational theory, and (5) knowledge and understanding of oneself as a consultant. Consultants can maintain a high level of professionalism by continuing their education, by attending professional conferences, by consulting with more experienced colleagues, and by obtaining the relevant credentials or licenses for the profession in which they expect to serve as a consultant.

Few counseling students have the opportunity to develop applied skills in consulting under competent supervision. For consultants to meet the demands of their position, it is critical that they receive training in specialized knowledge and skills (Newman, 1993). Brown (1993) believes that consultants should be exposed to a knowledge base in didactic settings, develop basic skills in practicum situations, and apply their knowledge and skills in field experiences. According to Brown, training in consultation skills lags far behind skills training in others areas of counseling. He considers consultation as "the forgotten child in the training of counselors." From his perspective, those who engage in consultation without proper training are unethical. Brown writes:

> It is relatively clear that counselors perceive themselves as functioning in the consultation role regardless of the training they have received. It is also abundantly clear that we as a professional group need to take a stand on the training of counselors and insist that counselors of the future be fully trained as consultants or that they refrain from engaging in the process. (p. 142)

Just as cultural awareness is critical in the practice of counseling, so is it basic to effective consultation. Jackson and Hayes (1993) state that a broader multicultural training program is needed for consultants. Consultants need training in diverse worldviews, an awareness of differences in reasoning patterns, an understanding of variations in communication patterns, and an awareness of one's capabilities to effect change. If students are not exposed to training in the multicultural dimensions of consultation, they will have only a limited ability to reach members of diverse racial, ethnic, and cultural backgrounds. Jackson and Hayes conclude: "To continue down the existing training and consulting path using monocultural philosophies and strategies, consultants, along with the profession of consultation, will be seen as ineffective, nonresponsive, and potentially identified as nonessential" (p. 147).

Relationship issues in consulting.   The consultee's interests and needs are paramount. The consulting relationship is based on an understanding and agreement between the consultant and the consultee on what the problem is, the goals for change, and the predicted outcomes of the interventions selected (ACA, 1995). Consultants should establish a clear contract with well-defined limits, respect their contract, and communicate its terms to all who are participating in consulting activities. Any changes in the contract should be made only through explicit agreement with staff members and the administration.

Remley (1993) recommends the use of written consultation contracts as a basis for setting the stage for successful relationships in consulting. Both consultants and consultees gain from written documents that spell out the essentials of the consultation relationship. The more specific a written contract is, the more useful the document will be to both parties. According to Remley, contracts are best structured by:

- clearly specifying the work to be completed by the consultant
- identifying any work products expected from the consultant
- establishing a time frame for completing the work
- identifying lines of authority and the person to whom the consultant is responsible
- establishing compensation arrangements, including the method of payment
- specifying any special arrangements agreed upon by the parties

A good contract is a form of legal protection for both the consultant and the consultee, but it can also assist both parties in developing a clear understanding of the terms of the consultation process. Written contracts can prevent misunderstandings.

A written contract can clarify the professional roles and responsibilities of consultants, reducing ambiguity. Dougherty (1995) cautions consultants to avoid tainting the consultation relationship with secondary roles such as counselor or supervisor. He admits that there is a fine line between where consultation ends and counseling begins, but it is a mistake to combine the roles of counselor and consultant and engage in a dual relationship.

Newman (1993) reminds us that consultants need to exert special care in maintaining appropriate boundaries, even if consultees request counseling. If it becomes evident that a consultee needs personal counseling, the course is to refer the consultee for appropriate professional help. For instance, school counselors should avoid discussing the personal concerns of a teacher or an administrator during consultation with that person. Ethical practice dictates that consultants monitor their interventions to avoid creating dependency or otherwise misusing their power.

An ethical consultant places top priority on the consultee's freedom of choice. Consultants have a responsibility to protect the freedom of consultees by declining to become involved in activities that require discussion of highly personal issues. If the consultation process is structured by a clear contract, inappropriate dual relatioships are unlikely to develop.

Rights of consultees.   Two central issues involving the rights of consultees are confidentiality and informed consent. Just as in any other professional relationship, absolute confidentiality cannot be guaranteed. The matter of who will have access to the consultant's findings should be established before gathering data. Consultants should remind staff members and administrators of the limits of confidentiality established during contract negotiations. Certain information that is given confidentially may be useful when it is presented anonymously to an administrator. Newman (1993) suggests that at a minimum consultants make certain that consultees clearly understand what and how information will be used, by whom, and for what purposes.

(1)   Consultants who work in schools may need to break confidentiality when there is abusive behavior on a consultee's part, such as a teacher's consistent violation of a school's policy regarding corporal punishment. Likewise, consultants who work in a residential care facility need to assume responsibility for protecting the residents, yet they may also have to report certain incidents or situations to others in the facility. In all settings, those who are participating in the consultation process have a right to know about the limits of confidentiality. It is the consultant's job to ensure that all participants clearly understand the parameters of confidentiality.

(2)   Ethical practice implies that consultants inform their consultees about the goals and purpose of consultation, the limits to confidentiality, the voluntary nature of consultation, the potential benefits, any potential risks, and the potential outcomes of intervention. Basic to informed consent is the notion that individuals have the freedom to choose from among various options, one of which is the freedom to decline to participate in the consultation process (Newman, 1993). As was mentioned in Chapter 4, informed consent is not exclusively accomplished at the outset of a relationship but is best achieved through a continuing discussion of relevant issues. Consultants should put themselves in the place of their consultees and ask themselves what they would want to know. For example, teachers should know if the consultant is keeping a list of those who seek consultation and should be told who has access to that list.

Issues involving consulting in groups.   Consultation is increasingly being done between a consultant and a group of consultees. The ethical guidelines for group work that are discussed in Chapter 13 apply here to the process of consulting in groups. When consultants use group process approaches, it is essential that they be competent in group consultation. Those who participate in consultation in groups have a right to know what will be expected of them. Matters such as self-disclosure, privacy, the boundary between work-related concerns and personal concerns, and the limits of confidentiality are all particularly important.

Three Case Examples of Consulting

◆   ***The case of Lynn.***   The principal of a school hires Lynn, a psychologist in private practice, to conduct a communications workshop focusing on improving interpersonal relationships between the faculty and the administration. The workshop is a two-day intensive group experience involving all teachers and the three administrators in the school. Participants are encouraged to openly express their concerns and difficulties and to focus on possible strategies for improving working conditions. The workshop seems to go well.

The following week, the principal calls Lynn and asks for a meeting. The principal agrees that the workshop seemed successful and says she would be interested in Lynn's assessment of the key faculty members whom she needs to pay closer attention to. She would like to know more about the natural leaders and the potential troublemakers. Lynn is asked to go through the list of teachers and make an assessment of each person's potential to be troublesome or helpful.

not part of agenda
contract so
no informed
consent of staff
confidentiality is
an issue, too

- What ethical issues, if any, are involved in this case?
- As the principal attended the workshop and basically heard everything, would it be permissible for Lynn to give her professional assessment of each person?
- The consultation contract was between the principal and Lynn. What rights, if any, does that fact give the principal?
- Because the teachers are being professionally assessed on the basis of their participation in the workshop, what were their rights regarding knowing in advance that this kind of assessment would be made and that it would be given to the principal? *They have every right — legally + ethically*
- Does informed consent require that all participants know exactly how the information they offer will be used? *yes*

♦ ***The case of Delilah.***   An airline management group is concerned about the loss of working hours because of on-the-job stress. Delilah is hired to provide stress-management skills to solve the problem. The contract calls for her to teach specific strategies such as relaxation, diet, exercise, aerobics, and visualization, with the stated goal of reducing stress and improving efficiency. In the process of teaching employees how to cope with stress, she discovers that many outside personal problems are contributing to their stress. She decides to alter her strategy to include several hours of group counseling to address the personal problems of the participants. In addition, she gives the participants three sources of referral for further professional help.

- Can a consultant unilaterally change the provisions of a contract? *no*
- Is it ethical for Delilah to ignore the personal problems that are contributing to inefficiency on the job because this information was not available to her when the contract was designed? *no*
- Does management have any rights to insist on the contract being strictly adhered to? What if management contends that personal problems are best dealt with separately and financed by the employees or their insurance company? *Yes. They'd be right — She should just give referrals —*
- Is Delilah now involved in a dual relationship as consultant and counselor? Is it unethical for her to hold further group sessions? *Yes.*

♦ ***A case of a hidden agenda.***   A state-funded agency employs a team of consultants to conduct human-relations training and staff development. Over time, these consultants earn a reputation for working effectively with the lower level staff. The director of the agency expresses a desire for the consultants to "work on" key members of the upper level staff who are identified as being particularly troublesome to the agency. The stipulation is that the focus on these key members is not to be disclosed; rather, the impression to be given is that the team is working to improve the overall efficiency to the staff.

♦ If the consultants accept this contract as it is written, are they being un-ethical? *they can't be open + honest about purposes + goals*
♦ If this hidden agenda is successfully carried out, overall efficiency will be enhanced and the entire agency benefits. Does the end justify the means? *no*
♦ Assume that a hidden agenda becomes evident to you during the course of a consulting workshop you are giving. What would be the ethical thing to do? Would you disclose to the members that you suspect a hidden agenda? Would you confront the director who had hired you? *yes*

Chapter Summary

Supervision and consultation are two roles that counselors are often asked to assume. It is clear that special training is needed to effectively perform the many functions required in these activities. Some of the key ethical issues associated with supervision and consultation involve carrying out professional roles and responsibilities, maintaining clear boundaries between roles, and avoiding the problems created by dual relationships.

Supervision is one way in which trainees learn how to apply their knowledge and skills to particular clinical situations. It is essential that supervisees receive regular feedback so that they have a basis for honing their skills. Effective supervision deals with the professional as a person and as a practitioner. It is not enough to focus on the trainee's skills, for the supervisory relationship is a personal process. Thus, the supervisee's dynamics are equally important in this process.

Consultation is a growing professional specialization that can be carried out with individuals and in small groups with diverse client populations in various work settings. Consultants help human-services workers deliver services to their clients more effectively. Thus, they focus on work-related concerns. Ethical and professional issues pertaining to consultation can be broken down into these areas: values, competence, training, the consulting relationship, the rights of consultees, and consulting in groups.

Suggested Activities

1. Role-play a situation that involves a supervisor's asking supervisees to get involved in therapy situations that are beyond the scope of their training and experience. One student in class can play the role of a persuasive supervisor who thinks that students will learn best by "jumping into the water and learning how to swim—or sink." The supervisor can ask trainees to

work with a family, lead a therapy group alone, or work with abused children. After the role playing, discuss the ethical and clinical issues involved, with a focus on ways to deal with inadequate supervision.

2. Set up another role-playing situation. In this case, the supervisor is difficult to reach and rarely keeps his or her appointments with the supervisees. One student can role-play the inaccessible supervisor, and several others can assume the roles of students who need to meet with their supervisor to discuss difficult cases.

3. Investigate some of the community agencies in your area to learn what supervision they offer to interns and to newly hired practitioners. Several students can form a panel to share the results.

4. Form an ethics committee in class to review the following cases dealing with supervision:

   ◆ a supervisor has made sexual offers to several supervisees
   ◆ a supervisor is accepting supervisees as clients in his or her private practice
   ◆ a supervisor makes it a practice to date former students in the program

   The ethics committee can present its case in class with appropriate courses of action for each problem area. The others in the class can interact with the committee by providing alternative viewpoints.

5. Interview a consultant to discover how this person was trained and what professional activities he or she typically performs. It would be useful for various students to interview consultants in different settings, such as businesses, public schools, agencies, and private practice. Ask the consultants to share some of the ethical dilemmas they have faced in their work. How did they deal with them?

6. Design a role-playing situation that involves consultation. At least one student assumes the role of consultant. A number of students can play the role of consultees who are seeking help from the consultant. Again, think of diverse settings to add some variety. Afterward, discuss the process involved.

7. Interview several clinical supervisors to determine what they consider to be the most pressing ethical and legal issues in the supervisory relationship. Some questions you might ask supervisors are: What are the rights of trainees? What are the main responsibilities of supervisors? To what degree should supervisors be held accountable for the welfare of the clients who are counseled by their trainees? What kind of specialized training have they had in supervision? Who is the proper focus of supervision—the client? the trainee? What are some common problems faced by supervisors in effectively carrying out their duties?

8. Assume that you are in a field placement as a counselor in a community agency. The administrators tell you that they do not want you to inform your clients that you are a student intern. They explain that your clients might feel that they were getting second-class service if they found out that you were in training. What would you say and do if you found yourself as

an intern in this situation? Would it be ethical to follow this directive and not inform your clients that you were a trainee and that you were receiving supervision? Do you agree or disagree with the rationale of the administrators? Might you accept the internship assignment under the terms outlined if you could not find any other field placements?

Chapter

10

Multicultural Perspectives and Diversity Issues

- Pre-Chapter Self-Inventory
- Introduction
- The Need for a Multicultural Emphasis
- Ethical Codes in Multicultural Counseling
- Cultural Values and Assumptions in Therapy
- Matching Client and Counselor
- Multicultural Training for Counselors
- Chapter Summary
- Suggested Activities

Pre-Chapter Self-Inventory

Directions: For each statement, indicate the response that most closely identifies your beliefs and attitudes. Use the following code:

5 = I *strongly agree* with this statement.
4 = I *agree* with this statement.
3 = I am *undecided* about this statement.
2 = I *disagree* with this statement.
1 = I *strongly disagree* with this statement.

_2_   1. Well-trained, sensitive, and self-aware therapists who do not impose their own values on clients are better qualified to be multicultural counselors.

_2_   2. To counsel effectively, I must be of the same ethnic background as my client.

_2_   3. Basically, all counseling interventions are multicultural.

_4_   4. I must challenge cultural stereotypes when they become obvious in counseling situations.

___   5. Contemporary counseling theories can be applied to people from all cultures.

___   6. A sensitive multicultural counselor is a spokesperson for the particular culture from which the client comes.

___   7. I will be able to examine my behavior and attitudes to determine the degree to which cultural bias might influence the interventions I make with clients.

___   8. Special guidelines are needed for counseling members of ethnic or racial minority groups.

___   9. Counselors must take into account the ethnic and cultural differences between themselves and their clients.

___ 10. The primary function of majority-group counselors is to alert their clients to the choices available to them in the mainstream culture.

___ 11. An effective counselor facilitates assimilation of the minority client into society.

___ 12. Ethical practice demands that counselors become familiar with the value systems of diverse cultural groups.

___ 13. I would have no trouble working with someone from a culture very different from mine, because we would be more alike than different.

___ 14. If I just listen to my clients, I will know all I need to know about their cultural background.

___ 15. Client resistance is typically encountered in multicultural counseling and must be eradicated before changes can take place.

___ 16. The ability to observe and understand nonverbal communication is an important component of multicultural counseling.

___ 17. Establishing a trusting relationship is more difficult when the counselor and the client come from different cultures.

___ 18. Unless practitioners have been educated about cultural differences, they cannot determine whether they are competent to work with diverse populations.

___ 19. As a condition for licensure, all counselors should have specialized training and supervised experience in multicultural counseling.

___ 20. At this point in my educational career I feel well prepared to counsel culturally diverse client populations.

Introduction

One of the major challenges facing counseling professionals is understanding the complex role that cultural diversity plays in their work. In a sense, all counseling interventions are multicultural. Clients and counselors bring to their relationship attitudes, values, and behaviors that can vary widely. One mistake is to deny the importance of these cultural variables in counseling; another is to overemphasize cultural differences to the extent that practitioners lose their naturalness and fail to make contact with their clients.

In this chapter we focus on the ethical implications of a multicultural perspective or lack thereof in the helping professions. To ensure that the terms we use in this chapter will have a precise meaning, we have provided specific definitions (see the box on page 319). We then introduce you to the need for a multicultural emphasis and suggest ways to avoid cultural tunnel vision and expand your consciousness. We focus on how your cultural values and your assumptions are likely to influence the manner in which you practice. We also consider what it means to be a culturally skilled counselor and how to provide training for multicultural counselors. This chapter is not a comprehensive treatment of multicultural counseling; the field is complex and is developing rapidly. Also, we do not treat separate ethnic groups, except by way of providing examples of some groups. We encourage you to expand your knowledge of the topics introduced here by acquiring further information on your own.

The Need for a Multicultural Emphasis

Cultural diversity is a fact of life in today's "global village," and counselors can no longer afford to ignore the issues involved in counseling culturally diverse populations. Multicultural counseling attempts to clarify the role of sociocultural forces in the origin, expression, and resolution of problems (Axelson, 1993). Das (1995) points out that culture influences every aspect of our lives, for it influences our view of social and psychological reality. Multicultural counseling is based on a number of premises identified here by Das (p. 45):

◆ All cultures represent meaningful ways of coping with the problems a particular group faces.

Key Terms

Culture, ethnicity, minority group, multiculturalism, multicultural counseling, diversity, ethnic-sensitive practice, racism, stereotypes, and the culturally encapsulated counselor are critical concepts for multicultural counseling. Take a few moments to acquaint yourself with the way these terms will be used in this chapter.

The word *culture* can be interpreted broadly, for it can be associated with a racial or ethnic group as well as with gender, religion, economic status, nationality, physical capacity or handicap, or affectional or sexual orientation. Pedersen (1994) describes culture as including demographic variables such as age, gender, and place of residence; status variables such as social, educational, and economic background; formal and informal affiliations; and the ethnographic variables of nationality, ethnicity, language, and religion. Considering culture from this broad perspective is particularly important for counselors, because culture represents the multiplicity of ways in which human beings adapt to their physical and social environment (Das, 1995).

Ethnicity is a sense of identity that stems from common ancestry, history, nationality, religion, and race. This unique social and cultural heritage provides cohesion and strength. It is a powerful unifying force that offers a sense of belonging and sharing based on commonality (Axelson, 1993; Lum, 1996).

Minority group has come to refer to any category of people who have been discriminated against or subjected to unequal treatment and oppression by society largely because of their group membership. These groups have been characterized as subordinate, dominated, and powerless. Thus, minority is often defined by the condition of oppression rather than by numerical criteria. Although the term *minority* has traditionally referred to national, racial, linguistic, and religious groups, it now also applies to women, gay men and lesbians, elderly people, people with physical handicaps, and those who are behaviorally deviant (Atkinson, Morten, & Sue, 1993; Lum, 1996).

Multiculturalism is a generic term that indicates any relationship between two or more diverse groups. *Cross-cultural, transcultural,* and *intercultural* are terms with similar meanings. We prefer *multicultural* because it more accurately reflects the complexity of culture but avoids any implied comparison. The multicultural perspective in human-service education takes into consideration the specific values, beliefs, and actions conditioned by a client's ethnicity, gender, religion, socioeconomic status, political views, lifestyle, geographic region, and historical experiences with the dominant culture (Wright, Coley, & Corey, 1989). Multiculturalism provides a conceptual framework that recognizes the complex diversity of a pluralistic society, while at the same time suggesting bridges of shared concern that bind culturally different individuals to one another (Pedersen, 1991).

Multicultural counseling is any counseling relationship in which the counselor and the client belong to different cultural groups, hold different assumptions about social reality, and subscribe to different worldviews (Das, 1995, p. 45). Arredondo and her colleagues (1996), who have operationalized a comprehensive set of multicultural competencies, write that multicultural counseling refers to approaches that integrate multicultural and culture-specific awareness, knowledge, and skills into counseling practices.

The United States is a pluralistic society, and all its citizens are ethnic, racial, and cultural beings. Arredondo and her colleagues (1996) suggest that multiculturalism focuses on ethnicity, race, and culture. In contrast, *diversity* refers to individual differences such as age, gender, sexual orientation, religion, and physical ability or disability. Both *multiculturalism* and *diversity* have been politicized in the United States in ways that have often been divisive, but these terms can equally represent positive assets in a pluralistic society.

(continued)

(continued)

Ethnic-sensitive practice goes beyond the concerns of the individual to address the consequences of racism, poverty, and discrimination on minority groups; it aims to change those institutions that perpetuate these conditions (Devore, 1985).

Racism is any pattern of behavior that denies access to opportunities or privileges to members of one racial group while perpetuating access to opportunities and privileges to members of another racial group (Ridley, 1989, 1995). Racism can operate on both individual and institutional levels.

Stereotypes are oversimplified and uncritical generalizations about individuals who are identified as belonging to a specific group.

The *culturally encapsulated counselor,* a concept introduced by Wrenn (1962, 1985), is characterized by:

- defining reality according to one set of cultural assumptions
- showing insensitivity to cultural variations among individuals
- accepting unreasoned assumptions without proof and without regard to rationality
- failing to evaluate other viewpoints and making little attempt to accommodate the behavior of others
- being trapped in one way of thinking that resists adaptation and rejects alternatives

Although counselors exhibiting these blatantly biased attitudes may be easily identified, many other well-intentioned helpers practice *unintentional racism* (Ridley, 1995). Practitioners who presume that they are free of any traces of racism seriously underestimate the impact of their own socialization. Whether these biased attitudes are intentional or unintentional, the result is harmful for both individuals and society. Pedersen (1994) believes that the key to recognizing unintentional racism lies in the willingness of practitioners to continually reexamine their underlying assumptions.

Note about names: There is some concern about how to refer appropriately to certain racial and ethnic groups. Preferred names tend to change. For instance, some alternate names for one group are Hispanic, Latino (Latina), Mexican American, or Chicana (Chicano). Realizing that there is no one "right" designation to fit any group, practitioners can show sensitivity to the fact that a name is important; they can ask their client how he or she would like to be identified.

- All counseling can be regarded as multicultural if culture is defined broadly to include not only race, ethnicity, and nationality but also gender, age, social class, sexual orientation, and disability.
- People seek counseling largely because of problems that emerge out of sociocultural conditions.
- Traditional counseling is a particular form of intervention developed in the West to cope with psychological distress.
- All cultures have developed formal or informal ways of dealing with human problems.

Whether a counselor is aware of it or not, cultural factors are an integral part of the counseling process.

The Problem of Cultural Tunnel Vision

A faculty member overheard one of our students inquiring about possibilities for a fieldwork placement in a community agency. The student remarked: "I don't want a placement where I'll have to work with poor people or minority groups." This brief statement revealed much about the student's attitudes and beliefs about both people and the helping professions. If we want students to become more culturally aware, it is essential that we encourage them to seek out people who are different from themselves.

Many students come into training with cultural tunnel vision. They have had limited cultural experiences, and in many cases they unwittingly impose their values on unsuspecting clients, assuming that everyone shares these values. At times, student helpers from the majority group have expressed the attitude, explicitly or implicitly, that racial and ethnic minorities are unresponsive to professional psychological intervention because of their lack of motivation to change or their "resistance" to seeking professional help.

Students are not alone in their susceptibility to cultural tunnel vision. Ridley (1995) develops the thesis that, ironic as it may seem, racism has been present in mental-health delivery systems for quite some time. Ridley states that studies from the 1950s to the present have documented enduring patterns of racism in mental-health-care delivery systems. The literature has examined the impact of racism on various racial groups and also the existence of racism in a variety of treatment settings.

Many clients have come to distrust helpers associated with the establishment or with social service agencies because of a history of unequal treatment. These clients may be slow to form trusting relationships with counselors who, because of their role, possess greater power than they do. Counselors may have difficulty identifying with these clients if they ignore the history behind this distrust. Helpers from all cultural groups need to honestly examine their own expectations and attitudes about the helping process. We are all culture-bound to some extent, and it takes a concerted effort for counselors to monitor their biases so that they do not impede the formation of helping relationships.

A good place for counselors to begin to move toward widening their encapsulated perspectives is to become more aware of their own culture. Knowing your own cultural framework provides a context for understanding how diverse cultures share common ground and also how to recognize areas of uniqueness. Pedersen (1994) puts this challenge well when he writes: "It is no longer possible for good counselors to ignore their own cultures or the cultures of their clients through encapsulation. However, until the multicultural perspective is understood as making the counselor's job easier instead of harder, and increasing rather than decreasing the quality of a counselor's life, little real change is likely to happen" (p. 22).

D. W. Sue and Sue (1990) are convinced that the field of clinical and counseling psychology has failed to meet the particular mental-health needs of ethnic minorities. Half of minority clients terminate counseling after only one contact with a therapist. Sue and Sue suggest that a basic reason for underutilization of services and early termination is the biased nature of the services themselves: "The services offered are frequently antagonistic or inappropriate to the life experiences of the culturally different client; they lack sensitivity and understanding, and they are oppressive and discriminating toward minority clients" (p. 7). From an ethical perspective, Sue and Sue maintain that mental-health professionals have a moral and professional responsibility to (1) become aware of and deal with the biases, stereotypes, and assumptions that undergird their practice; (2) became aware of the culturally different client's values and worldview; and (3) develop appropriate intervention strategies that take into account the social, cultural, historical, and environmental influences of culturally different clients.

There are other ways to interpret the underutilization of traditional psychotherapeutic services by minority clients. It may not be a Hispanic person's style to seek professional help quickly when faced with a problem. For example, consider Marco's experience of being torn between marrying a person selected by his parents and marrying a woman of his choice. He might first look for a solution within himself through contemplation. If he were unable to resolve his dilemma, he might seek assistance from a family member or a clergyperson. Then he might look to some of his friends for advice and support in making the best decision. If none of these approaches resulted in a satisfactory resolution of his problem, he might then turn to a mental-health professional for help. The fact that he did not seek counseling services sooner had little to do with his resistance or with insensitivity on the part of counselors; he was following a route that was congruent with his cultural background.

Some argue that minority clients who use counseling resources may lose their cultural values in the process. Culturally encapsulated counselors tend to mistakenly assume that a lack of assertiveness is a sign of dysfunctional behavior that should be changed. Merely labeling a behavior dysfunctional reflects a particular value orientation. Practitioners need to consider whether passivity is a problem from their client's perspective and whether assertiveness is a useful behavior that their client hopes to acquire.

Wood and Mallinckrodt (1990) recommend culturally sensitive assertiveness training for minority clients. But therapists who provide such training must be certain that gaining these interpersonal skills is a value shared by the client and not a goal imposed by the therapist. Counselors can initiate a dialogue about these issues with clients. "This openness and respect will help to ensure that the therapist will become, not another medium of cultural domination and discrimination, but rather the client's ally in more effective coping" (p. 10). Ideally, therapists will not merely tolerate the reality of cultural complexity but will also welcome and celebrate it.

The APA (1993) has developed a set of *Guidelines for Providers of Psychological Services to Ethnic, Linguistic, and Culturally Diverse Populations.* One of the provisions of this document is that regardless of their ethnic or racial background, service providers should be aware of how their own culture, life experiences, attitudes, values, and biases influence them. Additionally, practitioners are challenged to go beyond their cultural encapsulation and ask themselves: "Is it appropriate for me to view these clients any differently than I would if they were from my own ethnic or cultural group?" The APA's guidelines also challenge practitioners to respect the roles of family members and the community structures, hierarchies, values, and beliefs that are an integral part of the client's culture. Providers should identify resources in the family and the larger community and use them in delivering culturally sensitive services. For example, an entire Native American family may come to a clinic to provide support for an individual in distress because many of the healing practices found in Native American communities are centered in the family and the community.

Itai and McRae (1994) discuss the significance of counselors' understanding of cultural differences as a dimension of effectively reaching Japanese-American clients. Filial piety, or respect toward parents, is a basic value in Japanese-American and Chinese-American families. Children owe their parents obedience and are expected to respect and honor them. Children are taught how the rules of filial piety apply in many situations, and they understand the disappointment their parents will feel if they do not live up to their obligations. Much of daily behavior is influenced by a sense of guilt or shame for failing to live up to obligations imposed by others. Avoiding "losing face" is a motivational force to do what is expected.

In writing about Chinese-American cultural values and their impact on the counseling process, D. Sue and Sue (1991) identified several core traditional Chinese values. Self-determination and independence are valued less than family bonds and unity. Family communication patterns are based on cultural tradition and emphasize appropriate roles and status. Academic achievement and career development are very important, and individuals are taught to suppress strong emotions outside of the family. Counselors who do not understand or accept these values are likely to make the mistake of encouraging Chinese-American clients to change in directions that are not in harmony with their values.

Cultural sensitivity is not limited to one group but applies to all cultures. There is no sanctuary from cultural bias. All counselors must be vigilant to avoid using their own group as the standard by which to assess appropriate behavior. African-American counselors need to be aware of their possible prejudices toward Caucasian clients just as white counselors must be sensitive to their attitudes toward African-American clients. Indeed, African-American counselors also need to be aware of how their own cultural experiences and views are likely to influence their work with African-American clients. There can be even greater differences within the same cultural group than there are between different cultural groups.

Learning to Deal with Cultural Pluralism

Multiculturalism should be valued positively and not merely tolerated. Yet many of our mental-health organizations and educational institutions still take an ethnocentric view of the world (D. W. Sue, 1996b). To operate monoculturally and monolingually, as if all our clients were the same, is not in accord with reality, and it can result in unethical and ineffective practice.

Herr (1991) encourages counselors to take steps to deal effectively with cultural diversity and pluralism. He raises some excellent questions:

- How can counselors complement theories and practices that arise from Western approaches with those that arise from Eastern and other approaches?
- How can counselors become more familiar with the worldviews that different cultures reinforce?
- How can counselors help people of different cultures learn about majority norms, which are useful in some situations, without replacing their cultural pride and perspectives?
- How can counselors help majority clients face their own conscious and unconscious racism and sexism? How can counselors help their clients learn about and from minority cultures?
- How can minority counselors become aware of their own unconscious racism and sexism? How can they become less culturally encapsulated?
- What are some ways to provide cross-cultural counseling when the socialization of the client and the counselor are significantly different?

Understanding cultural pluralism begins with self-analysis, which is a long term task. D. W. Sue (1996a) contends that becoming multiculturally competent is best conceptualized as a life-long developmental process that requires continual education and training. Sue admits that realistically it is not possible to acquire an in-depth understanding of all the different cultural groups. Part of multicultural competence entails recognizing our limitations and is manifested in our willingness to (a) seek consultation, (b) seek continuing education, and (c) make referrals to a professional who is competent to work with a particular client population. Richardson and Molinaro (1996) maintain that when counselors learn about their own culture they are moving in the direction of acquiring multicultural competence. They add: "If a counselor accepts this challenge and engages in self-exploration, then learning about the race, cultures, and experiences of clients becomes a manageable process instead of an overwhelming and threatening one" (p. 241).

Ethical Codes in Multicultural Counseling

Most ethics codes mention the practitioner's responsibility to recognize the special needs of diverse client populations. For example, the preamble to the *Code of Ethics* of ACA (1995) calls for members to "recognize diversity in our society and embrace a cross-cultural approach in support of the worth, dignity, potential, and uniqueness of each individual." The ACA's nondiscrimination standard states:

> Counselors do not condone or engage in discrimination based on age, color, culture, disability, ethnic group, gender, race, religion, sexual orientation, marital status, or socioeconomic status. (A.2.a.)

A 2o

The ACA also calls upon counselors to respect differences:

Counselors will actively attempt to understand the diverse cultural backgrounds of the clients with whom they work. This includes, but is not limited to, learning how the counselor's own cultural/ethnic/racial identity impacts her or his values and beliefs about the counseling process. (A.2.b.)

In addition, specific ACA standards deal with diversity in most areas of theory, practice, training, and research.

In the most recent revision of the NASW's *Code of Ethics* (1996), cultural competence and recognition of social diversity are clearly linked to ethical practice. Two relevant guidelines are:

Social workers should have a knowledge base of their clients' cultures and be able to demonstrate competence in the provision of services that are sensitive to clients' cultures and to differences among people and cultural groups. (1.05.b.)

Social workers should obtain education about and seek to understand the nature of social diversity and oppression with respect to race, ethnicity, national origin, color, sex, sexual orientation, age, marital status, political belief, religion and mental or physical disability. (1.05.c.)

The APA ethics codes (1995) indicate that part of competence implies understanding diversity:

Where differences of age, gender, race, ethnicity, national origin, religion, sexual orientation, disability, language, or socioeconomic status significantly affect psychologists' work concerning particular individuals or groups, psychologists obtain the training, experience, consultation, or supervision necessary to ensure the competence of their services, or they make appropriate referrals. (1.08.)

Toward Diversity in Practice

Many therapeutic practices are biased against racial and ethnic minorities and women (D. W. Sue, Ivey, & Pedersen, 1996) and often reflect racism, sexism, and other forms of prejudice. D. W. Sue (1996b) puts this matter bluntly: "Rather than educate or heal, rather than offer enlightenment and freedom, and rather than allow for equal access and opportunities, historical and current practices have restricted, stereotyped, damaged, and oppressed the culturally different in our society" (p. 195). D. W. Sue and Sue (1990) contend that this ethnocentric bias has been destructive to the natural help-giving networks of minority communities. They suggest that helpers need to expand their perception of mental-health practices to include support systems such as family, friends, community, self-help programs, and occupational networks.

Counselors may misunderstand clients of a different sex, race, age, social class, or sexual orientation. If practitioners fail to integrate these diversity factors into their practice, they are infringing on the client's cultural autonomy and basic human rights, which will reduce the chance of establishing an effective therapeutic relationship. The failure to address these factors constitutes unethical practice (Cayleff, 1986; Ivey, 1990). Now let's consider two cases that illustrate some of the issues we have been exploring.

◆ **The case of Lee.**   Stacy, a Caucasian counselor, is a counselor at a university counseling center. A Vietnamese student, Lee, is assigned to her because of academic difficulties. Stacy observes that Lee is slow and deliberate in his conversational style, and she immediately signs him up for a class in English as a second language. In the course of their conversations, Lee discloses that his father is directing him toward a career in medicine, for which he thinks he is not suited. Stacy gives Lee a homework assignment, asking him to talk to his father and tell him that he no longer wants to pursue medicine and is going to follow a direction that appeals to him.

- ◆ Was the fact that Lee spoke slowly and deliberately an indication that he was deficient in English? Was the counselor insensitive in recommending an ESL class so hastily?
- ◆ Did the therapist's actions reveal respect for the roles of family members, hierarchies, values, and beliefs in the client's culture?
- ◆ Was Stacy too quick in making her assessments, considering that Lee was sent to the counseling center? Would it have made a difference if he had come voluntarily for guidance?
- ◆ How would you have handled this situation?

◆ **The case of Cynthia.**   An Asian counselor, Ling, has recently set up a private practice in a culturally mixed, upper-middle-class neighborhood. A Caucasian housewife, Cynthia, seeks Ling out for counseling. She is depressed, feels that life has little meaning, and feels enslaved by the needs of her husband and small children. When Ling asks about any recent events that could be contributing to her depression, she tells him that she has discussed with her husband her desire to return to school and pursue a career of her choosing. She told her husband that she felt stifled and needed to pursue her own interests. Her husband's response was to threaten a divorce if she followed through with her plans. Cynthia then consulted with her pastor, who pointed out her obligations to her family. Ling is aware of his own cultural biases, which include a strong commitment to family and to the role of the man as the head of the household. Although he shows empathy for Cynthia's struggle, he directs her toward considering postponing her own aspirations until her children have grown up. She surrenders to his direction because she feels guilty about asserting her own needs, and she is also fearful of being left alone. Ling then works with her to find other ways to add zest to her life that would not have such a radical impact on the family.

- ◆ Do you see any evidence of bias or unethical behavior in Ling's approach to this case?
- ◆ List some of the potential gender, age, and cultural issues in this case. How might you have addressed each of them?

- Should Ling have helped Cynthia explore the lack of meaning in her life? Was it unethical not to do so?
- Could Ling have acted any differently and still have been true to himself and his own cultural values?
- What might be the response of a feminist therapist?
- If Ling's client had been from a traditional Asian family, do you think Ling's approach would have been appropriate? Was this approach appropriate for Cynthia?
- Because Ling had different family values from Cynthia's, should he have referred her to another professional?
- If Ling had approached you for consultation, what advice might you have given him?
- Given what you know about your values, how might you have worked with Cynthia if she had been your client?

We suggest that you take a few moments to review the professional codes of ethics found in the Appendices to determine for yourself the degree to which they take cultural, ethnic, and racial dimensions into account. From a multicultural perspective, what are their shortcomings? To what degree do you think that most of them are culturally encapsulated? What revisions and additions can you think of as a basis for mental-health practitioners to function ethically in today's diverse world?

Cultural Values and Assumptions in Therapy

Eastern and Western are not just geographic terms but also represent philosophical, social, political, and cultural orientations. In this section we explore the difference between Western and Eastern assumptions about therapy, examine the importance of the counselor's values in multicultural therapy, and discuss the need for therapists to challenge stereotypical beliefs.

Western versus Eastern Values

Most contemporary theories of therapy and therapeutic practices are grounded in Western assumptions, yet most of the world differs from mainstream U.S. culture. Applying the Western model of therapy to Chinese culture does not work well. Likewise, the Western model also has major limitations when applied to Hispanics, Native Americans, African Americans, and Asian Americans. Professional psychological help is not a typical option for many minority groups. In fact, in most non-Western cultures informal groups of friends and relatives provide the supportive network. Informal counseling consists of the spontaneous outreach of caring people to others in need (Brammer, 1985).

Patterson (1985b, 1996) believes that Western methods can be useful despite cultural differences. Focusing on the universal factors that link all humanity, he contends that East and West must move toward each other:

Eastern cultures must change in the direction of greater concern for individual personal development. Western culture must move in the direction of greater concern for the influence of the individual upon others and . . . of cooperation in fostering personal development in others. (1985b, p. 188)

For him, the overemphasis on cultural diversity and training in specific techniques for various cultural groups "ignores the fact that we are rapidly becoming one world, with rapid communication and increasing interrelations among persons from varying cultures, leading to increasing homogeneity and a worldview representing the common humanity that binds all humans together as one species" (1996, p. 230).

Ho (1985), studying Asians' underuse of professional therapy, proposes a creative synthesis of collectivism and individualism whereby it is possible to draw from both worlds. Agreeing with Ho are Saeki and Borow (1985), who believe that the aim of treatment in both worlds is linked to striving for the good life as defined by the respective dominant cultures: "Eastern and Western systems both address the nature and control of intrapersonal conflict but do so in different ways" (p. 225). In the table at the top of page 329 we present the general characteristics that, according to Ho (1985), differentiate these two perspectives.

What are your reactions to the assignment of these particular values to these particular systems? Do you see any crossover? Now ask yourself these questions:

- To what degree is your value system an integration of both systems?
- Are you aware of holding any stereotypical beliefs and assumptions?
- Do you tend to downplay values different from your own?
- Do you assume that all your clients will be ready to engage in self-disclosure?
- How do you differentiate between resistance and a hesitancy that is culturally based?
- To what extent do you value assertiveness? Is this a value that you expect most of your clients to acquire? How might you react to clients who have no desire to be assertive?
- Do you agree with Patterson that it is not necessary, or desirable, to design new approaches for counseling clients from other cultures?

Think about these issues as you read about Dan's dilemma.

◆ ***The case of Dan.***   An Asian immigrant couple come to Dan, a marriage counselor in a small Midwestern city. They are concerned for the future of their marriage. The husband is quiet and controlled; the wife cries often but says little.

Dan has just completed a workshop in multicultural counseling. He is immediately conscious of their silence and is determined to respect this behavior. He is aware that in Asian cultures the wife typically defers to the husband, so he decides to be careful in prompting the wife to speak lest he be guilty of a

Comparison of Western and Eastern Systems (Ho, 1985)

West	East
Values	
Primacy of individual	Primacy of relationship
Democratic orientation	Authoritarian orientation
Nuclear family structure	Extended family structure
Emphasis on youth	Emphasis on maturity
Independence	Interdependence
Assertiveness	Compliance
Nonconformity	Conformity
Competition	Cooperation
Conflict	Harmony
Freedom	Security
Guiding Principles for Action	
Fulfillment of individual needs	Achievement of collective goals
Individual responsibility	Collective responsibility
Behavior Orientation	
Expression of feelings	Control of feelings
Uniqueness of individual	Uniformity
Self-actualization	Collective actualization
Time Orientation	
Future orientation	Traditionalism
Innovation	Conservatism
Ethical Orientation	
Morality anchored in person	Morality linked to relationships

cultural faux pas. The result is that Dan becomes silent and feels stifled and useless to them as a counselor.

- ◆ If you were confronted with Dan's dilemma, how would you deal with this couple?
- ◆ Even though the problem of marital discord seems straightforward, what potential cultural issues may Dan need to consider?
- ◆ What methods or techniques would you use to work with this couple?

Challenging Counselors' Stereotypical Beliefs

Counselors may think they are not biased, yet many hold stereotypical beliefs that could well affect their practice. Some examples include these statements: "Failure to change stems from a lack of motivation." "People have choices, and it is up to them to change their lives." Many people do not have a wide range of choices due to environmental factors beyond their control. To assume that all these people lack is motivation is simplistic in the extreme. Another often held assumption is that "talk therapy" works best. This ignores the fact that in many cultures people rely more on nonverbal expression.

Practitioners who counsel ethnic and racial minority clients without an awareness of their own stereotypical beliefs are likely to cause harm to their clients. Ethical practice in a multicultural context requires that counselors be aware of and sensitive to the unique cultural realities of their clients. Counselors who practice without this awareness and sensitivity risk engaging in unethical practice (Lee & Kurilla, 1997). Reflect on these issues as you consider these two case examples.

◆ **The case of Mac.**   Mac, a successful psychologist, has concerns about much of the multicultural movement. He sees it as more trendy than useful. "I do not impose my values. I do not tell clients what to do. I listen, and if I need to know something, I ask. How am I to know whether a Japanese-American client is more American than Japanese or vice versa unless I ask him? My belief is that the client will tell you all you need to know."

- ◆ What is your reaction to Mac's attitude?
- ◆ How would you determine the level of acculturation of a client?
- ◆ Is Mac burdening his client by asking him or her to educate him on culture issues?

Commentary.   We react not so much to what Mac says as to what is implied by what is said. Certainly, it is important for clients to tell counselors what they need to know. However, Mac seems to downplay the necessity for ongoing education and sensitivity to cultural issues. Formal education is not enough; we also need to listen to our clients. However, listening to our clients is not enough; we also need to be formally educated.

◆ **The case of Claudine.**   Claudine, a white counselor, takes over as director of a clinic that has a large percentage of Asian immigrants as clients. At a staff meeting she sums up her philosophy of counseling in this fashion: "People come to counseling to begin change or because they are already in the process of change. Our purpose is to challenge them to continue their change. This holds true whether the client is Euro-American, Asian, or some other minority. If clients are slow to speak, our job is to challenge them to speak, because the majority in American culture deals with problems through talking. Silence may be appropriate in Asian culture, but it does not work in this culture. The sooner clients learn this, the better for them."

- ◆ In what ways is Claudine culturally sensitive or culturally insensitive?
- ◆ Do you detect any signs of cultural bias?
- ◆ To what extent do you agree or disagree with Claudine, and why?

Assumptions about self-disclosure.   Counselors often assume that clients will be ready to talk about their intimate personal issues. This assumption ignores the fact that in some cultures self-disclosure is taboo and that some European ethic groups stress keeping problems "in the family."

Ridley (1984) asserts that individual verbal therapies often place African-American clients in a paradoxical situation. Although self-disclosure is typically considered to be essential for maximizing therapeutic outcomes, complex personal, interpersonal, and social factors may affect an African-American client's willingness to be open. In this light, the goals of most traditional "talk" therapies appear to be incompatible with the tendencies of many African-American clients.

Asian Americans are frequently described as the "most repressed of all clients" (D. W. Sue & Sue, 1985). However, such clients may in fact be holding true to their cultural background. How much value does "talk" therapy have for these clients?

Patterson (1985b, 1996) contends that unless clients are willing to verbalize and communicate their thoughts, feelings, attitudes, and perceptions, there is no basis for empathic understanding by the therapist. He asserts that the inability to self-disclose is something to be overcome, not accepted. Patterson (1996) writes: "The only way in which the counselor can enter the world of the client is with the permission of the client, who communicates the nature of his or her world to the counselor through self-disclosure. Thus, client self-disclosure is the sine qua non for counseling. Counselor respect and genuineness facilitate client self-disclosure" (p. 230).

The case of Lily.   Lily, a licensed counselor, has come to work in a family-life center that deals with many immigrant families. She often becomes impatient over the slow pace of her clients' disclosures. Lily decides to teach her clients by modeling for them. With one of her reticent couples she says: "My husband and I have many fights and disagreements. We express our feelings openly and clear the air. In fact, several years ago my husband had an affair, which put our relationship into a turmoil. I believe it was my ability to vent my anger and express my hurt that allowed me to work through this terrible event."

◆ What do you think of Lily's self-disclosure? Would such a disclosure be helpful to you if you were her client?

◆ Might you be inclined to make a similar type of disclosure to your clients? Why, or why not?

◆ What possible positive or negative outcomes might occur after such a disclosure?

◆ In your opinion, when, if ever, would such a disclosure be appropriate?

Assumptions about assertiveness.   Most counselors assume that clients are better off if they can behave in assertive ways, such as telling people directly what they think and what they want. In fact, much of therapy consists of teaching clients the skills to take an active stance toward life. D. W. Sue and Sue (1985) report a widespread view that Asian Americans are nonassertive and passive. They contend, however, that this assumption has not been supported by research. These authors emphasize that certain traditional counseling practices may act as barriers to effective multicultural helping, and they call for the use of intervention strategies that are congruent with the value orientation of Asian-American clients.

Assumptions about self-actualization and trusting relationships.

Another assumption made by mental-health professionals is that it is important for the individual to become a fully functioning person. A counselor may focus on what is good for the individual without regard for the impact of the individual's change on the significant people in that person's life or the impact of those significant people on the client. A creative synthesis between self-actualization and responsibility to the group may be a more realistic goal for some clients.   *more w/E than simply W perspective*

Another assumption pertains to the development of a trusting relationship. Mainstream Americans tend to form quick, though not necessarily deep, relationships and talk easily about their personal lives. This characteristic is reflected in most counseling approaches. Although counselors expect some resistance, they assume that clients will eventually be willing to explore personal issues. In many cultures this kind of a relationship takes a long time to develop. Many Asian American, Hispanics, and Native Americans have been brought up not to speak until spoken to, especially when they are with the elderly or with authority figures (D. W. Sue & Sue, 1990). A counselor may interpret the client's hesitancy to speak as resistance when it is only a sign of respect.

Assumptions about nonverbal behavior.

Many cultural expressions are subject to misinterpretation, including personal space, eye contact, handshaking, dress, formality of greeting, perspective on time, and so forth. Mainstream Americans frequently feel uncomfortable with periods of silence and tend to fill the air with words. In some cultures silence may be a sign of respect and politeness rather than a lack of a desire to continue to speak. The Japanese place value on indirectness and nonverbal communication. As Itai and McRae (1994) indicate, when working with Japanese-American clients, counselors need to understand the significance of silence. In Japanese culture, talking too much is viewed as impolite. Silence may be a reflection of boredom or confusion, or it may be an expression of resistance to what the counselor is asking of the client. Itai and McRae sugguest that counselors do well to pay attention to the subtle changes in nonverbal communication by the client so that they are able to understand the true meaning of silence and adopt appropriate counseling interventions to deal with the silence.

Western counselors are often systematically trained in attending skills, which include keeping an open posture, maintaining good eye contact, and leaning toward the client (Egan, 1994). Although these behaviors are aimed at creating a positive therapeutic relationship, individuals from certain ethnic groups may have difficulty responding positively or understanding the intent of such posturing. The Western counselor whose confrontational style involves direct eye contact, physical gestures, and probing personal questions may be seen as offensively intrusive by clients from many other cultures (Henkin, 1985).

In American culture eye contact is considered a sign of attentiveness and presence, and a lack thereof is viewed as being evasive. However, Devore (1985) cautions that Asians and Native Americans may view direct eye contact as a lack of respect. Thus, it is a mistake to prematurely label clients as "resistive" or "pathological" if they avoid eye contact and do not respond to the invitation of the attending behavior. In some cultures lack of eye contact may even be a sign of respect and good manners. In writing about Native Americans, Attneave (1985) indicates that direct eye-to-eye gaze generally indicates aggressiveness; in cross-gender encounters it usually means sexual aggressiveness. Counselors must acquire sensitivity to cultural differences to reduce the probability of miscommunication, misdiagnosis, and misinterpretation of behavior (Wolfgang, 1985, p. 100).

Assumptions about directness.   Western therapeutic approaches prize directness, yet in some cultures directness is a sign of rudeness and is something to be avoided. The counselor could assume that a lack of directness is evidence of pathology, or at least a sign of lack of assertiveness rather than a sign of respect. Although getting to the point immediately is a prized value in Western culture, clients from other cultures may prefer to delay or avoid dealing with their problems.

◆ ***The case of Miguel.***   Miguel, a Latino born in the United States, has completed his Ph.D. and is working at a community clinic in family therapy. In his training he has learned of the concept of triangulation, the tendency of two persons who are in conflict to involve a third person in their emotional system to reduce the stress. Miguel is on the watch for evidence of this tendency. While he is counseling a Latino family, the father says to his son, "Your mother wants you to show her more respect than you do and to obey her more." Miguel says to the mother, "Can you say this directly to your son yourself rather than speaking through your husband?" The room falls silent, and there is great discomfort.

- How might you have handled this situation differently, especially if you saw "triangulation" as leading to family pathology?
- Could the Western counseling theory of "triangulation" be an acceptable norm in another culture rather than something that needs to be changed?
- Miguel was counseling a family from his own ethnic background. What implications does his direct style have on his acceptance of his own ethnic roots? How does that influence the way he works with other Latino clients?

A personal illustration.   A few years ago Marianne Corey and Jerry Corey conducted a training workshop with counselors from a Latin American country. Marianne was accused by a male participant of being too direct and assertive. He had difficulty with Marianne's active leadership style and indicated that it was her place to defer to Jerry by letting him take the lead. Recognizing and respecting our cultural differences, we were able to arrive at a mutual understanding of different values.

Jerry had difficulty with the tardiness of the participants and had to accept the fact that we could not follow a rigid time schedule. Typically we have thought that if people were late or missed a session group cohesion would be difficult to maintain. Because the issue was openly discussed in this situation, however, the problem did not arise. We quickly learned that we had to adapt ourselves to the participants' view of time. To insist on interpreting such behavior as resistance would have been to ignore the cultural context.

Matching Client and Counselor

Does the counselor have to share the cultural background of the client to be effective? This is a difficult question to answer, and the research in this area is inconclusive. Some argue that successful cross-cultural counseling is highly improbable because of the cultural and racial barriers involved. Others argue that well-trained counselors, even though they differ from their clients, are capable of providing effective counseling. Pedersen (1991) recognizes the complex diversity of a pluralistic society, but also suggests bridges of shared concern that unite culturally different individuals. Counselor and client are both unique and similar. Patterson (1996) asserts that all counseling is multicultural. From his perspective, all clients belong to multiple groups that influence their perceptions, beliefs, attitudes, and behavior. To be effective, counselors must account for these multiple influences on behavior. This perspective allows room for counselors to effectively work with clients who differ from themselves in a number of significant respects.

A very different point of view is expressed by Markowitz (1994), who refers to the practices of a therapeutic group in New Zealand. This group believes that therapeutic conversations across cultural lines are inherently problematic. In their view, no outsider can overcome his or her own cultural biases and, therefore, will never be able to accurately judge another culture's understanding of what constitutes normal or abnormal, healthy or unhealthy behavior.

C. C. Lee (1997c) points out that one pitfall associated with multiculturalism is that some helping professionals may give up in exasperation, asking: "How can I really be effective with a client whose cultural background is different from mine?" When counselors are overly self-conscious about their ability to work with diverse client populations, they may become too analytical about what they say and do. Counselors who are afraid to face the differences between themselves and their clients, who refuse to accept the reality of these differences, who perceive such differences as problematic, or who are uncomfortable working out these differences are bound to fail. D. W. Sue and Sue (1990) describe culturally skilled counselors in this way:

> Counselors who are willing to address cultural differences directly are those who do not perceive them as impediments. Instead, counselors who view these differ-

ences as positive attributes will most likely meet and resolve the challenges that arise in cross-cultural counseling. Such an individual is a "culturally skilled counselor." (p. 172)

It is our position that counselors can learn to work with clients who differ from them in gender, race, culture, socioeconomic background, physical ability, age, or sexual orientation. But our stance is tempered by certain reservations and conditions. First, counselors need to have training in multicultural perspectives, both academic and experiential. Second, as in any other counseling situation, it is important that the client and the counselor agree to develop a working therapeutic relationship. Third, counselors are advised to be flexible in applying theories to specific situations. The counselor who has an open stance has a greater likelihood of success than someone who rigidly adheres to a single theoretical system. We support Ridley's (1989) contention that skillful counselors are able to focus on correct treatment goals and to employ a wide range of therapeutic techniques appropriately to specific presenting problems. Ridley believes that flexibility in using therapeutic techniques is probably the most important factor in effectively treating minority clients.

Fourth, the counselor should be open to being challenged and tested. In multicultural counseling there is a greater likelihood that clients will exhibit suspicion and distrust. Some African Americans perceive Euro-Americans as potential enemies unless proven otherwise. They may use many defenses as survival strategies to protect their true feelings. A Euro-American counselor may be perceived to be a symbol of the establishment. Even though the counselor has admirable motives, the client may distrust the counselor simply because he or she enjoys a position of dominance. Counselors who see themselves as culturally skilled and sensitive may find it difficult to withstand this kind of testing. If counselors became excessively defensive in such situations, they will probably lose the client. Clients may feel that they would have to reject their own culture to accept the counselor's values or solutions. To minority clients it may seem that a professional who is not part of the solution to their problem is really part of the problem.

Fifth, it becomes even more important in multicultural counseling situations for counselors to be aware of their own value systems, of potential stereotyping, and of any traces of prejudice. Earlier we described those culture-bound counselors who are unintentional racists. In some ways, such counselors can be more dangerous than those who are more open with their prejudices. According to Pedersen (1994), unintentional racists must be challenged either to become intentional racists or to modify their racist attitudes and behaviors. The key to changing unintentional racism lies in examining basic assumptions. Two forms of covert racism that Ridley (1995) identifies are color blindness and color consciousness. The counselor who says, "When I look at you, I see a person, not a black person," may encounter mistrust from clients who have difficulty believing that. This counselor's color blindness is an illusion based on the faulty assumption that the minority client is simply another client. Likewise, a counselor is not likely to earn credibility by saying, "If you were not black, you wouldn't have the problem you're facing." This is probably a case of color consciousness, which is an illusion based on the erroneous assumption that all of the client's problems come from being a member of an ethnic or racial minority. For a thought-provoking analysis of the role of racism in counseling practice, we suggest reading Ridley (1995).

Try to identify your own assumptions as you think about these questions:

- Does a counselor need to share the cultural background of the client to be effective?
- If you were to encounter considerable "testing" from a minority client, how do you think you would react? What are some ways in which you could work therapeutically, even though you feel defensive?
- What experiences have you had with discrimination? How do you think your own experiences could either help or hinder you in working with clients who have been discriminated against?

It may be difficult for minority clients to discuss their anger over prejudice with a counselor who is empathic to the point of condescension. E. M. J. Smith (1985a) writes that the life concerns of African-American women are both similar to and different from those of mainstream women, and she cautions counselors not to overgeneralize. One this issue Jones (1985) makes the point that a therapist's self-knowledge is at least as important as cultural understanding in effectively treating African-American clients. Jones concedes that culture and race do play a key role but adds that they should not be overplayed to the extent that they blur the unique individuality of the client.

Finally, counselors need to be aware of their own reactions to what they identify as unusual behavior. It is essential to determine whether such behavior is unusual within the minority client's cultural context. Minority clients may be suspicious and think people are out to get them. Rather than suffering from clinical paranoia, these clients may be reacting to the realities of an environment in which they have suffered oppression and prejudice. In such cases, this kind of response may be both normal and prudent.

As you read the following case, consider how could you increase your own sensitivity to individuals from cultural groups different from your own.

◆ **The case of John.**   John, who comes from a lower-middle-class neighborhood in an Eastern city, has struggled to get a college degree and has finally attained a master's degree in counseling. He is proud of his accomplishments, but he considers himself to be sensitive to his own background and to those who struggle with similar problems. He has moved to the West Coast and has been hired to work in a clinic in a neighborhood with a large minority population.

At the clinic John starts a group for troubled adolescents. His goals for this group are as follows: (1) to instill pride so that group members will see their present environment as an obstacle to be overcome, not suffered with; (2) to increase self-esteem and to challenge group members to fight the negativism they may encounter in their home environments; (3) to teach them to minimize their differences in terms of the larger community (for example, he points out

how some of their idioms and ways of speaking separate them from the majority and reinforce differences and stereotypes); and (4) to teach them how to
overcome obstacles in a nonsupportive environment.

John does not work very closely with other staff members. He views them
as being more interested in politics and red tape and as actually giving very little energy to working in the community. He has little to do with the families of
the adolescents, because he sees them as being too willing to accept handouts
and welfare and as not being very interested in becoming self-sufficient and
independent. He tells his group members: "What you have at home with your
families has obviously not worked for you. What you have in this group is the
opportunity to change and to have that change appreciated."

- Do you think John possesses the competencies necessary to qualify as a
  cross-cultural counselor? Why, or why not?
- Does John demonstrate an understanding of the unique needs of this minority group? If so, how?
- What, if any, cultural prejudices does John exhibit in the way he deals with
  group members? What prejudices, if any, do his goals for his adolescent
  group imply?
- What effect might it have had on his goals if John had become familiar with
  the environment of his group?
- What potential risks has John exposed his group members to after the group
  is finished?
- What difficulties might John encounter because of his attitude toward his
  colleagues in the clinic? Do you think he might be open to criticism from the
  parents? Explain.
- What stereotyping might John be doing in terms of his attitudes toward the
  parents of these adolescents?

Commentary.   John is a well-intentioned counselor who demonstrates an
almost complete lack of sensitivity to the particular needs of this minority community. We disagree with his axiom that simply because he could obtain a
graduate degree (against difficult odds) anybody could have the same success.
John made no attempt to become aware of the unique struggles or values of his
clients. He stereotyped the parents of his group members in a very indirect, but
powerful fashion. He imposed majority values in terms of language and up-
ward mobility. He set up potential conflicts between group members and their
families by the way he downplayed and labeled their families' value systems.
Even though this may be an extreme example of a well-intentioned but nevertheless insensitive counselor, John's attitude typifies the mentality of many
who come from the majority community to work with the minority community. This counselors' own struggles to achieve his goals did not necessarily
make him competent to deal with another's life situation. The counselor entering the minority community has at least as much to learn as to teach. If any real
work is to be done, it must be accomplished on a cooperative basis.

Multicultural Training for Counselors

Although referral is sometimes an appropriate course of action, it should not be viewed as a solution to the problem of inadequately trained counselors. Many agencies have practitioners whose cultural backgrounds are less diverse than the populations they serve. With the increasing number of culturally diverse clients seeking counseling, and with the decreasing number of resources to meet these needs, counselors may not have the luxury of referral. Therefore, we recommend that all counseling students, regardless of their racial or ethnic background, receive training in multicultural counseling and therapy (MCT).

S. P. Brown, Parham, and Yonker (1996) tell us that "a counselor may be acting irresponsibly if he or she fails to acquire the requisite training to treat diverse populations or rejects the client because of anxiety in treating a culturally diverse client" (p. 510). Although many training programs appear to be making efforts to instill cultural awareness in students, much remains to be done. As Ridley, Mendoza, and Kanitz (1994) point out, most programs now offer MCT. A single course is the most popular format, and programs offering more sophisticated, innovative, and comprehensive MCT training are still the exception. Likewise, Das (1995) informs us that 90% of counselor education programs include coursework in multicultural counseling. However, he adds that the quality and depth of this training in the majority of programs are not deemed sufficient to meet the growing mental-health needs of a culturally diverse population. Das further states that the single MCT course is frequently taught be an adjunct faculty and often lacks a strong conceptual framework tied to specific competencies.

Nuttall, Webber, and Sanchez (1996, p. 131) contend that the heart and soul of a quality multicultural training program depends on the competence, knowledge, and commitment of the faculty. The standards established by the Council for Accreditation of Counseling and Related Educational Programs (CACREP) require that programs provide curricular and experiential offerings in multicultural and pluralistic trends. The CACREP standards call for supervised practicum experiences that include people from the environments in which the trainee is preparing to work. Trainees should study ethnic groups, subcultures, the changing roles of women, sexism, urban and rural societies, cultural mores, spiritual issues, and differing life patterns.

Characteristics of the Culturally Skilled Counselor

D. W. Sue (1996b) identifies three primary goals for ethical multicultural practice. First, counselors need to become culturally aware of their own biases, values, and assumptions about human behavior. Second, counselors need to become increasingly aware of the cultural values, biases, and assumptions of the diverse groups with whom they are dealing. Third, counselors need to develop culturally appropriate intervention strategies for dealing with individuals and groups in a system.

Mental-health services can be delivered best if practitioners genuinely believe that their clients are basically psychologically healthy and are experiencing normal developmental struggles. C. C. Lee (1997b) contends that counseling services are enhanced when helpers recognize the cultural dynamics of their clients and have learned how to incorporate naturally occurring support systems into a range of interventions. For Lee, culturally responsive counseling is predicated on making full use of indigenous sources of helping.

The APA guidelines (1993) call for service providers to seek out educational and training experiences to enhance their understanding of the cultural, social, psychological, political, economic, and historical dimensions that are specific to the particular ethnic group being served. Furthermore, when counselors do not possess the knowledge and training to work appropriately and effectively with a given ethic group, they are urged to seek consultation with appropriate experts or make an appropriate referral, if necessary.

A major contribution to the counseling profession has been the development of multicultural competencies, which were initially formulated by D. W. Sue and colleagues (1982) and were later revised and expanded by D. W. Sue, Arredondo, and McDavis (1992). Most recently, Arredondo and her colleagues (1996) have updated and operationalized these competencies. The box on page 340 provides a condensed version of the essential attributes of culturally skilled counselors.*

In the early 1980s, D. W. Sue (1996a) requested that both the American Counseling Association and the American Psychological Association endorse the multicultural competencies that he and his colleagues formulated. According to Sue, defining multicultural competencies has stimulated considerable debate in the counseling profession because these competencies (a) provide a strong rationale for a multicultural perspective in the helping professions, (b) develop specific multicultural standards that define the culturally competent counselor, and (c) advocate a call for action in the implementation of standards for both ACA and APA. These competencies have been endorsed by the Association for Multicultural Counseling and Development (AMCD) and recently by the Association for Counselor Education and Supervision (ACES). Endorsement of these competencies demonstrates the increased interest among counselor educators and practitioners in actively pursuing cultural competence (D'Andrea & Arredondo, 1996).

◆ **The case of Talib.**   Talib, an immigrant from the Middle East, is a graduate student in a counseling program. During many class discussions, his views on gender roles become clear, yet he expresses his beliefs in a respectful and nondogmatic fashion. Talib's attitudes and beliefs about gender roles are that the man should be the provider and head of the home and that the woman is in charge of nurturance, which is a full-time job. Although not directly critical

---

*For the complete description of these competencies, along with explanatory statements, refer to "Operationalization of the Multicultural Counseling Competencies," by Arredondo, Toporek, Brown, Jones, Locke, Sanchez, and Stadler (1996), in the January 1996 edition of the *Journal of Multicultural Counseling and Development*.

Multicultural Counseling Competencies

I. Counselor Awareness of Own Cultural Values and Biases
   A. With respect to *attitudes and beliefs*, culturally skilled counselors:
      ◆ believe that cultural self-awareness and sensitivity to one's own cultural heritage is essential.
      ◆ are aware of how their own cultural background and experiences have influenced attitudes, values, and biases about psychological processes.
      ◆ are able to recognize the limits of their multicultural competencies and expertise.
      ◆ recognize their sources of discomfort with differences that exist between themselves and clients in terms of race, ethnicity, and culture.
   B. With respect to *knowledge*, culturally skilled counselors:
      ◆ have specific knowledge about their own racial and cultural heritage and how it personally and professionally affects their definitions of and biases about normality/abnormality and the process of counseling.
      ◆ possess knowledge and understanding about how oppression, racism, discrimination, and stereotyping affect them personally and in their work. This allows individuals to acknowledge their own racist attitudes, beliefs, and feelings.
      ◆ possess knowledge about their social impact on others.
   C. With respect to *skills*, culturally skilled counselors:
      ◆ seek out educational, consultative, and training experiences to improve their understanding and effectiveness in working with culturally different populations.
      ◆ are constantly seeking to understand themselves as racial and cultural beings and are actively seeking a nonracist identity.
II. Counselor Awareness of Client's Worldview
   A. With respect to *attitudes and beliefs*, culturally skilled counselors:
      ◆ are aware of their negative and positive emotional reactions toward other racial and ethnic groups that may prove detrimental to the counseling relationship. They are willing to contrast their own beliefs and attitudes with those of their culturally different clients in a nonjudgmental fashion.
      ◆ are aware of stereotypes and preconceived notions that they may hold toward other racial and ethnic minority groups.
   B. With respect to *knowledge*, culturally skilled counselors:
      ◆ possess specific knowledge and information about the particular group with which they are working.
      ◆ understand how race, culture, ethnicity, and so forth may affect personality formation, vocational choices, manifestation or psychological disorders, help-seeking behavior, and the appropriateness or inappropriateness of counseling approaches.
      ◆ understand and have knowledge about sociopolitical influences that impinge on the lives of racial and ethnic minorities.
   C. With respect to *skills*, culturally skilled counselors:
      ◆ familiarize themselves with relevant research and the latest findings regarding mental health and mental disorders that affect various ethnic and racial groups.
      ◆ become actively involved with minority individuals outside the counseling setting so that their perspective of minorities is more than an academic or helping exercise.
III. Culturally Appropriate Intervention Strategies
   A. With respect to *attitudes and beliefs*, culturally skilled counselors:
      ◆ respect clients' religious and spiritual beliefs and values, including attributions and taboos, because these affect worldview, psychosocial functioning, and expressions of distress.

(continued)

(continued)

- ◆ respect indigenous helping practices and respect help-giving networks among communities of color.
- ◆ value bilingualism and do not view another language as an impediment to counseling.

B. With respect to *knowledge,* culturally skilled counselors:

- ◆ have a clear and explicit knowledge and understanding of the generic characteristics of counseling and therapy and how they may clash with the cultural values of various cultural groups.
- ◆ are aware of institutional barriers that prevent minorities from using mental-health services.
- ◆ have knowledge of the potential bias in assessment instruments and use procedures and interpret findings in a way that recognizes the cultural and linguistic characteristics of clients.
- ◆ have knowledge of family structures, hierarchies, values, and beliefs from various cultural perspectives. They are knowledgeable about the community where a particular cultural group may reside and the resources in the community.
- ◆ are aware of relevant discriminatory practices at the social and the community level that may affect the psychological welfare of the population being served.

C. With respect to *skills,* culturally skilled counselors:

- ◆ are able to engage in a variety of verbal and nonverbal helping responses. They are able to send and receive both verbal and nonverbal messages accurately and appropriately. They are not tied to only one method or approach to helping but recognize that helping styles and approaches may be culture bound.
- ◆ are able to exercise institutional intervention skills on behalf of their clients. They can help clients determine whether a problem stems from racism or bias in others so that clients do not inappropriately personalize problems.
- ◆ are not averse to seeking consultation with traditional healers or religious and spiritual leaders and practitioners in the treatment of culturally different clients when appropriate.
- ◆ take responsibility for interacting in the language requested by the client and, if not feasible, make appropriate referrals.
- ◆ have training and expertise in the use of traditional assessment and testing instruments.
- ◆ attend to and work to eliminate biases, prejudices, and discriminatory contexts in conducting evaluations and providing interventions and develop sensitivity to issues of oppression, sexism, heterosexism, elitism, and racism.
- ◆ take responsibility for educating their clients to the processes of psychological intervention, such as goals, expectations, legal rights, and the counselor's orientation.

of his female classmates, Talib voices a concern that these students may be neglecting their family obligations by pursuing a graduate education. Talib bases his views not only on his cultural background but also by citing experts in this country who support his position that the absence of women in the home has been a major contributor to the breakdown of the family. There are many lively discussions between Talib and his classmates, many of whom hold very different attitudes regarding gender roles. Halfway through the semester, his instructor, Dr. Felice Good, asks Talib to come to her office after class. Dr. Good lets Talib know that she has grave concerns about his pursuing a career in counseling in this country with his present beliefs. She encourages him to consider another career if he is unable to change his "biased convictions" about the role of women. She tells him that unless he can open his thinking to more contemporary viewpoints he will surely encounter serious problems with clients and fellow professionals.

- ◆ If you were one of Talib's classmates, what would you want to say to him?
- ◆ What assumptions underlie Dr. Good's advice to Talib? Do you agree that Talib should consider other career options? Why, or why not?
- ◆ If you were a faculty member, what criteria would you use to determine that students are not suited for a program because of their values?
- ◆ How would you approach a person whose views seem very different from your own? Do you think Talib is gender biased?

Commentary.   Dr. Good seemed to assume that because Talib expressed strong convictions he was rigid and would impose his values on his clients. She did not communicate a respect for his value system along with her concern that Talib might impose his values on clients. She did not use this situation as a teaching tool in the classroom to explore the issue of value imposition.

Students who express strong values are often told that they should not work with certain clients. As a result, students may hesitate to expose their viewpoints if they differ from the "acceptable norm." In our view, a critical feature of MCT is the personal development of trainees, which includes helping them clarify a set of values and beliefs concerning culture that increases their chances of functioning effectively in multicultural situations. We try to teach students that having strong convictions is not the same as imposing them on others. Students must be aware of their value systems and be open to exploring them. However, they must not go into this profession to impose these values on others. Ridley and his colleagues (1994) contend that the scope of training should include both the personal and professional development of trainees. In defining a philosophy of MCT, they ask the following questions:

- ◆ How far do we go in shifting students' values and beliefs?
- ◆ How are we to assess the effects of such shifting?
- ◆ Do we have an ethical responsibility to influence trainees' values and beliefs, or is it an ethical violation of students' rights to their own personal beliefs?
- ◆ What are the implications for students who fail to conform to the accepted value system regarding human diversity?

Our Views on Multicultural Training

The first step in the process of acquiring multicultural counseling skills should be that students become involved in a self-exploratory class to help identify their cultural and ethnic blind spots. Ideally, this course would be required of all trainees in the mental-health professions and would be taught by someone with experience in multicultural issues. It is an ethical obligation of counselor educators to identify, and perhaps even screen out, those students who exhibit and maintain rigid notions of the way people ought to live, regardless of their cultural background. In addition to this introductory course, students should take at least one other course dealing exclusively with multicultural issues and minority groups.

It is also extremely important that a multicultural perspective be integrated throughout the curriculum. When teaching theories and techniques of counseling, for example, instructors can emphasize how such concepts and strategies can be adapted to the special needs of diverse client populations and how some theories may be quite inappropriate for culturally different clients. Wherever possible, representatives of diverse cultures can speak directly to the students about social, economic, and culture-specific factors that may affect mental-health treatment. In addition, we support C. C. Lee's (1997b) proposal for comprehensive and ongoing professional development experiences related to multicultural counseling. All counselors must have training in how to account for salient cultural dynamics in the therapeutic process.

Trainees should participate in at least one required internship in which they have multicultural experiences. Ideally, the agency supervisor will be well-versed in the cultural variables of that particular setting and also be skilled in cross-cultural understanding. Further, trainees should have access to both individual and group supervision on campus from a multiculturally qualified faculty member. Students should be encouraged to select supervised field placements and internships that will challenge them to work on gender issues, cultural concerns, developmental issues, and lifestyle differences. They will not learn to become effective multicultural counselors by working exclusively with clients with whom they are comfortable and who are "like them." We agree with C. C. Lee (1997b) that there is a limit to how much can be learned about cultural diversity from courses and workshops. Lee maintains that more can be learned by going out into the community and interacting with diverse groups of people who face a myriad of problems. Through well-selected internship experiences, trainees will not only expand their own consciousness but will also increase their knowledge of diverse groups and will have a basis for acquiring intervention skills.

Finally, we would highly recommend that trainees open themselves to people in other cultures through reading and travel. Students can also make use of films and videotapes and can attend seminars and workshops that focus on multicultural issues in the helping professions. Any experiences that will sensitize students to a broad range of life experiences and cultural values will contribute to their effectiveness as counselors. The film "The Color of Fear," by Lee Mun Wah, is a dramatic challenge to all of us to examine our presumed freedom from prejudice and bias.

As a way of getting the most from your training, we encourage you to accept your limitations and to be patient with yourself as you expand your vision of how your culture continues to influence the person you are today. It is not helpful to overwhelm yourself with all that you do not know. You will not become more effective in multicultural counseling by expecting that you must be completely knowledgeable about the cultural backgrounds of all your clients, by thinking that you should have a complete repertoire of skills, or by demanding perfection. Recognize and appreciate your efforts toward becoming a more effective person and counselor, and remember that becoming a multiculturally competent counselor is an ongoing process.

Chapter Summary

A number of writers have urged over the last decade that counselors learn about their own culture and become aware of how their experiences affect the way they work with others who are culturally different. By being ignorant of the values and attitudes of clients who are of a different race, age, sex, social class, or culture, therapists open themselves up to criticism. Imposing one's own vision of the world on clients not only leads to negative therapeutic outcomes but also constitutes unethical practice.

We are all limited by our cultural and ethnic experiences. But we can increase our awareness by direct contact with a variety of ethnic and cultural groups, by reading, by special course work, and by in-service professional workshops. It is essential that our practices be appropriate for the clients with whom we work. This entails modifying our theories and techniques to meet clients' unique needs and not rigidly applying interventions in the same manner to all clients. We encourage you to carefully examine your assumptions, attitudes, and values so that you can determine how they could influence your practice.

Suggested Activities

1. Select two or three cultures or races different from your own. What attitudes and beliefs about these cultures did you hold while growing up? How have your attitudes changed, if at all, and what contributed to the changes?
2. What values do you owe primarily to your culture? With the passing of time have any of your values changed, and, if so, how? How might these values influence the way you work with clients who are culturally different from you?
3. What cross-cultural life experiences have you had? Did you learn anything about your prejudices? What prejudices, if any, did you feel were directed at you? You might bring your experiences to class. Also, we suggest that you interview other students or faculty members who identify themselves as ethnically or culturally different from you. What might they teach you about differences that you as a counselor would need to take into consideration to work more effectively with them?
4. Invite speakers to class to talk about cross-cultural factors as they relate to values. Speakers representing special concerns of various ethnic groups can address the topic of certain values unique to their group and can discuss the implications of these values for counseling.
5. To what degree have your courses and field experience contributed to your ability to work effectively with people from other cultures? What training

experiences would you like to have to better prepare you for multicultural counseling?

6. Divide into groups of three in your class. One person role-plays a minority client. A second person assumes the counselor role. And the third person acts as an alter ego for the client, as the anticounselor. You might have the minority client be somewhat reluctant to speak. The counselor can deal with this silence by treating it as a form of resistance, using typical therapeutic strategies. During this time the anticounselor expresses the cultural meaning of the silence. Now, devise a way to deal with silence from this frame of reference without using traditional therapeutic techniques.

7. Minorities are often put under strong pressure to give up their beliefs and ways in favor of adopting the ideals and customs of the dominant culture. What do you think your approach would be in working with clients who feel such pressure? How might you work with clients who see their own ethnicity or cultural heritage as a handicap to be overcome?

8. "The Color of Fear," produced and directed by Lee Mun Wah, is an emotional and insightful portrayal of racism in America.* Its aim is to illustrate the type of dialogue and relationships needed if we are to have a truly multicultural society based on equality and trust. After viewing the film in class, share what it brought out in you.*

*"The Color of Fear" is available from Stir Fry Productions in Oakland, California. The Stir Fry Productions Company provides trained facilitators (in some areas) to assist with discussion after the film is shown.

Chapter

11

The Counselor
in the Community

- ◆ *Pre-Chapter Self-Inventory*

- ◆ *Introduction*

- ◆ *The Community Mental-Health Orientation*

- ◆ *Roles of Counselors Working in the Community*

- ◆ *The Use of Paraprofessionals*

- ◆ *Working within a System*

- ◆ *Chapter Summary*

- ◆ *Suggested Activities*

Pre-Chapter Self-Inventory

Directions: For each statement, indicate the response that most closely identifies your beliefs and attitudes. Use the following code:

5 = I *strongly agree* with this statement.
4 = I *agree* with this statement.
3 = I am *undecided* about this statement.
2 = I *disagree* with this statement.
1 = I *strongly disagree* with this statement.

_____ 1. It's important to include people from the client's environment in his or her treatment.

_____ 2. Counselors ought to take an active role in seeking solutions to the social and political conditions that are related to human suffering.

_____ 3. Mental-health experts should devote more of their energies to preventing emotional and behavioral disorders rather than treating them.

_____ 4. With increasing attention being paid to the community mental-health approach, the role of the professional must be expanded to include a variety of indirect services to clients as well as direct clinical services.

_____ 5. The use of paraprofessionals is a valuable and effective way to deal with the shortage of professional help.

_____ 6. Paraprofessionals who receive adequate training and close supervision are capable of providing most of the direct services that professionals now provide.

_____ 7. In working with a variety of client groups in the community, counselors must be skilled in out-of-office strategies such as outreach, consulting, advocacy, and working as an agent for change.

_____ 8. Human-services workers must understand the community in which they operate, including its needs, assets, and issues.

_____ 9. It's possible to work within the framework of a system and still do the things I'm convinced are most important.

_____ 10. When I think of working in an agency or institution, I feel a sense of powerlessness about initiating any real change in that organization.

_____ 11. I frequently have good ideas and proposals, and I see myself as being willing to do the work necessary to translate these plans into actual programs.

_____ 12. If I'm honest with myself, I can see that I might have a tendency to blame external sources for a failure on my part to do more professionally.

_____ 13. Although I might be unable to bring about major changes in an institution or system, I do feel confident that I can make changes within the boundaries of my own position.

_____ 14. I can see that I might fall into complacency and rarely question what I'm doing or how I could do my work more effectively.

_____ 15. It would be unethical to accept a position with an agency whose central aims I disagreed with philosophically.

___ 16. Human-service workers should be able to identify indigenous leaders in the community and work with them to improve conditions in the community.

___ 17. A central role in human services is the development of leadership among community members.

___ 18. As a professional working in the community, one of my main goals is to assist people in the community to develop their power and become increasingly self-reliant.

___ 19. As a counselor I'm part of a system, and I have a responsibility to work toward changing those aspects of the system that I think need changing.

___ 20. I feel a personal need for meaningful contact with colleagues so that I don't become excessively narrow in my thinking.

Introduction

Working with people who come for counseling is only one way in which professionals can use their skills to promote mental and emotional health. Many people would argue that professional helpers can foster real and lasting changes only if they have an impact on the total milieu of people's lives. The aspirations and difficulties of clients intertwine with those of many other people and, ultimately, with those of the community at large. In this chapter we focus on the community itself as the client.

Counselors have special responsibilities in the community. Ethical practice demands that interventions be designed that will reach client groups who need services. If counselors ignore community needs because such needs seem overwhelming, this too poses concerns. Certainly, counselors who turn away from critical challenges in a community are not demonstrating a spirit of aspirational ethics or making full use of their knowledge and skills to initiate change. Practitioners can make ripples within factions of the community even in small ways if they are committed to becoming change agents. It is essential that professionals focus on the capabilities and strengths within a community, for doing so empowers people in the community.

As a counselor, do you view the community as your client or the individual as your client? Do you believe you have a broader responsibility to address the conditions that create problems for individuals who come to see you? Whether or not you work in a community agency setting, you can benefit by knowing how to work with community resources. Examine your own commitment to community counseling by thinking about these questions:

- How are the social and psychological needs in your community met?
- Where can people go for the social and psychological services they need?
- What are the special needs of low-income people?
- What are some pressing economic needs in addition to mental-health concerns?

- If clients ask what resources are available to assist them, can you direct them?
- What forces within your community contribute to the problems individuals and groups are experiencing?
- What are the main assets in your community?
- What factors contribute to the strength and development of your community?
- What are the prevailing attitudes of people in your community about the range of mental-health services available to them?
- What role do you want to play in improving your community?

We begin this chapter by looking at the community mental-health movement, which focuses on ways of changing the environment rather than merely helping people adapt to their circumstances. Whereas the traditional approach to understanding and treating human problems focuses on resolution of internal conflicts as a pathway to individual change, the community approach focuses on ways of changing the environmental factors causing individual problems. This perspective is based on the premise that the community itself is the most appropriate focus of attention, rather than the individual. The "community as client" is a notion that Homan (1994) emphasizes:

> Just like an individual or a family, a community has resources and limitations. Communities have established coping mechanisms to deal with problems. To promote change in a community, the community must believe in its own ability to change and must take responsibility for its actions or inactions. (p. 23)

In some ways this chapter is a continuation of the previous chapter, which explored the ethical parameters of multicultural counseling. Counselors must move outside their traditional roles to meet the needs of diverse individuals and groups within a community. In addition, counselors are required to design interventions that go beyond the office.

Next we take up an issue of particular importance to the community worker, namely, how the system affects the counselor and how to survive while working in a system. In examining the counselor's relationship to both the community and the system, we address the ethical dimensions of practice. If counselors are unresponsive to the needs of the community, are they practicing ethically? If professionals allow the system in which they work to demoralize them, are they able to function optimally? Does taking a proactive stand on social issues that affect communities imply functioning at an aspirational level? The ethics codes of professional practice reinforce the practitioner's responsibility to the community and to society (see the box on page 350).

The Community Mental-Health Orientation

Because only a relatively small number of people can be reached effectively by traditional therapeutic approaches, many practitioners believe that innovative measures should be designed to reach underserved populations. The need for

Ethical Responsibilities to the Community and to Society

National Organization for Human Service Education (1995)

Human service professionals keep informed about current social issues as they affect the client and the community. They share that information with clients, groups and community as part of their work. (Statement 11)

Human service professionals act as advocates in addressing unmet client and community needs. Human service professionals provide a mechanism for identifying unmet client needs, calling attention to these needs, and assisting in planning and mobilizing to advocate for those needs at the local community level. (Statement 13)

Human service professionals advocate for the rights of all members of society, particularly those who are members of minorities and groups at which discriminatory practices have historically been directed. (Statement 16)

National Association of Social Workers (1996)

Social workers should engage in social and political action that seeks to ensure that all persons have equal access to the resources, employment, services, and opportunities that they require in order to meet their basic human needs and to develop fully. Social workers should be aware of the impact of the political arena on practice, and should advocate for changes in policy and legislation to improve social conditions in order to meet basic human needs and promote social justice. (6.04.a.)

Social workers should act to expand choice and opportunity for all persons, with special regard for vulnerable, disadvantaged, oppressed, and exploited persons and groups. (6.04.b.)

diverse and readily accessible treatment programs has been a key factor in the development of the community mental-health orientation. Counseling does not take place in a vacuum, isolated from the larger social and political influences of society (Dinkmeyer, 1991; Herr, 1991; Ivey & Rigazio-DiGilio, 1991; D. W. Sue & Sue, 1990). Environmental factors cause or contribute to the problems of many groups in society, and a process that considers both the individual and the environment is often most beneficial to clients.

Herr (1991) clearly presents a case for developing broader strategies that do not ignore sociopolitical factors. Changing client populations, society's pressing problems, and the impact of advanced technology challenge mental-health counselors to develop problem-solving techniques that draw from various disciplines (Brooks & Gerstein, 1990; Gerstein & Brooks, 1990; Ivey & Rigazio-DiGilio, 1991). Herr's comments reflect the traditional social work perspective of working with the "person in the environment." The mental-health professions are converging in their views of conditions that have multiple causes.

I. A. Lewis and Lewis (1989) define community counseling as "a multifaceted approach combining direct and indirect services to help community members live more effectively and to prevent the problems most frequently faced by those who use the services" (p. 10). They describe the activities that make up a comprehensive community counseling program as having the following four distinct facets:

1. Direct community services in the form of *preventive education* are geared to the population at large. Examples of these programs include life planning workshops, value clarification seminars, and interpersonal skills training. Because the emphasis is on prevention, these programs help people develop a wider range of competencies.

2. Indirect community services are attempts to change the social environment to meet the needs of the population as a whole and are carried out by influencing social policy. Community counseling deals with the victims of poverty, sexism, and racism, which typically leave people feeling powerless. The emphasis is on *influencing policymakers* and bringing about positive changes within the community.

3. Direct client services focus on *outreach activities* to a population that might be at risk for developing mental-health problems. Community counselors provide help to clients either facing crises or dealing with ongoing stressors that impair their coping ability. According to Herr (1991), one of the future challenges for the mental-health counselor will be to work with schools, churches, and employers to develop programs for employee assistance, substance-abuse treatment, and stress management for a variety of at-risk groups.

4. Indirect client services consist of *client advocacy*, which involves active intervention for and with an individual or a group. The community counselor works to empower disenfranchised groups that have become split off from the mainstream community; these include the unemployed, the homeless, the handicapped, and persons living with AIDS. In writing about challenges for the future, Herr (1991) predicts increased opportunities for mental-health counselors to play an advocacy role for individuals at risk. He believes that counselors need to work for effective day-care programs, interventions to deal with child abuse or spouse abuse, strategies for early identification and treatment, parent education, and formal programs to develop self-esteem and coping skills. The advocacy process is best conceived of as a way to assist groups who typically do not have power to move in the direction of acquiring tools to find and use resources, both within the community and within themselves.

Community counseling calls for practitioners who (a) are familiar with resources within the community that they can refer clients to, if necessary, (b) have a basic knowledge of the cultural background of their clients, (c) possess skills that can be used as needed by clients, and (d) have the ability to balance various roles as professionals.

Roles of Counselors Working in the Community

To meet the needs of many ethnic and culturally diverse clients, counselors must be willing to assume nontraditional roles. They might imagine themselves doing more outreach work with their clients. They could function in a public-housing tract, at a hospital bedside, at their workplace, or in other places where clients conduct their lives. The outreach approach may include both developmental and educational efforts, such as skills training, stress management, and consultation. This shift in the therapist's role truly involves a challenge, for the community counselor must go beyond the individual's problems to look for factors that contribute to these problems. The traditional approach tends to treat dysfunctions as belonging to the individual, with a corresponding tendency to teach people how to adjust to the "realities" of living in a society. In contrast, counselors working from a community perspective examine dysfunctional behavior by considering the contributing factors from the larger society. Rather than simply change the "problematic" individual, they attempt to change the dysfunctional system that is producing problems for individuals, families, and communities.

Alternative Counselor Roles

Sticking with a singular role, such as the one played by many traditional counselors with varying theoretical orientations, may have limitations in reaching certain clients. D. W. Sue, Ivey, and Pedersen (1996) stress the importance of flexibility when working in a community with many culturally different groups. Counselors' roles in these communities frequently involve larger social units, systems interventions, and prevention programs. Sue and his colleagues recommend that counselors who work in the community:

♦ recognize that no one person or group has a monopoly on the helping process
♦ use community resources as a way to enrich therapy
♦ supplement informal methods with formal methods of helping
♦ recognize that client problems are often best defined as residing in the family, group, or community
♦ work with client problems in their cultural context and attend to the network of support systems surrounding the client

Atkinson, Thompson, and Grant (1993) state that the role of psychotherapist is frequently inappropriately applied when working with racial or ethnic minority clients. Atkinson and his colleagues believe that the conventional role of psychotherapist is appropriate "only for a client who is highly acculturated and now wants relief from an existing problem that has an internal etiology" (p. 269). Other writers have criticized conventional approaches to therapy because they place undue responsibility on the minority client for his or her plight. At the extreme, some interventions blame client problems entirely on the client without regard for environmental factors that may be contributing to the client's problem. Community-oriented counselors emphasize the necessity of recognizing and dealing with environmental conditions that often create problems for ethnically diverse client groups. Atkinson, Morten, and Sue (1993) suggest that appropriate roles for counselors who work in the community include facilitators of self-help, outreach workers, counselors, consultants, ombudsmen, facilitators of indigenous support systems, and facilitators of indigenous healing methods. In selecting a role and strategies to use with racial or ethnic minority clients, Atkinson, Thompson, and Grant (1993) believe it is useful to take into account the client's level of acculturation, the locus of problem etiology, and the goal of counseling. Atkinson, Morten, and Sue (1993) and Atkinson, Thompson, and Grant (1993) identify a number of alternative roles for counselors. It is ethically incumbent on counselors who work in the community to assume some or all of these roles as needed to benefit their clients.

Change agent. Functioning in the role of change agents, counselors do what they can to confront and bring about change within the system that contributes to, if not creates, many of the problems clients face. In this role, counselors assist clients in recognizing oppressive forces in the community as a source of their problem. Counselors also teach clients strategies for dealing with these environmental problems. As change agents, counselors assist clients in developing power, particularly political power, to bring about change in the clients' social and physical environment.

Consultant. Operating as consultants, counselors can encourage ethnic minority clients to learn skills they can use to interact successfully with various forces within their community. In this role, the client and the counselor work in collegial fashion to address unhealthy forces within the system. As consultants, counselors can work with racial and ethnic minority clients to design preventive programs to reduce the negative impact of racism and oppression.

Adviser. This role is similar to that of consultant, except the counselor as adviser initiates the discussion with clients about ways to deal with environmental problems that contribute to their personal problems. For example, recent immigrants may need advice on coping with problems they will face in the job market or that their children may encounter at school.

Advocate. Because ethnic minority clients are often oppressed to some degree by the dominant society, they can be helped by counselors who are willing to speak on behalf of their clients. Counselors especially need to function as advocates for clients who are low in acculturation and who need remediation of a problem that results from discrimination and oppression.

Too often, counselors ignore the fact that before people can move toward growth and actualization their basic needs must be met. Psychotherapy can no longer afford to be tailor-made for the upper middle class. People who are unable to afford the services of professionals in private practice are entitled to adequate treatment. The community counseling approach serves people of all ages and backgrounds and with all types and degrees of problems. In community counseling, practitioners may find themselves performing some or all of these duties:

- developing abilities that help support the needs of minority groups in the community
- assisting client groups to become true partners with professionals in the development and delivery of services

- promoting community organization and development activities as funda-mental agency responsibilities and seeing that this is obviously reflected in agency budgets
- actively reaching out to people with special needs and initiating programs aimed at preventing problems rather than merely treating them
- drawing on and improving the skills of paraprofessionals and laypeople to help meet the many different needs of clients
- developing strategies to deal effectively with drug and alcohol abuse, child sexual and physical abuse, and domestic violence
- developing strategies that will empower the disenfranchised in the commu-nity
- consulting with a variety of social agencies about programs in gerontology, welfare, child care, and rehabilitation, and helping community workers apply psychological knowledge in their work
- evaluating human-services programs to assess agencies' intervention efforts
- advocating and assisting with public and private initiatives that promote the total well-being of clients
- working with members of a particular community to develop and build on community assets to promote communities and instill self-reliance

Homan (1994) describes some other options for counselors who hope to empower client groups. He admits that counselors may not be able to play a major role in changing negative conditions for clients, but they can take these specific actions:

- assist clients in understanding the forces in the environment that are caus-ing or contributing to their distress and help clients develop skills to con-front these forces
- identify those in a community who can play a major role in fostering change, which could include bringing similarly affected clients together or referring clients to other programs or other professionals
- bring the existence of harmful conditions to the attention of those who are in a position to act on that awareness

Facilitators of indigenous support systems.   All cultural groups have some form of social support aimed at preventing or remediating psychological and social problems. Many ethnically diverse clients, people in rural environ-ments, and older people would not consider seeking professional help. How-ever, they are willing to turn to social support systems within their own communities. Counselors should be aware of cultural factors that may be instrumental in contributing to a client's problem or resources that might help alleviate or solve the client's problem. Counselors can play an important role by encouraging clients to make full use of resources within their own commu-nities, including community centers, extended families, neighborhood social networks, ethnic churches, and ethnic advocacy groups. By directing clients to indigenous support systems, counselors can do a great deal to aid clients.

Facilitators of indigenous healing systems. Counselors need to learn what kinds of healing resources exist within a client's culture. In many cultures professional counselors have little hope of reaching individuals with problems, for these people are likely to put their trust in folk healers. If counselors are aware of indigenous resources, they can refer a client to a folk or spiritual healer from his or her culture. At times it may be difficult for counselors to adopt the worldview of their clients; in such instances it could be helpful to work with an indigenous healer. It may not be a question of conventional therapy *or* indigenous healing. Counselors can structure their activities to complement or augment, not replace, traditional healing resources.

Educating the Community

There are many reasons why people do not make use of available counseling resources: They may not be aware of their existence; they may not be able to afford these services; they may have misconceptions about the nature and purpose of counseling; they may be reluctant to recognize their problems; they may harbor the attitude that they should be able to take charge of their lives on their own; or they may perceive that these resources are not intended for them because the services are administered in a culturally insensitive way. One of the major barriers to clients not making use of social and psychological services is that access to these services is confusing.

One goal of the community approach is to educate the public and attempt to change the attitudes of the community about mental health. Many people still cling to a very narrow definition of mental illness. They make a clear demarcation between people whom they perceive as "abnormal" and those whom they perceive as "normal." Widespread misconceptions include the notion that once people suffer from any kind of emotional disturbance they can never be cured, the idea that people with emotional and behavioral disorders are merely deficient in "willpower," and the belief that the mentally ill are always dangerous and should be separated from the community lest they "contaminate" or harm others. Professionals face real challenges in combating these myths.

Some misconceptions about psychotherapy include the beliefs that it is only for people with extreme problems, that therapists provide clients with answers, that therapy is only for weak people, and that people should be able to solve their problems without professional help. These misconceptions often reinforce the fears people already have toward seeking professional assistance. Unless professionals actively work to present counseling services in a way that is understandable to the community at large, many people who could benefit from professional help may not seek it.

Influencing Policymakers

Mental-health programs can help communities find solutions for societal problems such as poverty, the plight of the homeless, AIDS, absent parents, child abuse, drive-by shootings, gang activities, crime, domestic violence, un-employment, tension and stress, alienation, addictions to drugs and alcohol, delinquency, and neglect of the elderly. These are merely a few of the formid-able challenges that communities face in preventing and treating human problems.

At times, these challenges facing community workers are overwhelming, especially with current constraints on funding. How can even those most ded-icated community workers continue to develop social programs if they are constantly faced with the likelihood that their programs will be cut back or canceled? There is little room for staff members to come up with innovative social programs when the agencies themselves are concerned with mere survival. A real challenge is to persuade those who control funding to spend at least as much of the government budget on prevention as they spend on punishment.

◆ ***The case of Susan.*** Susan is the director of a community clinic in an inner-city neighborhood. Her agency provides birth control counseling and funding for abortion for low-income women. As the time is approaching for her to submit her request for financing to the state government, she is con-tacted by a local politician who is adamantly opposed to abortion. He informs her that if she requests funding for abortion he will do everything in his power not only to deny the money but also to reduce the overall funding for the agency. Faced with the prospect of radically reduced funds, Susan omits her request for money for birth control and abortion services.

- ◆ In light of the threats that were made, did Susan act in the best interest of her community? Can you see any justification for her action? Was her deci-sion ethical?
- ◆ Would it be ethical for Susan to go along with the politician's request but later on, when the funding for the other programs was acquired, to divert some of the money for abortion services?
- ◆ How ethically bound was Susan to disclose the coercive attempts of the influential politician, even though it was only her word against his?
- ◆ What other strategies might Susan have used?

◆ ***The case of Natalie.*** Natalie is an intern with a community agency that provides counseling services to local elementary schools. She facilitates a group for children with behavioral problems. On one occasion the principal overheard one of the students expressing strong anger. The principal assumed control of the group, got into a verbal exchange with the child, and suspended him from school. When Natalie appealed to her clinical director, he angrily told her: "Back off, and don't you dare challenge the principal." He let her know in no uncertain terms that if she were to take action against the principal, the con-tract of providing counseling services to the school would be jeopardized, with the subsequent loss of funding to the clinic.

◆ What are the ethical considerations in this case?

◆ If you were Natalie, what would you do?

◆ If you were her supervisor, what would you say to her? What would you feel obligated to do, if anything?

How You Can Become Involved in the Community

It is easy for counselors to believe that they can effectively meet the needs of their clients through one-to-one sessions in an office, but many clients' needs are not met that way. We suggest that you consider your responsibility to teach clients to use the resources available to them in their communities. Here is a list of things you might do to link your clients to the environment in which they live. Rate each of these activities, using the following code:

A = I would do this *routinely.*

B = I would do this *occasionally.*

C = I would do this *rarely.*

___ 1. I would familiarize myself with available community resources so that I could refer my clients to appropriate sources of further help. I would follow up to see whether clients had been helped.

___ 2. With my clients' permission, I would contact people who had a direct influence on their lives.

___ 3. I would try to arrange sessions with clients and significant others so that they could explore ways of strengthening relationships.

___ 4. As part of the counseling process, I would teach my clients how to take advantage of the support systems in the community.

___ 5. I would work actively with groups that were trying to help themselves.

___ 6. I would work actively with groups that were trying to bring about change in the community.

___ 7. I would encourage efforts to make the community's helping network more responsive.

___ 8. I would use community leaders in setting up liaisons with other professional practitioners and agencies.

___ 9. I would train key people of various cultural groups in peer-counseling skills so that they could work with groups that might resist seeking professional services from an agency.

___ 10. I would help organize support for politicians who were actively involved in helping the community.

___ 11. I would work with agencies to determine which services need to be offered and how they might best be offered.

If you plan to go into one of the mental-health professions, you are likely to spend some time working in a community agency setting, and you will be working with many different facets within the community. If you were working in such a setting at this time, how prepared are you, both personally and academically, to assume a broader view of helping that encompasses being an agent for change within the community? What are some ways that you can learn what you will need to know to assume the role of an agent for change in the community? What skills do you already have that can be applied to community change? What specific skills will you need to acquire? What fears would you need to challenge to work effectively in the community? How might you translate your idealism into a practical set of strategies aimed at bringing about constructive change within the community? In addition to the options we have discussed here, can you think of some other ways you might help your clients?

The Use of Paraprofessionals

The question of how best to deliver psychological services to the people who are most in need of them is a controversial one. It is clear that there are not enough professionally licensed practitioners to meet the demand for psychological assistance. Moreover, mental-health services have not always been available to those unable to pay. Faced with these realities, many in the mental-health field have concluded that nonprofessionals should be given the training and supervision they need to provide some psychological services. Service agencies have discovered that paraprofessionals can indeed provide some services as effectively as full professionals, for much lower salaries.

Not all mental-health professionals are enthusiastic about the paraprofessional movement. Some point to the danger that inadequately trained people might do more harm than good. Others contend that the poor will receive inferior service. Still others fear that more and more paraprofessionals will be allowed to practice without the close supervision and intensive training they need. Some fear that their own jobs or income may be in jeopardized if paraprofessionals are allowed to provide services similar to those rendered by professionals.

Paraprofessionals fall into three general types of nontraditional mental-health workers:

1. Many community colleges offer two-year programs in the human services. Students in these programs receive specialized training that is aimed at preparing them to work in community mental-health centers, hospitals, and other human-service agencies. In addition, many colleges and universities have established four-year undergraduate programs in human services that stress practical experience, training, and supervision in mental-health work.

2. Lay volunteers from the community are also receiving training and supervision in therapeutic intervention with a wide range of clients. These volunteers work on hot lines, co-lead groups, and engage in other supportive activities.

3. The use of former patients is another way of meeting the increasing demand for mental-health services. Former addicts play a role through sub-

stance abuse programs in rehabilitating others who are addicted to drugs. Besides helping to alleviate the shortage of personnel, these nonprofessionals may actually be more effective in reaching certain people because they have experienced similar problems and learned to deal with them successfully.

A large part of the success of community mental-health programs will depend on these nontraditional workers' receiving the training and supervision they need to develop skills for effective intervention. In some instances, these workers may aid traditional practitioners, who are often trained in psychotherapeutic techniques but don't have sufficient experience or training in working with various racial, ethnic, and socioeconomic groups.

The trend toward the increased use of paraprofessionals means that professionals will have to assume new and expanding roles. Mental-health professionals can be expected to spend less time providing direct services to clients and more time teaching and consulting with community workers. In-service workshops for paraprofessionals and volunteer workers, educating the public about the nature of mental health, consulting, working as agents for change in the community, designing new programs, conducting research, and evaluating existing programs may all become part of the job for mental-health professionals.

Consultation is an approach that allows mental-health professionals to offer a wide array of assistance on the individual, group, institutional, and community levels. Much of the work of consulting in agencies deals with training paraprofessionals and even lay volunteer workers. For example, Marianne Corey provided training for lay helpers in a church group who did grief counseling. This consulting took the form of teaching volunteers basic listening and attending skills, ways to assess their limitations, and how and when to make appropriate referrals.

Working within a System

One of the major challenges for counselors who work in the community is to learn how to make the system work both for themselves as professionals and for the clients they serve. One of the reasons that working in a system can put an added strain on the counselor is that those providing financing may require monumental amounts of paperwork to justify continued funding. Another source of strain is the counselor's relationships with those who administer the agency or institution, who may have long forgotten the practicalities involved in providing direct services to clients. Conversely, practitioners who deal with clients directly may have little appreciation for the intricacies with which administrators must contend in managing their programs. If communication is inadequate, as it often is, tension is inevitable.

Many professionals struggle with the issue of how to work within a system while retaining their dignity, vitality, and convictions. The most important component in any effort to bring about change is your attitude. When people

focus on what cannot be changed, they promote powerlessness and helplessness. When they focus, instead, on the things that can be changed, they foster
a sense of power that allows for progress. Although working in any organization can be frustrating, counselors are sometimes too eager to put the blame on
institutions when their efforts to help others don't succeed. Conversely, counselors may blame clients too readily for problems associated with an inadequate system.

Although bureaucratic obstacles can certainly make it difficult to carry out
sound ideas, it is possible to work within an institution with dignity and self-
respect. The first step is honest self-examination in determining the degree
to which the "system" is actually hindering you as you try to put your ideas
into practice. Next, practitioners should evaluate the options they have in
responding to unacceptable circumstances. Homan (1994) raises some thought-
provoking questions in this regard:

◆ If you respond to the presence of disturbing social conditions within your
  midst by attempting to mainly soften the pain they cause, does this imply
  tolerance for these problems in the system?
◆ If you genuinely believe that your efforts make a difference, should you
  accept limitations on your efforts?
◆ To what degree is it your ethical responsibility to work toward shaping the
  system that shapes your practice?

Homan (1994) takes the position that simply tolerating problems within a
system is rarely gratifying and that workers gain professional satisfaction by
actively taking steps to promote positive changes:

> I believe that you do have options for challenging the circumstances that lead to the
> problems you confront. And I believe that you have options for creating conditions
> that permit you to do effective work. In my experience, workers who have acted
> thoughtfully and purposefully to confront and resolve systemic problems have
> produced many positive results. (p. 46)

Recognizing the need for action is the first step toward responding to unacceptable circumstances. Once a problem situation in a system has been identified, Homan suggests that you have four basic responses to chose from:

◆ You can change your perception by identifying the situation as acceptable.
◆ You can leave the situation, either by emotionally withdrawing or by physically leaving.
◆ You can recognize the situation as unacceptable and then decide to adjust to
  the situation.
◆ You can identify the situation as unacceptable and do what you can to
  change it.

Each of these actions has consequences for both you and your clients. If you
recognize that you do have choices in how you respond to unacceptable situations, there is an implied challenge to take action to change these circumstances. From an ethical perspective, you are expected to alert your employer

ACA
★
(D.1.c.)

to circumstances that may impair your ability to reach clients. ACA's (1995) standard states: "Counselors alert their employers to conditions that may be potentially disruptive or damaging to the counselor's professional responsibilities or that may limit their effectiveness" (D.1.c.).

Relationships between the Counselor and the Agency

In addition to their degrees, training, and professional competencies, counselors working in the community must also have the ability to deal with the rules and regulations of agencies. In speaking about agencies and organizations, we are referring to resources such as these:

- an AIDS hospice
- a city or county mental-health agency
- a free clinic
- a church counseling agency
- a school system (elementary or secondary)
- a college counseling center
- a health-promotion program
- a state mental hospital
- a community halfway house

Counselors typically have little say in the formulation of agency policies, yet they are limited in what they can do by the agency's rules and regulations. The system may be so cumbersome and difficult for clients to work with that the counselor has to assist them in obtaining resources through lobbying, advocacy, referrals, and networking.

As a counselor, you need to decide how you will work within a system and how you can be most effective. Investigate an agency's philosophy before you accept a position, and determine whether the agency's norms, values, and expectations coincide with what you expect from a position. When you accept a position in an agency, it is implied that you are able to support the philosophy and policies of that agency. If there is not a general congruence of values, you are almost certain to experience conflicts. An ACA (1995) ethical standard calls upon practitioners to work with their employers to change situations that impede professional functioning: "Counselors strive to reach agreement with employers as to acceptable standards of conduct that allow for changes in institutional policy conducive to the growth and development of clients" (D.1.I.).

★
(D.1.I.)

Counselors who are dissatisfied with an agency or the system may decide to subvert it in as many ways as they can. Others conform to institutional policies out of fear of losing their positions. Some find ways to make compromises between institutional demands and their personal requirements. Others find it impossible to retain their personal and professional dignity and still work within an institutional framework. It will be up to you to find your own answers to questions such as these:

- To what degree is my philosophy of helping compatible with the agency where I work?
- How can I meet the requirements of an institution and at the same time do what I most believe in?
- What stance will I take in dealing with a system?
- In what ways can I work to change a particular system?
- At what point does the price of attempting to work within an organized structure become too high?
- Can I work within an institutional framework and still retain my vitality?
- What special ethical obligations am I likely to face in working in a system?
- Am I serving my clients in the best way possible in private practice if I do not develop community contacts?

◆ ***The case of Ronnie.***   Ronnie, an African-American student, moved with his family into a mostly white community and attends high school there. Almost immediately, he becomes the butt of racial jokes and experiences social isolation. A teacher notices his isolation and sends him to the school counselor for remedial attention. It is evident to the counselor that Ronnie is being discriminated against, not only by many of the students but also by some of the faculty. The counselor has no reason to doubt the information provided by Ronnie, because she is aware of racism in the school and in the community. She determines that it would be much more practical to help Ronnie learn to ignore the prejudice than to try to change the racist attitudes of the school and the community.

- What do you think of the counselor's decision? What are its ethical ramifications? Does she have an ethical obligation to work to change community attitudes?
- To what set of values might the counselor be responding?
- What other courses of action could she have taken? What would you do in this situation?
- Does a school system have an ethical obligation to attempt to change attitudes of a community that discriminates against some of its citizens?
- By not addressing the problem, is the counselor part of the problem?

In this case, the counselor may be experiencing a conflict of values and may fear reprisals if she acts on values that are not shared by many in the community. She may want to do what is needed to promote the well-being of her client, yet she may be struggling with self-doubts and with anxiety about not being accepted by the faculty. If you were consulting with this counselor, what might you say to her?

The Tendency to Avoid Responsibility

We've alluded to the tendency to blame institutions for failing to implement effective programs. So often we hear the "If only it weren't for ___" argument, which absolves the speaker of responsibility and diminishes his or her personal power at the same time. Take a moment now to reflect on some typical statements of this kind and apply them to yourself. How likely are you to resort to these statements as a way of deflecting responsibility to external sources? Rate each one, using the following code:

A = I feel this way often, and I can hear myself making this statement frequently.
B = I feel this way at times, and I might be inclined to say this occasionally.
C = I rarely feel this way.
D = I can't see myself using this statement as a way of absolving myself of personal responsibility.

___ 1. You have to play politics if you want to get your programs through.
___ 2. I can't do what I really want to do because my director or supervisor wouldn't allow it.
___ 3. If the community were more receptive to mental-health programs, my projects would be far more successful than they are.
___ 4. I'm not succeeding because my clients aren't motivated.
___ 5. I can't really say what I think because I'd lose my job.
___ 6. The bureaucratic system makes it almost impossible to develop innovative and meaningful programs.
___ 7. A good community worker works with the system, not against it.
___ 8. I'm not free to pursue my own interests in my job because the institution dictates what my interests will be.
___ 9. The system makes it difficult to engage in the kind of counseling that would produce real change.
___ 10. My own individuality and professional identity must be subordinate to the policies of the institution if I expect to survive in the system.

What other statements might you make about your difficulties as a professional working in a system?

Counselors who put the blame on the system when they fail to act in accordance with their beliefs are bound to experience a growing sense of powerlessness. This feeling is sometimes expressed in words such as these: "I really can't change anything at all. I may as well just do what's expected and play the game." The temptation to submit to this stance of professional impotence constitutes a real ethical concern. It is an attitude that feeds on itself, to the detriment of clients.

Another way of evading personal responsibility is to settle into a cozy rut. Many counselors have found a niche in the system and have learned to survive with a minimum of effort. To remain comfortable, they continue to do the same thing over and over for weeks, months, and years. They rarely question the effectiveness of their efforts or give much thought to ways of reaching a greater number of people more effectively. They neither question the system in which they're involved nor develop new projects that would give them a change of pace. Although we appreciate their difficulties, this complacency is just as deadly a form of powerlessness as the defeated feeling of those who decide they can't really change things.

Both defeatism and complacency cheat clients. For this reason, we ask you to examine the ethics of counselors who become infected by these attitudes. And we encourage you to think about the following questions to clarify your position on ways in which you could increase your chances of assuming power within the system:

◆ What questions would you want to raise in a job interview?

◆ What ideas that you have wanted to put into practice have been resisted?

◆ What would you do if the organization for which you worked instituted a policy to which you were strongly opposed?

◆ What would you do if you believed strongly that certain changes needed to be made in your institution but your colleagues disagreed?

◆ What would you do if your supervisor continually blocked most of your activities despite your efforts to keep him or her informed of the reasons for them?

◆ How would you attempt to make contact with your colleagues if members of your staff seemed to work largely in isolation from one another?

◆ If your staff seemed to be divided by jealousies, hostilities, or unspoken conflicts, what do you think you would do?

◆ What do you consider to be the ethics involved in staying with a job after you've done everything you can to bring about change, but to no avail? (Consider that you have been asked to do things that are against your basic philosophy.)

Now let's look at two examples that illustrate some of the issues we've discussed in this chapter. Try to imagine yourself in each of these situations, and ask yourself how you would deal with them.

◆ **_The case of Sarah._**   Sarah works in a community mental health clinic, and most of her time is devoted to dealing with immediate crises. The more she works with people in crisis, the more she is convinced that the focus of her work should be on preventive programs designed to educate the public. Sarah comes to believe strongly that there would be far fewer clients in distress if people were effectively contacted and motivated to participate in growth-oriented educational programs. She develops detailed, logical, and convincing proposals for programs she would like to implement in the community, but they are consistently rejected by the director of her center. Because the clinic is partially funded by the government for the express purpose of crisis intervention, the director feels uneasy about approving any program that doesn't relate directly to this objective.

If you were in Sarah's place, what do you think you would do? Which of the following courses of action would you be likely to take?

___ I'd probably do what the director expected and complain that the bureaucratic structure inhibited imaginative programs.

___ Rather than taking the director's no as a final answer, I'd work toward a compromise. I'd do what was expected of me but find some way to make room for my special project. I'd work with the director until I convinced her to permit me to launch my program in some form.

___ If I couldn't do what I deemed important, I'd look for another job.

___ I'd involve clients in setting direction for the proposals and providing the necessary support to secure approval.

___ I'd examine the director's responses to see what merit they might have and incorporate them into my approach.

___ I'd get several other staff members together and pool our resources and look for ways to implement our program as a group.

◆ ***The case of Dermot.***   Dermot is a social worker in a school district. He is expected to devote most of his time to checking on children who are habitually truant and to do social-welfare work with dependent families. Although he knew his job description before he accepted the position, he now feels that his talents could be put to better use if he were allowed to do intensive counseling with families as units. Referral sources in the area are meager, and the families he works for cannot afford private treatment. Although he has the training to do the type of family counseling that he thinks is sorely needed, his school administrator makes it clear that any kind of therapy is outside the province of the school's responsibility. Dermot is told to confine himself to tracking down truant children, doing social work, and processing forms. If you were in Dermot's position, what do you think you would do?

___ Prior to taking action, I'd think about what the administrator needs in order to become an ally rather than an opponent.

___ I'd present a written plan to the local school board, showing that family counseling was needed and that public facilities were inadequate to meet this need.

___ I'd go ahead and do the family counseling without telling my administrator.

___ I wouldn't make waves, because I wouldn't want to lose my job.

Chapter Summary

The primary focus of this chapter has been on the importance of going beyond the limitations of one-to-one counseling. Counselors not only need to get involved in the community but also need to find ways to help their clients make the transition from individual counseling to their everyday lives. The community mental-health orientation is one way to meet the increasing demand for psychological services. Too often mental-health professionals have been denied the opportunity to devise programs that address the diverse needs of the community. Over the past few years some alternatives to conventional therapy have arisen, creating new roles for counselors and therapists.

You may be looking forward to a full-time career in a system. We think it is essential to consider how to make the system work *for* you and your clients rather than *against* you and your clients. If you treat people in a system as allies, the chances are increased that they will support your proposals for change. However, if you treat people as opponents, they are more likely to become your enemies and block actions you take to make changes in the system.

We challenge you to think of ways to accept the responsibility of surviving and working effectively in an organization and thus increasing your power as a person. Finally, we ask you to reflect on the major causes of disillusionment that often accompanies working in a system and to find creative ways to remain vital as a person and as a professional.

Suggested Activities

1. In small groups explore specific ways of becoming involved in the community or using community resources to assist you in working with your clients. After you've explored these issues, the class can reconvene to pool ideas.
2. Several students who are interested in the use of paraprofessionals in the human-services field can investigate the issue and present their results in the form of a panel discussion. The discussion can focus on the advantages and disadvantages of the use of paraprofessionals, current trends, and other issues the panel deems important.
3. An issue you may well face in your practice is how to get through the resistance that people have toward asking for psychological assistance. Ask yourself how you should respond to clients who have questions such as: "What will people think if they find out that I'm coming for professional help?" "Shouldn't I really be able to solve my problems on my own? Isn't it a sign of weakness that I need others to help me?" "Aren't most people who come to a community clinic really sick?" "Will I really be able to resolve my problems by consulting you?" After you've thought through your own responses, share them in dyads or in small groups.
4. How aware are you of the resources that exist in your community? Would you know where to refer clients for special help? How aware are you of the support systems that exist in your community? Individually or with other students, investigate a comprehensive community mental-health center in your area. In doing so, find the answers to questions such as these:
   - Where would you send a family who needed help?
   - What facilities are available to treat drug and alcohol abuse?
   - What kinds of crisis intervention are available? What are some common crises?
   - Are health and medical services available at the center?
   - What groups are offered?
   - Is individual counseling available? for whom? at what fee? long-term? short-term?
   - Where would you refer a couple seeking marital counseling?

- Are hot-line services available?
- What provisions are there for emergency situations?
- What do people have to do to qualify for help at the center?

5. Several students can interview a variety of professionals in the mental-health field about the major problems they encounter in their institution. What barriers do they meet when they attempt to implement programs? How do they deal with obstacles or red tape? How does the system affect them? Divide this task up so that a wide range of professionals and para-professionals are interviewed, including some who have been in the same job for a number of years and others who are just beginning. Compare the responses of experienced and inexperienced personnel without revealing the identities of the persons interviewed.

6. In small groups develop a list of skills human-service professionals need to have to work effectively in the community. Then have each group give an example of how those skills can be applied in community work. Discuss ways that you can best acquire or refine these skills.

7. Once you recognize the need for change within an organization, you've already taken an important step toward responding to an unacceptable situation. What other ways might you respond after recognizing that a problem exists within the organization for which you work? Identify skills you would need to have to make the desired changes. What are some ways that you can make changes in a system? How might you go about developing strategies for getting support from co-workers if you were interested in changing an agency?

8. Reflect on and discuss alternative roles human-service professionals might play when working in the community. Ask yourself which of the following roles you think you could assume as a community worker: (a) change agent, (b) consultant, (c) adviser, (d) advocate, (e) facilitator of indigenous support systems, or (f) facilitator of indigenous healing systems. In small groups discuss in which of these roles you'd feel least comfortable functioning. How could you learn to carry out professional roles in the community different from those in which you were trained?

Ethical Issues in Marital and Family Therapy

Pre-Chapter Self-Inventory

Directions: For each statement, indicate the response that most closely identifies your beliefs and attitudes. Use the following code:

5 = I *strongly agree* with this statement.
4 = I *agree* with this statement.
3 = I am *undecided* about this statement.
2 = I *disagree* with this statement.
1 = I *strongly disagree* with this statement.

___ 1. A person who comes from a troubled family is generally a poor candidate to become a good family therapist.

___ 2. I would never divulge in a family session any secrets given to me privately by one of the members.

___ 3. In practicing marriage counseling, I would see my clients only in conjoint therapy.

___ 4. Counselors have an ethical responsibility to encourage spouses to leave partners who are physically or psychologically abusive.

___ 5. I would not be willing to work with a couple in marital therapy if I knew that one of them had had an affair unbeknownst to the other.

___ 6. It is ethical for family therapists to use pressure and even coercion to get a reluctant client to participate in family therapy.

___ 7. Therapists who feel justified in imposing their own values on a couple or a family can do considerable harm.

___ 8. In couples or family therapy I would explain about confidentiality at the first session.

___ 9. Most family therapists, consciously or unconsciously, proselytize for maintaining a family way of life.

___ 10. There are ethical problems in treating only one member of a family.

___ 11. I would be willing to work with a single member of a family and eventually attempt to bring the entire family into therapy.

___ 12. Before accepting a family for treatment, I would obtain supervised training in working with families.

___ 13. Before working with families, I need to explore issues in my own family of origin.

___ 14. Skill in using family-therapy techniques is far more important to success in this area than knowing my own personal dynamics.

___ 15. I favor requiring continuing education in the field of marital and family therapy as a condition for renewal of a license in this area.

Introduction

Much of the practice of marital and family therapy rests on the foundation of systems theory. This theory views psychological problems as arising from within the individual's present environment and the intergenerational family system. Symptoms are believed to be an expression of dysfunctions within the system, which are often passed along through numerous generations. That the identified client's problem might be a symptom of how the system functions, not just a symptom of the individual's maladjustment and psychosocial development, was a revolutionary notion. The family systems perspective is grounded on the assumptions that a client's problematic behavior may (1) serve a function or purpose for the family, (2) be a function of the family's inability to operate productively, or (3) be a symptom of dysfunctional patterns handed down across generations. However, other theoretical frameworks also guide the practice of family therapy, including Bowen's multigenerational family therapy, Satir's human validation process model, Whitaker's experiential approach, structural family therapy, strategic family therapy, and the social construction models of family therapy (Corey, 1996b).

Goldenberg and Goldenberg (1996a) urge therapists to view all behavior, including the symptoms expressed by the individual, within the context of the family and society. Although traditional approaches to treating the individual have merit, it might be incumbent upon therapists to expand their perspectives by considering clients as members of their family, community, and society. The Goldenbergs claim that a systems orientation does not preclude dealing with the individual but does broaden the traditional emphasis to address the roles individuals play in the family.

The systems perspective views the family as a functioning entity that is more than the sum of its members. The family provides the context for understanding how individuals behave. Actions by any individual member influence all the other members, and their reactions have a reciprocal effect on the individual. For instance, an acting-out child may be expressing deep conflicts between the mother and the father and may actually be expressing the pain for an entire family. Family therapists often work with individuals, the couple, parents and children, several siblings together, the nuclear family, the family of origin, and social networks to get a better understanding of patterns that affect the entire system and to develop strategies for change (Everett, 1990).

Although contemporary marital and family therapists usually base their clinical practice on a foundation of systems theory, the majority of family therapists integrate concepts and techniques from various theoretical orientations to produce their own blend of methods based on their training, personality, and the population of families they serve (Hanna & Brown, 1995). Nichols and Schwartz (1995) also maintain that family therapy is moving toward integration. They put this trend as follows: "Today it no longer makes sense to study one and only one model and to neglect the insights of others. Family therapists are not only cross-fertilizing across models of family therapy, they are also adding concepts and methods from psychology to individual psychotherapy" (p. 536). This integration has made possible the emergence of graduate education and formal curricula in marital and family therapy (Everett, 1990).

Many master's programs in counseling now offer a specialization in relationship counseling or marital and family therapy. Components of the training program in marital and family therapy include the study of systems theory, an examination of family of origin, the use of live supervision, and an emphasis on ethical and professional issues specific to working with couples and families (R. L. Smith, 1993).

Many of the ethical issues we have already discussed take on special significance when therapists work with more than one client. Most graduate programs in marital and family therapy now require a separate course in ethics and the law pertaining to this specialization. There has been an increased emphasis on ethical, legal, and professional issues that are unique to a systems perspective. Some specific areas of ethical concern for family therapists that we will discuss in this chapter include therapist responsibility, confidentiality, client privilege, informed consent and the right to refuse treatment, therapist values, and training and supervision (Margolin, 1982). The professional practice of marital and family therapy is regulated by state laws, professional specialty guidelines, ethical codes, peer review, continuing education, managed care, and consultation (Goldenberg & Goldenberg, 1996a). We now turn to a discussion of the implications for the practice of family therapy of the ethical codes developed by the AAMFT (1991).

Ethical Standards in Marital and Family Therapy

The AAMFT *Code of Ethics* (1991) provides a framework for many of the ethical issues we will consider in this chapter. (Consult the Appendices for the complete code.) In addition to the AAMFT code, the *AAMFT Ethics Casebook* (Brock, 1994) is an excellent resource that applies the code to a variety of situations encountered by marriage and family therapists. The AAMFT code covers eight areas. We will discuss each of these areas briefly.

1. *Responsibility to clients.* "Marriage and family therapists advance the welfare of families and individuals. They respect the rights of those persons seeking their assistance, and make reasonable efforts to ensure that their services are used appropriately."

As the focus of therapy shifts from the individual to the family system, a new set of ethical questions is raised: Whose interests should the family therapist serve? To whom and for whom does the therapist have primary loyalty and responsibility? the identified patient? the separate family members as individuals? the family as a whole? The primary goal of family therapists has changed over the years from simply maintaining marital units to maximizing individual fulfillment within mutually satisfying marriages (Patten, Barnett, & Houlihan, 1991). By agreeing to become involved in family therapy, however, members can generally be expected to place a higher priority on the goals of therapy than on their own personal goals, and they may also have to relinquish a sense of privacy and confidentiality (Goldenberg & Goldenberg, 1996a). Other questions can also be raised: Should the therapist work with one client and then eventually attempt to bring the entire family into therapy? What is the proper course in cases involving reluctant children and adolescents?

2. *Confidentiality.* "Marriage and family therapists have unique confidentiality concerns because the client in a therapeutic relationship may be more than one person. Therapists respect and guard confidences of each individual client."

Confidentiality assumes unique significance in the practice of marital and family therapy. This issue arises within the family itself in deciding how to deal with secrets. Incest, extramarital affairs, contagious diseases, or physical or psychological abuse of a spouse or children may be involved. Should the therapist attempt to have families reveal all their secrets? What are the pros and cons of revealing a family secret when some members are likely to suffer from extreme anxiety if it is disclosed? Family therapists have different perspectives on maintaining confidentiality. Some treat all information they receive from a family member just as if the person were in individual therapy. Others refuse to see any member of the family separately, claiming that doing so fosters unproductive alliances and promotes the keeping of secrets. And others tell family members that they will exercise their own judgment about what to disclose from an individual session in a marital or family session.

3. *Professional competence and integrity.* "Marriage and family therapists maintain high standards of professional competence and integrity."

This principle implies that therapists will seek professional help when their own personal problems are likely to negatively affect their professional work or impair their clinical judgment. It also implies that they keep abreast of developments in the field through continuing education and clinical experiences. A single course or two in a graduate counseling program is hardly adequate preparation for functioning ethically and effectively as a counselor with couples or families. Some questions that can be productively explored are: How can therapists know when their own personal problems are likely to hamper their professional work? What are some ways in which therapists can best maintain their level of competence? How can therapists use their values in a constructive fashion?

4. *Responsibility to students, employees, and supervisees.* "Marriage and family therapists do not exploit the trust and dependency of students, employees, and supervisees."

The code cautions practitioners to avoid multiple relationships, which are likely to impair clinical judgment. As you saw in Chapter 7, perspectives differ on how best to handle dual relationships. Ryder and Hepworth (1990) suggest that the AAMFT dual relationship prohibition is undesirable because of the complex nature of such relationships in marital and family therapy. Not only are multiple relationships virtually impossible to eliminate, they contend, but even if it were possible, it would be a bad idea. Ryder and Hepworth are against making these complex relationships overly simple by legislation. Instead, they recommend that training and supervision include preparing students to deal with such complexity as well as teaching them how to deal with issues such as exploitation and power. Rather than condemning dual and multiple relationships as being harmful to clients, Tomm (1993) suggests that they can lead to increased counselor authenticity and can actually enhance the therapy process. Thus, prohibiting dual and multiple relationships is not the solution to the exploitation of clients or the misuse of power.

At this point you might consider these questions: What are your views about dual relationships as they apply to marital and family therapy? Do you agree with the AAMFT guideline that cautions against forming dual or multiple relationships? What are some multiple relationships that you might be faced with in working with couples or families? How would you weigh the potential benefits and the associated potential risks of such multiple relationships?

5. *Responsibility to research participants.* "Investigators respect the dignity and protect the welfare of participants in research and are aware of federal and state laws and regulations and professional standards governing the conduct of research."

Researchers must carefully consider the ethical aspects of any research proposal, making use of informed consent procedures and explaining to participants what is involved in any research project. If there is a conflict between research purposes and therapeutic purposes, how would you resolve it? What are some multicultural considerations in doing research in this area? Can marital and family therapists who do not conduct research be considered ethical? What obstacles do you see to doing research in this area?

6. *Responsibility to the profession.* "Marriage and family therapists respect the rights and responsibilities of professional colleagues and participate in activities which advance the goals of the profession."

Ethical practice requires measures of accountability that meet professional standards. It is expected that marriage and family therapists will contribute time to the betterment of society, including donating services. What would you say about the ethics of those marital and family therapists who do not contribute any of their professional time without a fee? What do you see as your ethical obligation to advance the goals of your profession? What activities do you participate in (or expect to participate in) for professional advancement?

7. *Fees.* "Marriage and family therapists make financial arrangements with clients, third party payers, and supervisees that are reasonably understandable and conform to accepted professional practices."

Marriage and family therapists do not accept payment for making referrals and do not exploit clients financially for services. They are truthful in representing facts to clients and to third parties regarding any services rendered. Ethical practice dictates a disclosure of fee policies at the onset of therapy. What steps would you take to inform your clients about your fee policies? What are some examples of your fee policies? Would you charge for missed appointments? What would you say about the ethics of a practitioner who charged a fee for making a referral to another professional? What are some ways in which clients can be exploited financially?

8. *Advertising.* "Marriage and family therapists engage in appropriate informational activities, including those that enable laypersons to choose professional services on an informed basis."

Ethical practice dictates that practitioners accurately represent their competence, education, training, and experience in marital and family therapy. Professional standards are used in announcing services. Therapists do not advertise themselves as specialists (for example, in sex therapy) without being able to support this claim by virtue of their education, training, and supervised experience. How would you propose to advertise your services? How might you promote yourself as a marital and family practitioner?

Ethical Problems for Family Therapists

Green and Hansen (1989) investigated the self-reported responses of family therapists to a variety of ethical dilemmas. Their results were similar to those found in a previous study (see Green & Hansen, 1986). Here is a list in rank order of areas that raised ethical concerns for family therapists:

1. treating the entire family
2. having values different from those of the family
3. treating the entire family after one member leaves
4. professional development activities
5. imposing therapist values—feminist
6. manipulating the family for therapeutic benefit
7. payment for services
8. decisions on marital status
9. reporting child abuse
10. supervision of trainees
11. balancing family and individual needs
12. consultation with other professionals
13. informed consent
14. testifying
15. working for an unethical organization
16. sharing research results

A number of ethical and legal considerations are unique to marital and family therapy. Because marital and family therapists focus on the family system as the client rather than on the individual's dynamics, potential ethical dilemmas can arise from the first session (Smith, Carlson, Stevens-Smith, & Dennison, 1995). Because of the increased complexity of their work, marital and family therapists are faced with more potential ethical conflicts than are practitioners who specialize in individual therapy. Some ethical concerns faced by marriage and family counselors are addressed by Huber (1994, p. 61):

- Can therapists automatically assume the right to define couples' and families' presenting problems in terms of their own therapeutic orientation?
- How much concerted effort can therapists exert in convening all significant family members for therapy sessions?
- Should willing individual marital partners or several family members seeking assistance go untreated because one individual refuses to participate?

- Under what situations, if any, should therapists impose their control on couples and families? If so, to what extent should they impose it in seeking change in the relationship system?
- How much intrasystem stress should be engendered or allowed to materialize in the pursuit of change?
- What are the ethical implications inherent in employing paradoxical procedures?
- How can the impact of working with couples and families within the larger context of service agency constraints be pursued ethically?

Results of a national survey on ethical practices.   Brock and Coufal (1994) report a study carried out to survey marriage and family therapists' self-reported compliance with the *AAMFT Ethics Code* and their attitudes toward its principles. The response rate was 54%, which itself indicated a high level of concern with ethical issues in the practice of marriage and family therapy. Brock and Coufal were interested in finding answers to these four questions:

- What is the clinical behavior of marriage and family therapists concerning issues of ethics?
- How does that behavior compare with what is stipulated by the *AAMFT Ethics Code*?
- Do marriage and family therapists support their code of ethics?
- How effective are the typical sources in establishing ethical standards?

Brock and Coufal (1994) found that most marriage and family therapy performed by AAMFT members generally adhered to the standards in the *AAMFT Code of Ethics*. With respect to the question of whether the code hampered the effectiveness of their therapy, 97% said it did not. The results showed that, overall, respondents behaved in accordance with the code and that they supported its provisions. The researchers concluded that "it is clear that practitioners endorse ethics as an important aspect of professional practice" (p. 40).

Brock and Coufal were interested in obtaining a preliminary idea of what might make up a standard of *prohibited practices* for marriage and family therapists. The criteria they used to identify standards was agreement by 90% of the respondents that they never engaged in a practice. Respondents reported *never engaging* in 24 practices (out of the 104 items on the self-report survey). These prohibited practices are:

- engage in petting or intimate kissing with client
- discuss a client by name with friends
- engage in sex with a supervisee or a student
- write drug prescriptions without medical license
- practice under the influence of alcohol or other drugs
- exaggerate or distort research findings
- claim clinical membership when an associate or student
- claim authorship beyond personal contribution
- disrobe in the presence of a client or clients

- falsely state credentials
- observe a couple engaging in sex during a session
- employ sexual surrogates with clients
- do custody evaluation without seeing the child
- conduct psychological testing without training
- hit, strike, or otherwise assault clients
- claim a practice specialty but have no training
- become sexually involved with a former client within one year of termination
- sign for hours a supervisee has not earned
- get paid to refer clients to someone
- urge spouses to engage in illegal sexual practice
- borrow money from a client
- engage in sexual behavior with an employee
- terminate therapy in order to have a sexual relationship
- prescribe a life-threatening symptom

As you review this list of prohibited practices, do you think they are all equally unethical? From your perspective, are certain behaviors higher up on the list of unethical practices? Identify the items that you consider to be "absolutely unethical." (On the first ten items, at least 90% of respondents said they never engage in the practice and at least 90% believed the practice to be absolutely unethical.)

The Brock and Coufal study revealed that marriage and family therapists have wide-ranging capacities for both ethical and unethical behavior. On the basis of this self-report inventory, it appears that most marriage and family therapists conform to the standards in the *AAMFT Ethics Code*. The survey did point out some direction for change. The findings revealed that improvement was needed in these specific areas:

- advising clients on marital status
- failing to obtain client consent to tape or observe sessions
- failing to report child abuse
- treating homosexuality as pathological
- failing to warn potential victims of lethal threats
- failing to participate in continuing education activities
- giving medical advice
- practicing when too tired or distressed
- providing therapy to students or supervisees
- tailoring diagnoses to meet insurance criteria
- failing to verify employee credentials
- failing to have research reviewed to protect human subjects

The above actions and omissions deviate from ethical standards of practice. These topics could fruitfully be addressed in training programs for students and supervisees and in continuing education programs for practitioners.

Contemporary Professional Issues

In this section we identify a few of the current professional issues in the practice of marital and family therapy. These include the personal, academic, and experiential qualifications necessary to practice in the field.

Personal Characteristics of the Family Therapist

In Chapter 2 we dealt with the significance of the personal characteristics of the therapist as a major factor in creating an effective therapeutic alliance. A number of writers consider the person of the therapist as the core issue in training family therapists. R. L. Smith (1994) states that training programs in marital and family therapy have experienced significant changes over the past several decades. He points out that trainees in marital and family therapy should be provided with opportunities to examine their personal and human skills first, develop basic counseling skills second, and learn and practice specialties such as systems theory and interventions in working with couples and families third.

Self-knowledge is particularly critical for family therapists, especially with regard to family-of-origin issues. When therapists work with a couple or a family, or with an individual who is sorting out a family-of-origin issue, their perceptions and reactions are bound to be influenced by their own family-of-origin issues. Therapists who are unaware of their own vulnerabilities are likely to misinterpret their clients or steer clients in a direction that will not arouse their own anxieties. Therapists who are aware of their own emotional issues are less likely to get entangled in the problems of their clients.

Many trainers of family therapists hold that a practitioner's mental health, as defined by relationships with his or her family of origin, has implications for professional training. It is assumed that trainees can benefit from an exploration of the dynamics of their family of origin because it enables them to relate more effectively to the families they will meet in their clinical practice.

Getz and Protinsky (1994) take the position that personal growth is an essential part of training for marriage and family counselors and that knowledge and skills cannot be separated from a helper's internal dynamics and use of self. They write: "Trainees can and should be referred for personal therapy, but their issues, when identified as affecting their work, are addressed preferably in training" (p. 183). Getz and Protinsky point to growing clinical evidence that a family-of-origin approach to supervision is a necessary dimension of training for therapists who want to work with families. They contend that the reactions of therapists to their clients' stories tend to reactivate therapists' old learned patterns of behavior and unresolved problems. Through studying their own family of origin, students are ultimately able to improve their ability to counsel families.

In writing on the personal training of family therapists, Aponte (1994) describes his person/practice model, which is based on the premise that therapy is a personal encounter within a professional framework. Although he acknowledges that theory and technique are essential to the professional practice of family therapy, he stresses that the process is affected wholly through the relationship between therapist and client. Above all, therapists must be skilled and sensitive clinicians. Knowledge and skills are of limited practical value if therapists are not able to use themselves as persons constructively in sessions with couples and families. For Aponte, training the person of the therapist calls for trainees to examine their personal issues in relation to the therapy they do: "The touching of therapists' and clients' lives in therapy beckons therapists to gain mastery of their personal selves in their clinical relationships" (p. 4).

Educational Requirements

Competence in marital and family therapy involves integrating theoretical knowledge, abilities in clinical assessment, and treatment techniques, which are acquired through both educational and supervisory experiences (Everett, 1990). Professionals who practice marital and family therapy come from diverse academic backgrounds. In an attempt to provide uniform structure to evaluate the quality of a professional's education and training, the AAMFT (1994) has established minimal educational standards and a set of training guidelines. To qualify for *clinical membership*, candidates must possess a master's or doctoral degree in marriage and family therapy, or its equivalent, preferably from an AAMFT-accredited educational institution. They are expected to have successfully completed appropriate graduate course work in both marriage and family studies and marriage and family therapy, to have had two years of professional work experience in marital and family therapy, and to have successfully completed at least 200 hours of supervision with a minimum of 1000 hours of work with marriage and family cases.

Training, supervision, and clinical experience. All marital and family training programs acknowledge that both conceptual knowledge and clinical skills are necessary to become a competent family therapist. As training programs have evolved, major didactic and experiential components have been identified. These general elements typically include the study of various systems theories, an examination of family-of-origin issues, the use of live supervision and direct feedback, and an emphasis on ethical issues specific to working with couples and families (R. L. Smith, 1993). In addition to these components of training, trainees are now likely to be exposed to a variety of current issues in the field of family therapy. Some of these include: (a) gender-sensitive models aimed at overcoming trainee gender bias and sex-role stereotyping; (b) a raised consciousness concerning the role of cultural and ethnic factors in influencing the outlooks and behaviors of individuals and families; (c) a knowledge of family law; and (d) an introduction to social constructionist perspectives on alternative therapist roles and the collaborative nature of family therapy (Goldenberg & Goldenberg, 1996a).

The training standards of the Council for Accreditation of Counseling and Related Educational Programs (CACREP) emphasize a set of core competencies considered necessary for all counselors who practice marital and family therapy. CACREP emphasizes the importance of examining and developing personal skills and becoming grounded in basic counseling skills prior to specialization. CACREP standards call for: knowledge and skill development in the foundations of counseling; focus on individual, marital, and family systems; training in systemic approaches to family therapy; extensive clinical instruction involving direct supervision of work with individuals, couples, and families; and an integration of individual counseling methods and systemic approaches in working with individuals, couples, and families (R. L. Smith et al., 1995).

We agree with a number of writers who give primary emphasis to the quality of supervised practice and clinical experience in the training of marital and family therapists. Academic knowledge comes alive in supervised practicum and internship, and trainees learn how to use and sharpen their intervention skills. Goldenberg and Goldenberg (1996a) assert that direct clinical contact with families is the most important component of professional training. It is through these encounters, under close supervision, that trainees develop their own styles of interacting with families. The Goldenbergs emphasize the need for students to work therapeutically with a variety of families from different ethnic and socioeconomic backgrounds who have various presenting problems. A program offering both comprehensive course work and clinical supervision provides the ideal learning situation.

Most graduate programs employ both didactic and experiential methods and supervised practice. Didactic methods include classroom lectures, readings, demonstrations, films and videotapes of family therapy sessions, role playing, and discussion. Clinical experience with families is of limited value without regularly scheduled supervisory sessions. Live supervision can be conducted by a supervisor who watches the sessions behind a one-way mirror and offers useful feedback and consultation to the trainee (Goldenberg & Goldenberg, 1996a). Family therapy trainees can also profit from the practice of co-therapy, which provides trainees with opportunities to work closely with a supervisor or a colleague. A great deal of the supervision can take place immediately after and between sessions.

Experiential methods include both personal therapy and working with one's own family of origin. A rationale for personal therapeutic experiences is that they enable trainees to increase their awareness of transference and countertransference. The AAMFT recommends such therapy. A rationale for exploring the family of origin is that it enables trainees to relate more effectively to the families they will meet in their clinical practice.

If counselors are seeing families as part of their work, and if their program did not adequately prepare them for competence in intervening with families, they are vulnerable to a malpractice suit for practicing outside the boundaries of their competence. Those practitioners who did not receive specialized training as students need to involve themselves in postgraduate in-service training or special workshops.

In his critique of the current state of training for marriage and family therapists, T. Patterson (1995) points out the lack of uniform standards of training for the many types of master's-level professionals who practice marriage and family therapy. Patterson believes that it is time to acknowledge the severe discrepancy that exists within the mental-health professions over the inconsistent standards and training that characterize the field of family therapy. Critical questions he identifies are: What do practitioners of marriage and family therapy hold in common? Does the field share enough of a focus to lead to a shared set of standards and thereby enhance its overall coherence and ethical status? Believing that professionals from the various disciplines could identify some common elements of training, skill, and experience essential to the practice of marriage and family therapy, Patterson contends that "it is never too late to enhance the integrity of the family field and to serve the interests of its students and, ultimately, the clients who will be served" (p. 20).

Family Therapy versus Individual Therapy: A Case to Consider

Ludwig is a counselor whose education and training have been exclusively in individual and group dynamics. He is presented with a client, Ella, whose difficulties indicate that much of her problem lies not just with her but with her entire family system. This realization comes to Ludwig after more than a dozen sessions with Ella, when he has already established a strong working relationship with her. Because he has no experience in family therapy, he ponders what to do. He thinks of referring Ella to a colleague who is well trained in family therapy, but he realizes that doing so could have a detrimental effect on her. One of Ella's problems has been a sense of abandonment by her parents. He wants to avoid giving her the impression that he, too, is abandoning her. He decides to stay with her and work with her individually. Much of the time is spent trying to understand the dynamics of the family members who are not present.

- ◆ Do you agree with Ludwig's clinical decision? Do you agree with his rationale?
- ◆ Even though Ludwig was practicing within the framework of his orientation and training, was he underestimating the limitations of that framework when part of Ella's problem was due to the family as a system? Was that ethical practice?
- ◆ Even though Ludwig was not trained as a family therapist, what if he had decided to see the entire family and attempted to do family therapy for the benefit of his client? Would that have been ethical?
- ◆ What if Ludwig had been trained in family systems but, when he suggested family sessions to Ella, she refused? What would you do if faced with such a dilemma?
- ◆ Assume that Ludwig decided to see each family member individually to learn how each viewed the family system. In this process he discovered a great discrepancy between Ella's description of the family and what the other family members said. Ludwig became convinced that his client was

either misreading the family or was not presenting an accurate description of her problem. What is your opinion of how he should then proceed? What theoretical rationale would you give for such a strategy?

Values in Marital and Family Therapy

In Chapter 3 we explored the impact of the therapist's values on the goals and direction of the therapeutic process. We now consider how values take on special significance in counseling couples and families. Values pertaining to marriage, the preservation of the family, divorce, traditional and nontraditional lifestyles, gender roles and the division of responsibility in the family, child rearing, and extramarital affairs can all influence the therapist's interventions. Counselors who, intentionally or unintentionally, impose their values on a couple or a family can do considerable harm.

It is crucial for therapists to understand how they might be biased against an individual or family whose views differ radically from their own. Goldenberg and Goldenberg (1996a) mention several ways that family therapists might make undue use of their influence: They may take sides with one member of the family against another; they may impose their values on family members; they may proselytize for maintaining a current marriage.

The value system of therapists has a crucial influence on their formulation and definition of the problems they see in a family, the goals and plans for therapy, and the direction the therapy takes. We want to emphasize again that it is not the function of any therapist to make decisions for clients. Family therapists should not decide how members of a family should change. The role of the therapist is to help family members see more clearly what they are doing, to help them make an honest evaluation of how well their present patterns are working for them, and to help and encourage them to make necessary changes.

In this section we invite you to think about your own values and to reflect on the impact that they are likely to have on the interventions you make with couples and families. To assist you in formulating your personal position on these issues, we provide a couple of cases to consider and raise value-laden issues that could affect the course of therapy.

◆ ***The case of Sharon.*** Suppose you have a 25-year-old client, Sharon, who says, "I'm never going to get married because I think marriage is a drag. I don't want kids, and I don't want to stay with one person forever." What follows are the inner dialogues of four therapists regarding her case.

Therapist A: She seems very selfish to me. With her attitude, it's probably a good idea that she doesn't intend to get married. I wonder why she's in therapy, anyway?

Therapist B: Well, she doesn't have to be married. Mental health doesn't necessarily require that one be married. I certainly would want to communicate to her that remaining single is acceptable. But I'd like to explore with her how she went about making this decision. I want to ensure that this is clearly what she wants to do and that it's not mainly a reaction to some painful situation in her life.

Therapist C: Why is she so down on marriage? I wonder if she's talking more about her family than marriage?

Therapist D: I feel sorry for her. She must have had some very painful experiences growing up. She must have had a terrible relationship with her father that prevents her from forming healthy relationships now. If I can only get to the underlying problem, I know she'll be able to overcome her negative experiences.

- What is your reaction to Sharon's statement?
- What is your reaction to each of the therapist's responses to her?
- What implied value is each therapist expressing?
- Why would you want to challenge (or accept) Sharon's decision?
- In what ways do you think you might work with Sharon differently from the four therapists? If you don't feel comfortable with a commitment to marriage and a family yourself, do you think you could be objective enough to help her explore some of the possibilities she might be overlooking?

◆ **The case of Frank and Judy.**   During the past few years Frank and Judy have experienced many conflicts in their marriage. Although they have made attempts to resolve their problems by themselves, they have finally decided to seek the help of a professional marriage counselor. Even though they have been thinking about divorce with increasing frequency, they still have some hope that they can achieve a satisfactory marriage.

We will present the approaches of three marriage counselors, each holding a different set of values pertaining to marriage and the family. As you read these responses, think about the degree to which they represent what you might say and do if you were counseling this couple.

Counselor A. This counselor believes that it is not her place to bring her values pertaining to the family into the sessions. She is fully aware of her biases regarding marriage and divorce, but she does not impose them or expose them in all cases. Her primary interest is to help Frank and Judy discover what is best for them as individuals and as a couple. She sees it as unethical to push her clients toward a definite course of action, and she lets them know that her job is to help them be honest with themselves.

- What are your reactions to this counselor's approach?
- Do you think it is possible for this counselor to keep her values out of the therapy process?

Counselor B. This counselor has been married three times herself. Although she believes in the institution, she is quick to maintain that far too many couples stay in their marriages and suffer unnecessarily. She explores with Judy and Frank the conflicts that they bring to the sessions. The counselor's interventions are leading them in the direction of divorce as the desired course of action, especially after they express this as an option. She suggests a trial separation and states her willingness to counsel them individually, with some joint sessions. When Frank brings up his guilt and reluctance to divorce because of the welfare of the children, the counselor confronts him with the harm that is being done to them by a destructive marriage. She tells him that it is too much of a burden to put on the children to keep the family together at any price.

◆ Do you see any ethical issues in this case? Is this counselor exposing or imposing her values?
◆ Do you think she should be a marriage counselor, given her bias and her background of three divorces?
◆ What interventions made by the counselor do you agree with? What are your areas of disagreement?

Counselor C. At the first session this counselor states his belief in the preservation of marriage and the family. He feels that many couples take the easy way out by divorcing too quickly in the face of difficulty. He says that most couples have unrealistically high expectations of what constitutes a "happy marriage." The counselor lets it be known that his experience continues to teach him that divorce rarely solves any problems but instead creates new problems that are often worse. The counselor urges Frank and Judy to consider the welfare of their three dependent children. He tells the couple of his bias toward saving the marriage so they can make an informed choice about initiating counseling with him.

◆ What are your personal reactions toward the orientation of this counselor?
◆ Is it ethical for him to state his bias so obviously?
◆ What if he were to keep his bias and values hidden from the couple and accept them into therapy? Do you think that he could work objectively with this couple? Why, or why not?

Commentary. This case illustrates that the value system of the counselor determines the direction counseling will take. The counselor who is dedicated to preserving marriage and family life is bound to function differently from the counselor who puts prime value on the welfare of an individual family member. What might be best for one family member might not necessarily be in the best interests of the entire family. It is essential, therefore, for counselors who work with couples and families to be aware of how their values influence the goals and procedures of therapy. Ethical practice should challenge clients to clarify their own values and to choose a course of action that is best for them.

Gender-Sensitive Marital and Family Therapy

Gender-sensitive marital and family therapy attempts to help both women and men overcome stereotyped gender roles. Sexist attitudes and patriarchal assumptions are examined for their impact on family relationships. With this approach, family therapy is conducted in an egalitarian fashion, and both therapist and client work collaboratively to empower individuals to choose roles rather than being limited by their gender (Goldenberg & Goldenberg, 1996a).

Both women and men are recipients of stereotyping and countertransference by therapists. Although the literature conveys the underlying message that men should be sensitive to women and vice versa, some female therapists are as biased toward their female clients as some men are. All therapists need to be aware of their values and beliefs about gender. In Chapter 10 we discussed the importance of counselors' being aware of how their culture has influenced their personality. We think that the ways in which people perceive gender likewise have a lot to do with their cultural background.

Challenging Traditional Gender Roles

Effective communication between therapists and their clients is often undermined by stereotypical views about how women and men think, feel, and behave. Counselors must be alert to the particular issues women and men struggle with and the ways their own views about gender might restrict clients to traditional roles. Counseling professionals should help both women and men to explore and challenge the stereotyped expectations that they behave in certain limited ways. Women may need assistance in overcoming internal barriers to autonomy, raising their self-esteem, and overcoming dependency. Men may need assistance in learning new ways to take responsibility for their own emotional lives.

Learning to make autonomous choices does not mean that women have to deny their needs for connection, and choosing to take care of oneself does not imply being unconcerned about others. Similarly, for men, learning to be more relational and sharing one's inner life does not mean a loss of independence and strength.

Autonomy sets the stage for healthy relating in a loving relationship. McBride (1990) writes: "As counselors, we need to encourage our female clients to choose to define themselves rather than be defined by others, to choose self-mastery rather than live up to the expectations of others, and to give themselves as much or more than they give to others" (p. 25). Although we are in basic agreement with McBride, we don't think the therapist should try to impose any set of values on women. Instead, the therapist can best function in the interests of female clients by challenging them to examine self-contradictions. The therapist's task is to help clients decide who and what they want to be, not what the therapist thinks they should be. Some clinicians might be uncomfortable supporting traditional roles for women for fear of perpetuating stereotypes and being labeled sexist. The point is that a woman does have choices and that her choices need to be supported by her therapist.

Gender Roles and Stereotypes

Good, Gilbert, and Scher (1990) discuss the value of integrating knowledge about the impact of gender into the practice of counseling women and men.

They advocate the use of "gender-aware therapy," which helps clients understand how societal conceptions of gender often limit their thinking, feeling, and behaving.

Counselors who work with couples and families can practice more ethically if they are aware of the history and impact of gender stereotyping as it is reflected in the socialization process in families. Effective practitioners must continually evaluate their own beliefs about appropriate family roles and responsibilities, child-rearing practices, multiple roles, and nontraditional vocations for women and men. Counselors also must have the knowledge to help their clients explore educational, vocational, and emotional goals that they previously deemed unreachable. The principles of gender-aware therapy have relevance for counselors as they help clients identify and work through gender concepts that have limited them.

L. S. Brown (1990) makes the point that a clinician's own countertransference responses to gender issues affect the assessment process, which further influences the way therapy is conducted. Some of her guidelines for incorporating gender concerns in assessment and therapy include inquiring into the meaning of femininity or masculinity for the client and guarding against the inappropriate imposition of gender-stereotyped values regarding healthy functioning. Including gender issues in the assessment process increases the chances of an unbiased assessment.

Feminist Perspective on Family Therapy

Feminists assert that our patriarchal society subjugates women, blames them for inadequate mothering, and expects them to accept their contribution to their problem. Feminist therapists integrate many theoretical orientations in their work with families. Their focus encourages a personal commitment to change gender inequity, and they espouse a vision of a future society that values equality between women and men. Avis (1986) states that feminist family therapists employ a wide range of interventions aimed at empowering women. Feminists are concerned about shifting the power balance between women and men in the family; they do so in a variety of ways, some of which include:

- placing the same demands for change on both women and men
- valuing women's requests for change
- challenging traditional roles whereby child rearing and housekeeping tasks are the primary functions of women and negotiating for a balanced distribution of these tasks
- expecting men to be concerned with parenting and homemaking
- focusing on the needs of women as individuals rather than focusing exclusively on the relationship
- challenging the patterns of male dominance and female subordination
- questioning gender-specific rules
- valuing women's work in the family

◆ valuing the expression of emotion and nurturance in both women and men
◆ requesting changes that alter roles

Enns (1993) believes that it is essential for feminist family therapists to affirm and value the roles women have traditionally played in the family. But beyond this, therapists should also support women's efforts to experience rewarding roles outside the family. Feminist family therapists use various interventions but recognize that none of these interventions is free of gender implications. They recognize the powerful impact that gender has on family relationships, and they make gender concerns central in the practice of family therapy. Indeed, gender is viewed as a primary organizing concept in working with families.

A Nonsexist Perspective on Family Therapy

Regardless of their particular theoretical orientations, it is incumbent upon family therapists to take whatever steps are necessary to account for gender issues in their practices and to become nonsexist family therapists. Margolin (1982) provides a number of recommendations on how to be a nonsexist family therapist and how to use the therapeutic process to challenge the oppressive consequences of stereotyped roles and expectations in the family. One recommendation is that family therapists examine their own behavior for unwitting comments and questions that imply that the wife and husband should perform specific roles and hold a specific status. For example, a therapist can show bias in subtle and nonverbal ways, such as looking at the wife when talking about rearing children or addressing the husband when talking about any important decisions that need to be made. Further, Margolin contends that family therapists are particularly vulnerable to the following biases: (1) assuming that remaining married would be the best choice for a woman, (2) demonstrating less interest in a woman's career than in a man's career, (3) encouraging couples to accept the belief that child rearing is solely the responsibility of the mother, (4) showing a different reaction to a wife's affair than to a husband's, and (5) giving more importance to satisfying the husband's needs than to satisfying the wife's needs. She raises two important questions dealing with the ethics of doing therapy with couples and families:

◆ How does the therapist respond when members of the family seem to agree that they want to work toward goals that (from the therapist's vantage point) are sexist in nature?
◆ To what extent does the therapist accept the family's definition of gender-role identities rather than trying to challenge and eventually change these attitudes?

As you read the case examples that follow, consider these guidelines: What are your values pertaining to gender, and how do these values influence your perception of these cases? How do you think your values might affect your manner of counseling in each case?

◆ ***The case of Marge and Fred.*** Marge and Fred come to marriage counseling to work on the stress they are experiencing in rearing their two adolescent sons. The couple direct the focus toward what their sons are doing and not doing. In the course of therapy, the counselor learns that both have full-time jobs outside the home. In addition, Marge has assumed another full-time job— mother and homemaker—but her husband refuses to share any domestic responsibilities. Marge doesn't question her dual career. Neither Marge nor Fred shows much interest in exploring the division of responsibilities in their relationship. Instead, they focus the sessions on getting advice about how to handle problems with their sons.

- ◆ Is it ethical for the therapist to focus only on the expressed concerns of Marge and Fred? Does the therapist have a responsibility to challenge this couple to look at how they have defined themselves and their relationship through assumptions about sex roles?
- ◆ If you were counseling this couple, what might you do? What are your values, and how do you think they would influence the interventions you might make in this case?
- ◆ What would you do with their presenting problem, their trouble with their sons? What else might the behavior of the sons imply?

As you think about this case and the following one, ask yourself how your values regarding traditional wives and mothers might affect your relationship with clients like Marge and Melody.

◆ ***The case of Melody.*** Melody, 38, is married and has returned to college to obtain a teaching credential. During the intake session she tells you that she is going through a lot of turmoil and is contemplating some major changes in her life. She has met a man who shares her interest and enthusiasm for school as well as many other aspects of her life. She is considering leaving her husband and children to pursue her own interests for a change.

The following statements represent responses counselors might have had to what Melody was saying, whether or not they actually voiced them to her. Which of these statements can you see yourself making to Melody? Which of them represent reactions you might have but would keep from her?
- ◆ "Perhaps this is a phase you're going through. It happens to a lot of women who return to college. Maybe you should slow down and think about it."
- ◆ "You'll never forgive yourself for leaving your children."
- ◆ "You may have regrets later on if you leave your children in such an impulsive fashion."
- ◆ "Many women in your position would be afraid to do what you're thinking about doing."
- ◆ "I hate to see you divorce without having some marriage counseling first to determine whether that's what you both want."
- ◆ "Maybe you ought to look at the prospects of living alone for a while. The idea of moving out of a relationship with your husband and right into a new relationship with another man concerns me."

If Melody were your client, which of your own values might influence your counseling with her? For example, what do you think of divorce? Would you want her to use divorce only as a last resort? How much do you value keeping her family intact?

◆ ***The case of Naomi.*** The White family (consisting of wife, husband, four children, and the wife's parents) has been involved in family therapy for several months. During one of the sessions, Naomi (the wife) expresses the desire to return to college to pursue a degree in law. This wish causes tremendous resistance on the part of every other member of her family. The husband says that he wants her to continue to be involved in his professional life and that, although he admires her ambitions, he simply feels that it would put too much strain on the entire family. Naomi's parents are shocked by their daughter's desire, viewing it as selfish, and they urge her to put the family's welfare first. The children express their desires for a full-time mother. Naomi feels great pressure from all sides, yet she seems committed to following through with her professional plans. She is aware of the sacrifices that would be associated with her studies, but she is asking for everyone in the family to make adjustments so that she can accomplish some goals that are important to her. She is convinced that her plans would not be detrimental to the family's welfare. The therapist shows an obvious bias by giving no support to Naomi's aspirations and by not asking the family to consider making any basic adjustments. Although the therapist does not openly say that she should give up her plans, his interventions have the result of reinforcing the family's resistance.

◆ Do you think this therapist is guilty of furthering gender-role stereotypes? *yes*
  Do his interventions show an interest in the well-being of the entire family? *no*
◆ Are there any other ethical issues in this case? If so, what are they?
◆ Being aware of your own bias regarding gender roles, how would you work with this family?
◆ Assume that the therapist had an obvious bias in favor of Naomi's plans and even pushed the family to learn to accept her right to an independent life. Do you see any ethical issue in this approach? Is it unavoidable for a therapist to take sides?

Responsibilities of Marital and Family Therapists

Margolin (1982) argues persuasively that difficult ethical questions confronted in individual therapy become even more complicated when a number of family members are seen together. She observes that the dilemma with multiple clients is that in some instances an intervention that serves one person's best interests could burden another family member or even be countertherapeutic. Under the family-systems model, for example, therapists do not focus their responsibility on the individual but on the family as a system. Such therapists avoid becoming agents of any one family member, believing that all family members contribute to the problems of the whole family. Ethical practice demands that therapists declare the nature of their commitments to each member of the family.

but how?

Therapist responsibilities are also a crucial issue in couple counseling or marriage counseling. This is especially true when the partners do not have a common purpose for seeking counseling. When one person wants divorce counseling and the other is coming to the sessions under the expectation of saving the marriage or improving the relationship, who is the primary client? How do therapists carry out their ethical responsibilities when the two persons in the relationship have different expectations?

In addition to clinical and ethical considerations, Margolin (1982) mentions legal provisions that can decide when the welfare of an individual takes precedence over that of a relationship. A clear example of a therapist's legal obligations is a case of child neglect or child abuse. The law requires family therapists to inform authorities if they suspect such abuse or become aware of it during the course of therapy. Even though reporting this situation may have negative consequences for the therapist's relationships with some members of the family, the therapist's ethical and legal responsibility is to help the threatened or injured person. It is clear that in some situations interventions to help an individual become more important than the goals of the family as a system, and clients should be informed of these situations during the initial session.

informed consent?!

Morrison, Layton, and Newman (1982) agree with Margolin's position that family therapists may face more ethical conflicts than most other therapists. Family therapists sometimes face accusations that they are the agents of the parents against the children, the children against the parents, or of one parent against the other. With so many possible conflicts, it is important for family therapists to know when to seek consultation.

The Responsibility to Consult

At times marriage and family therapists must struggle over the issue of when to consult with another professional. This is especially true of situations in which a person (or couple or family) is already involved in a professional relationship with a therapist and seeks the counsel of another therapist. What course of action would you take if a husband sought you out for private counseling while he and his wife were also seeing another therapist for marriage counseling? Would it be ethical to enter into a professional relationship with this man without the knowledge and consent of the other professional? What might you do or say if the husband told you that the reason for initiating contact with you was to get another opinion and perspective on his marital situation and that he did not see any point in contacting the other professional?

no

◆ ***An open-ended case.***   A couple is seeing a therapist for marriage counseling. The husband decides to quit the joint sessions and begins private sessions with another therapist. The wife remains in individual therapy with the original therapist. In the course of individual therapy, the husband comes to realize that he does not want to terminate the marriage after all. He persuades his wife to come with him for a joint session with his therapist to pursue the possibility of keeping the marriage intact.

- ◆ What are the ethical obligations of the husband's therapist? Does he have responsibility for consulting with the wife's therapist?
- ◆ Do the two therapists need to get permission from their clients to consult with each other?
- ◆ Would it be ethical for the husband's therapist to do marital therapy with the couple, ignoring the work being done by the wife's therapist?

Confidentiality in Marital and Family Therapy

The principle of confidentiality as it applies to marriage and family therapists entails that practitioners do not disclose what they have learned through the professional relationship except: (1) when mandated by law, such as in cases of physical or psychological child abuse, incest, child neglect, or abuse of the elderly; (2) when it is necessary to protect clients from harming themselves or to prevent a clear and immediate danger to others; (3) when the family therapist is a defendant in a civil, criminal, or disciplinary action arising from the therapy; or (4) when a waiver has previously been obtained in writing. If therapists use any material from their practice in teaching, lecturing, and writing, they take care to preserve the anonymity of their clients.

Therapists have differing views on the role of confidentiality when working with families. One view is that therapists should not divulge in a family session any information given to them by individuals in private sessions. In the case of marriage counseling, some practitioners are willing to see each spouse for individual sessions. Information given to them by one spouse is kept confidential. Other therapists, however, reserve the right to bring up certain issues in a joint session, even if one person mentioned the issue in a private session.

Some therapists who work with entire families go further. They have a policy of refusing to keep information secret that was shared individually. Their view is that secrets are counterproductive for open family therapy. Therefore, "hidden agendas" are seen as material that should be brought out into the open during a family session. Still another view is that therapists should inform their clients that any information given to them during private sessions will be divulged as they see fit in accordance with the greatest benefit for the couple or the family. These therapists reserve the right to use their professional judgment about whether to maintain individual confidences. In our opinion this latter approach is the most flexible; it avoids putting the counselor in the awkward position of having to either divulge secrets or keep secrets at the expense of the welfare of the family. As Margolin (1982) notes, therapists who have not promised confidentiality have more options and thus must carefully consider the therapeutic ramifications of their actions.

It is absolutely essential to ethical practice, however, that each marital and family therapist make his or her stand on confidentiality clear to each family member from the outset of therapy. Family members can then decide whether to participate in therapy and how much to disclose to the therapist. For example, a husband might disclose less in a private session if he knew that the therapist might bring these disclosures out in joint sessions.

◆ *A case of therapist quandary.*   A husband is involved in one-to-one therapy to resolve a number of personal conflicts, of which the state of his marriage is only one. Later, his wife comes in for some joint sessions. In their joint sessions much time is spent on how betrayed the wife feels over having discovered that her husband had an affair in the past. She is angry and hurt but has agreed to remain in the marriage and to come to these therapy sessions as long as the husband agrees not to resume the past affair or to initiate new ones. Reluctantly, the husband agrees to her demands. The therapist does not explicitly state her views about confidentiality, yet the husband assumes that she will keep to herself what she hears in both the wife's private sessions and his private sessions. During one of the joint sessions, the therapist does state her bias. She says that maintaining or initiating an affair is counterproductive if they both want to work on improving their marriage. The therapist states a strong preference that they agree not to have extramarital affairs.

In a later individual session the husband tells the therapist that he has begun a new affair. He brings this up privately with his therapist because he feels some guilt over not having lived up to the agreement. But he maintains that the affair is not negatively influencing his relationship with his wife and has helped him to tolerate many of the difficulties he has been experiencing in his marriage. He also asks that the therapist not mention this in a joint session, for he fears that his wife will leave him if she finds out that he is involved with another woman.

Think about these questions in deciding on the ethical course of action:

◆ The therapist has not explicitly stated her view of confidentiality. Is it ethical for her to bring up the husband's new affair in a joint session?

◆ How does the therapist handle her conviction regarding affairs in light of the fact that the husband tells her that it is actually enhancing, not interfering with, the marriage?

◆ Should the therapist attempt to persuade the husband to give up the affair? Should she persuade the client to bring up this matter himself in a joint session? Is the therapist colluding with the husband against the wife by not bringing up this matter?

◆ Should the therapist discontinue therapy with this couple because of her strong bias? If she does suggest termination and referral to another professional, might not this be tantamount to admitting to the wife that the husband is having an affair? What might the therapist say if the wife is upset over the suggestion of a referral and wants to know the reasons?

Informed Consent in Marital and Family Therapy

In Chapter 4 we examined the issue of informed consent and clients' rights within the framework of individual therapy. As Margolin (1982) notes, informed consent and the right to refuse treatment are also critical ethical issues in the practice of marital and family therapy. Before each individual agrees to participate in family therapy, it is essential that the counselor provide information about the purpose of therapy, typical procedures, the risks of negative outcomes, the possible benefits, the fee structure, the limits of confidentiality, the rights and responsibilities of clients, the option that a family member can withdraw at any time, and what can be expected from the therapist. When therapists take the time to obtain informed consent from everyone, they convey the message that no one member is the "identified patient" who is the source of all the family's problems. Although getting the informed consent of each member of the family is ideal from an ethical point of view, actually carrying out this practice may be difficult.

Most family therapists consider it essential that all members of the family participate. This bias raises ethical questions about exerting pressure on an individual to participate, even if that person is strongly against being involved. Although coercion of a reluctant person is generally viewed as unethical, many therapists strongly suggest that a reluctant family member participate for a session or two to determine what potential value there might be in family therapy. Some resistance can arise from a family member's feeling that he or she will be the main target of the sessions. This resistance can be lessened and perhaps even eliminated in a short period of time if the therapist refuses to allow the family to use one member as a scapegoat.

Patten and her colleagues (1991) and Haas and Alexander (1981) question the controversial strategy of withholding services until all participants are engaged in therapy. Haas and Alexander contend that the therapist who requires all members to participate in therapy may be cooperating with the most resistant family member in keeping the more willing members from beginning or continuing therapy as a family. Willing members can be put in an unfair position of being denied treatment unless they are able to persuade unwilling members to participate in family therapy. If an individual does not want to participate in family therapy, the therapist should explore other options for working with the family. Margolin (1982) thinks therapists with such a policy should have a list of referral sources where the part of the family willing to participate can receive treatment.

Protecting children's rights is typically made easier by treating the whole family (Haas & Alexander, 1981). Although parents retain the legal authority to consent to their children's treatment and to know what is occurring in individual therapy, this problem does not arise in family therapy because the parents are involved. The issue of informed consent should be open for family discussion. Haas and Alexander recommend that family therapists establish ground rules for dealing with matters such as family secrets and the privacy of individual members. If these rules are made part of the informed consent procedure at the initial sessions, issues of confidentiality are less likely to become a problem as therapy progresses. Goldenberg and Goldenberg (1996a) caution that therapists need to inform children in a way that they are likely to comprehend their role in the therapeutic process and then ask for their consent to participate. They add that it is essential to secure consent before videotaping or audiotaping, or observing families behind a one-way mirror.

Hare-Mustin (1980) observes that family therapy may be dangerous to one's health. Because it gives priority to the good of the entire family, it may not be in the best interests of individual family members. Further, by being required to participate in therapy, the members may have to subordinate their own goals and give up limited confidentiality. Hare-Mustin suggests that ethical practice demands minimizing these risks for individual members. This can be done by encouraging family members to question the goals of therapy so that they can understand how their own needs relate to the family's goals. Also, it is the therapist's responsibility to open for discussion the subject of how one member's goals are incompatible with family goals or perhaps even unacceptable to other members.

The implications of informed consent for family therapists and systems-oriented therapists are also discussed by Bray, Shepherd, and Hays (1985). These writers encourage therapists to tell prospective clients that they are looking beyond treating a specific and diagnosed problem to a broader view of the clients' health. Clients have a right to know that the family system will be the focus of the therapeutic process and to know about the practical implications of this theoretical perspective. Informed consent can be more complex than it appears. Many times families enter counseling with one person in the family being perceived as the one with the problem or the person causing the family distress. After therapy commences, however, the entire family becomes the focus of the therapist's intervention. Did these family members truly consent to become clients, or did they perceive their role as consultants? Family members should have opportunities to raise questions and know as clearly as possible what they are getting involved in when they enter family therapy.

Chapter Summary

The field of marital and family therapy is rapidly expanding and developing. With an expansion in educational programs comes the need for specialized training and experience. A thorough discussion of ethical issues must be part of all such programs. A few of these issues are determining who is the primary client, dealing with confidentiality, providing informed consent, counseling with minors, and exploring the role of values in family therapy.

The job of the therapist is to help the family or couple sort through their own values and not to influence them to conform to the therapist's value system. Likewise, a key ethical issue is the impact of the therapist's life experiences on his or her ability to practice effectively and objectively. For instance, if family therapists are bogged down by their own unfinished business with their family of origin or unresolved conflicts in their current family, it is not likely that they will be able to be therapeutic agents for other families. Therapists who are using their work as a way to fulfill their own needs or who have intense countertransference reactions toward particular family members may be blocking a family's progress. The ethical issues are clear in these cases.

As is true regarding all ethical issues, there is a significant relationship between sound ethical and clinical decision making. Family therapists may sometimes experience confusion, for example, regarding the ethical aspects of deciding who will attend family sessions. It is obvious, however, that such decisions cannot be made without a solid foundation in clinical theory and methodology. With increased knowledge and practical experience, therapists can make these ethical decisions with greater certainty. Being open to periodic supervision, seeking consultation when necessary, and being willing to participate in one's own therapy are some ways in which marital and family therapists can refine their clinical skills.

Suggested Activities

1. In the practice of marital and family therapy, informed consent is especially important. As a class discussion topic, explore some of these issues: What are the ethical implications of insisting that all members of a family participate in family therapy? What kind of information should a family therapist present from the outset to all those involved? Are there any ethical conflicts in focusing on the welfare of the entire family rather than on what might be in the best interests of an individual?

2. Investigate the status of regulating professional practice in marital and family therapy in your state. What are the academic and training requirements, if any, for certification or licensure in this field?

3. In a small group, discuss the major ethical problems facing marital and family therapists. Consider issues such as confidentiality, enforced therapy involving all family members, qualifications of effective family therapists, imposing the values of the therapist on a family, and practicing beyond one's competence.

4. Design a project to study your own family of origin. Interview as many relatives as you can. Look for patterns in your own relationships, including problems you currently struggle with, that stem from your family of origin. What advantages do you see in studying your own family as one way to prepare yourself for counseling families?

5. Imagine that you are participating on a board to establish standards—personal, academic, training, and experiential—for family therapists. What do you think the minimum requirements should be to prepare a trainee to work with families? What would your ideal training program for marital and family therapists look like?

Ethical Issues
in Group Work

Pre-Chapter Self-Inventory

Directions: For each statement, indicate the response that most closely identifies your beliefs and attitudes. Use the following code:

5 = I *strongly agree* with this statement.
4 = I *agree* with this statement.
3 = I am *undecided* about this statement.
2 = I *disagree* with this statement.
1 = I *strongly disagree* with this statement.

_____ 1. Groups are a second-rate therapeutic approach, used mainly as a way to cut costs.

_____ 2. Ethical practice requires that prospective group members be carefully screened and selected.

_____ 3. It's important to prepare members so that they can derive the maximum benefit from the group.

_____ 4. Requiring people to participate in a therapy group raises ethical issues.

_____ 5. It is unethical to allow a group to exert pressure on one of its members.

_____ 6. Confidentiality is less important in groups than it is in individual therapy.

_____ 7. Socializing among group members is almost always undesirable because it interferes with the functioning of the group.

_____ 8. One way of minimizing psychological risks to group participants is to negotiate contracts with the members.

_____ 9. A group leader has a responsibility to teach members how to translate what they've learned in the group to their outside lives.

_____ 10. It is unethical for counselor educators to lead groups of their students in training.

_____ 11. It is unethical for group leaders to employ a technique unless they are thoroughly trained in its use or under the supervision of an expert familiar with it.

_____ 12. It is the group leader's responsibility to make prospective members aware of their rights and responsibilities and to demystify the process of a group.

_____ 13. Group members should know that they have the right to leave the group at any time.

_____ 14. Before people enter a group, it is the leader's responsibility to discuss with them the personal risks involved, especially potential life changes, and help them explore their readiness to face these risks.

_____ 15. It is a sound practice to provide written ethical guidelines to group members in advance and discuss them in the first meeting.

Introduction

We are giving group work special attention, as we did marital and family therapy, because it raises unique ethical concerns. Practitioners who work with groups face a variety of situations that differ from those encountered in individual therapy. Groups have been increasing in popularity, and in many agencies and institutions they are the primary form of therapy. They are also considered to be the most cost-effective form of counseling. Along with this increased use of groups, there has been a rising ethical awareness.

In general, group therapy is as effective as individual therapy in bringing about change, and an expanding array of group techniques that are affordable and effective in overcoming a range of psychological and medical problems is now available (Sleek, 1995). Group therapy fits well into the managed care scene because groups can be designed to be brief and cost-effective treatments. In addition, groups provide a sense of community, which can be an antidote to an impersonal culture in which many clients live. The interpersonal learning that occurs in groups can accelerate a person's changes. However, most groups are time-limited and have fairly narrow goals. Many of the time-limited groups are aimed at symptomatic relief and teaching participants problem-solving strategies and interpersonal skills.

In our view, groups are often the treatment of choice, not a second-rate therapeutic approach. Many of the problems that bring people to counseling are rooted in interpersonal issues and involve difficulties forming or maintaining intimate relationships. Clients may be at a loss in knowing how to live well with the ones they love, and they often believe that their problems are unique and that they have few options to get out of deadening ruts. Groups provide a natural laboratory that demonstrates to people that they are not alone and that there is hope for creating a different life. Groups are powerful because long-term problems of group members may be played out in the group sessions, giving group members opportunities to try out different solutions.

Our illustrations of important ethical considerations are drawn from a broad spectrum of groups, including therapy groups, counseling groups, personal-growth groups, psychoeducational groups, educational groups, and structured groups. Obviously, these groups differ with respect to their member population, purpose, focus, and procedures, as well as in the level of training required for their leaders. Although these distinctions are important, the issues we discuss are common to most groups. Among the topics we discuss are the training of group leaders, co-leadership issues, the ethical issues surrounding group membership, confidentiality in groups, uses and abuses of group techniques, and issues concerning termination and follow-up.

Training and Supervision of Group Leaders

For competent group leaders to emerge, training programs must make group work a priority. Unfortunately, in some graduate training programs not even one group course is required. If a group course is required, it usually covers both the didactic and experiential aspects of group process. Training in group work tends to be didactic, is deficient in supervised group practice, and typically includes no more than one course (Conyne, 1996).

With proper training in group work, competent group practitioners will know their limitations and recognize the kinds of groups they are able to lead. Practitioners should familiarize themselves with referral resources and refrain from working with client populations that need special help beyond their level of competence. Competent group counselors should be able to explain to their clients the theory behind their group work and how their theory influences their practice. They should be able to present in clear language to the members the goals of the group and the relationship between the way they lead the group and their goals. Effective group leaders are able to conceptualize the group process and to relate what they do in a group to this model. Furthermore, responsible group workers are keenly aware of the importance of continuing their education. Even experienced professionals attend conventions and workshops, take courses, read, seek consultation and supervision, and get involved in special training programs from time to time.

Professional Training Standards*

The expanded "Professional Standards for the Training of Group Workers," (ASGW, 1991) specifies two levels of competencies and related training. First is a set of core *knowledge* and *skill competencies* that provide the foundation on which specialized training is built. At a minimum, one group course should be included in a training program, and it should be structured to help students acquire the basic knowledge and skills needed to facilitate a group. These group skills are best mastered through supervised practice, which should include observation and participation in a group experience.

Examples of group leaders' basic knowledge competencies are identifying one's strengths, weaknesses, and values; being able to describe the characteristics associated with the typical stages in a group's development; being able to describe the various roles and behaviors of group members; knowing the therapeutic factors at work in a group; understanding the importance of group and member evaluation; and being aware of the ethical issues special to group work.

Examples of skill competencies include being able to open and close group sessions, modeling appropriate behavior for group members, engaging in appropriate self-disclosure in the group, giving and receiving feedback, helping members attribute meaning to their experience, helping members integrate and apply their learning, and demonstrating the ability to apply the ACA (1995) *Code of Ethics and Standards of Practice* in group work.

* Adapted from "Professional Standards for the Training of Group Workers," adopted April 20, 1991, and reproduced by permission from *Together: Association for Specialists in Group Work, 20* (Fall 1991), 9–14. The ASGW is a division of the American Counseling Association, 5999 Stevenson Avenue, Alexandria, VA 22304.

Once counselor trainees have mastered these core knowledge and skills domains, they can acquire training in group work specializations in one or more of these four areas: (1) task/work groups, (2) guidance/psychoeducational groups, (3) counseling/interpersonal-problem-solving groups, and (4) psychotherapy/personality-reconstruction groups. The standards detail specific knowledge and skill competencies for these specialties and recommend the number of hours of supervised training necessary for each.

The training for *task/work groups* involves courses in the broad area of organizational development and management. It also includes course work in consultation. A minimum of 30 hours of supervised experience in leading or co-leading a task/work group is required.

The specialist training for *guidance/psychoeducation groups* involves course work in the broad area of community psychology, health promotion, marketing, consultation, and curriculum design. This specialty requires an additional 30 hours of supervised experience in leading or co-leading a guidance group in field practice.

The training for *counseling/interpersonal-problem-solving groups* should ideally include as much course work in group counseling as possible, with at least one course beyond the generalist level. A minimum of 45 hours of supervised experience in leading or co-leading a counseling group is required for this specialty.

The specialist training for *psychotherapy groups* consists of courses in the area of abnormal psychology, psychopathology, and diagnostic assessment to assure capabilities in working with more disturbed populations. A minimum of 45 hours of supervised experience working with therapy groups is required.

The core competencies and experiences delineated in the 1991 ASGW training standards are the foundation for training group workers. The standards of the Council for Accreditation of Counseling and Related Educational Programs (CACREP, 1994) that deal with group work reflect much of this material (Conyne, Wilson, Kline, Morran, & Ward, 1993). Attempts have been made to implement the ASGW recommendations with the CACREP standards, outlining supervised clinical experience obtained in both practicum and internship programs. The CACREP standards require experience in individual and group counseling under supervision and, consistent with the ASGW training standards, indicate that at least one fourth of direct service practicum be devoted to group work.

Whether core training in group work reflects minimal CACREP standards or the more specific ASGW standards, this training alone is not sufficient to prepare counselors for conducting groups on their own. Practitioners must still acquire training in a particular specialization in group work (Conyne, 1996). Dye (1996) believes that the ASGW training standards are realistic in defining minimum knowledge and skills and are valuable in differentiating between the major forms of group work. However, most graduate programs simply prepare counselors in the core competencies. Only some programs at the doctoral level offer the requisite courses and supervised training experiences necessary to acquire advanced competencies in any of the four group work specializations.

According to Dye, specialization generally takes place after completing a graduate program.

The current trend in training for group workers focuses on learning group processes by becoming involved in supervised experiences. Both direct participation in planned and supervised small groups and clinical experience in leading various groups under careful supervision are needed to equip leaders with the skills to meet the challenges of group work. However, Gumaer and Forrest (1995) recommend caution in group leader training to minimize the risk of malpractice. They state: "In our opinion, training standards and ethical guidelines for group therapists are inconsistent and vague, as are group therapy training practices. This creates uninformed practices that lead to group therapists' placing themselves in ethical and legal jeopardy" (p. 11).

Our Views on Training

Professional codes, legislative mandates, and institutional policies alone will not ensure competent group leadership. Group counselor trainees need to confront the typical dilemmas they will face in practice and learn ways to clarify their views on these issues. This can best be done by including ethics in the trainees' academic program as well as discussing ethical issues that grow out of the students' experiences in practicum, internship, and fieldwork. We have found that one effective way to teach ethical decision making is by presenting trainees with case vignettes of typical problems that occur in group situations and encouraging discussion of the ethical issues and pertinent guidelines. We tell both students and professionals who attend our workshops that they will not have the answers to many of the dilemmas they encounter in practice. Ethical decision making is an ongoing process that takes on new forms and increased meaning as practitioners gain experience. What is critical is that group leaders develop a receptivity to self-examination and to questioning the professionalism of their group practice.

We highly recommend at least three experiences as adjuncts to a training program for group workers: (1) personal (private) psychotherapy; (2) experience in group therapy, group counseling, or a personal-growth group; and (3) participation in a supervision and training group.

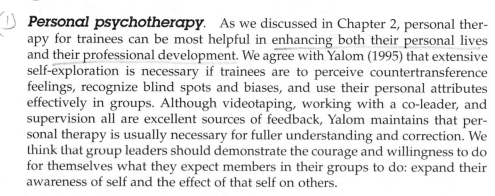

Personal psychotherapy. As we discussed in Chapter 2, personal therapy for trainees can be most helpful in enhancing both their personal lives and their professional development. We agree with Yalom (1995) that extensive self-exploration is necessary if trainees are to perceive countertransference feelings, recognize blind spots and biases, and use their personal attributes effectively in groups. Although videotaping, working with a co-leader, and supervision all are excellent sources of feedback, Yalom maintains that personal therapy is usually necessary for fuller understanding and correction. We think that group leaders should demonstrate the courage and willingness to do for themselves what they expect members in their groups to do: expand their awareness of self and the effect of that self on others.

(2)   **Self-exploration groups.**   As an adjunct to formal course work and internship training, participation in a therapeutic group can be extremely valuable. In addition to helping interns resolve personal conflicts and develop increased self-understanding, a personal-growth group can be a powerful teaching tool. One of the best ways to learn how to assist group members in their struggles is to work as a member of a group yourself. Yalom (1995) strongly recommends a group experience for trainees. Some of the benefits, he suggests, are experiencing the power of a group, learning what self-disclosure is about, coming to appreciate the difficulties involved in self-sharing, learning on an emotional level what one knows intellectually, and becoming aware of one's dependence on the leader's power and knowledge. He cites surveys indicating that 60% to 70% of group therapy training programs offer some type of personal-group experience. About half of these programs offer an optional group, and the other half a mandatory group.

(3)   **Participation in a training and supervisory group.**   We have found that workshops help group trainees develop the skills necessary for effective intervention. Also, interns can learn a great deal about their response to criticism, their competitiveness, their need for approval, their concerns over being competent, and their power struggles. In working with both university students learning about group approaches and professionals who want to upgrade their skills, we have found an intensive weekend workshop to be an effective format.

Ethical Issues in Training Group Counselors

Merta, Johnson, and McNeil (1995) conducted a national survey that provided some interesting insights into the nature and extent of group counselor training. Below are some findings:

◆ With respect to course work in group counseling, of the 262 programs in which a group counselor educator responded to the survey, 91% have a required course in group work.

◆ Many group counselor educators identify the purpose of their required group course as being introductory in nature rather than preparing students to be group counselors.

◆ Most of the counselor educators who teach group courses identify their theoretical or philosophical base as eclectic. A growing preference for eclecticism seems to be more accelerated for group work than for individual counseling.

◆ Only a minority of group counselor educators require participation in adjunct training or therapy groups, or in a supervised practicum, and only a minority use guest lectures or demonstrations.

◆ Less than half of those who teach group courses lead the experiential part in their group courses—and less than half of them lead outside groups.

♦ The most popular training component consists of didactic teaching methods (assigning readings and lectures); the most popular experiential component in class is role playing; and the most popular personal-growth experience is the adjunct experiential (personal-growth) group.

One controversial ethical issue in the preparation of group counselors pertains to the practice of combining experiential and didactic methods. Counselor educators who teach group courses do not appear to agree on the goals for combining therapeutic and training groups or on how students can best be evaluated (Forester-Miller & Duncan, 1990). Combining experiential and didactic approaches generally entails balancing multiple roles and responsibilities for instructors. Some of these roles are group facilitator, instructor, evaluator, and supervisor. Blending roles presents potential ethical problems, and various strategies are being employed to limit these problems in the preparation of group counselors. Merta, Wolfgang, and McNeil (1993) admit that no one training model or combination of safeguards is apt to solve the dilemma of protecting students from adverse dual relationships and at the same time provide them with the best possible training. It is challenging for those who teach group courses to learn ways to differentiate between experiential training workshops and counseling groups. At times it is difficult to draw clear distinctions between training workshops and counseling groups. It is essential that faculty who teach group courses or conduct training workshops for group workers monitor their practices by keeping the purpose of the training workshop clearly in mind.

In their article examining the ethical dilemma surrounding the use of experiential groups in training group counselors, Merta and Sisson (1991) conclude that counselor educators should consider the needs of the students, the program, and the profession. Experiential groups are an indispensable component in training, and Merta and Sisson offer the following eight recommendations for ethical practice in the preparation of group workers:

♦ Training programs should be surveyed nationally to determine how experiential groups are being used.
♦ The opinions of current trainees in group counseling can be useful in making ethical decisions.
♦ Although it is not appropriate that experiential groups become therapy groups, such groups need not be restricted to mere role-playing exercises.
♦ Because experiential groups are essential to the preparation of effective group counselors, participating in them should not be voluntary, nor should alternatives be provided for those who do not wish to become involved in these groups.
♦ It is preferable to have advanced students or practitioners from outside the department as leaders of experiential groups rather than the course instructor or other faculty members in the department.
♦ Students have a right to expect feedback regarding their performance in the experiential group.

◆ Instructors who teach group courses should meet with those who facilitate experiential groups for the purpose of discussing student progress in the group.
◆ Before enrolling in a program, students should be fully advised of the requirement of participating in an experiential group that encourages self-disclosure and personal exploration.

For a more detailed discussion of dual relationship controversies in the preparation of group counselors, see Herlihy and Corey (1997).

As you consider the training of group leaders, ponder these questions for yourself:

◆ Who is qualified to lead groups? What are the criteria for determining the competence of group leaders?
◆ What do you think of the training in clinical practice suggested in the ASGW's "Professional Standards for the Training of Group Workers"?
◆ What are some differences between a training group and a therapy group? Can you think of safeguards to minimize the potential risks of combining experiential and didactic methods?
◆ Does ethical practice demand that group leaders receive some form of personal therapy? Should this be group therapy or experience in a personal-growth group?
◆ How important are continuing education and training once trainees have completed a professional program?
◆ What are your reactions to the suggestions we offered for the training of group workers?

Co-Leadership

If you should decide to lead groups, you'll probably work with a co-leader at some time. We think there are many advantages to the co-leader model. The group can benefit from the insights and feedback of two leaders. The leaders can complement and balance each other. They can grow by discussing what goes on in the group and by observing each other's style, and together they can evaluate what has gone on in the group and plan for future sessions. Also, co-leaders can share the responsibilities. While one leader is working with a particular member, the other can be paying attention to others in the group.

The choice of a co-leader is crucial. A group can suffer if its leaders are not working effectively together. If much of the leaders' energies are directed at competing with each other or at some other power struggle or hidden agenda, there is little chance that the group will be effective.

Selection of a co-leader should involve more than attraction and liking. Each of the leaders should be secure enough that the group won't have to suffer as one or both of them try to "prove" themselves. We surely don't think it's essential that co-leaders always agree or share the same perceptions or interpretations; in fact, a group can be given vitality if co-leaders feel trusting enough to express their differences of opinion. Mutual respect and the ability to establish a relationship based on trust, cooperation, and support are most important. Also, each person should be autonomous and have his or her own style yet be able to work with the other leader as a team.

In our view it's essential for co-leaders to spend some time together immediately following a group session to assess what has happened. Similarly, we believe that they should meet at least briefly before each session to talk about anything that might affect their functioning in the group.

At this point we ask you to draw up your own guidelines for selecting a co-leader:

- What are the qualities you'd look for in a co-leader?
- What kind of person would you not want to lead with?
- If you found that you and your co-leader clashed on many issues and approached groups very differently, what do you think you'd do?
- What ethical implications are involved when a great deal of time during the sessions is taken up with power struggles and conflicts between the co-leaders?
- In what ways could you be most helpful to your co-leader?
- What kind of help would you expect to receive from your co-leader?

Ethical Issues in Group Membership

How can group leaders make potential members aware of the services they are providing? What information do clients have a right to expect before they decide to attend a group? People have a right to know what they are getting into before they make a commitment to become a part of any group. Informed consent requires that leaders make the members aware of their rights (as well as their responsibilities) as group participants.

 A case of informed consent. A group leader operates on the assumption that giving members information about her groups will ultimately be counterproductive. She does not tell them about the nature of the group process, the procedures she may use, or the best ways to get the maximum benefit from the group. She is concerned that members would focus on meeting her expectations. She does not emphasize defining goals and believes that members' uncertainty about what they want from the group will be good material to explore as part of the group process.

- Is this leader behaving unethically in not providing members with information about the goals of the group or the procedures she may use?
- What are some of the potential problems of providing too much information about a group before members enroll?
- What information do you think a member should have before deciding whether to participate in a group?

Screening and Selection of Group Members

Group leaders are faced with the difficult task of determining who should be included in a group and who should not. Are groups appropriate for all people? To put the question in another way, is it appropriate for *this* person to become a participant in *this* type of group, with *this* leader, at *this* time?

Assuming that not everyone will benefit from a group experience—and that some people will be psychologically harmed by certain group experiences—is it unethical to fail to screen prospective group candidates? Many group leaders do not screen participants, for various reasons. Some practitioners are theoretically opposed to the notion of using screening as a way of determining who is suitable for a group, and some maintain that they simply do not have the time to carry out effective screening. Others believe that ethical practice demands careful screening and preparation of all candidates.

Yalom (1995) argues that unless careful selection criteria are employed, group therapy clients may end up discouraged and may not be helped. He maintains that it is easier to identify the people who should be excluded from group therapy than those who should be included. Citing clinical studies, he lists the following as poor candidates for a heterogeneous outpatient intensive-therapy group: brain damaged people, paranoid individuals, hypochondriacs, those who are addicted to drugs or alcohol, acutely psychotic individuals, and antisocial personalities. In terms of criteria for inclusion, he contends that the client's level of motivation to work is the most important variable. From his perspective, groups are useful for people who have problems in the interpersonal domain, such as loneliness, inability to make or maintain intimate contacts, feelings of unlovability, fears of being assertive, and dependency issues. Clients who lack meaning in life, who suffer from diffuse anxiety, who are searching for an identity, who fear success, and who are compulsive workers might also profit from a group experience. The ethics code of ACA (1995) identifies the group leader's responsibility for screening prospective group members:

> Counselors screen prospective group counseling/therapy participants. To the extent possible, counselors select members whose needs and goals are compatible with goals of the group, who will not impede the group process, and whose well-being will not be jeopardized by the group experience. (A.9.a.)

Screening is most effective when the leader interviews the members and the members also have an opportunity to interview the leader. While prospective group members are being screened, they should be deciding whether they want to work with a particular leader and whether the group in question is suitable for them. Group candidates should not passively allow the matter to be decided for them by an expert. Practitioners should welcome the opportunity to respond to any questions or concerns that prospective members have, and they should actively encourage prospective members to raise questions about matters that will affect their participation. In some settings it is impractical to screen members prior to forming a group. In situations where it is not possible to conduct screening interviews, one alternative is to use the initial session to screen participants and to present informed consent guidelines.

Our experience has been that it is often difficult to predict who will benefit from a group experience. We realize that pre-group screening interviews are like any other interview, and some people will say what they think the interviewer expects. Those who are interviewed for a group often feel that they must sell themselves or that they are being evaluated and judged. Perhaps these feelings can be lessened somewhat if leaders emphasize that these interviews are really designed as a two-way process in which leaders and prospective members can decide together whether a particular group, with a particular leader, at a particular time is in the best interests of all concerned. Although we do have difficulty predicting who will benefit from a group, we have found screening interviews to be most helpful in excluding some people who we believed would probably have left the group with negative feelings or would have drained the group of the energy necessary for productive work.

Preparing Group Participants

To what extent are group counselors responsible for teaching participants to benefit from their group experience? Many practitioners do very little to prepare members systematically for a group. In fact, we know of some group workers who are opposed to systematic preparation on the ground that it would inhibit a group's spontaneity and autonomy. Others take the position that members must be provided with some structure to derive the maximum gains.

Yalom (1995) advocates exploring group members' misconceptions and expectations, predicting early problems, and providing a conceptual framework that includes guidelines for effective group behavior. He views this preparatory process as more than the dissemination of information. He contends that it reinforces the therapist's respect for the client, demonstrates that therapy is a collaborative venture, and shows that the therapist is willing to share his or her knowledge with the client. This cognitive approach to preparation has the goals of providing a rational explanation of the group process, clarifying how members are expected to behave, and raising expectations about what the group can accomplish.

In our training workshops we have seen much resistance that can be attributed to ignorance of group process and a misunderstanding of goals. Our preparation procedures apply to all types of groups, with some modifications. At both the screening session and the initial group meeting, we explore the members' expectations, clarify goals and objectives, discuss procedural details, explore the possible risks and values of group participation, and discuss guidelines for getting the most from a group experience (G. Corey, Corey, Callanan, & Russell, 1992; M. Corey & Corey, 1997). As part of member preparation we include a discussion of the values and limitations of groups, the psychological risks involved in group participation, and ways of minimizing these risks. We also allow time for dealing with misconceptions that people have about groups and for exploring any fears or resistances the members may have. In most of our groups members do have certain fears about what they will experience, and until we acknowledge these fears and talk about them, very little productive work can occur. Further, we ask members to spend time before they come to the group defining for themselves what they most want to achieve. To make their goals more concrete, we usually ask them to develop a contract that entails areas of concern on which they're willing to work in the group. We also ask them to do some reading and to write about their goals and about the significant turning points in their lives.

At this point, we ask you to write down some things you might do to prepare people for a group. What ethical concerns do you have regarding preparation? What do you think would occur if you did little in the way of preparing group members?

Involuntary Participation

Should group membership always be voluntary? Are there situations in which it is ethical to require or coerce people to participate in a group? How is informed consent especially critical in groups where attendance is mandatory?

Obviously, voluntary participation is an important beginning point for a successful group experience. Members will make significant changes only to the extent that they actively seek something for themselves. Unfortunately, not all groups are composed of clients who have chosen to be there. In some community agencies and inpatient facilities, the main therapeutic vehicle is group therapy. People receiving services may be required to attend group sessions, sometimes several times a week. This situation is somewhat akin to compulsory education—people can be forced to attend but not to learn.

When group participation is mandatory, much effort needs to be directed toward fully informing members of the nature and goals of the group, procedures to be used, the rights of members to decline certain activities, the limits of confidentiality, and what effect their level of participation in the group will have on critical decisions about them outside of the group. When attendance at group sessions is mandatory, group leaders must be certain that group members understand their rights and their responsibilities.

In the case that follows, consider the ethical issues involved in mandated group therapy, the failure to give members enough information to make decisions, and the use of pressure.

◆   *A case of an involuntary group.*   In a prison group an inexperienced leader senses that little progress is being made. In an attempt to lessen the members' resistance, she tells them that she does not want anybody to be part of the group who is not willing to participate freely in the sessions. She neglects to inform them that their refusal to attend group sessions will be documented and will be a factor in the decision about their release. Thus, the members are operating under the assumption that they have freedom of choice, yet they have not been given the information they need to make a real choice.

- Does this leader's desire for an effective group justify her practice? Why, or why not?
- Do you think members can benefit from a group experience even if they are required to attend? Why, or why not?
- What strategy might this leader have used to foster more effective group participation while still giving the members true freedom of choice?
- From an ethical perspective, is it required that members of an involuntary group give consent? To what degree should members be informed about the consequences of the quantity or quality of their participation in a group?

Freedom to Leave a Group

Once members make a commitment to be a part of a group, do they have the right to leave at any time they choose? Procedures for leaving a group should be explained to all members during the initial session. Ideally, the leader and the member cooperate to determine whether a group experience is proving to be productive or counterproductive. G. Corey, Corey, Callanan, and Russell (1992) take the position that clients have a responsibility to the leader and to other members to explain why they want to leave. There are several reasons for this policy. It can be deleterious to members to leave without having been able to discuss what they considered threatening or negative in the experience. Further, it is unfortunate for members to leave a group because of a misunderstanding about some feedback they have received. Such a termination can be harmful to group cohesion, for the members who remain may think that they caused a particular member's departure. We tell our members that they have an obligation to attend all sessions and to inform us and the group should they decide to withdraw. If members even consider withdrawing, we encourage them to bring this up for exploration in a session. We do not think it is ethical to use undue pressure to keep these members, and we are alert to other members' pressuring a person to stay.

Psychological Risks

The fact that groups can be powerful catalysts for personal change means that they are also risky. Although we don't think groups should be free of risks, ethical practice demands that group practitioners inform prospective participants of the potential hazards involved in the group experience. However, merely informing participants does not absolve leaders of all responsibility. Group leaders have an ethical responsibility to take precautionary measures to reduce unnecessary psychological risks. ACA's (1995) guidelines is: "In a group setting, counselors take reasonable precautions to protect clients from physical or psychological trauma" (A.9.b.). Certain safeguards can be taken during the course of a group to avoid disastrous outcomes. Here are some of the risks that participants should know about (M. Corey & Corey, 1997, pp. 31–34):

- Members may experience major disruptions in their lives as a result of their work in the group.
- Group participants are often encouraged to be completely open. In this quest for complete self-revelation, privacy is sometimes invaded.
- A related risk is group pressure. The participants' right not to explore certain issues or to stop at a certain point should be respected. Also, members should not be coerced into participating in an exercise.
- Scapegoating is another potential hazard in groups. Unchallenged projection and blaming can have dire effects on the target person.
- Confrontation can be used or misused in groups. Harmful attacks on others should not be permitted under the guise of "sharing."
- Even though a counselor may continue to stress the necessity not to discuss with outsiders what goes on in the group, there is no guarantee that all members will respect the confidential nature of their exchanges.
- People have occasionally been physically injured in groups as a result of engaging in physical techniques. Group counselors who introduce such techniques should have enough experience and training to understand the process and possible consequences of such work.

One way to minimize psychological risks in groups is to use a contract, in which leaders specify what their responsibilities are and members specify their commitment to the group by declaring what they're willing to do. If members and leaders operate under a contract that clarifies expectations, there is less chance for members to be exploited or damaged by a group experience.

Of course, a contract approach is not the only way to reduce potential risks, nor is it sufficient in itself to do so. One of the most important safeguards is the leader's training in group process. Group counselors have the major responsibility for preventing needless harm to members. To fulfill this role, group leaders should have a clear grasp of the boundaries of their competence. As a rule, leaders should conduct only those types of groups for which they have been sufficiently prepared. A counselor may be trained to lead a personal-growth or consciousness-raising group but be ill-prepared to embark on a therapy group. Sometimes people who have attended a few intensive groups become excited about doing this type of group as leaders, even though they have had little or no training or supervision. Oftentimes they are in over their heads and unable to cope with what emerges in the group. Working with an experienced co-leader is one good way to learn and also a way to reduce potential risks.

Confidentiality in Groups

The ethical, legal, and professional aspects of confidentiality (discussed in Chapter 5) have a different application in group situations. Are members of a group under the same ethical and legal obligations as the group leader not to disclose the identities of other members or the content of what was shared in the group? The legal concept of privileged communication generally does not apply in a group setting, unless there has been a statutory exception. Therefore, group counselors have the responsibility of informing members of the limits of confidentiality within the group setting, their responsibilities to other group members, and the absence of legal privilege concerning what is shared in a group (Anderson, 1996). A few states have statutes that specifically ensure privacy in group, marital, and family therapy. These states grant privileged communications when third parties are present if the persons are instrumental in treatment, which is true of group therapy (VandeCreek, Knapp, & Herzog, 1988). Members do have an ethical obligation to respect the communications of others in the group.

How to encourage confidentiality.   The ACA (1995) standard on confidentiality in group work is: "In group work, counselors clearly define confidentiality and the parameters for the specific group being entered, explain its importance, and discuss the difficulties related to confidentiality involved in group work. The fact that confidentiality cannot be guaranteed is clearly communicated to group members" (B.2.a.). Although most writers on ethical issues in group work make the point that confidentiality cannot be guaranteed, they also talk about the importance of teaching group members to avoid breaking confidences. Confidentiality in group situations is difficult to enforce. Because members cannot assume that anything they say or hear in the group will remain confidential, they should be able to make an informed choice about how much to reveal.

It is our position that leaders need periodically to reaffirm to group members the importance of not discussing with outsiders what has occurred in the group. In our own groups we talk with each prospective member about the necessity of maintaining confidentiality to establish the trust and cohesion required if participants are to reveal themselves in significant ways. We discuss this point during the screening interviews, again during the pregroup or initial meetings, at times during the course of a group when it seems appropriate, and again at termination. Most people do not maliciously attempt to hurt others by talking with people outside the group about specific members. However, it's tempting for members to share their experiences with other people, and in so doing they sometimes make inappropriate disclosures. Because of this tendency to want to share with outsiders, we repeatedly caution participants in any type of group about how easily and unintentionally the confidentiality of the group can be compromised.

If you were to lead any type of group, which of the following measures might you take to ensure confidentiality? Check any of the statements that apply:

_✓_ I'd repeatedly mention the importance of confidentiality.

_✓_ I'd require group members to sign a statement saying that they would maintain the confidential character of the group.

_✓_ I'd let members know that they would be asked to leave the group if they violated confidentiality.

_____✓ I'd have a document describing the dimensions of confidentiality to which all the members could refer.

_____ With the permission and knowledge of the members, I'd tape-record all the sessions.

_____ I'd say very little about confidentiality and leave it up to group members to decide how they would deal with the issue.

Exceptions to confidentiality. Group counselors have a responsibility to define clearly what confidentiality means, explain its importance, and inform members of the difficulties involved in enforcing it. Although group counselors are expected to stress the importance of confidentiality and set a norm, they are also expected to inform members about its limits. For example, if members pose a danger to themselves or to others, the group leader would be ethically and legally obliged to breach confidentiality. The other limitations for confidentiality, which were discussed in Chapter 5, also apply to group work.

It is a good practice for group workers to give a written statement to each member outlining the nature, purposes, and limitations of confidentiality and acknowledging specific situations that would require the breaching of confidences. It seems that such straightforwardness with members from the outset does a great deal to create trust, for at least members know the consequences of certain revelations to the group.

Of course, it is imperative that those who lead groups become familiar with the state laws that have an impact on their practice. For instance, since 1967, all states have had mandatory child abuse reporting laws. Several states also have mandatory elder abuse and dependent adult abuse reporting laws. The great majority, with the exception of a couple of states, currently have laws requiring counselors to report clients' threats to harm themselves or others.

If you lead a group at a correctional institution or a psychiatric hospital, you may have to record in a member's chart certain behaviors or verbalizations that he or she exhibits in the group. At the same time, your responsibility to your clients requires you to inform them that you are documenting their verbalizations and behaviors and that this information is accessible to other staff (G. Corey, Williams, & Moline, 1995).

Confidentiality with minors. Corey, Williams, and Moline (1995) address specific problems related to confidentiality in doing group work with children and adolescents. Do parents have a right to information that is disclosed by their children in a group? The answer to that question depends on whether we are looking at it from a legal, ethical, or professional viewpoint. State laws differ regarding counseling minors. It is important for group leaders to be well aware of the laws related to working with minors in the state where they are practicing. Circumstances in which a minor may seek professional help without parental consent, defining an emancipated minor, or the rights of parents (or legal guardians) to have access to the records regarding the professional help received by their minor child vary according to state statutes.

According to Arthur and Swanson (1993), parents and guardians have the legal right to communications between the minor and the counselor. There are exceptions to this general rule. Legally, if minors can seek or refuse treatment, they may be considered competent to decide what disclosures, if any, they want to share with others. Arthur and Swanson recommend that in cases where the minor's right to confidentiality is merely implied by a legal statute, it is wise for counselors to seek consultation and legal advice before releasing information if the minor refuses to sign a confidentiality waiver.

Before any minor enters a group, it is a good practice to obtain written permission from the parents. Such a statement should include a brief description of the purpose of the group, the importance of confidentiality as a prerequisite to accomplishing these purposes, and your intention not to violate any confidences. Although it may be useful to give parents information about their child, this can be done without violating confidences. One useful practice to protect the privacy of what goes on in the group is to provide information to parents in a session with the child present. It is also helpful to inform and discuss with minors their concerns in advance, especially over what the therapist might tell their parents. Such practices can strengthen the child's trust in the counselor.

Group leaders have a responsibility in groups that involve children and adolescents to take measures to increase the chances that confidentiality will be kept. It is important to work cooperatively with parents and legal guardians as well as to enlist the trust of the young people. It is also useful to teach minors, using a vocabulary that they are capable of understanding, about the nature, purposes, and limitations of confidentiality. It is a good idea for leaders to encourage members to initiate discussions on confidentiality whenever this becomes an issue for them.

Values in Group Counseling

Group counselors should be aware of their own values and the potential impact they have on the interventions they are likely to make. However, group counselors are sometimes timid about making their values known, lest they influence the direction that the members are likely to take. Group counselors must consider when it might be appropriate to expose their beliefs, decisions, life experiences, and values. The key issue is that leaders should not short-circuit the members' exploration. Rather, the leader's central function is to help members find answers that are congruent with their own values.

From our perspective, the leader's function is to challenge members to evaluate their behavior to determine how it is working for them, not to advise members on the proper course to adopt. If members come to the realization that what they are doing is not serving them well, it is appropriate for the leader to challenge them to develop alternative ways of behaving that will enable them to reach their goals. Group leader behaviors that are hallmarks of ethical, professional, and effective practice include: (a) demonstrating acceptance of the person of the client; (b) avoiding responding to sarcastic remarks with sarcasm; (c) educating the members about group process; (d) being honest with members rather than harboring hidden agendas; (e) avoiding judgments and labeling of members, and instead describing the behavior of members; (f) stating observations and hunches in a tentative way rather than dogmatically; (g) letting members who are difficult know how they are affecting them in a nonblaming way; (h) detecting their own countertransference reactions; (i) avoiding misusing their power; (j) providing both support and caring confrontations; and (k) avoiding meeting their own needs at the expense of the members (M. Corey & Corey, 1993).

An awareness of cultural diversity is particularly important for group work. In Chapter 10 we discussed the characteristics of the culturally skilled counselor. The self-awareness, knowledge, and skill competencies that we described in that chapter certainly apply to practitioners who work in groups. In working with groups characterized by diversity, counselors need to be aware of the assumptions they make about ethnic and cultural groups, and they should adapt their practices to the needs of the members. They need to be watchful of tendencies to treat people on the basis of stereotypes. It is critical that leaders become aware of their biases based on age, disability, ethnicity, gender, race, religion, or sexual orientation.

We suggest that you refer to the discussion of value conflicts in Chapter 3 and consider specific areas in which you might be inclined to impose your values in the groups you lead. Reflect on any tendencies you may have to lead your clients in a certain direction and think about ways to minimize the chances of imposing your values on them.

Uses and Abuses of Group Techniques

Group techniques can be used to facilitate the movement of a group and to deepen and intensify certain feelings. We think leaders should have a clear rationale for using each technique. This is an area in which theory can be a useful guide for practice.

Techniques can also be abused or used in unethical ways. Some ways leaders might employ techniques unethically are:

- using techniques with which they are unfamiliar
- using techniques to serve their own hidden agendas or to enhance their power
- using techniques whose sole purpose is to create an intense atmosphere because of the leader's need for intensity
- using techniques to pressure members or in other ways deprive them of their dignity

We use these guidelines in our practice to avoid abusing techniques in a group:

Proper Guidelines

- Techniques used should have a therapeutic purpose and be grounded in some theoretical framework.
- The client's self-exploration and self-understanding should be fostered.
- Techniques are devised for each unique client situation, and they assist the client in exploring some form of new behavior.
- Leaders should modify their techniques so that they are suitable for the client's cultural and ethnic background.
- Techniques are not used to cover up the leader's incompetence; rather, they are used to enhance the group process.
- Techniques are introduced in a timely and sensitive manner, and they are abandoned if they are not working.
- The tone of a leader is consistently invitational; members are given the freedom either to participate in or to skip a given experiment.
- Leaders should only use techniques they are familiar with, and they should be aware of the potential impact of these techniques.

Although it is unrealistic to expect that leaders will always know exactly what will result from an intervention, they should know how to cope with unexpected outcomes. For example, guided fantasies into times of loneliness as a child or physical exercises designed to release anger can lead to intense emotional experiences. If leaders use such techniques, they must be ready to deal with any emotional release. It is essential that group counselors become aware of the potential for encouraging catharsis to fulfill their own needs. Some leaders may enjoy seeing people express anger because they would like to be able to do so themselves. They may push members to get into contact with angry feelings by developing techniques to bring out such feelings and to focus the group on anger. Although these are legitimate feelings, for surely most of us are at times angry, expressing anger in the group may satisfy the leader's agenda rather than being therapeutic for the member. This question ought to be raised frequently: "Whose needs are primary, and whose needs are being met—the members' or the leader's?"

Therapist Competence

How can leaders determine whether they are competent to use a certain technique? Although some leaders who have received training in the use of a technique may hesitate to use it (out of fear of making a mistake), other overly confident leaders may not have any reservations about trying out new techniques. It is useful if leaders have experienced these techniques as members of a group and have a clear rationale for using them. Group counselors should be able to articulate a theoretical orientation that guides the interventions they make in their groups.

◆ *A case of an inexperienced leader.*   An inexperienced group leader has recently graduated from a master's degree program in counseling. As a part of his job as a community mental-health counselor, he organizes a weekly two-hour group. He realizes that his training in group approaches is limited, so he decides to attend a weekend workshop on body therapy. He does some intense personal work himself at the workshop, and he comes away impressed with the power of what he has witnessed. He is eager to meet his group on Tuesday evening so that he can try out some of these techniques. (He has not been trained in these techniques in graduate school, nor is he receiving any direct supervision in the group that he is leading.)

At the next session of the group a member says, "I feel a lot of pain and anger, and I don't know how to deal with these feelings." The leader intervenes by having the member lie down. He pushes on the client's abdomen and encourages her to scream, kick, shout, and release all the feelings that she's been keeping locked up inside of her. The client becomes pale, and her breathing becomes shallow and fast. She describes tingling sensations in her arms, a numbness, and a tight mouth, and she says that she is scared and cannot breathe. The leader encourages her to stay with it and get out all those pent-up feelings that are choking her up. At the same time others in the group seem frightened, and some are angry with the leader for pushing the client.

- Do you think a leader is competent to use body-oriented techniques after one weekend workshop? *no*
- Was this leader's behavior inappropriate, unethical, or both? *yes, both* If the leader had had a qualified supervisor at the session, would your answer be different?
- How can a group leader determine when he or she is adequately trained in the use of a technique? *training + supervision*

Unfinished Business

Another major issue pertaining to the use of group techniques relates to providing immediate help for any group member who shows extreme distress during or at the end of a group session, especially if techniques were used to elicit intense emotions. Although some "unfinished business" promotes growth, there is an ethical issue in the use of a technique that incites strong emotional reactions if the client is abandoned at the end of a session because time has run out. Leaders must take care to allow enough time to deal adequately with the reactions that were stimulated in a session. Techniques should not be introduced in a session when there is not enough time to work through the feelings that might result or in a setting where there is no privacy or where the physical setup would make it harmful to employ certain techniques.

Our position on the ethical use of techniques is that group leaders need to learn about potential adverse effects. One way for group leaders to learn is by taking part in groups themselves. By being a group member and first experiencing a range of techniques, a therapist can develop a healthy respect for using techniques appropriately to meet clients' needs. In our training workshops for group leaders we encourage spontaneity and inventiveness in the use of techniques, but we also stress the importance of striking a balance between creativity and irresponsible bravado. The reputation of group work has suffered from the actions of irresponsible practitioners, mostly those who use techniques randomly without a clear rationale. If the group leader has a sound academic background, has had extensive supervised group experience, has participated in his or her own therapy or personal-growth experience, and has a basic respect for clients, he or she is not likely to abuse techniques.

The Consultation and Referral Process

Group counselors need to be aware of their limitations in working with certain types of clients. The willingness to consult with other professionals demonstrates good faith on the practitioner's part. It is a good practice for leaders to explain to members their policies about consultation. When are they likely to consult? When they do consult, what measures do they take to protect confidentiality? Are they willing to have between-session consultations with group members? When and how might they refer? Here are some guidelines pertaining to the consultation and referral process:

- It is a good idea for members to bring the issues that were discussed during between-session consultations into the group, if appropriate.
- Group counselors should seek consultation and supervision when they are faced with ethical concerns or difficulties that interfere with their carrying out their leadership functions.
- Leaders should develop a sensitivity to making appropriate referrals.
- Leaders can learn about the resources within the community and help members make use of these resources.

As we discussed earlier, one way to protect against a malpractice suit is to demonstrate that consultation procedures were used in dealing with an ethical dilemma. If group leaders consult supervisors or other professionals, they are demonstrating good clinical practice, adhering to ethical guidelines, and minimizing their chances of malpractice.

Issues Concerning Termination

The termination phase of a group provides an opportunity for members to clarify the meaning of their experience, to consolidate the gains they've made, and to make decisions about the new behaviors they want to carry away from the group and apply to their everyday lives. The following professional issues and questions are involved in the termination of a group:

- What responsibilities do group leaders have for assisting participants to develop a conceptual framework that will make sense of, integrate, and consolidate what they've learned in their group?

- To what degree is it the leader's responsibility to ensure that members aren't left with excessive unfinished business at the end of the group?
- How can group leaders help participants translate what they've learned as a result of the group into their daily lives? Should leaders assume that this translation will occur automatically, or must they prepare members for generalizing their learning?

As a stage in the life of the group, termination has its own meaning and significance. Yalom (1995) observes that therapy group members tend to avoid the difficult work of terminating by ignoring or denying their concerns about it; therefore, it is the leader's task to keep them focused on the ending of their group. His view is that termination is an integral part of the therapeutic process, which if properly understood and managed can be a major force in promoting and maintaining change. In addition, therapists need to look at their own feelings about the termination process, for they sometimes unnecessarily delay a member's termination because of their own perfectionistic expectations or their lack of faith in their client's ability to function effectively without the group.

Follow-Up and Evaluation

How can leaders help members evaluate the effectiveness of their group experience? What kind of follow-up could be provided after the termination of any group? Throughout the life of a group, group leaders assist members in assessing their own progress and monitor their style of modeling. In this sense, evaluation is an ongoing process whereby members are taught how to determine if the group is helping them attain their personal goals.

Once a group has ended, follow-up group sessions provide an opportunity to evaluate both the process and the outcomes of a group experience. In our opinion, follow-up activities are useful to the members and the group counselor as well. Both short-term follow-up (after one month) and long-term follow-up (after three months to a year) can be invaluable measures of accountability. Because the members know that they will be coming together to evaluate their progress toward their goals, they are more willing to work actively at making changes. Participants can develop contracts during the final sessions involving actions to be taken between the termination and the follow-up session (or sessions). These sessions are valuable not only because they offer the leader an opportunity to evaluate the effectiveness of the group but also because they provide members with the opportunity to gain a more realistic assessment of the group's impact. Members have a chance to express and work through their reactions to the group experience, and they can report on the degree to which they have fulfilled their contracts since they left the group. They also have a chance to receive additional feedback and reinforcement from the other members. (For more discussion on termination issues, see M. Corey and Corey, 1997.)

Chapter Summary

Along with the growing popularity of group approaches to counseling and therapy comes a need for ethical and professional guidelines for those who lead groups. There are many types of groups, and there are many possible uses of groups in various settings. In this chapter we have discussed issues that are related to most groups. Some of these issues are: How does a leader's theoretical view of groups influence the way a group is structured? What are some key elements in recruiting, screening, selecting, and preparing group members? What ethical, professional, legal, and practical issues concerning confidentiality are involved in any type of group? To what degree should participants be prepared for a group before the group begins? What are some ethical issues in the selection and training of group leaders? In what ways can group techniques be used or abused? What responsibility do group leaders have in terms of follow-up and evaluation? With respect to these and other issues, we have stressed the importance of formulating your own views on ethical practice in leading groups.

Suggested Activities

1. Replicate the initial session of a group. Two students can volunteer to be co-leaders, and approximately ten other students can become group members. Assume that the group is a personal-growth group that will meet for a predetermined number of weeks. The co-leaders' job is to orient and prepare the members by describing the group's purpose, by giving an overview of group process concepts, and by talking about ground rules for effective group participation. If time allows, members can express any fears and expectations they have about being involved in the group, and they can also raise questions they would like to explore. This exercise is designed to give you practice in dealing with concerns that both group leaders and members often have at the beginning of a group.

2. Practice conducting screening interviews for potential group members. One person volunteers to conduct interviews, and another student can role-play a potential group member. Allow about ten minutes for the interview. Afterward, the prospective client can talk about what it was like to be interviewed, and the group leader can share his or her experience. This exercise can be done with the entire class watching, in small groups, or in dyads.

3. Suppose you're expected as part of your job to lead a group composed of people who are required to be part of the group and who really don't want to be there. How will the nature of the group affect your approach? What might you do differently with this group compared with a group of people who want the experience? This is a good situation to role-play in class, with several students playing the reluctant members while others practice dealing with them.

4. You're leading a counseling group with high school students on their campus. One day a member comes to the group obviously under the influence of drugs. He is incoherent and disruptive. How do you deal with him? What might you say or do? Discuss in class how you would deal with this situation, or demonstrate how you might respond by having a fellow student role-play the part of the adolescent.

5. Again, assume that you're leading a high school counseling group. An angry father who gave written permission for his son's participation comes to your office and demands to know what's going on in your group. He is convinced that his son's participation in the group is an invasion of family privacy. As a group leader, how would you deal with his anger? To make the situation more real and interesting, have someone role-play the father.

6. Selecting a good co-leader for a group is important, for not all matches of co-leaders are productive. Form dyads and negotiate with your partner to determine whether the two of you would be effective if you were to lead a group together. You might discuss matters such as potential power struggles, competitiveness, compatibility of views and philosophy, your differing styles and how they might complement or interfere with each other, and other issues that you think would have a bearing on your ability to work as a team.

7. Form a panel in class to explore the uses and abuses of group techniques. The panel can look at specific ways in which group techniques can be used to enhance learning, as well as ways in which they can be misused.

Some Concluding Ideas about Ethical Thinking

We've raised some of the ethical and professional issues that you are likely to encounter in your counseling practice. Instead of providing answers, we've tried to stimulate you to think about your own guidelines for professional practice and to initiate a process of thinking that you can apply to the many other issues you will face as a counselor.

If there is one fundamental question that can serve to tie together all the issues we've discussed, it is this: "Who has the right to counsel another person?" This question can be the focal point of your reflection on ethical and professional issues. It can also be the basis of your self-examination whenever you have concerns about clients. You can continue to ask yourself, "What makes me think that I can help anyone? What do I have to offer the people I'm counseling? Am I doing in my own life what I'm encouraging my clients to do?" If you answer these questions honestly, at times you may be troubled. You may feel that you have no right to counsel others, perhaps because your own life isn't always the model you would like it to be for your clients. Yet this occasional self-doubt is far less damaging, in our view, than a failure to examine these questions. Complacency will stifle your growth as a counselor; honest self-examination, although more difficult, will make you a more effective therapist.

We want to close our discussion by returning to the theme that has guided us throughout this book—namely, that developing a sense of professional and ethical responsibility is a task that is never really finished. There are no final or universal answers to many of the questions we have posed. For ourselves, we hope we never fall into the deadening trap of thinking that we "have it made" and no longer need to reexamine our assumptions and practices. We've found that the issues raised in this book have demanded periodic reflection and an openness to change. Thus, although we hope you've given careful thought to your own ethical and professional guidelines, we also hope you'll be willing to rethink your positions as you gain more experience.

Refer to the self-assessment at the end of Chapter 1, which surveys your attitudes about ethical and professional issues. We suggest that you cover your initial answers and retake the inventory now that you've come to the end of the course. Then you can compare your responses to see whether your thinking has changed. In addition, we suggest that you circle the ten questions that are most significant to you or that you're most interested in pursuing further. Bring these to class, and discuss them in small groups. Afterward, a survey can be conducted to get some idea of the issues that were most important to the students in your class.

As a way to review this book and the course you are completing, write down a few of the most important things you have learned. You might also write down some of the questions that this book and your course have left unanswered for you. After you've made your two lists, form small groups and exchange ideas with other students. This can be an excellent way to get some sense of the most crucial areas and topics that were explored by your fellow students and a fine way to wrap up the course.

Once the course is over, where can you go from here? How can you maintain the process of reflection that you've begun in this course? One excellent way to keep yourself alive intellectually is to develop a reading program. We suggest that you begin by selecting some of the books that we've listed in the References. We'd also like to suggest that you dip into this book again from time to time. It can be valuable to reread various chapters as you take different courses that deal with the issues we've considered. In addition, periodically reexamining your responses can stimulate your thinking and provide a measure of your professional and intellectual growth. We hope you'll find other ways to make this book meaningful as you continue your search for your own direction.

References

Adair, J. G., Dushenko, T. W., & Lindsay, R. C. L. (1985). Ethical regulations and their impact on research practice. *American Psychologist, 40*(1), 59–72.

*Ahia, C. E., & Martin, D. (1993). *The danger-to-self-or-others exception to confidentiality.* Alexandria, VA: American Counseling Association.

Akamatsu, T. J. (1988). Intimate relationships with former clients: National survey of attitudes and behavior among practitioners. *Professional Psychology: Research and Practice, 19*(4), 454–458.

*Albright, D. E., & Hazler, R. J. (1995). A right to die? Ethical dilemmas of euthanasia. *Counseling and Values, 39*(3), 177–189.

American Counseling Association (l995). *Code of ethics and standards of practice.* Alexandria, VA: Author.

American Association for Marriage and Family Therapy. (1991). *AAMFT code of ethics.* Washington, DC: Author.

American Association for Marriage and Family Therapy. (1994). *Membership requirements and applications.* Washington, DC: Author.

American Psychiatric Association. (1994). *Diagnostic and statistical manual of mental disorders* (4th ed.). Washington, DC: Author.

American Psychological Association. (1985). *White paper on duty to protect.* Washington, DC: Author.

American Psychological Association. (1995). *Ethical principles of psychologists and code of conduct.* Washington, DC: Author.

American Psychological Association. (1993). Guidelines for providers of psychological services to ethnic, linguistic, and culturally diverse populations. *American Psychologist, 48*(1), 45–48.

American School Counselor Association. (1992). *Ethical standards for school counselors.* Alexandria, VA: Author.

*Anderson, B. S. (1996). *The counselor and the law* (4th ed.). Alexandria, VA: American Counseling Association.

*Anderson, S. K., & Kitchener, K. S. (1996). Nonromantic, nonsexual posttherapy relationships between psychologists and former clients: An exploratory study of critical incidents. *Professional Psychology: Research and Practice, 27*(1), 59–66.

*Aponte, H. J. (1994). How personal can training get? *Journal of Marital and Family Therapy, 20*(1), 3–15.

*Arredondo, P., Toporek, R., Brown, S., Jones, J., Locke, D., Sanchez, J., & Stadler, H. A. (1996). Operationalization of multicultural counseling competencies. *Journal of Multicultural Counseling and Development, 24*(1), 42–78.

*Books and articles marked with an asterisk are suggested for further study.

*Arthur, G. L., & Swanson, C. D. (1993). *Confidentiality and privileged communication.* Alexandria, VA: American Counseling Association.

Association for Counselor Education and Supervision. (1993, Summer). Ethical guidelines for counseling supervisors. *Spectrum, 53*(4), 3–8.

Association for Specialists in Group Work. (1989). *Ethical guidelines for group counselors.* Alexandria, VA: Author.

Association for Specialists in Group Work. (1991, Fall). Professional standards for the training of group workers. *Together: Association for Specialists in Group Work, 20,* 9–14.

*Atkinson, D. R., Morten, G., & Sue, D. W. (Eds.). (1993). *Counseling American minorities: A cross-cultural perspective* (4th ed.). Dubuque, IA: Brown and Benchmark.

*Atkinson, D. R., Thompson, C. E., & Grant, S. K. (1993). A three-dimensional model for counseling racial/ethnic minorities. *The Counseling Psychologist, 21*(2), 257–277.

Attneave, C. L. (1985). Practical counseling with American Indian and Alaska native clients. In P. Pedersen (Ed.), *Handbook of cross-cultural counseling and therapy* (pp. 135–140). Westport, CT: Greenwood Press.

*Austad, C. S. (1996). *Is long-term psychotherapy unethical? Toward a social ethic in an era of managed care.* San Francisco, CA: Jossey-Bass.

Austin, K. M., Moline, M. M., & Williams, G. T. (1990). *Confronting malpractice: Legal and ethical dilemmas in psychotherapy.* Newbury Park, CA: Sage.

Avis, J. M. (1986). Feminist issues in family therapy. In F. P. Piercy, D. H. Sprenkle, & Associates (Eds.), *Family therapy sourcebook* (pp. 213–242). New York: Guilford Press.

*Axelson, J. A. (1993). *Counseling and development in a multicultural society* (2nd ed.). Pacific Grove, CA: Brooks/Cole.

Bartell, P. A., & Rubin, L. J. (1990). Dangerous liaisons: Sexual intimacies in supervision. *Professional Psychology: Research and Practice, 21*(6), 442–450.

*Bates, C. M., & Brodsky, A. M. (1989). *Sex in the therapy hour. A case of professional incest.* New York: Guilford Press.

Baumrind, D. (1985). Research using intentional deception. *American Psychologist, 40*(2), 165–174.

*Becvar, D. S. (1994). Can spiritual yearnings and therapeutic goals be melded? *Family Therapy News,* 13–14.

Bednar, R. L., Bednar, S. C., Lambert, M. J., & Waite, D. R. (1991). *Psychotherapy with high-risk clients: Legal and professional standards.* Pacific Grove, CA: Brooks/Cole.

*Bennett, B. E., Bricklin, P. M., & VandeCreek, L. (1994). Response to Lazarus's "How certain boundaries and ethics diminish therapeutic effectiveness." *Ethics and Behavior, 4*(3), 263–266.

*Bennett, B. E., Bryant, B. K., VandenBos, G. R., & Greenwood, A. (1990). *Professional liability and risk management.* Washington, DC: American Psychological Association.

*Benningfield, A. B. (1994). The impaired therapist. In G. W. Brock (Ed.), *American Association for Marriage and Family Therapy ethics casebook* (pp. 131–139). Washington, DC: American Association for Marriage and Family Therapy.

Bergin, A. E. (1991). Values and religious issues in psychotherapy and mental health. *American Psychology, 46*(4), 393–403.

Bergin, A. E., & Jensen, J. P. (1990). Religiosity of psychotherapists: A national survey. *Psychotherapy, 27*(1), 3–7.

Berman, A. L., & Jobes, D. A. (1991). *Adolescent suicide: Assessment and intervention.* Washington, DC: American Psychological Association.

Bernard, J. L., & Jara, C. S. (1986). The failure of clinical psychology graduate students to apply understood ethical principles. *Professional Psychology: Research and Practice, 17*(4), 313–315.

Bernard, J. M. (1994). Multicultural supervision: A reaction to Leong and Wagner, Cook, Priest, and Fukuyama. *Counselor Education and Supervision, 34*(2), 159–171.

*Bernard, J. M., & Goodyear, R. K. (1992). *Fundamentals of clinical supervision.* Boston, MA: Allyn & Bacon.

Bersoff, D. N. (1994). Explicit ambiguity: The 1992 ethics code as an oxymoron. *Professional Psychology: Research and Practice, 25*(4), 382–387.

*Bersoff, D. N. (1995). *Ethical conflicts in psychology.* Washington, DC: American Psychological Association.

Bersoff, D. N. (1996). The virtue of principle ethics. *The Counseling Psychologist, 24*(1), 86–91.

Bishop, D. R. (1992). Religious values as cross-cultural issues in counseling. *Counseling and Values, 36,* 179–191.

Blanck, R. R., & DeLeon, P. H. (1996). Managed care: Strongly conflicting views. *Professional Psychology: Research and Practice, 27*(4), 323–324.

Board of Behavioral Science Examiners. (1989, November/December). Sex should never be a part of therapy. *The California Therapist,* pp. 21–28.

Bonger, B. (1991). *The suicidal patient: Clinical and legal standards of care.* Washington, DC: American Psychological Association.

Borders, L. D. (1991). A systematic approach to peer group supervision. *Journal of Counseling and Development, 69*(3), 248–252.

Borys, D. S. (1994). Maintaining therapeutic boundaries: The motive is therapeutic effectiveness, not defensive practice. *Ethics and Behavior, 4*(3), 267–273.

Borys, D. S., & Pope, K. S. (1989). Dual relationships between therapist and client: A national study of psychologists, psychiatrists, and social workers. *Professional Psychology: Research and Practice, 20*(5), 283–293.

Bouhoutsos, J., Holroyd, J., Lerman, H., Forer, B. R., & Greenberg, M. (1983). Sexual intimacy between psychotherapists and patients. *Professional Psychology: Research and Practice, 14*(2), 185–196.

Bowen, N. H., Bahrick, A. S., & Enns, C. Z. (1991). A feminist response to empowerment. *Journal of Counseling and Development, 69*(3), 228.

Bowman, V. E., Hatley, L. D., Bowman, R. (1995). Faculty-student relationships: The dual role controversy. *Counselor Education and Supervision, 24*(3), 232–242.

*Brace, K. (1997). Ethical considerations in the development of counseling goals. In *The Hatherleigh guide to ethics in therapy* (pp. 17–35). New York: Hatherleigh Press.

Bradley, L. J. (1995). Certification and licensure issues. *Journal of Counseling and Development, 74*(2), 185–186.

Brammer, L. M. (1985). Nonformal support in cross-cultural counseling and therapy. In P. Pedersen (Ed.), *Handbook of cross-cultural counseling and therapy* (pp. 87–92). Westport, CT: Greenwood Press.

Brammer, L. M., Shostrom, E. L., & Abrego, P. J. (1989). *Therapeutic psychology: Fundamentals of counseling and psychotherapy* (5th ed.). Englewood Cliffs, NJ: Prentice-Hall.

Bray, J. H., Shepherd, J. N., & Hays, J. R. (1985). Legal and ethical issues in informed consent to psychotherapy. *American Journal of Family Therapy, 13*(2), 50–60.

*Brock, G. W. (Ed.). (1994). *American Association for Marriage and Family Therapy ethics casebook.* Washington, DC: American Association for Marriage and Family Therapy.

Brock, G. W., & Coufal, J. D. (1994). A national survey of the ethical practices and attitudes of marriage and family therapists. In G. W. Brock (Ed.), *American Association for Marriage and Family Therapy ethics casebook* (pp. 27–48). Washington, DC: American Association for Marriage and Family Therapy.

*Brodsky, A. M. (1986). The distressed psychologist: Sexual intimacies and exploitation. In R. R. Kilburg, P. E. Nathan, & R. W. Thoreson (Eds.), *Professionals in distress: Issues, syndromes, and solutions in psychology* (pp. 153–172). Washington, DC: American Psychological Association.

Brooks, D. K., & Gerstein, L. H. (1990). Counselor credentialing and interprofessional collaboration. *Journal of Counseling and Development, 68*(5), 477–484.

Broskowski, A. (1991). Current mental health care environments: Why managed care is necessary. *Professional Psychology: Research and Practice, 22*(1) 6–14.

Brown, D. (1993). Training consultants: A call to action. *Journal of Counseling and Development, 72*(2), 139–143.

Brown, L. S. (1990). Taking account of gender in the clinical assessment interview. *Professional Psychology: Research and Practice, 21*(1), 12–17.

Brown, L. S. (1994). Concrete boundaries and the problem of literal-mindedness: A response to Lazarus. *Ethics and Behavior, 4*(3), 275–281.

Brown, S. P., Parham, T. A., & Yonker, R. (1996). Influence of a cross-cultural training course on racial identity attitudes of white women and men: Preliminary perspective. *Journal of Counseling and Development, 74*(5), 510–516.

Buhrke, R. A., & Douce, L. A. (1991). Training issues for counseling psychologists in working with lesbian women and gay men. *The Counseling Psychologist, 19*(2), 216–234.

Burke, M. T., & Miranti, J. G. (1992). *Ethical and spiritual values in counseling.* Alexandria, VA: American Association for Counseling and Development.

*Burke, M. T., & Miranti, J. G. (Eds.). (1995). *Counseling: The spiritual dimension.* Alexandria, VA: American Counseling Association.

Burke, M. T., & Miranti, J. G. (1996). *Summit on spirituality.* Presentation at the Association for Counselor Education and Supervision, Portland, Oregon.

Calfee, B. E. (1996). Legally defensive client record keeping. *Directions in Mental Health Counseling, 6,* 1–10.

*Calfee, B. E. (1997). Lawsuit prevention techniques. In *The Hatherleigh guide to ethics in therapy* (pp. 109–125). New York: Hatherleigh Press.

California Association of Marriage and Family Therapists. (1995, November/December). Disciplinary Actions. *The California Therapist, 7*(6), 24–25.

California Association of Marriage and Family Therapists. (1996a, March/April). Disciplinary Actions. *The California Therapist, 8*(2), 18.

California Association of Marriage and Family Therapists (1996b, May/June). Disciplinary Actions. *The California Therapist, 8*(3), 25–26.

California Association of Marriage and Family Therapists. (1996c, July/August). Disciplinary Actions. *The California Therapist, 8*(4), 34.

California Department of Consumer Affairs. (undated). *Professional therapy never includes sex* (pamphlet). Sacramento: Author.

*Canter, M. B., Bennett, B. E., Jones, S. E., & Nagy, T. F. (1994). *Ethics for psychologists: A commentary on the APA ethics code.* Washington, DC: American Psychological Association.

Cayleff, S. E. (1986). Ethical issues in counseling gender, race, and culturally distinct groups. *Journal of Counseling and Development, 64*(5), 345–347.

Chauvin, J. C., & Remley, T. P. (1996). Responding to allegations of unethical conduct. *Journal of Counseling and Development, 74*(6), 563–568.

Cohen, E. D. (1997). Ethical standards in counseling sexually active clients with HIV. In *The Hatherleigh guide to ethics in therapy* (pp. 211–233). New York: Hatherleigh Press.

Coleman, H. L. K. (1996). Portfolio assessment of multicultural counseling competency. *The Counseling Psychologist, 24*(2), 216–229.

*Coleman, E., & Schaefer, S. (1986). Boundaries of sex and intimacy between client and counselor. *Journal of Counseling and Development, 64*(5), 341–344.

Committee on Women in Psychology, American Psychological Association. (1989). If sex enters into the psychotherapy relationship. *Professional Psychology: Research and Practice, 20*(2), 112–115.

Conyne, R. K. (1996). The Association for Specialists in Group Work Training Standards: Some Considerations and Suggestions for Training. *Journal for Specialists in Group Work, 21*(3), 155–162.

Conyne, R. K., Wilson, F. R., Kline, W. B., Morran, D. K., & Ward, D. E. (1993). Training group workers: Implications of the new ASGW training standards for training and practice. *Journal for Specialists in Group Work, 18*(1), 11–23.

*Cook, D. A. (1994). Racial identity in supervision. *Counselor Education and Supervision, 34*(2), 132–141.

Corey, G. (1995). *Theory and practice of group counseling* (4th ed.) and *Manual.* Pacific Grove, CA: Brooks/Cole.

Corey, G. (1996a). *Case approach to counseling and psychotherapy* (4th ed.). Pacific Grove, CA: Brooks/Cole.

Corey, G. (1996b). *Theory and practice of counseling and psychotherapy* (4th ed.) and *Manual.* Pacific Grove, CA: Brooks/Cole.

Corey, G., Corey, C., & Corey, H. (1997). *Living and learning.* Belmont, CA: Wadsworth.

Corey, G., & Corey, M. (1997). *I never knew I had a choice* (6th ed.). Pacific Grove, CA: Brooks/Cole.

Corey, G., Corey, M., Callanan, P., & Russell, J. M. (1992). *Group techniques* (2nd ed.). Pacific Grove, CA: Brooks/Cole.

Corey, G., & Herlihy, B. (1993). Dual relationships: Associated risks and potential benefits. *Ethical Issues in Professional Counseling, 1*(1), 3–11.

Corey, G., & Herlihy, B. (1996a). Client rights and informed consent. In B. Herlihy & G. Corey (Eds.), *ACA ethical standards casebook* (5th ed.) (pp. 181–183). Alexandria, VA: American Counseling Association.

Corey, G., & Herlihy, B. (1996b). Competence. In B. Herlihy & G. Corey (Eds.), *ACA ethical standards casebook* (5th ed.) (pp. 217–220). Alexandria, VA: American Counseling Association.

Corey, G., & Herlihy, B. (1996c). Counselor training and supervision. In B. Herlihy & G. Corey (Eds.), *ACA ethical standards casebook* (5th ed.) (pp. 275–278). Alexandria, VA: American Counseling Association.

Corey, G., & Herlihy, B. (1996b). Dual/multiple relationships: Toward a consensus of thinking. In *The Hatherleigh guide to ethics in therapy* (pp. 183–194). New York: Hatherleigh Press.

*Corey, G., Williams, G. T., & Moline, M. E. (1995). Ethical and legal issues in group counseling. *Ethics and Behavior, 5*(2), 161–183.

Corey, M., & Corey, G. (1993). Difficult group members—difficult group leaders. *New York State Association for Counseling and Development, 8*(2), 9–24.

Corey, M., & Corey, G. (1997). *Groups: Process and practice* (5th ed.). Pacific Grove, CA: Brooks/Cole.

Cormier, L. S., & Bernard, J. M. (1982). Ethical and legal responsibilities of clinical supervisors. *Personnel and Guidance Journal, 60*(8), 486–490.

Corsini, R., & Wedding, D. (1995). *Current Psychotherapies* (5th ed.). Itasca, IL: F. E. Peacock.

*Costa, L., & Altekruse, M. (1994). Duty-to-warn guidelines for mental health counselors. *Journal of Counseling and Development, 72*(4), 346–350.

Council for Accreditation of Counseling and Related Educational Programs. (1994). *CACREP accreditation standards and procedures manual.* Alexandria, VA: Author.

Crawford, R. L. (1994). *Avoiding counselor malpractice.* Alexandria, VA: American Counseling Association.

Cummings, N. A. (1990). The credentialing of professional psychologists and its implication for the other mental health disciplines. *Journal of Counseling and Development, 68*(5), 485–490.

Cummings, N. A. (1995). Impact of managed care on employment and training: A primer for survival. *Professional Psychology: Research and Practice, 26*(1), 10–15.

Custer, G. (1994, November) Can universities be liable for incompetent grads? *APA Monitor, 25*(11), 7.

D'Andrea, M., & Arredondo, P. (1996, December). ACES formally endorses multicultural counseling competencies. *Counseling Today,* p. 29.

Das, A. K. (1995). Rethinking multicultural counseling: Implications for counselor education. *Journal of Counseling and Development, 74*(1), 45–52.

Davis, J. W. (1981). Counselor licensure: Overskill? *Personnel and Guidance Journal, 60*(2), 83–85.

Dean, L. A., & Meadows, M. E. (1995). College counseling: Union and intersection. *Journal of Counseling and Development, 74*(2) 139–142.

Department of Consumer Affairs. (1990). *Professional therapy never includes sex.* Sacramento, CA: Author.

Deutsch, C. J. (1984). Self-reported sources of stress among psychotherapists. *Professional Psychology: Research and Practice, 15*(6), 833–845.

Devore, W. (1985). Developing ethnic sensitivity for the counseling process: A social-work perspective. In P. Pedersen (Ed.), *Handbook of cross-cultural counseling and therapy* (pp. 93–98). Westport, CT: Greenwood Press.

Dinkmeyer, D. (1991). Mental health counseling: A psychoeducational approach. *Journal of Mental Health Counseling, 13*(1), 37–42.

Donigian, J. (1991). Dual relationships: An ethical issue. *Together, 19*(2), 6–7.

Dougherty, A. M. (1992). Ethical issues in consultation. *Elementary School Guidance and Counseling, 26,* 214–220.

Dougherty, A. M. (1995). *Consultation: Practice and perspectives in school and community settings* (2nd ed.). Pacific Grove, CA: Brooks/Cole.

Dye, H. A. (1996). Afterword: Confirmations, contrasts, and conjecture. *Journal for Specialists in Group Work, 21*(3), 178–180.

Eberlein, L. (1987). Introducing ethics to beginning psychologists: A problem-solving approach. *Professional Psychology: Research and Practice, 18*(4), 353–359.

Egan, G. (1994). *The skilled helper: A problem-management approach to helping* (5th ed.). Pacific Grove, CA: Brooks/Cole.

Emerson, S., & Markos, P. A. (1996). Signs and symptoms of the impaired counselor. *Journal of Humanistic Education and Development, 34,* 108–117.

Engels, D. W., Minor, C. W., Sampson, J. P., & Splete, H. H. (1995). Career counseling specialty: History, development, and prospect. *Journal of Counseling and Development, 74*(2), 134–138.

Enns, C. Z. (1993). Twenty years of feminist counseling and therapy. *The Counseling Psychologist, 21*(1), 3–87.

Erickson, S. H. (1993). Ethics and confidentiality in AIDS counseling: A professional dilemma. *Journal of Mental Health Counseling, 15*(2), 118–131.

Essandoh, P. K. (1996). Multicultural counseling as the "fourth force." *The Counseling Psychologist, 24*(1), 126–137.

Everett, C. A. (1990). The field of marital and family therapy. *Journal of Counseling and Development, 68*(5), 498–502.

Everstine, L., Everstine, D. S., Heymann, G. M., True, R. H., Frey, D. H., Johnson, H. G., & Seiden, R. H. (1980). Privacy and confidentiality in psychotherapy. *American Psychologist, 35*(9), 828–840.

Falk, P. J. (1989). Lesbian mothers: Psychosocial assumptions in family law. *American Psychologist, 44*(6), 941–947.

Farber, B. A. (1983a). Psychotherapists' perceptions of stressful patient behavior. *Professional Psychology: Research and Practice, 14*(5), 697–705.

Farber, B. A. (1983b). *Stress and burnout in the human service professions.* New York: Pergamon Press.

Farrugia, D. (1993). Exploring the counselor's role in "right to die" decisions. *Counseling and Values, 37*(2), 61–70.

Fassinger, R. E. (1991a). Counseling lesbian women and gay men. *The Counseling Psychologist, 19*(2), 156.

Fassinger, R. E. (1991b). The hidden minority: Issues and challenges in working with lesbian women and gay men. *The Counseling Psychologist, 19*(2), 157–176.

Favier, C. M., Eisengart, S., & Colonna, R. (1995). *The counselor intern's handbook.* Pacific Grove, CA: Brooks/Cole.

Favier, C. M., & O'Brien, E. M. (1993). Assessment of religious beliefs form. *Counseling and Values, 37*(3), 176–178.

Fogel, M. S. (1990, May/June). Supervisors should not dominate but doubt, reflect, innovate. *Family Therapy News,* pp. 5–6.

Foos, J. A., Ottens, A. J., & Hill, L. K. (1991). Managed mental health: A primer for counselors. *Journal of Counseling and Development, 69*(4), 332–336.

Forester-Miller, H. (1997). Rural communities: Can dual relationships be avoided? In B. Herlihy & G. Corey (Eds.), *Boundary issues in counseling: Multiple roles and responsibilities* (pp. 99–100). Alexandria, VA: American Counseling Association.

*Forester-Miller, H., & Davis, T. E. (1995). *A practitioner's guide to ethical decision making.* Alexandria, VA: American Counseling Association.

Forester-Miller, H., & Duncan, J. A. (1990). The ethics of dual relationships in the training of group counselors. *Journal for Specialists in Group Work, 15*(2), 88–93.

Foster, S. (1996, January). The consequences of violating the "forbidden zone." *Counseling Today,* p. 24.

Fraser, J. S. (1996). All that glitters is not always gold: Medical offset effects and managed behavioral health care. *Professional Psychology: Research and Practice, 27*(4), 335–344.

Fremon, C. (1991, January 27). Love and death. *Los Angeles Times Magazine,* pp. 17–35.

Fretz, B. R., & Mills, D. H. (1980). *Licensing and certification of psychologists and counselors.* San Francisco: Jossey-Bass.

*Fujimura, L. E., Weis, D. M., & Cochran, J. R. (1985). Suicide: Dynamics and implications for counseling. *Journal of Counseling and Development, 63*(10), 612–615.

Fukuyama, M. A. (1990). Taking a universal approach to multicultural counseling. *Counselor Education and Supervision, 30*(1), 6–17.

*Fukuyama, M. A. (1994). Critical incidents in multicultural counseling: A phenomenological approach to supervision research. *Counselor Education and Supervision, 34*(2), 142–151.

*Fulero, S. M. (1988). *Tarasoff.* 10 years later. *Professional Psychology: Research and Practice, 19*(2), 184–190.

Gabbard, G. (1994). Teetering on the precipice: A commentary on Lazarus's "How certain boundaries and ethics diminish therapeutic effectiveness." *Ethics and Behavior, 4*(3), 283–286.

Gabbard, G. O. (1995, April). What are boundaries in psychotherapy? *The Menninger Letter, 3*(4), 1–2.

Gabbard, G. O. (Ed.). (1989). *Sexual exploitation in professional relationships.* Washington, DC: American Psychiatric Association.

Gallessich, J. (1982). *The profession and practice of consultation.* San Francisco: Jossey-Bass.

Garcia, A. (1990). An examination of the social work profession's efforts to achieve legal regulation. *Journal of Counseling and Development, 68*(5), 491–497.

Gelso, C. J., & Carter, J. A. (1985). The relationship in counseling and psychotherapy: Components, consequences, and theoretical antecedents. *The Counseling Psychologist, 13*(2), 155–243.

*Genia, V. (1994). Secular psychotherapists and religious clients: Professional considerations and recommendations. *Journal of Counseling and Development, 72*(4), 395–398.

Gerstein, L. H., & Brooks, D. K. (1990). Introduction for a special feature. The helping professions' challenge: Credentialing and interdisciplinary collaboration. *Journal of Counseling and Development, 68*(5), 475–476.

Getz, J. G., & Protinsky, H. O. (1994). Training marriage and family counselors: A family-of-origin approach. *Counselor Education and Supervision, 33*(3), 183–200.

*Gill-Wigal, J., & Heaton, J. A. (1996). Managing sexual attraction in the therapeutic relationship. *Directions in Mental Health Counseling, 6*(8), 4–15.

Gilliland, B. E., & James, R. K. (1997). *Crisis intervention strategies* (3rd ed.). Pacific Grove, CA: Brooks/Cole.

Glaser, R. D., & Thorpe, J. S. (1986). Unethical intimacy: A survey of sexual contact and advances between psychology educators and female graduate students. *American Psychologist, 41*(1), 42–51.

Glosoff, H. L., Corey, G., & Herlihy, B. (1996). Dual relationships. In B. Herlihy & G. Corey, (Eds.). *ACA ethical standards casebook* (5th ed.) (pp. 251–257). Alexandria, VA: American Counseling Association.

Goldberg, J. R. (1994). Spirituality, religion and secular values: What role in psychotherapy? *Family Therapy Newsletter*, pp. 1–17.

Goldenberg, I., & Goldenberg, H. (1996a). *Family therapy: An overview* (4th. ed.). Pacific Grove, CA: Brooks/Cole.

Goldenberg, I., & Goldenberg, H. (1996b). *My self in family context: A personal journal.* Pacific Grove, CA: Brooks/Cole.

Good, G. E., Gilbert, L. A., & Scher, M. (1990). Gender aware therapy: A synthesis of feminist therapy and knowledge about gender. *Journal of Counseling and Development, 68*(4), 376–380.

*Goodman, R. W., & Carpenter-White, A. (1996). The family autobiography assignment: Some ethical considerations. *Counselor Education and Supervision, 35*(3), 230–238.

Gottlieb, M. C. (1990). Accusations of sexual misconduct: Assisting in the complaint process. *Professional Psychology: Research and Practice, 21*(6), 455–461.

Gottlieb, M. C. (1994). Ethical decision making, boundaries, and treatment effectiveness: A reprise. *Ethics and Behavior, 4*(3), 287–293.

Gray, L. A., & Harding, A. I. (1988). Confidentiality limits with clients who have the AIDS virus. *Journal of Counseling and Development, 66*(5), 219–223.

Green, S. L., & Hansen, J. C. (1986). Ethical dilemmas in family therapy. *Journal of Marital and Family Therapy, 12*(3), 225–230.

Green, S. L., & Hansen, J. C. (1989). Ethical dilemmas faced by family therapists. *Journal of Marital and Family Therapy, 15*(2), 149–158.

Greenhut, M. (1991, May/June). Professional networking: The downward spiral to "health." *The California Therapist*, pp. 47–48.

*Grimm, D. W. (1994). Therapist spiritual and religious values in psychotherapy. *Counseling and Values, 38*(3), 154–164.

Gumaer, J., & Forrest, A. (1995). Avoiding conflict in group therapy: Ethical and legal issues in group training and practice. *Directions in Mental Health Counseling, 5*(5), 4–15.

Gutheil, T G. (1989, November/December). Patient-therapist sexual relations. *The California Therapist*, pp. 29–31.

Gutheil, T. G. (1994). Discussion of Lazarus's "How certain boundaries and ethics diminish therapeutic effectiveness." *Ethics and Behavior, 4*(3), 295–298.

*Gutheil, T. G., & Gabbard, G. O. (1993). The concept of boundaries in clinical practice: Theoretical and risk-management dimensions. *American Journal of Psychiatry, 150*(2), 188–196.

*Guy, J. D. (1987). *The personal life of the psychotherapists.* New York: Wiley.

Guy, J. D., & Liaboe, G. P. (1986a). The impact of conducting psychotherapy upon the interpersonal relationships of the psychotherapist. *Professional Psychology: Research and Practice, 17*(2), 111–114.

Guy, J. D., & Liaboe, G. P. (1986b). Personal therapy for the experienced psychotherapist: A discussion of its usefulness and utilization. *The Clinical Psychologist, 39*(1), 20–23.

Guy, J. D., Poelstra, P. L., & Stark, M. J. (1989). Personal distress and therapeutic effectiveness: National survey of psychologists practicing psychotherapy. *Professional Psychology: Research and Practice, 20*(1), 48–50.

*Guy, J. D., Stark, M. J., & Poelstra, P. L. (1988). Personal therapy for psychotherapists before and after entering professional practice. *Professional Psychology: Research and Practice, 19*(4), 474–476.

Haas, L. J., & Alexander, J. R. (1981). *Ethical and legal issues in family therapy.* Paper presented at the meeting of the American Psychological Association, Los Angeles.

Haas, L. J., & Cummings, N. A. (1991). Managed outpatient mental health plans: Clinical, ethical, and practical guidelines for participation. *Professional Psychology: Research and Practice, 22*(1), 45–51.

Hall, L. A. (1996). Bartering: A payment methodology whose time has come again or an unethical practice? *Family Therapy News, 27*(4), 7, 19.

Hamann, E. E. (1994). Clinicians and diagnosis: Ethical concerns and clinical competence. *Journal of Counseling and Development, 72*(3), 259–260.

*Hammel, G. A., Olkin, R., & Taube, D. O. (1996). Student-educator sex in clinical and counseling psychology doctoral training. *Professional Psychology: Research and Practice, 27*(1), 93–97.

Handelsman, M. M. (1986a). Ethics training at the master's level: A national survey. *Professional Psychology: Research and Practice, 17*(1), 24–26.

Handelsman, M. M. (1986b). Problems with ethics training by "osmosis." *Professional Psychology: Research and Practice, 17*(4), 371–372.

Handelsman, M. M. (1990). Do written consent forms influence clients' first impressions of therapists? *Professional Psychology: Research and Practice, 21*(6), 451–454.

Handelsman, M. M., & Galvin, M. D. (1988). Facilitating informed consent for outpatient psychotherapy: A suggested written format. *Professional Psychology: Research and Practice, 19*(2), 223–225.

Handelsman, M. M., Kemper, M. B., Kesson-Craig, P., McLain, J., & Johnsrud, C. (1986). Use, content, and readability of written informed consent forms for treatment. *Professional Psychology: Research and Practice, 17*(6), 514–518.

Hanna, S. M., & Brown, J. H. (1995). *The practice of family therapy: Key elements across models.* Pacific Grove, CA: Brooks/Cole.

Hare-Mustin, R. T. (1980). Family therapy may be dangerous to your health. *Professional Psychology, 11*(6), 935–938.

Harrar, W. R., VandeCreek, L., & Knapp, S. (1990). Ethical and legal aspects of clinical supervision. *Professional Psychology: Research and Practice, 21*(1), 37–41.

Hatherleigh guide to ethics in therapy. (1997). New York: Hatherleigh Press.

Hedges, L. E. (1993, July/August). In praise of dual relationships. Part II: Essential dual relatedness in developmental psychotherapy. *The California Therapist,* pp. 42–46.

Heiden, J. M. (1993). Preview-prevent: A training strategy to prevent counselor-client sexual relationships. *Counselor Education and Supervision, 33*(1), 53–60.

Hendrix, D. H. (1991). Ethics and intrafamily confidentiality in counseling with children. *Journal of Mental Health Counseling, 13*(3), 323–333.

Henkin, W. A. (1985). Toward counseling the Japanese in America: A cross-cultural primer. *Journal of Counseling and Development, 63*(8), 500–503.

Herlihy, B. (1996). When a colleague is impaired: The individual counselor's response. *Journal of Humanistic Education and Development, 34,* 118–127.

Herlihy, B., & Corey, G. (1992). *Dual relationships in counseling.* Alexandria, VA: American Counseling Association.

Herlihy, B., & Corey, G. (1994). Codes of ethics as catalysts for improving practice. *Ethical Issues in Professional Counseling, 2*(3), 2–12.

*Herlihy, B., & Corey, G. (1996a). *ACA Ethical standards casebook* (5th ed.). Alexandria, VA: American Counseling Association.

Herlihy, B., & Corey, G. (1996b). Confidentiality. In B. Herlihy & G. Corey (Eds.), *ACA ethical standards casebook* (5th ed.) (pp. 205–209). Alexandria, VA: American Counseling Association.

Herlihy, B., & Corey, G. (1996c). Working with multiple clients. In B. Herlihy & G. Corey (Eds.), *ACA ethical standards casebook* (5th ed.) (pp. 229–233). Alexandria, VA: American Counseling Association.

*Herlihy, B., & Corey, G. (1997). *Boundary issues in counseling: Multiple roles and responsibilities*. Alexandria, VA: American Counseling Association.

*Herlihy, B., & Remley, T. P. (1995). Unified ethical standards: A challenge for professionalism. *Journal of Counseling and Development, 74*(2), 130–133.

Herr, E. L. (1991). Challenges to mental health counselors in a dynamic society: Macrostrategies in the profession. *Journal of Mental Health Counseling, 13*(1), 6–20.

Hersch, L. (1995). Adapting to health care reform and managed care: Three strategies for survival and growth. *Professional Psychology: Research and Practice, 26*(1), 16–26.

*Hill, M., Glaser, K., & Harden, J. (1995). A feminist model for ethical decision making. In E. J. Rave & C. C. Larsen (Eds.), *Ethical decision making in therapy: Feminist perspectives* (pp. 18–37). New York: Guilford Press.

Hinnefeld, B., & Towers, K. D. (1996). Supreme Court ruling upholds psychotherapist-patient privilege. *Practitioner Focus, 9*(2), 4, 18.

Ho, D. Y. E. (1985). Cultural values and professional issues in clinical psychology: Implications from the Hong Kong experience. *American Psychologist, 40*(11), 1212–1218.

Hoffman, M. A. (1991a). Counseling the HIV-infected client: A psychosocial model for assessment and intervention. *The Counseling Psychologist, 19*(4), 467–542.

Hoffman, M. A. (1991b). Training mental health counselors for the AIDS crisis. *Journal of Mental Health Counseling, 13*(2), 264–269.

Holroyd, J., & Bouhoutsos, J. C. (1985). Sources of bias in reporting effects of sexual contact with patients. *Professional Psychology: Research and Practice, 16*(5), 701–709.

Holroyd, J. C., & Brodsky, A. (1980). Does touching patients lead to sexual intercourse? *Professional Psychology, 11*(5), 807–811.

Holub, E. A., & Lee, S. S. (1990). Therapists' use of nonerotic physical contact: Ethical concerns. *Professional Psychology: Research and Practice, 21*(2), 115–117.

Holzman, L. A., Searight, H. R., & Hughes, H. M. (1996). Clinical psychology graduate students and personal psychotherapy: Results of an exploratory study. *Professional Psychology: Research and Practice, 27*(1), 98–101.

*Homan, M. (1994). *Promoting community change: Making it happen in the real world*. Pacific Grove, CA: Brooks/Cole.

Hosie, T. W. (1995). Counseling specialties: A case of basic preparation rather than advanced specialization. *Journal of Counseling and Development, 74*(2), 177–180.

*Hotelling, K. (1988). Ethical, legal, and administrative options to address sexual relationships between counselor and client. *Journal of Counseling and Development, 67*(4), 233–237.

Hotelling, K. (1991). Sexual harassment: A problem shielded by silence. *Journal of Counseling and Development, 69*(6), 497–501.

Howard, S. (1991). Organizational resources for addressing sexual harassment. *Journal of Counseling and Development, 69*(6), 507–511.

Huber, C. H. (1994). *Ethical, legal, and professional issues in the practice of marriage and family therapy* (2nd ed.). New York: Macmillan.

*Huey, W. (1996). Counseling minor clients. In B. Herlihy & G. Corey (Eds.), *ACA ethical standards casebook* (5th ed.) (pp. 241–245). Alexandria, VA: American Counseling Association.

Humphrey, F. (1994). Dual relations. In G. W. Brock (Ed.), *American Association for Marriage and Family Therapy ethics casebook* (pp. 115–124). Washington, DC: American Association for Marriage and Family Therapy.

*Hwang, P. O. (1995). *Other-esteem: A creative response to a society obsessed with promoting the self*. San Diego, CA: Black Forrest Press.

Ibrahim, F. A. (1986). *Cultural encapsulation of the APA ethical principles.* Unpublished manuscript, University of Connecticut, Storrs.

Ibrahim, F. A. (1996). A multicultural perspective on principle and virtue ethics. *The Counseling Psychologist, 24*(1), 78–85.

*Ibrahim, E. A., & Arredondo, R M. (1990). Ethical issues in multicultural counseling. In B. Herlihy & L. B. Golden (Eds.), *AACD ethical standards casebook* (4th ed.) (pp. 137–145). Alexandria, VA: American Association for Counseling and Development.

Imber, S. D., Glanz, L. M., Elkin, I., Sotsky, S. M., Boyer, J. L., & Leber, W. R. (1986). Ethical issues in psychotherapy research: Problems in a collaborative clinical trials study. *American Psychologist, 41*(2), 137–146.

*International Association for Marriage and Family Counselors. (1993). *Ethical code for International Association for Marriage and Family Counselors.* Alexandria, VA: Author.

*Itai, G., & McRae, C. (1994). Counseling older Japanese American clients: An overview and observations. *Journal of Counseling and Development, 72*(4), 373–377.

Ivey, A. E. (1990). *Developmental strategies for helpers: Individual, family, and network interventions.* Pacific Grove, CA: Brooks/Cole.

Ivey, A. E., & Rigazio-DiGilio, S. A. (1991). Toward a developmental practice of mental health counseling. Strategies for training, practice, and political unity. *Journal of Mental Health Counseling, 13*(1), 21–36.

Ivey, A. E., Ivey, M. B., & Simek-Morgan, L. (1997). *Counseling and psychotherapy: A multicultural perspective* (4th ed.). Boston: Allyn and Bacon.

Jackson, D. N., & Hayes, D. H. (1993). Multicultural issues in consultation. *Journal of Counseling and Development, 72*(2), 144–147.

*Jensen, J. P., & Bergin, A. E. (1988). Mental health values of professional therapists: A national interdisciplinary survey. *Professional Psychology: Research and Practice, 19*(3), 290–297.

Jones, C. L., & Higuchi, A. (1996). Landmark New Jersey lawsuit challenges 'no cause' termination. *Practitioner Focus, 9*(2), 1, 13.

Jones, E. E. (1985). Psychotherapy and counseling with black clients. In P. Pedersen (Ed.), *Handbook of cross-cultural counseling and therapy.* Westport, CT: Greenwood Press.

Jones, L. (1996). *HIV/AIDS: What to do about it.* Pacific Grove, CA: Brooks/Cole.

Jordan, A. E., & Meara, N. M. (1990). Ethics and the professional practice of psychologists: The role of virtues and principles. *Professional Psychology: Research and Practice, 21*(2), 107–114.

Jourard, S. (1968). *Disclosing man to himself.* Princeton, NJ: Van Nostrand.

Jourard, S. (1971). *The transparent self* (rev. ed.). New York: Van Nostrand.

*Kain, C. D. (1996). *Positive HIV affirmative counseling.* Alexandria, VA: American Counseling Association.

*Kaiser, T. L. (1997). *Supervisory relationships: Exploring the human element.* Pacific Grove, CA: Brooks/Cole.

Kalichman, S. C., & Craig, M. E. (1991). Professional psychologists' decisions to report suspected child abuse: Clinician and situation influences. *Professional Psychology: Research and Practice, 22*(1), 84–89.

Karon, B. P. (1995). Provision of psychotherapy under managed health care: A growing crisis and national nightmare. *Professional Psychology: Research and Practice, 26*(1), 5–9.

*Keith-Spiegel, P., & Koocher, G. (1985). *Ethics in psychology: Professional standards and cases.* New York: Random House.

Kelly, E. W. (1994). The role of religion and spirituality in counselor education: A national survey. *Counselor Education and Supervision, 33*(4), 227–237.

Kelly, E. W. (1995a). Counselor values: A national survey. *Journal of Counseling and Development, 73*(6), 648–653.

*Kelly, E. W. (1995b). *Spirituality and religion in counseling and psychotherapy.* Alexandria, VA: American Counseling Association.

*Kiser, J. D. (1996). Counselors and the legalization of physician-assisted suicide. *Counseling and Values, 40*(2), 127–131.

Kiser, J. D., & Korpi, K. N. (1996). The need for ethical reasoning regarding physician-assisted suicide. *Counseling Today,* p. 28.

Kitchener, K. S. (1984). Intuition, critical evaluation and ethical principles: The foundation for ethical decisions in counseling psychology. *The Counseling Psychologist, 12*(3), 43–55.

*Kitchener, K. S. (1996). There is more to ethics than principles. *The Counseling Psychologist, 24*(1), 92–97.

Kitchener, K. S., & Harding, S. S. (1990). Dual role relationships. In B. Herlihy & L. B. Golden (Eds.), *AACD ethical standards casebook* (4th ed.) (pp. 146–154). Alexandria, VA: American Association for Counseling and Development.

Knapp, S., & VandeCreek, L. (1982). *Tarasoff.* Five years later. *Professional Psychology, 13*(4), 511–516.

Knapp, S., & VandeCreek, L. (1990). Application of the duty to protect to HIV-positive patients. *Professional Psychology: Research and Practice, 21*(3), 161–166.

Kottler, J. A. (1993). *On being a therapist* (rev. ed.). San Francisco: Jossey-Bass.

*Kottler, J. A. (Ed.). (1997). *Finding your way as a counselor.* Alexandria, VA: American Counseling Association.

Kramer, S. A. (1990). *Positive endings in psychotherapy: Bringing meaningful closure to therapeutic relationships.* San Francisco: Jossey-Bass.

*Kurpius, S. E. R. (1997). Current ethical issues in the practice of psychology. In *The Hatherleigh guide to ethics in therapy* (pp. 1–16). New York: Hatherleigh Press.

Lamb, D. H., Clark, C., Drumheller, P., Frizzell, K., & Surrey, L. (1989). Applying *Tarasoff* to AIDS-related psychotherapy issues. *Professional Psychology: Research and Practice, 20*(1), 37–43.

Lambert, M. J., & Cattani-Thompson, K. (1996). Current findings regarding the effectiveness of counseling: Implications for practice. *Journal of Counseling and Development, 74*(6), 601–608.

Lanning, W. (1997). Ethical codes and responsible decision-making. In J. A. Kottler (Ed.), *Finding your way as a counselor* (pp. 111–113). Alexandria, VA: American Counseling Association.

Laughran, W., & Bakken, G. M. (1984). The psychotherapist's responsibility toward third parties under current California law. *Western State University Law Review, 12*(1), 1–33.

Lazarus, A. A. (1990). Can psychotherapists transcend the shackles of their training and superstitions? *Journal of Clinical Psychology, 46*(3), 351–358.

*Lazarus, A. A. (1994a). How certain boundaries and ethics diminish therapeutic effectiveness. *Ethics and Behavior, 4*(3), 255–261.

*Lazarus, A. A. (1994b). The illusion of the therapist's power and the patient's fragility: My rejoinder. *Ethics and Behavior, 4*(3), 299–306.

Leahy, M. J., & Szymanski, E. M. (1995). Rehabilitation counseling: Evolution and current status. *Journal of Counseling and Development, 74*(2) 163–166.

*Lee, C. C. (1997a). Cultural dynamics: Their importance in culturally responsive counseling. In C. C. Lee (Ed.), *Multicultural issues in counseling: New approaches to diversity* (pp. 15–30). Alexandria, VA: American Counseling Association.

*Lee, C. C. (1997b). New approaches to diversity: Implications for professional counselor training and research. In C. C. Lee (Ed.), *Multicultural issues in counseling: New approaches to diversity* (pp. 353–360). Alexandria, VA: American Counseling Association.

*Lee, C. C. (1997c). The promise and pitfalls of multicultural counseling. In C. C. Lee (Ed.), *Multicultural issues in counseling: New approachs to diversity* (pp. 3–13). Alexandria, VA: American Counseling Association.

*Lee, C. C., & Kurilla, V. (1997). Ethics and multiculturalism: The challenge of diversity. In *The Hatherleigh guide to ethics in therapy* (pp. 235–248). New York: Hatherleigh Press.

Lee, C. C., & Richardson, B. L. (1991a). *Multicultural issues in counseling. New approaches to diversity.* Alexandria, VA: American Association for Counseling and Development.

Lee, C. C., & Richardson, B. L. (1991b). Problems and pitfalls of multicultural counseling. In C. C. Lee & B. L. Richardson (Eds.), *Multicultural issues in counseling: New approaches to diversity* (pp. 3–9). Alexandria, VA: American Association for Counseling and Development.

Leong, F. T. L., & Wagner, N. S. (1994). Cross-cultural counseling supervision: What do we know? What do we need to know? *Counselor Education and Supervision, 34*(2), 117–131.

Lewis, G. J., Greenburg, S. L., & Hatch, D. B. (1988). Peer consultation groups for psychologists in private practice: A national survey. *Professional Psychology: Research and Practice, 19*(1), 81–86.

Lewis, I. A., & Lewis, M. D. (1989). *Community counseling.* Pacific Grove, CA: Brooks/Cole.

Lindsey, R. I. (1984). Informed consent and deception in psychotherapy research: An ethical analysis. *The Counseling Psychologist, 12*(3), 79–86.

Lien, C. (1993). The ethics of the sliding scale. *Journal of Mental Health Counseling, 15*(3), 334–341.

Loar, L. (1995). Brief therapy with difficult clients. *Directions in Mental Health Counseling, 5*(12), 3–11.

Loewenberg, E. & Dolgoff, R. (1992). *Ethical decisions for social work practice* (4th ed.). Itasca, IL: F. E. Peacock.

Locke, D. C. (1990). A not so provincial view of multicultural counseling. *Counselor Education and Supervision, 30*(1), 18–25.

*Lum, D. (1996). *Social work practice and people of color. A process-stage approach* (3rd ed.). Pacific Grove, CA: Brooks/Cole.

Mabe, A. R., & Rollin, S. A. (1986). The role of a code of ethical standards in counseling. *Journal of Counseling and Development, 64*(5), 294–297.

*Mappes, D. C., Robb, G. P., & Engels, D. W. (1985). Conflicts between ethics and law in counseling and psychotherapy. *Journal of Counseling and Development, 64*(4), 246–252.

Margolin, G. (1982). Ethical and legal considerations in marital and family therapy. *American Psychologist, 37*(7), 788–801.

Marino, T. W. (1996). The challenging task of making counseling services relevant to more populations. *Counseling Today,* pp. 1, 6.

Markowitz, L. M. (1994). The cross-currents of multiculturalism. *The Family Therapy Networker, 18*(4), 18–69.

*Mattson, D. L. (1994). Religious counseling: To be used, not feared. *Counseling and Values, 38*(3), 187–192.

McBride, M. C. (1990). Autonomy and the struggle for female identity: Implications for counseling women. *Journal of Counseling and Development, 69*(1), 22–26.

McCarthy, P., Sugden, S., Koker, M., Lamendola, F., Maurer, S. & Renninger, S. (1995). A practical guide to informed consent in clinical supervision. *Counselor Education and Supervision, 35*(2), 130–138.

McGuire, J., Nieri, D., Abbott, D., Sheridan, K., & Fisher, R. (1995). Do *Tarasoff* principles apply in AIDS-related psychotherapy? Ethical decision making and the role of therapist homophobia and perceived client dangerousness. *Professional Psychology: Research and Practice, 26*(6), 608–611.

McRae, M. B., & Johnson, S. D. (1991). Toward training for competence in multicultural counselor education. *Journal of Counseling and Development, 70*(1), 131–135.

*Meara, N. M., Schmidt, L. D., & Day, J. D. (1996). Principles and virtues: A foundation for ethical decisions, policies, and character. *The Counseling Psychologist, 24*(1), 4–77.

Melton, G. B. (1981a). Children's participation in treatment planning: Psychological and legal issues. *Professional Psychology, 12*(2), 246–252.

Melton, G. B. (1981b). Effects of a state law permitting minors to consent to psychotherapy. *Professional Psychology, 12*(5), 647–654.

Melton, G. B. (1988). Ethical and legal issues in AIDS-related practice. *American Psychologist, 43*(11), 941–947.

Merta, R. J., Johnson, P., & McNeil, K. (1995). Updated research on group work: Educators, course work, theory, and teaching methods. *Journal for Specialists in Group Work, 20*(3), 143–150.

Merta, R. J., & Sisson, J. A. (1991). The experiential group: An ethical and professional dilemma. *Journal for Specialists in Group Work, 16*(4), 236–245.

*Merta, R. J., Wolfgang, L., & McNeil, K. (1993). Five models for using the experiential group in the preparation of group counselors. *Journal for Specialists in Group Work, 18*(4), 200–207.

*Miller, G. M., & Larrabee, M. J. (1995). Sexual intimacy in counselor education and supervision: A national survey. *Counselor Education and Supervision, 34*(4), 332–343.

Miller, G. M., & Wooten, H. R. (1995). Sports counseling: A new counseling specialty area. *Journal of Counseling and Development, 74*(2), 172–173.

*Miller, I. J. (1996). Managed health care is harmful to outpatient mental health services: A call for accountability. *Professional Psychology: Research and Practice, 27*(4), 349–363.

Miranti, J., & Burke, M. T. (1995). Spirituality: An integral component of the counseling process. In M. T. Burke & J. G. Miranti (Eds.), *Counseling: The spiritual dimension.* (pp. 1–3). Alexandria, VA: American Counseling Association.

Monahan, J. (1993). Limiting therapist exposure to *Tarasoff* liability: Guidelines for risk containment. *American Psychologist, 48*(4), 242–250.

Morrison, C. F. (1989). AIDS: Ethical implications for psychological intervention. *Professional Psychology: Research and Practice, 20*(3), 166–171.

Morrison, J. Layton, B., & Newman, J. (1982). Ethical conflict in clinical decision making: A challenge for family therapists. In J. Hansen (Ed.), *Values, ethics, legalities and the family therapist.* Rockville, MD: Aspen.

Morrissey, M. (1996). Supreme court extends confidentiality privilege. *Counseling Today,* pp. 1, 6, 10.

Myers, J. E. (1995a). From "forgotten and ignored" to standards and certification: Gerontological counseling comes of age. *Journal of Counseling and Development, 74*(2), 143–149.

Myers, J. E. (1995b). Specialties in counseling: Rich heritage or force for fragmentation? *Journal of Counseling and Development, 74*(2), 115–116.

National Association of Social Workers. (1994). Client self-determination in end-of-life decisions. *Social Work Speaks: NASW Policy Statements* (3rd ed.) (pp. 58–61). Washington, DC: Author.

National Association of Social Workers. (1996). *Code of ethics.* Washington, DC: Author.

National Board for Certified Counselors. (1989). *Code of ethics.* Greensboro, NC: Author.

National Board for Certified Counselors. (1993). *Specialty certification 1994.* Greensboro, NC: Author.

National Career Development Association. (1987). *National Career Development Association ethical standards.* Alexandria, VA: Author.

National Organization for Human Service Education. (1995). *Ethical standards of the National Organization for Human Service Education.* Author.

Newman, J. L. (1993). Ethical issues in consultation. *Journal of Counseling and Development, 72*(2), 148–156.

Newman, R. (1996). Supreme court affirms privilege. *APA Monitor, 27*(8), 44.

Newman, R., & Bricklin, P. M. (1991). Parameters of managed mental health care: Legal, ethical, and professional guidelines. *Professional Psychology: Research and Practice, 22*(1), 26–35.

Nichols, M. P., & Schwartz, R. C. (1995). *Family therapy: Concepts and methods* (3rd ed.). Boston: Allyn and Bacon.

Nicolai, K. M., & Scott, N. A. (1994). Provision of confidentiality information and its relation to child abuse reporting. *Professional Psychology: Research and Practice, 25*(2),154–160.

Nuttall, E. V., Webber, J. J., & Sanchez, W. (1996). MCT theory and implications for training. In D. W. Sue, A. E. Ivey, & P. B. Pedersen (Eds.), *A theory of multicultural counseling and therapy*. Pacific Grove, CA: Brooks/Cole.

*Olarte, S. W. (1997). Sexual boundary violations. In *The Hatherleigh guide to ethics in therapy* (pp. 195–209). New York: Hatherleigh Press.

Overholser, J. C. (1991). The Socratic method as a technique in psychotherapy supervision. *Professional Psychology: Research and Practice, 22*(1), 68–74.

Page, R. C., & Bailey, J. B. (1995). Addictions counseling certification: An emerging counseling specialty. *Journal of Counseling and Development, 74*(2), 167–171.

Paisley, P. O., & Borders, L. D. (1995). School counseling: An evolving specialty. *Journal of Counseling and Development, 74*(2), 150–153.

Paradise, L. V. & Siegelwaks, B. (1982). Ethical training for group leaders. *Journal for Specialists in Group Work, 7*(3), 162–166.

Pate, R. H. (1995). Certification of specialties: Not if, but how. *Journal of Counseling and Development, 74*(2), 181–184.

Pate, R. H. (1996). *Jaffee v. Redmond:* A primer on privilege. *NBCC NewsNotes, 13*(1), 1–4.

Patten, C., Barnett, I., & Houlihan, D. (1991). Ethics in marital and family therapy: A review of the literature. *Professional Psychology: Research and Practice, 22*(2), 171–175.

Patterson, C. H. (1985a). New light for counseling theory. *Journal of Counseling and Development, 63*(6), 349–350.

Patterson, C. H. (1985b). *The therapeutic relationship: Foundations for an eclectic psychotherapy*. Pacific Grove, CA: Brooks/Cole.

Patterson, C. H. (1989). Values in counseling and psychotherapy. *Counseling and Values, 33*, 164–176.

Patterson, C. H. (1996). Multicultural counseling: From diversity to universality. *Journal of Counseling and Development, 74*(3), 227–231.

Patterson, T. (1995). Macro-ethics: The current state of the family field. *The Family Psychologist*, pp. 18–20.

Pedersen, P. (1991). Multiculturalism as a generic approach to counseling. *Journal of Counseling and Development, 70*(1), 6–12.

Pedersen, P. (1994). *A handbook for developing multicultural awareness.* (2nd ed.). Alexandria, VA: American Counseling Association.

Pedersen, P. (1996). The importance of both similarities and differences in multicultural counseling: Reaction to C. H. Patterson. *Journal of Counseling and Development, 74*(3), 236–237.

*Pedersen, P. B., Draguns, J., Lonner, W., & Trimble, J. (Eds.). (1996). *Counseling across cultures* (4th ed.). Thousand Oaks, CA: Sage.

*Perlin, M. L. (1997). The "duty to protect" others from violence. In *The Hatherleigh guide to ethics in therapy* (pp. 127–146). New York: Hatherleigh Press.

*Phillips, D. G. (1997). Legal and ethical issues in the era of managed care. In R. M. Alperin & D. G. Phillips (Eds.), *The impact of managed care on the practice of psychotherapy: Innovation, implementation, and controversy* (pp. 171–184). New York: Brunner/Mazel.

*Ponterotto, J. G., Casas, J. M., Suzuki, L. A., & Alexander, C. M. (1995). *Handbook of multicultural counseling*. Thousand Oaks, CA: Sage.

Pope, K. S. (1985a, April). Dual relationships: A violation of ethical, legal, and clinical standards. *California State Psychologist, 20*(3), 3–5.

Pope, K. S. (1985b, July/August). The suicidal client: Guidelines for assessment and treatment. *California State Psychologist, 20*(5), 3–7.

Pope, K. S. (1987). Preventing therapist-patient sexual intimacy: Therapy for a therapist at risk. *Professional Psychology: Research and Practice, 18*(6), 624–628.

Pope, K. S. (1988). How clients are harmed by sexual contact with mental health professionals: The syndrome and its prevalence. *Journal of Counseling and Development, 67*(4), 222–226.

Pope, K. S. (1990a). Ethical and malpractice issues in hospital practice. *American Psychologist, 45*(9), 1066–1070.

Pope, K. S. (1990b). Therapist-patient sex as sex abuse: Six scientific, professional, and practical dilemmas in addressing victimization and rehabilitation. *Professional Psychology: Research and Practice, 21*(4), 227–239.

*Pope, K. S., & Bouhoutsos, J. C. (1986). *Sexual intimacy between therapists and patients.* New York: Praeger.

*Pope, K. S., Keith-Spiegel, P., & Tabachnick, B. G. (1986). Sexual attraction to clients: The human therapist and the (sometimes) inhuman training system. *American Psychologist, 41*(2), 147–158.

*Pope, K. S., Sonne, J. L., & Holroyd, J. (1993). *Sexual feelings in psychotherapy: Explorations for therapists and therapists-in-training.* Washington, DC: American Psychological Association.

Pope, K. S., & Tabachnick, B. G. (1994). Therapists as patients: A national survey of psychologists' experiences, problems, and beliefs. *Professional Psychology Research and Practice, 25*(3), 247–258.

*Pope, K. S., Tabachnick, B. G., & Keith-Spiegel, P. (1987). Ethics of practice: The beliefs and behaviors of psychologists as therapists. *American Psychologist, 42*(11), 993–1006.

Pope, K. S., & Vasquez, M. J. T. (1991). *Ethics in psychotherapy and counseling: A practical guide for psychologists.* San Francisco: Jossey-Bass.

*Priest, R. (1994). Minority supervisor and majority supervisee: Another perspective of clinical reality. *Counselor Education and Supervision, 34*(2), 152–158.

Prieto, L. R. (1996). Group supervision: Still widely practiced but poorly understood. *Counselor Education and Supervision, 35*(4), 295–307.

Rabinowitz, E. E. (1991). The male-to-male-embrace: Breaking the touch taboo in a men's therapy group. *Journal of Counseling and Development, 69*(6), 574–576.

Remley, T. P. (1990). Counseling records: Legal and ethical issues. In B. Herlihy & L. B. Golden (Eds.), *AACD ethical standards casebook* (4th ed.) (pp. 162–169). Alexandria, VA: American Association for Counseling and Development.

Remley, T. P. (1991). *Preparing for court appearances.* Alexandria, VA: American Association for Counseling and Development.

Remley, T. P. (1993). Consultation contracts. *Journal of Counseling and Development, 72*(2), 157–158.

Remley, T. P. (1995). A proposed alternative to the licensing of specialties in counseling. *Journal of Counseling and Development, 74*(2) 126–129.

Remley, T. P. (1996). The relationship between law and ethics. In B. Herlihy & G. Corey, (Eds.), *ACA ethical standards casebook* (5th ed.) (pp. 285–292). Alexandria, VA: American Counseling Association.

*Remley, T. P., Herlihy, B., & Herlihy, S. B. (1997). The U.S. Supreme Court decision in *Jaffee v. Redmond:* Implications for counselors. *Journal of Counseling and Development, 75*(3), 213–218.

Richardson, L. M., & Austad, C. S. (1991). Realities of mental health practice in managed-care settings. *Professional Psychology: Research and Practice, 22*(1), 52–59.

Richardson, T. Q., & Molinaro, K. L. (1996). White counselor self-awareness: A prerequisite for developing multicultural competence. *Journal of Counseling and Development, 74*(3), 238–242.

Ridley, C. R. (1984). Clinical treatment of the nondisclosing black client: A therapeutic paradox. *American Psychologist, 39*(11), 1234–1244.

Ridley, C. R. (1985). Imperatives for ethnic and cultural relevance in psychology training programs. *Professional Psychology: Research and Practice, 16*(5), 611–622.

Ridley, C. R. (1989). Racism in counseling as an adversive behavioral process. In P. Pedersen, J. Draguns, W. Lormer, & J. Trimble (Eds.), *Counseling across cultures* (3rd ed.) (pp. 55–77). Honolulu: University of Hawaii Press.

*Ridley, C. R. (1995). *Overcoming unintentional racism in counseling and therapy: A practitioner's guide to intentional intervention.* Thousand Oaks, CA: Sage.

*Ridley, C. R., Mendoza, D. W., & Kanitz, B. E. (1994). Multicultural training: Reexamination, operationalization, and integration. *The Counseling Psychologist, 22*(2), 227–289.

Riger, S. (1991). Gender dilemmas in sexual harassment: Policies and procedures. *American Psychologist, 46*(5), 497–505.

Ritter, K. Y., & O'Neill, C. W. (1989). Moving through loss: The spiritual journey of gay men and lesbian women. *Journal of Counseling and Development, 68*(1), 9–15.

Robinson, S. E., & Gross, D. R. (1985). Ethics of consultation: The Canterville ghost. *The Counseling Psychologist, 13*(3), 444–465.

Rodolfa, E. R., Kitzrow, M., Vohra, S., & Wilson, B. (1990). Training interns to respond to sexual dilemmas. *Professional Psychology: Research and Practice, 21*(4), 313–315.

Rogers, C. (1961). *On becoming a person.* Boston: Houghton Mifflin.

Rogers, C. (1980). *A way of being.* Boston: Houghton Mifflin.

Rubel, C. S. (1996). Managed cost systems and the adapting therapist. *Family Therapy News, 27*(3), 1–10.

*Rutter, P. (1989). *Sex in the forbidden zone.* Los Angeles: J. P. Tarcher.

Ryder, R., & Hepworth, J. (1990). AAMFT ethical code: "Dual relationships." *Journal of Marital and Family Therapy, 16*(2), 127–132.

Saeki, C., & Borow, H. (1985). Counseling and psychotherapy: East and West. In P. Pedersen (Ed.), *Handbook of cross-cultural counseling and therapy* (pp. 223–229). Westport, CT: Greenwood Press.

*St. Germaine, J. (1993). Dual relationships: What's wrong with them? *American Counselor, 2*(3), 25–30.

Salisbury, W. A., & Kinnier, R. T. (1996). Posttermination friendship between counselors and clients. *Journal of Counseling and Development, 74*(5), 495–500.

Sanders, J. R., & Keith-Spiegel, P. (1980). Formal and informal adjudication of ethics complaints against psychologists. *American Psychologist, 3*(12), 1096–1105.

Schaffer, S. J. (1997). Don't be aloof about record-keeping; it may be your best liability coverage. *The National Psychologist, 6*(1), 21.

Schank, J. A., & Skovholt, T. M. (1997). Dual-relationship dilemmas of rural and small-community psychologists. *Professional Psychology: Research and Practice, 28*(1), 44–49.

Seppa, N. (1996, August). Supreme court protects patient-therapist privilege. *APA Monitor, 27*(8), 39.

Shannon, J. W., & Woods, W. J. (1991). Affirmative psychotherapy for gay men. *The Counseling Psychologist, 19*(2), 197–215.

Sharf, R. S. (1996). *Theories of psychotherapy and counseling: Concepts and cases.* Pacific Grove, CA: Brooks/Cole.

Sherry, R. (1991). Ethical issues in the conduct of supervision. *The Counseling Psychologist, 19*(4), 566–584.

Shore, K. (1996). Managed care: An alternative view. *Professional Psychology: Research and Practice, 27*(4), 323–324.

Sinacore-Guinn, A. L. (1995). The diagnostic window: Culture- and gender-sensitive diagnosis and training. *Counselor Education and Supervision, 35*(1), 18–31.

Skorupa, J., & Agresti, A. A. (1993). Ethical beliefs about burnout and continued professional practice. *Professional Psychology: Research and Practice, 24*(3), 281–285.

Slater, B. R. (1988). Essential issues in working with lesbian and gay male youths. *Professional Psychology: Research and Practice, 19*(2), 226–235.

Sleek, S. (1994, December). Ethical dilemmas plague rural practice. *APA Monitor,* pp. 26–27.

Sleek, S. (1995, July). Group therapy: tapping the power of teamwork. *APA Monitor, 26*(7), 1, 38–39.

Sleek, S. (1996, April). Ensuring accuracy in clinical decisions. *APA Monitor, 26*(4), 30.

*Slimp, P. A., & Burian, B. K. (1994). Multiple role relationships during internship: Consequences and recommendations. *Professional Psychology: Research and Practice, 25*(1), 39–45.

*Smith, D., & Fitzpatrick, M. (1995). Patient-therapist boundary issues: An integrative review of theory and research. *Professional Psychology: Research and Practice, 26*(5), 499–506.

Smith, E. M. J. (1985a). Counseling black women. In P. Pedersen (Ed.), *Handbook of cross-cultural counseling and therapy* (pp. 181–187). Westport, CT: Greenwood Press.

Smith, E. M. J. (1985b). Ethnic minorities: Life stress, social support, and mental health issues. *The Counseling Psychologist, 13*(4), 537–579.

Smith, H. B., & Robinson, G. P. (1995). Mental health counseling: Past, present, and future. *Journal of Counseling and Development, 74*(2), 158–162.

Smith, R. L. (1993). Training in marriage and family counseling and therapy: Current status and challenges. *Counselor Education and Supervision, 33*(2), 89–102.

Smith, R. L. (1994). Directions in marriage and family graduate level training. *Counselor Education and Supervision, 34*(3), 180–183.

Smith, R. L., Carlson, J., Stevens-Smith, P., & Dennison, M. (1995). Marriage and family counseling. *Journal of Counseling and Development, 74*(2), 154–157.

Smith, T. S., McGuire, J. M., Abbott, D. W, & Blau, B. I. (1991). Clinical ethical decision making: An investigation of the rationales used to justify doing less than one believes one should. *Professional Psychology: Research and Practice, 22*(3), 235–239.

Sobocinski, M. R. (1990). Ethical principles in the counseling of gay and lesbian adolescents: Issues of autonomy, competence, and confidentiality. *Professional Psychology: Research and Practice, 21*(4), 240–247.

Somberg, D. R., Stone, G. L., & Claiborn, C. D. (1993). Informed consent: Therapists' beliefs and practices. *Professional Psychology: Research and Practice, 24*(2), 153–159.

*Sommers-Flanagan, J., & Sommers-Flanagan, R. (1995). Intake interviewing with suicidal patients: A systematic approach. *Professional Psychology: Research and Practice, 26*(1), 41–47.

Sonne, J. L., & Pope, K. S. (1991). Treating victims of therapist-patient sexual involvement. *Psychotherapy, 28,* 174–187.

Stadler, H. A. (1986a). Making hard choices: Clarifying controversial ethical issues. *Counseling and Human Development, 19*(1), 1–10.

*Stadler, H. A. (1986b). To counsel or not to counsel: The ethical dilemma of dual relationships. *Journal of Counseling and Human Service Professions, 1*(1), 134–140.

Stadler, H. A. (1990a). Confidentiality. In B. Herlihy & L. B. Golden (Eds.), *AACD ethical standards casebook* (4th ed.) (pp. 102–110). Alexandria, VA: American Association for Counseling and Development.

Stadler, H. A. (1990b). Counselor impairment. In B. Herlihy & L. B. Golden (Eds.), *AACD ethical standards casebook* (4th ed.) (pp. 177–187). Alexandria, VA: American Association for Counseling and Development.

Stake, J. E., & Oliver, J. (1991). Sexual contact and touching between therapist and client: A survey of psychologists' attitudes and behavior. *Professional Psychology: Research and Practice, 22*(4), 297–307.

*Storm, C. L. (1994). Defensive supervision: Balancing ethical responsibility with vulnerability. In G. W. Brock (Ed.), *American Association for Marriage and Family Therapy ethics casebook* (pp. 173–190). Washington, DC: American Association for Marriage and Family Therapy.

Strasburger, L. H., Jorgenson, L., & Sutherland, P. (1992). The prevention of psychotherapist sexual misconduct: Avoiding the slippery slope. *American Journal of Psychotherapy, 46,* 544–555.

Stromberg, C., & Dellinger, A. (1993, December). Malpractice and other professional liability. *The Psychologist's Legal Update.* Washington, DC: National Register of Health Service Providers in Psychology.

Stromberg, C., Schneider, J., & Joondeph, B. (1993, August). Dealing with potentially dangerous patients. *The Psychologist's Legal Update.* Washington, DC: National Register of Health Service Providers in Psychology.

Stromberg, C., and his colleagues in the Law Firm of Hogan & Hartson of Washington, DC. (1993, April). Privacy, confidentiality and privilege. *The Psychologist's Legal Update.* Washington, DC: National Register of Health Service Providers in Psychology.

Sue, D., & Sue, D. W. (1991). Counseling strategies for Chinese Americans. In C. C. Lee & B. L. Richardson (Eds.), *Multicultural issues in counseling: New approaches to diversity* (pp. 79–90). Alexandria, VA: American Association for Counseling and Development.

Sue, D. W. (1996a). ACES endorsement of the multicultural counseling competencies: Do we have the courage? *ACES Spectrum Newsletter, 57*(1), pp. 9–10.

Sue, D. W. (1996b). Ethical issues in multicultural counseling. In B. Herlihy & G. Corey (Eds.), *ACA ethical standards casebook* (5th ed.) (pp. 193–197). Alexandria, VA: American Counseling Association.

*Sue, D. W. (1997). Multicultural perspectives on multiple relationships. In B. Herlihy & G. Corey (Eds.), *Boundary issues in counseling: Multiple roles and responsibilites* (pp. 106–109). Alexandria, VA: American Counseling Association.

*Sue, D. W., Arredondo, P., & McDavis, R. J. (1992). Multicultural counseling competencies and standards: A call to the profession. *Journal of Counseling and Development, 70*(4), 477–486.

Sue, D. W., Bernier, J. E., Durran, A., Feinberg, L., Pedersen, P., Smith, E. J., & Nuttall, E. V. (1982). Position paper: Cross-cultural counseling competencies. *The Counseling Psychologist, 10*(2), 45–52.

*Sue, D. W., Ivey, A. E., & Pedersen, P. B. (1996). *A theory of multicultural counseling and therapy.* Pacific Grove, CA: Brooks/Cole.

Sue, D. W., & Sue, D. (1985). Asian Americans and Pacific Islanders. In P. Pedersen (Ed.), *Handbook of cross-cultural counseling and therapy* (pp. 141–146). Westport, CT: Greenwood Press.

*Sue, D. W., & Sue, D. (1990). *Counseling the culturally different: Theory and practice* (2nd ed.). New York: Wiley.

*Sumerel, M. B., & Borders, L. D. (1996). Addressing personal issues in supervision: Impact on counselors' experience level on various aspects of the supervisory relationship. *Counselor Education and Supervision, 35*(4), 268–286.

Summit on Spirituality. (1995, December). *Counseling Today,* p. 30.

Swanson, C. (1983). The law and the counselor. In J. Brown & B. Pate (Eds.), *Being a counselor: Directions and challenges.* Pacific Grove, CA: Brooks/Cole.

Sweeney, T. J. (1995). Accreditation, credentialing, professionalization: The role of specialties. *Journal of Counseling and Development, 74*(2), 117–125.

*Swenson, L. C. (1997). *Psychology and law for the helping professions.* Pacific Grove, CA: Brooks/Cole.

Szasz, T. (1974). *The myth of mental illness: Foundations of a theory of personal conduct* (rev. ed.). New York: Harper & Row.

*Szasz, T. (1986). The case against suicide prevention. *American Psychologist, 41*(7), 806–812.

Tabachnick, B. G., Keith-Spiegel, P., & Pope, K. S. (1991). Ethics of teaching: Beliefs and behaviors of psychologists as educators. *American Psychologist, 46*(5), 506–515.

Tennyson, W. W., & Strom, S. A. (1986). Beyond professional standards: Developing responsibleness. *Journal of Counseling and Development, 64*(5), 298–302.

Tjeltveit, A. C. (1986). The ethics of value conversion in psychotherapy: Appropriate and inappropriate therapist influence on client values. *Clinical Psychology Review, 6,* 515–537.

Tokunaga, H. T. (1984). Ethical issues in consultation: An evaluative review. *Professional Psychology: Research and Practice, 15*(6), 811–821.

*Tomm, K. (1993, January/February). The ethics of dual relationships. *The California Therapist,* pp. 7–19.

Totten, G., Lamb, D. H., & Reeder, G. D. (1990). *Tarasoff* and confidentiality in AIDS-related psychotherapy. *Professional Psychology: Research and Practice, 21*(3), 155–160.

Truscott, D., Evans, J., & Mansell, S. (1995). Outpatient psychotherapy with dangerous clients: A model for clinical decision making. *Psychology: Research and Practice, 26*(5), 484–490.

*Tyler, J. M., & Tyler, C. L. (1997). Ethics in supervision: Managing supervisee rights and supervisor responsibilities. In *The Hatherleigh guide to ethics in therapy* (pp. 75–95). New York: Hatherleigh Press.

Tymchuk, A. J. (1981). Ethical decision making and psychological treatment. *Journal of Psychiatric Treatment and Evaluation, 3,* 507–513.

VandeCreek, L., & Knapp, S. (1994). Ethical and legal issues. In F. M. Dattilio & A. Freeman (Eds.), *Cognitive-behavioral strategies in crisis intervention* (pp. 362–373). New York: Guilford Press.

VandeCreek, L., Knapp, S., & Herzog, C. (1987). Malpractice risks in the treatment of dangerous patients. *Psychotherapy, 24*(2), 145–153.

VandeCreek, L., Knapp, S., & Herzog, C. (1988). Privileged communication for social workers. *Social Casework: The Journal of Contemporary Social Work, 69,* 28–34.

*Vasquez, M. J. T. (1988). Counselor-client sexual contact: Implications for ethics training. *Journal of Counseling and Development, 67*(4), 238–241.

Vasquez, M. J. T. (1992). Psychologist as clinical supervisor: Promoting ethical practice. *Professional Psychology: Research and Practice, 23*(3), 196–202.

*Vasquez, M. J. T. (1996). Will virtue ethics improve ethical conduct in multicultural settings and interactions? *The Counseling Psychologist, 24*(1), 98–104.

*Walden, S. L. (1997). The counselor/client partnership in ethical practice. In B. Herlihy & G. Corey (Eds.), *Boundary issues in counseling: Multiple roles and responsibilities* (pp. 40–47). Alexandria, VA: American Counseling Association.

Watkins, C. E. (1983). Transference phenomena in the counseling situation. *Personnel and Guidance Journal, 62*(4), 206–210.

Watkins, C. E. (1985). Countertransference: Its impact on the counseling situation. *Journal of Counseling and Development, 63*(6), 356–359.

Weinrach, S. G., & Thomas, K. R. (1996). The counseling profession's commitment to diversity-sensitive counseling: A critical reassessment. *Journal of Counseling and Development, 74*(5), 472–477.

Welfel, E. R., & Lipsitz, N. E. (1984). The ethical behavior of professional psychologists: A critical analysis of the research. *The Counseling Psychologist, 12*(3), 31–42.

Werth, J. L., & Carney, J. (1994). Incorporating HIV-related issues into graduate student training. *Professional Psychology: Research and Practice, 25*(4), 458–465.

*Wheeler, N., & Bertram, B. (1994). Legal aspects of counseling: Avoiding lawsuits and legal problems. (Workshop material and video seminar). Alexandria, VA: American Counseling Association.

Whiston, S. C., & Emerson, S. (1989). Ethical implications for supervisors in counseling of trainees. *Counselor Education and Supervision, 28*(4), 318–325.

White, J. L., & Parham, T. A. (1990). *The psychology of blacks: An African-American perspective* (2nd ed.). Englewood Cliffs, NJ: Prentice-Hall.

*Willison, B. G., & Masson, R. L. (1986). The role of touch in therapy: An adjunct to communication. *Journal of Counseling and Development, 64*(8), 497–500.

Wise, R. S., Lowery, S., & Silverglade, L. (1989). Personal counseling for counselors in training: Guidelines for supervisors. *Counselor Education and Supervision, 28*(4), 326–336.

Wittmer, J., & Remley, T. P., Jr. (1994, Summer). A counselor-client contract, *NBCC NewsNotes, 11*(1), 12.

Wolfgang, A. (1985). The function and importance of nonverbal behavior in intercultural counseling. In P. Pedersen (Ed.), *Handbook of cross-cultural counseling and therapy* (pp. 99–105). Westport, CT: Greenwood Press.

Wood, P. S., & Mallinckrodt, B. (1990). Culturally sensitive assertiveness training for ethnic minority clients. *Professional Psychology: Research and Practice, 21*(1), 5–11.

*Wrenn, C. G. (1962). The culturally encapsulated counselor. *Harvard Educational Review, 32,* 444–449.

Wrenn, C. G. (1985). Afterword: The culturally encapsulated counselor revisited. In P. Pedersen (Ed.), *Handbook of cross-cultural counseling and therapy* (pp. 323–329). Westport, CT: Greenwood Press.

Wright, J., Coley, S., & Corey, G. (1989, May). Challenges facing human services education today. *Journal of Counseling and Human Service Professions, 3*(2), 3–11.

Wubbolding, R. E. (1991). Professional issues: Consultation and ethics Part II. *Journal of Reality Therapy, 10*(2), 55–59.

*Wubbolding, R. E. (1996). Working with suicidal clients. In B. Herlihy & G. Corey (Eds.), *ACA ethical standards casebook* (5th ed.) (pp. 267–274). Alexandria, VA: American Counseling Association.

*Wylie, M. S. (1995). Diagnosing for dollars? *The Family Therapy Networker, 19*(3), 22–69.

Yalom, I. (1995). *The theory and practice of group psychotherapy* (4th ed.). New York: Basic Books.

Younggren, J. N. (1993). Ethical issues in religious psychotherapy. *Register Report, 19*(4), 1–8.

Youngstrom, N. (1991a, July). Lesbians and gay men still find bias in therapy. *APA Monitor,* pp. 24–25.

Youngstrom, N. (1991b, July). Mandatory reporting deters sex treatment. *APA Monitor,* p. 35.

Zimpfer, D. G., & DeTrude, J. C. (1990). Follow-up of doctoral graduates in counseling. *Journal of Counseling and Development, 69*(l), 51–56.

Appendices

- A. *Codes of Ethics and Standards of Practice*, American Counseling Association (ACA, 1995)

- B. *Ethical Principles of Psychologists and Code of Conduct*, American Psychological Association (APA, 1995)

- C. *Code of Ethics*, National Association of Social Workers (NASW, 1996)

- D. *AAMFT Code of Ethics*, American Association for Marriage and Family Therapy (AAMFT, 1991)

- E. *Ethical Standards of Human Service Professionals*, National Organization for Human Service Education (NOHSE, 1995)

- F. A Guide to Professional Organizations

A. Codes of Ethics and Standards of Practice, American Counseling Association (ACA, 1995)

PREAMBLE

The American Counseling Association is an educational, scientific and professional organization whose members are dedicated to the enhancement of human development throughout the life span. Association members recognize diversity in our society and embrace a cross-cultural approach in support of the worth, dignity, potential, and uniqueness of each individual.

The specification of a code of ethics enables the association to clarify to current and future members, and to those served by members, the nature of the ethical responsibilities held in common by its members. As the code of ethics of the association, this document establishes principles that define the ethical behavior of association members. All members of the American Counseling Association are required to adhere to the Code of Ethics and the Standards of Practice. The Code of Ethics will serve as the basis for processing ethical complaints initiated against members of the association.

Section A: The counseling relationship

A.1. CLIENT WELFARE
   a. *Primary Responsibility.*
      The primary responsibility of counselors is to respect the dignity and to promote the welfare of clients.

   b. *Positive Growth and Development.*
      Counselors encourage client growth and development in ways that foster the clients' interest and welfare; counselors avoid fostering dependent counseling relationships.
   c. *Counseling Plans.*
      Counselors and their clients work jointly in devising integrated, individual counseling plans that offer reasonable promise of success and are consistent with abilities and circumstances of clients. Counselors and clients regularly review counseling plans to ensure their continued viability and effectiveness, respecting clients' freedom of choice. (See A.3.b.)
   d. *Family Involvement.*
      Counselors recognize that families are usually important in clients' lives and strive to enlist family understanding and involvement as a positive resource, when appropriate.
   e. *Career and Employment Needs.*
      Counselors work with their clients in considering employment in jobs and circumstances that are consistent with the clients' overall abilities, vocational limitations, physical restrictions, general temperament, interest and aptitude patterns, social skills, education, general qualifications, and other relevant characteristics

and needs. Counselors neither place nor participate in placing clients in positions that will result in damaging the interest and the welfare of clients, employers, or the public.

A.2. RESPECTING DIVERSITY

a. *Nondiscrimination.*

Counselors do not condone or engage in discrimination based on age, color, culture, disability, ethnic group, gender, race, religion, sexual orientation, marital status, or socioeconomic status. (See C.5.a., C.5.b., and D.1.i.)

b. *Respecting Differences.*

Counselors will actively attempt to understand the diverse cultural backgrounds of the clients with whom they work. This includes, but is not limited to, learning how the counselor's own cultural/ethnic/racial identity impacts her/his values and beliefs about the counseling process. (See E.8. and F.2.i.)

A.3. CLIENT RIGHTS

a. *Disclosure to Clients.*

When counseling is initiated, and throughout the counseling process as necessary, counselors inform clients of the purposes, goals, techniques, procedures, limitations, potential risks and benefits of services to be performed, and other pertinent information. Counselors take steps to ensure that clients understand the implications of diagnosis, the intended use of tests and reports, fees, and billing arrangements. Clients have the right to expect confidentiality and to be provided with an explanation of its limitations, including supervision and/or treatment team professionals; to obtain clear information about their case records; to participate in the ongoing counseling plans; and to refuse any recommended services and be advised of the consequences of such refusal. (See E.5.a. and G.2.)

b. *Freedom of Choice.*

Counselors offer clients the freedom to choose whether to enter into a counseling relationship and to determine which professional(s) will provide counseling. Restrictions that limit choices of clients are fully explained. (See A.1.c.)

c. *Inability to Give Consent.*

When counseling minors or persons unable to give voluntary informed consent, counselors act in these clients' best interests. (See B.3.)

A.4. CLIENTS SERVED BY OTHERS

If a client is receiving services from another mental health professional, counselors, with client consent, inform the professional persons already involved and develop clear agreements to avoid confusion and conflict for the client. (See C.6.c.)

A.5. PERSONAL NEEDS AND VALUES

a. *Personal Needs.*

In the counseling relationship, counselors are aware of the intimacy and responsibilities inherent in the counseling relationship, maintain respect for clients, and avoid actions that seek to meet their personal needs at the expense of clients.

b. *Personal Values.*

Counselors are aware of their own values, attitudes, beliefs, and behaviors and how these apply in a diverse society, and avoid imposing their values on clients. (See C.5.a.)

A.6. DUAL RELATIONSHIPS

a. *Avoid When Possible.*

Counselors are aware of their influential positions with respect to clients, and they avoid exploiting the trust and dependency of clients. Counselors make every effort to avoid dual relationships with clients that could impair professional judgment or increase the risk of harm to clients. (Examples of such relationships include, but are not limited to, familial, social, financial, business, or close personal relationships with clients.) When a dual relationship cannot be avoided, counselors take appropriate professional precautions such as informed consent, consultation, supervision, and documentation to ensure that judgment is not impaired and no exploitation occurs. (See F.1.b.)

b. *Superior/Subordinate Relationships.*

Counselors do not accept as clients superiors or subordinates with whom they have administrative, supervisory, or evaluative relationships.

A.7.   SEXUAL INTIMACIES WITH CLIENTS

a. *Current Clients.*

Counselors do not have any type of sexual intimacies with clients and do not counsel persons with whom they have had a sexual relationship.

b. *Former Clients.*

Counselors do not engage in sexual intimacies with former clients within a minimum of two years after terminating the counseling relationship. Counselors who engage in such relationships after two years following termination have the responsibility to thoroughly examine and document that such relations did not have an exploitative nature, based on factors such as duration of counseling, amount of time since counseling, termination circumstances, client's personal history and mental status, adverse impact on the client, and actions by the counselor suggesting a plan to initiate a sexual relationship with the client after termination.

A.8.   MULTIPLE CLIENTS

When counselors agree to provide counseling services to two or more persons who have a relationship (such as husband and wife, or parents and children), counselors clarify at the outset which person or persons are clients and the nature of the relationships they will have with each involved person. If it becomes apparent that counselors may be called upon to perform potentially conflicting roles, they clarify, adjust, or withdraw from roles appropriately. (See B.2. and B.4.d.)

A.9.   GROUP WORK

a. *Screening.*

Counselors screen prospective group counseling/therapy participants. To the extent possible, counselors select members whose needs and goals are compatible with goals of the group, who will not impede the group process, and whose well-being will not be jeopardized by the group experience.

b. *Protecting Clients.*

In a group setting, counselors take reasonable precautions to protect clients from physical or psychological trauma.

A.10.   FEES AND BARTERING (See D.3 a. and D.3.b.)

a. *Advance Understanding.*

Counselors clearly explain to clients, prior to entering the counseling relationship, all financial arrangements related to professional services including the use of collection agencies or legal measures for nonpayment. (A.11.c.)

b. *Establishing Fees.*

In establishing fees for professional counseling services, counselors consider the financial status of clients and locality. In the event that the established fee structure is inappropriate for a client, assistance is provided in attempting to find comparable services of acceptable cost. (See A.10.d., D.3.a., and D.3.b.)

c. *Bartering Discouraged.*

Counselors ordinarily refrain from accepting goods or services from clients in return for counseling services because such arrangements create inherent potential for conflicts, exploitation, and distortion of the professional relationship. Counselors may participate in bartering only if the relationship is not exploitive, if the client requests it, if a clear written contract is established, and if such arrangements are an accepted practice among professionals in the community. (See A.6.a.)

d. *Pro Bono Service.*

Counselors contribute to society by devoting a portion of their professional activity to services for which there is little or no financial return (pro bono).

A.11.   TERMINATION AND REFERRAL

a. *Abandonment Prohibited.*

Counselors do not abandon or neglect clients in counseling. Counselors assist in making appropriate arrangements for the continuation of treatment, when necessary, during interruptions such as vacations, and following termination.

b. *Inability to Assist Clients.*

If counselors determine an inability to be of professional assistance to clients, they avoid entering or immediately terminate a counseling relationship. Counselors are knowledgeable about referral resources and suggest appropriate alternatives. If clients decline the suggested referral, counselors should discontinue the relationship.

   c. *Appropriate Termination.*

     Counselors terminate a counseling relationship, securing client agreement when possible, when it is reasonably clear that the client is no longer benefiting, when services are no longer required, when counseling no longer serves the client's needs or interests, when clients do not pay fees charged, or when agency or institution limits do not allow provision of further counseling services. (See A.10.b. and C.2.g.)

A.12. COMPUTER TECHNOLOGY

   a. *Use of Computers.*

     When computer applications are used in counseling services, counselors ensure that: (1) the client is intellectually, emotionally, and physically capable of using the computer application; (2) the computer application is appropriate for the needs of the client; (3) the client understands the purpose and operation of the computer applications; and (4) a follow-up of client use of a computer application is provided to correct possible misconceptions, discover inappropriate use, and assess subsequent needs.

   b. *Explanation of Limitations.*

     Counselors ensure that clients are provided information as a part of the counseling relationship that adequately explains the limitations of computer technology.

   c. *Access to Computer Applications.*

     Counselors provide for equal access to computer applications in counseling services. (See A.2.a.)

Section B: Confidentiality

B.1. RIGHT TO PRIVACY

   a. *Respect for Privacy.*

     Counselors respect their clients' right to privacy and avoid illegal and unwar-

ranted disclosures of confidential information. (See A.3.a. and B.6.a.)

   b. *Client Waiver.*

     The right to privacy may be waived by the client or their legally recognized representative.

   c. *Exceptions.*

     The general requirement that counselors keep information confidential does not apply when disclosure is required to prevent clear and imminent danger to the client or others or when legal requirements demand that confidential information be revealed. Counselors consult with other professionals when in doubt as to the validity of an exception.

   d. *Contagious, Fatal Diseases.*

     A counselor who receives information confirming that a client has a disease commonly known to be both communicable and fatal is justified in disclosing information to an identifiable third party, who by his or her relationship with the client is at a high risk of contracting the disease. Prior to making a disclosure the counselor should ascertain that the client has not already informed the third party about his or her disease and that the client is not intending to inform the third party in the immediate future. (See B.1.c and B.1.f)

   e. *Court Ordered Disclosure.* *see privilege because its a legal term.*

     When court ordered to release confidential information without a client's permission, counselors request to the court that the disclosure not be required due to potential harm to the client or counseling relationship. (See B.1.c.)

   f. *Minimal Disclosure.*

     When circumstances require the disclosure of confidential information, only essential information is revealed. To the extent possible, clients are informed before confidential information is disclosed.

   g. *Explanation of Limitations.*

     When counseling is initiated and throughout the counseling process as necessary, counselors inform clients of the limitations of confidentiality and identify foreseeable situations in which confidentiality must be breached. (See G.2.a.)

h. *Subordinates.*

Counselors make every effort to ensure that privacy and confidentiality of clients are maintained by subordinates including employees, supervisees, clerical assistants, and volunteers. (See B.1.a.)

i. *Treatment Teams.*

If client treatment will involve a continued review by a treatment team, the client will be informed of the team's existence and composition.

B.2.   GROUPS AND FAMILIES

a. *Group Work.*

In group work, counselors clearly define confidentiality and the parameters for the specific group being entered, explain its importance, and discuss the difficulties related to confidentiality involved in group work. The fact that confidentiality cannot be guaranteed is clearly communicated to group members.

b. *Family Counseling.*

In family counseling, information about one family member cannot be disclosed to another member without permission. Counselors protect the privacy rights of each family member. (See A.8., B.3., and B.4.d.)

B.3.   MINOR OR INCOMPETENT CLIENTS

When counseling clients who are minors or individuals who are unable to give voluntary, informed consent, parents or guardians may be included in the counseling process as appropriate. Counselors act in the best interests of clients and take measures to safeguard confidentiality. (See A.3.c.)

B.4.   RECORDS

a. *Requirement of Records.*

Counselors maintain records necessary for rendering professional services to their clients and as required by laws, regulations, or agency or institution procedures.

b. *Confidentiality of Records.*

Counselors are responsible for securing the safety and confidentiality of any counseling records they create, maintain, trans-

fer, or destroy whether the records are written, taped, computerized, or stored in any other medium. (See B.1.a.)

c. *Permission to Record or Observe.*

Counselors obtain permission from clients prior to electronically recording or observing sessions. (See A.3.a.)

d. *Client Access.*

Counselors recognize that counseling records are kept for the benefit of clients, and therefore provide access to records and copies of records when requested by competent clients, unless the records contain information that may be misleading and detrimental to the client. In situations involving multiple clients. access to records is limited to those parts of records that do not include confidential information related to another client. (See A.8., B.1.a., and B.2.b.)

e. *Disclosure or Transfer.*

Counselors obtain written permission from clients to disclose or transfer records to legitimate third parties unless exceptions to confidentiality exist as listed in Section B. 1. Steps are taken to ensure that receivers of counseling records are sensitive to their confidential nature.

B.5.   RESEARCH AND TRAINING

a. *Data Disguise Required.*

Use of data derived from counseling relationships for purposes of training, research, or publication is confined to content that is disguised to ensure the anonymity of the individuals involved. (See B.1.g. and G.3.d.)

b. *Agreement for Identification.*

Identification of a client in a presentation or publication is permissible only when the client has reviewed the material and has agreed to its presentation or publication. (See G.3.d.)

B.6.   CONSULTATION

a. *Respect for Privacy.*

Information obtained in a consulting relationship is discussed for professional purposes only with persons clearly concerned with the case. Written and oral reports present data germane to the purposes of the consultation, and every effort is made to protect client identity and avoid undue invasion of privacy.

b. *Cooperating Agencies.*

Before sharing information, counselors make efforts to ensure that there are defined policies in other agencies serving the counselor's clients that effectively protect the confidentiality of information.

Section C: Professional responsibility

C.1.   STANDARDS KNOWLEDGE

Counselors have a responsibility to read, understand, and follow the Code of Ethics and the Standards of Practice.

C.2.   PROFESSIONAL COMPETENCE

a. *Boundaries of Competence.*

Counselors practice only within the boundaries of their competence, based on their education, training, supervised experience, state and national professional credentials, and appropriate professional experience. Counselors will demonstrate a commitment to gain knowledge, personal awareness, sensitivity, and skills pertinent to working with a diverse client population.

b. *New Specialty Areas of Practice.*

Counselors practice in specialty areas new to them only after appropriate education, training, and supervised experience. While developing skills in new specialty areas, counselors take steps to ensure the competence of their work and to protect others from possible harm.

c. *Qualified for Employment.*

Counselors accept employment only for positions for which they are qualified by education, training, supervised experience, state and national professional credentials, and appropriate professional experience. Counselors hire for professional counseling positions only individuals who are qualified and competent.

d. *Monitor Effectiveness.*

Counselors continually monitor their effectiveness as professionals and take steps to improve when necessary. Coun-

selors in private practice take reasonable steps to seek out peer supervision to evaluate their efficacy as counselors.

e. *Ethical Issues Consultation.*

Counselors take reasonable steps to consult with other counselors or related professionals when they have questions regarding their ethical obligations or professional practice. (See H.1)

f. *Continuing Education.*

Counselors recognize the need for continuing education to maintain a reasonable level of awareness of current scientific and professional information in their fields of activity. They take steps to maintain competence in the skills they use, are open to new procedures, and keep current with the diverse and/or special populations with whom they work.

g. *Impairment.*

Counselors refrain from offering or accepting professional services when their physical, mental, or emotional problems are likely to harm a client or others. They are alert to the signs of impairment, seek assistance for problems, and, if necessary, limit, suspend, or terminate their professional responsibilities. (See A.11.c.)

C.3.   ADVERTISING AND SOLICITING CLIENTS

a. *Accurate Advertising.*

There are no restrictions on advertising by counselors except those that can be specifically justified to protect the public from deceptive practices. Counselors advertise or represent their services to the public by identifying their credentials in an accurate manner that is not false, misleading, deceptive, or fraudulent. Counselors may only advertise the highest degree earned which is in counseling or a closely related field from a college or university that was accredited when the degree was awarded by one of the regional accrediting bodies recognized by the Council on Postsecondary Accreditation.

b. *Testimonials.*

Counselors who use testimonials do not solicit them from clients or other persons who, because of their particular circumstances, may be vulnerable to undue influence.

c. *Statements by Others.*

Counselors make reasonable efforts to ensure that statements made by others about them or the profession of counseling are accurate.

d. *Recruiting through Employment.*

Counselors do not use their places of employment or institutional affiliation to recruit or gain clients, supervisees, or consultees for their private practices. (See C.5.e.)

e. *Products and Training Advertisements.*

Counselors who develop products related to their profession or conduct workshops or training events ensure that the advertisements concerning these products or events are accurate and disclose adequate information for consumers to make informed choices.

f. *Promoting to Those Served.*

Counselors do not use counseling, teaching, training, or supervisory relationships to promote their products or training events in a manner that is deceptive or would exert undue influence on individuals who may be vulnerable. Counselors may adopt textbooks they have authored for instruction purposes.

g. *Professional Association Involvement.*

Counselors actively participate in local, state, and national associations that foster the development and improvement of counseling.

C.4. CREDENTIALS

a. *Credentials Claimed.*

Counselors claim or imply only professional credentials possessed and are responsible for correcting any known misrepresentations of their credentials by others. Professional credentials include graduate degrees in counseling or closely related mental health fields, accreditation of graduate programs, national voluntary certifications, government issued certifications or licenses, ACA professional membership, or any other credential that might indicate to the public specialized knowledge or expertise in counseling.

b. *ACA Professional Membership.*

ACA professional members may announce to the public their membership status. Regular members may not announce their ACA membership in a manner that might imply they are credentialed counselors.

c. *Credential Guidelines.*

Counselors follow the guidelines for use of credentials that have been established by the entities that issue the credentials.

d. *Misrepresentation of Credentials.*

Counselors do not attribute more to their credentials than the credentials represent, and do not imply that other counselors are not qualified because they do not possess certain credentials.

e. *Doctoral Degrees from Other Fields.*

Counselors who hold a master's degree in counseling or a closely related mental health field, but hold a doctoral degree from other than counseling or a closely related field do not use the title "Dr." in their practices and do not announce to the public in relation to their practice or status as a counselor that they hold a doctorate.

C.5. PUBLIC RESPONSIBILITY

a. *Nondiscrimination.*

Counselors do not discriminate against clients, students, or supervisees in a manner that has a negative impact based on their age, color, culture, disability, ethnic group, gender, race, religion, sexual orientation, or socioeconomic status, or for any other reason. (See A.2.a.)

b. *Sexual Harassment.*

Counselors do not engage in sexual harassment. Sexual harassment is defined as sexual solicitation, physical advances, or verbal or nonverbal conduct that is sexual in nature, that occurs in connection with professional activities or roles, and that either: (1) is unwelcome, is offensive, or creates a hostile workplace environment, and counselors know or are told this; or (2) is sufficiently severe or intense to be perceived as harassment to a reasonable person in the context. Sexual harassment can consist of a single intense or severe act or multiple persistent or pervasive acts.

c. *Reports to Third Parties.*

Counselors are accurate, honest, and unbiased in reporting their professional activities and judgments to appropriate third parties including courts, health insurance companies, those who are the recipients of evaluation reports, and others. (See B.1.g.)

d. *Media Presentations.*

When counselors provide advice or comment by means of public lectures, demonstrations, radio or television programs, prerecorded tapes, printed articles, mailed material, or other media, they take reasonable precautions to ensure that (1) the statements are based on appropriate professional counseling literature and practice; (2) the statements are otherwise consistent with the Code of Ethics and the Standards of Practice; and (3) the recipients of the information are not encouraged to infer that a professional counseling relationship has been established. (See C.6.b.)

e. *Unjustified Gains.*

Counselors do not use their professional positions to seek or receive unjustified personal gains, sexual favors, unfair advantage, or unearned goods or services. (See C.3.d.)

C.6. RESPONSIBILITY TO OTHER PROFESSIONALS

a. *Different Approaches.*

Counselors are respectful of approaches to professional counseling that differ from their own. Counselors know and take into account the traditions and practices of other professional groups with which they work.

b. *Personal Public Statements.*

When making personal statements in a public context, counselors clarify that they are speaking from their personal perspectives and that they are not speaking on behalf of all counselors or the profession. (See C.5.d.)

c. *Clients Served by Others.*

When counselors learn that their clients are in a professional relationship with another mental health professional, they request release from clients to inform the other professionals and strive to establish positive and collaborative professional relationships. (See A.4.)

Section D: Relationships with other professionals

D.1. RELATIONSHIPS WITH EMPLOYERS AND EMPLOYEES

a. *Role Definition.*

Counselors define and describe for their employers and employees the parameters and levels of their professional roles.

b. *Agreements.*

Counselors establish working agreements with supervisors, colleagues, and subordinates regarding counseling or clinical relationships, confidentiality, adherence to professional standards, distinction between public and private material, maintenance and dissemination of recorded information, workload, and accountability. Working agreements in each instance are specified and made known to those concerned.

c. *Negative Conditions.*

Counselors alert their employers to conditions that may be potentially disruptive or damaging to the counselor's professional responsibilities or that may limit their effectiveness.

d. *Evaluation.*

Counselors submit regularly to professional review and evaluation by their supervisor or the appropriate representative of the employer.

e. *In-Service.*

Counselors are responsible for in-service development of self and staff.

f. *Goals.*

Counselors inform their staff of goals and programs.

g. *Practices.*

Counselors provide personnel and agency practices that respect and enhance the rights and welfare of each employee and recipient of agency services. Counselors strive to maintain the highest levels of professional services.

h. *Personnel Selection and Assignment.*

Counselors select competent staff and assign responsibilities compatible with their skills and experiences.

i. *Discrimination.*

Counselors, as either employers or employees, do not engage in or condone practices that are inhumane, illegal, or unjustifiable (such as considerations based on age, color, culture, disability, ethnic group, gender, race, religion, sexual orientation, or socioeconomic status) in hiring, promotion, or training. (See A.2.a. and C.5.b.)

j. *Professional Conduct.*

Counselors have a responsibility both to clients and to the agency or institution within which services are performed to maintain high standards of professional conduct.

k. *Exploitive Relationships.*

Counselors do not engage in exploitive relationships with individuals over whom they have supervisory, evaluative, or instructional control or authority.

l. *Employer Policies.*

The acceptance of employment in an agency or institution implies that counselors are in agreement with its general policies and principles. Counselors strive to reach agreement with employers as to acceptable standards of conduct that allow for changes in institutional policy conducive to the growth and development of clients.

D.2.   CONSULTATION (See B.6.)

a. *Consultation as an Option.*

Counselors may choose to consult with any other professionally competent persons about their clients. In choosing consultants, counselors avoid placing the consultant in a conflict of interest situation that would preclude the consultant being a proper party to the counselor's efforts to help the client. Should counselors be engaged in a work setting that compromises this consultation standard, they consult with other professionals whenever possible to consider justifiable alternatives.

b. *Consultant Competency.*

Counselors are reasonably certain that they have or the organization represented has the necessary competencies and resources for giving the kind of consulting services needed and that appropriate referral resources are available.

c. *Understanding with Clients.*

When providing consultation, counselors attempt to develop with their clients a clear understanding of problem definition, goals for change, and predicted consequences of interventions selected.

d. *Consultant Goals.*

The consulting relationship is one in which client adaptability and growth toward self-direction are consistently encouraged and cultivated. (See A.1.b.)

D.3.   FEES FOR REFERRAL

a. *Accepting Fees from Agency Clients.*

Counselors refuse a private fee or other remuneration for rendering services to persons who are entitled to such services through the counselor's employing agency or institution. The policies of a particular agency may make explicit provisions for agency clients to receive counseling services from members of its staff in private practice. In such instances, the clients must be informed of other options open to them should they seek private counseling services. (See A.10.a., A.11.b., and C.3.d.)

b. *Referral Fees.*

Counselors do not accept a referral fee from other professionals.

D.4.   SUBCONTRACTOR ARRANGEMENTS

When counselors work as subcontractors for counseling services for a third party, they have a duty to inform clients of the limitations of confidentiality that the organization may place on counselors in providing counseling services to clients. The limits of such confidentiality ordinarily are discussed as part of the intake session. (See B.1.e. and B.1.f.)

Section E: Evaluation, assessment, and interpretation

E.1.   GENERAL

a. *Appraisal Techniques.*

The primary purpose of educational and psychological assessment is to provide measures that are objective and interpretable in either comparative or absolute terms. Counselors recognize the need to interpret the statements in this section as applying to the whole range of appraisal techniques, including test and nontest data.

b. *Client Welfare.*

Counselors promote the welfare and best interests of the client in the development, publication, and utilization of educational and psychological assessment techniques. They do not misuse assessment results and interpretations and take reasonable steps to prevent others from misusing the information these techniques provide. They respect the client's right to know the results, the interpretations made, and the bases for their conclusions and recommendations.

E.2.   COMPETENCE TO USE AND INTERPRET TESTS

a. *Limits of Competence.*

Counselors recognize the limits of their competence and perform only those testing and assessment services for which they have been trained. They are familiar with reliability, validity, related standardization, error of measurement, and proper application of any technique utilized. Counselors using computer-based test interpretations are trained in the construct being measured and the specific instrument being used prior to using this type of computer application. Counselors take reasonable measures to ensure the proper use of psychological assessment techniques by persons under their supervision.

b. *Appropriate Use.*

Counselors are responsible for the appropriate application, scoring, interpretation, and use of assessment instruments, whether they score and interpret such tests themselves or use computerized or other services.

c. *Decisions Based on Results.*

Counselors responsible for decisions involving individuals or policies that are based on assessment results have a thorough understanding of educational and psychological measurement, including validation criteria, test research, and guidelines for test development and use.

d. *Accurate Information.*

Counselors provide accurate information and avoid false claims or misconceptions when making statements about assessment instruments or techniques. Special efforts are made to avoid unwarranted connotations of such terms as IQ and grade equivalent scores. (See C.5.c.)

E.3.   INFORMED CONSENT

a. *Explanation to Clients.*

Prior to assessment, counselors explain the nature and purposes of assessment and the specific use of results in language the client (or other legally authorized person on behalf of the client) can understand, unless an explicit exception to this right has been agreed upon in advance. Regardless of whether scoring and interpretation are completed by counselors, by assistants, or by computer or other outside services, counselors take reasonable steps to ensure that appropriate explanations are given to the client.

b. *Recipients of Results.*

The examinee's welfare, explicit understanding, and prior agreement determine the recipients of test results. Counselors include accurate and appropriate interpretations with any release of individual or group test results. (See B.1.a. and C.5.c.)

E.4.   RELEASE OF INFORMATION TO
COMPETENT PROFESSIONALS

a. *Misuse of Results.*

Counselors do not misuse assessment results, including test results, and interpretations, and take reasonable steps to prevent the misuse of such by others. (See C.5.c.)

b. *Release of Raw Data.*

Counselors ordinarily release data (e.g. protocols, counseling or interview notes, or questionnaires) in which the client is identified only with the consent of the client or the client's legal representative. Such data are usually released only to persons recognized by counselors as competent to interpret the data. (See B.1.a.)

E.5.   PROPER DIAGNOSIS OF MENTAL DISORDERS

a. *Proper Diagnosis.*

Counselors take special care to provide proper diagnosis of mental disorders. Assessment techniques (including personal interview) used to determine client care (e.g., locus of treatment, type of treatment, or recommended follow-up) are carefully selected and appropriately used. (See A.3.a. and C.5.c.)

b. *Cultural Sensitivity.*

Counselors recognize that culture affects the manner in which clients' problems are defined. Clients' socioeconomic and cultural experience is considered when diagnosing mental disorders.

E.6.   TEST SELECTION

a. *Appropriateness of Instruments.*

Counselors carefully consider the validity, reliability, psychometric limitations, and appropriateness of instruments when selecting tests for use in a given situation or with a particular client.

b. *Culturally Diverse Populations.*

Counselors are cautious when selecting tests for culturally diverse populations to avoid inappropriateness of testing that may be outside of socialized behavioral or cognitive patterns.

E.7.   CONDITIONS OF TEST ADMINISTRATION

a. *Administration Conditions.*

Counselors administer tests under the same conditions that were established in their standardization. When tests are not administered under standard conditions or when unusual behavior or irregularities occur during the testing session, those conditions are noted in interpretation, and the results may be designated as invalid or of questionable validity.

b. *Computer Administration.*

Counselors are responsible for ensuring that administration programs function properly to provide clients with accurate results when a computer or other electronic methods are used for test administration. (See A.12.b.)

c. *Unsupervised Test-Taking.*

Counselors do not permit unsupervised or inadequately supervised use of tests or assessments unless the tests or assessments are designed, intended, and validated for self administration and/or scoring.

d. *Disclosure of Favorable Conditions.*

Prior to test administration, conditions that produce most favorable test results are made known to the examinee.

E.8.   DIVERSITY IN TESTING

Counselors are cautious in using assessment techniques, making evaluations, and interpreting the performance of populations not represented in the norm group on which an instrument was standardized. They recognize the effects of age, color, culture, disability, ethnic group, gender, race, religion, sexual orientation, and socioeconomic status on test administration and interpretation and place test results in proper perspective with other relevant factors. (See A.2.a.)

E.9.   TEST SCORING AND INTERPRETATION

a. *Reporting Reservations.*

In reporting assessment results, counselors indicate any reservations that exist regarding validity or reliability because of the circumstances of the assessment or the inappropriateness of the norms for the person tested.

b. *Research Instruments.*

Counselors exercise caution when interpreting the results of research instruments possessing insufficient technical data to support respondent results. The specific purposes for the use of such instruments are stated explicitly to the examinee.

c. *Testing Services.*

Counselors who provide test scoring and test interpretation services to support the assessment process confirm the validity of such interpretations. They accurately describe the purpose, norms, validity, reliability, and applications of the procedures and any special qualifications applicable to their use. The public offering of an automated test interpretations service is considered a professional-to-professional consultation. The formal responsibility of the consultant is to the consultee, but the ultimate and overriding responsibility is to the client.

E.10. TEST SECURITY

Counselors maintain the integrity and security of tests and other assessment techniques consistent with legal and contractual obligations. Counselors do not appropriate, reproduce, or modify published tests or parts thereof without acknowledgment and permission from the publisher.

E.11. OBSOLETE TESTS AND OUTDATED TEST RESULTS

Counselors do not use data or test results that are obsolete or outdated for the current purpose. Counselors make every effort to prevent the misuse of obsolete measures and test data by others.

E.12. TEST CONSTRUCTION

Counselors use established scientific procedures, relevant standards, and current professional knowledge for test design in the development, publication, and utilization of educational and psychological assessment techniques.

Section F: Teaching, training, and supervision

F. 1. COUNSELOR EDUCATORS AND TRAINERS

a. *Educators as Teachers and Practitioners.*
Counselors who are responsible for developing, implementing, and supervising educational programs are skilled as teachers and practitioners. They are knowledgeable regarding the ethical, legal, and regulatory aspects of the profession, are skilled in applying that knowledge, and make students and supervisees aware of their responsibilities. Counselors conduct counselor education and training programs in an ethical manner and serve as role models for professional behavior. Counselor educators should make an effort to infuse material related to human diversity into all courses and/or workshops that are designed to promote the development of professional counselors.

b. *Relationship Boundaries with Students and Supervisees.*
Counselors clearly define and maintain ethical, professional, and social relationship boundaries with their students and supervisees. They are aware of the differential in power that exists and the student's or supervisee's possible incomprehension of that power differential. Counselors explain to students and supervisees the potential for the relationship to become exploitive.

c. *Sexual Relationships.*
Counselors do not engage in sexual relationships with students or supervisees and do not subject them to sexual harassment. (See A.6. and C.5.b)

d. *Contributions to Research.*
Counselors give credit to students or supervisees for their contributions to research and scholarly projects. Credit is given through coauthorship, acknowledgment, footnote statement, or other appropriate means, in accordance with such contributions. (See G.4.b. and G.4.c.)

e. *Close Relatives.*
Counselors do not accept close relatives as students or supervisees.

f. *Supervision Preparation.*
Counselors who offer clinical supervision services are adequately prepared in supervision methods and techniques. Counselors who are doctoral students serving as practicum or internship supervisors to master's level students are adequately prepared and supervised by the training program.

g. *Responsibility for Services to Clients.*
Counselors who supervise the counseling services of others take reasonable measures to ensure that counseling services provided to clients are professional.

h. *Endorsement.*
Counselors do not endorse students or supervisees for certification, licensure, employment, or completion of an academic or training program if they believe students or supervisees are not qualified for the endorsement. Counselors take reasonable steps to assist students or supervisees who are not qualified for endorsement to become qualified.

F.2.   COUNSELOR EDUCATION AND
        TRAINING PROGRAMS
    a. *Orientation.*

    Prior to admission, counselors orient prospective students to the counselor education or training program's expectations, including but not limited to the following: (1) the type and level of skill acquisition required for successful completion of the training, (2) subject matter to be covered, (3) basis for evaluation, (4) training components that encourage self-growth or self-disclosure as part of the training process, (5) the type of supervision settings and requirements of the sites for required clinical field experiences, (6) student and supervisee evaluation and dismissal policies and procedures, and (7) up-to-date employment prospects for graduates.

    b. *Integration of Study and Practice.*

    Counselors establish counselor education and training programs that integrate academic study and supervised practice.

    c. *Evaluation.*

    Counselors clearly state to students and supervisees, in advance of training, the levels of competency expected, appraisal methods, and timing of evaluations for both didactic and experiential components. Counselors provide students and supervisees with periodic performance appraisal and evaluation feedback throughout the training program.

    d. *Teaching Ethics.*

    Counselors make students and supervisees aware of the ethical responsibilities and standards of the profession and the students' and supervisees' ethical responsibilities to the profession. (See C.1. and F.3.e.)

    e. *Peer Relationships.*

    When students or supervisees are assigned to lead counseling groups or provide clinical supervision for their peers, counselors take steps to ensure that students and supervisees placed in these roles do not have personal or adverse relationships with peers and that they understand they have the same ethical obligations as counselor educators, trainers, and supervisors. Counselors make every effort to ensure that the rights of peers are not compromised when students or supervisees are assigned to lead counseling groups or provide clinical supervision.

    f. *Varied Theoretical Positions.*

    Counselors present varied theoretical positions so that students and supervisees may make comparisons and have opportunities to develop their own positions. Counselors provide information concerning the scientific bases of professional practice. (See C.6.a.)

    g. *Field Placements.*

    Counselors develop clear policies within their training program regarding field placement and other clinical experiences. Counselors provide clearly stated roles and responsibilities for the student or supervisee, the site supervisor, and the program supervisor. They confirm that site supervisors are qualified to provide supervision and are informed of their professional and ethical responsibilities in this role.

    h. *Dual Relationships as Supervisors.*

    Counselors avoid dual relationships such as performing the role of site supervisor and training program supervisor in the student's or supervisee's training program. Counselors do not accept any form of professional services, fees, commissions, reimbursement, or remuneration from a site for student or supervisee placement.

    i. *Diversity in Programs.*

    Counselors are responsive to their institution's and program's recruitment and retention needs for training program administrators, faculty, and students with diverse backgrounds and special needs. (See A.2.a.)

F.3.   STUDENTS AND SUPERVISEES
    a. *Limitations.*

    Counselors, through ongoing evaluation and appraisal, are aware of the academic and personal limitations of students and supervisees that might impede performance. Counselors assist students and supervisees in securing remedial assistance when needed, and dismiss from the training program supervisees who are unable to provide competent service due to academic or personal limitations. Counselors seek professional consultation and document their decision to dismiss or refer students or supervisees for assistance. Counselors assure that students and supervisees have recourse to address decisions made, to require them to seek assistance, or to dismiss them.

b. *Self-Growth Experiences.*
Counselors use professional judgment when designing training experiences conducted by the counselors themselves that require student and supervisee self-growth or self-disclosure. Safeguards are provided so that students and supervisees are aware of the ramifications their self-disclosure may have on counselors whose primary role as teacher, trainer, or supervisor requires acting on ethical obligations to the profession. Evaluative components of experiential training experiences explicitly delineate predetermined academic standards that are separate and not dependent on the student's level of self-disclosure. (See A.6.)

c. *Counseling for Students and Supervisees.*
If students or supervisees request counseling, supervisors or counselor educators provide them with acceptable referrals. Supervisors or counselor educators do not serve as counselor to students or supervisees over whom they hold administrative, teaching, or evaluative roles unless this is a brief role associated with a training experience. (See A.6.b.)

d. *Clients of Students and Supervisees.*
Counselors make every effort to ensure that the clients at field placements are aware of the services rendered and the qualifications of the students and supervisees rendering those services. Clients receive professional disclosure information and are informed of the limits of confidentiality. Client permission is obtained in order for the students and supervisees to use any information concerning the counseling relationship in the training process. (See B.1.e.)

e. *Standards for Students and Supervisees.*
Students and supervisees preparing to become counselors adhere to the Code of Ethics and the Standards of Practice. Students and supervisees have the same obligations to clients as those required of counselors. (See H.1.)

Section G: Research and publication

G .1. RESEARCH RESPONSIBILITIES

a. *Use of Human Subjects.*
Counselors plan. design, conduct, and report research in a manner consistent with pertinent ethical principles, federal and state laws, host institutional regulations, and scientific standards governing research with human subjects. Counselors design and conduct research that reflects cultural sensitivity appropriateness.

b. *Deviation from Standard Practices.*
Counselors seek consultation and observe stringent safeguards to protect the rights of research participants when a research problem suggests a deviation from standard acceptable practices. (See B.6.)

c. *Precautions to Avoid Injury.*
Counselors who conduct research with human subjects are responsible for the subjects' welfare throughout the experiment and take reasonable precautions to avoid causing injurious psychological, physical, or social effects to their subjects.

d. *Principal Researcher Responsibility.*
The ultimate responsibility for ethical research practice lies with the principal researcher. All others involved in the research activities share ethical obligations and full responsibility for their own actions.

e. *Minimal Interference.*
Counselors take reasonable precautions to avoid causing disruptions in subjects' lives due to participation in research.

f. *Diversity.*
Counselors are sensitive to diversity and research issues with special populations.

They seek consultation when appropriate. (See A.2.a. and B.6.)

G.2. INFORMED CONSENT

a. *Topics Disclosed.*

In obtaining informed consent for research, counselors use language that is understandable to research participants and that: (1) accurately explains the purpose and procedures to be followed; (2) identifies any procedures that are experimental or relatively untried; (3) describes the attendant discomforts and risks; (4) describes the benefits or changes in individuals or organizations that might be reasonably expected; (5) discloses appropriate alternative procedures that would be advantageous for subjects; (6) offers to answer any inquiries concerning the procedures; (7) describes any limitations on confidentiality; and (8) instructs that subjects are free to withdraw their consent and to discontinue participation in the project at any time. (See B.1.f.)

b. *Deception.*

Counselors do not conduct research involving deception unless alternative procedures are not feasible and the prospective value of the research justifies the deception. When the methodological requirements of a study necessitate concealment or deception, the investigator is required to explain clearly the reasons for this action as soon as possible.

c. *Voluntary Participation.*

Participation in research is typically voluntary and without any penalty for refusal to participate. Involuntary participation is appropriate only when it can be demonstrated that participation will have no harmful effects on subjects and is essential to the investigation.

d. *Confidentiality of Information.*

Information obtained about research participants during the course of an investigation is confidential. When the possibility exists that others may obtain access to such information, ethical research practice requires that the possibility, together with the plans for protecting confidentiality, be explained to participants as a part of the procedure for obtaining informed consent. (See B.1.e.)

e. *Persons Incapable of Giving Informed Consent.*

When a person is incapable of giving informed consent, counselors provide an appropriate explanation, obtain agreement for participation and obtain appropriate consent from a legally authorized person.

f. *Commitments to Participants.*

Counselors take reasonable measures to honor all commitments to research participants.

g. *Explanations after Data Collection.*

After data are collected, counselors provide participants with full clarification of the nature of the study to remove any misconceptions. Where scientific or human values justify delaying or withholding information, counselors take reasonable measures to avoid causing harm.

h. *Agreements to Cooperate.*

Counselors who agree to cooperate with another individual in research or publication incur an obligation to cooperate as promised in terms of punctuality of performance and with regard to the completeness and accuracy of the information required.

i. *Informed Consent for Sponsors.*

In the pursuit of research, counselors give sponsors, institutions, and publication channels the same respect and opportunity for giving informed consent that they accord to individual research participants. Counselors are aware of their obligation to future research workers and ensure that host institutions are given feedback information and proper acknowledgment.

G.3. REPORTING RESULTS

a. *Information Affecting Outcome.*

When reporting research results, counselors explicitly mention all variables and conditions known to the investigator that may have affected the outcome of a study or the interpretation of data.

b. *Accurate Results.*

Counselors plan, conduct, and report research accurately and in a manner that minimizes the possibility that results will be misleading. They provide thorough discussions of the limitations of their data and alternative hypotheses. Counselors do not engage in fraudulent research, distort data, misrepresent data, or deliberately bias their results.

c. *Obligation to Report Unfavorable Results.*
Counselors communicate to other counselors the results of any research judged to be of professional value. Results that reflect unfavorably on institutions, programs, services, prevailing opinions, or vested interests are not withheld.

d. *Identity of Subjects.*
Counselors who supply data, aid in the research of another person, report research results, or make original data available take due care to disguise the identity of respective subjects in the absence of specific authorization from the subjects to do otherwise. (See B.1.g. and B.5.a.)

e. *Replication Studies.*
Counselors are obligated to make available sufficient original research data to qualified professionals who may wish to replicate the study.

G.4. PUBLICATION

a. *Recognition of Others.*
When conducting and reporting research, counselors are familiar with and give recognition to previous work on the topic, observe copyright laws, and give full credit to those to whom credit is due. (See F.1.d. and G.4.c.)

b. *Contributors.*
Counselors give credit through joint authorship, acknowledgment, footnote statements, or other appropriate means to those who have contributed significantly to research or concept development in accordance with such contributions. The principal contributor is listed first and minor technical or professional contributions are acknowledged in notes or introductory statements.

c. *Student Research.*
For an article that is substantially based on a student's dissertation or thesis, the student is listed as the principal author. (See F.1.d. and G.4.a.)

d. *Duplicate Submission.*
Counselors submit manuscripts for consideration to only one journal at a time. Manuscripts that are published in whole or in substantial part in another journal or published work are not submitted for publication without acknowledgment and permission from the previous publication.

e. *Professional Review.*
Counselors who review material submitted for publication, research, or other scholarly purposes respect the confidentiality and proprietary rights of those who submitted it.

Section H: Resolving ethical issues

H.1. KNOWLEDGE OF STANDARDS
Counselors are familiar with the Code of Ethics and the Standards of Practice and other applicable ethics codes from other professional organizations of which they are members, or from certification and licensure bodies. Lack of knowledge or misunderstanding of an ethical responsibility is not a defense against a charge of unethical conduct. (See F.3.c.)

H.2. SUSPECTED VIOLATIONS

a. *Ethical Behavior Expected.*
Counselors expect professional associates to adhere to the Code of Ethics. When counselors possess reasonable cause that raises doubts as to whether a counselor is acting in an ethical manner, they take appropriate action. (See H.2.d. and H.2.e.)

b. *Consultation.*
When uncertain as to whether a particular situation or course of action may be in violation of the Code of Ethics, counselors consult with other counselors who are knowledgeable about ethics, with colleagues, or with appropriate authorities.

c. *Organization Conflicts.*
If the demands of an organization with which counselors are affiliated pose a conflict with the Code of Ethics, counselors specify the nature of such conflicts and express to their supervisors or other responsible officials their commitment to the Code of Ethics. When possible, coun-

selors work toward change within the organization to allow full adherence to the Code of Ethics.

d. *Informal Resolution.*

When counselors have reasonable cause to believe that another counselor is violating an ethical standard, they attempt to first resolve the issue informally with the other counselor if feasible, providing that such action does not violate confidentiality rights that may be involved.

e. *Reporting Suspected Violations.*

When an informal resolution is not appropriate or feasible, counselors, upon reasonable cause, take action such as reporting the suspected ethical violation to state or national ethics committees, unless this action conflicts with confidentiality rights that cannot be resolved.

f. *Unwarranted Complaints.*

Counselors do not initiate, participate in, or encourage the filing of ethics complaints that are unwarranted or intend to harm a counselor rather than to protect clients or the public.

H.3.   COOPERATION WITH ETHICS COMMITTEES

Counselors assist in the process of enforcing the Code of Ethics. Counselors cooperate with investigations, proceedings, and requirements of the ACA Ethics Committee or ethics committees of other duly constituted associations or boards having jurisdiction over those charged with a violation. Counselors are familiar with the ACA Policies and Procedures and use it as a reference in assisting the enforcement of the Code of Ethics.

STANDARDS OF PRACTICE

All members of the American Counseling Association (ACA) are required to adhere to the Standards of Practice and the Code of Ethics. The Standards of Practice represent minimal behavioral statements of the Code of Ethics. Members should refer to the applicable section of the Code of Ethics for further interpretation and amplification of the applicable Standard of Practice.

Section A: The counseling relationship

STANDARD OF PRACTICE ONE (SP-1)
  NONDISCRIMINATION

Counselors respect diversity and must not discriminate against clients because of age, color, culture, disability, ethnic group, gender, race, religion, sexual orientation, marital status, or socioeconomic status. (See A.2.a.)

STANDARD OF PRACTICE TWO (SP-2)
DISCLOSURE TO CLIENTS

Counselors must adequately inform clients, preferably in writing, regarding the counseling process and counseling relationship at or before the time it begins and throughout the relationship. (See A.3.a.)

STANDARD OF PRACTICE THREE (SP-3)
DUAL RELATIONSHIPS

Counselors must make every effort to avoid dual relationships with clients that could impair their professional judgment or increase the risk of harm to clients. When a dual relationship cannot be avoided, counselors must take appropriate steps to ensure that judgment is not impaired and that no exploitation occurs. (See A.6.a. and A.6.b.)

STANDARD OF PRACTICE FOUR (SP-4)
SEXUAL INTIMACIES WITH CLIENTS

Counselors must not engage in any type of sexual intimacies with current clients and must not engage in sexual intimacies with former clients within a minimum of two years after terminating the counseling relationship. Counselors who engage in such relationship after two years following termination have the responsibility to thoroughly examine and document that such relations did not have an exploitative nature.

STANDARD OF PRACTICE FIVE (SP-5)
PROTECTING CLIENTS DURING GROUP WORK

Counselors must take steps to protect clients from physical or psychological trauma resulting from interactions during group work. (See A.9.b.)

STANDARD OF PRACTICE SIX (SP-6)
ADVANCE UNDERSTANDING OF FEES

Counselors must explain to clients, prior to their entering the counseling relationship, financial arrangements related to professional services. (See A.10. a-d. and A.11.c.)

STANDARD OF PRACTICE SEVEN (SP-7)

TERMINATION

Counselors must assist in making appropriate arrangements for the continuation of treatment of clients, when necessary, following termination of counseling relationships. (See A.11.a.)

STANDARD OF PRACTICE EIGHT (SP-8)

INABILITY TO ASSIST CLIENTS

Counselors must avoid entering or immediately terminate a counseling relationship if it is determined that they are unable to be of professional assistance to a client. The counselor may assist in making an appropriate referral for the client. (See A.11.b.)

STANDARD OF PRACTICE FOURTEEN (SP-14)

PERMISSION TO RECORD OR OBSERVE

Counselors must obtain prior consent from clients in order to electronically record or observe sessions. (See B.4.c.)

STANDARD OF PRACTICE FIFTEEN (SP-15)

DISCLOSURE OR TRANSFER OF RECORDS

Counselors must obtain client consent to disclose or transfer records to third parties, unless exceptions listed in SP-9 exist. (See B.4.e.)

STANDARD OF PRACTICE SIXTEEN (SP-16)

DATA DISGUISE REQUIRED

Counselors must disguise the identity of the client when using data for training, research, or publication. (See B.5.a.)

Section B: Confidentiality

STANDARD OF PRACTICE NINE (SP-9)

CONFIDENTIALITY REQUIREMENT

Counselors must keep information related to counseling services confidential unless disclosure is in the best interest of clients, is required for the welfare of others, or is required by law. When disclosure is required, only information that is essential is revealed and the client is informed of such disclosure. (See B.1. a.-f.)

STANDARD OF PRACTICE TEN (SP-10)

CONFIDENTIALITY REQUIREMENTS FOR SUBORDINATES

Counselors must take measures to ensure that privacy and confidentiality of clients are maintained by subordinates. (See B.1.h.)

STANDARD OF PRACTICE ELEVEN (SP-11)

CONFIDENTIALITY IN GROUP WORK

Counselors must clearly communicate to group members that confidentiality cannot be guaranteed in group work. (See B.2.a.)

STANDARD OF PRACTICE TWELVE (SP-12)

CONFIDENTIALITY IN FAMILY COUNSELING

Counselors must not disclose information about one family member in counseling to another family member without prior consent. (See B.2.b.)

STANDARD OF PRACTICE THIRTEEN (SP-13)

CONFIDENTIALITY OF RECORDS

Counselors must maintain appropriate confidentiality in creating, storing, accessing, transferring, and disposing of counseling records. (See B.4.b.)

Section C: Professional responsibility

STANDARD OF PRACTICE SEVENTEEN (SP-17)

BOUNDARIES OF COMPETENCE

Counselors must practice only within the boundaries of their competence. (See C.2.a.)

STANDARD OF PRACTICE EIGHTEEN (SP-18)

CONTINUING EDUCATION

Counselors must engage in continuing education to maintain their professional competence. (See C.2.f.)

STANDARD OF PRACTICE NINETEEN (SP-19)

IMPAIRMENT OF PROFESSIONALS

Counselors must refrain from offering professional services when their personal problems or conflicts may cause harm to a client or others. (See C.2.g.)

STANDARD OF PRACTICE TWENTY (SP-20)

ACCURATE ADVERTISING

Counselors must accurately represent their credentials and services when advertising. (See C.3.a.)

STANDARD OF PRACTICE TWENTY-ONE (SP-21)

RECRUITING THROUGH EMPLOYMENT

Counselors must not use their place of employment or institutional affiliation to recruit clients for their private practices. (See C.3.d.)

STANDARD OF PRACTICE TWENTY-TWO (SP-22)

CREDENTIALS CLAIMED

Counselors must claim or imply only professional credentials possessed and must correct any known misrepresentations of their credentials by others. (See C.4.a.)

STANDARD OF PRACTICE TWENTY-THREE (SP-23)
SEXUAL HARASSMENT

Counselors must not engage in sexual harassment. (See C.5.b.)

STANDARD OF PRACTICE TWENTY-FOUR (SP-24)
UNJUSTIFIED GAINS

Counselors must not use their professional positions to seek or receive unjustified personal gains, sexual favors, unfair advantage, or unearned goods or services. (See C.5.e.)

STANDARD OF PRACTICE TWENTY-FIVE (SP-25)
CLIENTS SERVED BY OTHERS

With the consent of the client, counselors must inform other mental health professionals serving the same client that a counseling relationship between the counselor and client exists. (See C.6.c.)

STANDARD OF PRACTICE TWENTY-SIX (SP-26)
NEGATIVE EMPLOYMENT CONDITIONS

Counselors must alert their employers to institutional policy or conditions that may be potentially disruptive or damaging to the counselor's professional responsibilities, or that may limit their effectiveness or deny clients' rights. (See D.1.c.)

STANDARD OF PRACTICE TWENTY-SEVEN (SP-27)
PERSONNEL SELECTION AND ASSIGNMENT

Counselors must select competent staff and must assign responsibilities compatible with staff skills and experiences. (See D.1.h.)

STANDARD OF PRACTICE TWENTY-EIGHT (SP-28)
EXPLOITIVE RELATIONSHIPS WITH SUBORDINATES

Counselors must not engage in exploitive relationships with individuals over whom they have supervisory, evaluative, or instructional control or authority. (See D.1.k.)

Section D: Relationship with other professionals

STANDARD OF PRACTICE TWENTY-NINE (SP-29)
ACCEPTING FEES FROM AGENCY CLIENTS

Counselors must not accept fees or other remuneration for consultation with persons entitled to such services through the counselor's employing agency or institution. (See D.3.a.)

STANDARD OF PRACTICE THIRTY (SP-30)
REFERRAL FEES

Counselors must not accept referral fees. (See D.3.b.)

Section E: Evaluation, assessment, and interpretation

STANDARD OF PRACTICE THIRTY-ONE (SP-31)
LIMITS OF COMPETENCE

Counselors must perform only testing and assessment services for which they are competent. Counselors must not allow the use of psychological assessment techniques by unqualified persons under their supervision. (See E.2.a.)

STANDARD OF PRACTICE THIRTY-TWO (SP-32)
APPROPRIATE USE OF ASSESSMENT INSTRUMENTS

Counselors must use assessment instruments in the manner for which they were intended. (See E.2.b.)

STANDARD OF PRACTICE THIRTY-THREE (SP-33)
ASSESSMENT EXPLANATIONS TO CLIENTS

Counselors must provide explanations to clients prior to assessment about the nature and purposes of assessment and the specific uses of results. (See E.3.a.)

STANDARD OF PRACTICE THIRTY-FOUR (SP-34)
RECIPIENTS OF TEST RESULTS

Counselors must ensure that accurate and appropriate interpretations accompany any release of testing and assessment information. (See E.3.b.)

STANDARD OF PRACTICE THIRTY-FIVE (SP-35)
OBSOLETE TESTS AND OUTDATED TEST RESULTS

Counselors must not base their assessment or intervention decisions or recommendations on data or test results that are obsolete or outdated for the current purpose. (See E.11.)

Section F: Teaching, training, and supervision

STANDARD OF PRACTICE THIRTY-SIX (SP-36)
SEXUAL RELATIONSHIPS WITH STUDENTS OR SUPERVISEES

Counselors must not engage in sexual relationships with their students and supervisees. (See F.1.c.)

STANDARD OF PRACTICE THIRTY-SEVEN (SP-37)
CREDIT FOR CONTRIBUTIONS TO RESEARCH

Counselors must give credit to students or supervisees for their contributions to research and scholarly projects. (See F.1.d.)

STANDARD OF PRACTICE THIRTY-EIGHT (SP-38)
SUPERVISION PREPARATION

Counselors who offer clinical supervision services must be trained and prepared in supervision methods and techniques. (See F.1.f.)

STANDARD OF PRACTICE THIRTY-NINE (SP-39)

EVALUATION INFORMATION

Counselors must clearly state to students and supervisees in advance of training, the levels of competency expected, appraisal methods, and timing of evaluations. Counselors must provide students and supervisees with periodic performance appraisal and evaluation feedback throughout the training program. (See F.2.c.)

STANDARD OF PRACTICE FORTY (SP-40)

PEER RELATIONSHIPS IN TRAINING

Counselors must make every effort to ensure that the rights of peers are not violated when students and supervisees are assigned to lead counseling groups or provide clinical supervision. (See F.2.e.)

STANDARD OF PRACTICE FORTY-ONE (SP-41)

LIMITATIONS OF STUDENTS AND SUPERVISEES

Counselors must assist students and supervisees in securing remedial assistance, when needed, and must dismiss from the training program students and supervisees who are unable to provide competent service due to academic or personal limitations. (See F.3.a.)

STANDARD OF PRACTICE FORTY-TWO (SP-42)

SELF-GROWTH EXPERIENCES

Counselors who conduct experiences for students or supervisees that include self-growth or self-disclosure must inform participants of counselors' ethical obligations to the profession and must not grade participants based on their nonacademic performance. (See F.3.b.)

STANDARD OF PRACTICE FORTY-THREE (SP-43)

STANDARDS FOR STUDENTS AND SUPERVISEES

Students and supervisees preparing to become counselors must adhere to the Code of Ethics and the Standards of Practice of counselors. (See F.3.e.)

Section G: Research and publication

STANDARD OF PRACTICE FORTH-FOUR (SP-44)

PRECAUTIONS TO AVOID INJURY IN RESEARCH

Counselors must avoid causing physical, social, or psychological harm or injury to subjects in research. (See G.1.c.)

STANDARD OF PRACTICE FORTY-FIVE (SP-45)

CONFIDENTIALITY OF RESEARCH INFORMATION

Counselors must keep confidential information obtained about research participants. (See G.2.d.)

STANDARD OF PRACTICE FORTY-SIX (SP-46)

INFORMATION AFFECTING RESEARCH OUTCOME

Counselors must report all variables and conditions known to the investigator that may have affected research data or outcomes. (See G.3.a.)

STANDARD OF PRACTICE FORTY-SEVEN (SP-47)

ACCURATE RESEARCH RESULTS

Counselors must not distort or misrepresent research data, nor fabricate or intentionally bias research results. (See G.3.b.)

STANDARD OF PRACTICE FORTY-EIGHT (SP-48)

PUBLICATION CONTRIBUTORS

Counselors must give appropriate credit to those who have contributed to research. (See G.4.a. and G.4.b.)

Section H: Resolving ethical issues

STANDARD OF PRACTICE FORTY-NINE (SP-49)

ETHICAL BEHAVIOR EXPECTED

Counselors must take appropriate action when they possess reasonable cause that raises doubts as to whether counselors or other mental health professionals are acting in an ethical manner. (See H.2.a.)

STANDARD OF PRACTICE FIFTY (SP-50)

UNWARRANTED COMPLAINTS

Counselors must not initiate, participate in, or encourage the filings of ethics complaints that are unwarranted or intended to harm a mental health professional rather than to protect clients or the public. (See H.2.f.)

STANDARD OF PRACTICE FIFTY-ONE (SP-51)

COOPERATION WITH ETHICS COMMITTEES

Counselors must cooperate with investigations, proceedings, and requirements of the ACA Ethics Committee or ethics committees of other duly constituted associations or boards having jurisdiction over those charged with a violation. (See H.3.)

B. *Ethical Principles of Psychologists and Code of Conduct, American Psychological Association (APA, 1995)*

INTRODUCTION

The American Psychological Association's (APA's) Ethical Principles of Psychologists and Code of Conduct (hereinafter referred to as the Ethics Code) consists of an Introduction, a Preamble, six General Principles (A–F), and specific Ethical Standards. The Introduction discusses the intent, organization, procedural considerations, and scope of application of the Ethics Code. The Preamble and General Principles are *aspirational* goals to guide psychologists toward the highest ideals of psychology. Although the Preamble and General Principles are not themselves enforceable rules, they should be considered by psychologists in arriving at an ethical course of action and may be considered by ethics bodies in interpreting the Ethical Standards. The Ethical Standards set forth *enforceable* rules for conduct as psychologists. Most of the Ethical Standards are written broadly, in order to apply to psychologists in varied roles, although the application of an Ethical Standard may vary depending on the context. The Ethical Standards are not exhaustive. The fact that a given conduct is not specifically addressed by the Ethics Code does not mean that it is necessarily either ethical or unethical.

Membership in the APA commits members to adhere to the APA Ethics Code and to the rules and procedures used to implement it. Psychologists and students, whether or not they are APA members, should be aware that the Ethics Code may be applied to them by state psychology boards, courts, or other public bodies.

This Ethics Code applies only to psychologists' work-related activities, that is, activities that are part of the psychologists' scientific and professional functions or that are psychological in nature. It includes the clinical or counseling practice of psychology, research, teaching, supervision of trainees, development of assessment instruments, conducting assessments, educational counseling, organizational consulting, social intervention, administration, and other activities as well. These work-related activities can be distinguished from the purely private conduct of a psychologist, which ordinarily is not within the purview of the Ethics Code.

The Ethics Code is intended to provide standards of professional conduct that can be applied by the APA and by other bodies that choose to adopt them. Whether or not a psychologist has violated the Ethics Code does not by itself determine whether he or she is legally liable in a court action, whether a contract is enforceable, or whether other legal consequences occur. These results are based on legal rather than ethical rules. However, compliance with or violation of the Ethics Code may be admissible as evidence in some legal proceedings, depending on the circumstances.

In the process of making decisions regarding their professional behavior, psychologists must consider this Ethics Code, in addition to applicable laws and psychology board regulations. If the

Ethics Code establishes a higher standard of conduct than is required by law, psychologists must meet the higher ethical standard. If the Ethics Code standard appears to conflict with the requirements of law, then psychologists make known their commitment to the Ethics Code and take steps to resolve the conflict in a responsible manner. If neither law nor the Ethics Code resolves an issue, psychologists should consider other professional materials[1] and the dictates of their own conscience, as well as seek consultation with others within the field when this is practical.

The procedures for filing, investigating, and resolving complaints of unethical conduct are described in the current Rules and Procedures of the APA Ethics Committee. The actions that APA may take for violations of the Ethics Code include actions such as reprimand, censure, termination of APA membership, and referral of the matter to other bodies. Complainants who seek remedies such as monetary damages in alleging ethical violations by a psychologist must resort to private negotiation, administrative bodies, or the courts. Actions that violate the Ethics Code may lead to the imposition of sanctions on a psychologist by bodies other than APA, including state psychological associations, other professional groups, psychology boards, other state or federal agencies, and payors for health services. In addition to actions for violation of the Ethics Code, the APA Bylaws provide that APA may take action against a member after his or her conviction of a felony, expulsion or suspension from an affiliated state psychological association, or suspension or loss of licensure.

PREAMBLE

Psychologists work to develop a valid and reliable body of scientific knowledge based on research. They may apply that knowledge to human behavior in a variety of contexts. In doing so, they perform many roles, such as researcher, educator, diagnostician, therapist, supervisor, consultant, administrator, social interventionist, and expert witness. Their goal is to broaden knowledge of behavior and, where appropriate, to apply it pragmatically to improve the condition of both the individual and society. Psychologists respect the central importance of freedom of inquiry and expression in research, teaching, and publication. They also strive to help the public in developing informed judgments and choices concerning human behavior. This Ethics Code provides a common set of values upon which psychologists build their professional and scientific work.

This Code is intended to provide both the general principles and the decision rules to cover most situations encountered by psychologists. It has as its primary goal the welfare and protection of the individuals and groups with whom psychologists work. It is the individual responsibility of each psychologist to aspire to the highest possible standards of conduct. Psychologists respect and protect human and civil rights, and do not knowingly participate in or condone unfair discriminatory practices.

The development of a dynamic set of ethical standards for a psychologist's work-related conduct requires a personal commitment to a lifelong effort to act ethically; to encourage ethical behavior by students, supervisees, employees, and colleagues, as appropriate; and to consult with others, as needed, concerning ethical problems. Each psychologist supplements, but does not violate, the Ethics Code's values and rules on the basis of guidance drawn from personal values, culture, and experience.

[1]Professional materials that are most helpful in this regard are guidelines and standards that have been adopted or endorsed by professional psychological organizations. Such guidelines and standards, whether adopted by the American Psychological Association (APA) or its Divisions, are not enforceable as such by this Ethics Code, but are of educative value to psychologists, courts, and professional bodies. Such materials include, but are not limited to, the APA's *General Guidelines for Providers of Psychological Services* (1987), *Specialty Guidelines for the Delivery of Services by Clinical Psychologists, Counseling Psychologists Industrial/Organizational Psychologists, and School Psychologists* (1981), *Guidelines for Computer Based Tests and Interpretations* (1987), *Standards for Educational and Psychological Testing* (1985), *Ethical Principles in the Conduct of Research With Human Participants* (1982), *Guidelines for Ethical Conduct in the Care and Use of Animals* (1986), *Guidelines for Providers of Psychological Services to Ethnic, Linguistic, and Culturally Diverse Populations* (1990), and *Publication Manual of the American Psychological Association* (3rd ed., 1983). Materials not adopted by APA as a whole include the APA Division 41 (Forensic Psychology)/ American Psychology–Law Society's *Specialty Guidelines for Forensic Psychologists* (1991).

GENERAL PRINCIPLES

Principle A: Competence

Psychologists strive to maintain high standards of competence in their work. They recognize the boundaries of their particular competencies and the limitations of their expertise. They provide only those services and use only those techniques for which they are qualified by education, training, or experience. Psychologists are cognizant of the fact that the competencies required in serving, teaching, and/or studying groups of people vary with the distinctive characteristics of those groups. In those areas in which recognized professional standards do not yet exist, psychologists exercise careful judgment and take appropriate precautions to protect the welfare of those with whom they work. They maintain knowledge of relevant scientific and professional information related to the services they render, and they recognize the need for ongoing education. Psychologists make appropriate use of scientific, professional, technical, and administrative resources.

Principle B: Integrity

Psychologists seek to promote integrity in the science, teaching, and practice of psychology. In these activities psychologists are honest, fair, and respectful of others. In describing or reporting their qualifications, services, products, fees, research, or teaching, they do not make statements that are false, misleading, or deceptive. Psychologists strive to be aware of their own belief systems, values, needs, and limitations and the effect of these on their work. To the extent feasible, they attempt to clarify for relevant parties the roles they are performing and to function appropriately in accordance with those roles. Psychologists avoid improper and potentially harmful dual relationships.

Principle C: Professional and scientific responsibility

Psychologists uphold professional standards of conduct, clarify their professional roles and obligations, accept appropriate responsibility for their behavior, and adapt their methods to the needs of different populations. Psychologists consult with, refer to, or cooperate with other professionals and institutions to the extent needed to serve the best interests of their patients, clients, or other recipients of their services. Psychologists' moral standards and conduct are personal matters to the same degree as is true for any other person, except as psychologists' conduct may compromise their professional responsibilities or reduce the public's trust in psychology and psychologists. Psychologists are concerned about the ethical compliance of their colleagues' scientific and professional conduct. When appropriate, they consult with colleagues in order to prevent or avoid unethical conduct.

Principle D: Respect for people's rights and dignity

Psychologists accord appropriate respect to the fundamental rights, dignity, and worth of all people. They respect the rights of individuals to privacy, confidentiality, self-determination, and autonomy, mindful that legal and other obligations may lead to inconsistency and conflict with the exercise of these rights. Psychologists are aware of cultural, individual, and role differences, including those due to age, gender, race, ethnicity, national origin, religion, sexual orientation, disability, language, and socioeconomic status. Psychologists try to eliminate the effect on their work of biases based on those factors, and they do not knowingly participate in or condone unfair discriminatory practices.

Principle E: Concern for others' welfare

Psychologists seek to contribute to the welfare of those with whom they interact professionally. In their professional actions, psychologists weigh the welfare and rights of their patients or clients, students, supervisees, human research participants, and other affected persons, and the welfare of animal subjects of research. When conflicts occur among psychologists' obligations or concerns, they attempt to resolve these conflicts and to perform their roles in a responsible fashion that avoids or minimizes harm. Psychologists are sensitive to real and ascribed differences in power between themselves and others, and they do not exploit or mislead other people during or after professional relationships.

Principle F: Social responsibility

Psychologists are aware of their professional and scientific responsibilities to the community and the society in which they work and live. They apply and make public their knowledge of psychology in order to contribute to human welfare. Psychologists are concerned about and work to mitigate the causes of human suffering. When undertaking research, they strive to advance human welfare and the science of psychology. Psychologists try to avoid misuse of their work. Psychologists comply with the law and encourage the development of law and social policy that serve the interests of their patients and clients and the public. They are encouraged to contribute a portion of their professional time for little or no personal advantage.

ETHICAL STANDARDS

1. General standards

These General Standards are potentially applicable to the professional and scientific activities of all psychologists.

1.01 Applicability of the Ethics Code
The activity of a psychologist subject to the Ethics Code may be reviewed under these Ethical Standards only if the activity is part of his or her work-related functions or the activity is psychological in nature. Personal activities having no connection to or effect on psychological roles are not subject to the Ethics Code.

1.02 Relationship of Ethics and Law
If psychologists' ethical responsibilities conflict with law, psychologists make known their commitment to the Ethics Code and take steps to resolve the conflict in a responsible manner.

1.03 Professional and Scientific Relationship
Psychologists provide diagnostic, therapeutic, teaching, research, supervisory, consultative, or other psychological services only in the context of a defined professional or scientific relationship or role. (See also Standards 2.01. Evaluation, Diagnosis, and Interventions in Professional Context, and 7.02, Forensic Assessments.)

1.04 Boundaries of Competence

a. Psychologists provide services, teach, and conduct research only within the boundaries of their competence, based on their education, training, supervised experience, or appropriate professional experience.

b. Psychologists provide services, teach, or conduct research in new areas or involving new techniques only after first undertaking appropriate study, training, supervision, and/or consultation from persons who are competent in those areas or techniques.

c. In those emerging areas in which generally recognized standards for preparatory training do not yet exist, psychologists nevertheless take reasonable steps to ensure the competence of their work and to protect patients, clients, students, research participants, and others from harm.

1.05 Maintaining Expertise
Psychologists who engage in assessment, therapy, teaching, research, organizational consulting, or other professional activities maintain a reasonable level of awareness of current scientific and professional information in their fields of activity, and undertake ongoing efforts to maintain competence in the skills they use.

1.06 Basis for Scientific and Professional Judgments
Psychologists rely on scientifically and professionally derived knowledge when making scientific or professional judgments or when engaging in scholarly or professional endeavors.

1.07 Describing the Nature and Results of Psychological Services
a. When psychologists provide assessment, evaluation, treatment, counseling, supervision, teaching, consultation, research, or other psychological services to an individual, a group, or an organization, they provide, using language that is reasonably understandable to the recipient of those services, appropriate information beforehand about the nature of such services and appropriate information later about results and conclusions. (See also Standard 2.09, Explaining Assessment Results.)

b. If psychologists will be precluded by law or by organizational roles from providing such information to particular individuals or groups, they so inform those individuals or groups at the outset of the service.

1.08 Human Differences

Where differences of age, gender, race, ethnicity, national origin, religion, sexual orientation, disability, language, or socioeconomic status significantly affect psychologists' work concerning particular individuals or groups, psychologists obtain the training, experience, consultation, or supervision necessary to ensure the competence of their services, or they make appropriate referrals.

1.09 Respecting Others

In their work-related activities, psychologists respect the rights of others to hold values, attitudes, and opinions that differ from their own.

1.10 Nondiscrimination

In their work-related activities, psychologists do not engage in unfair discrimination based on age, gender, race, ethnicity, national origin, religion, sexual orientation, disability, socioeconomic status, or any basis proscribed by law.

1.11 Sexual Harassment

a. Psychologists do not engage in sexual harassment. Sexual harassment is sexual solicitation, physical advances, or verbal or nonverbal conduct that is sexual in nature, that occurs in connection with the psychologists' activities or roles as a psychologist, and that either: (1) is unwelcome, is offensive, or creates a hostile workplace environment, and the psychologist knows or is told this; or (2) is sufficiently severe or intense to be abusive to a reasonable person in the context. Sexual harassment can consist of a single intense or severe act or of multiple persistent or pervasive acts.

b. Psychologists accord sexual-harassment complainants and respondents dignity and respect. Psychologists do not participate in denying a person academic admittance or advancement, employment, tenure, or promotion, based solely upon their having made, or their being the sub-

ject of, sexual-harassment charges. This does not preclude taking action based upon the outcome of such proceedings or consideration of other appropriate information.

1.12 Other Harassment

Psychologists do not knowingly engage in behavior that is harassing or demeaning to persons with whom they interact in their work based on factors such as those persons' age, gender, race, ethnicity, national origin, religion, sexual orientation, disability, language, or socioeconomic status.

1.13 Personal Problems and Conflicts

a. Psychologists recognize that their personal problems and conflicts may interfere with their effectiveness. Accordingly, they refrain from undertaking an activity when they know or should know that their personal problems are likely to lead to harm to a patient, client, colleague, student, research participant, or other person to whom they may owe a professional or scientific obligation.

b. In addition, psychologists have an obligation to be alert to signs of, and to obtain assistance for, their personal problems at an early stage, in order to prevent significantly impaired performance.

c. When psychologists become aware of personal problems that may interfere with their performing work-related duties adequately, they take appropriate measures, such as obtaining professional consultation or assistance, and determine whether they should limit, suspend, or terminate their work-related duties.

1.14 Avoiding Harm

Psychologists take reasonable steps to avoid harming their patients or clients, research participants, students, and others with whom they work, and minimize harm where it is foreseeable and unavoidable.

1.15 Misuse of Psychologists' Influence

Because psychologists' scientific and professional judgments and actions may affect the lives of others, they are alert to and guard against personal, financial, social, organizational, or political factors that might lead to misuse of their influence.

1.16 Misuse of Psychologists' Work

  a. Psychologists do not participate in activities in which it appears likely that their skills or data will be misused by others, unless corrective mechanisms are available. (See also Standard 7.04, Truthfulness and Candor.)

  b. If psychologists learn of misuse or misrepresentation of their work, they take reasonable steps to correct or minimize the misuse or misrepresentation.

1.17 Multiple Relationships

  a. In many communities and situations, it may not be feasible or reasonable for psychologists to avoid social or other nonprofessional contacts with persons such as patients, clients, students, supervisees, or research participants. Psychologists must always be sensitive to the potential harmful effects of other contacts on their work and on those persons with whom they deal. A psychologist refrains from entering into or promising another personal, scientific, professional, financial, or other relationship with such persons if it appears likely that such a relationship reasonably might impair the psychologist's objectivity or otherwise interfere with the psychologist's effectively performing his or her functions as a psychologist, or might harm or exploit the other party.

  b. Likewise, whenever feasible, a psychologist refrains from taking on professional or scientific obligations when preexisting relationships would create a risk of such harm.

  c. If a psychologist finds that, due to unforeseen factors, a potentially harmful multiple relationship has arisen, the psychologist attempts to resolve it with due regard for the best interests of the affected person and maximal compliance with the Ethics Code.

1.18 Barter (with Patients or Clients)

  Psychologists ordinarily refrain from accepting goods, services, or other nonmonetary remuneration from patients or clients in return for psychological services because such arrangements create inherent potential for conflicts, exploitation, and distortion of the professional relationship. A psychologist may participate in bartering *only* if (1) it is not clinically contraindicated, *and* (2) the relationship is not exploitative. (See also Standards 1.17, Multiple Relationships, and 1.25, Fees and Financial Arrangements.)

1.19 Exploitative Relationships

  a. Psychologists do not exploit persons over whom they have supervisory, evaluative, or other authority such as students, supervisees, employees, research participants, and clients or patients. (See also Standards 4.05–4.07 regarding sexual involvement with clients or patients.)

  b. Psychologists do not engage in sexual relationships with students or supervisees in training over whom the psychologist has evaluative or direct authority, because such relationships are so likely to impair judgment or be exploitative.

1.20 Consultations and Referrals

  a. Psychologists arrange for appropriate consultations and referrals based principally on the best interests of their patients or clients, with appropriate consent, and subject to other relevant considerations, including applicable law and contractual obligations. (See also Standards 5.01, Discussing the Limits of Confidentiality, and 5.06, Consultations.)

  b. When indicated and professionally appropriate, psychologists cooperate with other professionals in order to serve their patients or clients effectively and appropriately.

  c. Psychologists' referral practices are consistent with law.

1.21 Third-Party Requests for Services

  a. When a psychologist agrees to provide services to a person or entity at the request of a third party, the psychologist clarifies to the extent feasible, at the outset of the service, the nature of the relationship with each party. This clarification includes the role of the psychologist (such as therapist, organizational consultant, diagnostician, or expert witness), the probable uses of the services provided or the information obtained, and the fact that there may be limits to confidentiality.

b. If there is a foreseeable risk of the psychologist's being called upon to perform conflicting roles because of the involvement of a third party, the psychologist clarifies the nature and direction of his or her responsibilities, keeps all parties appropriately informed as matters develop, and resolves the situation in accordance with this Ethics Code.

1.22 Delegation to and Supervision of Subordinates

a. Psychologists delegate to their employees, supervisees, and research assistants only those responsibilities that such persons can reasonably be expected to perform competently, on the basis of their education, training, or experience, either independently or with the level of supervision being provided.

b. Psychologists provide proper training and supervision to their employees or supervisees and take reasonable steps to see that such persons perform services responsibly, competently, and ethically.

c. If institutional policies, procedures, or practices prevent fulfillment of this obligation, psychologists attempt to modify their role or to correct the situation to the extent feasible.

1.23 Documentation of Professional and Scientific Work

a. Psychologists appropriately document their professional and scientific work in order to facilitate provision of services later by them or by other professionals, to ensure accountability, and to meet other requirements of institutions or the law.

b. When psychologists have reason to believe that records of their professional services will be used in legal proceedings involving recipients of or participants in their work, they have a responsibility to create and maintain documentation in the kind of detail and quality that would be consistent with reasonable scrutiny in an adjudicative forum. (See also Standard 7.01, Professionalism, under Forensic Activities.)

1.24 Records and Data

Psychologists create, maintain, disseminate, store, retain, and dispose of records and data relating to their research, practice, and other work in accordance with law and in a manner that permits compliance with the requirements of this Ethics Code. (See also Standard 5.04, Maintenance of Records.)

1.25 Fees and Financial Arrangements

a. As early as is feasible in a professional or scientific relationship, the psychologist and the patient, client, or other appropriate recipient of psychological services reach an agreement specifying the compensation and the billing arrangements.

b. Psychologists do not exploit recipients of services or payors with respect to fees.

c. Psychologists' fee practices are consistent with law.

d. Psychologists do not misrepresent their fees.

e. If limitations to services can be anticipated because of limitations in financing, this is discussed with the patient, client, or other appropriate recipient of services as early as is feasible. (See also Standard 4.08, Interruption of Services.)

f. If the patient, client, or other recipient of services does not pay for services as agreed, and if the psychologist wishes to use collection agencies or legal measures to collect the fees, the psychologist first informs the person that such measures will be taken and provides that person an opportunity to make prompt payment. (See also Standard 5.11, Withholding Records for Nonpayment.)

1.26 Accuracy in Reports to Payors and Funding Sources

In their reports to payors for services or sources of research funding, psychologists accurately state the nature of the research or service provided, the fees or charges, and where applicable, the identity of the provider, the findings, and the diagnosis. (See also Standard 5.05, Disclosures.)

1.27 Referrals and Fees

When a psychologist pays, receives payment from, or divides fees with another professional other than in an employer–employee relationship, the payment to each is based on the services (clinical, consultative, administrative, or other) provided and is not based on the referral itself.

2. Evaluation, assessment, or intervention

2.01 Evaluation, Diagnosis, and Interventions in Professional Context
   a. Psychologists perform evaluations, diagnostic services, or interventions only within the context of a defined professional relationship. (See also Standard 1.03, Professional and Scientific Relationship.)
   b. Psychologists' assessments, recommendations, reports, and psychological diagnostic or evaluative statements are based on information and techniques (including personal interviews of the individual when appropriate) sufficient to provide appropriate substantiation for their findings. (See also Standard 7.02, Forensic Assessments.)

2.02 Competence and Appropriate Use of Assessments and Interventions
   a. Psychologists who develop, administer, score, interpret, or use psychological assessment techniques, interviews, tests, or instruments do so in a manner and for purposes that are appropriate in light of the research on or evidence of the usefulness and proper application of the techniques.
   b. Psychologists refrain from misuse of assessment techniques, interventions, results, and interpretations and take reasonable steps to prevent others from misusing the information these techniques provide. This includes refraining from releasing raw test results or raw data to persons, other than to patients or clients as appropriate, who are not qualified to use such information. (See also Standards 1.02, Relationship of Ethics and Law, and 1.04, Boundaries of Competence.)

2.03 Test Construction
   Psychologists who develop and conduct research with tests and other assessment techniques use scientific procedures and current professional knowledge for test design, standardization, validation, reduction or elimination of bias, and recommendations for use.

2.04 Use of Assessment in General and With Special Populations
   a. Psychologists who perform interventions or administer, score, interpret, or use assessment techniques are familiar with the reliability, validation, and related standardization or outcome studies of, and proper applications and uses of, the techniques they use.
   b. Psychologists recognize limits to the certainty with which diagnoses, judgments, or predictions can be made about individuals.
   c. Psychologists attempt to identify situations in which particular interventions or assessment techniques or norms may not be applicable or may require adjustment in administration or interpretation because of factors such as individuals' gender, age, race, ethnicity, national origin, religion, sexual orientation, disability, language, or socioeconomic status.

2.05 Interpreting Assessment Results
   When interpreting assessment results, including automated interpretations, psychologists take into account the various test factors and characteristics of the person being assessed that might affect psychologists' judgments or reduce the accuracy of their interpretations. They indicate any significant reservations they have about the accuracy or limitations of their interpretations.

2.06 Unqualified Persons
   Psychologists do not promote the use of psychological assessment techniques by unqualified persons. (See also Standard 1.22, Delegation to and Supervision of Subordinates.)

2.07 Obsolete Tests and Outdated Test Results
   a. Psychologists do not base their assessment or intervention decisions or recommendations on data or test results that are outdated for the current purpose.
   b. Similarly, psychologists do not base such decisions or recommendations on tests and measures that are obsolete and not useful for the current purpose.

2.08 Test Scoring and Interpretation Services
   a. Psychologists who offer assessment or scoring procedures to other professionals

accurately describe the purpose, norms, validity, reliability, and applications of the procedures and any special qualifications applicable to their use.

b. Psychologists select scoring and interpretation services (including automated services) on the basis of evidence of the validity of the program and procedures as well as on other appropriate considerations.

c. Psychologists retain appropriate responsibility for the appropriate application, interpretation, and use of assessment instruments, whether they score and interpret such tests themselves or use automated or other services.

2.09 Explaining Assessment Results
Unless the nature of the relationship is clearly explained to the person being assessed in advance and precludes provision of an explanation of results (such as in some organizational consulting, preemployment or security screenings, and forensic evaluations), psychologists ensure that an explanation of the results is provided using language that is reasonably understandable to the person assessed or to another legally authorized person on behalf of the client. Regardless of whether the scoring and interpretation are done by the psychologist, by assistants, or by automated or other outside services, psychologists take reasonable steps to ensure that appropriate explanations of results are given.

2.10 Maintaining Test Security
Psychologists make reasonable efforts to maintain the integrity and security of tests and other assessment techniques consistent with law, contractual obligations, and in a manner that permits compliance with the requirements of this Ethics Code. (See also Standard 1.02, Relationship of Ethics and Law.)

3. Advertising and other public statements

3.01 Definition of Public Statements
Psychologists comply with this Ethics Code in public statements relating to their professional services, products, or publications or to the field of psychology. Public statements include but are not limited to paid or unpaid advertising, brochures, printed matter, directory listings, personal resumes or curricula vitae, interviews or comments for use in media, statements in legal proceedings, lectures and public oral presentations, and published materials.

3.02 Statements by Others
a. Psychologists who engage others to create or place public statements that promote their professional practice, products, or activities retain professional responsibility for such statements.

b. In addition, psychologists make reasonable efforts to prevent others whom they do not control (such as employers, publishers, sponsors, organizational clients, and representatives of the print or broadcast media) from making deceptive statements concerning psychologists' practice or professional or scientific activities.

c. If psychologists learn of deceptive statements about their work made by others, psychologists make reasonable efforts to correct such statements.

d. Psychologists do not compensate employees of press, radio, television, or other communication media in return for publicity in a news item.

e. A paid advertisement relating to the psychologist's activities must be identified as such, unless it is already apparent from the context.

3.03 Avoidance of False or Deceptive Statements
a. Psychologists do not make public statements that are false, deceptive, misleading, or fraudulent, either because of what they state, convey, or suggest or because of what they omit, concerning their research, practice, or other work activities or those of persons or organizations with which they are affiliated. As examples (and not in limitation) of this standard, psychologists do not make false or deceptive statements concerning (1) their training, experience, or competence; (2) their academic degrees; (3) their credentials; (4) their institutional or association affiliations; (5) their services; (6) the scientific or clinical basis for, or results or degree of success of, their ser-

vices; (7) their fees; or (8) their publications or research findings. (See also Standards 6.15, Deception in Research, and 6.18, Providing Participants With Information About the Study.)

b. Psychologists claim as credentials for their psychological work, only degrees that (1) were earned from a regionally accredited educational institution or (2) were the basis for psychology licensure by the state in which they practice.

3.04 Media Presentations

When psychologists provide advice or comment by means of public lectures, demonstrations, radio or television programs, prerecorded tapes, printed articles, mailed material, or other media, they take reasonable precautions to ensure that (1) the statements are based on appropriate psychological literature and practice, (2) the statements are otherwise consistent with this Ethics Code, and (3) the recipients of the information are not encouraged to infer that a relationship has been established with them personally.

3.05 Testimonials

Psychologists do not solicit testimonials from current psychotherapy clients or patients or other persons who because of their particular circumstances are vulnerable to undue influence.

3.06 In-Person Solicitation

Psychologists do not engage, directly or through agents, in uninvited in-person solicitation of business from actual or potential psychotherapy patients or clients or other persons who because of their particular circumstances are vulnerable to undue influence. However, this does not preclude attempting to implement appropriate collateral contacts with significant others for the purpose of benefiting an already engaged therapy patient.

4. Therapy

4.01 Structuring the Relationship

a. Psychologists discuss with clients or patients as early as is feasible in the therapeutic relationship appropriate issues, such as the nature and anticipated course

of therapy, fees, and confidentiality. (See also Standards 1.25, Fees and Financial Arrangements, and 5.01, Discussing the Limits of Confidentiality.)

b. When the psychologist's work with clients or patients will be supervised, the above discussion includes that fact, and the name of the supervisor, when the supervisor has legal responsibility for the case.

c. When the therapist is a student intern, the client or patient is informed of that fact.

d. Psychologists make reasonable efforts to answer patients' questions and to avoid apparent misunderstandings about therapy. Whenever possible, psychologists provide oral and/or written information, using language that is reasonably understandable to the patient or client.

4.02 Informed Consent to Therapy

a. Psychologists obtain appropriate informed consent to therapy or related procedures, using language that is reasonably understandable to participants. The content of informed consent will vary depending on many circumstances; however, informed consent generally implies that the person (1) has the capacity to consent, (2) has been informed of significant information concerning the procedure, (3) has freely and without undue influence expressed consent, and (4) consent has been appropriately documented.

b. When persons are legally incapable of giving informed consent, psychologists obtain informed permission from a legally authorized person, if such substitute consent is permitted by law.

c. In addition, psychologists (1) inform those persons who are legally incapable of giving informed consent about the proposed interventions in a manner commensurate with the persons' psychological capacities, (2) seek their assent to those interventions, and (3) consider such persons' preferences and best interests.

4.03 Couple and Family Relationships

a. When a psychologist agrees to provide services to several persons who have a relationship (such as husband and wife or parents and children), the psychologist attempts to clarify at the outset (1) which of the individuals are patients or clients and (2) the relationship the psychologist will have with each person. This clarification includes the role of the psychologist and the probable uses of the services provided or the information obtained. (See also Standard 5.01, Discussing the Limits of Confidentiality.)

b. As soon as it becomes apparent that the psychologist may be called on to perform potentially conflicting roles (such as marital counselor to husband and wife, and then witness for one party in a divorce proceeding), the psychologist attempts to clarify and adjust, or withdraw from, roles appropriately. (See also Standard 7.03, Clarification of Role, under Forensic Activities.)

4.04 Providing Mental Health Services to Those Served by Others

In deciding whether to offer or provide services to those already receiving mental health services elsewhere, psychologists carefully consider the treatment issues and the potential patient's or client's welfare. The psychologist discusses these issues with the patient or client, or another legally authorized person on behalf of the client, in order to minimize the risk of confusion and conflict, consults with the other service providers when appropriate, and proceeds with caution and sensitivity to the therapeutic issues.

4.05 Sexual Intimacies with Current Patients or Clients

Psychologists do not engage in sexual intimacies with current patients or clients.

4.06 Therapy with Former Sexual Partners

Psychologists do not accept as therapy patients or clients persons with whom they have engaged in sexual intimacies.

4.07 Sexual Intimacies with Former Therapy Patients

a. Psychologists do not engage in sexual intimacies with a former therapy patient or client for at least two years after cessation or termination of professional services.

b. Because sexual intimacies with a former therapy patient or client are so frequently harmful to the patient or client, and be-cause such intimacies undermine public confidence in the psychology profession and thereby deter the public's use of needed services, psychologists do not engage in sexual intimacies with former therapy patients and clients even after a two-year interval except in the most unusual circumstances. The psychologist who engages in such activity after the two years following cessation or termination of treatment bears the burden of demonstrating that there has been no exploitation, in light of all relevant factors, including (1) the amount of time that has passed since therapy terminated, (2) the nature and duration of the therapy, (3) the circumstances of termination, (4) the patient's or client's personal history, (5) the patient's or client's current mental status, (6) the likelihood of adverse impact on the patient or client and others, and (7) any statements or actions made by the therapist during the course of therapy suggesting or inviting the possibility of a posttermination sexual or romantic relationship with the patient or client. (See also Standard 1.17, Multiple Relationships.)

4.08 Interruption of Services

a. Psychologists make reasonable efforts to plan for facilitating care in the event that psychological services are interrupted by factors such as the psychologist's illness, death, unavailability, or relocation or by the client's relocation or financial limitations. (See also Standard 5.09, Preserving Records and Data.)

b. When entering into employment or contractual relationships, psychologists provide for orderly and appropriate resolution of responsibility for patient or client care in the event that the employment or contractual relationship ends, with paramount consideration given to the welfare of the patient or client.

4.09 Terminating the Professional Relationship

a. Psychologists do not abandon patients or clients. (See also Standard 1.25e, under Fees and Financial Arrangements.)

b. Psychologists terminate a professional relationship when it becomes reasonably clear that the patient or client no longer needs the service, is not benefiting, or is being harmed by continued service.

c. Prior to termination for whatever reason, except where precluded by the patient's or client's conduct, the psychologist discusses the patients' or clients' views and needs, provides appropriate pretermination counseling, suggests alternative service providers as appropriate, and takes other reasonable steps to facilitate transfer of responsibility to another provider if the patient or client needs one immediately.

5. Privacy and confidentiality

These Standards are potentially applicable to the professional and scientific activities of all psychologists.

5.01 Discussing the Limits of Confidentiality

a. Psychologists discuss with persons and organizations with whom they establish a scientific or professional relationship (including, to the extent feasible, minors and their legal representatives) (1) the relevant limitations on confidentiality, including limitations where applicable in group, marital, and family therapy or in organizational consulting, and (2) the foreseeable uses of the information generated through their services.

b. Unless it is not feasible or is contraindicated, the discussion of confidentiality occurs at the outset of the relationship and thereafter as new circumstances may warrant.

c. Permission for electronic recording of interviews is secured from clients and patients.

5.02 Maintaining Confidentiality
Psychologists have a primary obligation and take reasonable precautions to respect the confidentiality rights of those with whom they work or consult, recognizing that confidentiality may be established by law, institutional rules, or professional or scientific relationships. (See also Standard 6.26, Professional Reviewers.)

5.03 Minimizing Intrusions on Privacy

a. In order to minimize intrusions on privacy, psychologists include in written and oral reports, consultations, and the like only information germane to the purpose for which the communication is made.

b. Psychologists discuss confidential information obtained in clinical or consulting relationships, or evaluative data concerning patients, individual or organizational clients, students, research participants, supervisees, and employees, only for appropriate scientific or professional purposes and only with persons clearly concerned with such matters.

5.04 Maintenance of Records
Psychologists maintain appropriate confidentiality in creating, storing, accessing, transferring, and disposing of records under their control, whether these are written, automated, or in any other medium. Psychologists maintain and dispose of records in accordance with law and in a manner that permits compliance with the requirements of this Ethics Code.

5.05 Disclosures

a. Psychologists disclose confidential information without the consent of the individual only as mandated by law, or where permitted by law for a valid purpose, such as (1) to provide needed professional services to the patient or the individual or organizational client, (2) to obtain appropriate professional consultations, (3) to protect the patient or client or others from harm, or (4) to obtain payment for services, in which instance disclosure is limited to the minimum that is necessary to achieve the purpose.

b. Psychologists also may disclose confidential information with the appropriate consent of the patient or the individual or organizational client (or of another legally authorized person on behalf of the patient or client), unless prohibited by law.

5.06 Consultations
When consulting with colleagues, (1) psychologists do not share confidential information that reasonably could lead to the identification of a patient, client, research participant, or other person or organization with

whom they have a confidential relationship unless they have obtained the prior consent of the person or organization or the disclosure cannot be avoided, and (2) they share information only to the extent necessary to achieve the purposes of the consultation. (See also Standard 5.02, Maintaining Confidentiality.)

5.07 Confidential Information in Databases
   a. If confidential information concerning recipients of psychological services is to be entered into databases or systems of records available to persons whose access has not been consented to by the recipient, then psychologists use coding or other techniques to avoid the inclusion of personal identifiers.
   b. If a research protocol approved by an institutional review board or similar body requires the inclusion of personal identifiers, such identifiers are deleted before the information is made accessible to persons other than those of whom the subject was advised.
   c. If such deletion is not feasible, then before psychologists transfer such data to others or review such data collected by others, they take reasonable steps to determine that appropriate consent of personally identifiable individuals has been obtained.

5.08 Use of Confidential Information for Didactic or Other Purposes
   a. Psychologists do not disclose in their writings, lectures, or other public media, confidential, personally identifiable information concerning their patients, individual or organizational clients, students, research participants, or other recipients of their services that they obtained during the course of their work, unless the person or organization has consented in writing or unless there is other ethical or legal authorization for doing so.
   b. Ordinarily, in such scientific and professional presentations, psychologists disguise confidential information concerning such persons or organizations so that they are not individually identifiable to others

and so that discussions do not cause harm to subjects who might identify themselves.

5.09 Preserving Records and Data
   A psychologist makes plans in advance so that confidentiality of records and data is protected in the event of the psychologist's death, incapacity, or withdrawal from the position or practice.

5.10 Ownership of Records and Data
   Recognizing that ownership of records and data is governed by legal principles, psychologists take reasonable and lawful steps so that records and data remain available to the extent needed to serve the best interests of patients, individual or organizational clients, research participants, or appropriate others.

5.11 Withholding Records for Nonpayment
   Psychologists may not withhold records under their control that are requested and imminently needed for a patient's or client's treatment solely because payment has not been received, except as otherwise provided by law.

6. Teaching, training supervision, research, and publishing

6.01 Design of Education and Training Programs
   Psychologists who are responsible for education and training programs seek to ensure that the programs are competently designed, provide the proper experiences, and meet the requirements for licensure, certification, or other goals for which claims are made by the program.

6.02 Descriptions of Education and Training Programs
   a. Psychologists responsible for education and training programs seek to ensure that there is a current and accurate description of the program content, training goals and objectives, and requirements that must be met for satisfactory completion of the program. This information must be made readily available to all interested parties.
   b. Psychologists seek to ensure that statements concerning their course outlines are accurate and not misleading, particularly regarding the subject matter to be covered, bases for evaluating progress, and the

nature of course experiences. (See also Standard 3.03, Avoidance of False or Deceptive Statements.)

c. To the degree to which they exercise control, psychologists responsible for announcements, catalogs, brochures, or advertisements describing workshops, seminars, or other non-degree-granting educational programs ensure that they accurately describe the audience for which the program is intended, the educational objectives, the presenters, and the fees involved.

6.03 Accuracy and Objectivity in Teaching

a. When engaged in teaching or training, psychologists present psychological information accurately and with a reasonable degree of objectivity.

b. When engaged in teaching or training, psychologists recognize the power they hold over students or supervisees and therefore make reasonable efforts to avoid engaging in conduct that is personally demeaning to students or supervisees. (See also Standards 1.09, Respecting Others, and 1.12, Other Harassment.

6.04 Limitation on Teaching

Psychologists do not teach the use of techniques or procedures that require specialized training, licensure, or expertise, including but not limited to hypnosis, biofeedback, and projective techniques, to individuals who lack the prerequisite training, legal scope of practice, or expertise.

6.05 Assessing Student and Supervisee Performance

a. In academic and supervisory relationships, psychologists establish an appropriate process for providing feedback to students and supervisees.

b. Psychologists evaluate students and supervisees on the basis of their actual performance on relevant and established program requirements.

6.06 Planning Research

a. Psychologists design, conduct, and report research in accordance with recognized standards of scientific competence and ethical research.

b. Psychologists plan their research so as to minimize the possibility that results will be misleading.

c. In planning research, psychologists consider its ethical acceptability under the Ethics Code. If an ethical issue is unclear, psychologists seek to resolve the issue through consultation with institutional review boards, animal care and use committees, peer consultations, or other proper mechanisms.

d. Psychologists take reasonable steps to implement appropriate protections for the rights and welfare of human participants, other persons affected by the research, and the welfare of animal subjects.

6.07 Responsibility

a. Psychologists conduct research competently and with due concern for the dignity and welfare of the participants.

b. Psychologists are responsible for the ethical conduct of research conducted by them or by others under their supervision or control.

c. Researchers and assistants are permitted to perform only those tasks for which they are appropriately trained and prepared.

d. As part of the process of development and implementation of research projects, psychologists consult those with expertise concerning any special population under investigation or most likely to be affected.

6.08 Compliance with Law and Standards

Psychologists plan and conduct research in a manner consistent with federal and state law and regulations, as well as professional standards governing the conduct of research, and particularly those standards governing research with human participants and animal subjects.

6.09 Institutional Approval

Psychologists obtain from host institutions or organizations appropriate approval prior to conducting research, and they provide accurate information about their research proposals. They conduct the research in accordance with the approved research protocol.

6.10 Research Responsibilities

Prior to conducting research (except research

involving only anonymous surveys, naturalistic observations, or similar research), psychologists enter into an agreement with participants that clarifies the nature of the research and the responsibilities of each party.

6.11 Informed Consent to Research

a. Psychologists use language that is reasonably understandable to research participants in obtaining their appropriate informed consent (except as provided in Standard 6.12, Dispensing With Informed Consent). Such informed consent is appropriately documented.

b. Using language that is reasonably understandable to participants, psychologists inform participants of the nature of the research; they inform participants that they are free to participate or to decline to participate or to withdraw from the research; they explain the foreseeable consequences of declining or withdrawing; they inform participants of significant factors that may be expected to influence their willingness to participate (such as risks, discomfort, adverse effects, or limitations on confidentiality, except as provided in Standard 6.15, Deception in Research); and they explain other aspects about which the prospective participants inquire.

c. When psychologists conduct research with individuals such as students or subordinates, psychologists take special care to protect the prospective participants from adverse consequences of declining or withdrawing from participation.

d. When research participation is a course requirement or opportunity for extra credit, the prospective participant is given the choice of equitable alternative activities.

e. For persons who are legally incapable of giving informed consent, psychologists nevertheless (1) provide an appropriate explanation, (2) obtain the participant's assent, and (3) obtain appropriate permission from a legally authorized person, if such substitute consent is permitted by law.

6.12 Dispensing with Informed Consent

Before determining that planned research (such as research involving only anonymous questionnaires, naturalistic observations, or certain kinds of archival research) does not require the informed consent of research participants, psychologists consider applicable regulations and institutional review board requirements, and they consult with colleagues as appropriate.

6.13 Informed Consent in Research Filming or Recording

Psychologists obtain informed consent from research participants prior to filming or recording them in any form, unless the research involves simply naturalistic observations in public places and it is not anticipated that the recording will be used in a manner that could cause personal identification or harm.

6.14 Offering Inducements for Research Participants

a. In offering professional services as an inducement to obtain research participants, psychologists make clear the nature of the services, as well as the risks, obligations, and limitations. (See also Standard 1.18, Barter [With Patients or Clients].)

b. Psychologists do not offer excessive or inappropriate financial or other inducements to obtain research participants, particularly when it might tend to coerce participation.

6.15 Deception in Research

a. Psychologists do not conduct a study involving deception unless they have determined that the use of deceptive techniques is justified by the study's prospective scientific, educational, or applied value and that equally effective alternative procedures that do not use deception are not feasible.

b. Psychologists never deceive research participants about significant aspects that would affect their willingness to participate, such as physical risks, discomfort, or unpleasant emotional experiences.

c. Any other deception that is an integral feature of the design and conduct of an experiment must be explained to participants as early as is feasible, preferably at the conclusion of their participation, but no later than at the conclusion of the research. (See also Standard 6.18, Providing Participants With Information About the Study.)

6.16 Sharing and Utilizing Data

Psychologists inform research participants of their anticipated sharing or further use of personally identifiable research data and of the possibility of unanticipated future uses.

6.17 Minimizing Invasiveness

In conducting research, psychologists interfere with the participants or milieu from which data are collected only in a manner that is warranted by an appropriate research design and that is consistent with psychologists' roles as scientific investigators.

6.18 Providing Participants with Information about the Study

a. Psychologists provide a prompt opportunity for participants to obtain appropriate information about the nature, results, and conclusions of the research, and psychologists attempt to correct any misconceptions that participants may have.

b. If scientific or humane values justify delaying or withholding this information, psychologists take reasonable measures to reduce the risk of harm.

6.19 Honoring Commitments

Psychologists take reasonable measures to honor all commitments they have made to research participants.

6.20 Care and Use of Animals in Research

a. Psychologists who conduct research involving animals treat them humanely.

b. Psychologists acquire, care for, use, and dispose of animals in compliance with current federal, state, and local laws and regulations, and with professional standards.

c. Psychologists trained in research methods and experienced in the care of laboratory animals supervise all procedures involving animals and are responsible for ensuring appropriate consideration of their comfort, health, and humane treatment.

d. Psychologists ensure that all individuals using animals under their supervision have received instruction in research methods and in the care, maintenance, and handling of the species being used, to the extent appropriate to their role.

e. Responsibilities and activities of individuals assisting in a research project are consistent with their respective competencies.

f. Psychologists make reasonable efforts to minimize the discomfort, infection, illness, and pain of animal subjects.

g. A procedure subjecting animals to pain, stress, or privation is used only when an alternative procedure is unavailable and the goal is justified by its prospective scientific, educational, or applied value.

h. Surgical procedures are performed under appropriate anesthesia; techniques to avoid infection and minimize pain are followed during and after surgery.

i. When it is appropriate that the animal's life be terminated, it is done rapidly, with an effort to minimize pain, and in accordance with accepted procedures.

6.21 Reporting of Results

a. Psychologists do not fabricate data or falsify results in their publications.

b. If psychologists discover significant errors in their published data, they take reasonable steps to correct such errors in a correction, retraction, erratum, or other appropriate publication means.

6.22 Plagiarism

Psychologists do not present substantial portions or elements of another's work or data as their own, even if the other work or data source is cited occasionally.

6.23 Publication Credit

a. Psychologists take responsibility and credit, including authorship credit, only for work they have actually performed or to which they have contributed.

b. Principal authorship and other publication credits accurately reflect the relative scientific or professional contributions of the individuals involved, regardless of their relative status. Mere possession of an institutional position, such as Department Chair, does not justify authorship credit. Minor contributions to the research or to the writing for publications are appropriately acknowledged, such as in footnotes or in an introductory statement.

c. A student is usually listed as principal author on any multiple-authored article that is substantially based on the student's dissertation or thesis.

6.24 Duplicate Publication of Data

Psychologists do not publish, as original data, data that have been previously published. This does not preclude republishing data when they are accompanied by proper acknowledgment.

6.25 Sharing Data

After research results are published, psychologists do not withhold the data on which their conclusions are based from other competent professionals who seek to verify the substantive claims through reanalysis and who intend to use such data only for that purpose, provided that the confidentiality of the participants can be protected and unless legal rights concerning proprietary data preclude their release.

6.26 Professional Reviewers

Psychologists who review material submitted for publication, grant, or other research proposal review respect the confidentiality of and the proprietary rights in such information of those who submitted it.

7. Forensic activities

7.01 Professionalism

Psychologists who perform forensic functions, such as assessments, interviews, consultations, reports, or expert testimony, must comply with all other provisions of this Ethics Code to the extent that they apply to such activities. In addition, psychologists base their forensic work on appropriate knowledge of and competence in the areas underlying such work, including specialized knowledge concerning special populations. (See also Standards 1.06, Basis for Scientific and Professional Judgments; 1.08, Human Differences; 1.15, Misuse of Psychologists' Influence; and 1.23, Documentation of Professional and Scientific Work.)

7.02 Forensic Assessments

a. Psychologists' forensic assessments, recommendations, and reports are based on information and techniques (including personal interviews of the individual, when appropriate) sufficient to provide appropriate substantiation for their findings. (See also Standards 1.03, Professional and Scientific Relationship; 1.23, Documentation of Professional and Scientific Work; 2.01, Evaluation, Diagnosis, and Interventions in Professional Context; and 2.05, Interpreting Assessment Results.)

b. Except as noted in c, below, psychologists provide written or oral forensic reports or testimony of the psychological characteristics of an individual only after they have conducted an examination of the individual adequate to support their statements or conclusions.

c. When, despite reasonable efforts, such an examination is not feasible, psychologists clarify the impact of their limited information on the reliability and validity of their reports and testimony, and they appropriately limit the nature and extent of their conclusions or recommendations.

7.03 Clarification of Role

In most circumstances, psychologists avoid performing multiple and potentially conflicting roles in forensic matters. When psychologists may be called on to serve in more than one role in a legal proceeding—for example, as consultant or expert for one party or for the court and as a fact witness—they clarify role expectations and the extent of confidentiality in advance to the extent feasible, and thereafter as changes occur, in order to avoid compromising their professional judgment and objectivity and in order to avoid misleading others regarding their role.

7.04 Truthfulness and Candor

a. In forensic testimony and reports, psychologists testify truthfully, honestly, and candidly and, consistent with applicable legal procedures, describe fairly the bases for their testimony and conclusions.

b. Whenever necessary to avoid misleading, psychologists acknowledge the limits of their data or conclusions.

7.05 Prior Relationships

A prior professional relationship with a party does not preclude psychologists from testifying as fact witnesses or from testifying to their services to the extent permitted by applicable law. Psychologists appropriately take into account ways in which the prior relationship might affect their professional objectivity or opinions and disclose the potential conflict to the relevant parties.

7.06 Compliance with Law and Rules

In performing forensic roles, psychologists are reasonably familiar with the rules governing their roles. Psychologists are aware of the occasionally competing demands placed upon them by these principles and the requirements of the court system, and attempt to resolve these conflicts by making known their commitment to this Ethics Code and taking steps to resolve the conflict in a responsible manner. (See also Standard 1.02, Relationship of Ethics and Law.)

8. Resolving ethical issues

8.01 Familiarity with Ethics Code

Psychologists have an obligation to be familiar with this Ethics Code, other applicable ethics codes, and their application to psychologists' work. Lack of awareness or misunderstanding of an ethical standard is not itself a defense to a charge of unethical conduct.

8.02 Confronting Ethical Issues

When a psychologist is uncertain whether a particular situation or course of action would violate this Ethics Code, the psychologist ordinarily consults with other psychologists knowledgeable about ethical issues, with state or national psychology ethics committees, or with other appropriate authorities in order to choose a proper response.

8.03 Conflicts Between Ethics and Organizational Demands

If the demands of an organization with which psychologists are affiliated conflict with this Ethics Code, psychologists clarify the nature of the conflict, make known their commitment to the Ethics Code, and to the extent feasible, seek to resolve the conflict in a way that permits the fullest adherence to the Ethics Code.

8.04 Informal Resolution of Ethical Violations

When psychologists believe that there may have been an ethical violation by another psychologist, they attempt to resolve the issue by bringing it to the attention of that individual if an informal resolution appears appropriate and the intervention does not violate any confidentiality rights that may be involved.

8.05 Reporting Ethical Violations

If an apparent ethical violation is not appropriate for informal resolution under Standard 8.04 or is not resolved properly in that fashion, psychologists take further action appropriate to the situation, unless such action conflicts with confidentiality rights in ways that cannot be resolved. Such action might include referral to state or national committees on professional ethics or to state licensing boards.

8.06 Cooperating with Ethics Committees

Psychologists cooperate in ethics investigations, proceedings, and resulting requirements of the APA or any affiliated state psychological association to which they belong. In doing so, they make reasonable efforts to resolve any issues as to confidentiality. Failure to cooperate is itself an ethics violation.

8.07 Improper Complaints

Psychologists do not file or encourage the filing of ethics complaints that are frivolous and are intended to harm the respondent rather than to protect the public.

C. *Code of Ethics*, National Association of Social Workers (NASW, 1996)

OVERVIEW

The National Association of Social Workers Code of Ethics is intended to serve as a guide to the everyday professional conduct of social workers. This code includes four sections. Section one, "Preamble," summarizes the social work profession's mission and core values. Section two, "Purpose of the Code of Ethics," provides an overview of the Code's main functions and a brief guide for dealing with ethical issues or dilemmas in social work practice. Section three, "Ethical Principles," presents broad ethical principles, based on social work's core values, that inform social work practice. The final section, "Ethical Standards," includes specific ethical standards to guide social workers' conduct and to provide a basis for adjudication.

PREAMBLE

The primary mission of the social work profession is to enhance human well-being and help meet basic human needs of all people, with particular attention to the needs and empowerment of people who are vulnerable, oppressed and living in poverty. An historic and defining feature of social work is the profession's focus on individual well-being in a social context and the well-being of society. Fundamental to social work is attention to the environmental forces that create, contribute to, and address problems in living.

Social workers promote social justice and social change with and on behalf of clients. 'Clients' is used inclusively to refer to individuals, families, groups, organizations, and communities. Social workers are sensitive to cultural and ethnic diversity and strive to end discrimination, oppression, poverty, and other forms of social injustice. These activities may be in the form of direct practice, community organizing, supervision, consultation, administration, advocacy, social and political action, policy development and implementation, education, and research and evaluation. Social workers seek to enhance the capacity of people to address their own needs. Social workers also seek to promote the responsiveness of organizations, communities, and other social institutions to individuals' needs and social problems.

The mission of the social work profession is rooted in a set of core values. These core values, embraced by social workers throughout the profession's history, are the foundation of social work's unique purpose and perspective:

- Service
- Social justice
- Dignity and worth of the person
- Importance of human relationships
- Integrity
- Competence

The constellation of these core values reflect what is unique to the social work profession. Core values, and the principles which flow from them, must be balanced within the context and complexity of the human experience.

PURPOSE OF THE CODE OF ETHICS

Professional ethics are at the core of social work. The profession has an obligation to articulate its basic values, ethical principles, and ethical standards. The NASW Code of Ethics sets forth values, principles, and standards to guide social workers' conduct. The code of ethics is relevant to all social workers and social work students, regardless of their professional functions, the settings in which they work, or the populations they serve.

This NASW Code of Ethics serves six purposes:

♦ The code identifies core values on which social work's mission is based.
♦ The code summarizes broad ethical principles that reflect the profession's core values and establishes a set of specific ethical standards that should be used to guide social work practice.
♦ The code of ethics is designed to help social workers identify relevant considerations when professional obligations conflict or ethical uncertainties arise.
♦ The code provides ethical standards to which the general public can hold the social work profession accountable.
♦ The code socializes practitioners new to the field to social work's mission, values, ethical principles, and ethical standards.
♦ The code articulates standards that the social work profession itself can use to assess whether social workers have engaged in unethical conduct. NASW has formal procedures to adjudicate ethics complaints filed against its members.[1] In subscribing to this code social workers are required to cooperate in its implementation, participate in NASW adjudication proceedings, and abide by any NASW disciplinary rulings or sanctions based on it.

This code offers a set of values, principles, and standards to guide decision making and conduct when ethical issues arise. It does not provide a set of rules that prescribe how social workers should act in all situations. Specific applications of the code must take into account the context in which it is being considered and the possibility of conflicts among the code's values, principles, and standards. Ethical responsibilities flow from all human relationships, from the personal and familial to the social and professional.

Further, the code of ethics does not specify which values, principles, and standards are most important and ought to outweigh others in instances when they conflict. Reasonable differences of opinion can and do exist among social workers with respect to the ways in which values, ethical principles, and ethical standards should be rank-ordered when they conflict. Ethical decision making in a given situation must apply the informed judgment of the individual social worker and should also consider how the issues would be judged in a peer review process where the ethical standards of the profession would be applied.

Ethical decision making is a process. There are many instances in social work where simple answers are not available to resolve complex ethical issues. Social workers should take into consideration all the values, principles, and standards in this code that are relevant to any situation in which ethical judgment is warranted. Social workers' decisions and actions should be consistent with the spirit as well as the letter of this code.

In addition to this code, there are many other sources of information about ethical thinking that may be useful. Social workers should consider ethical theory and principles generally, social work theory and research, laws, regulations, agency policies, and other relevant codes of ethics, recognizing that among codes of ethics social workers should consider the NASW Code of Ethics as their primary source. Social workers also should be aware of the impact on ethical decision making of their clients' and their own personal values, cultural and religious beliefs, and practices. They should be aware of any conflicts between personal and professional values and deal with them responsibly. For additional guidance social workers should consult relevant literature on professional ethics and ethical decision making, and seek appropriate consultation when faced with ethical dilemmas. This may involve consultation with an agency-based or social work organization's ethics

[1]For information on NASW adjudication procedures, see *NASW Procedures for the Adjudication of Grievances*.

committee, regulatory body, knowledgeable colleagues, supervisors, or legal counsel.

Instances may arise where social workers' ethical obligations conflict with agency policies, relevant laws or regulations. When such conflicts occur, social workers must make a responsible effort to resolve the conflict in a manner that is consistent with the values, principles, and standards expressed in this code. If a reasonable resolution of the conflict does not appear possible, social workers should seek proper consultation before making a decision.

This code of ethics is to be used by NASW and by other individuals, agencies, organizations, and bodies (such as licensing and regulatory boards, professional liability insurance providers, courts of law, agency boards of directors, government agencies, and other professional groups) that choose to adopt it or use it as a frame of reference. Violation of standards in this code does not automatically imply legal liability or violation of the law. Such determination can only be made in the context of legal and judicial proceedings. Alleged violations of the code would be subject to a peer review process. Such processes are generally separate from legal or administrative procedures and insulated from legal review or proceedings in order to allow the profession to counsel and/or discipline its own members.

A code of ethics cannot guarantee ethical behavior. Moreover, a code of ethics cannot resolve all ethical issues or disputes, or capture the richness and complexity involved in striving to make responsible choices within a moral community. Rather a code of ethics sets forth values, ethical principles and ethical standards to which professionals aspire and by which their actions can be judged. Socials workers' ethical behavior should result from their personal commitment to engage in ethical practice. This code reflects the commitment of all social workers to uphold the profession's values and to act ethically. Principles and standards must be applied by individuals of good character who discern moral questions and, in good faith, seek to make reliable ethical judgments.

ETHICAL PRINCIPLES

The following broad ethical principles are based on social work's core values of: service, social justice, dignity and worth of the person, importance of human relationships, integrity, and competence. These principles set forth ideals to which all social workers should aspire.

VALUE: *Service*

Ethical Principle: *Social workers' primary goal is to help people in need and to address social problems.*

Social workers elevate service to others above self-interest. Social workers draw on their knowledge, values, and skills to help people in need and to address social problems. Social workers are encouraged to volunteer some portion of their professional skills with no expectation of significant financial return (pro bono service).

VALUE: *Social Justice*

Ethical Principle: *Social workers challenge social injustice.*

Social workers pursue social change, particularly with and on behalf of vulnerable and oppressed individuals and groups of people. Social workers' social change efforts are focused primarily on issues of poverty, unemployment, discrimination, and other forms of social injustice. These activities seek to promote sensitivity to and knowledge about oppression, and cultural and ethnic diversity. Social workers strive to ensure equality of opportunity, access to needed information, services, resources, and meaningful participation in decision making for all people.

VALUE: *Dignity and Worth of the Person*

Ethical Principle: *Social workers respect the inherent dignity and worth of the person.*

Social workers treat each person in a caring and respectful fashion, mindful of individual differences and cultural and ethnic diversity. Social workers promote clients' socially responsible self-determination. Social workers seek to enhance clients' capacity and opportunity to change and to address their own needs. Social workers are cognizant of their dual responsibility to clients and to the broader society. They seek to resolve conflicts between clients' and the broader society's interests in a socially responsible manner consistent with the values, ethical principles, and ethical standards of the profession.

VALUE: *Importance of Human Relationships*

Ethical Principle: *Social workers recognize the central importance of human relationships.*

Social workers understand that relationships between and among people are an important vehicle for change. Social workers engage people as partners in the helping process. Social workers seek to strengthen relationships among people in a purposeful effort to promote, restore, maintain, and enhance the well-being of individuals, families, social groups, organizations, and communities.

VALUE: *Integrity*

Ethical Principle: *Social workers behave in a trustworthy manner.*

Social workers are continually aware of the profession's mission, values, ethical principles, and ethical standards, and practice in a manner consistent with them. Social workers act honestly and responsibly and promote ethical practices on the part of the organizations with which they are affiliated.

VALUE: *Competence*

Ethical Principle: *Social workers practice within their areas of competence and develop and enhance their professional expertise.*

Social workers continually strive to increase their professional knowledge and skills and to apply them in practice. Social workers should aspire to contribute to the knowledge base of the profession.

ETHICAL STANDARDS

The following ethical standards are relevant to the professional activities of all social workers. These standards concern: (1) social workers' ethical responsibilities to clients, (2) social workers' ethical responsibilities to colleagues, (3) social workers' ethical responsibilities in practice settings, (4) social workers' ethical responsibilities as professionals, (5) social workers' ethical responsibilities to the profession, and (6) social workers' ethical responsibilities to the broader society.

Some of the standards that follow are enforceable guidelines for professional conduct and some are more aspirational in nature. The extent to which each standard is enforceable is a matter of professional judgment to be exercised by those responsible for reviewing alleged violations of ethical standards.

1. Social workers' ethical responsibilities to clients

1.01 Commitment to Clients

Social workers' primary responsibility is to promote well-being of clients. In general, clients' interests are primary. However, social workers' responsibility to the larger society or specific legal obligations may on limited occasions supercede the loyalty owed clients and clients should be so advised. (Examples include when a social worker is required by law to report that a client has abused a child or has threatened to harm self or others.)

1.02 Self-Determination

Social workers respect and promote the right of clients to self-determination and assist clients in their efforts to identify and clarify their goals. Social workers may limit clients' right to self-determination when, in their professional judgment, clients' actions or potential actions pose a serious, foreseeable, and imminent risk to themselves or others.

1.03 Informed Consent

a. Social workers should provide services to clients only in the context of a professional relationship based, when appropriate, on valid informed consent. Social workers should use clear and understandable language to inform clients of the purpose of the service, risks related to the service, limits to service because of the requirements of a third-party payor, relevant costs, reasonable alternatives, clients' right to refuse or withdraw consent, and the time frame covered by the consent. Social workers should provide clients with an opportunity to ask questions.

b. In instances where clients are not literate or have difficulty understanding the primary language used in the practice setting, social workers should take steps to ensure clients' comprehension. This may include providing clients with a detailed verbal explanation or arranging for a qualified interpreter and/or translator whenever possible.

c. In instances where clients lack the capacity to provide informed consent, social workers should protect clients' interests by seeking permission from an appropriate third party, informing clients consistent with their level of understanding. In such instances social workers should seek to ensure that the third party acts in a manner consistent with clients' wishes and interests. Social workers should take reasonable steps to enhance such clients' ability to give informed consent.

d. In instances where clients are receiving services involuntarily, social workers should provide information about the nature and extent of services, and of the extent of clients' rights to refuse service.

e. Social workers who provide services via electronic mediums (such as computers, telephone, radio, and television) should inform recipients of the limitations and risks associated with such services.

f. Social workers should obtain clients' informed consent before audiotaping or videotaping clients, or permitting third party observation of clients who are receiving services.

1.04 Competence

a. Social workers should provide services and represent themselves as competent only within the boundaries of their education, training, license, certification, consultation received, supervised experience, or other relevant professional experience.

b. Social workers should provide services in substantive areas or use intervention techniques or approaches that are new to them only after engaging in appropriate study, training, consultation, and/or supervision from persons who are competent in those interventions or techniques.

c. When generally recognized standards do not exist with respect to an emerging area of practice, social workers should exercise careful judgment and take responsible steps—including appropriate education, research, training, consultation, and supervision—to ensure the competence of their work and to protect clients from harm.

1.05 Cultural Competence and Social Diversity

a. Social workers should understand culture and its function in human behavior and society, recognizing the strengths that exist in all cultures.

b. Social workers should have a knowledge base of their clients' cultures and be able to demonstrate competence in the provision of services that are sensitive to clients' cultures and to differences among people and cultural groups.

c. Social workers should obtain education about and seek to understand the nature of social diversity and oppression with respect to race, ethnicity, national origin, color, sex, sexual orientation, age, marital status, political belief, religion and mental or physical disability.

1.06 Conflicts of Interest

a. Social workers should be alert to and avoid conflicts of interest that interfere with the exercise of professional discretion and impartial judgment. Social workers should inform clients when a real or potential conflict of interest arises and take responsible steps to resolve the issue in a manner that makes the clients' interests primary and protects clients' interests to the greatest extent possible. In some cases, protecting clients' interests may require termination of the professional relationship with proper referral of the client.

b. Social workers should not take unfair advantage of any professional relationship or exploit others to further their personal, religious, political, or business interests.

c. Social workers should not engage in dual or multiple relationships with clients or former clients in which there is a risk of exploitation or potential harm to the client. In instances when dual or multiple relationships are unavoidable, social workers should take steps to protect clients and are responsible for setting clear, appropriate, and culturally sensitive boundaries. (Dual or multiple relationships occur when social workers relate to clients in more than one relationship, whether professional, social, or business. Dual or multiple relationships can occur simultaneously or consecutively.)

d. When social workers provide services to two or more persons who have a relationship with each other (for example, couples, family members), social workers should clarify with all parties which individuals will be considered clients and the nature of social workers' professional obligations to the various individuals who are receiving services. Social workers who anticipate a conflict of interest among the individuals receiving services, or who anticipate having to perform in potentially conflicting roles (for example, when a social worker is asked to testify in a child custody dispute or divorce proceedings involving clients), should clarify their role with the parties involved and take appropriate action to minimize any conflict of interest.

1.07 Privacy and Confidentiality

a. Social workers should respect clients' right to privacy. Social workers should not solicit private information from clients unless it is essential to providing service or conducting social work evaluation or research. Once private information is shared, standards of confidentiality apply.

b. Social workers may disclose confidential information when appropriate with a valid consent from a client, or a person legally authorized to consent on behalf of a client.

c. Social workers should protect the confidentiality of all information obtained in the course of professional service, except for compelling professional reasons. The general expectation that social workers will keep information confidential does not apply when disclosure is necessary to prevent serious, foreseeable, and imminent harm to a client or other identifiable person or when laws or regulations require disclosure without a client's consent. In all instances, social workers should disclose the least amount of confidential information necessary to achieve the desired purpose; only information that is directly relevant to the purpose for which the disclosure is made should be revealed.

d. Social workers should inform clients, to the extent possible, about the disclosure of confidential information and the potential consequences and, when feasible, before the disclosure is made. This applies whether social workers disclose confidential information as a result of a legal requirement or based on client consent.

e. Social workers should discuss with clients and other interested parties the nature of confidentiality and limitations of clients' right to confidentiality. Social workers should review with clients circumstances where confidential information may be requested and where disclosure of confidential information may be legally required. This discussion should occur as soon as possible in the social worker-client relationship and as needed throughout the course of the relationship.

f. When social workers provide counseling services to families, couples, or groups, social workers should seek agreement among the parties involved concerning each individual's right to confidentiality and obligation to preserve the confidentiality of information shared by others. Social workers should inform participants in family, couples, or group counseling that social workers cannot guarantee that all participants will honor such agreements.

g. Social workers should inform clients involved in family, couples, marital, or group counseling of the social worker's, employer's, and/or agency's policy concerning the social worker's disclosure of confidential information among the parties involved in the counseling.

h. Social workers should not discuss confidential information to third party payors, unless clients have authorized such disclosure.

i. Social workers should not disclose confidential information in any setting unless privacy can be assured. Social workers should not discuss confidential information in public or semi-public areas (such as hallways, waiting rooms, elevators, and restaurants).

j. Social workers should protect the confidentiality of clients during legal proceedings to the extent permitted by law. When a court of law or other legally authorized body orders social workers to disclose confidential or privileged information without a client's consent and such disclosure could cause harm to the client, social workers should request that the court withdraw or limit the order as narrowly as possible and/or maintain the records under seal, unavailable for public inspection.

k. Social workers should protect the confidentiality of clients when responding to requests from members of the media.

l. Social workers should protect the confidentiality of clients' written and electronic records and other sensitive information. Social workers should take reasonable steps to ensure that clients' records are stored in a secure location and that clients' records are not available to others who are not authorized to have access.

m. Social workers should take precautions to ensure and maintain the confidentiality of information transmitted to other parties through the use of computers, electronic mail, facsimile machines, telephones and telephone answering machines, and other electronic or computer technology. Disclosure of identifying information should be avoided whenever possible.

n. Social workers should transfer or dispose of clients' records in a manner that protects clients' confidentiality and is consistent with state statutes governing records and social work licensure.

o. Social workers should take reasonable precautions to protect client confidentiality in the event of the social worker's termination of practice, incapacitation, or death.

p. Social workers should not disclose identifying information when discussing clients for teaching or training purposes, unless the client has consented to disclosure of confidential information.

q. Social workers should not disclose identifying information when discussing clients with consultants, unless the client has consented to disclosure information or there is a compelling need for such disclosure.

r. Social workers should protect the confidentiality of deceased clients consistent with the preceding standards.

1.08 Access to Records

a. Social workers should provide clients with reasonable access to records concerning them. Social workers who are concerned that clients' access to their records could cause serious misunderstanding or harm to the client should provide assistance in interpreting the records and consultation with the client regarding the records. Social workers should limit client access to social work records, or portions of clients' records, only in exceptional circumstances when there is compelling evidence that such access would cause serious harm to the client. Both the client's request and the rationale for withholding some or all of the record should be documented in the client's file.

b. When providing clients with access to their records, social workers should take steps to protect the confidentiality of other individuals identified or discussed in such records.

1.09 Sexual Relationships

a. Social workers should under no circumstances engage in sexual activities or sexual contact with current clients, whether such contact is consensual or forced.

b. Social workers should not engage in sexual activities or sexual contact with clients' relatives or other individuals with whom clients maintain a close, personal relationship where there is a risk of exploitation or potential harm to the client. Sexual activity or sexual contact with clients' relatives or other individuals with whom clients maintain a personal relationship has the potential to be harmful to the client and may make it difficult for the social worker and client to maintain appropriate professional boundaries. Social workers—not their clients, their clients' relatives or other individuals with whom the client maintains a personal relationship—assume the full burden for setting clear, appropriate and culturally sensitive boundaries.

c. Social workers should not engage in sexual activities or sexual contact with former clients because of the potential for harm to the client. If social workers engage in conduct contrary to this prohibition or claim that an exception to this prohibition is warranted due to extraordinary circumstances, it is social workers—not their clients—who assume the full burden of demonstrating that the former client has not been exploited, coerced, or manipulated, intentionally or unintentionally.

d. Social workers should not provide clinical services to individuals with whom they have had a prior sexual relationship. Providing clinical services to a former sexual partner has the potential to be harmful to the individual and is likely to make it difficult for the social worker and individual to maintain appropriate professional boundaries.

1.10 Physical Contact

Social workers should not engage in physical contact with clients where there is a possibility of psychological harm to the client as a result of the contact (such as cradling or caressing clients). Social workers who engage in appropriate physical contact with clients are responsible for setting clear, appropriate, and culturally sensitive boundaries that govern such physical contact.

1.11 Sexual Harassment

Social workers should not sexually harass clients. Sexual harassment includes sexual advances, sexual solicitation, requests for sexual favors, and other verbal or physical conduct of a sexual nature.

1.12 Derogatory Language

Social workers should not use derogatory language in their written or verbal communications to or about clients. Social workers should use accurate and respectful language in all communications to and about clients.

1.13 Payment for Services

a. When setting fees, social workers should ensure that the fees are fair, reasonable, and commensurate with the service performed. Consideration should be given to the client's ability to pay.

b. Social workers should avoid accepting goods or services from clients as payment for professional services. Bartering arrangements, particularly involving services, create the potential for conflicts of interest, exploitation, and inappropriate boundaries in social workers' relationships with clients. Social workers should explore and may participate in bartering only in very limited circumstances where it can be demonstrated that such arrangements are an accepted practice among professionals in the local community, considered to be essential for the provision of service, negotiated without coercion and entered into at the client's initiative and with the client's informed consent. Social workers who accept goods or services from clients as payment for professional services assume the full burden of demonstrating that this arrangement will not be detrimental to the client or the professional relationship.

c. Social workers should not solicit a private fee or other remuneration for providing services to clients who are entitled to such available services through the social workers' employer or agency.

1.14 Clients Who Lack Decision-Making Capacity

When social workers act on behalf of clients who lack the capacity to make informed decisions, social workers should take reasonable steps to safeguard the interests and rights of those clients.

1.15 Interruption of Services

Social workers should make reasonable efforts to ensure continuity of services in the event that they are interrupted by factors such as unavailability, relocation, illness, disability, or death.

1.16 Termination of Services

a. Social workers should terminate services to clients, and professional relationships with them, when such services and relationships are no longer required or no longer serve the clients' needs or interests.

b. Social workers should take reasonable steps to avoid abandoning clients who are still in need of services. Social workers should withdraw services precipitously only under unusual circumstances, giving careful consideration to all factors in the situation and taking care to minimize possible adverse effects. Social workers should assist in making appropriate arrangements for continuation of services when necessary.

c. Social workers in fee-for-service settings may terminate services to clients who are not paying an overdue balance if the financial contractual arrangements have been made clear to the client, if the client does not pose an imminent danger to self or others, and if the clinical and other consequences of the current non-payment have been addressed and discussed with the client.

d. Social workers should not terminate services to pursue a social, financial, or sexual relationship with a client.

e. Social workers who anticipate the termination or interruption of services to clients should notify clients promptly and seek the transfer, referral, or continuation of services in relation to the clients' needs and preferences.

f. Social workers who are leaving an employment setting should inform clients of appropriate options for the continuation of service and their benefits and risks.

2. Social workers' ethical responsibilities to colleagues

2.01 Respect
   a. Social workers should treat colleagues with respect, and represent accurately and fairly the qualifications, views, and obligations of colleagues.

   b. Social workers should avoid unwarranted negative criticism of colleagues with clients or with other professionals. Unwarranted negative criticism may include demeaning comments that refer to colleagues' level of competence or to individuals' attributes such as race, ethnicity, national origin, color, age, religion, sex, sexual orientation, marital status, political belief, mental or physical disability, or any

other preference, personal characteristic, or status.

   c. Social workers should cooperate with social work colleagues and with colleagues of other professions when it serves the well-being of clients.

2.02 Confidentiality with Colleagues
Social workers should respect confidential information shared by colleagues in the course of their professional relationships and transactions. Social workers should ensure that such colleagues understand social workers' obligation to respect confidentiality and any exceptions related to it.

2.03 Interdisciplinary Collaboration
   a. Social workers who are members of an interdisciplinary team should participate in and contribute to decisions that affect the well-being of clients by drawing on the perspectives, values, and experiences of the social work profession. Professional and ethical obligations of the interdisciplinary team as a whole and of its individual members should be clearly established.

   b. Social workers for whom a team decision raises ethical concerns should attempt to resolve the disagreement through appropriate channels. If the disagreement cannot be resolved social workers should pursue other avenues to address their concerns, consistent with client well-being.

2.04 Disputes Involving Colleagues
   a. Social workers should not take advantage of a dispute between a colleague and employer to obtain a position or otherwise advance the social worker's own interests.

   b. Social workers should not exploit clients in a dispute with a colleague or engage clients in any inappropriate discussion of a social worker's conflict with a colleague.

2.05 Consultation
   a. Social workers should seek advice and counsel of colleagues whenever such consultation is in the best interests of clients.

   b. Social workers should keep informed of colleagues' areas of expertise and competencies. Social workers should seek consultation only from colleagues who have demonstrated knowledge, expertise and competence related to the subject of the consultation.

c. When consulting with colleagues about clients, social workers should disclose the least amount of information necessary to achieve the purposes of the consultation.

2.06 Referral for Services

a. Social workers should refer clients to other professionals when other professionals' specialized knowledge or expertise is needed to serve clients fully, or when social workers believe they are not being effective or making reasonable progress with clients and additional service is required.

b. Social workers who refer clients to other professionals should take appropriate steps to facilitate an orderly transfer of responsibility. Social workers who refer clients to other professionals should disclose, with clients' consent, all pertinent information to the new service providers.

c. Social workers are prohibited from giving or receiving payment for a referral when no professional service is provided by the referring social worker.

2.07 Sexual Relationships

a. Social workers who function as supervisors or educators should not engage in sexual activities or contact with supervisees, students, trainees, or other colleagues over whom they exercise professional authority.

b. Social workers should avoid engaging in sexual relationships with colleagues where there is potential for a conflict of interest. Social workers who become involved in, or anticipate becoming involved in, a sexual relationship with a colleague have a duty to transfer professional responsibilities when necessary, in order to avoid a conflict of interest.

2.08 Sexual Harassment

Social workers should not engage in any sexual harassment of supervisees, students, trainees, or colleagues. Sexual harassment includes sexual advances, sexual solicitation, requests for sexual favors, and other verbal or physical conduct of a sexual nature.

2.09 Impairment of Colleagues

a. Social workers who have direct knowledge of a social worker colleague's impairment which is due to personal problems, psychosocial distress, substance abuse, or mental health difficulties, and which interferes with practice effectiveness, should consult with that colleague when feasible and assist the colleague in taking remedial action.

b. Social workers who believe that a social work colleague's impairment interferes with practice effectiveness and that the colleague has not taken adequate steps to address the impairment should take action through appropriate channels established by employers, agencies, NASW, licensing and regulatory bodies, and other professional organizations.

2.10 Incompetence of Colleagues

a. Social workers who have direct knowledge of a social work colleague's incompetence should consult with that colleague when feasible and assist the colleague in taking remedial action.

b. Social workers who believe that a social work colleague is incompetent and has not taken adequate steps to address the incompetence should take action through appropriate channels established by employers, agencies, NASW, licensing and regulatory bodies, and other professional organizations.

2.11 Unethical Conduct of Colleagues

a. Social workers should take adequate measures to discourage, prevent, expose, and correct the unethical conduct of colleagues.

b. Social workers should be knowledgeable about established policies and procedures for handling concerns about colleagues' unethical behavior. Social workers should be familiar with national, state, and local procedures for handling ethics complaints. These include policies and procedures created by NASW, licensing and regulatory bodies, employers, agencies, and other professional organizations.

c. Social workers who believe that a colleague has acted unethically should seek resolution by discussing their concerns with the colleague when feasible and when such discussion is likely to be productive.

d. When necessary, social workers who believe that a colleague has acted unethically should take action through appropriate formal channels (such as contacting a state licensing board or regulatory body, NASW committee on inquiry, or other professional ethics committees).

e. Social workers should defend and assist colleagues who are unjustly charged with unethical conduct.

3. Social workers' ethical responsibilities in practice settings

3.01 Supervision and Consultation

a. Social workers who provide supervision or consultation should have the necessary knowledge and skill to supervise or consult appropriately and should do so only within their areas of knowledge and competence.

b. Social workers who provide supervision or consultation are responsible for setting clear, appropriate, and culturally sensitive boundaries.

c. Social workers should not engage in any dual or multiple relationships with supervisees in which there is a risk of exploitation of or potential harm to the supervisee.

d. Social workers who provide supervision should evaluate supervisees' performance in a manner that is fair and respectful.

3.02 Education and Training

a. Social workers who function as educators, field instructors for students, or trainers should provide instruction only within their areas of knowledge and competence, and should provide instruction based on the most current information and knowledge available in the profession.

b. Social workers who function as educators or field instructors for students should evaluate students' performance in a manner that is fair and respectful.

c. Social workers who function as educators or field instructors for students should

take reasonable steps to ensure that clients are routinely informed when services are being provided by students.

d. Social workers who function as educators or field instructors for students should not engage in any dual or multiple relationships with students in which there is a risk of exploitation or potential harm to the student. Social work educators and field instructors are responsible for setting clear, appropriate, and culturally sensitive boundaries.

3.03 Performance Evaluation

Social workers who have the responsibility for evaluating the performance of others should fulfill such responsibility in a fair and considerate manner, and on the basis of clearly stated criteria.

3.04 Client Records

a. Social workers should take reasonable steps to ensure that documentation in records is accurate and reflective of the services provided.

b. Social workers should include sufficient and timely documentation in records to facilitate the delivery of services and to ensure continuity of services provided to clients in the future.

c. Social workers' documentation should protect clients' privacy to the extent that is possible and appropriate, and should include only that information that is directly relevant to the delivery of services.

d. Social workers should store records following the termination of service to ensure reasonable future access. Records should be maintained for the number of years required by state statutes or relevant contracts.

3.05 Billing

Social workers should establish and maintain billing practices that accurately reflect the nature and extent of services provided, and by whom the service was provided in the practice setting.

3.06 Client Transfer

a. When an individual who is receiving services from another agency or colleague contacts a social worker for services, the social worker should carefully consider the client's needs before agreeing to provide services. In order to minimize possible confusion and conflict, social workers should discuss with potential clients the nature of their current relationship with other service providers and the implications, including possible benefits or risks, of entering into a relationship with a new service provider.

b. If a new client has been served by another agency or colleague, social workers should discuss with the client whether consultation with the previous service provider is in the client's best interest.

3.07 Administration

a. Social work administration should advocate within and outside of their agencies for adequate resources to meet clients' needs.

b. Social workers should advocate for resource allocation procedures that are open and fair. When not all clients' needs can be met, an allocation procedure should be developed that is non-discriminatory and based on appropriate and consistently applied principles.

c. Social workers who are administrators should take reasonable steps to ensure that adequate agency or organizational resources are available to provide appropriate staff supervision.

d. Social work administrators should take reasonable steps to ensure that the working environment for which they are responsible is consistent with and encourages compliance with the NASW Code of Ethics. Social work administrators should take reasonable steps to eliminate any conditions in their organizations that violate, interfere with, or discourage compliance with the Code of Ethics.

3.08 Continuing Education and Staff Development

Social work administrators and supervisors should take reasonable steps to provide or arrange for continuing education and staff development for all staff for whom they are responsible. Continuing education and staff development should address current knowledge and emerging developments related to social work practice and ethics.

3.09 Commitments to Employers

a. Social workers generally should adhere to commitments made to employers and employing organizations.

b. Social workers should work to improve employing agencies' policies and procedures, and the efficiency and effectiveness of their services.

c. Social workers should take reasonable steps to ensure that employers are aware of social workers' ethical obligations as set forth in the NASW Code of Ethics and their implications for social work practice.

d. Social workers should not allow an employing organization's policies, procedures, regulations, or administrative orders to interfere with their ethical practice of social work. Social workers should take reasonable steps to ensure that their employing organizations' practices are consistent with the NASW Code of Ethics.

e. Social workers should act to prevent and eliminate discrimination in the employing organization's work assignments and in its employment policies and practices.

f. Social workers should accept employment or arrange student field placements only in organizations where fair personnel practices are exercised.

g. Social workers should be diligent stewards of the resources of their employing organizations, wisely conserving funds where appropriate, and never misappropriating funds or using them for unintended purposes.

3.10 Labor-Management Disputes

a. Social workers may engage in organized action, including the formation of and participation in labor unions, to improve services to clients and working conditions.

b. The actions of social workers who are involved in labor-management disputes, job actions, or labor strikes should be guided by the profession's values, ethical principles, and ethical standards. Reasonable differences of opinion exist among social workers concerning their primary obligation as professionals during an actual or threatened labor strike or job action. Social workers should carefully examine relevant issues and their possible impact on clients before deciding on a course of action.

4. Social workers' ethical responsibilities as professionals

4.01 Competence
  a. Social workers should accept responsibility or employment only on the basis of existing competence or the intention to acquire the necessary competence.
  b. Social workers should strive to become and remain proficient in professional practice and the performance of professional functions. Social workers should critically examine, and keep current with, emerging knowledge relevant to social work. Social workers should routinely review professional literature and participate in continuing education relevant to social work practice and social work ethics.
  c. Social workers should base practice on recognized knowledge, including empirically-based knowledge, relevant to social work and social work ethics.

4.02 Discrimination
  Social workers should not practice, condone, facilitate, or collaborate with any form of discrimination on the basis of race, ethnicity, national origin, color, age, religion, sex, sexual orientation, marital status, political belief, or mental or physical disability.

4.03 Private Conduct
  Social workers' should not permit their private conduct to interfere with their ability to fulfill their professional responsibilities.

4.04 Dishonesty, Fraud, and Deception
  Social workers should not participate in, condone, or be associated with dishonesty, fraud, or deception.

4.05 Impairment
  a. Social workers should not allow their own personal problems, psychosocial distress, legal problems, substance abuse, or mental health difficulties to interfere with their professional judgment and performance or jeopardize the best interests of those for whom they have a professional responsibility.
  b. Social workers whose personal problems, psychosocial distress, legal problems, substance abuse, or mental health difficulties interfere with their professional judgment and performance should immediately seek consultation and take appropriate remedial action by seeking professional help, making adjustments in workload, terminating practice, or taking any other steps necessary to protect clients and others.

4.06 Misrepresentation
  a. Social workers should make clear distinctions between statements made and actions engaged in as a private individual and as a representative of the social work profession, a professional social work organization, or of the social worker's employing agency.
  b. Social workers who speak on behalf of professional social work organizations should accurately represent the official and authorized positions of the organizations.
  c. Social workers should ensure that their representations to clients, agencies, and the public of professional qualifications, credentials, education, competence, affiliations, services provided, or results to be achieved are accurate. Social workers should claim only those relevant professional credentials they actually possess and take steps to correct any inaccuracies or misrepresentations of their credentials by others.

4.07 Solicitations
  a. Social workers should not engage in uninvited solicitation of potential clients who, because of their circumstances, are vulnerable to undue influence, manipulation, or coercion.
  b. Social workers should not engage in solicitation of testimonial endorsements (including solicitation of consent to use a client's prior statement as a testimonial endorsement) from current clients or from

other persons who, because of their particular circumstances, are vulnerable to undue influence.

4.08 Acknowledging Credit

a. Social workers should take responsibility and credit, including authorship credit, only for work they have actually performed and to which they have contributed.

b. Social workers should honestly acknowledge the work of and the contributions made by others.

5. Social workers' ethical responsibilities to the social work profession

5.01 Integrity of Profession

a. Social workers should work toward the maintenance and promotion of high standards of practice.

b. Social workers should uphold and advance the values, ethics, knowledge, and mission of the profession. Social workers should protect, enhance, and improve the integrity of the profession through appropriate study and research, active discussion, and responsible criticism of the profession.

c. Social workers should contribute time and professional expertise to activities that promote respect for the value, integrity, and competence of the social work profession. These activities may include teaching, research, consultation, service, legislative testimony, presentations in the community and participation in their professional organizations.

d. Social workers should contribute to the knowledge base of social work and share with colleagues their knowledge related to practice, research, and ethics. Social workers should seek to contribute to the profession's literature and to share their knowledge at professional meetings and conferences.

e. Social workers should act to prevent the unauthorized and unqualified practice of social work.

5.02 Evaluation Research

a. Social workers should monitor and evaluate policies, the implementation of programs, and practice interventions.

b. Social workers should promote and facilitate evaluation and research in order to contribute to the development of knowledge.

c. Social workers should critically examine and keep current with emerging knowledge relevant to social work and fully utilize evaluation and research evidence in their professional practice.

d. Social workers engaged in evaluation or research should consider carefully possible consequences and should follow guidelines developed for the protection of evaluation and research participants. Appropriate institutional review boards should be consulted.

e. Social workers engaged in evaluation or research should obtain voluntary and written informed consent from participants, when appropriate, without any implied or actual deprivation or penalty for refusal to participate, without undue inducement to participate, and with due regard for participants' well-being, privacy and dignity. Informed consent should include information about the nature, extent, and duration of the participation requested and disclosure of the risks and benefits of participation in the research.

f. When evaluation or research participants are incapable of giving informed consent, social workers should provide an appropriate explanation to them, obtain the participant's assent, and obtain consent from an appropriate proxy.

g. Social workers should never design or conduct evaluation or research that does not use consent procedures, such as certain forms of naturalistic observation and/or archival research, unless rigorous and responsible review of the research has found it to be justified because of its prospective scientific yield, educational, or applied value and unless equally effective alternative procedures that do not involve waiver of consent are not feasible.

h. Social workers should inform participants of their rights to withdraw from evaluation and research at any time without penalty.

i. Social workers should take appropriate steps to ensure that participants in evaluation and research have access to appropriate supportive services.

j. Social workers engaged in evaluation or research should protect participants from unwarranted physical or mental distress, harm, danger, or deprivation.

k. Social workers engaged in the evaluation of services should discuss collected information only for professional purposes and only with persons professionally concerned with this information.

l. Social workers engaged in evaluation or research should ensure the anonymity or confidentiality of participants and the data obtained from them. Social workers should inform participants of any limits of confidentiality, the measures that will be taken to ensure confidentiality, and when any records containing research data will be destroyed.

m. Social workers who report evaluation and research results should protect participants' confidentiality by omitting identifying information unless proper consent has been obtained authorizing disclosures.

n. Social workers should report evaluation and research findings accurately. They should not fabricate or falsify and should take steps to correct any errors later found in published data using standard publication methods.

o. Social workers engaged in evaluation or research should be alert to and avoid conflicts of interest and dual relationships with participants, should inform participants when a real or potential conflict of interest arises, and should take steps to resolve the issue in a manner that makes participants' interests primary.

p. Social workers should educate themselves, their students, and colleagues about responsible research practices.

6. Social workers' ethical responsibilities to the broader society

6.01 Social Welfare

Social workers should promote the general welfare of society, from local to global levels, and the development of people, their communities, and their environment. Social workers should advocate for living conditions conducive to the fulfillment of basic human needs and promote social, economic, political, and cultural values and institutions that are compatible with the realization of social justice.

6.02 Public Participation

Social workers should facilitate informed participants by the public in shaping social policies and institutions.

6.03 Public Emergencies

Social workers should provide appropriate professional services in public emergencies, to the greatest extent possible.

6.04 Social and Political Action

a. Social workers should engage in social and political action that seeks to ensure that all persons have equal access to the resources, employment, services, and opportunities that they require in order to meet their basic human needs and to develop fully. Social workers should be aware of the impact of the political arena on practice, and should advocate for changes in policy and legislation to improve social conditions in order to meet basic human needs and promote social justice.

b. Social workers should act to expand choice and opportunity for all persons, with special regard for vulnerable, disadvantaged, oppressed, and exploited persons and groups.

c. Social workers should promote conditions that encourage respect for the diversity of cultures and social diversity within the United States and globally. Social workers should promote policies and practices that demonstrate respect for difference, support the expansion of cultural knowledge and resources, advocate for programs and institutions that demonstrate cultural competence, and promote policies that safeguard the rights of and confirm equity and social justice for all people.

d. Social workers should act to prevent and eliminate domination, exploitation, and discrimination against any person, group, or class on the basis of race, ethnicity, national origin, color, age, religion, sex, sexual orientation, marital status, political belief, mental or physical disability, or any other preference, personal characteristic, or status.

D. *AAMFT Code of Ethics,* American Association for Marriage and Family Therapy (AAMFT, 1991)

The Board of Directors of the American Association for Marriage and Family Therapy (AAMFT) hereby promulgates, pursuant to Article 2, Section 2.013 of the Association's By-laws, the Revised AAMFT Code of Ethics, effective August 1, 1991.

The AAMFT Code of Ethics is binding on Members of AAMFT in all membership categories, AAMFT Approved Supervisors, and applicants for membership and the Approved Supervisor designation (hereafter, AAMFT Member).

If an AAMFT Member resigns in anticipation of, or during the course of an ethics investigation, the Ethics Committee will complete its investigation. Any publication of action taken by the Association will include the fact that the Member attempted to resign during the investigation.

Marriage and family therapists are strongly encouraged to report alleged unethical behavior of colleagues to appropriate professional associations and state regulatory bodies.

1. RESPONSIBILITY TO CLIENTS

Marriage and family therapists advance the welfare of families and individuals. They respect the rights of those persons seeking their assistance, and make reason able efforts to ensure that their services are used appropriately.

1.1 Marriage and family therapists do not discriminate against or refuse professional service to anyone on the basis of race, gender, religion, national origin, or sexual orientation.

1.2 Marriage and family therapists are aware of their influential position with respect to clients, and they avoid exploiting the trust and dependency of such persons. Therapists, therefore, make every effort to avoid dual relationships with clients that could impair professional judgment or increase the risk of exploitation. When a dual relationship cannot be avoided, therapists take appropriate professional precautions to ensure judgment is not impaired and no exploitation occurs. Examples of such dual relationships include, but are not limited to, business or close personal relationships with clients. Sexual intimacy with clients is prohibited. Sexual intimacy with former clients for two years following the termination of therapy is prohibited.

1.3 Marriage and family therapists do not use their professional relationships with clients to further their own interests.

1.4 Marriage and family therapists respect the right of clients to make decisions and help them to understand the consequences of these decisions. Therapists clearly advise a client that a decision on marital status is the responsibility of the client.

1.5 Marriage and family therapists continue therapeutic relationships only so long as it is reasonably clear that clients are benefiting from the relationship.

1.6 Marriage and family therapists assist persons in obtaining other therapeutic services if the therapist is unable or unwilling, for appropriate reasons, to provide professional help.

1.7 Marriage and family therapists do not abandon or neglect clients in treatment without making reasonable arrangements for the continuation of such treatment.

1.8 Marriage and family therapists obtain written informed consent from clients before videotaping, audiorecording, or permitting third party observation.

2. CONFIDENTIALITY

Marriage and family therapists have unique confidentiality concerns because the client in a therapeutic relationship may be more than one person. Therapists respect and guard confidences of each individual client.

2.1 Marriage and family therapists may not disclose client confidences except: (a) as mandated by law; (b) to prevent a clear and immediate danger to a person or persons; (c) where the therapist is a defendant in a civil, criminal, or disciplinary action arising from the therapy (in which case client confidences may be disclosed only in the course of that action); or (d) if there is a waiver previously obtained in writing, and then such information may be revealed only in accordance with the terms of the waiver. In circumstances where more than one person in a family receives therapy, each such family member who is legally competent to execute a waiver must agree to the waiver required by subparagraph (d). Without such a waiver from each family member legally competent to execute a waiver, a therapist cannot disclose information received from any family member.

2.2 Marriage and family therapists use client and/or clinical materials in teaching, writing, and public presentations only if a written waiver has been obtained in accordance with Subprinciple 2.1(d), or when appropriate steps have been taken to protect client identity and confidentiality.

2.3 Marriage and family therapists store or dispose of client records in ways that maintain confidentiality.

3. PROFESSIONAL COMPETENCE AND INTEGRITY

Marriage and family therapists maintain high standards of professional competence and integrity.

3.1 Marriage and family therapists are in violation of this Code and subject to termination of membership or other appropriate action if they: (a) are convicted of any felony; (b) are convicted of a misdemeanor related to their qualifications or functions; (c) engage in conduct which could lead to conviction of a felony, or a misdemeanor related to their qualifications or functions; (d) are expelled from or disciplined by other professional organizations; (e) have their licenses or certificates suspended or revoked or are otherwise disciplined by regulatory bodies; (f) are no longer competent to practice marriage and family therapy because they are impaired due to physical or mental causes or the abuse of alcohol or other substances; or (g) fail to cooperate with the Association at any point from the inception of an ethical complaint through the completion of all proceedings regarding that complaint.

3.2 Marriage and family therapists seek appropriate professional assistance for their personal problems or conflicts that may impair work performance or clinical judgment.

3.3 Marriage and family therapists, as teachers, supervisors, and researchers, are dedicated to high standards of scholarship and present accurate information.

3.4 Marriage and family therapists remain abreast of new developments in family therapy knowledge and practice through educational activities.

3.5 Marriage and family therapists do not engage in sexual or other harassment or exploitation of clients, students, trainees, supervisees, employees, colleagues, research subjects, or actual or potential witnesses or complainants in investigations and ethical proceedings.

3.6   Marriage and family therapists do not diagnose, treat, or advise on problems outside the recognized boundaries of their competence.

3.7   Marriage and family therapists make efforts to prevent the distortion or misuse of their clinical and research findings.

3.8   Marriage and family therapists, because of their ability to influence and alter the lives of others, exercise special care when making public their professional recommendations and opinions through testimony or other public statements.

4. RESPONSIBILITY TO STUDENTS, EMPLOYEES, AND SUPERVISEES

Marriage and family therapists do not exploit the trust and dependency of students, employees, and supervisees.

4.1   Marriage and family therapists are aware of their influential position with respect to students, employees, and supervisees, and they avoid exploiting the trust and dependency of such persons. Therapists, therefore, make every effort to avoid dual relationships that could impair professional judgment or increase the risk of exploitation. When a dual relationship cannot be avoided, therapists take appropriate professional precautions to ensure judgment is not impaired and no exploitation occurs. Examples of such dual relationships include, but are not limited to, business or close personal relationships with students, employees, or supervisees. Provision of therapy to students, employees, or supervisees is prohibited. Sexual intimacy with students or supervisees is prohibited.

4.2   Marriage and family therapists do not permit students, employees, or supervisees to perform or to hold themselves out as competent to perform professional services beyond their training, level of experience, and competence.

4.3   Marriage and family therapists do not disclose supervisee confidences except: (a) as mandated by law; (b) to prevent a clear and immediate danger to a person or persons; (c) where the therapist is a defendant in a civil, criminal, or disciplinary action arising from the supervision (in which case supervisee confidences may be disclosed only in the course of that action); (d) in educational or training settings where there are multiple supervisors, and then only to other professional colleagues who share responsibility for the training of the supervisee; or (e) if there is a waiver previously obtained in writing, and then such information may be revealed only in accordance with the terms of the waiver.

5. RESPONSIBILITY TO RESEARCH PARTICIPANTS

Investigators respect the dignity and protect the welfare of participants in research and are aware of federal and state laws and regulations and professional standards governing the conduct of research.

5.1   Investigators are responsible for making careful examinations of ethical acceptability in planning studies. To the extent that services to research participants may be compromised by participation in research, investigators seek the ethical advice of qualified professionals not directly involved in the investigation and observe safeguards to protect the rights of research participants.

5.2   Investigators requesting participants' involvement in research inform them of all aspects of the research that might reasonably be expected to influence willingness to participate. Investigators are especially sensitive to the possibility of diminished consent when participants are also receiving clinical services, have impairments which limit understanding and/or communication, or when participants are children.

5.3   Investigators respect participants' freedom to decline participation in or to withdraw from a research study at any time. This obligation requires special thought and consideration when investigators or other members of the research team are in positions of authority or influence over participants. Marriage and family therapists, therefore, make every effort to avoid dual relationships with research participants that could impair professional judgments or increase the risk of exploitation.

5.4   Information obtained about a research participant during the course of an investigation is confidential unless there is a waiver previously obtained in writing. When the possibility exists that others, including family members, may obtain access to such information, this possibility, together with the plan for protecting confidentiality, is explained as part of the procedure for obtaining informed consent.

6. RESPONSIBILITY TO THE PROFESSION

Marriage and family therapists respect the rights and responsibilities of professional colleagues and participate in activities which advance the goals of the profession.

6.1   Marriage and family therapists remain accountable to the standards of the profession when acting as members or employees of organizations.

6.2   Marriage and family therapists assign publication credit to those who have contributed to a publication in proportion to their contributions and in accordance with customary professional publication practices.

6.3   Marriage and family therapists who are the authors of books or other materials that are published or distributed cite persons to whom credit for original ideas is due.

6.4   Marriage and family therapists who are the authors of books or other materials published or distributed by an organization take reasonable precautions to ensure that the organization promotes and advertises the materials accurately and factually.

6.5   Marriage and family therapists participate in activities that contribute to a better community and society, including devoting a portion of their professional activity to services for which there is little or no financial return.

6.6   Marriage and family therapists are concerned with developing laws and regulations pertaining to marriage and family therapy that serve the public interest, and with altering such laws and regulations that are not in the public interest.

6.7   Marriage and family therapists encourage public participation in the design and delivery of professional services and in the regulation of practitioners.

7. FINANCIAL ARRANGEMENTS

Marriage and family therapists make financial arrangements with clients, third party payors, and supervisees that are reasonably understandable and conform to accepted professional practices.

7.1   Marriage and family therapists do not offer or accept payment for referrals.

7.2   Marriage and family therapists do not charge excessive fees for services.

7.3   Marriage and family therapists disclose their fees to clients and supervisees at the beginning of services.

7.4   Marriage and family therapists represent facts truthfully to clients, third party payors, and supervisees regarding services rendered.

8. ADVERTISING

Marriage and family therapists engage in appropriate informational activities, including those that enable laypersons to choose professional services on an informed basis.

General advertising

8.1   Marriage and family therapists accurately represent their competence, education, training, and experience relevant to their practice of marriage and family therapy.

8.2   Marriage and family therapists assure that advertisements and publications in any media (such as directories, announcements, business cards, newspapers, radio, television, and facsimiles) convey information that is necessary for the public to make an appropriate selection of professional services. Information could include: (a) office information, such as name, address, telephone number, credit card acceptability, fees, languages spoken, and office hours; (b) appropriate degrees, state licensure and/or certification, and AAMFT Clinical Member status; and (c) description of practice. (For requirements for advertising under the AAMFT name, logo, and/or the abbreviated initials AAMFT, see Subprinciple 8.15, below.)

8.3 Marriage and family therapists do not use a name which could mislead the public concerning the identity, responsibility, source, and status of those practicing under that name and do not hold themselves out as being partners or associates of a firm if they are not.

8.4 Marriage and family therapists do not use any professional identification (such as a business card, office sign, letterhead, or telephone or association directory listing) if it includes a statement or claim that is false, fraudulent, misleading, or deceptive. A statement is false, fraudulent, misleading, or deceptive if it (a) contains a material misrepresentation of fact; (b) fails to state any material fact necessary to make the statement, in light of all circumstances, not misleading; or (c) is intended to or is likely to create an unjustified expectation.

8.5 Marriage and family therapists correct, wherever possible, false, misleading, or inaccurate information and representations made by others concerning the therapist's qualifications, services, or products.

8.6 Marriage and family therapists make certain that the qualifications of persons in their employ are represented in a manner that is not false, misleading, or deceptive.

8.7 Marriage and family therapists may represent themselves as specializing within a limited area of marriage and family therapy, but only if they have the education and supervised experience in settings which meet recognized professional standards to practice in that specialty area.

Advertising using AAMFT designations

8.8 The AAMFT designations of Clinical Member, Approved Supervisor, and Fellow may be used in public information or advertising materials only by persons holding such designations. Persons holding such designations may, for example, advertise in the following manner:

- ◆ *Jane Doe, Ph.D., a Clinical Member of the American Association for Marriage and Family Therapy.*

Alternately, the advertisement could read:
- ◆ *Jane Doe, Ph.D., AAMFT Clinical Member.*
- ◆ *John Doe, Ph.D., an Approved Supervisor of the American Association for Marriage and Family Therapy.*

Alternately, the advertisement could read:
- ◆ *John Doe, Ph.D., AAMFT Approved Supervisor.*
- ◆ *Jane Doe, Ph.D., a Fellow of the American Association for Marriage and Family Therapy.*

Alternately, the advertisement could read:
- ◆ *Jane Doe, Ph.D., AAMFT Fellow.*

More than one designation may be used if held by the AAMFT Member.

8.9 Marriage and family therapists who hold the AAMFT Approved Supervisor or the Fellow designation may not represent the designation as an advanced clinical status.

8.10 Student, Associate, and Affiliate Members may not use their AAMFT membership status in public information or advertising materials. Such listings on professional resumes are not considered advertisements.

8.11 Persons applying for AAMFT membership may not list their application status on any resume or advertisement.

8.12 In conjunction with the AAMFT membership, marriage and family therapists claim as evidence of educational qualifications only those degrees (a) from regionally accredited institutions or (b) from institutions recognized by states which license or certify marriage and family therapists, but only if such state regulation is recognized by AAMFT.

8.13 Marriage and family therapists may not use the initials AAMFT following their name in the manner of an academic degree.

8.14 Marriage and family therapists may not use the AAMFT name, logo, and/or the abbreviated initials AAMFT or make any other such representation which would imply that they speak for or represent the Association. The Association is the sole owner of its name, logo, and the abbreviated initials AAMFT. Its committees and divisions, operating as such, may use the name, logo, and/or the abbreviated initials AAMFT in accordance with AAMFT policies.

8.15 Authorized advertisements of Clinical Members under the AAMFT name, log, and/or the abbreviated initials AAMFT may include the following: the Clinical Member's name, degree, license or certificate held when required by state law, name of business, address, and telephone number. If a business is listed, it must follow, not precede the Clinical Member's name. Such listings may not include AAMFT offices held by the Clinical Member, nor any specializations, since such a listing under the AAMFT name, logo, and/or the abbreviated initials, AAMFT, would imply that this specialization has been credentialed by AAMFT.

8.16 Marriage and family therapists use their membership in AAMFT only in connection with their clinical and professional activities.

8.17 Only AAMFT divisions and programs accredited by the AAMFT Commission on Accreditation for Marriage and Family Therapy Education, not businesses nor organizations, may use any AAMFT-related designation or affiliation in public information or advertising materials, and then only in accordance with AAMFT policies.

8.18 Programs accredited by the AAMFT Commission on Accreditation for Marriage and Family Therapy Education may not use the AAMFT name, logo, and/or the abbreviated initials AAMFT. Instead, they may have printed on their stationery and other appropriate materials a statement such as:

The (name of program) of the (name of institution) is accredited by the AAMFT Commission on Accreditation for Marriage and Family Therapy Education.

8.19 Programs not accredited by the AAMFT Commission on Accreditation for Marriage and Family Therapy Education may not use the AAMFT name, logo, and/or the abbreviated initials AAMFT. They may not state in printed program materials, program advertisements, and student advisement that their courses and training opportunities are accepted by AAMFT to meet AAMFT membership requirements.

E. *Ethical Standards of Human Service Professionals*, National Organization for Human Service Education (NOHSE, 1995)

PREAMBLE

Human services is a profession developing in response to and in anticipation of the direction of human needs and human problems in the late twentieth century. Characterized particularly by an appreciation of human beings in all of their diversity, human services offers assistance to its clients within the context of their community and environment. Human service professionals, regardless of whether they are students, faculty or practitioners, promote and encourage the unique values and characteristics of human services. In so doing human service professionals uphold the integrity and ethics of the profession, partake in constructive criticism of the profession, promote client and community well-being, and enhance their own professional growth.

The ethical guidelines presented are a set of standards of conduct which the human service professional considers in ethical and professional decision making It is hoped that these guidelines will be of assistance when the human service professional is challenged by difficult ethical dilemmas. Although ethical codes are not legal documents, they may be used to assist in the adjudication of issues related to ethical human service behavior.

Human service professionals function in many ways and carry out many roles. They enter into professional-client relationships with individuals, families, groups and communities who are all referred to as "clients: in these standards. Among their roles are caregiver, case manager, broker, teacher/educator, behavior changer, consultant, outreach professional, mobilizer, advocate, community planner, community change organizer, evaluator and administrator.[1] The following standards are written with these multi-faceted roles in mind.

THE HUMAN SERVICE PROFESSIONAL'S RESPONSIBILITY TO CLIENTS

STATEMENT 1 Human service professionals negotiate with clients the purpose, goals, and nature of the helping relationship prior to its onset, as well as inform clients of the limitations of the proposed relationship.

STATEMENT 2 Human service professionals respect the integrity and welfare of the client at all times. Each client is treated with respect, acceptance and dignity.

STATEMENT 3 Human service professionals protect the client's right to privacy and confidentiality except when such confidentiality would cause harm to the client or others, when agency guidelines state otherwise, or under other stated conditions (e.g., local, state, or federal laws). Professionals inform clients of the limits of confidentiality prior to the onset of the helping relationship.

[1]Southern Regional Education Board. *Roles and Functions for Mental Health Workers: A Report of a Symposium*. Atlanta, GA: Community Mental Health Worker Project, 1967.

STATEMENT 4 If it is suspected that danger or harm may occur to the client or to others as a result of a client's behavior, the human service professional acts in an appropriate and professional manner to protect the safety of those individuals. This may involve seeking consultation, supervision, and/or breaking the confidentiality of the relationship.

STATEMENT 5 Human service professionals protect the integrity, safety, and security of client records. All written client information that is shared with other professionals, except in the course of professional supervision, must have the client's prior written consent.

STATEMENT 6 Human service professionals are aware that in their relationships with clients power and status are unequal. Therefore they recognize that dual or multiple relationships may increase the risk of harm to, or exploitation of, clients, and may impair their professional judgment. However, in some communities and situations it may not be feasible to avoid social or other nonprofessional contact with clients. Human service professionals support the trust implicit in the helping relationship by avoiding dual relationships that may impair professional judgment, increase the risk of harm to clients or lead to exploitation.

STATEMENT 7 Sexual relationships with current clients are not considered to be in the best interest of the client and are prohibited. Sexual relationships with previous clients are considered dual relationships and are addressed in Statement 6 (above).

STATEMENT 8 The client's right to self-determination is protected by human service professionals. They recognize the client's right to receive or refuse services.

STATEMENT 9 Human service professionals recognize and build on client strengths.

THE HUMAN SERVICE PROFESSIONAL'S RESPONSIBILITY TO THE COMMUNITY AND SOCIETY

STATEMENT 10 Human service professionals are aware of local, state, and federal laws. They advocate for change in regulations and statutes when such legislation conflicts with ethical guidelines and/or client rights. Where laws are harmful to individuals, groups or communities, human service professionals consider the conflict between the values of obeying the law and the values of serving people and may decide to initiate social action.

STATEMENT 11 Human service professionals keep informed about current social issues as they affect the client and the community. They share that information with clients, groups and community as part of their work.

STATEMENT 12 Human service professionals understand the complex interaction between individuals, their families, the communities in which they live, and society.

STATEMENT 13 Human service professionals act as advocates in addressing unmet client and community needs. Human service professionals provide a mechanism for identifying unmet client needs, calling attention to these needs, and assisting in planning and mobilizing to advocate for those needs at the local community level.

STATEMENT 14 Human service professionals represent their qualifications to the public accurately.

STATEMENT 15 Human service professionals describe the effectiveness of programs, treatments, and/or techniques accurately.

STATEMENT 16 Human service professionals advocate for the rights of all members of society, particularly those who are members of minorities and groups at which discriminatory practices have historically been directed.

STATEMENT 17 Human service professionals provide services without discrimination or preference based on age, ethnicity, culture, race, disability, gender, religion, sexual orientation or socioeconomic status.

STATEMENT 18 Human service professionals are knowledgeable about the cultures and communities within which they practice. They are aware of multiculturalism in society and its impact on the community as well as individuals within the community. They respect individuals and groups, their cultures and beliefs.

STATEMENT 19 Human service professionals are aware of their own cultural backgrounds, beliefs, and values, recognizing the potential for impact on their relationships with others.

STATEMENT 20 Human service professionals are aware of sociopolitical issues that differentially affect clients from diverse backgrounds.

STATEMENT 21 Human service professionals seek the training, experience, education and supervision necessary to ensure their effectiveness in working with culturally diverse client populations.

THE HUMAN SERVICE PROFESSIONAL'S RESPONSIBILITY TO COLLEAGUES

STATEMENT 22 Human service professionals avoid duplicating another professional's helping relationship with a client. They consult with other professionals who are assisting the client in a different type of relationship when it is in the best interest of the client to do so.

STATEMENT 23 When a human service professional has a conflict with a colleague, he or she first seeks out the colleague in an attempt to manage the problem. If necessary, the professional then seeks the assistance of supervisors, consultants or other professionals in efforts to manage the problem.

STATEMENT 24 Human service professionals respond appropriately to unethical behavior of colleagues. Usually this means initially talking directly with the colleague and, if no resolution is forthcoming, reporting the colleague's behavior to supervisory or administrative staff and/or the professional organization(s) to which the colleague belongs.

STATEMENT 25 All consultations between human service professionals are kept confidential unless to do so would result in harm to clients or communities.

THE HUMAN SERVICE PROFESSIONAL'S RESPONSIBILITY TO THE PROFESSION

STATEMENT 26 Human service professionals know the limit and scope of their professional knowledge and offer services only within their knowledge and skill base.

STATEMENT 27 Human service professionals seek appropriate consultation and supervision to assist in decision making when there are legal, ethical or other dilemmas.

STATEMENT 28 Human service professionals act with integrity, honesty, genuineness, and objectivity.

STATEMENT 29 Human service professionals promote cooperation among related disciplines (e.g., psychology, counseling, social work, nursing, family and consumer sciences, medicine, education) to foster professional growth and interests within the various fields.

STATEMENT 30 Human service professionals promote the continuing development of their profession. They encourage membership in professional associations, support research endeavors, foster educational advancement, advocate for appropriate legislative actions, and participate in other related professional activities.

STATEMENT 31 Human service professionals continually seek out new and effective approaches to enhance their professional abilities.

THE HUMAN SERVICE PROFESSIONAL'S RESPONSIBILITY TO EMPLOYERS

STATEMENT 32 Human service professionals adhere to commitments made to their employer.

STATEMENT 33 Human service professionals participate in efforts to establish and maintain employment conditions which are conducive to high quality client services. They assist in evaluating the effectiveness of the agency through reliable and valid assessment measures.

STATEMENT 34 When a conflict arises between fulfilling the responsibility to the employer and the responsibility to the client, human service professionals advise both of the conflict and work conjointly with all involved to manage the conflict.

THE HUMAN SERVICE PROFESSIONAL'S RESPONSIBILITY TO SELF

STATEMENT 35 Human service professionals strive to personify those characteristics typically associated with the profession (e.g., accountability, respect for others, genuineness, empathy, pragmatism).

STATEMENT 36 Human service professionals foster self-awareness and personal growth in themselves. They recognize that when professionals are aware of their own values, attitudes, cultural background, and personal needs, the process of helping others is less likely to be negatively impacted by those factors.

STATEMENT 37 Human service professionals recognize a commitment to lifelong learning and continually upgrade knowledge and skills to serve the populations better.

F. A Guide to Professional Organizations

It is a good idea while a student to begin your identification with state, regional, and national professional associations. To assist you in learning about student memberships, here is a list of the major national professional organizations, along with a summary of student membership benefits.

American Counseling Association (ACA)

The ACA has 56 state branches and four regional branch assemblies. Students qualify for a special annual membership rate of $59.50 and half the rate for membership in any of the 16 member associations or divisions. Student memberships are available to both undergraduate and graduate students enrolled at least half-time or more at the college level.

ACA membership provides many benefits, including a subscription to the *Journal of Counseling and Development* and a monthly newspaper entitled *Counseling Today,* eligibility for professional liability insurance programs, legal defense services, and professional development through workshops and conventions. A copy of ACA's *Code of Ethics and Standards of Practice* (1995) is available. ACA puts out a resource catalog that provides information on the various aspects of the counseling profession, as well as giving detailed information about membership, journals, books, home-study programs, videotapes, audiotapes, and liability insurance. For further information, contact:

American Counseling Association
5999 Stevenson Avenue
Alexandria, VA 22304-3300
Telephone: (703) 823-9800 or (800) 347-6647

National Board for Certified Counselors (NBCC)

The NBCC offers a certification program for counselors. National Certified Counselors (NCCs) meet the generic professional standards established by the board and agree to abide by the *NBCC Code of Ethics.* NCCs work in a variety of educational and social service settings such as schools, private practice, mental-health agencies, correctional facilities, community agencies, rehabilitation agencies, and business and industry. To qualify for an NCC, candidates must meet the minimum educational and professional counseling experience requirements established by the NBCC. For a copy of the *NBCC Code of Ethics* and further information about becoming a National Certified Counselor, contact:

National Board for Certified Counselors
3-D Terrace Way
Greensboro, NC 27403
Telephone: (910) 547-0607
(800) 398-5389 (Application request line)

National Organization for Human Service Education (NOHSE)

The National Organization for Human Service Education's (NOHSE) focus includes supporting and promoting improvements in direct service, public education, program development, planning and evaluation, administration, and public policy. Members are drawn from diverse disciplines— mental health, child care, social services, gerontology, recreation, corrections, and developmental disabilities. Membership is open to human-service educators, students, fieldwork supervisors, and direct-care professionals. Student membership is $15 per year, which includes a subscription to the newsletter (the *Link*), the yearly journal (*Human Services Education*), and a discount price for the yearly conference (held in October). For further information about membership in the National Organization for Human Service Education, contact:

> Douglas A Whyte,
> Membership Chair of NOHSE
> Membership, NOHSE
> Community College of Philadelphia
> 1700 Spring Garden Street
> Philadelphia, PA 19130-3991
> Telephone: (215) 751-8522 or (215) 751-8000

American Association for Marriage and Family Therapy (AAMFT)

The AAMFT has a student membership category. You must obtain an official application, including the names of at least two Clinical Members from whom the association can request official endorsements. You also need a statement signed by the coordinator or director of a graduate program in marital and family therapy in a regionally accredited educational institution verifying your current enrollment. Student membership may be held until receipt of a qualifying graduate degree, or for a maximum of five years. Members receive the *Journal of Marital and Family Therapy*, which is published four times a year, and a subscription to six issues yearly of *Family Therapy News*. For a copy of the AAMFT Code of Ethics, membership applications, and further information, write to:

> American Association for Marriage and
> Family Therapy
> 1133 Fifteenth Street, N.W., Suite 300
> Washington, DC 20005-2710
> Telephone: (202) 452-0109

National Association of Social Workers (NASW)

NASW membership is open to all professional social workers. The NASW Press, which produces *Social Work* and the *NASW News* as membership benefits, is a major service in professional development. NASW publishes a number of pamphlets regarding practice standards; the following publications are currently available:

- *Standards and Guidelines for Social Work Case Management for the Functionally Impaired*
- *Standards for the Practice of Clinical Social Work*
- *Standards for Social Work in Health Care Settings*
- *Standards for Social Work Practice in Child Protection*
- *Standards for Social Work Services in Long-Term Care Facilities*
- *Standards for Social Work Services in Schools*

For a copy of any of the above pamphlets, or for a copy of the *The National Association of Social Workers Code of Ethics* (1996), or for information on membership categories and benefits, write to:

> National Association of Social Workers
> 750 First Street, NE, Suite 700
> Washington, DC 20002-4241
> Telephone: (202) 408-8600 or (800) 638-8799
> FAX (202) 336-8312

American Psychological Association

The APA has a Student Affiliates category rather than student membership. Journals and subscriptions are extra. Each year in mid-August or late August the APA holds a national convention. For further information or for a copy of the *Ethical Principles of Psychologists and Code of Conduct* (1995), write to:

> American Psychological Association
> 1200 17th Street, N.W.
> Washington, DC 20036
> Telephone: (202) 955-7600

In addition to the national organization there are seven regional divisions, each of which has an annual convention. For addresses or information about student membership in any of them, contact the main office of the APA or see a copy of the association's monthly journal, *American Psychologist*.

A number of APA publications may be of interest to you. The following can be ordered from:

American Psychological Association, Order Department
P.O. Box 2710
Hyattsville, MD 20784-0710
Telephone: (703) 247-7705

1. *Specialty Guidelines for Delivery of Services by Psychologists*
   ◆ "Delivery of Services by Clinical Psychologists"
   ◆ "Delivery of Services by Counseling Psychologists"
   ◆ "Delivery of Services by School Psychologists"
   ◆ "Delivery of Services by Industrial/Organizational Psychologists"
2. *Careers in Psychology* (pamphlet)
3. *How to Manage Your Career in Psychology*
4. *Is Psychology the Major for You? Planning for Your Undergraduate Years*
5. *Graduate Study in Psychology and Associated Fields.* Information on graduate programs in the United States and Canada, including staff/student statistics, financial aid deadlines, tuition, teaching opportunities, housing, degree requirements, and program goals.
6. *Preparing for Graduate Study: Not for Seniors Only!*
7. *Ethnic Minority Perspectives on Clinical Training and Services in Psychology*
8. *Toward Ethnic Diversification in Psychology Education and Training*
9. *Ethical Principles in the Conduct of Research with Human Participants*
10. *Standards for Educational and Psychological Testing.* Revised standards for evaluating the quality of tests, testing practices, and the effects of test use. There are also chapters on licensure and certification and program evaluation. New in this edition are chapters on testing linguistic minorities and the rights of test takers.

American Psychoanalytic Association

The American Psychoanalytic Association approved a code of ethics in 1975 and revised it in 1983. Some of its sections deal with relationships with patients and colleagues, protection of confidentiality, fees, dispensing drugs, consultation, sexual misconduct, remedial measures for the psychoanalyst, and safeguarding the public and the profession. These principles of ethics can be secured by writing to:

American Psychoanalytic Association
309 East 49th Street
New York, NY 10017

American Psychiatric Association

This organization has a code of ethics entitled "Principles of Medical Ethics, with Annotations Especially Applicable to Psychiatry." The address of this organization is:

1400 K Street, NW
Washington, DC 20005
(202) 682-6000

Sociological Practice Association

The Sociological Practice Association is the professional organization of clinical and applied sociologists. Clinical sociology is sociological intervention. Clinical sociologists have specialty areas such as organizations, health and illness, forensic sociology, aging, and comparative social systems. They work as action researchers, organizational development specialists, sociotherapists, conflict interventionists, social policy implementers, and consultants. For information regarding certification instructions and for a copy of the "Ethical Standards of Sociological Practitioners," contact:

Sociological Practice Association
RD2, Box 141A
Chester, NY 10918

Name Index

Subject Index

Abandonment, as ethical issue, 121–122, 142, 145
Abortion counseling, 74, 75
Accountability, 373
Acquired immune deficiency syndrome (AIDS), 76–77, 91, 94, 101, 105, 183, 184, 186, 187, 189, 190, 191, 192, 266, 351, 355, 361
Adolescents, 73–74, 81, 133–137, 177, 371
Advertising, 373–374
Advice giving, 51–52, 413
Advocacy, in community counseling, 351, 353
Alcoholics Anonymous, 79, 80
American Association for Marriage and Family Therapy (AAMFT), 6, 8, 9, 30, 31, 120, 124, 156, 227, 228, 248, 252, 253, 267, 282, 301, 371, 372, 373, 375, 376, 379
  Code of Ethics, 498–507
  membership requirements and applications, 378
  summary of benefits and address, 509
American Counseling Association (ACA), 4, 5, 6, 8, 9, 11, 12, 13, 14, 30, 41, 63, 71, 82, 94, 99, 113, 120, 122, 126, 134, 156, 161, 186, 208, 210, 211, 215, 218, 227, 235, 248, 252, 253, 261, 267, 271, 273, 274, 275, 276, 282, 292, 293, 296, 299, 300, 308, 309, 324, 325, 339, 361, 399, 406, 409, 411
  Code of Ethics and Standards of Practice, 444–463
  summary of benefits and address, 508

American Psychoanalytic Association, summary of benefits and address, 510
American Psychological Association (APA), 4, 5, 6, 7, 9, 30, 37, 41, 63, 99, 100, 113, 120, 125, 126, 156, 158, 209, 210, 211, 215, 227, 235, 248, 267, 301, 308, 322, 325, 339
  Ethical Principles of Psychologists and Code of Conduct, 464–481
  summary of benefits and address, 509–510
Assertiveness, and multicultural counseling, 322, 329, 331–332
Association for Counselor Education and Supervision (ACES), 291, 292, 293, 298, 301, 339
Association for Multicultural Counseling and Development (AMCD), 339
Association for Specialists in Group Work (ASGW), 399, 400, 401, 404
Association for Spiritual, Ethical, Religious Values in Counseling (ASERVIC), 82
Attitudes and beliefs about professional and ethical issues, inventory of, 19–29
Autonomy, 12

Bartering, 229, 234–238
Behavioral therapy, 202
Beneficence, 13
Board of Behavioral Science Examiners, 246
Board of Psychology, 246
Bradley Center v. *Wessner*, 167–168

Breach of contract, 115, 140
Burnout, 33, 58, 62, 63, 64

California Association of Marriage and Family Therapists (CAMFT), 53, 246, 247
Catharsis, in groups, 415
Certification, 277, 278
Child abuse, 179, 180, 249, 351, 354, 355–356, 372, 389, 390
Child and adolescent counseling:
  confidentiality, 137, 159–160
  protecting from harm, 179–183
  working with reluctant clients, 371
Child Protective Services, 180, 181, 182
Client-centered therapy, 204, 210
Client dependence, 52–56
Clients:
  African-American, 180, 194, 196, 323, 327, 331, 335, 336, 362
  Asian-American, 89, 194, 196, 238, 327, 328, 330, 331, 332, 333
  bartering for professional services, 234–238
  boundary management and multiple relationships, 223–263
  Caucasian, 323, 326
  Chicano, 320
  children and adolescents, 73–74, 133–137, 371
  Chinese-American, 323
  dangerous, 169–171, 199
  dependent, 52–56
  difficult, 51, 135
  dual relationships with, 144, 234, 238–241
  elderly, 78–79
  erotic contact with, 245–256

TO THE OWNER OF THIS BOOK:

We hope that, as you read *Issues and Ethics in the Helping Professions*, 5th Edition, you found yourself challenged to clarify your positions on the issues we've raised. Only through your comments and the comments of others can we assess the impact of this book and improve it in the future.

School and address: _____

Instructor's name: _____

1. In what class did you use this book? _____

2. What did you like *most* about this book? _____

_____

_____

3. What did you like *least* about this book? _____

_____

_____

4. How useful were the pre-chapter inventories and the other inventories within the chapters?

_____

_____

5. How useful were the cases and examples in helping you formulate and clarify your thoughts on the issues? _____

_____

6. How valuable were the end-of-chapter activities and exercises? _____

_____

7. What issues that we explored were most relevant to you? _____

_____

8.   What topics do you think should be expanded or added to this book in future editions?

_____

_____

9. In the space below or in a separate letter, please write any other comments about the book you'd like to make. We welcome your suggestions! Thank you for taking the time to write to us.

Optional:

Your name: _____ Date: _____

May Brooks/Cole quote you, either in promotion for *Issues and Ethics in the Helping Professions,* Fifth Edition, or in future publishing ventures?

Yes: _____ No: _____

Sincerely,

Gerald Corey
Marianne Schneider Corey
Patrick Callanan

FOLD HERE

FOLD HERE

→ Tell Kerry
   → 9:00 bedtime
      (aloud) read-time
   → tell approx. when you'll
      be home.

* Frankl books

P140 } duty
        breach of duty
          injury
            causation rule
              malpractice

P146

Safeguard against malpractice
  · practice w/in competency
  · be pers. + prof honest + open
  · seek consultation — the c.
    underst. risk management
       techniques.